VOICES
OF YUGOSLAV JEWRY

SUNY Series in Anthropology and Judaic Studies
Walter P. Zenner, Editor

VOICES
OF YUGOSLAV JEWRY

PAUL BENJAMIN GORDIEJEW

STATE UNIVERSITY OF NEW YORK PRESS

Published by
State University of New York Press, Albany

Printed in the United States of America

For information, address the State University of New York Press, State University Plaza, Albany, N.Y. 12246

Production by Diane Ganeles
Marketing by Anne Valentine

Library of Congress Cataloging-in-Publication Data

Gordiejew, Paul Benjamin, 1954–
Voices of Yugoslav Jewry / Paul Benjamin Gordiejew.
p. cm. — (SUNY series in anthropology and Judaic studies)
Includes bibliographical references and index.
ISBN 0-7914-4021-4 (hc : alk. paper). — ISBN 0-7914-4022-2 (pb : alk. paper)
1. Jews—Yugoslavia—History. 2. Holocaust, Jewish (1939–1945)—Yugoslavia. 3. Yugoslavia—Ethnic relations. I. Title. II. Series.
DS135.Y8G67 1999
949.7'004924—dc21 98-3405
CIP

10 9 8 7 6 5 4 3 2 1

To my mother and
the memory of my father.
Many, many thanks.

CONTENTS

Acknowledgments / ix

Preface / xiii

Introduction / 1

1. History and Identity / 21

2. Before and after the Holocaust / 39

3. The Collective Voice of Submergence / 91

4. An Experiment in Secular Jewishness / 179

5. Voices of Yugoslav Jewry / 201

6. Forward into the Past / 347

7. Theoretical Musings: What Is a (Yugoslav) Jew? / 409

Appendix / 433

Notes / 437

Bibliography / 445

Index / 469

ACKNOWLEDGMENTS

The production of this book was not a solo effort. Many individuals contributed in different ways along the path toward the final product, and I want to thank them all.

First I want to thank Arthur Tuden for sticking with me throughout the duration of the project. He was, and still is, always prepared to discuss issues relating to the dynamics of ethnicity and identity. On numerous occasions he passed on fresh and stimulating theoretical insights. I also want to thank him for his humanity. He understood that such projects are always undertaken within the human context with all its vicissitudes.

Thanks are due to the members of my dissertation committee at the University of Pittsburgh: Robert Hayden, Alexander Orbach, Richard Scaglion, and Rubie Watson. Each made a valuable contribution to my doctoral dissertation, which served as the basis for the book.

Fieldwork is a necessary but expensive undertaking in the discipline of anthropology. I was fortunate to benefit from the financial support of various organizations and individuals. The International Research and Exchanges Board (IREX) provided fourteen months of generous funding. Especially gracious to me were program officers Marie Schulte and Regina Kay. Thanks also to the federal exchange partner in the former Yugoslavia for its financial contribution. The Center for Russian and East European Studies at the University of Pittsburgh contributed funding for separate research trips to Yugoslavia. Robert Donnorummo and Ronald Linden, who have directed the Center for many years, have always stood behind me. I thank them. Also in Pittsburgh, the United Jewish Federation contributed generously toward research and writing. I would like to single out Dr. Sidney Busis for showing interest in my work and facilitating the funding process. In addition, I want to thank Ms. Ruth Schacter and Steve Landes and the members of the Endowment Committee for twice deeming my project worthy of support. Thanks, also, to Steve Zupcic of the University of Pittsburgh, who has been an excellent facilitator and resource. A Nationality Rooms scholarship permitted me to visit and acquaint myself with Yugoslavia before beginning longterm fieldwork. I thank Ms. Maxine Bruhns, who does a superb job running that program, and the Rukavina family for providing, in honor of their parents, the actual funds for the scholarship. It was during that first trip that I initiated contact with the Jews of Yugoslavia.

Thanks to my peers at the University of Pittsburgh, for contributing critical comments on my work—Debbie Fiedler, Ellen Madono, Lipika Mazumdar, Lila Shaara, Martha Terry, and Michael Tickner. From our sessions together I gained insights into the cultures of Japan, India, Homestead (PA), Mexico, and Papua New Guinea. I value their friendship even more.

Last but far from least among those who contributed financial and emotional support toward the project are members of my family—my mother, Ludmila, and my siblings and their spouses, Joel and Beth Gordiejew and Anna and Ed Kostaroff. I cannot thank enough my mother, who never tired standing with me and providing endless encouragement and my late father, Peter, who is a true hero to me.

Financial support allowed me to carry out fieldwork in Yugoslavia, but it did not produce this book. Many other, more personal factors, were significant along the way. I want to thank all of my informants in Yugoslavia, some of whom have died—Vilma Market, a survivor of much and one who demonstrated the gift of helping others; Katarina Adanaja, a most gracious lady; Šemaja Avramović, a child of Dorćol: Samuel Elazar, collector and recorder of Sephardi folklore. A very special thanks to Davor Salom, who also became a friend; once again, to the late Vilma Market, who supplied me with literature on the Jews of Yugoslavia; to Milica Kraus Mihailović, curator of the Jewish Historical Museum, who arranged interviews for me; to Dr. Lavoslav Kadelburg, former president of the Federation of Jewish Communities of Yugoslavia; to David Albahari, Rabbi Cadik Danon, Dunja Sprajč, Srđan Matić, Dijamanta Kovačević, Silvana and Dušan Mladinov, and to Dolores Moreno for providing housing in Split. Many thanks to Erna Samakov who provided me with a great room in the center of

Belgrade during my third stay. A special thanks to the Grečić family in Novi Beograd—Dr. Vladimir Grečić and his wife Ljubinka, Ljubinka's mother, Dragica, who graciously opened her home to me on two separate trips, and Liz and Ljuba.

Back in the United States, my Pittsburgh affines and friends played no small part in the journey. Boris and Henrietta Rock have welcomed me in their home and shared many necessary and desirable things—housing, good eastern European home cooking, and friendship. Dr. Douglas and Elizabeth Shields have done likewise for all my years in Pittsburgh. David and Margaret Shields welcomed me into their family. Some of the writing took place in their home. Thanks to Grace for sharing a year of fieldwork with me in Yugoslavia. I hope we will remember fondly a beautiful land before the strife and killing started.

Arthur and Agnes Tuden have provided continual support and encouragement. I appreciate all the good advice and friendship. Many of the discussions on subjects in the book took place in their kitchen. Thanks, also, to two more residents of Denniston Avenue, Annie and Benjamin Preis, who have shared some of the wonders of life with me as I completed the book.

A special word of thanks to my sister Anna and her husband Ed, for opening up their Michigan home to me and allowing me to write. I also want to thank Carolyn, Ted, and Cathryn for loving and helping their uncle through a difficult time.

Finally, I appreciate the help of all the people at SUNY Press. Thanks to Professor Walter Zenner, the editor of the Anthropology and Judaic Studies series, for thinking enough of an early manuscript to get the process underway. Many thanks to Zina Lawrence, Jennie Doling, and Diane Ganeles for answering my questions and facilitating the entire review and production process. I wish to include Christine Worden, who preceded Ms. Lawrence, and all others at SUNY Press involved in the production of this book. Many thanks, as well, to the anonymous reviewers, for their criticisms and gracious remarks.

PREFACE

"Being Where?"[1]

As visitors and natives walk along the boulevards and streets of Belgrade, they are hard pressed to see any signs of Jewish life, either the life that now is or the vibrant life that once was. A persistent search in this Balkan city might lead the more curious observer to the Jevrejski Dom on 7th of July Street with its barely legible Hebrew inscription at the top of the building,[2] or to the walled Sephardi cemetery located beside Belgrade's New Cemetery, or by chance to the remaining synagogue on Birjuzova Street within sight of the dome of the Serbian Patriarchate's Saborna Crkva.[3] A walk down into what was the Sephardi Jewish quarter of Dorćol along the Danube, where the Jews were called *Los de abajo*, "those from below," reveals the continued presence of a Jevrejska ulica.[4] But no longer are there any Jews on Jewish Street. The familiar rhythm of a specifically Jewish life, with its sites, smells, and sounds and the images these elements gave rise to, was extinguished a half century ago in the Holocaust. The rhythm was not suddenly abandoned by its practitioners. It was dealt a deathblow by the German and domestic fascists who sought to annihilate all traces of Jewish existence. Following the war many of the surviving traces of that rhythm were abandoned voluntarily as many of the Jewish survivors sought enthusiastically to submerge themselves in the New Yugoslavia of Tito and his Partisans. It was into this seemingly empty, or at least fragmented, cultural landscape that I arrived to study Yugoslav Jewish identity.

As other anthropologists have discovered recently, I found that I could not conduct or write a classical ethnography with its familiar methods, forms, and categories—immersion into indigenous culture through participant observation ("hanging out with the natives"), delineation of kinship charts, descriptions of domestic structures, and so on. Culture itself, as described in the classical literature, appeared to be found nowhere. Later, I came to realize that my fieldwork and writing experiences had placed me in the company of an increasing number of ethnographers who, their particular assumptions and a priori frameworks notwithstanding, have also confronted fragmented ethnographic realities and once full but now nearly empty cultural spaces. Jonathan Boyarin (1991) recognized that the dislocated Polish Jews of Paris were a fragmented community experiencing the disjuncture that comes from losing the hope of a utopian future after already having abandoned their past or having been cut off from it. In the elderly Jews of Venice, California, Barbara Myerhoff (1978) witnessed behavioral patterns that she could only describe as bricolage, the shreds-and-patches of a cultural past woven together to meet the needs of an isolated old-age existence. In contending with the fragmented realities of his field situation in the Philippines, Jean-Paul Dumont (1992:1) represents them in his ethnographic text as vignettes, "a plurality of images . . . that superimpose themselves upon each other to create an out-of-focus ensemble, since cultural contours are never sharp and stories never straight, neither those [one] hear[s] nor those [one is] told." By presenting the fragmented realities to the reader in ways that are not artificially made coherent by the writer, the reader likewise experiences what the ethnographer confronted in the field. The ethnographic text, thus, serves as an analog of how, through organization and writing, the ethnographer has dealt with the ethnographic reality. The reader is thereby "forced into experiencing the intellectual discomfort, the emotional disquiet, the unsettling challenge of shattered certitudes that appear as obbligati in anthropological fieldwork" (ibid:6). Like the experience the folklorist John Dorst (1989:10) had in describing the suburban community of Chadds Ford, Pennsylvania, I too had "little hope of finding an indisputable [ethnic community] whether in hard facts of geography or in a sociology of community."

The ethnographic reality that I confronted in the field, which partially remained in my memories and which I partially represented in the field notes I brought back home, led me to radically reorient myself from writing a classical ethnography to an ethnography of concepts, symbols, and personal narratives. The narratives were based partly upon my own partial knowledge and interpretation of my encounters with individuals and their words, and partly upon the collaborative efforts of my informants and me in constructing what Myerhoff has called ethno-persons. My informants provided the fragmented autobiographical narratives and, with their proneness to reflexivity, contributed to interpretation as well.

What exactly was this ethnographic reality that I confronted? How did it attach itself to my analytical framework and to my manner of (re)presenting the Jews of Yugoslavia in this text? How has it shaped my description, analysis, and presentation? I have referred to the ethnographic reality that my informants confront as a fragmented cultural landscape, with places in it that may be empty. It follows that, for me, the outsider, this cultural landscape appeared even more barren, for to enter the worlds of my informants I had to rely upon their statements, their memories, and their imaginations. There was no ongoing Jewish life into which I could immerse myself and thereby begin to know the concrete realities of everyday life and sense the material images that infuse newness and creativity into that life. One solution would have been to contain my observations to the narrowly contained sphere of organized Jewish life, where in fact certain structures and patterns could be detected, but this would have given the mistaken impression of the existence of a well-bounded, homogenous, and clearly defined community. But only a minority of the Jewish population participated regularly in organized Jewish life. Being a Jew in Yugoslavia thus meant something much less bounded and defined.

Against the fragmented contours of the Yugoslav Jewish cultural landscape, I, the anthropologist, confronted a population characterized by what it had lost, had abandoned, or had taken away from it, by a population whose members confronted disjuncture in themselves and in others and whose shared cultural space had been reduced to a cultural program constructed by the organized community or to a conceptual sphere that required no regular participation in a social or even a ritual community.

This study explores the conjunctures and disjunctures of Yugoslav Jewish transformations and the multiplicity that characterizes individual quests for identity and meaning. What is presented is a study of a symbolic more than a social community. It is an example of the construction and affirmation of a particular pattern of symbolic accomodation displayed by the organized community. I have termed this pattern, submergence. Within this symbolic community individuals attempt to bring some order into their lives by patching together a makeshift identity, with parts of their Jewishness self-selected, other parts imposed upon them, and still other parts embedded in their consciousness through a process of transference. Peter Berger (1974:64) has written, "Through most of human history, individuals lived in life-worlds that were more or less unified. . . . For the individual this meant quite simply that the *same* integrative symbols permeated the various sectors of his everyday life." As the individual narratives presented in chapter 5 show, the Jews of the postwar years were no longer guided by the integrative symbols that constitute a Jewish tradition. Of course, as individuals they could have chosen to follow the single path of the organized Jewish community and be guided by the key symbols of the newly invented Titoist tradition, and indeed some did. But the narratives reveal to us that these individuals were guided less by an authoritative and integrated symbol system and more by private symbols that they themselves selected or created. It was these latter symbols that pointed inward and thus provided a sense of meaning and internal coherence, or perhaps, for some, tension and struggle. Some of the symbols were externally situated as *krajputaše* or landmarks along individual Jewish paths of existence.

The Jews of Yugoslavia have been a population caught in the middle, and thus the metaphor of the acrobat performing a balancing act used by one of my informants is an appropriate one. I, too, have been caught in the middle between an empirical anthropology and an interpretive anthropology. I agree with O'Meara (1989) that there is room for both approaches in anthropology. For this study, because of the ethnographic reality I confronted in Yugoslavia, I had no choice but to rely heavily on the subjectivity of informants' statements, which I could not check against the empirical data that come from observing concrete persons in everyday life. However, I have also strived to present the causal factors that created such a truncated and barren cultural landscape in which this population is situated and through which its members move.

INTRODUCTION

The historical and contemporary complexities and diversity of the former Yugoslavia present significant problems to anthropologists and other social scientists interested in macro- and microlevel processes of history, identity, and change. This study focused on one ethnic population that historically has been dispersed throughout what was the state of Yugoslavia and consequently has been exposed to various and often conflicting political movements, nationalist and internationalist ideologies, and cultural systems. Not only has this population, the Jews of Yugoslavia, who are now the Jews of Bosnia, Croatia, Macedonia, Serbia, and Slovenia, lived in regions that possess different histories and national mythologies, it also lived on the border of warring empires and came to reflect features of both the foreign rulers and the indigenous ruled. The purpose of the study was to examine both the individual and collective forms and meanings Yugoslav Jewish identities have taken as a result of and in response to historical transformations and the communal imaginings that have sprung from them, the most recent being the destruction of Yugoslavia and the projects of national reconstruction that followed in the wake.

Although never a large population, the Jews of Yugoslavia enjoyed a traditionally Jewish albeit acculturated life style before the First World War and a less traditional but still vibrant existence before the Second World War.[1] A single cataclysmic event in history, motivated by a racist ideology (Mosse 1980) and implemented through a program of genocide, wiped out four-fifths of the Yugoslav Jewish population and changed its complexion forever. Other concurrent historical processes—a world war, a civil war, a socialist revolution, followed in the postwar years by five waves of emigration and a program of building a socialist state and a socialist culture—also left their impressions on this population. Faced with the aftermath of a destruction that cut them off from everything that was most meaningful to them, these Jews, maimed and crippled though they were, could have disappeared altogether without a trace. If they had, that would have been the end of Jewish history in this part of the Balkans. There would be no story to tell, for there would be no living voices. But Jews resolved to rise from the destruction, to sift through the remaining fragments, and to stitch together a community and individual lives. In what may now be called the Titoist postwar period, the Jewish community initiated an experiment in secular Jewishness whose intent was to reconstitute the Jewish community, but in so doing to submerge it simultaneously within the new socialist system. More recently, following in the wake of the fall of state socialism throughout eastern Europe, the Titoist system underwent erosion and a violent collapse. With these changes came a Jewish resurgence that sprang from diverse sources and manifested itself in different forms.

Given the rapid changes that created greater uncertainty, the Jews of Yugoslavia again faced the dilemma of finding solutions for a problematic and often ambiguous Jewish identity in a period of crisis and major historical transition. The historical past, a time when the vast majority of Jews was guided by tradition, was long gone. Their numbers were reduced drastically by genocide, warfare, ethnic cleansing, assimilation, and emigration. With the collapse of state socialism, the Jewish community no longer could feel the security of submergence within the structure once offered by the relative political stability of Titoism and the symbolic pillars upon which it rested. Accompanying political discontent and erosion were confrontation and conflict, rapid social change, and uncertainty about the future. The problem of the study was to describe and interpret how the Jews of Yugoslavia, as individuals and as a community, have responded to the changes within and outside their population, including the most recent dilemma associated with the violent transition to independent political states. First in the relative political stability of Titoist Yugoslavia, and now in the rapidly changing and volatile political and social context, how have Jews used, manipulated, negotiated, communicated, refashioned, or ignored Jewish identity in their public and private lives? Is identity as manifested by these individuals a phenomenon of history, of politics, of population profile and social context, of natural primordial attachments that together constitute a basic group identity, or is it a dialectical phenomenon arising from the convergence of cultural and political dynamics? In addition, this study examined the effect that transition itself, particularly one whose anti-structural[2] characteristics tend toward the uncontrolled and chaotic, has had on the Jews in diverse regions of a fragmented land. In this transition, where the rules of interethnic interaction were changed, how did non-Jewish actors symbolically manipulate the Jews and Jewish symbols in the transitional processes of national re-creation, presentation, and contestation?

A Panoramic View of the Research Setting

Fieldwork for this study of Jewish identity was initiated in what at the time was the multinational and multiethnic state of socialist Yugoslavia, which spanned a large part of the peninsula that has long served as a crossroads between the European West and the Asian East, the Mediterranean South and the European North. Given its strategic location and the divisive nature of its mountainous and riverine topography, the land on which socialist Yugoslavia rested has long been a region in which diverse ethnic populations have mingled, sometimes mixing and sometimes not. Entrance into this land was easy, thus inviting foreign rulers to extend their dominion over the indigenous peoples and the foreign minorities (e.g., Greeks, Armenians, Jews) who sought economic opportunity and perhaps respite from persecution. But once inside this land, conquerors and migrants found travel and communication across regions difficult because of the mountainous terrain. The rugged terrain notwithstanding, this was a land that was neither demographically stable nor ethnically and religiously tidy. Short-term and long-term movements occurred with regularity. Even the common correspondence of Croats with Roman Catholicism and Serbs with Eastern Orthodoxy did not fully solidify in certain regions until the eighteenth century (Hammel 1993). However, the impact of centuries of foreign domination, which did solidify existing divisions or create new ones among indigenous populations, contributed to producing a geographical area marked by stark and pervasive contrasts. Thus, before Yugoslavia came into existence in 1918, the process of "tidying up" the ethnic map was largely a process imposed by foreign rulers, whether of the kind who came to conquer and rule or who deliberated peace treaties at conference tables in faraway places.

The land which the socialist state of Yugoslavia occupied has had not one but several histories, each inscribed in memories, oral traditions, museum displays, and written histories. The paths that these populations have chosen and continue to take today are, in no small part, influenced by what happened in the past. This is not to say that these peoples have never broken with the past. They have. Perhaps the more interesting questions are: When do people break from the past? What do they break with more easily? What do they resist breaking away from? What happens when they try to break away? Only by examining cultural histories can we find the clues that will help us answer such questions. The demise of socialist Yugoslavia has shown us that the past, however interpreted, is a part of the consciousness of these peoples. Why, in fact, did certain features of the past become such an essentialized part of identity in the present (see Comaroff and Comaroff 1992; Wilson 1994)? Although the past may not be what directly has caused the ethnic divisions and conflicts of socialist and post-socialist Yugoslavia, the past is often selectively invoked and manipulated by ethnopolitical actors. These actors are often successful because the past is deeply felt by the populace. This is apparent because people respond to the historical symbols and myths that have been recontextualized for contemporary conditions and political aims. The Serbs, for example, have succeeded in taking the fatalities of their past—their slaughter at the hands of the advancing Ottoman Turks on Kosovo Polje, "the Field of Blackbirds," their great losses during the retreat of the Serbian army toward the Adriatic Sea in 1915, and their slaughter by the German Wehrmacht and Croatian Ustasha during the Second World War—and placing them into the core of their Nationhood. What else could serve the interest of the Nation any better? What else could move its people more (see Anderson 1991)?

What kinds of histories have contributed to creating the contrasts found in Yugoslavia? What kinds of myths have been written and told that render these same histories selectively, thereby contributing to both collective remembering of the so-called glorious past or times of martyrdom and collective forgetting of the inglorious moments of the past? As an example of the former, both Serbs and Croats have emphasized the histories of their respective independent native states in medieval times. Likewise, both have emphasized histories of resented domination by foreign powers. The elements of these histories are similar: contamination, loss, and preservation of continuity.

Indigenous rule and foreign domination are important in understanding the prevailing perceptions and interethnic relations of the present, both for the larger and smaller ethnic populations. The position of a small and dispersed ethnic population like the Jews has been and continues to be influenced by its direct relationships with other, particularly larger and stronger, ethnic populations. Also, the patterns of relationships among other ethnic populations, particularly the Serb-Croat relationship, have had an impact on the position of smaller populations. For populations dispersed among the various *nacije* ("nation" peoples), their position was especially complex and, potentially, internally disruptive. For instance, the recent fragmentation of socialist Yugoslavia has fragmented the Jews of Yugoslavia. In Bosnia-Hercegovina the fragmentation has threatened the very existence of Bosnian and Sarajevo Jewry as entities. About four hundred Jews remained in besieged Sarajevo. Among the four hundred, not all of whom were registered members of the Sarajevo Jewish community, were those intent on remaining in Sarajevo because they believed in the independent Bosnian state and are proud of the nearly four and one-half centuries of continuous (except for 1941–45) Jewish existence in Bosnia (Stephen Schwartz, personal communication).

After about seventy years of being politically united, the latest "Yugoslav experiment" (Rusinow 1977) in the form of the Socialist Federal Republic of Yugoslavia fell short in bridging the divisions rooted in different political and cultural histories, despite the genuine efforts, the formulaic, almost magiclike rhetoric, and the various performances that were intended to either foster or symbolically represent the brotherhood and unity of the Yugoslav peoples. The historical cleavages continued to be a real and perceived basis of difference and underlying friction. Associated with the different histories have been diverse political systems and ideologies, economic policies, communication systems, religions, worldviews, languages and dialects, nationalisms, and geo-political orientations. Yugoslavia was a fragile society built upon and/or characterized by: histories of foreign rule and domination that divided its peoples; migrations and resettlements; wars, including two World Wars; national and ideological revolutions; fusions and fissions; marked tripartite religious division (quadripartite, in the case of Bosnia); national myths and myth-making; genocide and fratricide; powerful historical memories; various nationalisms and nationalist ideologies with opposing cultural and political goals; Tito and his brand of socialism; the feature of occupying a geographical and ideological space betwixt-and-between. All of this diversity has affected the historical positions occupied by the Jews of Yugoslavia, and it continues to affect their lives today. What is needed is a political and cultural history that will inform our understanding of how these factors contribute to identity formation and transformation. Chapters 1 through 3 are a step in this direction, but I do not want to pretend that they can substitute for such a history.

Only the much larger former Soviet Union matched Yugoslavia in ethnic diversity in this part of the world. The two countries shared other features as well. But there were great differences between the two lands. For example, whereas the ethnic Russians commanded the absolute majority in the Soviet state, no one ethnic group in Yugoslavia enjoyed such dominance in socialist Yugoslavia. Several ethnic populations, however, perceived the Serbs, the largest Yugoslav population, as a threat to their own ethnic autonomy because of the Serbs' overrepresentation in key institutions such as the Yugoslav National Army (JNA) and as harboring hegemonistic motivations. For a balanced historically based view of the Serbian minority's position within Croatia, and the basis of the Croats' resentment of that position, I refer the reader to Ivo Goldstein's article in *East European Reporter* (1990).

Religious cleavages are critical to understanding ethnic ascriptions and dynamics in Yugoslavia. Traditionally religion has been a marker of ethnic identity, and vice-versa. That is, to be Catholic was to be a Croat, or, to be a Croat was be Catholic; to be Orthodox was to be a Serb, and to be a Serb was to be Orthodox.[3] Historically, there was a meeting of the great civilizations of Judaism, Christianity (Eastern Orthodox and Roman Catholic), and Islam in this land. Because of the relatively small number of Jews who lived in the land in any one historical period, the influence of Judaism was felt the least of the three. The line of the Orthodox-Catholic division crosses through the central part of the country. This schism was not everywhere felt the same. In frontier zones, especially, each variant felt the pull of the other. Conversions took place. At first the Orthodox variant appeared to possess the greater magnetic attraction of the two (Banac 1984). The Christian-Muslim division did not gradually disappear with the decline of the Ottoman Turkish Empire. In fact, its presence today divides the Serbs and Muslims in war-torn Bosnia and Hercegovina. During my fieldwork this cleavage was most evident in the ethnic conflict in the Province of Kosovo between the once Christian Serbs and the Muslim Albanians. Today this region has exploded into much greater violence than occurred there in 1981. In addition, ethnically and religiously mixed Macedonia is one candidate for violence. At stake in Macedonia is not only peaceful coexistence among the ethnic groups in the new state, but also the struggles over the legitimacy of Macedonian peoplehood and all that attaches to it, such as the very use of the labels "Macedonia" and "Macedonian" (Danforth 1995). It should be noted that the Yugoslav Muslims of Bosnia-Hercegovina became one of the nation peoples of socialist Yugoslavia in the 1960s. Nowhere else in the world did such an ethnoreligious entity exist as a political nation and nationality. The Yugoslav Muslim nation was recognized as a nation together with the other five nation peoples of Yugoslavia: the Serbs, Croats, Slovenes, Macedonians, and the Montenegrins. Intrareligious cleavages were also strong in Yugoslavia, particularly between the Orthodox Serbs, Montenegrins, and Macedonians, and the Catholic Croats and Orthodox Serbs. Titoist political motivations played a part in producing internal religious schism. Protestant churches also had congregations in Yugoslavia, but they represented a very small percentage of all religious groups.

With the rise of modern nationalism in this part of the world, the nationalist ideologies and movements of the Yugoslav peoples took different forms. The strategies that they adopted grew out of their diverse experiences under different empires. The Serbs exhibited a popular nationalism, the Slovenes a bourgeois nationalism, and the Croats a combination of aristocratic and bureaucratic nationalism. As Sugar points out, these "vying nationalisms of three disparate peoples had to be reconciled within one state structure" (Sugar 1969:53–54). All three, however, were influenced in their own way by romantic nationalisms of the nineteenth century. "Without a doubt, nationalism represent[ed] the most important domestic phenomenon in Yugoslavia" (Starr 1982:237). After being politically united for over seventy years, particularistic ethnic nationalisms overwhelmed any supranational Yugoslavism. What underlined the various nationalisms were two basic opposite orientations—integration and autonomy. The Slovenes and the Croats, and the Bosnians and the Macedonians all opted for the latter, while the Serbs and Montenegrins fought for a form of integration, though non-Serbs would claim that integration is really a code word for Serbian dominance and hegemony.

Yugoslavia was the first Communist state to depart from the parent Soviet model. Tito and his advisors created a true variant after experimenting initially with Stalinist structure and policies. Its betwixt-and-between status became evident in several ways. Politically Tito was a founder of the Non-Aligned Movement, whose aim was not to bow to either Moscow or Washington. But the Titoist Yugoslavs were also pragmatists and used their non-aligned status to their competitive advantage. Playing off one superpower against the other in their implementation of market socialism, they benefitted economically and politically from the capitalists of the West and the communists of the East. Nor did the Yugoslavs break their ties with the East. Political and economic ties with the Arab world grew stronger and stronger. Yugoslavia, however, often was aligned with the Soviet Bloc states, such as when it severed diplomatic relations with Israel in 1967.

As the political and economic structure of socialist Yugoslavia moved from a centrist, unitarist model to one that was deliberately more and more decentralized, the structure and maneuvering of the Communist Party elites followed this pattern. As decentralization became patterned to a great extent along ethnic lines, government and Party elites, whose position of power depended increasingly on regional and republic-level interests, began to represent those interests above the interests of the federation. This pattern existed long before the historical changes that have brought the collapse of the Marxist-socialist state in Eastern Europe. In Yugoslavia, decentralization in the form of (con)federalization had nothing to do with the Communist Party losing or relinquishing control. Rather, the Communist rulers created a structure in which the Party itself became divided along ethnic lines. The arena for and the populations participating in the competition for scarce resources were set within the constitutional structure of the Yugoslav state. That such competition would set entire ethnic populations rather than classes against one another was fixed in a document, particularly in the 1974 Constitution. Such a process did not develop along the lines of Marxist principles of historical determinism. The persistence of ethnic cleavages and feelings of relative deprivation were felt by political elites and the populace. Acknowledging that ethnic cleavages were real and not about to disappear quickly, Tito and his advisors acted as pragmatists and continued to implement strategies of circumvention (Neal 1984). The idealism that emerged from the victorious aftermath of the Partisan War and the bold break with the Soviet Union had given way to pragmatic solutions that served to maintain the political order. By 1970 the reigning plausibility structure of Titoism, which in this case really was a superstructure, was being seriously tested by nationalism from within.

The history of this land can be described as a history of weddings, divorces, and adoptions. Sometimes coercion played a part; other times the fusions were voluntary. The latest divorce has been a violent, bloody one. There were three experiments with the "Yugoslav Idea" itself, that is, three efforts to create unity out of diversity. The first was a kind of pan-Slavism that grew out of nineteenth century romantic nationalism. The second was the creation of the Kingdom of Serbs, Croats and Slovenes in 1918, which was more than just the artificial creation of a postwar peace conference. There were both Serbian and Croatian advocates of the union. The last was the socialist Yugoslavia of Tito. All three experiments ultimately failed. None managed to overcome the diversity and to unite the diverse elements for long. A fourth experiment does not seem probable in the near future.

Jews in the Yugoslav Mosaic

The Jews lived in all six republics and the two provinces of the Federal Republic of Socialist Yugoslavia. Thus, in a sense, the diasporic Jews lived diasporically within the state as well. The greatest concentrations were located in three cities that have long been centers of Jewish life—Belgrade, the capital of Yugoslavia and of Serbia, Zagreb, the capital of Croatia, and Sarajevo, the capital of Bosnia-Hercegovina. These three cities are important for comparative reasons because they reflect historical divisions that had produced diverse social systems and fostered different cultural orientations. According to Harriet Pass Freidenreich (1979), Zagreb reflected the European West, for it fell under the control of the Habsburg Empire. Sarajevo reflected the Oriental East, as it was under the control of the Ottoman Turks for nearly five hundred years. Since Belgrade's fortunes or misfortunes swung back and forth between the Austrians and the Ottomans, this city which sits at the confluence of the Danube and Sava Rivers came to reflect shades of both. This description of the three cities was accurate. Visitors to these cities could sense contrasts in such forms as architecture, cuisine, appearance, and music. But perhaps this classic division hides the complexities, overemphasizes the differences, and underemphasizes the similarities wrought by the historical transformations that began during the nineteenth century, when Ottoman influence was waning and European influence was rising.

More recently with respect to these traditional divisions, the respective ethnic populations have engaged in various campaigns that have deliberately sought to cleanse their territories of "alien" influences. In 1994, no longer could I find anywhere in Belgrade a cup of that thick, dark brew called *turska kafa* ("Turkish coffee"). I did drink many cups of *crna kafa* ("black coffee") that looked and tasted just like the *turska kafa* I drank at the sidewalk cafes on previous trips. Of course, these campaigns that set out to purge the cultural terrain of foreign influences or reminders have cut a much wider swath than the name for a kind of coffee. Churches and mosques have been destroyed, houses burned, and masses of people killed or moved. These have been the most recent strategies in "tidying up" the ethnic map.

Belgrade served as the primary site of fieldwork. Research was also conducted in Sarajevo and Zagreb, with more limited fieldwork carried out in other cities where Jews lived and which reflected regional differences: Split, located in the Dalmatian region of the Adriatic coast; Subotica, located in near the Hungarian border in the Province of Vojvodina; and Borovo, adjacent to Vukovar, in the Slavonian region of Croatia. In the late 1980s Jewish communities still existed in other cities throughout the former Yugoslavia: Skopje in Macedonia; Novi Sad in the Vojvodina; Niš in Serbia; Zemun just across the river from Belgrade; Osijek in Slavonian Croatia; Rijeka in Istria; Ljubljana in Slovenia. No longer was there a community in Kosovo, as only several Jews remained in that conflict zone. Lastly, I include in my setting those sites that had social and cultural significance for the Yugoslav Jews. Such sites included: the Pirovac camp, located in the town of Pirovac on the Adriatic coast between the cities of Split and Zadar; Djakovo, a pilgrimage site in the Slavonian region of Croatia; Sajmište, a commemoration site across the Sava River from Belgrade.

Confronting and Responding to the Ethnographic Reality

The fieldwork for this study was carried out during three historical phases: the socialist phase (1985–86), the year of transition (1989), and the post-socialist phase (1994). During my initial and longest fieldwork stay, difficulties in trying to implement traditional ethnographic methodologies led me to question the sociocultural existence of the Jewish community that I set out to study. Problems of methodological implementation became problems of theoretical reorientation and exploration. Consequently, my attention was turned to exploring what were individualistic processes of identity formation and transformation. Rather than social boundary as a central focus, a truncated pattern of ethnicity and individuated forms and meanings of identity captured my attention. Both my informants and I faced, where identity is concerned, familiar epistemological questions. All of them asserted their Jewishness, even though for some doubt about their identity surfaced along the way. But the deeper confrontation, whether conscious or not, was with the questions, what makes us Jews and how do we (and perhaps others) know? As an outsider, I was asking, "Who are these people? What makes them Jews? How do they know? How do others know? How do I know?" In presenting the narratives that describe how my informants confronted and dealt with their metaphysical and epistemological dilemmas, I have chosen not to be constrained by a position that denies validity to any particular sphere of knowledge.

Entrance into the world of my population was not a smooth one. I felt that I had not gained acceptance into the community until many months had passed. Contributing to the methodological obstacles I faced during my first extended stay was an inaccessibility to households in which Jews lived. Several interviews were held on the premises of the Jewish community or in a public place, such as a hotel restaurant.

As an anthropologist the problem I encountered was the paucity of opportunities to observe and participate in a process called "Jewish life" over extended time periods. There was no daily life cycle to observe, the absence of which constrained the development of the traditional dyadic tie between anthropologist and informant. What did exist as Jewish life was located in organized events, and these were intermittent or irregular, and not always held in the same city. Even in the country Jewish identity had a transnational form. Given such ethnographic conditions, how could I have described a "living population," at least one whose continuity and survival were self-contained or self-sufficient? Ethnic life did not appear to flow from a consensual culture or from social relations that constituted traditional forms of social organization or even new forms based on political or economic interest, but rather by means of (1) an organized community, held together by a central organization, the Federation of Jewish Communities of Yugoslavia, (2) prominent individuals who brought prestige and recognition to the population, (3) a tiny remnant of believers and traditional ritualists, (4) the experiences of individuals, and (5) external actors who attempted to appropriate and manipulate Jewish symbols for their own instrumental purposes. In contrast, missing or eroded components included (a) a traditional belief system, (b) rites of passage, (c) explicit communal norms and sanctions, (d) traditional units of social organization, and (e) extra-communal associations.

Furthermore, people knew that I was a foreigner. Some were curious about the questions that I asked them. One informant, wondering why I was asking so many political questions, simply could not believe that I was an anthropologist. There were those who believed I was a spy, my key informant disclosed to me just before my departure from Belgrade. He told me that an invented Jewish kinship tie would have facilitated entrance and acceptance. In my contacts with the Yugoslav Jews, I discovered that indeed "certain groups are more circumspect than others in their dealings with outsiders" (Watson 1974). But, in addition, what if those who shared certain ingroup characteristics (e.g., descent, self-ascription, ritual participation) are also treated as outsiders while attending communal events? If such individuals experienced difficulty in penetrating communal social boundaries, and they did, then what does a true outsider, an American anthropologist, experience? The keys to comprehending this problem lies in the history, structure, and character of the "community" itself.

What did all of this mean for me, the anthropologist? In short, I was unable to study a living population or group as anthropologists traditionally have defined such a unit. One alternative was to become a salvage anthropologist, trying to preserve fragments of the past, but this was unattractive to me. It was more interesting to find that the task of salvage anthropology was being carried out by the Yugoslav Jews themselves. The other alternative, to reiterate, was to turn a methodological problem into a theoretical and ethnological one. Is there a Jewish community in Yugoslavia? Does a community encapsulate only those individuals who share face-to-face relations? Or, must a community be defined in social terms? Are they Jews? What makes them Jews? A description and an analysis of the Jews of Yugoslavia required a methodological and theoretical refocusing from reliance on participant-observation to a multimethod approach, and from what once were collective worldviews and traditions to what had become largely individual experiences and private symbols of identity.

The Population of Study

The population from which Jewish informants and respondents were selected consists of the global population of Yugoslav Jews. For the purpose of the study, the Yugoslav Jewish population encompassed all Jews living in socialist and former Yugoslavia, all Jews born in Yugoslavia but now living elsewhere, and certain individuals now deceased. At the populational level, a broad definition of who is a Jew was been applied. This broad definition includes criteria of ascription and descent, either matrilineal or patrilineal. Membership in a local Jewish community was not a criterion, since certain non-Jewish kin were also members and not all Jews chose to belong to such an organization.

Although a case could be made for considering the Jews of different regions of socialist Yugoslavia as distinct populations rather than one population, I opted to use a multilevel approach. Since the primary units of analysis for this study were the organized community (*zajednica*), which was not limited to one local community (*opština*), and the individual, and because I elicited data from and pertaining to different regions, I refer to the population of Yugoslav Jews. On another level I identified, in a limited way, regional differences that were reflected in the minds and behaviors of these individuals and the communities to which they belong. Is a Jew from Belgrade different from a Jew in Croatia or Bosnia? In making regional comparisons, particularly when speaking of collectivities rather than individuals, I would like to compare populations. But this approach introduces potential problems. First of all, the Sephardi-Ashkenazi division in place before the Second World War collapsed largely because of demographic changes. Also, the considerable internal migration in the immediate postwar years resulted in further integration not only of Sephardim and Ashkenazim, but also of Jews from different regions. Furthermore, as I show in chapter 3, political motivations contributed to eliminating differences that might have detracted from communal unity. Thus, to make valid and reliable comparisons between postwar communities, a number of variables would have to be controlled. Since controlled comparisons were not made, any comparisons that I make above the level of the individual are intuitive and exploratory and should be accepted as such.

I met many of my informants while maintaining a presence on the premises of the Federation of Jewish Communities of Yugoslavia, attending various communal events in different parts of the country, and going to the Belgrade synagogue for the Friday evening services. I was introduced to two excellent informants through acquaintances of my wife. One of these became a *veza* relationship of *poznanstvo*.[4] A Montenegrin friend led me to two other individuals who could be classified as "on the fringe" of Jewish life.[5] These were the kinds of Jewish individuals whom I wanted to include as part of my sample. The "friend of a friend" method turned out to be an excellent way to meet new people. Although I did not always target whom I wanted to talk to, my informants and respondents constituted a variable if not representative sample of the Yugoslav Jewish population.

A total of sixty-three individuals constitute the primary sample of the study. Table 1.1 presents a breakdown by generation, gender, region, occupational category, and degree of communal participation. Included in the secondary sample were (1) individuals with whom I talked casually and observed but did not formally interview, (2) certain deceased individuals who were prominent in Yugoslav Jewish life (e.g., Albert Vajs), and (3) individuals who completed questionnaires administered by the Federation ("My Family" questionnaire N = 37; "Ritual & Customs" questionnaire N = 31; Youth questionnaire N = 1).

Several non-Jews with ties to Yugoslav Jews were interviewed: Ljubomir Tadić, president of the Society of Serbian-Jewish Friendship and well-known academic; Vuk Drašković, writer-turned-politician; Sobodan Nešović, Moša Pijade's official biographer; and a young Montenegrin man who wanted to convert. More casual conversations were held with other non-Jews.

A number of my informants are identified by their actual names, while an effort has been made to protect the identities of certain others. The conception of what constitutes sensitive data may or may not be shared by the anthropologist and his or her informants. Since my population was very small, I wanted to protect my informants. However, it is impossible to construct a protective net that can conceal or protect every identity in such a small population. Several of my informants were public figures who have been interviewed by the press. No attempt was made to conceal identities when the source of the information was part of the public domain (e.g., magazines, newspapers, books). In addition, no attempt was made to conceal the identities of some of the prominent officials in the community.

Table 1.1
Description of Primary Sample

Feature	*Number (n)*	*Percentage (%)*
Total Sample (1)	63	100
Gender		
Female	24	38
Male	39	62
Generation		
Senior	34	54
Middle	21	33
Youth	8	13
Current Residence (2)		
Belgrade	44	70
Zagreb	10	16
Sarajevo	3	5
Other	6	9
Occupational Category		
Arts & Sciences (writing, publishing, broadcasting, music, academic)	15	24
Free Profession	6	10
Business	6	10
JC Administration	9	14
JC Professional	4	6
Students	6	10
Religious Specialist	1	2
Diplomat (retired)	1	2
Other/Unknown	15	24
Degree of Communal Participation		
High predom. secular	22	52
High predom. religious	4	10
High both spheres	8	19
"Expert" contribution	4	10
Little or None	4	10

(1) This sample includes all individuals of Yugoslav Jewish descent who were formally interviewed and/or who completed a questionnaire. Excluded are individuals with whom I established a relationship but did not formally interview and individuals who were a part of two group interviews that I conducted, one with an exclusively women's group in Split and one with Jewish youth in Belgrade (4 males, 1 female).

The fieldwork for this study was carried out between October 1985 and October 1986, during a two-month period (April–May) in 1989, and a three-week period in September 1994. The study has three timeframes. The ethnographic focus of the study is on the post-Second World War period of socialist Yugoslavia, with the primary emphasis on the periods of my research visits (1985–86; 1989; 1994). The entire description and analysis of the postwar period extends from 1945 to 1994. The timeframe of focus is placed within the broader timeframe of the presence of Jews in the Balkans.

Methodological and Epistemological Framework

Participant observation was used in a limited way whenever or wherever possible. Since no longer are there any Jewish quarters or a daily cycle of Jewish life, participant observation was limited mostly to distinct Jewish spheres of interaction or to events in which Jews participated. These include synagogue services, holiday celebrations in the community, burials and commemorations in the Jewish cemeteries, pilgrimages, annual meetings, gatherings and seminars, and the summer camp. During my visits I conducted research in all of these spheres. There were other spheres of interaction or events that were covered in my data collection. These include bookstores, restaurants, and public meetings.

Because of the limitations imposed on participant observation, I was forced to rely heavily on interviewing, casual conversations, and printed materials. Observing social relations on a regular basis outside the sphere of formal organizations (e.g., Federation of Jewish Communities of Yugoslavia, local communities) was very difficult if not impossible. The interviews helped to elicit self-definitions of identity, experiences and symbols of personal significance, and fragments of individual worldviews.

Content analysis served as an important method of analysis. Content was differentiated according to whether or not it was published or printed within the Jewish community. Content that was published or printed within the community was further categorized into primary and secondary data. Memos and minutes of meetings were categorized as primary, as was the *Jevrejski Pregled* (Jewish Review) and the *Biltens* (Bulletins) of the Belgrade, Zagreb, and Sarajevo communities. The Jewish community also published books and academic journals (*Jevrejski Almanah*, *Zbornik*). Some of this material can be categorized as primary data (articles, short stories, and poems written by Yugoslav Jews).

Data were collected from several questionnaires that had been administered by the Jewish community in the past. Existing questionnaires from which I collected data were the *Rituals Customs Questionnaire*, the *Moja Porodica* ("My Family") Questionnaire, and the *Youth Questionnaire*. My analysis of these sources was selective rather than exhaustive; there is opportunity for further research using the data elicited by these instruments. An effort was made to distribute, through a student, a questionnaire designed for Jews of Yugoslav descent now living in Israel. Given the absentee nature of this kind of research, it turned out to be a dismal failure, with only one questionnaire returned. The individual who responded, however, is a well-known man who immigrated to Israel before the Second World War. In addition, I mailed a questionnaire to several individuals, six of whom completed and returned it to me. Lastly, demographic and sociocultural self-report data were gathered from a computer printout of the results of the survey conducted by the Federation in 1985.

Populational, social structural and cultural variables were all given considerable attention in trying to understand Yugoslav Jewish identities. Certainly, if demographic trends had been much different, it is highly probable that Jewish institutions and culture would have been affected differently. Population size, age structure, natural growth rate, and density were all variables that influenced the overall profile of the Jewish population and its capacity for ethnic maintenance and reproduction. Yet, taken either synchronically or diachronically, material and structural variables do not explain everything or even what is most important about this population.

I assumed at the outset that certain internal states and personal experiences of my informants, together with the competing sociocultural systems and ideologies with which they had contact, were the primary conditioning variables influencing individual identities. However, material and structural factors cannot be ignored. Most recently, political fragmentation and war must be included as critical factors that have influenced yet another transformation of Jewish identity.

In determining what were the significant features of Yugoslav Jewishness, I started with anthropologists who argue that there is something internal, call it a cognitive or mental orientation, a worldview, or an ontological and epistemological framework, that is the primary mover behind the actions and interactions of human beings. I departed from this notion of culture if and when it failed to accept the fact that individuals often deviate from the prescriptions and proscriptions located not only in their minds, but also in texts (including charters), oral traditions, myths, rituals, and formal and informal social relations. Some deviate more, some less. Some see their behavior as a deviation, while others do not. Perhaps the deviations themselves come to be incorporated internally into a shared consciousness, even if only in a dyadic relationship, and manifested externally through expressive cultural forms. To study the real world of deviations, I moved to an interpretive approach that examined individual variations of Jewish identity. That was the ethnographic reality of the Yugoslav Jews that I confronted.

The Organization of the Chapters

Chapter 1, "History and Identity," examines how collective identity was formed and informed by two kinds of history. There were the historical processes over which the Jews had little or no control but which contributed to transforming and shaping their identities. It is such a history that has produced irreversible effects. The second kind of history entailed a process whereby the postwar Jewish community rendered a past that could be accommodated with the history that was being written by the new rulers of socialist Yugoslavia. This latter history-making helped fashion Jewish identity out of various tangible and intangible elements.

Chapter 2, "Before and After the Holocaust" contrasts the prewar and post-Second World War population profiles of the Jewish population. It is suggested that a particular population profile can facilitiate or constrain the capacity for ethnic maintenance, transmission, and reproduction. Jewish identity is analyzed on the collective, familial, and individual levels. I demonstrate that, although fractures were already very apparent, particularly along generational lines, a pattern of structural integration continued to characterize Yugoslav Jewry before the Second World War. Truncation, in contrast to integration, was a post-Second World War pattern that reflected significant demographic decimation and sociocultural erosion on all three of these levels. Particularly striking in the case of the Yugoslav Jews was the absence of the specifically Jewish family and household, which traditionally linked the individual to the community. The truncated structure of the Yugoslav Jews, thus, reflected a much condensed organized community at the top, wide variation on the individual level, and a striking gap in the middle.

Chapter 3, "The Collective Voice of Submergence," describes the pattern of submergence that characterized the collective level of the population, the organized Jewish community. Submergence was a synthesis of features of the Jewish sociocultural system and the key symbols of the invented tradition of the socialist system, in which the former were subordinate to but perceived to be compatible with the latter. It involved participating simultaneously in constructing a socialist state and in creating a secular Jewishness. Submergence was the product of historical antecedents, a vulnerable demographic structure, sociocultural erosion, the process of societal transformation in a multiethnic state directed by a dominant political elite, and the direction of Jewish leaders sympathetic to the goals and values of the rulers of the new state.

Chapter 4 describes the Yugoslav Jewish community's "Experiment in Secular Jewishness." While submergence was a process of accommodation oriented to the state, the experiment in secular Jewishness was oriented to the community itself. The question was, can the Jewish community survive without its religious base? Given the highly secular nature of the community in socialist Yugoslavia, the conditions were in place to test for the "success" or "failure" of the experiment.

In contrast to chapters 3 and 4, which present the unified voice of submergence, chapter 5, "Voices of Yugoslav Jewry," presents a range of individual voices, some of which blended with the unified voice of submergence, but most of which were quite distinctive. Though distinctive, most were never heard as public voices. Through the individual narratives we can see how different individuals sought to solve the dilemmas of being (who am I?), knowing (how do I know?) and showing their Jewish identities. For many older Jews, experiences and memories of the past provided orientation for the present. It was by acts of traditional or secular commitment that some individuals affirmed or reaffirmed their Jewishness. For others, solving these dilemmas and coming to terms with their own identities involved a personal quest during which they appropriated or constructed private symbols of Jewishness. In some cases, when an individual engaged in cultural production (e.g., produced a text) or displayed his or her Jewishness in some other way, the once private symbols and themes became public ones. For all individuals, though in varying degrees, the source of Jewishness, the pursuit, selection and incorporation of Jewishness into their lives, and the product(s) of this process were necessarily fragmented.

Chapter 6, "Forward into the Past," examines the effect of the latest major political change on Jewish identity. Resurgence of Jewishness in its various forms, including those imposed from without, is the product of the transitional conditions that characterize the ongoing historical changes in the former Yugoslavia and eastern Europe as a whole. These conditions, which in this part of the world are associated with the demise of monolithic socialism and the proliferation of political, social, and economic crises, are fertile soil for ethnicities that exhibit increased diversity, visibility, ambiguity, escape, symbolic power of the weak, and confrontation over contested claims. When the political and symbolic orders of Tito's socialism, within which the organized community had chosen to submerge itself, began to erode, the community and individual Jews could not resist being influenced by the phase of transition that ensued. Resurgent ethnicity is essentially an anti-structural phenomenon, for it has neither an integrated Jewish tradition nor an intact socialist system to sustain it, and it reflects the instability of the present as it works its way toward an uncertain future.

Chapter 7, "Theoretical Musings: What is a (Yugoslav) Jew?", constitutes a self-designed labyrinth that allows me to wander across theoretical terrains in search of a more integrated understanding of the collective and individual self.

Although the book is a coherent unit, certain chapters can be read on their own terms. Chapter 5 is the flesh and spirit of the book, revealing from a range of individual narratives or "voices" the protean self of the Jews of Yugoslavia. If there is one chapter that can stand alone and speak to diverse readers, this is the one. For readers who are particularly interested in understanding the recent destruction of Yugoslavia, chapter 6 addresses issues of the collapse and how the historical processes associated with it have irreversibly affected the Jewish population. I have placed a discussion of the theoretical problems at the end of the book, in chapter 7, for readers who are interested in how the present study can be integrated with other works dealing with issues of self and identity.

1

HISTORY AND IDENTITY

> We are never more than the co-authors of our own narratives. Only in fantasy do we live what story we please. . . . We enter upon a stage which we did not design and we find ourselves part of an action that was not of our making (MacIntyre 1984: 213).

> I am [a] Jew from the older generation, soon to be the oldest. What little I know about Jewishness I received from religious parents. We heard about the history of the Jews in religion classes from the great rabbi Moric Levi, and our general orientation in Judaism we received in Hashomer Hatzair.[1] But much of that is forgotten (*Bilten* (JOS) 3 (1989):41).

There is the history that helps make the present, and there is the history that helps make the past. Both kinds of history, the history that actually happened and the history that is told, written, rewritten, displayed, reenacted, and used are essential to understanding Jewish identities at different times and places. Very real objective historical processes imposed themselves on the Yugoslav Jews, and the survivors among them in turn responded to the new conditions in which they found themselves in socialist Yugoslavia by selecting those elements from their past which could be refashioned in a manner that accommodated political and cultural goals. In the postwar period, they too helped coauthor the mythology of the New Yugoslavia, especially those narratives in which Jews played active roles in the National Liberation Struggle of 1941–1945. But they also chose to remember the horrors of history by ritually mourning those who did not survive the Holocaust. It is in such collective and also individual acts of mourning lost family members and friends that we can see that history is not just the construction of the present. Rather, using the words of one young Serbian writer, "sometimes time has irreversible effects" (Longinović 1996: 213). The Jews of postwar Yugoslavia, both the flesh-and-blood ones that I saw and knew and those I encountered in the texts of Yugoslav Jewish writers, "grappl[ed] with time and its irreversible effects on life" (ibid).

This chapter has several aims. The first is to present briefly the historical processes that were significant in shaping Jewish identities. I describe some of the major continuities and discontinuities, together with the uniformities and variations, in Jewish life across time and place on the territory which the state of Yugoslavia once occupied. However, it is not my intent to write a single history or multiple histories of Jewish life in this part of the Balkan Peninsula, nor would this endeavor fall within the scope and aim of the book.[2] The formation and expression of a collective Jewish identity during the socialist period entailed a process of selecting and emphasizing those historical elements that could be integrated into their new conceptions about their place in Yugoslav and Jewish history and in the new state. In this chapter I single out these elements and describe them more fully in the chapters that follow. Another aim of this chapter, also supporting my general argument that identity cannot be understood or even exist apart from history, is to claim that both Jewish commonality and difference can be understood with a narrative conception of history. There is a narrative, or story, that many Jews share. And, given the diasporic nature of the Jewish past and present, even within the Balkans, various Jewish settlements have been part of the narratives of other peoples. Thus, there are stories that we as single groups tell, and there are stories that several groups tell together. From this perspective it is easier to grasp identity as incorporating both difference and similarity.

Jews in the Balkans

The exact time and place of Jewish settlement in what became Yugoslavia is unknown. Different theories based on scraps of evidence found in various sources have been expounded. Although such evidence points to a Jewish presence during Greek domination, more solid material evidence based on archeological finds confirms permanent Jewish settlement during Roman rule (Mirć

1957–58). The Jews are, chronologically, a more indigenous ethnic population than the Slavic populations to this region, even though the distinctiveness of the ancient Oriental and Romaniot, and later, Byzantine, Jews was erased by the demographic and cultural vitality of Sephardi Jews who began settling there in the sixteenth century. With the above chronology in mind, the Jews cannot be considered a more foreign element, as strangers in the land of the South Slavs. However, chronology or time is not the only or strongest factor used in classifying populations as indigenous or foreign. Demographic composition and trends, power relations, wealth, and culture (including cultural goals and mythologizing the past to attain these goals) carry far greater weight in the construction of such cultural classifications and in determining place in such schemes. Given these factors over time, the Jews acted mainly as marginal players in the political, social, and economic spheres of society, though in certain urban areas they were far from marginal. Nevertheless, despite small numbers, low profile, and limited impact, their long continuous presence provided them with a sense of stability and legitimacy. They felt that they belonged and were a part of Yugoslav history. No one group has complete authorship of a historical narrative that can be called Yugoslav or Balkan history. As far as the Jews are concerned, they entered upon the Balkan stage at different times and began participating in the narratives of other peoples. Likewise, the other peoples participated in the ongoing Jewish narrative.

Various migrations from different points of origin have influenced immensely the course of Jewish history in what would become Yugoslavia in the twentieth century. Three branches of the Jewish people settled on this territory—Romaniot, Ashkenazi, and Sephardi.

The Romaniot branch of Jewry, which came from the Near East, was the first to settle in this area. Very little is known about Jews who lived on the Balkan Peninsula B.C.E. Of those who arrived with Roman expansion two thousand years ago, some may have been slaves while others followed Roman armies in order to flee persecution in Palestine and seek a better, quieter life elsewhere. It seems that once in the Balkans, the Jews were given freedom of movement. The archeological record suggests that they were not drawn to a single area. The best evidence of actual communal settlements come from Dalmatia, then the Roman colony of Illyricum, where the Roman emperor Diocletian had his summer palace, and from Macedonia, where they exhibited both Near

Eastern and Hellenistic features. In the Macedonian town of Bitolj the Jews were referred to as *Levantini* or *Mizrahi* ("from the East"). The latter became the surname of several Jewish families (Jevrejski Istorijski Muzej, 1978, 32). The significance of these findings and their presentation is that Jewish presence in this area since antiquity has been confirmed (see exhibit catalogues *Jevreji u Jugoslaviji* (1988) or *Jews in Yugoslavia* (English edition), 1989).

The Jews on what became Yugoslav territories lived in conditions that diverged from the general European patterns. For example, although the Jews in the Ottoman Empire belonged to the subordinate *raya* category, they lived under more tolerable conditions than did the Jews in the Habsburg Empire or Russia.[3] In fact, Jews from the north sought refuge in Ottoman lands from pogroms and persecutions inflicted by Crusade forces and local peoples. Later, the Ottoman Sultan Bayazid II welcomed the influx of Jewish refugees expelled from Spain and Portugal. It is significant that Jews did not flee from Ottoman lands to other regions. All of the above facts have not escaped the writers of postwar Yugoslav Jewish historiography, who have given high marks to the Ottoman rulers' treatment of the Jews. However, certain writers (e.g., Pinto, S. 1954; Pinto, A. 1986) have pointed out that Jewish life on the periphery of the Ottoman Empire, such as in Bosnia, depended largely on the disposition of local rulers towards the Jews. And it was not always favorable.

The influx of the Sephardi Jews expelled from Spain in 1492 and from Portugal a few years later was the most significant mass immigration of Jews into the Balkans. These Iberian Jews did not immigrate into a nation but rather into an empire of many ethnic peoples. The rulers of the Ottoman Empire welcomed these displaced Jews, knowing that their expansionist goals would benefit from the expertise that these Jews could provide them in critical areas such as munitions, medicine, trade, and administration. Those Jews already living in Ottoman lands were too few in number to make a significant contribution and did not have the specific skills and knowledge coveted by the Ottoman rulers.

In the Ottoman Empire the Jews, together with the Serbs and other Christian populations, were a *dhimmi* (protected minority community) people of the Book, subordinate to the dominant Muslims. The Muslim rulers gave local Jewish and other ethnoconfessional communities relative autonomy as long as they paid the necessary taxes and did not disrupt the Ottoman rule. Local communities governed themselves in more than just religious affairs.

Jewish communal courts handled cases involving all aspects of life. Individual Jews, however, were brought occasionally before Muslim *sheriat* courts, though not as witnesses. These cases were most often related to economic life (Levi 1969; Pinto 1954).[4] The Jews may have had an advantage over other populations because of the valued resources they provided the rulers. As elsewhere, here, too, they sought a close tie with the rulers. To facilitate this process the Jews and other subordinate peoples in the empire created "foundation myths" in an attempt to place themselves nearer to the Ottoman ruler and thereby secure their position and gain advantage in the multiethnic empire (Braude 1982).[5] As historian Harriet Pass Freidenreich points out, "Until the late nineteenth century, the Sephardi communities in Belgrade and Sarajevo displayed an extremely traditional and patriarchal character" (1979:6). These communities were close-knit, keeping most of their non-economic activities confined to the Jewish quarter. Although ethnic isolation had been strengthened by the Ottoman's theocractic system of rule, the Jews reinforced their separation by opting for isolation in a system that was not characterized by the European pattern of enforced ghetto settlement. These Jews were not forced to live in a sealed off ghetto. If they had the means, they were free to settle outside the concentrated Jewish quarter. By no means, however, were these Jews immune to the processes of cultural borrowing and acculturation. After all, they had not avoided secular learning while in Spain. Although they retained much of their Spanish heritage and followed the Judaic tradition, their life style had "become strongly influenced by the oriental environment" (ibid.). This was evident in their appearance, cuisine, dwellings, music, and vocabulary.[6]

The Jews were an urban rather than rural population, though their economic position as middlemen took them into the countryside. Before Serbian independence much of their competition came from other non-indigenous minorities, particularly from the Greeks and Armenians who, like the Jews, were engaged in trade and commerce and lived in the towns. The Serbian urban class had been wiped out by the Ottomans, and only began to re-form following the Serbian uprisings in the nineteenth century. With Serbian autonomy (1830) and, later, independence from Ottoman rule, the status of the Jews changed. Although some postwar Jews and Serbs depict a past Serbia as free of antisemitism, the Jews lived at the mercy of individual rulers who adopted, at times, anti-Jewish measures. Also, Serbian businessmen who feared Jewish economic competition initiated a campaign to rid the Serbian interior of Jewish settlement. As Freidenreich (ibid:31) notes, "None of these [discriminatory] laws applied to the Jews of Belgrade, who constituted more than half of the Jewish population of Serbia." However, she continues, "these unfortunate incidents did have a considerable effect on the Jewish community of Belgrade because, on the one hand, most of the Jewish businessmen who left the provincial towns came to the capital in generally impoverished circumstances, and on the other hand, some Jews left Belgrade at this time out of fear of possible future measures" (ibid.).

Although not restricted as to where they could settle, distinct settlement patterns nevertheless emerged. Jewish settlers tended to encapsulate themselves in quarters, particularly near the central business district. In time, residence patterns within cities reflected class differences among the Jews. For centuries the Jews of Belgrade lived in a quarter (*mahala* or, simply, *mala*) called Dorćol, located by the Danube river banks in the lower part of the city. The Jewish individual who was born or lived in this quarter is still affectionately referred to as "a child of Dorćol." Only a few such individuals remain alive. In time some of the economically more prosperous Jews began to move out of Dorćol and settle in higher parts of the city (Zerek) which were adjacent to or within the central business district or *čaršija*. In the Ladino language (Judeo-Spanish, Judezmo) the Jews of Dorćol were called *Los de abajo* ("those from below") and the Jews of Zerek and the *čaršija* as *Los de arriba* ("those from above") (Alkalaj 1961–1962). Thus, the spatial move of residence to a higher point in the city was considered a move of upward social mobility. Some of the living descendants of these Jews still live in Belgrade.

Ashkenazi Jews from the central and northern parts of Europe began arriving during the twelfth century. They fled persecution and intolerable conditions in the northern lands. The onset of the Crusades in the eleventh century, in particular, spurred such migration to the Balkan south. Ashkenazi migration to this region continued until the twentieth century. The greatest influx of Ashkenazi Jews occurred in the nineteenth century into Habsburg lands (Croatia, Slavonia, Vojvodina). Having been banished for more than two centuries, the Jews were permitted to return to these lands after Emperor Josif II issued the Edit of Toleration in 1781 (Freidenreich 1979:42; see also Glesinger 1954).

The place of the Jews in the Habsburg Empire was less secure than that of their mostly Sephardi counterparts in Ottoman lands.

As a subordinate ethnic and religious minority, they were tolerated and allowed to practice their religion. However, though situated outside the mainstream of society by external imposition and self-isolation, their internal communal affairs were more subject to state interference and control (Freidenreich 1979; see also Gross 1988). Unlike the Jews in the Ottoman Empire who shared a tolerated but subordinate religious status in the Muslim theocracy with the Slavic Orthodox and Catholic non-Muslim peoples, the Habsburg Jews lived with indigenous peoples who shared the Roman Catholic religion of the foreign rulers.

Most of the Ashkenazi Jews abandoned Yiddish and spoke the language(s) of the foreign rulers, that is, German and/or Hungarian. Prior to the onset of Jewish emancipation, the Jews in these territories tended to acculturate toward the ruling rather than the surrounding indigenous nations. This pattern changed following Jewish emancipation in the second half of the nineteenth century and during the struggle to consolidate civil rights and equality. Then the reference groups became the South Slavic host nations. One indicator of this reorientation was the slavicization of first names, especially for girls (Freidenreich 1979).

The Ashkenazi Jews in these territories were exposed to liberalization considerably earlier than were Jews in former Ottoman lands. One manifestation of this liberalizing trend was the religious split that developed within the Ashkenazim branch between the Neologues (Reformed) and the Orthodox. The latter was a small but dedicated minority. When the Federation of Jewish Religious Communities was established in 1919, they refused to join and formed their own association instead (Freidenreich 1979; *Spomenica,* 1969).

The contrast between Ottoman and Habsburg lands was great. They did not share a common history, except if one includes the numerous conflicts between the two great powers, especially in the border zone. The legacy of this split is visible today in a myriad of ways. It is visible in the divisions of religion, political values, historical memory, nationalistic expression, language, geographical orientation, and identity. It was one land mass and precariously remained one country composed of many different worlds and peoples until its final collapse in 1991 (ibid:1). In the past the Jews of different regions mirrored these divisions. Harriet Pass Freidenreich, whose historical description of interwar Yugoslav Jewry stimulated my interest in the diversity among Jews, expressed it best:

> This dichotomy [between the Sephardi and Ashkenazi Jews] mirrored to a certain extent the conflict between Serbs and Croats, the East and the West, which has always caused considerable tension within the country. Just as the Serbs accepted the Eastern Orthodox variant of Christianity and the influence of Byzantium, and the Croats accepted Catholicism and the dominance of Rome, so the Sephardim generally adopted the Babylonian model within Judaism and the Ashkenazim the Palestinian (ibid:7).

The prewar Jewish population was characterized by increasing class stratification. Overall, most Jews fell into the middle class, but there were also wealthy Jews (e.g., industrialists, bankers), working-class Jews, and a growing number of poor Jews. The increase in the Jewish poor seemed to alarm the community as a whole. Class polarization was particularly evident in the central region of Bosnia. Austrian occupation of Bosnia-Hercegovina prevented that region's economic conditions from deteriorating to the degree that they did in Macedonia. As a result of remaining within the underdeveloped Ottoman Empire until the Balkan Wars in 1912–1913, Macedonian Jewry was far more impoverished as a whole than Jews living in other regions. Of the 823 families living in Bitolj in 1932, 267 families were poor and 331 were in "utter poverty" (Oren 1971:54). This is yet another area of life in which the Jews reflected regional differences in Yugoslavia as a whole. To the Ashkenazi Jews of Croatia and the Vojvodina, the Sephardim of the Macedonian cities of Skopje and Bitolj were a cultural continent apart. Dr. Rudolph Buchwald, who was the General-Secretary of the Zionist Federation in Yugoslavia, wrote a report of his visit to these cities in 1936. The report was entitled,"Via the Jewish Neighborhoods of Southern Serbia." He saw that world in the following way:

> I encountered them amid a volume of tongues and multiplicity of folk styles, . . . amidst the horrendous noise of the Levant. . . . These Jews walked around amid all this, wearing their kaftans and fezes, with a special kind of nobility. . . . These Jews who were so strange and yet so dear and near. . . . They were recipients of the influences of various cultures that penetrated the area—whether of Byzantium and Hellenism . . . or the Turkish and the Albanian, whether

> the Serbian or the Bulgarian. Each of them leaving behind a residue and having inscribed its impression on them. Nevertheless they preserved their unique qualities as Jews and fashioned a special Jewish type that exists nowhere else the wide world over (Buchwald 1936:36, quoted in Oren 1971:58).

Both Bosnia and Macedonia had been important administrative and trade centers during earlier historical periods. The fate of these centers followed the decay and collapse of the imperial powers that controlled them. Many Macedonian Jews chose emigration as a solution. Another deciding factor in Bosnia, in particular, after its occupation by Austria in 1878, was the transformation of political economy. For example, the numerous artisans of the region who had practiced their crafts for generations found themselves on the periphery of economic development after the introduction of industrial capital and of a new system of government. Migrating into Bosnia following the occupation were significant numbers of Ashkenazi Jews from mostly Slavic speaking Central European lands. Having been under the Austrian system and speaking German, these new arrivals were immediately prepared to contribute to the capitalistic and administrative development of the region. From the beginning a class division along Ashkenazi and Sephardi lines began to develop. The poor Jews belonged to the Sephardi branch. The class division was reinforced by the tendency of the Sephardi and Ashkenazi Jews to establish independent communal organizations and synagogues (Freidenreich 1979).

It is important to add that Jews helped other Jews through the charitable support distributed through social welfare and ritual organizations, patron-client relationships, and through the contributions of money, food, and clothing provided by individuals and families. Some of these gifts were distributed periodically by way of customs associated with certain holidays or festivals. No repayment was required, although the giver and receiver shared a tacit understanding that once the latter became established or raised out of impoverishment he, too, would become a giver. This generalized form of reciprocity was practiced in the community. Jews who could not afford to pay the communal tax were exempted. Another effort aimed at the poor Jews, particularly those of Macedonia, was to campaign for funds that would enable them to resettle in Palestine (see Oren 1971).

Balkan Jewry

An American folklorist has written a comprehensive study of a Balkan Jewish population. In *From Sofija to Jaffa: The Jews of Bulgaria and Israel*, a book which follows Bulgarian Jewry from the first century to their present lives in Israel, Guy Haskell (1994) provides a sweeping history of these Jews. He devotes separate chapters to the pre-Ottoman period, the Ottoman (1389–1878) and post-Ottoman periods (1878–1940), and the war years (1940–1944). Haskell relies for this historical description on written sources, which he approaches critically, as well as on informants. Most of the ethnographic focus, however, is on Bulgarian Jews now living in Israel. One of Guy Haskell's theoretical aims is to derive what he calls the "components of [Bulgarian and Bulgarian-Israeli] identity." Reflecting on my own preparation and initial fieldwork, I believe that my original aim was similar to Haskell's—to derive a set of features of Yugoslav Jewish identity. What I found, however, is something other than what I would call "the components of Yugoslav Jewish identity." Where the present work converges with Haskell's is in showing how "pivotal collective experiences . . . have influenced the identity of the group as a whole. . . . paying careful attention to those events, ideas, and cultural transformations that influence ethnic identity [in the present]" (Haskell 1994:72). Although the present study shares with Haskell's the general aim of describing and explaining transformations of the identities of a Balkan Jewish population, our historical and ethnographic approaches and emphases diverge considerably. We have written complementary but very different books on two Jewish populations that occupy the place of footnotes in Jewish historiography.

Guy Haskell provides a more comprehensive historical treatment of Bulgarian Jewry than the present study does of Yugoslav Jewry. I thus recommend that readers seeking a fuller historical understanding of Balkan Jewry as a whole, as seen through the anthropological lens, read *From Sofija to Jaffa*. It should be noted, however, that Haskell argues for the uniqueness of the Jews of Bulgaria. Hence, readers should proceed cautiously when attempting to generalize from Bulgarian Jewry to other Jewish populations in the Balkans. This caution certainly applies to the Jews of Yugoslavia, whose histories both converge with and diverge from the history of Bulgarian Jewry. Thus, I suggest that Haskell's historical rendering should be read together with works that focus specifically on Yugoslavia, such as Harriet Pass Freidenreich's *The Jews of Yugoslavia.*

Haskell writes, "Although Bulgarian Jewry shares many historical and cultural features with other Balkan Sephardim, its singular demographic make-up and historical experience created a people whose attitudes, culture, and relationship to gentile society were unique, and resulted in the dramatic cultural and social transformations and events during the last century which have no parallel in Jewish social and political history." Were they in fact unique in this regard? Certainly, Ottoman rule over Bulgaria, Serbia, and Bosnia created many similar conditions for its Jewish communities. As a people of the Book, the Jews were a protected religious minority. Furthermore, as city dwellers, they sustained more contact with the other urbanites, the Muslim rulers and other ethnic minorities, than they did with the indigenous Christian populations in the countryside. At times, the indigenous Slavs associated Jews with the Muslim rulers, which sometimes led to Jewish flight. As Haskell notes, the Ottoman rulers "provided its Jewish population with a measure of security and protection unmatched anywhere in Christian Europe" (ibid:77). The large number of Sephardim were welcomed by Sultan Bayazid into the empire. Moreover, they entered when the empire was at its peak. As the empire began to erode after the sixteenth century, many of its Jewish communities also experienced a loss of vigor. Perhaps more than Bulgarian Jewry, who lived closer to the Ottoman center, Serbian and particularly Bosnian Jews lived on the periphery of the eroded empire and were more likely to fall victim to the capricious whims of local rulers. But the Jews of Bulgaria and other regions were not exempt from such threats. Haskell tells us that "[w]ith the decline of Ottoman power came a decline in Ottoman tolerance, and several discriminatory decrees were issued restricting Jewish rights. In 1592 and 1598, Prince Michael of Wallachia crossed the Danube and laid waste Vidin, Pleven, and Nikopol. Nikopol was burned to the ground, in Vidin two synagogues were destroyed, and both communities were decimated" (ibid:82). In Serbia, too, Belgrade changed hands several times between the Ottomans and Habsburgs in various wars, and the city's Jews inevitably suffered from both sides. Haskell is perhaps right on target when he writes that with the decline of and corruption in the Empire "a general malaise set in among the Jews of the Balkans" (ibid:82). At this time the once potent Sephardi culture brought from the Iberian Peninsula, which integrated religious and non-religious components began its own decline. In his book Haskell proceeds to show how the Jews of Bulgaria filled the vacuum in Jewish life created by what he specifies as a spiritual and educational decline (ibid:84).

If we compare Bulgarian and Serbian Jewry, we may find that some of the uniqueness claimed for Bulgarian Jewry withers away. Unlike Bulgaria's homogeneous Jewish population, however, Serbia had distinctive Sephardi and Ashkenazi populations, and for purposes of comparison of the kind Haskell invites we must keep them separate. On the whole, Sephardi and Ashkenazi communities in Belgrade were not only different because of separate institutions, but also because of how their members saw the Serbs and in turn how the Serbs saw them. When Serbs referred to the Jews of Serbia as *naši Jevreji* ("our Jews"), they had mainly Sephardi Jews in mind. Thus, the Sephardi experience in Belgrade was similar to that of Bulgarian Jewry in terms of general acceptance by both ethnic populations in Bulgaria and in Serbian Belgrade.

The Ethnogenesis of the Yugoslav Jewish Community

Based on the Law on the Jewish Religious Community established in 1929, the Jews in interwar Yugoslavia "formally constituted a state-recognized religious body patterned on the Central European model" (Freidenreich 1979:72). The Law of 1929 defined the duties of the Sephardi, Neologue, and Orthodox religious communities.[7] It also legalized Jewish holidays for Jews in government service and the military, and for Jewish students. Individual Jews could belong to the Sephardi, Neologue Ashkenazi, or Orthodox Religious Community. Membership, in theory, was "compulsory by law for all adherents of the Jewish faith residing in the country. . . . Withdrawal . . . was possible only by conversion to another religion or by moving elsewhere" (ibid:73). Even before the war, however, not everyone was a member of one of these communities. Despite this fact it remains that before the war, religion was the primary distinguishing marker of ethnic descent for both Jews and non-Jews. The two were often synonymous identifications. Even Jews who sought national integration with larger nationalities retained their Jewish religious affiliation. They called themselves "Serbs (or Croats) of the Mosaic faith." Although legally the Jews constituted a religious community, the state recognized them as a national minority with the right to establish various institutions and associations (Vajs 1954).

Although there was considerable acculturation and even assimilation between the world wars, the Jews of that period can be distinguished from other populations on more than just religious criteria. Structurally, they represent a demographic and socioeconomic contrast to other populations. The Jews were urbanites while their host populations were predominately rural and peasant. Despite representing less than half of one percent of the total population, their urban presence was as high as twenty times that percentage, thus giving them a voice in municipal politics and economics. In some cities their presence was sufficiently strong to influence the balance of power on certain political issues. The occupational distributions of Jews and non-Jews reflected the urban-rural dichotomy. Whereas 76 percent of the active non-Jewish population were engaged in agriculture, forestry, and fishing, only a minuscule 0.6 percent of the Jewish population were associated with these occupational categories. Fifty-nine percent of the active Jewish population fell within the category of commerce, credit, and communication, but only four percent of the non-Jewish population did so. Proportionately, Jews were represented twice as high in the category of public services, free professions, and military, although relatively few pursued military careers (Freidenreich 1979:219). In contrast to the other populations, the Slovenes excluded, the Jews enjoyed near universal literacy. Because of their declining birthrate during the twentieth century, Jewish children were not overrepresented in the elementary schools, but in higher education Jewish students were overrepresented in medicine, law, engineering, philosophy, and music (ibid:64–66).

The Shared Features of Yugoslav Jewry

The Jews of Yugoslavia in all of their diversity have shared certain commonalities with one another and together constitute a part of the wider collectivity called the Jewish People—*Am Israel.* For many, perhaps most, this unifying feature of peoplehood, which can also be understood as the narrative or story of the Jews, overrides the numerous differentiating features within Jewry (Elazar 1989). But as Anthony Cohen (1985) demonstrates in *The Symbolic Construction of Community*, underneath shared symbols such as the "Jewish People" or the "Jewish Community" or even "Jewish

Narrative" is found a wide range of meanings carried by individual members and subgroups, as each interpretation is mediated by a different set of social statuses, experiences, and locations. Furthermore, it cannot be overlooked that the Jewish narrative(s) unfolded and overlapped with the narratives of other peoples. No one people writes its own complete story. To understand this basic commonality of peoplehood, thus, we must begin with the understanding that there exists often bewildering complexity and difference beneath the shared symbolic forms. While acknowledging the mediating processes involved in the construction of the symbolic community, that is a community united more by integrative symbols than social institutions, it can be shown that the Jewish community is unified by the written and ongoing narrative that is Jewish history. It is a community that has lived and is continuing to live a story. But as stated earlier, no one can boast of complete authorship of such a narrative (see MacIntyre 1984). Moreover, different peoples participate in each other's narratives, and thus every group is part of multiple narratives. Keeping this in mind we cannot speak about an unconstrained refashioning of identity.

We can examine several elements of the historical narrative of the Jewish people. First of all, the written account itself—from the selection of the founding ancestor to tribal development, the giving of the law, and state development—not only serves as a charter and model for behavior, but it also tells a story. The story is not just a medium through which to communicate moral principles, but to describe people, events, social transformations, displacements, defeats, victories, and suffering. That the text itself, that which contains the story, retains its significance for the remnant of practicing religious Jews of Belgrade is evident in various forms and activities, perhaps most dramatically on Simhat Torah,[8] when the Torah scrolls are paraded around the synagogue and are touched and kissed by the congregants. Through their reenactment in such rituals the different events in the story have been remembered. The Simhat Torah rituals highlight God giving the Law to the Jewish people and the people delighting in the Law. I witnessed this reenactment in the highly secular Belgrade community. Even there the ritual flame had not been entirely extinguished. The written account provides a description of the ritually sealed covenant between God and this People. Many Jews continue to believe that the covenant gave the Jews a messianic purpose and mission, although their interpretations of the purpose vary according to beliefs and political orientations. Others try to explain away this purpose by substituting materialist or other interpretive methodologies. What is significant despite the spectrum of belief and unbelief is the ritual, spiritual, or at least conceptual, hold that this convenant has had and continues to have over the Jewish People, including those few members who lived in Yugoslavia and now live in its successor states. This I found to be true even for those who might describe themselves as agnostic or atheist in relation to the Jewish Charter (Torah and Tanakh). They responded that knowing they are the descendants of Abraham is important to them and that they "continue to feel the imprint of the covenant." Jewish activist and past president of the Zagreb Jewish community, Slavko Goldstein, a secular oriented Jew, more than acknowledged the importance of the Bible when he wrote:

> Only the original source, the Bible, is incontestable. In the Old Testament are rooted the powerful myths of one, almighty Lord, of the chosen people, of the Covenant with God, of the promised land, of the Messiah who was to come when it was the most necessary. When the disbelief of recent times diluted the power of religion and myth, their place was taken by the power of biblical history, literature, philosophy, the moral code. Never exhausted and ever open to new interpretations, the Bible has become the Book for all times and of all nations but above all, it has remained the Book of the people that made it and founded on it their cult of the Book (Goldstein 1989:13).

Anthropological observers of Jewish ethnicity concur with Goldstein regarding the Jewish charter. Handelman and Handelman (1990:195) have commented that "the most enduring and influential template of [model for] Jewish culture is the Hebrew Bible, together with related commentaries, liturgies, legends, folk traditions, and festivals. They constitute a corpus of knowledge and experience, . . . encoded in the Hebrew Bible."

The story is incomplete without the sacred landscape of the Promised Land, Palestine, Israel. This part of the story as told from within the land or in exile or diaspora has remained significant for millennia. Jews carried with them into the Balkan Diaspora a nostalgic sentiment for the ancient Jewish state and the hope of rebirth, long before the mass Zionist movements of the twentieth century. In Yugoslavia this sentiment was dramatically demonstrated by the story about a Sarajevo rabbi by the name of Rav

Danon, who died in Hercegovina in the nineteenth century on route to Palestine.[9] His grave is the only one in the area, and on the anniversary of his death Bosnian Jewish pilgrims traveled to the site and held a *limud*.[10] Such pilgrimages continued well after the Second World War. Other pre-Zionist accounts demonstrate the nostalgic or mystical tie to the land. The Zemun rabbi Jehuda Alkalaj, for example, has been called a forerunner of Zionist orientation.[11] The story of Rav Danon is a story about movement toward the land; it is about going back, unlike exile, which highlights the opposite condition of not being in or not moving toward the land. This is often referred to as the exilic condition, which may involve movement away from the land, displacement, and de-territorialization. This condition continued to be felt and was manifested in the statements of the Jews of postwar Yugoslavia. One community leader spoke about carrying that ancient fate. Another noted how the Jews are classified as *neki drugi* ("someone else") or *nešto drugo* ("something else") (Albahari 1990). The Jews' historical statuses, or lack of them, raise important anthropological questions concerning how groups that experience de-territorialization and dislocation become categorized in the "national order of things" (see Malkki 1995).

Jewish customs and symbolic activities are closely tied to the Jewish religion. It is extremely difficult to express Jewishness without using or invoking such symbols. Secular Yugoslav Jews acknowledged that, even though they themselves are not religious, religious symbols and institutions like the synagogue are important for the maintenance of both Jewish life and identity. It is worth noting that the survival of Jewish communities is associated with the presence of some semblance of religious practice, though there may be Yugoslav Jewish individuals who may disagree with this thesis.[12] One secular Jewish leader acknowledged that "the only thing that can save the [Yugoslav Jewish] ethnic group is *religion*." The Jewish community of socialist Yugoslavia can be classified as predominantly secular, but a tiny practicing religious remnant remained. It is impossible to state what the Yugoslav Jewish community would have been without such a remnant, but there is some evidence that suggests Jewish existence cannot thrive or even continue without any Jewish ritual. The case of Chinese Jewry suggests that the loss of Jewish religious practices was associated with the complete assimilation of the Chinese Jews into their host society. Rhee (1973) hypothesized that Jewish entrance into the civil service, which required the adoption of Confucianism, contributed to the attenuation of the Judaic religion in China. Although the Yugoslav Jews had not broken completely with religious practice and symbolic forms, their conscious orientation toward secularism provided sufficient conditions for "testing" whether their "experiment in secular Jewishness" had successfully replaced Judaism. At the same time we must acknowledge that the presence of religious life, however contracted and neglected, can fulfill functions of ethnic preservation and thus help to ensure continuity.

A Persistent People

The Jews are an ancient people whose history continues to unfold. As a people, they have not been reduced to "writing history." The Jews are a persistent people that have survived generation after generation for four thousand years despite the absence of a Jewish state and despite restrictions and persecutions of various kind and scale in the lands where they settled following the last great dispersion that began with the destruction of Jerusalem and the Second Temple in 70 C.E. Spicer (1971) has argued that such opposition is the primary ingredient that characterizes a persistent people. Certainly opposition has been a ubiquitous feature of Jewish life. Whether or not the oppositional process was the primary factor behind the persistence of the Yugoslav Jews is examined below. It is sufficient to state here that opposition in its more coercive and violent forms was not the factor it was elsewhere in Europe, with the exception of the years 1941–1945. What is certain is that Jews have persisted continuously for about two thousand years on the territory that became Yugoslavia. On that basis alone they can be described as a persistent people.

The Jews are a historical people also in the sense that their view of the world is historical rather than cosmological (Berger 1967). Specific historical events and persons define this general historical orientation. To the Jews, Abraham, Moses and Jacob certainly have more substance than Hercules, Perseus, and Agamemnon. It is, thus, more difficult to conceive the Jewish people in Berger's terms, as a "mythologically conceived collectivity" (ibid:117–118). I do, however, see grounds for defining the Jews of Yugoslavia, on one level, as a "conceptual community" or a "symbolic community" (Cohen 1985).

The Significant Materials of Yugoslav Jewish Identity

Significance is defined as those elements in the past that the Yugoslav Jews themselves considered important for conceptualizing Jewishness and reconstructing a Jewish community in the postwar years. They were the elements that the Yugoslav Jews, selected and then displayed in various forms. I elicited such significant elements, the materials out of which a postwar collective identity was fashioned, from published chronologies, publication topics, museum and exhibit topics, interviews, and cultural performances; that is, from what they have said or written, what they have done, and what they have displayed. A sampling of such elements would include: transformational events (e.g., wars), social movements (e.g., Zionist movement, Communist movement), ideologies (e.g., fascism, Titoist socialism, nationalism).

The Yugoslav Jews reflected their own internal diversity and the external diversity of the various foreign rulers and indigenous peoples with whom they came into contact. In the words of one community leader, the Yugoslav Jews "resemble the rest of the Yugoslavs. Just as contemporary Yugoslavia still carries the stamp of its history, its cultural traditions and the material civilization of the Ottoman Empire, Austro-Hungarian Empire, and the Venetian Republic, so the Yugoslav Jews carry the fading marks of Sephardi and Ashkenazi cultures, through which [the following] levels of influence clearly were deposited: Serbian enlightenment, Croatian Illyrianism, Hungarian regeneration, the Young Turk movement, emancipation, national awakening and liberation. And also: the Holocaust and racist persecutions which were repulsed and destroyed in the National War of Liberation with the noticeable contribution of Yugoslav Jewry" (Mošić 1987:45).

2

BEFORE AND AFTER THE HOLOCAUST

> Sometimes I think we are the last Jews in this city, the four of us. . . . [One] can't raise a family here anymore. Children no longer have a basic orientation in life. No longer can you teach them what a street is, what a square is, what a courtyard is . . . and if there is no system, then there also is no family. Do you know what held the Jews together? The family. A system. Law. Torah. And where are Jews disappearing? In places where there is no Torah. . . . When I was young, I lived for Shabbat. But who celebrates Shabbat today? Who lights candles today? Therefore I say that we probably are the last Jews in the city. When I enter your home I sense that scent of the family which disappeared from my nostrils long ago . . . (Albahari 1983:116).

Throughout Jewish history in the Balkans population change resulting from natural growth and decline, migration, war, displacement, and natural disaster has occurred, but none has rivaled the catastrophic change that struck the Jews during the years 1941–1945 when an ideologically motivated population policy of genocide was implemented. Demographically and socioculturally, these years mark the before and after period of Yugoslav Jewish existence.

The pre- and post-Second World War patterns of ethnicity are compared and contrasted in this chapter. In so doing the sudden impact of the historical imposition of genocide upon the Jews is seen as the major event that nearly obliterated a small but vital population and left it vulnerable to larger and more powerful forces operating at war's end. Relatedly, by comparing the population profiles of the two historical periods, before and after the Holocaust, we can see more sharply how population variables constrained the process of communal regeneration. In short, in this chapter the following questions are asked: What kind of Jewish existence was supported by the population profile of prewar Yugoslav Jewry? How was Jewish culture maintained, reproduced, and transmitted? Given demographic change of cataclysmic proportion and the impact of political transformation, what kind of ethnic responses became possible and which were selected within the parameters of the postwar population profile?

Although the primary aim of this chapter is to show the structural effects of disjuncture and massive dislocation, the secondary aim is to demonstrate that there was significant continuity in political orientation between the prewar and postwar periods. A discernible movement to the political left was occurring among the younger generation of Jews and thereby creating a capacity for submergence into the future socialist state. The actual process and structure of submergence is described in the following chapter.

Population Profiles

Prewar and postwar population profiles are described and contrasted according to demographic profile, sociocultural composition and integration, and degree to which particular ethnic markers remained intact or had eroded. Sociocultural composition refers to (1) social units and spheres of activity, (2) ritual-symbolic markers associated with time and space, people, events, rituals, and objects, and (3) ideational components such as beliefs, values, and cultural goals. A tri-level model is used to assist in conceptualizing sociocultural composition and degree of integration on and across the collective, familial, and individual levels of the Yugoslav Jewish population.[1]

The forms, capacity for, and extent of sociocultural reproduction, maintenance, and transmission are important factors to consider when examining structures and processes of identity formation and transformation. How did each of the two radically different population profiles of the Yugoslav Jewish community—the integrated, multi-institutional, and multi-ideological prewar pattern and the truncated, eroded, uni-institutional, and uni-ideological postwar pattern that emerged in the aftermath of the Holocaust—facilitate or constrain ethnic maintenance, transmission, and reproduction?

Prewar Demographic Composition and Trends

It is impossible to describe a stable population profile from the day Jews began arriving in this part of the Balkan Peninsula to the eve of World War II. As described earlier, Jews arrived at different times and from different places, settling under different rulers and political conditions. Here I will describe briefly the population profile of pre-Second World War, especially interwar,Yugoslav Jewry and will show that the prewar profile provided a greater capacity to support a traditional, albeit increasingly a secularized and identity-oriented Jewishness. All three levels of the Jewish community—collective, familial, and individual—were integrated, even as strain from internal and external pressures was apparent and various social and ideological fractures were gradually transforming the population.

At its height the population size of Yugoslav Jewry numbered about 76,000, rather small compared to Jewish populations in neighboring lands. The actual number of Jews in Yugoslavia on the eve of the Second World War swelled to about 82,000 after the influx of Jewish refugees from Central Europe. This Balkan territory once again became a refuge for Jews fleeing intolerable conditions in northern lands, but this time the refuge was to be short-lived for fascism traveled south quickly. The indigenous population of 76,000 was dispersed throughout the country, with the largest percentages, in ranked order, living in interior Croatia and Slavonia, Vojvodina, Bosnia and Hercegovina, Serbia, and Macedonia. Forty percent of the Jewish population lived in the cities of Zagreb (Croatia), Belgrade (Serbia), and Sarajevo (Bosnia). Considerable Jewish settlements existed in Bitolj (Macedonia), Novi Sad (Vojvodina), Subotica (Vojvodina), Osijek (Slavonia), and other towns.

Virtually all of the Jews lived in cities and larger towns, whereas 80 percent of the indigenous populations were peasants engaged in agriculture, forestry, and fishing (Freidenreich 1979:219). This contrast made the visibility and contribution of Jews in urban life and development especially evident. As late as 1940 when Jews comprised only 0.46 percent of the total Yugoslav population, they comprised 4.2 percent of the population of Belgrade, 5.8 percent of the population of Zagreb, 9.1 percent of the populations of Sarajevo and Bitolj, 6.4 percent of the population of Novi Sad, and 5.4 percent of the population of Subotica (*Spomenica,* 1970:80). Thus, absolute population size alone may not be most indicative of the kind and intensity of ethnicity maintained and displayed by a population. Other factors, examined below, such as relative size in urban areas and economic concentration, tell us more about the relative vitality and integration of Jewish sociocultural life before the devastation of war and genocide struck this population.

Population size and concentration did not remain stable until steady growth ensued toward the end of the nineteenth century. Jewish settlements long had been exposed to the vicissitudes of nature and to numerous human interventions. Floods, fires, epidemics, illnesses, wars, evacuations, and forced resettlements intervened to disrupt demographic and sociocultural composition at different points in time. The Jews of Belgrade occupied an especially vulnerable position, living in a low part of the city, *Jalija,*[2] which occasionally received the flood waters of the Danube River. Even more dangerous and consequential for demographic and sociocultural stability was Belgrade's strategic position between the Ottoman and Habsburg Empires. Belgrade passed hands from the Turks to the Austrians, and then back again to the Turks. Every time a military change would occur, a change in the status of the Jews would follow. Such vulnerability was not conducive to steady growth or stability. In the nineteenth century when the Serbs revolted against the Ottoman Turks and won a measure of independence, Jewish existence was affected by the favorable and unfavorable policies of individual rulers (Vinaver 1955–1956; Kovačević 1959–1960; Pinto, S. 1954).

Before the Second World War, Macedonian Jewry was reduced drastically. Having become relatively impoverished as a consequence of the decline of the Ottoman Empire and the political turmoil in the region (e.g., Balkan Wars, World War I), many of these Jews emigrated to the United States, Chile, and Argentina. Bitolj alone had a population of over 7,000 reduced to under 4,000 by such outmigration (Freidenreich 1979).

Prewar Population Profile and Ethnic Capacity

Certain writers contend that until the emancipation of the Jews the Jewish religion as practiced in the diaspora made all Jews socially and culturally more alike than different (Elazar 1989). Even after emancipation in the latter half of the nineteenth century and following its political and organizational unification immediately after the formation of Yugoslavia in 1918, the Jewish population as a whole was characterized by diversity and division by political orientation, ethnic branch, religious rite, language, class, and customs. Despite such internal variation the Jewish religion continued to distinguish the Jews from all the surrounding peoples and provided the mechanisms by which Jewish tradition was maintained, reproduced, and could be transmitted to the next generation, even though a significant generational shift away from that tradition became especially pronounced in the decade leading up to the Second World War. On the other hand, as noted in a memorial volume published by the postwar Federation of Jewish Communities of Yugoslavia, there was also a (perhaps modest) return to religion in the late 1930s (*Spomenica*, 1970). An increasing number of Jewish lives, particularly among the youth, no longer were guided by the prescriptions and proscriptions of the Judaic religion. Nevertheless, the critical point in regard to ethnic capacity is that the ritual-symbolic order and the religious infrastructure that undergirded that order were strained but intact, integrated across three levels of the population, and available to all Jews who desired to participate in Jewish rituals. They even touched the lives of the youth and intellectuals who opted for new forms of Jewishness, such as the Zionist-Marxist synthesis propagated by Hashomer Hatzair. In short, Jewish identity was integrated insofar as the structural supports were in place, as were the ritual-symbolic markers, on all three levels of the Jewish community. Moreover, a significant proportion of this integrated collectivity remained to keep Jewish tradition viable for the current generation and probably for the next had not war intervened. With regard to ritual-symbolic activities, particular attention was paid to rites and customs associated with the domains of kinship, commensality, and purification, and religious rites in general. In actual practice these domains are not exclusive. Each of the three levels is discussed next.

The Collective Level

Population size was not the most important variable before the war, although it certainly contributed to sociocultural composition and manifestation. For example, the larger prewar Jewish population and communities allowed their members to add to and elaborate on their material culture. As Freidenreich (1979) notes, the record of interwar Yugoslav Jewry indicates positive expansion of communal activities. Although individual communities faced financial crises before the war, the Yugoslav Jews as a whole sustained themselves by their own revenues collected by means of taxation, payments for ritual services, and donations. They were not dependent on foreign Jewish support. Expansion sometimes proceeded in spite of real financial difficulties, as when the Sarajevo Sephardi community forged ahead with plans to construct a large synagogue, a massive undertaking in 1930. Also, the wealthier regions helped to sustain the poorest communities located in the central and southern regions of the country. It is also worth noting that the Yugoslav Jewish community as a whole, via the Federation of Jewish Religious Communities of Yugoslavia, supported several thousand refugees from Central Europe in the 1930s. Although small in absolute number, this was a population that was extremely well organized and able to deal with the social needs of its poorer communities and individual members.

The communities supported full-time rabbis and other specialists. There was a chief rabbinate and two rabbinical synods (Neologue and Orthodox) in the country. In the larger cities several synagogues operated. In Bitolj alone before World War I eight could be found. Four were destroyed, including the central synagogue, *Kahal Kadosh Portugal* (Oren 1971:49). In Sarajevo eight synagogues operated between the wars, seven Sephardi and one Ashkenazi (*The Jews in Yugoslavia*, 1989, 73). Burial societies (Hevra Kaddisha) for both men and women performed functions associated with death, charity, and even exchange in marriage. Larger institutions such as schools and even a hospital and an old-age home were built and maintained.

Various voluntary organizations were created to meet the diverse social needs, cultural interests, and ideological orientations of the population. In Belgrade and Sarajevo, for example, about fifteen such organizations operated between the wars (ibid:88–89). Various newspapers and magazines were published. The Yugoslav Jewish community was thus a multi-institutional population. As its members began to be attracted to and accepted secular ideologies alongside the Judaic religion, it became, also, in Parkin's (1974) terms, a multi-ideological collectivity. That there was considerable variation allowed within the state during the interwar period certainly contributed to the variation exhibited within the organizational framework of the Jewish population. Various conflicts took place between various segments of the population, such as between assimilationists and Zionists and the so-called traditionalists and progressives.

Before the Second World War many ethnic markers were still present on the collective level, though change was occurring at varying rates in different regions of the country, which influenced the degree of intactness or erosion of these markers. In the Sephardi communities of Bosnia and Macedonia traditional life remained strong until the Second World War. One indicator of their cultural conservatism was the low degree of linguistic acculturation. In Macedonia and Bosnia, Ladino continued to be spoken by most or many Jews (Freidenreich 1979). Universal participation in ritual activities, however, had become a practice of the past, and certain ritual activities were being discarded or left to the older generation. In fact, in the Sephardi community of Sarajevo there seemed to be only two extremes, the observant older generation and the non-observant youth generation. Perhaps one exception to this generational split in Sarajevo was the experiment of liberalization conducted by the transplanted Bulgarian rabbi, Abraham Kapon, who introduced choir singing during silent congregational prayer. Thus, the temple in which he served earned the nickname *Il Kal di los Mudos*—the Synagogue of the Mute. Rabbi Kapon introduced other modern elements into his services. For example, the women in attendance no longer had to sit behind a thick grating. Reflecting his influence, his temple was also referred to as the *Il Kal de Kapon*—the Kapon Synagogue. Typically, the ritual observance of the Sephardim of Serbia and Bosnia was more traditional than that of the Jews of former Habsburg lands. The Sephardi mode of modernization was reflected in external forms such as the architecture of their synagogues (Freidenreich 1979:87). Meanwhile, in the Neologue communities of Croatia and Vojvodina, a larger percentage of Jews were non-observant. The largest synagogue in Zagreb had a seating capacity of only three hundred in a community of about ten thousand Jews. Even in Neologue strongholds like Zagreb, however, Neologue religious liberalism did not go uncriticized. An article in the Zagreb Jewish press condemned changes in the main synagogue as "sinful" (Heim 1919, quoted in Freidenreich 1979:89–90). The author wrote:

> Last Saturday there was a religious service in our synagogue with a completely new face: for minutes a man could think that he was in some parish church, and not in a Jewish synagogue. The *haftorah* [prophetic portion] was read silently and not recited aloud, and at that time—they played the organ, either to increase the impression that one was in church or to amuse the congregation which was bored. *Tefila* [the standing prayer] was not repeated, but

> the cantor also read silently—or didn't read, who would know? And then most important the reading of the Torah [Bible] was cut in half . . . (ibid.).

Zagreb's small Orthodox community maintained a distinctive identity and organizational structure. The life of the community was governed by ritual prescriptions and proscriptions. A member of the community was not permitted to occupy a communal position if he did not "keep the Sabbath and holidays according to the *Shulhan Arukh*," if he did not "maintain ritual bathing practices as in the *Shulhan Arukh*," or if he "made use of non-Orthodox Jewish facilities, such as butchers, synagogues, etc., " and he could not vote if his wife did not cover her own hair (Freidenreich 1979:75).

What characterized the collective level was not solely persistence or change but rather the general persistence of tradition and change in the forms of sociocultural strain and erosion, particularly among the young, and of conscious secular reformulation or abandonment for a secular ideology.

The Familial Level

Until the outbreak of World War II the Jewish family was intact and linked the individual to the community. Thus, the inclusion of the family as a viable unit of the tri-level model reflected a pattern of integration, which can be contrasted with the truncated pattern that came to characterize the postwar collectivity following the virtual destruction of this institution. The presence, function, and strength of the family as a specifically Jewish unit of ritual and cultural transmission were the basis for an integrated pattern of Jewishness. Children of less- or non-observant households usually had friends belonging to other households whose members were ritually observant and served as cultural models for them. Even non-traditional households usually were not without a few ethnic markers, such as foods and special meals. If nothing else, all members of the household were Jews and social relations extended to other Jews, both friends and shopkeepers. This was especially true for Jews living in Jewish quarters and neighborhoods, where holiday celebrations often spilled out onto the streets.

There were 17,370 Jewish families with an average of 4.11 members in 1938 (Perera 1968–1970:136). Given the high ethnic endogamy that continued to be practiced by Yugoslav Jews, these social units were ethnically homogeneous. Thus, young Jews were presented with no dilemma in selecting an ethnic line of descent. One was born into a Jewish family with two Jewish parents. Opting out of Jewish life was motivated by politics, not kinship. Endogamy was high even within the separate branches of Sephardim and Ashkenazim, although this practice was beginning to break down in the twentieth century, especially on the side of the Ashkenazi Jews (Pinto, A. 1987; see Freidenreich 1979).

The prewar Jewish family was a ritual unit and the household a ritual sphere in which various rites and customs were observed in varying degrees of intactness and intensity. Most important was the family's observance of the Sabbath. Preparation for this weekly holiday began one or two days before, for no baking or cooking was permitted on the Sabbath itself. The mother baked the special Sabbath bread (*hallah*, *barhes* [Ashk.]), *pitikas* (Seph.) and prepared other special foods (e.g., *sholet*—cooked beans with meat; *pastel*—filled pastry). Lighting fires on the Sabbath was proscribed. Many older Jews maintained this custom. Just before sundown on Friday the *shammash* would make his rounds of the Jewish quarter in Štip (Macedonia), and from each courtyard he would shout in Ladino: *Asindjendo ke ja es tarde*! ("It's late! Light your fires!") (Sion 1985, quoted in Jevrejski Istorijski Muzej, 1986:19). If a fire had to be started, or a light switched on, on the Sabbath itself, a non-Jew, referred to as the *Shabbes-goy* (Ashk.) or *fatija* (Seph.) would perform this act. Sometimes the entire family attended the synagogue, but usually just the males went. It was in the household that the family celebrated the Sabbath and other holidays as a kinship unit. By observing the Sabbath (Shabbat, Shabbes) the family was living according to the Jewish rhythm of life. On a weekly basis it was a period of time set apart from the ordinary flow of time. Reinforcing this separation from ordinary time were the special rites, customs, and objects associated with the Sabbath celebration. During its observance of the Sabbath the family engaged in rites of commensality, purification, and kinship. The end of the Sabbath typically was marked by the *Havdalah* rite, also called *Avdole*, *Havdole* (Ashkenazi), *Avdala* (Sephardi) (Jevrejski Istorijski Muzej, 1986).

The Individual Level

As previously noted, the Jewish individual did not choose his or her ethnic line of descent. She or he was born into a homogeneous Jewish family and became a member of a homogeneous Jewish household in which Jewish tradition may or may not have been strictly observed. The parents registered their child in the local community or *opština*. Only after emancipation did individual Jews begin declaring themselves as Jews by religion and as Serbs or Croats by nationality. Before emancipation there was no such dual affiliation. Declaring oneself as something other than Jewish, however, had nothing to do with mixed descent, for Jews continued to practice endogamy after emancipation and their push toward greater integration with the society in which they lived. The Jewish individual was also a member of a legally established Jewish religious community. In addition, the individual participated in one or more Jewish institutions or organizations. He attended Jewish schools, joined Jewish societies, and participated in Jewish voluntary organizations.

Before the war the individual level was marked by the rites of passage associated with the life cycle. Rites associated with all stages of the life cycle—birth, puberty, marriage, death—were practiced. Jewish boys were circumcised (*berit milah*) at eight days; they had their bar mitzvah when they turned thirteen; they were married under a *huppah;* and their bodies were prepared for burial according to Jewish custom and buried in a Jewish cemetery. Not only were all of these life cycle rites intact and practiced, there was a complex of more or less elaborate customs and rituals surrounding each stage. Jewish customs had long been powerful mechanisms that regulated behavior. Two Sephardi sayings that express their power are: *bolje da propadne selo nego običaji* ("it's better that a village perish rather than do customs") and *običaj je jači od medvjeda* ("custom is stronger than a lion") (Pinto 1987:34). Avram Pinto, who has described the Bosnian Jewish past in a book and many colorful aspects of that life in many short tales that have been published in *Jevrejski Pregled,* has written that "the customs were stronger than all of the written laws" (ibid.).

The stage of marriage can be used to show one such complex of customs. Bosnia was a region of the country that retained most traditional customs until the Second World War. There, for example, marriage involved more than just a wedding ceremony. A matchmaker or *kazamentero* was enlisted to find an appropriate mate. Several prominent male and female matchmakers could be called upon. Males felt cultural pressure to marry by twenty-three years of age, and females by sixteen or seventeen. The bride's family was obligated to provide the groom with a dowry (*dota* in Spanish; *miraz* in Serbian/Croatian). Families too poor to put together a dowry were helped by different Jewish societies such as the burial society *Hevra Kaddisha*. In addition to the dowry presentation by the bride's family to the son-in-law (*zet*), the groom's family also presented gifts to the bride's family. Thus, an exchange of goods passed between the two families. Two days before the wedding the prospective bride (*vjernica*) took a ritual bath in the *mikveh*. This particular purification rite was called *tevilah* (Hebrew). In Sarajevo the Jewish community purchased for their sole use a part of the Gazi Husrevbegov *hamam* or public bath (Pinto 1987). In Bitolj, in what was part of southern Serbia, the groom was concealed in his house for eight days before the wedding (Buchwald 1936, in Oren 1971). A marriage contract, called a *ketubbah*, was prepared. The *ketubbah* was a legal document fully recognized by the civil court and the Jewish communal court, the *Bet-din*. The complete contents of the dowry received by the groom or son-in-law (*zet*) were written into the marriage contract. If a man divorced his wife, he was required to return the goods to the bride's family. The wedding ceremony itself was a religious affair. There were no civil weddings in Bosnia. Couples travelled to Novi Sad in Vojvodina to have a civil wedding. The bride and groom stood under a canopy called a *huppah*. The bride was subjected to a test of her virginity. If the bride was found to not be a virgin, the husband had grounds for divorcing her (Pinto 1987). The Sephardim of Belgrade had the same custom before World War I. But within one generation the custom was discontinued.

Furthermore, institutions and specialists—rabbis/*hakhamim*, cantors/*hazzanim*, *mohalim*, *shohetim*, teachers—were available to facilitiate instruction, liturgical rituals, and rites of passages. Nearly all Jewish boys received some religious instruction, even if they did not attend a Jewish school. According to a survey conducted in 1985, seventy-four percent of postwar Jewish respondents, fifty years of age and older, indicated that they had received some religious instruction. This percentage would be certainly higher if only those over the age of sixty or sixty-five were considered. In some places rabbis taught a religion class in a non-Jewish school. In this way, when it came time for the *bar mitzvah*, boys had some familiarity with religion and Hebrew.

The fact that the individual was part of a Jewish family and a Jewish community that collectively participated in the life cycle celebrations further reinforced the individual's place in the family and community and integrated the entire collectivity. It was not a matter of the autonomous individual undergoing only an individual passage. Rather it was an individual becoming incorporated into a community and a community reaffirming that it was an integrated, cohesive whole.

The Prewar Pattern: Fragmenting but Integrated

The demographic and sociocultural data demonstrate a strained but still integrated pattern of Jewishness. On and across the collective, familial, and individual levels, Jewish social units and ritual-symbolic markers were present and viable. Particularly critical is the presence of the Jewish family as a viable Jewish institution and as a vital link connecting the collective and individual levels. The family is arguably the most important social institution of the Jews.

Also important in the prewar model is the relative intactness of many key social units, the ritual infrastructure, and ritual-symbolic markers. Jewish calendrical (*moed*) time continued to set the rhythm for much of Jewish life. Even non-religious Jews were affected by this rhythm, even if it meant only eating special meals and foods during certain times of the year. After all, individuals may have severed ties with the organized community, as some did for political reasons, but they remained connected to their families, friends, and neighborhoods. Jewish spheres outside of the local communal organization or *opština* (*kehilla*) were varied. Different needs, interests, and orientations could be met and accommodated within one of many voluntary organizations.

On the other hand, change and erosion cannot be ignored. In many places certain rites and customs were abandoned or began to erode after the First World War. Behaviors associated with the concept of purity were declining. For example, adherence to dietary prescriptions and proscriptions was in decline before the war. In a subsample (n=31) that I examined, taken from a larger sample of Jewish individuals who completed a questionnaire distributed by the Federation's Jewish Historical Museum, about fifty percent of the respondents came from pre-Second World War families that practiced the dietary laws of *kashrut*. Ritual bathing, too, had eroded to the point where it was associated with the grandparental generation and the small Orthodox community.

The Capacity for Submergence

Submergence into socialist Yugoslavia, which is described in detail in the following chapter as a structure of political and symbolic integration with the socialist state, was not just suddenly cast upon or adopted by the postwar Jewish community. Rather, submergence was a part of larger historical processes, some of which were entered into voluntarily, while others fell outside the control of the community. These processes produced a greater capacity for submergence and provided a historical and existential basis for creating a foundational myth; that is, a myth that would place these Jews closer to the revolutionary founders and rulers of the New Yugoslavia. For many of the senior generation leaders and activists of the postwar community, this part of their past was the beginning of the transformational process of becoming both a different kind of Jew and a different kind of Yugoslav. The wartime experience intensified and accelerated the transformation process for those in the prewar movement. For most Jews and other peoples, however, the wartime period was the beginning of their political transformation. The primary purpose of this chapter has been to show the break between the prewar and postwar periods. In this section, however, it is important to show that there were also significant links in political orientation between the prewar, wartime, and postwar periods. For instance, many of the leaders of the highly secularized postwar Jewish community participated in the prewar Jewish youth movement and/or in the National Liberation Struggle.

With emancipation in the second half of the nineteenth century came the first collective break with the traditional past and the beginning of a major transformation of the Jews of these South Slavic lands. Before emancipation some Jewish individuals acted autonomously, but usually they did so within the boundaries of the community. What ensued followed general patterns of modernity (Bell 1980; Berger 1967), but with particular Yugoslav Jewish manifestations. For the first time, Jews had legal access to spheres of life previously denied them. Immediately they began to seek entrance into these spheres. Emancipation accelerated acculturation and initiated various degrees of assimilation. The process of cultural erosion began or accelerated, resulting in the loss or erosion of ethnic markers of distinctiveness. For example, linguistic distinctiveness eroded. Integrationist tendencies were particularly strong until Zionism began to make its influence felt in the late 1920s, which then sparked new forms of integrationism and synthesis. Some sought a synthetic solution in a dual national-religious affiliation, while others sought to create an ethnic-political synthesis. A smaller number of individuals chose to part with their

Jewishness in varying degrees and devote their lives to achieving Communist goals. Some opted for a complete break with their Jewish past, while others retained ties with the Jewish world. Even some of the most radical and revolutionary individuals did not sever all ties with the Jewish community. Joza Baruh of the revolutionary Baruh family received rooms, which he turned into art studios, and a scholarship from the Jewish community, which he used to study painting in Paris (Jevrejski Istorijski Muzej, 1976). Olga Alkalaj, the aunt of one of my Belgrade informants, used her skills as a lawyer to assist the Communist movement. In the end, she chose to return to Belgrade, where she died with other Jews as a victim of the Holocaust (Dedijer 1961).

Following Emancipation the previously less-differentiated sacred-secular whole began to divide into more distinct spheres of life. Gradually the secular side of Jewish life began to dominate. Greater portions of the communities' budgets began to be allotted to non-religious activities during the interwar period. Secularization continued to grow stronger, especially among the youth and intellectual segments of the population. Even within the sacred or religious sphere, change began to shape in the form of theological and external forms of liberalization, such as the Christian features of organs and choirs introduced into Jewish synagogues.

That these post-Emancipation processes clearly were unfolding before the Second World War cannot be denied, even though, as I have showed, traditional institutions and rituals remained viable on all three levels of the Jewish community. The processes of change, however, were placing a strain on traditional Jewish life. Sociocultural erosion and decay were well underway. The authority of religious law (*Halakhah*) and tradition was being undermined. Jewish individuals and communities confronted new ideas and problems which, in turn, created new dilemmas, including the dilemma, even crisis, of identity (see Freidenreich 1979, particularly chapter 8, "The Crisis of Identity"). The development of a varied and active secular cultural life replaced what had been the holistic existence of communal life.

Particularly important to note is which segments of the population were moving away from tradition and toward secular forms most rapidly. These segments were a large part of the youth generation and of the intellectuals. A minority of these, including the children of upper class families, opted to leave the Jewish milieu and join the illegal Communist Party. Most of the youth, as indicated below, remained tied to the Jewish community or one of its voluntary organizations. What Schatz (1991:46–47) writes about the Polish Jewish radicals is true for the Yugoslav Jewish radicals: "Despite their rejection of the old world, however, they were still its product." Although their rejection of much of their cultural heritage contributed to weakening its power over them, they also drew upon this heritage, particularly its messianism, while striving to remake themselves and society.

Movement to the Political Left

The Yugoslav Jewish progressive tradition, which has been made an important part of the postwar Jewish community's mythology and the foundation of the senior generation's collective identity as a secular and politically progressive generation, can be divided into the prewar and wartime periods. The prewar period can be divided further into two periods: 1918–1932 and 1933–1941 (Romano 1980). This tradition encompasses all progressive, radical, and revolutionary movements and activities within and outside the sphere of the Jewish community. The Jews who composed the progressive generation, mainly youth and a segment of the intellectuals and workers, did not form a cohesive unit. They chose between different life paths. One path that remained within the Jewish community is often referred to as the Jewish Youth Movement, while the path outside the Jewish community was the Communist movement, also referred to as the revolutionary movement of the working class. Those in the Jewish youth movement belonged largely to Zionist youth organizations. A significant number of Jewish individuals who had been on the former path crossed over onto the second path before the onset of the war, while an even greater number crossed over at the beginning of the National Liberation Struggle. By showing actual Jewish involvement in the prewar progressive and revolutionary movement (about two times their proportion in the population), in the wartime resistance and political revolution (about three to four times their number in the initial period), and in postwar socialist construction, the postwar community, particularly its senior generation, created not only a mythology but also demonstrated the historical continuity of a progressive generation from its emergence to its wartime participation to its socialist activism after the war.

In the earlier prewar period, 1918–1932, Jews as individuals began participating in progressive political movements and activities, including in the illegal Communist Party, which was banned after 1920 following a very respectable showing in the parliamentary election. Their absolute numbers were small, but their proportionate contribution was not insignificant. Jews were usually among those tried and sentenced for illegal political activity or suspicion of it. Among them were those known as *ilegalci*, individuals who were constantly on the run from the police. The best known Jewish *ilegalac* was the Communist revolutionary Moša Pijade. Several Jews from Yugoslav territories even participated in the October Revolution in 1917 and in the Hungarian Revolution two years later. Jewish participation in the organization and radicalization of the union movement was also significant (ibid.).

After 1932 a greater number of Jews moved to the political left in the decade before the Second World War. Possible reasons behind this movement are given below. Taking part in this movement were mostly the Jewish youth, Jewish intellectuals, and some of the Jewish workers and Jewish poor, mostly in Sarajevo, where Jewish social stratification differed from other regions in which large concentrations of Jews lived. Above all it was a generational shift. The movement to the left in the 1930s was discernible in the emergence of a generation of youth, representing mostly the middle and upper classes, with the exception of Sarajevo because of its class polarization and political activism of its citizens. A politicized generation came into being, united by Jewish descent and a left-wing orientation. Until the disintegration of socialist Yugoslavia, this generation would remain intact as members of the broader progressive tradition but internally divided by choice of life path; that is, the choice of remaining within or outside the Jewish community, although some from the latter path did begin to participate in the community after the immediate postwar years. A word of caution is in order. Given the small number of Jews in Yugoslavia even before the war, comparisons with the Jewish left-wing experience elsewhere in Eastern Europe are somewhat limited. The radical generation of Polish Communists, for example, represented over twenty percent of the Communist movement in Poland (Schatz 1991). This was a distinct demographic, sociological, and political phenomenon from the vantage point of both Jews and non-Jews. In Yugoslavia, where the Communist Party was illegal, it is unknown exactly how many Jews were in the Party. Their participation was not insignificant but outsiders did not see it as a collective phenomenon, and perhaps neither did the Jews until after the war while in the process of constructing a collective representation of themselves and securing a place in the new socialist order.

Before proceeding to discuss the possible precipitants of Jewish progressive or left-wing activity, I will explain what *progressive* meant to these Jews. They have used this term to describe themselves in the prewar and postwar periods. First, it must be remembered that not long before, certainly before the emancipation of the Jews in the latter half of the nineteenth century, the Jewish response to injustice and hostility reflected their minority and subordinate position in society. They pleaded, paid large sums of money, isolated themselves, and sought economic niches that other populations avoided. Now, some began to challenge and confront, and to work toward changing the existing system, even though the position of the Jewish population as a whole was quite good. Furthermore, they were prepared to go outside of the community and outside of their immediate cultural tradition to accomplish this. Going outside of their cultural tradition did not necessarily entail abandoning every aspect of it. Reinterpretation and synthesis were two ways of accomplishing this. The term *progressive* is a key linguistic symbol that the Jews of Yugoslavia used to subsume left-wing ideas and activities carried out within and outside the Jewish community. Since Jews were associated with both spheres, both can be placed within the progressive tradition mythologized by the postwar Jewish community. The response formulated and acted out within the community and the one formulated and implemented outside the community were different, but they shared common ground. What many of the progressive youth in Zionist organizations and some Jewish intellectuals shared with those who pursued radicalism and change outside of the community was a left-wing, even Marxist, political orientation. What divided these Jews was their position on the nationality issue (Freidenreich 1979). For some, Marxism and Zionism were compatible, and thus they believed a synthesis was possible. For others, Marxism and Zionism were antithetical. In the postwar period, certain individuals (see Albahari 1984) of this latter ideological persuasion clearly stated this position, even, perhaps, to the extent of denying the synthesis between Zionism and Marxism that had operated within the Jewish movement and produced a significant number of Party members.

Jews who chose to work within the community may have introduced a radical ideology into Jewish life, but they avoided direct confrontation with the government, and most had no intention of bringing a political revolution to Yugoslavia. They did not seek to overthrow the government. Most of all they wanted to remain Jews and as Jews to seek synthetic solutions to the dilemmas and crises of life. They were also committed to creating a Jewish state in Palestine based on socialist principles. Those who had joined the Communist movement as members or sympathizers did seek to accomplish political revolution and societal transformation. They considered themselves Yugoslavs rather than Jews. An unknown number of Jews wanted to achieve both Jewish and global emancipation (Freidenreich 1979).

There is no simple, univariate explanation of why Jews joined and/or participated in left-wing movements. Several interacting factors precipitated this movement to the left among the Jews of Yugoslavia, particularly among a generation of Jewish youth, what is today's senior generation. Not all of these factors had the same influence or degree of influence on Jews living in the different regions of the country or on individuals within particular regions. Rather, they had a permutational effect on individuals.

On the surface the conditions in which the Jews found themselves did not seem to favor a broad movement to the left, and, indeed, there was no large movement to join the progressive movement until the 1930s. The position of the Jewish community in interwar Yugoslavia was very good compared to that of Jewish communities in Central Europe. The state treated the Jews favorably, even in regard to their Zionist activities, which the Jews were allowed to pursue freely. Neither the authorities nor the Jews saw these activities as incompatible with Yugoslav loyalties. Most Yugoslav Jewish Zionists contributed money but had no intention of emigrating to Palestine (ibid.). The Jewish communities were allowed to pursue their own cultural programs and free to practice the Jewish religion. There were instances of antisemitism and instances of anti-Jewish measures, particularly in the first years after Yugoslavia was founded, but there were no antisemitic laws or organized movements until just before the Second World War. Some of the interwar parties exhibited antisemitism, but their platforms were weighted with other issues.[3] The central Serb-Croat conflict overshadowed all other conflicts. Interethnic relations were generally good or tolerant in the perceptions of the Jews, especially where the Sephardi Jews were concerned. The Serbs called them "our Jews," which was the title of a book, *Naši Jevreji* (Dimitrijević and Stojanović), published in 1940, the product of Serbian and Jewish collaboration. The surrounding host populations often did not perceive the Ashkenazi Jews in the same way. Also, the Ashkenazim, more than the Sephardim, sought the path of assimilation but found that the host society placed limits on this process.

The Sephardim sought a more balanced integration into general society. These differences were reflected in their interpretation of Zionism. The Ashkenazim favored a more Palestine-centered Zionism, while the Sephardi espoused a form of diasporic nationalism. They believed that Jewish existence was viable outside of a Jewish state. After all, they were the descendants of Jews who had settled in these lands more than four centuries ago and had developed a tie to the land that was not easily severed.[4] On the whole, the Jews enjoyed economic well-being. The majority of the Jewish population belonged to the middle and upper classes. Although they could not avoid the economic difficulties of the global depression, many had sufficient resources to survive the crisis. Jewish self-help organizations and practices helped to alleviate some of the economic suffering of the Macedonian and Bosnian Jews. Moreover, Jewish life expanded rather than diminished during the interwar years (Freidenreich 1979). Considering all of these factors together, the material and political well-being of most of the Jewish population was generally favorable. Furthermore, it appeared that until the late 1930s there was no immediate threat to the Yugoslav Jews from within the country. If anything, one might hypothesize that their class position would be an obstacle whenever they tried to join the Communist-led revolutionary movement. In certain instances it probably was. The community documents only one such case that occurred during the war (*Jevreji u Jugoslaviji*, 1988).

The movement to the left was precipitated by external conditions and by transformations and responses to change in the Jewish community itself. I will deal with the internal Jewish factors first, that is, with Jewish culture and social structure. Did Jewish socialization patterns allow for deviation and adaptability to new conditions, for individualism, and so forth? This requires further study because the postwar mythology tends to underemphasize choices that did not lead to participation in the movement. Was there a potential for secular messianism? That is, did the Jewish progressives and radicals draw upon, consciously or not, something in their culture and collective experience that facilitated such a movement? How did Jewish culture influence the movement? Not only the Jewish present, but also the Jewish past and Jewish future (visions of the future, cultural goals) must be considered as conditioning the selections individuals and groups make. Jews who became secularized after emancipation may have moved away from religious practice, but they continued to live from the cultural capital of Judaism (see Finestein 1977). Secular Zionism, for example, cannot be separated from what is religious or sacred to the Jews (e.g., the land of Israel). Or, perhaps the ambivalence, tensions, and uncertainties created by the meeting of different traditions motivated these Jews to work toward resolving them by joining the progressive movement.

How did social structural conditions within the Jewish population influence the movement to the left? With the exception of Sarajevo, membership in the working and poor classes did not appear to have precipitated such movement. Most Jewish members of the proletariat and lower classes were apolitical. In fact, it is membership in the middle and upper classes that is correlated to the Jewish movement to the left. Yugoslav Jews, in contrast to most of the Yugoslav population, were urban, literate, well educated, and mobile. Soon after gaining civil rights, prosperous Jewish businessmen began to send their sons to the best universities in Yugoslavia and abroad. In Yugoslavia, this meant the University of Zagreb in Croatia and the University of Belgrade in Serbia, and abroad it often meant schools in either Prague or Vienna. While pursuing their university education these Jewish students were exposed to left-wing ideas. After their return to their hometowns, many of these students served as change agents in their Jewish communities (Freidenreich 1979; Koš 1976; Romano 1980).

Family background alone does not appear to have been an independent precipitant, since members of the same family sometimes went in different ideological and political directions. While the revolutionary Moša Pijade was imprisoned and beaten for his Communist activities, his older brother Uziel, according to Pijade biographer Slobodan Nešović (1968), supported the political parties in power, as did the majority of Jews until a dictatorship was imposed by King Alexander in 1929.[5] In some cases, however, such as in the famous revolutionary family of Baruhs from Belgrade's Jewish quarter of Dorćol, the family was obviously a significant contributing factor. Family background factors that did contribute to choice of life path include patterns of socialization. Parents and/or older siblings encouraged educational pursuits and intellectual curiosity. Multilingualism was encouraged. Moša Pijade's early socialization included an immersion in the German and Serbian languages, which served him well when translating Marx's *Das Kapital*. Since multilingualism contributed to the development of interethnic communicability, perhaps it contributed to the formation of greater ethnic tolerance, which was highly valued by the Jews and a goal of the prewar Communists.

Was region a significant factor? Although the degree of progressive or revolutionary activity was not uniform by region, region alone cannot be considered a primary precipitant because Jews from all regions of the country joined the movement. Perhaps the one regional exception was Macedonia, where poverty and cultural conservatism were much higher, and where considerable outmigration occurred.

Perhaps more than the past or present it was their cultural and/or political vision of the future that most strongly motivated members of this younger generation of Jews to join left-wing organizations and movements. Given their subordinate place in the community and the growing difficulty of emigration to Palestine, they lacked the power to control the present, particularly in implementing their Zionist-Socialist vision. By establishing agricultural training centers in Yugoslavia, they tried to prepare for emigration to Palestine. The Communist Party offered a vision of the future that was attractive to them and a program of immediate action. Being young, they believed that they could be the catalysts for change and also be among the ones who would reap the fruits of the struggle for change. The future, thus, may have moved them more than the past or present, insofar as the Jewish community itself was concerned.

External conditions, particularly societal stratification along political, economic, and ethnic lines, were also important. As citizens of Yugoslavia and as members of a tiny minority population, the Jews were influenced by societal conditions. In the economic sphere, the global economic crisis had hit the small retail traders and craftsmen of Sarajevo especially hard. Unlike most other cities of significant Jewish concentration, class polarization in Sarajevo was quite pronounced. Poverty was a major problem in that community, as it affected 398 Jewish families with 1,700 persons, 1,116 of whom earned nothing (Finci 1966:191). Politically, instability characterized the country. First, power was not distributed evenly by region or by ethnic nation. Peoples' perceptions of this imbalance, which varied in their accuracy, only exacerbated the problem. The Yugoslav Idea of a unified South Slavic state evaporated quickly. That political parties acted in effect as national interest groups did nothing to facilitate federal(ist) solutions. Such ethnopolitical maneuvering and open hostility precluded the development of any kind of Yugoslav identity. The situation in the country deteriorated to the point where, in 1929, the Serbian King Alexander dissolved the parliamentary democracy and instituted a dictatorship, which seemingly only confirmed the suspicions and claims made by non-Serbs of Serbian control and dominance. Whether or not the Serbs were as dominant as the non-Serbs claim will not be pursued here.[6] Underlying this political instability was the growing discontent among many non-Serbs and incidents of violence directed at ethnic opponents. During this period the Communist Party of Yugoslavia, operating as an illegal underground movement, was kept in check by the government, which sometimes took excessive measures against the Communists and their sympathizers. The government and the courts treated the Jews in the revolutionary movement as Communists and not as Jews.

To reiterate, the position of the Jewish community as a whole during most of the interwar period was relatively good. The state, with the Serbian monarchy at the head, treated the Jews quite favorably (see Freidenreich 1979). Antisemitism had no broad, organized form in interwar Yugoslavia until just before the Second World War when two antisemitic laws were introduced, and thus it cannot be posited as a major precipitant of Yugoslav Jewish radicalism, that is, unless the situation of the Jews elsewhere in Europe is taken into account. The question is, how precarious did the Yugoslav Jews perceive their own situation to be? During the 1930s fascism began increasingly to penetrate Yugoslav boundaries. They knew the situation in Europe was becoming more grave. The arrival of several thousand Jewish refugees in Yugoslavia was visible proof that the Jewish situation throughout the continent was precarious.

Another precipitant was the Communist Party's success at political socialization and self-representation. Within Yugoslavia itself the Communist Party successfully attracted segments of the Jewish population by infiltrating Jewish youth organizations and by representing itself as sharing Jewish interests and as a defender of the Jews. The more that Jewish individuals felt removed from Jewish society and integrated into the movement led by the Party, the stronger they felt the problems of general society to be their own. Certainly once in the Communist movement these feelings were intensified. By circulating its workers among different regions, the Party successfully fostered a Yugoslavist orientation, which among many Jews was already strong, while every other political party and movement showed divisive tendencies (Djilas

1991). Such Yugoslavism was very attractive to many Jews, less so to others. It was a potential solution to any identity crisis, especially for those in multiethnic areas, but because it was never accepted by other peoples it never became a viable alternative. Rebecca West describes this Yugoslavist orientation in *The Black Lamb and Grey Falcon*. She describes a Jewish couple from Split, Dalmatia who "seemed outside the Splitchani tradition" and who "put its trust in synthesis and centralization." A benevolent unifying force would help to accomplish this synthesis (1982).

There was also a psychological side to the movement to the left. According to Zvi Loker, who emigrated to Israel in the 1930s, the particular Jewish frustration "originated to a considerable extent in the situation prevailing in Jewish society and in the Zionist movement" (1976:75). The younger Jews thought that the older Jews, who controlled the communal organizations, were failing to meet the needs of the younger generation, which had moved away from religion and tradition and toward a left-wing Zionist orientation. At the same time it was difficult to obtain the necessary emigration visa to leave Yugoslavia for Palestine. Despite the creation of preparatory training centers in Yugoslavia, these young people grew increasingly frustrated because they were unable to put their particular socialist-Zionist synthesis into practice. Loker writes that the "outcome of all this frustration was that youth in various Zionist movements turned to more radical pursuits, including the revolutionary movement. Some enlisted in the International Brigade. It was hoped that these would satisfy the desire for immediate and practical action" (ibid.).

Although not every young Jew joined the revolutionary path of the progressive movement, most of those who made that choice belonged to the younger generation. When age is considered together with various permutations of factors such as level of education and location of study, intellectual curiosity, interest group affiliation, personal ties with ideologically significant others, degree of integration in Yugoslav society, degree of Yugoslavist orientation, and sociocultural factors, there appears to be a strong relationship with involvement in revolutionary and radical activity. Since Jews joined the Communist movement and the Partisans as individuals, determining which of the above factors are most significant must take into account the contingencies each individual faced and the choices she or he made. A focus on individual choices does not mean group patterns are nonexistent. Positing such group patterns is, beyond a certain point, more difficult for Yugoslav Jews because of their small number, their dispersal across ethnic regions, and a lack of documentation because the Communist Party was illegal and because once they joined they often abandoned ethnic identity.

Life Paths

In the interwar period Jewish youth tended to fall into three general categories: the Zionists, the Communists, and the apolitical. "The son or daughter of a wealthy integrationist was likely to turn to communism or else become committed to a profession; the children of middle-class parents [both Ashkenazim and Sephardim] often became Zionists, especially socialist-Zionists of the Hashomer Hatzair variety; the lower classes for the most part were apolitical" (Freidenreich 1979:163). Together, the Communist youth, the working-class members of *Matatja* in Sarajevo and the middle-class members of Hashomer Hatzair composed the Jewish progressive generation. What joined them was their left-wing, Marxist orientation. Each of these segments, however, diverged on the nationality issue, and each selected different life paths, although there was significant crossover from the two paths within the Jewish Youth Movement to the Communist path. What eventually brought together all three paths was the National Liberation Struggle. After the wartime period of convergence, individual Jews selected one of two paths, the path that kept them tied to the Jewish community and the path that remained, for the most part, outside the community. After the immediate postwar years, there was some return on the part of Jews who had chosen the latter path. This included Jews who had occupied government positions or were career army officers who only became active in Jewish communal life after retirement. In addition, certain prominent individuals who had chosen to remain outside of the community occasionally had contact with the community. For example, the famous Jewish conductor and director of the Peoples' Liberation Theater, Oskar Danon, performed at special events such as the anniversary celebration hosted by the Sarajevo Jewish community in 1966.

Organized Jewish youth activity only began in the South Slavic lands in the first decade of the twentieth century. By the time the first Zionist youth organizations were established in Yugoslavia, various transformations were already underway. The Jews were seeking integration into Yugoslav society. Young people were pursuing secular fields of education and subsequently entering the free professions as well as the arts and sciences. "In Yugoslavia, as in western Europe, Zionism was to a large extent a postassimilationist phenomenon and attracted to its ranks those who had already broken away from Judaism, who were seeking a solution to their identity crisis in the concept of a Jewish people" (ibid:159).[7] The Zionist organizations functioned "to stimulate Jewish national consciousness at least among the younger generation" (ibid:154).[8]

The Zionist youth federation was at first "slightly left-of-center, but not particularly Palestine centered" (ibid:165). As in the parent Zionist Federation, there was internal factionalism in the youth federation, with certain segments, including Ahdut Hatzofim, withdrawing because they believed it was insufficiently Zionist. First established as a radical subsidiary of the youth federation, the Ahdut Hatzofim (scout union) became "emphatically Palestine centered, advocating socialist principles and eventual *aliya* to Palestine" (ibid.). Ahdut Hatzofim later reconciled with the youth federation. Freidenreich writes:

> From that point on the left-wing dominated the federation and imposed its Palestine-centered philosophy upon the entire federation. In 1931 Ahdut Hatzofim changed into Histadrut Hashomer Hatzair and belonged officially to the international Hashomer Hatzair movement, which was Marxist and radical Zionist in orientation and stressed *halutziut*, or pioneer emigration to Palestine to work primarily in agriculture. . . . By 1938 Hashomer Hatzair had 1,374 members . . . in all parts of Yugoslavia (ibid:167).

These young people had a cultural goal or vision, perhaps just nostalgia, of Jews together again in a common state. The cultural sentiments connected with the land of Israel had not died. Zionism began to put this cultural goal, or these nostalgic sentiments, into ideological and political form. Zionist activity objectified the cultural vision. The secular strand of political Zionism has been interpreted as secular messianism. As such Zionism for the generation of secular and progressive Jewish youth became both a cultural and political goal. This generation then adopted socialist and Marxist ideas and practices to achieve this goal. They went outside of their cultural tradition to create a synthesis. Those young people within this generation who carried a more Yugoslavist or internationalist view were willing to submit to political centralization and a benevolent unifying force (West 1982) to lead the way. For a significant number this meant the Communist Party of Yugoslavia.

The Zionist youth movement had the effect of blurring historical divisions and distinctions still prevalent in the older generations. One social indicator was the increasing number of marriages between Sephardim and Ashkenazim in Sarajevo between 1908 and 1940 (from 5% of total marriages to 8% to 14% of all Jewish marriages in Sarajevo; the figures are even more striking when seen as percentages of marriages involving Ashkenazim in Sarajevo: 10% to 20% to almost 40%) (Freidenreich 1979:152–153).[9]

In Sarajevo children of middle-class Sephardi families tended to join Hashomer Hatzair, while youth from lower classes tended to join *Matatja*, a Jewish working youth association. It fell outside the exclusively Zionist sphere. *Matatja* was "the most important exception to the general rule of Zionist preponderance in Yugoslav Jewish youth organizations" (ibid:167). When it began in 1923 it had between eighty to one hundred members. Seven years later it had six hundred fifty, and the number continued to increase. *Matatja* was composed of several sections—music, literary, cultural, sports, etc. These young Jews rejected the philosophies of the other local Jewish youth organizations, both Zionist and Sephardist, on account of their predominantly middle-class, intellectual orientation. *Matatja's* orientation and program appealed to the less-educated working-class segments, the young artisans, commercial assistants, and workers. While the association was overwhelming Sephardi, it never identified itself with the Sephardi movement. Actually, in the early 1930s the cultural section devoted much of its attention to Zionist topics and tried to increase Jewish nationalist awareness among its members, but toward the end of the decade, the major subject under discussion was Marxist doctrine. Claims have been made that *Matatja* became a Communist cover organization, which is indeed plausible. Some members were secretly associated with the underground Communist movement and tried to use the club as a basis for operations and propaganda. In 1936 several members were arrested for suspected Communist activities and thereafter the organization came under constant police surveillance. In 1939 the authorities forced it to disband, allegedly for not abiding by its statutes but in reality for Communist affiliations. A year later, however, it was allowed to reconstitute itself under the supervision of the Sephardi communal executive. An organization like *Matatja* could only have been possible in a town such as Sarajevo, with a large Jewish working-class population and strong Jewish consciousness (ibid:167–168). "The association was Jewish by membership and by conviction; it was not integrationist, not Zionist, and not even Sephardist. It seemingly rejected all the ideologies of their elders and helped pave the way for the future Yugoslavia" (ibid:168; see Koš 1976 for a further description of *Matatja* from the perspective of a Jew from Sarajevo).

Gams (1975:50) writes that the Jewish youth movement in the form of these organizations provided many cadres to the Communist movement because their ideas and forms of socialization were similar to those of the Yugoslav Communist Youth Association (SKOJ). Some joined the movement before the war, and many more joined at the beginning of the war. It is significant that many Hashomer Hatzair members joined the Partisans soon after the German occupation of Yugoslavia. For example, the entire Belgrade branch of Hashomer Hatzair joined. They "fought for a Jewish as well as a Yugoslav cause" (Freidenreich 1979:168–169). The Jews in the Novi Sad branch of Hashomer Hatzair requested to enter the movement as a Jewish group, but the Communist Party of Yugoslavia resisted such overtures. Having been denied entrance as a group, these young Jews from Novi Sad who managed to survive the early German onslaught joined and participated as individuals (Kovač 1975). Neither the postwar authorities nor publications published outside the Jewish Community acknowledge these Jewish-Zionist movements, and thus the Jewish contribution to progressive activities has gone largely unnoticed (Loker:1977:105).

Because the Jewish population of Yugoslavia was small (about 0.5%), Jewish participation in the Communist movement was less than that of Jews in other East European countries, but, "their role in helping to lay the foundations for the future Yugoslavia was of some significance" (Freidenreich 1979:179). There was "a sizable group of younger Jews who played an active role in the illegal Communist Party, which functioned as an underground movement after 1921" (ibid:178). The exact number is difficult to establish, since membership was secret and Jews were not counted separately in their midst (ibid.). If their numerical contribution is considered relative to their percentage of the total population, this significance becomes more apparent. Whereas they represented slightly less than 0.5 percent of the Yugoslav population, they represented about five percent of the defendants in political trials, and even more in Belgrade and Sarajevo. They represented about three percent of the Communists serving terms in the Lepoglava and Sremska Mitrovica prisons (*The Jews in Yugoslavia,* 1989:105).

Another indicator, described below, is Jewish participation in the Spanish Civil War. There is no doubt that their contribution was significant to the postwar community, which has included it as an integral part of their mythology and collective identity.

Yugoslav Jewish Volunteers in the Spanish Civil War

Thirty-four Yugoslav Jews participated in the Spanish Civil War. While Jews constituted only 0.5 percent of the Yugoslav population, they contributed over two percent of the volunteers (Loker 1976:71; Romano 1980). Loker provides information about the background, motivation, and subsequent political activities of these Jewish volunteers.

The Yugoslav Jewish volunteers represented a spectrum of occupations. About one-third were workers. Others included physicians, commercial employees, and journalists. There were also five students among them. Twenty-nine were men. Two-thirds were Ashkenazi. The majority were from Croatia and Slovenia, the most industrialized part of the country. Zagreb was the focus of revolutionary agitation. The northwestern corner of Yugoslavia was also closest to the Austrian border and Vienna, which was the center of Comintern activities in the 1930s. Twenty-five of the thirty-four were active members of the Communist Party, while the remaining nine had no party affiliation. Of the twenty-five Communists, at least nine are known to have been members of Jewish youth organizations (mostly Hashomer Hatzair) before they joined the League of Communist Youth (Loker 1976:72, 76).

Many of the Jewish volunteers did not see themselves as Jews, but as cosmopolitans and universalists. Only a few knew anything of Judaism, and most had drifted away from Zionism. They had no language of their own, such as the Yiddish spoken by the Polish and other Jews. For members of the Communist Party the directive to enlist as volunteers was decisive. Some shared the realization of the need to make a stand against fascism. Some were simply young idealists. In the group were individuals without any affiliation who just responded to events or to specific appeals. There were adventurers of all kinds, and "somewhat emotional intellectuals" who came to solve problems of their own but had little understanding of the Spanish problem itself (ibid:75, 77).

There is a clear relationship between participation in the Spanish Civil War and subsequent military and political activity. This is true for Jews and other Yugoslav peoples. Whereas in the Soviet

Union veterans of the Spanish Civil War were purged by Stalin, in Yugoslavia Tito admired the veterans and deployed them in various capacities. Some of these veterans became generals. Four Jewish veterans became National Heroes of Yugoslavia. Loker writes:

> It is thus quite understandable that not a few of the more talented of Jewish youth in the Balkans found in the War in Spain full scope for their revolutionary activities, and were convinced that any future communist regimes would provide a solution to the "Jewish question". When World War Two erupted, many of them joined the anti-fascist struggle and some attained high positions in the people's democracies which arose after the defeat of Hitlerism (ibid:76).

The Break in Jewish Existence

Fascism had begun to infiltrate Yugoslav society in the 1930s. Certain restrictions on the Jews were put into effect in 1940. The number of Jews allowed to enroll in universities was restricted. The Jews were virtually taken out of certain businesses. Antisemitism grew more visible and organized. Thousands of Jewish refugees fleeing fascism in Central Europe entered Yugoslavia, many of whom wanted to reach Palestine but never did.

The Second World War brought a disruption of catastrophic dimensions to the Jews of Yugoslavia, as it did to the rest of European Jewry. Change was abrupt. Fighting as Partisans and as soldiers in the National Liberation War, approximately 1,300 Jews died through the war years. Most of the 67,500 or 82 percent who died during the war, however, died from the implementation of German Nazism and domestic fascism that resulted in the well-documented and substantiated genocide upon the Jews. They died by shooting, gassing, hanging, starvation, and other means, within and outside various concentration camps located in Yugoslavia (about 39,000) and abroad (24,000) (*The Jews in Yugoslavia*, 1989). Many who died as victims of the Jewish Holocaust did not have sufficient time to join the Yugoslav resistance. Serbia, in particular, was overwhelmed by German forces very early and very quickly, and the German Wehrmacht 100:1 reprisal policy for every German soldier killed was most severe on the Jews, who were targeted even above the Serbs, who also fell under the same policy. Many of the Jews in Croatia (Jews in Dalmatia were under Italian occupation until the capitulation of Italy in September 1943) and Bosnia and Hercegovina died at the hands of the Ustasha, a domestic fascist group that ruled the Independent State of Croatia (NDH) and carried out heinous crimes (see books published by the Yugoslav Jewish community: Levntal 1957; Pinto and Pinto 1972; 1974; *Sećanja Jevreja na Logor Jasenovac*, 1972; Romano 1980). About 24,000 of Yugoslavia's Jews died in the Jasenovac camp, located on the territory of the NDH. The acts of genocide in Yugoslavia and elsewhere (Yugoslav Jews were transported to and murdered in such concentration camps as Auschwitz and Treblinka) transformed the Yugoslav Jewish population to a minuscule size and more. These acts removed individuals, many of whom were specialists, who could help maintain an intact and integrated sociocultural system and who could be strong competitors in certain interethnic spheres of life (e.g., business, medicine, law). Many of these had roles that defined them as the gatekeepers of Jewish tradition. These were Jews who both guarded Jewish tradition and passed it on. They were ritual specialists, educators, community leaders and activists, parents, and grandparents. Together they operated on the three levels of the collectivity and thus helped to maintain an integrated pattern of Jewish ethnicity.

The suddenness of change was significant in different ways. There was no gradual decline of traditional Jewish life. Most of those who were old enough and had had the opportunity to observe and participate in Jewish ritual had forsaken it, while those born after the war never had the chance to experience or even see it firsthand. For them, there was nothing to forsake. The line of continuity had been broken, or at least so it seemed. Certainly the line had attenuated dangerously. The leaders of the organized community embarked on a new line, setting the experiment of secular Jewishness in motion, submerging the community in the process. Many individual Jews, however, having been cut off from the line of continuity and the cycle of determined time (*moed*), were left to create private symbols of Jewishness in selective, autonomous moments or to abandon Jewishness altogether except, perhaps, in a declarative way.

Organized postwar emigration between 1948 and 1952 cut the surviving population in half. Among those emigrants was the majority of a generation that had the potential of producing children and thereby adding to the population size and, at least for a time, maintaining more Jewish families. Without this generation fewer infants were born, the skewed age distribution became even more pronounced, and the senior generation of the 1980s felt no push from below to remove it from its position of communal influence and power.

In addition to the direct causes of change in the population profile, less direct factors such as participation in the revolution and socialist state-building that followed are important to consider. Less direct factors are important when examining, for example, patterns of self-ascription (e.g., on censuses). It is clear that there were many more Jews in postwar Yugoslavia than declared themselves on official state censuses. War, genocide, and emigration losses do not provide complete answers for such demographic discrepancies, nor do they provide a complete explanation of the major patterns of ethnic response (submergence, individuation) selected by Jews in the postwar period. Certain minuscule Jewish populations have managed to maintain traditional rituals and customs (see Abraham 1989 for a description of how the Indian Jewish communities have maintained traditional practices in spite of their minuscule sizes).

Postwar Demographic Composition

It is impossible to determine the precise number of Jews who lived in socialist Yugoslavia. No doubt more Jews lived in the country than declared themselves on official censuses. There was considerable fluctuation of declaration on the censuses themselves, including the sharp increase from 2,100 in 1961 to 4,811 in 1971 and the sharp decrease from 1971 to 1981. In search of an explanation, it may be asked what might have intensified feelings of Jewish belonging during the interim years. The apparent answer appears to be the 1967 Six Day War in Israel, an event that shook the Jews not only in Israel but throughout the world. Based on other data sources we know that the number of 4,811 was much closer to the actual population size. The total population size of approximately 6,000 to 6,500 as estimated by the organized community remained relatively stable since the last emigration wave in 1952. It is interesting that ten years after the 1971 census the total number of Jews declaring themselves as Jews dropped below even the 1961 figure, so that at first glance the 1971 total appears to be an anomaly in Jewish census declaration. But is it? A more plausible explanation for the dramatic increase may be computer error, for the increase appears only in the Republic of Croatia.

However, Marko Perić (1980), the Yugoslav Jewish demographer, still lists 4,811 in his table.

In order to obtain closer and more reliable estimates of the total population size of Yugoslav Jewry, other data sources were examined. The Jewish calendar or *Luach* published and distributed annually by the Federation of Jewish Communities of Yugoslavia always included a numerical survey of membership size of each community and surrounding cities. However, an enumeration of the membership was not conducted annually. The compiler of the calendar, Rabbi of Yugoslavia, Cadik Danon, noted that an update was needed in the 1980s.

Jews and non-Jewish spouses and children were eligible for membership in the organized Jewish community. With this in mind, non-Jewish members and nonmembers must be factored in or out, depending on one's analytical goals. If the total number of Jews is being estimated, then, obviously non-Jews must be excluded from the tally. If I can estimate, based on a 1985 survey conducted by the Federation, that 88 percent of community members were Jewish, then according to the *Luach* of 1984–1985 a total population of slightly more than 5,500 Jews lived in the country. However, another problem arises in that not all Jews were registered members of local Jewish communities. How many Jews chose not to register as members of a Jewish community? No one knows what the true number was. How many of their offspring considered themselves to be Jews? The original director of the 1985 survey estimated the total number of Jews to be 10,000, the highest estimate that I heard while in Yugoslavia. The rabbi put the figure somewhat lower, at about 5,500, which, understandably, is closer to the *Luach* figure he compiled. The lowest total estimate I heard was 1,500. The great disparity in estimates of population size, one informant told me, suggests something about the ambiguous nature of Jewish identity in Yugoslavia. Perhaps the best that I can do is estimate that the population size fell somewhere between the membership size, which includes some non-Jews (approximately 10%), and the highest estimate of 10,000. This number would be about 7,000–7,500, which would equal the membership plus the estimated 2,000 assimilated and unaffiliated Jews. In 1980, for every 10,000 Jews in the world, five lived in Yugoslavia, but for every 10,000 Yugoslav citizens, only 2.6 Jews lived in Yugoslavia (Levi 1983). The Jews of Yugoslavia comprised less than one percent of the Yugoslav population. Was ethnic salience, not to say maintenance and reproduction, possible in such a tiny population?

At issue is not just a twelvefold reduction in absolute population size. Even before the Second World War the Jews comprised less than one percent (0.46) of the Yugoslav population. Relative population size is critical. Because of the decimation of the Jewish population and the mass postwar migration of other Yugoslav populations to the cities in the 1950s, the Jews ceased to be a visible urban presence. Also critical was the reduction or elimination of critical segments of the population—the gatekeepers, the guardians of tradition. Community leaders, religious specialists, educators, and wealthy business persons were lost, never to be replaced. The loss of such diverse specialists had a profound impact on the kind of ethnicity that could be supported in the socialist Yugoslav state. State control over the economy also contributed to this process by virtually removing the Jews as distinct players in the economic arena. Also, no longer was their position in society defined and regulated by a special law. In short, the Jews of Yugoslavia had lost much of their sociocultural visibility and distinction.

Size, then, may place certain limits on ethnic manifestation, but it does not preclude it. Jewish communities in most cities and towns before the Second World War were not large, but their members maintained and reproduced a traditional infrastructure and belief system for those who desired to live a distinct Jewish life in their generation. Perhaps where size is most important is in the economic and political spheres where there is interethnic competition or a need to justify receiving certain resources. It is also important for material demonstration and public visibility. Also, not just size but the distributions of particular categories of people in a population were important (e.g., age, sex, occupation, ritual expertise). The Jews were markedly elderly, had a low birthrate, had little economic viability, and lacked ritual specialists. It is therefore not surprising that they asked themselves, "Are we the final generation?" The critical issue of reproduction was both demographic and cultural. Could they perpetuate themselves biologically and culturally? Size and ritual are related, but size does not necessarily preclude ritual performance once the minimum ten adult males that form the prayer quorum is achieved. In the postwar period, however, the factor of choice entered the picture. The presence of ten or more adult Jewish men in a location no longer meant a prayer quorum would definitely convene. Individual men chose whether or not to participate, and very few men chose to be ritually active. The skewed elderly age structure is another factor that compounded the relationship between size and ritual performance.

Some were too old and ill to attend the synagogue, and the community provided no transportation, at least not in Belgrade. In addition, some individuals chose to practice a privatized form of religion.

The collapse of formal divisions and factions, the results of postwar socioeconomic and political leveling, and the increased influence of a unifying central institution, the Federation of Jewish Communities of Yugoslavia, contributed to greater uniformity which, in turn, reduced the impact of size reduction. Furthermore, many Yugoslav Jews shared the common experience and/or memory of the recent tragic past, and a large number participated in the culture of memorialism. This, too, contributed to greater unity and uniformity.

Jews were distributed in cities throughout all six republics and the two autonomous provinces of Yugoslavia. However, very few resided in Montenegro, where there never were many Jews, or in Macedonia and Kosovo, where substantial Jewish communities could be found before the war.

By examining proportions of the total for both the 1981 Census and the 1988–1989 *Luach*, it can be determined whether or not the low number of individuals who declared themselves as Jews in the 1981 census matches proportionately the Jewish membership figures when broken down by republic and province. For example, for the 1981 state census, 25 percent of those who declared themselves as Jews lived in Bosnia-Hercegovina. The *Luach* figures show that 24 percent of the total registered membership lived in Bosnia-Hercegovina. Proportionately the figures are all very or fairly close except for those of the Vojvodina,[10] where a high percentage of Jews-by-descent declared themselves as Jews on the 1981 census—12 percent higher than the next highest group, the Jews of Croatia, and 19 percent higher than the third highest group, the Jews of Bosnia-Hercegovina. When I compared the total of the census and the total of the membership, I found when dividing the lower census figure (1384) into the higher membership number (5419) that the total number of individuals who declared themselves as Jews was only 26 percent of the total membership as enumerated in the *Luach*.[11] If I make a similar comparison by dividing the census figure of 1,384 into the lower estimate (5,500) of total Jews in Yugoslavia, the percentage of declared Jews drops to 20 percent, and to only 14 percent if I use the higher estimate of 10,000.

In the 1980s most of the Yugoslav Jews were concentrated within the republics of Serbia (32%), Croatia (29%), and Bosnia-

Hercegovina (23.7%), and a majority of these were further localized within the cities of Belgrade, Zagreb, and Sarajevo. Belgrade contained the largest population of Jews (1,598 or 30%), followed by Sarajevo (1,090 or 20%) and Zagreb (1.028 or 19%). If we combine these cities with their surrounding areas, we find that 32 percent of the Jewish communal membership lived in or near Belgrade, 21 percent in or near Sarajevo, and 20 percent in or near Zagreb. Seventy-three percent of all members lived in or near these three urban centers, compared to the approximately 40 percent that lived in these three cities before the war. Thus, Belgrade, Sarajevo, and Zagreb remained the three major locations of Jewish concentration, though strikingly more so after the war. Given the membership figures I can estimate that less than one percent of all the Belgrade communal membership (and perhaps of the total Jewish population in Serbia?) lived outside of the geographical area of Belgrade and surrounding cities such as Zemun and Pančevo. Therefore, if one was Jewish or married to a Jew and lived in Serbia, she or he probably lived in or near Belgrade. Jews in Croatia were more dispersed. Of the total registered membership in Croatia, 13.6 percent lived in Dalmatia (4% of the total membership), while 15.2 percent lived in the eastern region of Slavonia, primarily in the city of Osijek.

Before the Second World War large numbers of Jews lived in Macedonia (7,762) and in the Vojvodina, which included the Banat, Bačka, and Baranja regions (20,200). In Macedonia only 112 registered communal members remained. Nearly all of these resided in the capital of Skopje, once a thriving Jewish city. No longer are there any Jews in the city of Bitolj where 3,350 lived just before the war and more than twice that number about a decade before the war. In the Vojvodina there were 613 registered members, and over 70 percent of these lived in Novi Sad and Subotica combined. Nearly all of the Jews have left the crisis region of Kosovo, which had about 1,000 Jews, and a handful of Jewish individuals remained in Montenegro (5 declared on the 1981 census), which never had many Jews (about 300 before the war). That the number of registered communal members was zero for Kosovo and Montenegro was partly due to the absence of any organized community in those areas of the country. In Slovenia there were 83 registered members, with the majority of those in the capital of Ljubljana.

Based on distributions in the state census of 1981, it is evident that relatively large concentrations of Jews continued to live in sections of the city called *Stari Grad* ("Old City") or in one of the other sections near the central business district. But a movement away from the center of the city can also be detected. In both Belgrade and Sarajevo substantial numbers of Jewish residents lived in the outlying suburbs of New Belgrade and New Sarajevo. Belgraders refer to the highrise apartments of New Belgrade as "sleeping boxes," a derogatory reference to the breakdown of traditional urban patterns and social relations.

Marko Perić (1980) notes that only 40 percent of the respondents in the Federation's 1971–1972 survey were born in the same republic in which they were living at the time of the survey and in which they had lived before the war in 1940. Of the total born in Bosnia-Hercegovina, 64 percent continued to live there; 82 percent continued to live in Croatia, 85 percent in Serbia Proper (without the two autonomous provinces of Vojvodina and Kosovo), 70 percent in Vojvodina, 31 percent in Slovenia, and 17 percent in Macedonia. These figures show that the highest percentage of out-migration was from Macedonia, Slovenia, and Bosnia-Hercegovina. Many Jews from Macedonia (49%) and Bosnia-Hercegovina migrated to Belgrade. Migration results taken from the 1985 survey show that only 27 percent of the respondents were living in the same republic in which they were born or living before the war.

Such postwar internal migration changed the composition of local Jewish communities. Postwar local communities were not simply smaller and weaker survivals of prewar communities. For example, out of the 1,200 Jews in Belgrade in 1945, only 250–300 were Belgradian Jews (Perera 1968–1970:139). The extremely high fatality count is the primary explanation. The Jews of Belgrade were among the first victims of the Second World War. Belgrade was the first city that the Germans declared free of Jews (Browning 1985). In addition, after the war many Jews did not return to their old homes that had been destroyed and to businesses that no longer existed, but they started their lives anew in larger cities where other Jews were likely to be found and where their chances of finding work were greater. Subotica was an exception to this pattern. In a survey in which 282 of the 298 (94%) of the members were interviewed, 146 were born in Subotica and 60 were born in other places in the Vojvodina. Of the 282, 222 listed Hungarian as their maternal language; only 44 listed Serbo-Croatian (Jelić 1984).

Postwar communal heterogeneity caused by internal migration appears to have made certain local communities more Yugoslav than regional in composition. Politically, as a community they tended not to favor one ethnic population over another. Some but by no means all of the newcomers to Belgrade, for example, were less supportive of the Serbian position vis-à-vis the other ethnic nations than prewar Belgraders. It is significant that the Federation of Jewish Communities of Yugoslavia was located in Belgrade. This institution was intended to represent all of the local Jewish communities. Most of the officers of the Federation, except for the presidents of the three largest communities who served as vice-presidents, were required to live in Belgrade.

Females outnumbered males in the Yugoslav Jewish population. In the 1985 Federation survey Jewish females accounted for 58 percent (total females, 55%) of the sample, while Jewish males accounted for 42 percent (total males, 45%) of the sample for a sex ratio of 138 females to 100 males (138:100). The reason for the difference between the sexes has its roots in the senior generation. When considering only the 55 and older respondents, we find that 65 percent are females and 35 percent males, which is a sex ratio of 186 females to 100 males (186:100), a disparity of almost two females for every male. These sex ratios are much higher than the balanced overall sex ratio of 104:101 in the Yugoslav population.

Women may have outnumbered men in the senior generation by nearly two to one (2:1), but men continued to occupy most of the key leadership positions, a disparity which did not go unnoticed in the Belgrade community. The disparity was discussed in the community's now defunct newsletter, the *Bilten* (Bulletin). During my fieldwork men occupied most of the leadership positions in various spheres of the organized community—presidents, vice-presidents, publishing, financial, camping, religious, and so on. Thus, a gender division existed on the federational level especially, but also was visible on the local community level. On the whole, however, women have been more active than men in communal life, with much of their contribution made through the Women's Section and the Social Committee.

Survey age data from 1985, which the survey analyst grouped into four categories (0–19; 20–39; 40–59; 60 and older), revealed the following age structure: the 60 and older age category was the largest (44% for Jews only; 42% for community members; 38% for total sample) by a significant margin, which indicates a markedly elderly Yugoslav Jewish population; the second largest category, 20–39, consisted of 23 percent of the Jewish respondents, 24 percent of the respondents who were members of the Jewish community, and 25 percent of the total respondents; the third largest category was the 0–19 (17%–19%), while the smallest category was the 40–45 (16%–19%). The upper half of this last category included the aforementioned "missing half-generation" which was lost to emigration and also the lack of births during the war years. When the age data are broken down into sixteen smaller categories, three distinct generational categories emerge: 75 and older; 35–39; 5–10. The age categories located between each of these categories contain far fewer persons. The structure appears to be three-generational with missing "half-generations" in between the three largest categories.

Above all else it is the large number of elderly Jews that is indicated by the available data. The 1971–72 data indicated an elderly to children age ratio of three to one (3:1). This is particularly striking when compared to the ratio in the total Yugoslav population in which there were twice the number of children as there were elderly. Whereas 29 percent of the Jews were 60 or older in 1971, only 12 percent of the total Yugoslav population fell into that age category. The 15 and younger category contained 27 percent of the total Yugoslav population, while less than 10 percent of the Jewish 1971 survey sample was included in this category (Perić 1980).

Power and influence have been concentrated in the most senior generation. The members of this generation were alive before the war and thus had both the knowledge and experience of Jewish life. In their careers they were either well established or retired. This allowed them to devote more of their time to the community. In the Belgrade community there were few communal activists below 60 years of age. The mean age of the Executive Council, for example, was 61.5 years of age in 1983. Of the 39 members of the Council, 14 were 71 years of age or older, and 12 were between 61 and 70 years of age. Only eight were 50 years old or younger (Levi 1983). Many were sympathetic to the political transformation of Yugoslav society and wanted to build a more secular Jewish community. Lastly, they felt no push from younger Jews on their status in the community. In terms of age alone this concentration of power and leadership in the oldest generation created a problem of succession. The large number of elderly Jews meant high mortality and morbidity. Individuals from the most active generation who were once active in Jewish life could participate no longer because of poor health.

Although mild oscillation is visible in certain years, there was a steady overall decline in the Jewish birthrate in the postwar years (*Jevrejski Pregled* 38 (1–2), 1987). By the 1980s there was an average of less than two births for each Jewish woman who gave birth, which reflected the general trend in Jewish communities outside Israel (Levi 1983). At the same time that the birthrate was declining, the mortality rate climbed steadily. The high rate of mortality reflected the large number of Jewish elderly. More than mortality is involved in examining attrition and delineating its impact. Two kinds of attrition must be considered. Morbidity removes individuals from active participation in communal life. Since there are so many older Jews, many of whom were once active in Jewish life, morbidity is a critical factor affecting Jewish life.

About 7,500 of the survivors emigrated to Israel in five emigration waves from 1948 to 1952. This was a great reduction of an already demographically decimated population. Particularly significant was the loss of a childbearing generation that would have strengthened the Yugoslav Jewish community demographically and socioculturally had it remained in Yugoslavia. A segment of the emigrant population represented the missing half-generation that fell just below the senior generation.

Demographic composition cannot ignore the attrition that resulted because of assimilation and non-membership in the organized Jewish community. Although the true number of Jews in these attritional categories is unknown, even the estimated loss of ten percent can be significant in such a tiny population. Certainly the estimated figure of 2,000, if accurate, would be an even more significant loss. Recent events suggest that there were more Jews in the country than some had estimated. Many Jews who were not registered in the organized Jewish community took advantage of the opportunity to evacuate Bosnia and Hercegovina because of the war. Ivica Čerešnješ, the president of the Sarajevo Jewish community, estimates that one-third to one-half of Bosnian Jews were not registered (Schwartz 1992, personal communication).

In short, the data, disregarding for the moment the cultural goals and wills of the actors, pointed to a bleak future. The Second World War and Holocaust transformed the demographic composition of the Jewish population to the point of making it vulnerable to extinction. Subsequent social practices such as ethnic exogamy did not reverse the havoc caused by the above historical events, but only pointed to an uncertain future.

Postwar Population Profile and Ethnic Capacity

The Familial Level and the Pattern of Truncation

Truncation characterized the postwar sociocultural profile of Yugoslav Jewry. Truncation is a pattern that indicates the absence or erosion of sociocultural integration between different levels of an ethnic collectivity, thereby reducing the ethnic capacity for sociocultural maintenance, reproduction, and transmission. The postwar Yugoslav Jewish profile was truncated precisely because the Jewish family that historically had linked the individual to the collective level of community life ceased to be a viable Jewish unit capable of functioning in those ways.

The removal of the Jewish family-household as a ritual unit and as an agent of and setting for Jewish cultural reproduction and transmission contributed to or served as a catalyst for sociocultural erosion, contraction, and redefinition of Jewishness on the other two levels as well. For example, individual rites of passage, which also provide times of family and community celebration, were almost nonexistent, except for the final passage of death. Does such a pattern of truncation necessarily lead to ethnic nonviability and eventual extinction, or does it allow for ethnic reformulation? Certainly the Yugoslav Jews recognized that they were a demographically weak population and were no longer capable of regaining the ethnic capacity of the prewar community, although, as Abraham (1989) has shown for the Indian Jewish communities, it is possible for a demographically weak community to maintain traditional practices. The Yugoslav Jews did confront the possibility of their extinction as a distinct Jewish group. They chose, however, not to intervene by attempting to reverse certain demographic trends. Instead, as I describe more fully in chapters 3 and 4, they chose to experiment with a reformulated Jewishness within the framework of a strong centralized organization and the "cultural program" carried out within its sphere of activity.

On the surface, at least, the causes of truncation are easily identified. Underlying all of these causes was the demographic decimation of the Yugoslav Jewish population resulting from genocide, war, emigration, and subsequently, the practice of ethnic exogamy and establishment of heterogeneous households and assimilation of one kind or another. Families and entire extended kinship units were completely or partially obliterated. Finding someone who did not lose close kinspersons would be difficult, since about eighty percent of the Jewish population was killed. Furthermore, many survivors who were capable of producing offspring did not return after the war or emigrated between 1948–1952. Given their absence the reproductive capacity of the Jewish population declined further. Those who chose to remain in Yugoslavia faced an increasingly shrinking Jewish spouse pool.

Marrying out, thus, was not necessarily in the immediate postwar years a decision of preference but of availability for those below the senior generation and for older individuals seeking new mates. Although with demographic decimation the conditions for truncation had been set, the actual practice of exogamy (marrying a non-Jew) set the process of truncation in motion. As the number of ethnically mixed marriages and consequently heterogeneous households grew, the pattern of truncation became more firmly entrenched. No longer were such marriages and households considered to be cultural or statistical aberrations.

In 1938 there were 17,370 Yugoslav Jewish families with an average of 4.11 members. In 1964 only 3,220 Jewish families with an average of 1.89 members remained. In many cases only one or two individual members of large families survived the war. Most of these were older and did not establish new families (Perera 1968–1970:142–143). The formation of families of procreation was sometimes delayed because of housing shortages. Young adults tended to remain in their parents' households well into their twenties, perhaps even their thirties. The number of new households dropped from 438 between 1946–1955 to a low of 184 between 1956–1965, then the number increased to 245 between 1966–1975 before again dropping to 205 between 1976–1985 (*Demographic Survey,* 1985).

The practice of marrying non-Jews and the creation of new households with children from this kind of union does not, however, necessarily result in sociocultural truncation. Other variables influence whether or not truncation will result. Some in-marrying partners become active participants in the ethnic life of their spouse's group. The mother of one of my informants converted to Judaism before the war during her first marriage. He attributes receiving Jewish feeling from his mother. However, there are limits to such inclusion, particularly if the non-Jewish spouse does not formally convert.

As stated, the postwar marriage practice has been one of ethnic exogamy, because of the smaller probability of finding a mate who is Jewish and of individual preference and choice. In Belgrade, for example, in 1983 there were 158 registered men in the 20–40 age category. There were 66 women in the 20–29 age category, and this number included those who were already married (Levi 1983). Despite the shortage of prospective younger aged Jewish spouses, such marriages have taken place occasionally. Limited exogamy may not pose a great threat to a population's survival if the population is large or powerful. The Yugoslav Jews, however, were one of Yugoslavia's smallest populations. As an organized community they offered certain advantages (e.g., travel) that might have attracted an in-marrying spouse, but to fully appropriate those advantages a formal conversion was required, and that act has been rare (0.27% of respondents in the 1985 Survey). Still, about 12 percent of the membership was non-Jewish (*Demographic Survey*, 1985) which constituted a significant segment that cannot be overlooked.

The kinship ideology stopped operating as a regulator of spouse selection. That came about not only because of demographic constraints, but also because of ideological change. Ethnic exogamy became acceptable in the new state in which a key symbol was the "Brotherhood and Unity of the Yugoslav Peoples" For its part, the organized community did not attempt to curtail such practice but instead adopted a non-interventionist approach.

With regard to descent as reflected in the 1985 survey, 74 percent of the respondents specified that they have a Jewish father, and 66 percent that they have a Jewish mother. Respondents whose parents are both Jewish constituted 52 percent of the sample. Excluding the senior generation would have produced a much lower percentage. Those whose father only is Jewish constituted 21 percent; those whose mother only is Jewish constituted 14 percent; those whose parents are not Jewish constituted 12 percent of the sample. There is some variation by local community. The Subotica community had an exceptionally high percentage of members whose parents are both Jewish (about 85%).

Of the 576 families registered with the Belgrade Jewish community in 1983, 120 or 23 percent included parents who are Jewish or half-Jewish, while 456 or 77 percent have mixed parentage. Stevan Levi, past president of the Belgrade community, stated that the high number of ethnically mixed marriages has its "objective and subjective reasons." Without the large number of elderly who married before the war, or perhaps immediately after, the number of mixed marriages likely would have been even higher, though such marriages did not characterize only the younger Jews. Mixed marriages obviously influence how children will be socialized. Questions are raised. Who will be the primary agent of socialization, the

Jewish or non-Jewish parent? What norms will the child be taught to adhere to? Which group will become the child's reference group? What kind of knowledge will the child be encouraged to learn? Who will be the significant others for the child? In what settings will learning occur? Will the child be socialized primarily by the restricted code or by the nonrestricted code which recognizes feelings and abstract principles more than authority and structured roles (Douglas 1973)? In Yugoslavia, as elsewhere, just because a Jewish parent was in the home did not necessarily mean the child would be raised as a Jew. Conversely, a non-Jewish parent may have choosen to expose the child to as many things Jewish as is possible in the Yugoslav setting. Because of the dispersed nature of Jewish sites and activities in Yugoslavia and abroad, this may have been an attractive alternative for either or both parents. Since most youth and children who participated were half-Jews by descent, exogamous marriages did not automatically lead to leaving the community.

The Collective Level

The Yugoslav Jewish population was demographically decimated by the Second World War. This wartime decimation (82%) was compounded by (1) the emigration of about half of the survivors, (2) assimilation/non-membership in the organized community (estimates of 10% and 2,000), (3) the pattern of truncation, (4) the loss of specialists and gatekeepers of tradition, (5) the procedure of recording dual affiliation on state censuses, and (6) the noninterference of the organized community in reversing certain trends. Furthermore, the rural-urban migration of other populations contributed to the loss of the Jewish urban presence. Lastly, the socioeconomic leveling and transformation of the Jewish population contributed to the disappearance or attenuation of significant contrasts between Jews and non-Jews.

Because of the demographic decimation, together with such contributing factors as the new political conditions and the organized community's orientation and priorities, the organizational framework and sociocultural composition of Yugoslav Jewry changed considerably. On the collective level, there had been a reduction and erosion of Jewish social units and spheres of activity (see Table 1 in Appendix for a comprehensive contrast between the prewar and the postwar population profile). No longer could the 121 local communities of the prewar era be maintained. Only 35 were revived after the war, and by 1985 there were 32. Far fewer than these 32 had active programs for their membership. The following local communities sent representatives to the Conference of Communities: Belgrade, Zagreb, Sarajevo, Novi Sad, Osijek, Subotica, Skopje, Split, Rijeka, Ljubljana.

No longer was there a multi-institutional, multi-ideological, multi-branch, multi-rite, and multi-class profile. In place before the war was a strong extra-communal organizational structure that reflected wide intra-populational variation by sex, age, class, ethnic branch, religiosity, political orientation, and interest, whereas the structure and ideological orientation of the postwar organized community reflected organizational centralization and ideological and performative uniformity. Given their prewar and wartime experience, and faced with demographic decimation, truncation, and sociocultural erosion in a radically transformed society, the Yugoslav Jews chose to pursue reformulation rather than succumb to complete assimilation and, ultimately, extinction. While adopting a non-interventionist approach toward demographic trends and composition that portended a bleak future and a similar attitude toward many traditional rituals and customs, they selected two separate but interrelated reformulative ethnic responses: secular Jewishness and political-symbolic submergence in Titoism. Among those who desired to be a part of the organized community there seemed to be general agreement on this policy of seeking a close tie with the new rulers while remaining Jews. Submergence entailed being voluntarily saturated in Titoism, but a strong organizational framework would be the foundation and mechanism of Jewish maintenance.

Within the postwar local community or *opština*, both structural continuities and differences between the prewar and postwar periods can be discerned. An executive board, a broader communal council, and various committees oriented toward different spheres of communal life (e.g., financial, social-welfare, cultural) constituted the communal structure. Open elections were held. A relatively small group, mostly composed of influential men, maintained positions of leadership. But there were important differences. The postwar community was based on voluntary membership, and as such it was a voluntary organization. Whereas before the war a graduated tax structure based on wealth was in effect, postwar members paid only a nominal annual membership fee. Although prewar local communities experienced serious economic crises, they were essentially autonomous units that obtained their revenue from the taxation of their members, which included fees for ritual purposes. During the interwar period a considerable portion of their budgets was designated for religious and ritual purposes, though the allotments for these declined over the years. In Zagreb, for instance, whose Neologue community was generally nonobservant, over fifty percent of the 1926 budget was designated for religious and ritual purposes. The percentage had dropped to less than one-third of the total budget by 1937, which was still a considerable amount by postwar standards (Freidenreich 1979:81). In the more observant Sephardi and Orthodox communities the percentage was certainly higher. The postwar local communities, in contrast, were voluntary organizations, dependent on outside support from the Federation which, in turn, was dependent on financial support from foreign Jewish organizations like the American Joint Distribution Committee and the Memorial Foundation for Jewish Culture. No longer did religion and ritual occupy places of priority in communal life. Other spheres, as ranked by one of my informants who occupied a high-level position in the Federation, had higher priority and hence commanded a greater portion of the budget.

The religious and ritual infrastructure had largely eroded. Most of the prewar communities had their own synagogues, cemeteries, and ritual specialists, but during my initial fieldwork only three synagogues held weekly Shabbat services. The Belgrade and Zagreb communities provided Erev Shabbat (Friday evening) services, while the Subotica community was the sole community that held a Sabbath day service. Attendance for Friday evening services was low. In Belgrade I calculated an average of twenty-three persons who attended the weekly service during the course of my fieldwork, and not all of these were Jews. It took the 180th anniversary celebration of the Zagreb Jewish community in 1986, which was attended by guests from abroad and from around Yugoslavia, to fill the Zagreb synagogue. It was the largest attendance for an Erev Shabbat service in Zagreb since 1941. Other communities operated their synagogues for certain holidays, but they had to import the single rabbi or one of the few other ritual specialists in the country, or they were forced to import someone from abroad. For two decades until 1968 the Yugoslav Jews had only one practicing rabbi, Menahem Romano, who lived in Sarajevo. He died in 1968 and was not replaced until 1973 when Cadik Danon, a prewar graduate of the Middle Theological School of Sarajevo, wartime *prvoborac* (participant in the Partisan uprising from the beginning) and retired diplomat, agreed to serve as the Rabbi of Yugoslavia. On two separate occasions the Federation sent a young man abroad, once to Israel and once to London, for rabbinical study. These attempts to educate young men to meet the ritual needs of the population failed. More recently, one of my informants, a convert to Judaism, was sent to Israel for rabbinical study and, when I last saw him, was nearing the completion of his studies. In addition, the rabbi trained several young men from Belgrade to serve as *hazzanim* (predmolitelji, prayer leaders). Another outcome of the drastic reduction in population size and in the number of viable communities was the deterioration of Jewish cemeteries, a matter of great concern to the community.

Other spheres of Jewish life were never or only barely reestablished. Two Jewish kindergartens operated for a time in Zagreb and Belgrade. The community managed to reestablish a home for the aged, one of the best facilities of its kind in the country. Like the old-age home, the Pirovac summer camp, also under the auspices of the Federation of Jewish Communities of Yugoslavia, stands witness not to the strength of Yugoslav Jewry but rather to the efforts of a minuscule community to withstand the pressures of a vulnerable population profile and total assimilation.

The Individual Level

The most glaring absence from postwar Jewish life on the individual level are the rites of passage of the life cycle. Jewish rituals associated with birth, coming of age, and marriage are extremely rare. During my fieldwork I observed only one synagogue wedding of a foreign couple. Two circumcisions were performed, not on eight-day-old infants, as prescribed by Jewish law, but on two university students, one of whom was a convert to Judaism. The circumciser was not a Jewish *mohel* but a hospital physician. The *bar mitzvah*, the rite of passage into adulthood (manhood) and thus into eligibility for the male prayer quorum or *minyan*, did not occur during my stay, although two informants told me that this rite would occur in the future. The *gabai* of the Belgrade synagogue approached me while I was sitting in a pew on Yom Kippur and informed me that one of the boys who had attended the service would have a bar mitzvah. The second, a resident of Subotica, known as the most religious of the remaining communities, told me that his two sons would undergo this rite of passage into manhood. In addition to the rites themselves, the customs associated with the life stages have also either disappeared completely or been eroded considerably. Only death ritual remains strong, although most aspects of it no longer are performed.

For Yugoslav Jews, both the first and last name can be important ethnic markers that sets them apart from the South Slavic and other populations. This symbolic marker, too, underwent erosion. When a Jewish woman married out she took the family name of her husband. An informant did describe a case of children of an intermarried Jewish woman wanting to take their mother's maiden Jewish name, but that was no doubt an exception. Another generational pattern of naming could be detected. In certain obituaries one could read the names of three generations of the same family. There were cases in which an individual was given a Slavic name by his or her parents and as a parent gave a Jewish name to his or her own children.

Even before the war some Jews slavicized their names by adding the common suffix *-ić* out of patriotism or because of their integrationist orientation. They saw themselves as Serbs or Croats by nationality and Jews by religion. After the war several Jews changed their entire name out of loyalty to the new state (e.g., Velimir Drechsler to Marko Perić). Individuals who changed their name were not necessarily more assimilated than those who kept their Jewish names. In such cases, name changing did not contribute to cutting off the individual from the community, but it did contribute to overall symbolic erosion. Yet another public symbol became eroded and distinctiveness was weakened, especially in a country like Yugoslavia, where ethno-linguistic patterns of naming were so ubiquitous.

The Limited Options Offered by Truncation

Given the truncated pattern that removed the family-household as a viable Jewish unit and sphere of activity, the individual Jew who wanted to maintain and/or pursue his or her Jewishness was left with two options or alternative responses to the new circumstances of Yugoslav society. One option was to participate in the organized Jewish community, which had taken over some of the functions and activities performed by the Jewish family before the war. The organized Jewish community, however, differed in many respects from what it had been earlier. It had become more centralized and uniform. Class and political variation had been leveled. The leadership explicitly stated that the community was pursuing secular Jewishness, simultaneously submerging itself in the new political and symbolic order of Titoism. It was a program of reconstruction in the face of demographic decimation and socio-cultural erosion and truncation. Religion and eroded ritual practices were not entirely ignored, but they had lost their place of priority and importance. What rites and customs were retained, including those traditionally associated with the family, were now taken over by the organized community. The individual who desired to be a part of a Jewish collectivity, thus, no longer could connect with one of a number of extra-communal Jewish organizations that represented his or her own interests and ideological persuasion, but could only be a part of a collectivity guided by a leadership elite that directed the community on one particular course. The other option was to attempt to pursue Jewishness through self-constitution or self-situation, that is, an individuated Jewishness.

Continuous to Discontinuous Time

Although before the war Jewish life was changing in various ways, the Jewish calendar or rhythm of life continued to influence the lives of the Jews. This was especially true for religious Jews, but non-religious Jews were affected by the holiday festivities as well. The surrounding population saw that the Jews did or did not behave in certain ways on particular days. Thus, both the Jews and the non-Jews were aware of the flow of Jewish time. Living according to the annual Jewish cycle of life called for regular times of reemergence and social visibility. The postwar Jews, in contrast, were far less influenced by the Jewish calendar. The calendar influenced most Jews minimally or not at all. Jewish social visibility in the postwar years emerged primarily in two ways. First, Jews were visible during commemoration rites because they were key participants in many of these rites and were memorialized in them as victims of fascism and as fallen fighters. Second, Jews became more visible during times of threat or crisis.

Problems of Postwar Enumeration and Jewish Declaration

The first postwar census of the Yugoslav population was conducted in 1948. In this census there were 6,853 Jews, which indicates that a little more than half of the registered communal members declared themselves as Jews. The number of individuals who declared themselves as Jews on that and subsequent state censuses was far smaller than the true number of Jews. The

Yugoslav Jewish demographer Perić (1970) explains that a significant number did not want to declare themselves as Jews because of the horrible fate Jews suffered during the Second World War just because of their ethnic origin. Many declared a dual identity, such as Serb-Jew, but census statisticians counted only the first designation. Because of such census tallying a part of the already decimated Jewish population was "lost" in the censuses. When Perić delved deeper into the census results he found an interesting, and, to him, apparently disturbing, discrepancy in the statistical treatment of dual identity responses. When Jews declared *Serb-Jew* only *Serb* was recorded. This procedure was not consistent when applied to other nationalities. When *Serb-Montenegrin* or *Serb-Gypsy* was declared, the second designation was recorded and counted. Perić suggested that perhaps the statisticians, who work with a mass of information and large figures, simply overlooked this inconsistency because of the relative and absolute small number of Jews (ibid:21–22).

The categories of nationality and religion were both included in the census of 1953. It is interesting that in 1953, the year following the fifth and final emigration wave, more Jews declared themselves by religion (2,565) than by nationality (2,307) (Perić 1973:269). It is unclear whether a particular segment of the population chose to declare by religion. Most likely the oldest generation was well represented in this declarative category. Thereafter the category of religion was eliminated from the state census. The Federation was the Federation of Jewish Religious Communities until "Religious" was removed in the 1950s, despite more Jews declaring themselves by religion than by nationality on the 1953 census.

In declaring oneself on postwar censuses in the new socialist state, an individual had a constitutional right (Article 33) to refrain from declaring any nationality, as well as other options. The option of declaring oneself as a Yugoslav was available and saw a tremendous increase from the 1971 to the 1981 census. It is highly probable that a significant percentage of Jews opted for this declaration. The meanings attached to such a declaration is another matter, and different explanations can be found (Rusinow 1989; *Yugoslav Life,* November 1988). The census itself does not reveal the motivation behind the declaration, although motivation can be intuitively surmised by relating census declaration to contemporary conditions and trends together with the variable of region. Declaration by region of residence was yet another option available to the postwar citizen of Yugoslavia, though few chose it. The number of Jews who declared themselves by either of these options is unknown.

In Yugoslavia the most popular option of declaring nationality was one's actual ethnic descent, although in ethnically heterogeneous households the element of personal choice further complicated the population profile. Different members of the same household could declare different nationalities or census options. This was especially true for individual members of minority groups, particularly members of the so-called *etničke grupe*, defined as very small nationality groups without their own territory. Of such populations, the Jews were probably the most dispersed and thus had the most options. Members of such groups could declare themselves in one or more ways. Individuals could declare themselves according to the descent group into which they were born. In cases of ethnically divided descent, the bilateral descent principle could operate in different ways.

The traditional descent principle of the dominant ethnic population could have been used to determine or select ethnic origin. South Slavic groups traditionally reckoned descent patrilineally. Thus, Jews in Yugoslavia, if selecting the principle of the host population, may have used patrilineality to establish ethnic descent. The Jewish individual who wanted to declare him- or herself as a Jew, and whose only Jewish parent was the father, may have invoked patrilineality, the South Slavic descent principle. According to the Bible genealogical descent was reckoned patrilineally or matrilineally, depending on the intent of the genealogist. Jewish *Halakhic* tradition, on the other hand, recognizes matrilineal descent in reckoning ethnic origin.[12] If an individual wished to declare as a Jew and only his or her mother was Jewish, matrilineality was invoked. Another option was declaring according to the descent group of a grandparent, when this group was different from the group of either parent. Declaring themselves according to the dominant ethnic population of the region (particularly Serbian or Croatian) was another option. Yet another option was to refuse to declare any of the Yugoslav nationalities. Lastly, individuals may have declared themselves by something besides nationality or citizenship.

The main descent principle underlying all of the options was flexibility. Both within the Yugoslav Jewish world and in Yugoslav society, reckoning Jewish descent through the only Jewish parent, regardless of sex, was acceptable and created no problems of membership in the organized Jewish community.

The options open to individuals were problematic for enumeration on surveys conducted by the organized Jewish community itself. The large number of exogamous marriages and ethnically heterogeneous households had introduced the element of self-ascription and choice. Households included both Jews and non-Jews. Children could declare differently. Parents put little or no pressure on their children to declare a certain nationality. Other individuals, such as educators and census takers, did pressure Jewish individuals to declare in certain ways. As noted, within Yugoslavia Jews had the flexibility to declare themselves as Jews and be accepted as such even when Halakhic criteria were not met. Such flexibility was sanctioned by the organized community. Most other Yugoslavs knew too little about Jews to make their own judgments or respond to individual claims. When attending Jewish events in foreign countries, however, some Yugoslav Jewish youth complained that other Jews viewed them with reservation, if not suspicion, as an organization of friends of Jews. Furthermore, for various reasons self-ascription sometimes changed. Some individuals never were told that they were Jews and only discovered their Jewish origin sometime after childhood. Conversely, some whose ethnic background was never in doubt chose at some turning point in life to declare themselves as something other than Jewish, even if acknowledging Jewish descent. Such cases exist. One of my respondents made a public break with the organized Jewish community when he was about sixteen years old. He began to consider himself a Yugoslav. His Jewishness became an entirely private matter.

Problems associated with demographic enumeration and analysis were further complicated because membership in the community was voluntary. Before the war every individual was theoretically a member of the Jewish religious community. The difference from other religions was the Jewish community's legal status as a religious community and not a nationality. After the war, non-Jewish kin became members of local Jewish communities. Included in this category, for example, are non-Jewish widows and widowers. What emerges in official censuses and in surveys is considerable fluctuation in declaration and the reasons for it must be found in association with the context of individual lives and that of the population as a whole.

There was also the problem of the "lost," "marginal," and assimilated Jews. After the Second World War not all Jews declared themselves as Jews and, consequently, they did not register in any of the local reconstituted Jewish communities. A significant number of Jews did acknowledge their Jewish origins, but they chose not to become members of the communities. Between 1958 and 1965 efforts were launched by the organized community to determine the number of Jews who were not members. In each of four such enumerations the percentage of non-registered Jews was close to 10 percent (Perera 1968–1970). I also have seen a much greater figure (2,000), which would have put the non-registered percentage at over 20 percent. Some of these may participate in certain communal activities without becoming formal members, while others may participate in the small Jewish world through personal networks that include Jews. These individuals were included in my Yugoslav Jewish study population, regardless of whether or not their names appeared on a formal membership list. How to enumerate such persons, however, was problematic. Given these Jews on the periphery of the institutional Yugoslav Jewish world, estimates of the size and composition of the Yugoslav Jewish population varied. As individuals, however, many were accessible through personal ties. Complicating the problem still further was the active participation of Jews who chose not to be members of a Jewish community. Some of these nonmembers even occupied board positions in the organized community.

3

THE COLLECTIVE VOICE OF SUBMERGENCE

> From the time of their reorganization after the war until today, the Federation and the local Jewish communities have always accepted as one of their responsibilities the task of stimulating Yugoslav Jews in the direction of the widest possible support of the construction of socialist Yugoslavia. This is an expression of the desire and disposition of the majority of Jews. Otherwise there existed the [task] of reeducating that small number who had yet to come to a full understanding of the new Yugoslav reality (Vajs 1954:29).

This chapter presents the collective voice of the Jews of socialist Yugoslavia, particularly that of the organized Jewish community, which comprised the Federation of Jewish Communities of Yugoslavia and its satellite local Jewish communities.[1] This was the voice that sounded in my ears before the dismemberment of socialist Yugoslavia. I describe and analyze it as I heard it. It was the voice of submergence, by which I mean a voice that blended with the larger, stronger, and penetrating voice of the rulers of socialist Yugoslavia. In submerging, the Jewish voice was not lost completely in the dominant voice, but at times it was hard to hear its distinctiveness.

In submerging itself in the emerging invented tradition of socialist Yugoslavia, the Jewish community reimagined and represented itself through the lens of the newly legitimated ideology. The leaders of the community chose to establish a secure place within the new state and its symbolic order. In so doing a transposition took place. The Jewish community repositioned itself. Titoist ideology became the new constant with which the Jewish community sought to refashion itself.

The Links between Wartime Participation and Postwar Leadership

For all individuals in postwar socialist Yugoslavia, Jews and non-Jews alike, participation in the National Liberation Struggle (NOB) was an important criterion for good standing and advancement. For the Jewish population as a whole, the participation of many of its members in the NOB demononstrated to the new rulers that it had achieved a place in the new society. It was contingent upon the Jewish community's own initiative, however, to gather and show evidence of participation. And so it did, designating this task a communal priority. In pursuing this aim, the community also wanted to refute the myth that cast the Jews in the role of unresisting sheep being led to the slaughter. The Jews of Yugoslavia wanted to show the other side of their war experience, that of the Jewish fighter, saboteur, and revolutionary hero. Although accomplished quietly through its publishing activity, the Jewish community also contested the claims of non-Jewish individuals who wrote that Jews were underrepresented in the NOB (see *Zbornik*). The Jewish community believed that it had indeed secured for itself an acknowledged place in socialist Yugoslavia.

Because of or despite being targeted by the Germans and Ustasha, a significant number of Jews joined the NOB at different periods and contributed at various levels in the National Liberation Army (NOV) and the National Liberation Movement (NOP). Proportionately, Jews were represented three to four times greater in the Partisan uprisings than their percentage of the total population (Romano 1980). Facilitating their entrance were their prewar contacts with the Communist and revolutionary movement and their preparedness for conflict which they had received from their Marxist training. Many who had joined the Communist Youth or Communist Party before the war accepted the most dangerous assignments in urban areas, where they were at double risk as Communists and Jews.

Much of the task of documenting the Jewish contribution to the NOB was taken up by the Jews themselves. Jews inside and outside the framework of the organized community contributed to this effort. This task was significant for several reasons. As noted, the postwar Jewish community wanted to put to rest the myth of the Jews as the sheep being led to the slaughter. In its place they represented themselves as the fighters, military commanders, *prvoborci*, and national heroes who had distinguished themselves in the struggle of resistance and revolution. By demonstrating their disproportionately great participation in the face of many obstacles put in their way, they not only silenced certain individuals who either ignored Jewish participation or portrayed it as less than it was (e.g., Tito's biographer Vladimir Dedijer) (ibid.), but they also showed that they had won and deserved a place in the new Titoist order.

Part of the problem of Jewish participation in the NOB stems from how individual Jews identified themselves and how they were identified by others. The editors of the Federation's *Zbornik* volumes I and III state that the Jewish fighters were regarded as belonging to the Yugoslav ethnic groups among whom they lived. They write, "It is true that many Jewish fighters declared themselves as belonging to these nationalities, and were by many other criteria accepted as in fact part of these nationalities. However, according to certain criteria, they were also Jews" (Loker 1977:105–106). As noted elsewhere, Jews could join the Partisans only as individuals; the Communist Party did not permit them to join as groups of Jews. Once in Partisan units, Jewish individuals often adopted non-Jewish nicknames for the purpose of protecting themselves and their units, but this also tended to associate them with other nationalities. Some Jews changed their names out of patriotism.

The Jews contributed an exceptionally high proportion of medical personnel to the Yugoslav National Liberation War. The largest segment (21%) of Jews in the NOV consisted of doctors and other medical personnel. Altogether, there were 1,022 Jewish medical persons, of whom 167 died. One reason for such high participation was that the Germans and the Ustashi exempted them during the first year of the war in order to fight epidemics. Another reason was that many were in the prewar revolutionary movement and thus had ties to the Partisans. Over fifty percent of all Jewish medical personnel participated in the NOV, which, as stated in an exhibit catalogue, was "proof of the readiness on the part of Yugoslav Jewry to fight or at least to help in the struggle against Nazism when the opportunity was offered" (*The Jews in Yugoslavia*, 1989, 122). There was a great shortage of doctors during the war, hence the Jewish medical contribution was critical. In 1939 Jews constituted 22 percent of all doctors in the country, while in 1942, 56 percent (40/73) of all doctors in the Partisan medical corps were Jews (ibid:129). The Jewish participation would have been greater, had many doctors not been transported to concentration camps, where about 435 Jewish doctors died (Romano 1973:129).

It is significant that before the war many Jewish medical students were politically progressive and members of either the Communist Youth Organization or the Communist Party. Pavle Pap

Table 3.1
Yugoslav Jewish POWs and Postwar Communal Position or Role

Name	*Position or Sphere of Activity*
Still Alive in 1985	
Lavoslav Kadelburg	President, SJOJ, 1964–92; VP, SJOJ
Aleksandar Levi	SJOJ Dep. Pres., Editor, *Jewish Review*
Stevan Levi	President, Belgrade JC, VP, SJOJ
Josip Presburger	Activist
Andrija Gams	Jewish Historical Museum
Slavko Zvezdić	President, Split JC (later, hon. Pres.)
Isak-Bata Amar	Activist, Belgrade
Rafailo Blam	Activist, Belgrade
Oto Centner	Pres. Curatorship of L. Švarc Home
Deceased at Time of Research	
Albert Vajs	President, SJOJ, 1948–64

was among these at the University of Belgrade. Pap (*Šilja)* was the only Jew besides Moša Pijade selected to be a member of the Central Committee of the Communist Party. Medical persons were among the organizers of the uprising (ibid:124).

There were about 350–400 Yugoslav Jewish reserve officers in prisoner-of-war (POW) camps in Germany. During their internment many were involved in the antifascist and communist movements as they operated in the camps. Among these POWs were several individuals who would come to occupy key positions in the postwar Jewish community. This link between POW status and postwar Jewish activism and leadership is quite apparent.

Just as experience in the National Liberation Struggle was linked to status and advancement in Yugoslav society (Denitch 1976; Taylor 1987), so too it appears to have been linked to leadership position in the postwar Jewish community.[2] Since a significant number of Yugoslav Jewish POWs were engaged in antifascist or Communist political activities during their internment in Germany, they were acknowledged as participants in the NOB. It is interesting that they were discussing plans for reconstruction of the Jewish community while still interned (Presburger 1975; Vajs 1954). Although Tables 3.1 and 3.2 do not present an exhaustive list of POWs and NOB participants who became lead-

Table 3.2
Yugoslav Jews (1) in NOB and Postwar Communal Position or Role

Name and Year Joined NOB	*Communal Position/Role*
Beginning of Uprising	
Cadik Danon	Rabbi of Yugoslavia
Dragan Volner	Pres. JOZ
Jaša Romano	Council of JHM
Vera Dojč	VP JOZ
Later	
Andrija Preger NOP '42	Pres. Cult. Comm., SJOJ, EC
Egon Štark NOP '41 (2)	Pres. JONS, EC
Benjamin Samakovlija NOV '41	Pres. JOSk
Bencion Levi NOP '42	Pres. JOB, SJOJ
Isak Levi	Pres. JOSa, SJOJ
Slavko Goldstein NOP '42 (2)	Pres. JOZ, SJOJ
Samuel Elazar NOP '42	Pres. JOSa
After Sept. 8, 1943 (Capitul. of Italy)	
Jaša Almuli NOV '44 (2)	Pres. JOB, SJOJ
Tina Finci NOV '43	Pres. WS, SJOJ, EC
Aleksandar Mošić NOV '43	Dep. Pres., SJOJ, EC
Silvana Mladinov NOV '43	Pres. JOSp
Pavle Šosberger BOR, NOV '44	EC
Eta Najfeld NOV '44	Soc. Comm., SJOJ, EC
Mile Salom NOV '43	JOB positions
Eduard Tauber NOV '4	Pres. JOSp, EC
Lea Sorger NOV '44	
Eugen Verber NOV '44	Cult. Comm., SJOJ, EC
Wartime Experience and/or Year Joined NOB Unknown	
Aleksandar Švarc	Pres. JOL

(1) = alive in 1985
(2) = prewar SKOJ or CPY

ers in the postwar Jewish community, they illustrate this significant link. Table 3.1 shows the link between POW internment and postwar position in the community for several key individuals still alive in 1985. Table 3.2 does the same for non-POWs who participated in the NOB.

Submergence

Submergence was a synthesis of a Jewish memorial culture and a newly invented socialist culture in which the former accommodated itself with the latter. While helping to build the New Yugoslavia, the Jewish survivors simultaneously participated in the narrower experiment of creating a secular Jewish community. Participating in these two tasks allowed the Yugoslav Jews to shuttle between, and even simultaneously occupy, the Jewish and the Yugoslav poles of life and the points in-between. That is, submergence allowed for simultaneous participation in two different but historically convergent symbolic universes.

Submergence displayed qualities of the dramaturgical performance and discipline described by the sociologist Erving Goffman (1957). That is, it entailed a kind of role-playing on the part of the organized Jewish community. To the new rulers the Yugoslav Jews conveyed an intense desire to fit in, to be an integral part of the new order. Even during the interwar period in Yugoslavia, the Jews indicated how much they wanted to fit in by adopting the nationality of the dominant group of the region or by taking a strong Yugoslavist orientation. The prewar inclination toward Yugoslavism carried over into the postwar Yugoslav state. Driven by their desire to find a place in the new order, they set out to publicly display their loyalty and conformity. They were prepared to be Yugoslav to the degree to which many of the other nationalities were not.[3] The performances were dramaturgical in the sense that they followed a fixed order. Many of the same verbal themes and utterances were repeated regularly, thus giving the appearance of scripting. Dramaturgical discipline was also important for the performance to accomplish its goals. What was not said, not shown, and not done was just as critical as what was said, shown, and done.

The conception of submergence is found in the words of the Yugoslav Jews themselves. Albert Vajs, the president of the Federation of Jewish Communities of Yugoslavia from 1948 until his death in 1964, described the Jewish community as a distinct unit, but as one "saturated with the spirit and deeds of that socialist country" (1955:13). Vajs' description connotes an altered state of consciousness. That is indeed what submergence was, although the altered state was the result of a symbolic and not a physiological transformation. Jewish life was not just different in socialist Yugoslavia; it was qualitatively different. Vajs goes on to state that such a saturation did not result in losing but in strengthening Jewish identity. Clearly, thus, the intent was not to discard Jewishness, but to reformulate it into something qualitatively different from what it had been, at least for a period of time. This latter point is not insignificant. Altered states are often temporary states. Their history had informed them that change was a constant in their lives. They had always been affected by change from without and no doubt would be again.

The Political and Symbolic Orders of the New Yugoslavia

To successfully complete a transformation of Yugoslav society following the consolidation of power, the new socialist rulers first had to uproot the old order and substitute a new order in its place. Not only did this entail constructing a new political order, but also a new symbolic order with its constituent language, objects, and performances placed within a new flow of time. They thus engaged in inventing a tradition (Hobsbawm 1983) that would serve to mobilize the populace and institutionalize wartime slogans and popular front organizations.

The National War of Liberation and Yugoslav Revolution, or simply, Partisan War, culminated in a new set of power relations. There began a revolutionary transfer of power during the chaos of 1941–45. The Yugoslav Communists consolidated their power more quickly than any Communist Party had done previously (Djilas 1991). Before the war the Communist Party was a small, close-knit cadre party, illegal since 1920. Although in the decade preceding the war its membership had grown, there were only about 12,000 members in 1941. It was the Party's ability to successfully exploit what was for its leaders a fortuitous mix of extraordinary circumstances that allowed them to take power.

The successful revolutionary strategy included mobilizing the sole multiethnic resistance force. This resistance force became the basis for the People's Army whose political commissars preached ethnic reconciliation. This army included representatives from all of the major ethnic populations at all levels of the resistance and Party organization. Much of the rhetoric concerning wartime and postwar goals was couched in non-Communist language, thus encouraging greater inclusivism. The composition of this army and the proselytization of Party members led to an expansion of membership in the Communist Party and the Communist youth organization. The Partisan leadership had promised an equality for all Yugoslav peoples.

In socialist Yugoslavia, power became consolidated in the Communist Party, and within that party in the hands of a political elite, a group of about 1,200 individuals on the federal and republic levels (Denitch 1976:8). Any opposition in the early years was dealt with either violently or in a manner that physically isolated those branded as enemies of the state. Until 1950, two years after the break with the Soviet Union and expulsion from the Cominform on the traditional Serbian holiday of Vidovdan, the Yugoslav system could be described as Stalinist.

Out of the National Liberation Struggle and its revolutionary cadres a new political order was established. The bases of power in the new political order included a charismatic leader—Tito, a political elite, referred to as "the club of 1941," the Communist Party of Yugoslavia (changed in 1952 to the League of Communists of Yugoslavia (SKJ) and its youth branch, the Association of Communist Youth of Yugoslavia (SKOJ)), the Socialist Alliance of Yugoslav Working Peoples (SAWPY), the Association of Veterans of the National War of Liberation (SUBNOR), the state structure at the federal, republic, local government levels, and the Constitution and legal system.

The attainment and the distribution of power in socialist Yugoslavia were associated with several criteria. The greater the number of criteria met by an individual, the greater were the chances of success as defined by the new socialist rulers. First, there was the criterion of experience in the Partisan War (NOB, NOV, NOP). Several ranked levels were associated with this criterion. The year one joined the war was extremely critical to establishing status. The top rank or level of NOB participation included veterans of the original uprising in June 1941 (*prvoborci*), those holding a National Hero medal, and major underground activists. There were about 24,000 people in this group still alive in the 1970s. The next level included the category of individuals who joined the NOB before September 9, 1943, the day Italy capitulated. About 300,000 of this group were alive in the mid-1970s.

Individuals in these two top-level groups were rewarded with special social benefits, such as pensions, employment, and housing. The third level included all other veterans, with the addition of those who "helped." Also important was the military rank one attained, in the following order: (1) colonel or higher, (2) officer or commissar, (3) soldier to lieutenant, and the decorations one received (ibid:87). The second major criterion was membership in the Communist Party. Denitch (ibid:82) writes that party membership was related to participation in the social system and to social mobility, but the causal relationship is not clear. Immediately after the war Party membership, especially when combined with wartime achievements, was related to opportunity for and speed of individual achievement and upward mobility (ibid.). Party seniority was positively related to what one's status had been in the Partisan army (ibid:86–87). The year that one joined and one's political function were important factors associated with party membership. Additional important criteria included prewar political activity, political education, state honors and awards, age (old enough to have been in the Partisans), occupation, and gender, with males wielding more power than females.

The new Titoist rulers consolidated power by first eliminating their opposition, the "enemies of the state," all whom they deemed to be fascists, nationalists, and capitalists. Later, their campaign of ideological cleansing was extended to those they labeled Stalinists, Cominformists, religious nationalists, and whomever else they considered a threat to the new order. Creating distinctiveness and a new identity apart from both the Old Yugoslavia and the Soviet model of state socialism helped establish legitimacy and authority. Undeterred in attaining their goals, the rulers used various methods of keeping their power, authority, and legitimacy. Particularly in the early years after the Second World War, considerable physical coercion or threat of coercion was used. The rulers even maintained concentration camps where they detained persons whom they proclaimed enemies of the state (see chapter 6).

Construction of the new symbolic order began during the National Liberation Struggle. The key symbols of the New Yugoslavia formed the basis of a new cultural tradition upon which a new community could be created. In listing the key symbols I follow Ortner's (1973) analytical distinction between key symbols that summarize and those that elaborate. Summarizing symbols sum up, express, and represent for the participants in an emotionally powerful and relatively undifferentiated way what the system means to them. "They operate to compound and synthesize a complex system of ideas, to "summarize" them under a unitary form which "stands for" the system as a whole" (ibid:1340).

Symbolic manipulation or management was a major means of maintaining power and establishing legitimacy. Specifically, to accomplish these aims the rulers used a special language (including a "national patriotic myth which constitute[d] the justification for the legitimacy of the movement" (Denitch 1976:14) and a new set of calendrical rituals and ceremonies, which the new rulers believed would detach people from their religious traditions. It was believed that reordering time would help accomplish the latter. There were also proscriptions regarding the use of the key symbols. Importantly, the new rulers controlled the state's communications network and the system of education. Mass socialization and dissemination were thus in their hands.

The summarizing symbols of the new symbolic order, the "six pillars" of the invented tradition of Titoism, included: (1) Tito, (2) the Communist Party, (3) National Liberation Struggle, (4) Brotherhood and Unity, (5) Socialist Self-Management, and (6) Non-Alignment.

At the core was Tito himself, the dominant and unifying symbol of the entire order. Tito, or "Walter," his underground name, was a prewar legendary figure. He was the revolutionary founder. The origin myth of the New Yugoslavia is inexplicable without the creator. Later, Tito become an active symbol of stability, continuity, unity, and conflict resolution. In Tito, the symbol, were condensed all of the other symbols of the order. All else emanated from Tito, and all else ultimately could be traced back to Tito. From Tito the man, the legend, and the symbol was created the ideology of Titoism, the first variant of the Soviet parent model of socialism. Titoism enjoyed magiclike control over most of the population well into the 1980s. Even though tarnished during the erosion and dismemberment of socialist Yugoslavia, the symbolic presence of Tito had not been entirely eradicated, especially in certain regions (e.g., Macedonia) and among certain groups (e.g., elderly NOB veterans). Nevertheless, it cannot be overlooked that after his death Tito's symbolic grip over the Yugoslav peoples gradually eroded. With his physical demise began the dissolution of the entire symbolic order. Here we have an ideological framework and a symbolic order that were not greater than the individual. As we now know, viable states cannot be built upon the immortality strivings of great men (see Lifton 1968). Such men die, and with the passing of time their symbolic power withers with them.

Titoism had legitimacy as a unifying structure on one level and as an ideological framework on another level. The symbolic order reflected and actively supported both. As Ortner (1973) has conceptually laid out, symbols can be strategies for action. In fact, the Titoist symbolic order, not the ideological framework or political structure, became the most potent force in the Yugoslav system. There were no losses to be suffered in invoking the NOB to stir the memories and emotions of the Yugoslav peoples. And, what could be more noble than the "brotherhood and unity" of all Yugoslav peoples? Its legitimacy was based on its actual success in mobilizing persons from all of Yugoslavia's ethnic populations to resist a foreign occupier who intended on imposing an unwanted ideology, and on its temporary symbolic success in ideologically veiling the roots of ethnic conflicts by constantly invoking "brotherhood and unity." Perhaps Tito believed that by reiterating this slogan enough times and in enough places ethnic mistrust would fade away. Initially he adhered to the Marxist belief that ethnic attachments and sentiments indeed would fade away, and so he set out to construct a new Yugoslav being and a new Yugoslav culture. Not much later he abandoned this identity building project for the principle of equality (*jednakost*) in all things, even to the point of reinterpreting the past in a manner that would preclude any particular ethnic population from being singled out as contributing more or less to the revolution and the building of the New Yugoslavia. Trials may have been held after the war, but as far as who gave more or lost more in the war, there was to be no such accounting as the competitive "counting of graves" which transpired when Yugoslavia began gasping its last breaths in 1990–1991. Under Tito, Yugoslav culture did not mean a national culture, but rather a common socialist experience, a common socialist reality, and common socialist aspirations. In addition, Tito's real successes established legitimacy because of the conditions under which Titoism was created—a world war, a civil war, and later in 1948 the bold break from Stalin. The fact that a political revolution occurred under such conditions made it more acceptable to a population which did not want to experience such violence and yet again the yoke of foreign rule. With only about 12,000 Party members at the start of the war, the country certainly was not about to hand over power to a small and illegal cadre party. That Titoism emerged during a clearly demarcated historical period also provided it with historicity. It was not the product of the minds of ideologues. Titoism was based on a revolution, but it covered a much broader base that incorporated most if not all of the Yugoslav peoples. Few were alienated initially. Even the atrocities committed by Yugoslav peoples on one another were veiled by the myths, symbols, and ceremonies connected in some way with the National Liberation Struggle and the slogan-turned-ethos of brotherhood and unity that sprung from it. There was no attempt to deal directly with this tragic historical memory. The graves were not to be counted, nor were the bodies to be displayed and given burials. What actually had happened and the memory of it was instead obfuscated by the mystifications of the language and performances of the symbolic order. In short, the rulers attempted to manipulate the memories of the peoples they ruled.

Elaborating symbols "work in the opposite direction, providing vehicles for sorting out complex and undifferentiated feelings and ideas, making them comprehensible to oneself, communicable to others, and translatable into orderly action" (Ortner 1973:1340). They provide cognitive and affective categories for entire worldviews or for specific orientations. The National Liberation Struggle, for example, was to provide categories for a successful multinational society, for the solution of ethnic conflicts, and for the ideals of freedom, unity, and equality. As "strategies for action," elaborating symbols provide "programs for orderly social action in relation to culturally defined goals" (ibid.).

Some examples of symbols of the new symbolic order that carried "conceptual elaborating power" (ibid.) were as follows: (1) for the summarizing symbol National Liberation Struggle (NOB): *pale borce* (fallen fighters), *žrtve fašizma* (victims of fascism), *partizani* (Partisans), *prvoborci* (fighters at the beginning of the uprising), National Heroes, revolution, revolutionary inheritance, *borba* (struggle), *oslobodjenje* (liberation), national liberation, social liberation, *hrabrost* (courage), *čojstvo* (manliness, manly virtue[4]), *junaštvo* (heroism), *čast* (honor), *neprijatelj* (enemy), *sloboda* (freedom); for the summarizing symbol of Socialist Construction: New Yugoslavia, revolutionary inheritance, *jedinstvo* (unity), *jednakost* (equality), *za lepu budućnost* (for a beautiful future), building new relationships, chosen path, path created by the KPJ and Tito, guarantee for the future, enemies, new period of freedom. It should be noted that many of the elaborating symbols were associated with the summarizing symbols.

The "strategies for action" are those symbolic forms and activities by which the key symbols, both summarizing and elaborating, are manifested. For example, the *govor* or formal speech was a means of communicating the key symbols through language. The commemoration of fallen fighters and victims of fascism was a symbolic activity that manifested the key symbols through performance, material objects, language, and time orientation. In all the strategies employed, the aim was to evoke certain emotions that could be harnessed for motivating people to think and act in certain ways.

The Phase of Incorporation into the New Yugoslavia

Collective Incorporation

Three highly symbolic events that took place in the span of one and one-half months at the end of 1944 following the liberation of Belgrade symbolically marked the incorporation of the postwar Jewish community into the New Yugoslavia.

Van Gennep's tripartite structure of rites of passage can be extended to describe the transformation of the Yugoslav Jews. The phase of separation is associated with the Nazi occupation of Yugoslavia and the separation of the Jews as a People marked for mass extermination. As a physical sign of their status and determined fate, they were forced to wear yellow badges and sent like cattle to various death camps. The war period of 1941–1945 served as the liminal period in which the Nazi occupiers and their Yugoslav collaborators attempted to level and destroy the entire Jewish population, first by herding them into concentration camps and then by murdering them. Even before the "Final Solution" was systematically implemented, the Jews in Serbia were especially singled out as targets of German reprisals (Browning 1985). Their plans, however, did not entirely succeed. Over 5,000 Yugoslav Jews managed, sooner or later, to join the resistance or People's Army, and the Jewish fighter-Partisan was born. Through the experience of genocide Jews died, and through the experience of armed resistance and revolutionary activity Jews were transformed as individuals and as a collectivity. The three symbolic events served as the rites of incorporation, acknowledging the transformation and establishing the place of the Jews in the new society.

The first event took place on 22 October 1944. On this date in newly liberated Belgrade, prewar Federation President Fridrih Pops, who had managed to escape detection during the war, hung the "Federation of Jewish Communities of Yugoslavia" tablet on the Federation's building on Zmaj Jovine Street in central Belgrade (Levi 1989; Vajs 1954; 1955–1956). This was the first act of public renewal. It declared that the Jews of Yugoslavia were intent on remaining in the country and reestablishing a community.

The second event occurred about one week later, on 1 November 1944. The Conference of Jewish Communities convened and decided to unite the Sephardi and Ashkenazi branches, thereby demonstrating that "Brotherhood and Unity" as the solution to Yugoslavia's National Question (i.e., ethnic divisions and conflicts) would be immediately instituted and practiced within the Jewish community itself (ibid.). The primary ethnic conflict, exacerbated by the wartime atrocities, was between the Serbs and Croats. Jews lived among both of these peoples and had strongly identified with the cultures of both; hence, the decision to unify the two Jewish branches sent a strong symbolic message to the new rulers and the entire country.

The initiators of the above two events were the Jews themselves. They sent a message to other Jews and to the new rulers. It was the rulers, however, that initiated the third symbolic event of incorporation. The event took place on December 4, 1944. On this day Moša Pijade, revolutionary leader and child of Jewish Dorćol, led a contingent of AVNOJ members, NOV officers, and representatives of the new Yugoslav government in a visit to the Belgrade synagogue where services continue to be held today (ibid.). One eyewitness recalled the event: "Attention was given to one man who walked into the temple. He was wearing a Partisan shirt. . . . Weeping women held him by the hands and shoulders from all sides. The man was deeply moved. Tears could be seen behind his glasses. The man was Moša Pijade" (Džumhur 1986: 51–52). By visiting the synagogue the rulers publicly acknowledged the Jewish community. Moreover, the fact that the visit was made to the synagogue, a Jewish religious site, marked the Jewish community as a special case. This act of special benevolence continued to characterize the relationship between the rulers and the Jewish community. It is significant to note that the traditional religious elements of the Jews were thereafter not politicized, which was not the case in other religious groups. Evidence of this special benevolence was apparent in the community's publishing activity. Despite the anti-Zionist position of the state, the postwar community published information about the close tie that had existed between

Zionism and Marxism in certain Jewish youth organizations before the war. The tie was interpreted as a positive one. Such information was never censured as far as I know.

Individual Incorporation: A Transformed Jew Returns Home

I have described the war years as a phase of transformation. The transformation was abrupt. Much of it was involuntary, initiated by outside forces. The past was being taken away from many who were not ready to relinquish it. Others parted with the past voluntarily, on their own terms which were strongly influenced by the conditions of the war and revolution. This latter category of Jews, in particular, was being transformed into "something else." For many, by war's end, the transformation was nearly complete. They were prepared for incorporation into the New Yugoslavia and for participation in the phase of socialist construction. Jakob Papo, a Sephardi Jew from Sarajevo, was one such transformed individual. What follows is part-translation, part-paraphrase of part of Jakob Papo's own account of his return and incorporation into the New Yugoslavia, after having spent four years in a German prisoner-of-war camp (Papo 1988:45–48):

> It is the end of the war. The prisoners are running away from the Germans. Some are running away with the Germans.
>
> One morning the extraordinary happened. I see the French POWs running away. Where? Why? The Russians are in the city! I grabbed the first bicycle that I saw and peddled along a road until I came to a city and saw the army—the Red Army! Freedom, freedom for the people! That was the first picture that freedom gave me.
>
> Those few days that I remained in Germany I didn't know what was happening. I was always with the soldiers of the Red Army. They accepted me completely, primarily because of Tito, of whom they had all heard and knew as the legendary leader of the Yugoslav Partisans. I was among my own, free, happy.
>
> I didn't think about the future or the past. I was happy with what the revolution had accomplished, that there is freedom and I am living in that freedom.

But, I wanted to return to my homeland, to my home, to my birthplace, my Sarajevo, and so I went.

Things did not unfold as I wanted them to. With difficulty I got to Prague. I met some students there from Sarajevo who recognized me. Our Yugoslav mission in Prague arranged for me to work on the repatriation of our citizens, especially the POWS. I accepted the assignment. I knew what we wanted to accomplish, because we had fought for that even before the war. I knew what to say and do in order that the POWs and all our citizens would desire to return to Yugoslavia. [For Jakob Papo the significant "We" (or "They") meant all those who had fought to liberate Yugoslavia.]

It was a long trip back to Sarajevo, with transfers in Subotica and Belgrade. In Belgrade I met some old friends and ate familiar food. Everything was joyful. Still, occasionally, in the evenings, I would get those unwanted thoughts. Mixed together was the memory of the known past and the fear of an unknown future. My mother had died in the Djakovo concentration camp. She was taken there with my younger brother who was 11 years old. My sister was taken to another camp, and my father to yet another. I knew this. Twice my mother had written to me from Djakovo. Then one day I received the official word: "Your mother died, and your brother was taken to an unknown destination." [Papo never informs the reader that they are Jews.] Four years have passed. I would think about it, then it would go away, and then again I would think about it. But the train I sat in rattled on about freedom, sun, and the fatigue of the living, and I was fortunate.

The train arrived in Sarajevo at night. I sat down in the streetcar and left for the Cathedral, to my old neighborhood. I went immediately. My gait, at first firm and lively, became slower and more difficult. The houses looked more or less the same, and people went about as before. However, there were strangers everywhere, even in the house where I had lived before the war. I found myself again by the Cathedral. Now what? I sat down on the edge of the sidewalk, on top of my haversack in which I carried all of my belongings. It was night. Where would I spend the night? Only at that moment did I fully grasp that I no longer had anyone from my family. Mother and father, brother and sister—all killed in Ustasha camps. I had known before. Still, only then, sitting alone on the street, I understood and felt how that reality hurt and how difficult it was. I told myself that millions of people had died and were killed in camps, and that I wasn't the only one in that position. But I had to be relieved of my hurt. I was terribly unhappy and full of dread at that moment.

The next day I again traveled along Takovska Street to the house in which I had lived before the war. Before the war the house had been dilapidated, but now it was fixed up, looking like new. I didn't go inside. I didn't ask if they knew anything about my family. I didn't even go to the neighbors. I did not have the will or the strength.

In those first days I wandered around the city, which for four years had been trampled upon by fascism. Pictures from the past and present flashed before me and in me.

Before the war there were many unemployed people on the streets of Sarajevo, people dressed in ragged clothes. Now many people still wear such clothes, but they no longer just wander aimlessly. They walk as if they have a fixed destination, as if they are going to work.

I walk further into the city. I walk past a bookstore, the same one that had been selling *Mein Kampf* before the war. I now see the new edition of the history of the SKPB. The delight that overcame me prompted me to buy it. I spent my last dinar that they had given me to survive the first days of my return. I didn't regret it because we had lived to see this kind of book sold publicly.

I walked further. I passed by many places that held childhood memories for me. I stopped for a long time by Golubinjaka. We often went there to shop. I stood there for a long time, just gazing, and the memories within me just reeled off like film.

I then began to think about what I would do for work and how I would live. I had no qualifications. I had not even completed middle school. During the student strikes in the Technical School in Sarajevo in 1937, I had been arrested and expelled from all the middle schools in the country, losing the right to take even private examinations. Nevertheless, I not only must, I want to, work. I don't want to study. I don't want anyone to support me or to help me. I went straight to the People's City Council (GNO) and offered my services to work. I had no friends there, but I recognized many people, even met some people. I didn't tell them that I had no work, that I was without a home and without money. They employed me immediately, without any reservations. I worked first in the Commission for Repatriation, and then in the Housing Department. I didn't watch the clock when I worked. When I was not working I took trips into the countryside. I then understood that all the stories about how the POWs would be badly received were all wrong. I read the words of Comrade Tito: "In 1941 you went into war having decided that you would give your lives for the fatherland. It was not your fault. . . . You in the POW camps were also on the front. You fulfilled your duties there, only that you were unable to fulfill them with guns in your hand. But you remained faithful to the new, democratic, federative Yugoslavia."

The days, filled with work and rest, passed by quickly. Before long I met Veso Jovanović on the street. He asked me nothing, but he escorted me to the Public Prosecutor's Office where he worked. He arranged for me to take a job there. Everything went quickly. The workers accepted me as one of their own, sincerely, comradely. Most knew me from before the war. I was then accepted into the membership of the Communist Party of Yugoslavia and was selected to be a workers' representative. At the time I had not even graduated from middle school, while my comrades were university graduates from the Law Faculty. I knew that I couldn't do it like this, but it was difficult for me to think about studying. But one day Veso and the other comrades kicked me out of the office, saying" "Go now and study and don't dare to return until you graduate." I put all my energies into studying and in a short time I took all of my examinations. Later I enrolled in the Law Faculty.

In my memory of that period, I especially remember two things. First, I remember the great enthusiasm in the work place and in work activities. No one watched the clock or

> was concerned about taking breaks or resting. No one called it temporary work. We accepted it as completely normal to work as long as the job required it. And we used our free time for various work activities [reconstruction projects]. Who among the older generations doesn't remember the work activities in [the village]? Second, I remember the powerful comradeship and sense of mutual belonging among people. People competed to see who would work more and better. Our roots were not in our ancestors but in ourselves. Those were wonderful days, full of youthful pride and enthusiasm.
>
> That is how I came back to my city. I stayed in Sarajevo and never wanted to leave (Papo 1988:45–48).

Reimagining the Jewish Community in the New Yugoslavia

For those who had emerged from the rubble of the Second World War, the outcomes of the resistance to a fascist aggressor and occupying power, a civil war, and a political revolution, created a capacity to see the world in a new way. The new rulers imagined a Yugoslavia undergirded by a new tradition, and they set out to build it. At this point, some key questions come to mind. Within this phase of imagining and constructing the brotherhood and unity of Yugoslav peoples, what places were assigned to the small, powerless minorities? Were such minorities a part of the newly imagined community? Furthermore, did the surviving Jewish community reimagine its own identity at the same time? Did it participate in the imagining of the larger Yugoslav community? Did it place itself closer to or further away from the images recalled or created by the new rulers? Why was their reimagining of the Jewish community closer to the imaginings of Titoist Yugoslavia and further from or even opposed to the more recent imaginings of the Serbs, Croats, Bosnian Muslims, and Slovenes?

Historical processes and events had dealt the Jewish community a severe blow of death and destruction. Ethnic forms, however, emerge not only from dynamic historical processes but also are shaped by the responses of the ethnic actors themselves. How did the Jews of socialist Yugoslavia reimagine and refashion themselves out of the fragments of cultural materials that survived together with the structures that constrained their actions? The organized Jewish community responded in two related ways, one directed inward and the other directed outward. These responses, which I have termed an "experiment in secular Jewishness" and "submergence," corresponded to the twofold task of the Jewish community as stated by Federation President Albert Vajs. Vajs (1954; 1955–56) declared that the members of the Jewish community were to participate simultaneously in rebuilding the decimated Jewish community and in constructing a socialist society.

These aims did not change with Vajs' successor, Lavoslav Kadelburg. From the first to the fourth decade after the war, the overall stated purpose remained constant. The Jewish community of the New Yugoslavia was to be constant in aim. That is, it was to strive to remain Jewish, which entailed, according to Kadelburg, ethnic maintenance (*održanje*), ethnic continuity (*kontinuitet*), and ethnic existence or being (*postojanje*) (Kadelburg 1970). To meet its first aim the Jewish community was to be elastic in strategy; that is, adaptable, flexible, and even amalgamable.[5] Jewish continuity would be continued by the decimated community. There was no intention of breaking "thousands of years of continuity" (Vajs 1955–56:12), but the means of ethnic maintenance would be predominantly secular and the essence or being of the collectivity would likewise be something "qualitatively new."

According to Vajs, the overwhelming majority quickly entered into social, political, economic, and cultural life, that is, in the construction of the new socialist state (1954:29). Vajs noted that "only a small number of Jews stood on the sidelines," and an "unknown number violated the interests of the new state" (ibid.). From these statements we know that there were dissenters, those who were less sympathetic or totally unsympathetic to postwar societal transformation. The postwar literature published by the community, however, does not indicate any ideological struggle. Given the new conditions, especially in the immediate postwar years, such opposition becoming public was unlikely because of the early political rigidity and because the Jewish community was concerned primarily with social welfare and infrastructural renewal. That some ideological dissent existed is indicated by an Israeli of Yugoslav descent. He dismisses the conclusion implied by one author that there was virtually no ideological variation or dissent after the war. My own hypothesis is that most of those who were less sympathetic or opposed to the new rulers and their social order emigrated or chose not to make their personal ideological orientation a divisive issue in the community. One of the motivating reasons behind such emigration was to flee the new political order. Yugoslav Jewish sources tend to euphemize the issue when they explain that Jews left for "personal reasons" (Loker 1976). The "dissenters" who remained were among those who carved their own life paths of significance on which they lived their lives or hoped to discover answers to questions of identity and place in Yugoslav society.

The following statements made by Albert Vajs explicitly declare the aims and purposes of the postwar Jewish community:

> We returned to the liberated land with the decisive aim to participate in her reconstruction and in the renewal of our own broader community (Vajs 1955–56:13).
>
> [We do not intend] to live in any kind of isolation, but rather to participate fully in the struggles and aims of a land in which we are citizens; not to separate ourselves from what is the common responsibility and the common rights of all citizens of socialist Yugoslavia. However, we want to be and can be conscious Jews . . . (ibid:13–14).
>
> Our Jewish community is a living and active part of Yugoslavia and of Jewish reality today and for the future (ibid:14).

Submergence provided the postwar Jews with their "rightful place" in the new order. They were not, therefore, in Mary Douglas' (1979) terms, "matter out of place." Related to structure is visibility. For the rulers and participants in the commemorative ceremonies, they were made visible by the symbolic statuses that they occupied, those of "fallen warriors," "victims of fascism," revolutionary heroes, and *prvoborci.* Their participation in the National Liberation Struggle and their willingness to participate in societal transformation gave them a place in the the New Yugoslavia.

Why did they even seek such symbolic representation? First, they believed that they had the responsibility and duty "not to forget" and to transmit this obligation to their descendants. Second, it provided an opportunity to show publicly the degree of Jewish participation in the National Liberation Struggle. Third, it provided an opportunity to balance their victim and warrior statuses.

The new rulers preached ethnic reconciliation. The solution to Yugoslavia's national question, they proclaimed, was in institutionalizing the "brotherhood and unity" and "brotherhood and equality" forged during the National War of Liberation. In accord with proclamations in the 1950s that the national question had been resolved in Yugoslavia, Federation of Jewish Communities President Albert Vajs wrote, "In the New Yugoslavia there was no, and today there is no, kind of 'Jewish Problem'" (Vajs 1954:29).

Obtaining security was certainly high on the list of the Jewish community's aims, given the recent genocide carried out upon the Jews in Yugoslavia and other European countries. The Titoist legal system laid down a strict law prohibiting discrimination on ethnic grounds. Any breach of this law brought severe penalties.

> The protection of national rights is given by the government and regulations which have wiped out the remains of instigations of national, racial or religious hatred by means of severe penalties. The strict measures against the few, most verbal, antisemitic excesses did not have only an exemplary character but were a reflection of the decisiveness of government organs to drastically crush such provocations at the root (*Spomenica*, 1970:131).

The organized community was given autonomy in their efforts to remain Jews in the new society. That this was attained was seen in the continuation of a Jewish cycle of life, non-interference in publishing about the Zionist-socialist prewar connection even when Zionism was denounced as racism, and in the continuance of the tie with the Yugoslav Jews in Israel. The state did not try to isolate the Yugoslav Jews from Jewish organizations abroad. Such ties were continuous, even after the diplomatic break with Israel in 1967. The Yugoslav Jews claimed they never felt isolated from world Jewry. For example, the East European and western Jewish communities and organizations were brought together for the first time in Sarajevo during the 1966 celebration of the 400th anniversary of the arrival of the Jews in Bosnia and Hercegovina.

The organized Jewish community fostered and maintained contacts with influential institutions and individuals. It was believed, for example, that the president of the Federation of Jewish Communities should have such contacts. One individual leader stated that the Jews should not act as a special interest group. However, the same individual wrote about the importance of keeping good ties with individual sociopolitical organizations on issues that interest both sides and for receiving occasional material assistance for individual projects (Levi 1989:21).

Having chosen to reject the Judaic belief system, or never having been socialized into it, and having joined the progressive movement which incorporated Marxist ideas, many of the Yugoslav Jews shared at least a part of the belief system of the rulers. Certainly they shared many of the values proclaimed to characterize socialist Yugoslavia, such as freedom, justice, equality, and toleration. In regard to the last of these, Lowie (1954:327) wrote: "The Jews, because of their history of persecutions, forced migrations, etc. have come to value tolerance. Thus, if it takes, for a period, a "militant cult of tolerance" to make intolerant human beings tolerant, then that is preferable."

The New Yugoslavia did not take sides in global conflicts (i.e., Cold War). It chose coexistence over total catastrophe, the only two alternatives, according to Albert Vajs (Vajs 1955–56:8–9). This, in turn, left room for optimism, which was certainly high in the first decade after the war (see ibid.).

The Jews took the early intent of creating a Yugoslav nation and identity seriously. Even when this goal was abandoned, the Jewish community and many Jewish individuals continued to be Yugoslavist in orientation, even in identity. In this regard they were overachievers. They wanted to be good Yugoslavs. As one informant described the Federation President Kadelburg, "He is a great Jew, but a great Yugoslav, too." The fact that the Jews continued to be dispersed throughout the country made this orientation particularly attractive. It promoted unity within the community as well as in society.

In 1948, the year that Tito broke with the Cominform, Yugoslavia was among the first member states of the United Nations to recognize the state of Israel. The state also assisted in the emigration of some 8,000 Jews to Israel between 1948–1952. The formation of the non-alignment movement, which initiated a closer tie to the Arab world, and the diplomatic break with Israel in 1967, made it difficult for the Yugoslav Jews to speak openly about their feelings about Israel and Zionism. Nevertheless, the community never severed ties with Israel, particularly with the Association of Yugoslav Jews in Israel (*Hitahdut Olej Jugoslavije*).

Constraints existed, but most of these, were also submerged, not talked about, or relegated to the private spheres of life. There were Jews who wanted either to remain invisible as Jews or to assimilate completely out of fear. Other Jews had other reasons for concealing their Jewishness. For example, in connection with formal membership in the Jewish community, the "fear of being put on another list" has been mentioned. The break in diplomatic relations between Yugoslavia and Israel was a potential constraint, together with Yugoslavia's general foreign policy which favored states hostile to Israel. With such political shifts, no doubt disillusionment with the visible results of Titoism and with the ideology itself set in for many.

For most Jews who remained in Yugoslavia, the incentives to submerge in socialist Yugoslavia far outweighed any constraints. Even for those who had not participated in the resistance struggle or were not members of the Communist Party, the new state offered societal goals they believed in, those of equality, tolerance, punishment of discrimination, and freedom of cultural expression. Moreover, they were free to leave the country at any time, which set them apart from the rest of Eastern Europe.

Submergence into Socialist Yugoslavia

In the sections that follow I will describe the Jewish community's association with and/or participation in the political and symbolic orders of socialist Yugoslavia. Although analytically these orders are treated as distinct, in reality they are inextricably connected by various links. *Svečanosti*, a common class of both festive and solemn symbolic performances which mediated between the two orders in an open, public way, provided one such link.

Association with the Bases of Power

When an ethnic community establishes a tie to the rulers, submergence does not necessarily follow. Historically, various Jewish communities have actively sought to establish and to foster ties with their foreign rulers and have not in the process lost their distinctiveness. The rulers, on their part, welcomed the knowledge and skills of Jewish individuals (e.g., "court Jews") but looked upon the Jewish collectivity as a whole with suspicion. There have always been cases of individuals submerging in other cultures, but historically documented cases of collective Jewish submergence are rare. One such case for which documentation is available pertains to the Jews of China (Rhee 1973). When examining the tie to the rulers, more than the mere existence of some kind of association must be established. In the case of the postwar Jewish community of Yugoslavia, the quality, scope, and depth of that tie set within specific historical conditions help explain the submerged nature of the association. However, it is only when the community's place in both the political and symbolic orders is described that the full extent of submergence is understood.

Although the various institutional links to persons, offices, and organizations of power had a symbolic dimension, each of the links served as a structural support of the place of the Jewish community in Yugoslav society. These links were largely associations with the loci of power. Primarily because of its demographic composition the Yugoslav Jewish community by itself was politically and economically impotent and as such not an active and independent player in the power relations among Yugoslav peoples. Association with the loci of power, however, has its rewards, and these rewards, such as security and a place in the new structure, were valued resources that a decimated and vulnerable population actively sought to obtain. The Yugoslav Jews, as some of my informants and respondents indicated, believed that success in life comes from membership in a certain group or in certain groups. They exhibited this orientation in their patterns of formal and informal association with the following bases of power in socialist Yugoslav society.

Standing high above all of the other power holders was Tito himself. Tito was no ordinary ruler. He was *the* Ruler. Tito as a dominant and key symbol was described above. Here, as a power holder, Tito wore many hats. Tito was the President of the Socialist Federative Republic of Yugoslavia, later given the title of President for life (he was succeeded by a Presidency of eight, not by a President); he was the General Secretary of the Communist Party; he was the Marshall of the Yugoslav National Army; he was a world statesman and the co-founder of the non-aligned movement; he was also Comrade Tito, one of the People. With all of his titles and positions, Tito covered all of the bases of power in domestic and international spheres. By association with Tito, the Jewish community was not only linked to the most powerful person in the state, it was by association linked to the apex of power in the federal government, the Party, and the military. For the Jews, thus, Tito was not only, as shown elsewhere, a condensed symbol, he was also a base of condensed power.

The Jewish association with Tito was created before the war and later sustained during the course of his life. His longest held job outside of politics was in a mill owned by Samuel Polak, a Jew from Croatia (Beloff 1985). He and the famous prewar revolutionary Moša Pijade met in the Sremska Mitrovic prison, where the two men began a lifelong friendship and political partnership. During the course of the prewar movement, the National Liberation Struggle, and the postwar state, Pijade never lost the favor of Tito. As the principal translator of Marx's *Das Kapital*[6] and other works of literature, Pijade was extremely well versed in Marxist ideology, and he passed his knowledge on to Tito. Pijade has been described as the ideological mentor to Tito (Beloff 1985; Nešović 1994). Pijade, as I have described above, served in numerous capacities for Tito, including the vice presidency of the postwar state. Other Jews had personal ties to Tito. Pavle Pap, the only Jew besides Moša Pijade to have been a member of the Central Committee of the Communist Party of Yugoslavia, certainly had contacts with Tito. The uncle of one of my informants was Tito's personal physician during the war. I have already described the striking contribution of Jewish medical personnel to the war effort.

Anthropologists have shown that in certain societies individuals and groups have sought ways to place themselves closer to the founding ancestor, to a paramount chief, or to the line of descent that would benefit them most. Tito was the founder-hero of socialist Yugoslavia, a new society that was ostensibly being transformed into a brotherhood of Yugoslav peoples. Whether the brotherhood in question was a sociological or solely a symbolic one, existing only during a ritual phase of time, benefit accrued to those who could demonstrate close association with the founder and his prewar Communist or wartime Partisan line of descent. Socialist rulers such as Tito and his political elite repeatedly used the idiom of kinship in their rhetoric. It became part of the standardized symbolic language of the new society. In a society with divisions and conflicts that had been swept under the rhetorical rug of "brotherhood and unity," the various symbolic forms and activities whose intent it was to unite and consolidate became even more important. Tito himself never ceased reiterating the Partisan War slogan-turned-founding ethos of "brotherhood and unity," believing the words, if repeated often enough, had magiclike qualities that would transform the fragile political union into a solid one. Like Tito, the Jews were pro-Yugoslavist. They, too, regularly reiterated the slogan of "brotherhood and unity." They knew that Tito was Yugoslavist in orientation, but as time went on and elites became nationalized, they could trust fewer other leaders to have such an orientation.

Through the Jewish individuals who joined the uprising from the very beginning, the Jewish community had an association with what was known as the "club of 1941." These early Partisans or *prvoborci* were awarded the *Spomenica 1941*, which bestowed upon them rewards and privileges related to jobs and housing. In absolute numbers, not many Jews were in this group. It is known that 150 Jewish survivors were awarded the *Spomenica 1941*, which gave them access to a privileged life style. Cadik Danon, who occupied the post of Rabbi of Yugoslavia, was a *prvoborac* who took up a career as a diplomat in the foreign ministry rather than resuming his prewar rabbinical service. Given the representation of Jews in the earliest phase of the resistance, this number would have been much higher had more Jews survived the war.

Although it is impossible to state a figure summarizing Jewish membership in the Communist Party, it was probably significant. The president of the Federation of Jewish Communities of Yugoslavia indicated that the Jewish membership in the Party immediately after the war was about twenty percent. With the emigration of one-half of the survivors, the percentage was surely higher for those who were more sympathetic to the socialist transformation and thus chose to remain. Besides the wartime experience, the transformed occupational structure of the Jewish population was related to membership in the Party. After the war a significant number of Jews occupied government or government-related jobs. Also, many remained in the military following the war and made careers there. Career enhancement was certainly related to membership in the Party. This was probably the strongest motivation for those below the senior generation, that is, those who were very young during the war or born after the war. These post-Partisan generations carried neither the prewar Jewish progressive tradition nor the Partisan experience of the Second World War. They possessed neither the revolutionary tradition of their fathers nor the Torah tradition of their grandfathers.

Not everyone joined the Communist Party. There were individuals who were invited to join but refused. They did not lose their jobs, but did lose such privileges as traveling abroad on business. Others whose wartime or immediate postwar enthusiasm attracted them to the Party dropped out at some point. It is, however, difficult to draw generalizations about the Yugoslav Jews as a whole when considering motivations. Some onetime fervent Communists became disillusioned with Yugoslav socialist social reality, while in the same period certain young adults without the direct experience and memory of the war became socialists of one persuasion or another. Whatever the actual percentage of Jewish membership in or of individual orientation toward the Party, the significant ethnographic reality was that the organized community repeatedly acknowledged what it perceived to be the accomplishment and continual leading role of the Party in Yugoslav society.

The Jewish population had one of its members, Moša Pijade, at the very top of the power elite and federal government. Until his death in an airplane accident in the 1950s, Pijade occupied the vice-presidency of the federal government. Some prominent Jews severed their ties with the Jewish community completely. However, Moša Pijade, one of the most powerful men in the country because of his prewar and wartime revolutionary achievements, his relationship to Tito, and his official position, was not one of these. However, according to his biographer, Pijade was against any Jewish individuals seeking his support based on their common tie of ethnic descent (Nešović 1994).

At the federal level there were other Jews who occupied high administrative posts in the postwar period. Dr. Lavoslav Kadelburg, president of the Federation of Jewish Communities of Yugoslavia since 1964, occupied top-level posts. Yugoslavia's only rabbi, Cadik Danon, served in high foreign service posts after the war. Leo Mates served as the Yugoslav ambassador to the United Nations, and Aleksander Demajo as the ambassador to Bolivia. Several Jews also served in the government positions below the federal level. In addition, unlike before the war, a significant number of Jews occupied various positions as government administrators and employees.

A considerable number of Jews remained in the military after the Second World War. This contributed to the overall transformation of the Jewish population's occupational structure. Relatively few Jews had pursued military careers before the war. At an international dinner party attended by Tito and one of my informants, a foreign guest asked my informant, "Mrs. Adanja, is there antisemitism in Yugoslavia?" To this inquiry my informant, in good humor, replied, "Well, you know, Mr. K, there are more Jewish generals in Yugoslavia than there are in Israel." And it was true. Fourteen Jews rose to the rank of general in the Yugoslav military, including Roza Papo, the first female general. All of these severed completely or did not renew their ties to the community until after their retirement from the army. Some of the returnees were given military funerals in the Jewish cemetery. These funerals were events that displayed submergence in a uniquely Jewish sphere.

The Jewish community maintained an association with the Socialist Alliance of Working Peoples of Yugoslavia (SAWPY). The following words are found in the Memorial Book (*Spomenica,* 1970:132), which commemorated the fiftieth anniversary of the Federation of Jewish Communities of Yugoslavia:

> We established the most active cooperation with the sociopolitical organizations, especially with SAWPY (Socialist Alliance of Working Peoples of Yugoslavia) and SUBNOR. This cooperation was reflected in the inclusion of our Federation and communities in sociopolitical activities in the country and abroad, in joint declarations against fascism and neonazism, in struggles for human rights and against all discrimination, and in expressing together our respect for the fallen fighters and victims of fascism in the Second World War and other wars.

The numerous interest groups were all part of SAWPY and were referred to as sociopolitical organizations and institutions. The Partisan War Veterans' Association, identified by the acronym SUBNOR, was the most significant of these organizations with which the organized community had maintained a formal and informal tie. On the informal level, Jewish veterans of the National War of Liberation maintained relationships with non-Jewish veterans, primarily through local SUBNOR chapters. On the formal level, the organized community maintained a ritual tie with various local SUBNOR chapters. SUBNOR representatives participated in all of the commemoration ceremonies that were an integral part of Yugoslav and Yugoslav Jewish ritual cycles.

The organized community also used its association with SUBNOR politically to protect its own interests. In one meeting a member of the committee proposed that all individuals with ties to SUBNOR write letters to focus attention on a matter of particular interest to the Jewish community (*Zapisnik,* May 1984).

The community sometimes invoked the Yugoslav constitution and law when it perceived it was under attack by certain individuals in Yugoslav society. Being aware of the symbolic weight of the law, the community leaders invoked it and rationally presented their position. Also significant is the fact that several individuals occupied high legal offices in socialist Yugoslavia, including service on various supreme courts.

Symbolic Symmetry

Submergence was a process that established a structure of symbolic symmetry (Kugelmass 1988) between the organized Jewish community and the socialist Yugoslav state. Higher symbolic symmetry results when a greater number of key symbols are shared between two entities than are not shared and when the potential for symbolic asymmetry is concealed or controlled from within one or both entities. The higher the symbolic symmetry the more integrated or submerged a community was in the symbolic order of socialist Yugoslavia. As demonstrated below, the Jewish community exhibited high symbolic symmetry. Conversely, symbolic asymmetry set definable, visible boundaries between the state and a community, thereby contributing to a more distinctive identity apart from the state.

The Yugoslav Jews contributed to the creation of certain key symbols that formed the new symbolic order. During the war many Jews, above their proportion of the population, contributed to the NOP and fought in the NOV, that is, they participated in the Partisan War and Yugoslav Socialist Revolution. At least ten (I have seen different figures) Jews were proclaimed National Heroes of Yugoslavia. Hundreds of others were decorated, some several times. As best they could and as conditions allowed, Jews from all over the country joined the Partisans and, as such, reflected the multiethnic composition of the resistance force and the rallying slogan of "brotherhood and unity." After the war most of those who remained in the country were sympathetic to the goals of the new society and contributed to the process of socialist construction and the activities of political legitimation. Creators do not easily discard or part with their creations. This was the case for the Jews of Yugoslavia.

The key symbols of the New Yugoslavia held "much cultural interest" (Ortner 1973) for the Jews of Yugoslavia, particularly for the organized Jewish community. The Yugoslav Jews themselves said that the key symbols of the new state were important and significant. This was evident by the space devoted to these symbols in various communal publications (*Jevrejski Pregled*, *Jevrejski Almanah*, *Zbornik*, *Bilten*, *Spomenice)*, in public speeches (*govori*), and to some extent in their material culture. What they may have thought or what meanings they attached to these symbols was not always as clear. There was variability of beliefs, opinions, and variations that, for the most part, remained private during collective performances. An extremely high degree of collective uniformity marked performances that were directed outward or that included participants who were outsiders. Most important in exhibiting submergence was the outward form. Individuals may have said things that deviated from the collective representation, but they did not do this in a public forum, and certainly not as participants in the performance. What the community did say about Tito can be used as an index of their interest. Following Tito's death in 1980 the Jewish community published a special supplement to the *Jewish Review* as a memorial to the deceased leader. In this memorial supplement the community expressed the extent of Tito's stature and significance when they referred to him as "the colossal symbol who became a living legend" (*Jevrejski Pregled*, Special Supplement, 1980).

The key symbols were manifested in different forms, activities, and contexts. They emerged in print, speeches, commemorations, anniversary celebrations, concerts, exhibitions, and formal meetings. Greater cultural elaboration marked these symbols. One indication of this was that they were all made a part of the mythology of the New Yugoslavia, constantly reiterated and expressed in mundane context, but especially in ritual context. They were both mythologized and sacralized. For example, there was Tito the man, and there was Tito the living legend, Tito the colossal symbol, Marshall Tito, President Tito, General Secretary Tito, Tito's Way, Tito's Work, Tito's ideals, Tito the creator of brotherhood and unity, and Tito the creator of a socialist inheritance. Both Tito's birthday (Day of Youth) and death anniversary were ritually observed. Various representations of Tito were everywhere, symbolizing his omnipresence in Yugoslav life. The Jewish community joined with everyone else in this cultural elaboration of the hero-founder of the New Yugoslavia.

Finally, there were certain cultural restrictions surrounding these symbols. This criterion was observed mainly in the organized community by what was not said about the key symbols. In my perusal of communal publications and documents from various board meetings, I found nothing that suggested criticism of Tito, the National War of Liberation, Brotherhood and Unity, or of the key symbols associated with socialist construction (Brotherhood and Equality, Self-Management, Non-Alignment). This strongly suggests that the Jewish community at least publicly adhered to the proscription regarding criticism of these symbols.

Associated with the above means of exhibiting symbolic symmetry and thereby submergence is symbolic control and manipulation. Whoever occupies a position from which certain symbols can be controlled and thus manipulated has the distinct advantage of influencing and directing change or of supporting the status quo. In the postwar Jewish community the group that had such control remained relatively small, which is apparent from a check of leaders and activists across time. The great majority of these, though not all, were secular oriented and sympathetic to Titoism.

In the case of the Yugoslav Jewish community, I do not want to imply that there were significant power struggles after the war or that coercive means were used to emphasize certain spheres of Jewish life and to weaken others. Symbolic manipulation in the community fueled little if any public dissent. It was no secret that the postwar community leaders embarked on a course that emphasized secular content, forms, and activities. Religious forms were not attacked, at least not directly. Virulent atheism did not characterize the leaders or the members, all of whom believed that extremes were to be avoided, but the features of the Judaic tradition were deemphasized through symbolic means, particularly by manipulating language. Religion, for example, still had its place in Jewish life, but it was now, in this new historical period in which all Yugoslav peoples were united by a "common socialist consciousness," primarily for the *few, elderly* Jews who had been raised in the traditional way and could not or would not part with it (Kadelburg 1970). In fact, synagogue attendance was characterized by the old and few. In this sense, the statement reflected what was actually happening in the synagogue. The war had taken its toll on the religious infrastructure. For many years there had been only one rabbi in the entire country, Menhahem Romano in Sarajevo. Between 1968 and 1973 the community was without a practicing rabbi. Thus, for many of the ritualists, it was not a matter of losing what they had, but of gaining something which had been lost. Such provision could come only through the secular leadership, for the religious life of the community fell within the institutionalized structure of the Religious Section of the community. Still, the statement regarding the "few" and "elderly" also involved symbolic manipulation. The symbolic association that was being made did not reflect a temporary pattern of synagogue attendance but implied instead an irreversible pattern. Certainly it did not encourage participation in that sphere of Jewish life. Symbolic manipulation also occurred when many of the secular leaders chose to avoid the synagogue and events that were deemed "religious." Also, the word "religious" was removed from the official title of the Federation. On the other hand the leaders did not ignore the needs of the religious Jews. They made several attempts to send young men from the community abroad for religious training. Two of these attempts failed. The third, in the person of one of my informants, has been a success.

The Language of Submergence

The language of submergence incorporated a wide range of linguistic symbols and forms, from single words and familiar acronyms to the myths that composed the entire mythology of the Titoist state. In-between these two extremes the language of submergence included phrases, slogans, inscriptions, oaths, songs, hymns, poems, books, stage and film dramas, speeches, eulogies, and legends. In saturating society with the key symbols through these different speech forms, the rulers intended to reach both the mind and the emotions of their followers.

There were many single words, word-sets and acronyms associated with Titoism that were familiar to the populace. First, some of the key summarizing symbols were designated by a single word and/or an acronym: Tito, NOB (National Liberation Struggle), KPJ (Communist Party of Yugoslavia or simply, the Party), SKJ (League of Communists of Yugoslavia, the new name for the Party beginning in 1952), Non-Alignment, Self-Management. Likewise, many of the key elaborating symbols were so represented: revolution (*revolucija*), liberation (*oslobodjenje*), struggle (*borba)*, freedom (*sloboda*), Partisans (*Partizani*), *prvoborci*, and so on (see Tables 3.3 and 3.5). Many of the above words were combined with one or more additional words. Examples include Tito's Way, Tito's Work, Tito's ideas, socialist self-management, liberation struggle, revolutionary inheritance, and revolutionary hero.

The slogan of "Brotherhood and Unity" (*Bratstvo i Jedinstvo*), a key summarizing symbol, originated during the Partisan War and was invoked repeatedly until the late 1980s in the Jewish community. Tito used this slogan in almost all of his public speeches. It was proclaimed that the solution of Yugoslavia's ethnic divisions and conflicts depended on the continuation of the "brotherhood and unity of Yugoslav peoples" that emerged during the war and that was later purportedly institutionalized in the federational structure of the new Yugoslav state.

Table 3.3
A Componential Comparison of Jewish Participation in Four Commemorative *Svečanosti* (1)

	Commemorations			
	Djakovo	*Ledine*	*Sajmište*	*Yom ha-Sho'ah*
Fixed Order				
Pozdrav (greeting)	+	+	+	+
Term of address	+	+	+	
Govor (Jewish)	+	+		+
Govor (non-Jewish)	+	+	+	
Thanks to the state	+	+		
Spomen	+	+	+	+
Počast/Minute of Silence (Paying homage)	+	+		+
Parting w/ deceased	+	+	+	+
Music	+	+	+	+
Poetry/Dramat. Reading	+		+	
Povorka (Processional)	+	+		+
Wreath laying	+	+	+	+
Flower laying	+	+		+
Grave visitation	+			+
Kaddish	+			+
El Male Rahamim	+			+
Limud	+			
Prijem (Reception)	+	+		
Distribution of Awards	+	+		
Participants				
Size of gathering	Mid	Sm	Lg	Sm
SJOJ	+	+	+	+
JO(s)	+	+	+	+
Rabbi	+			+
Local government	+	+	+	
LCY				
Socio-political org.	+	+	+	
SUBNOR (Vets. of NOB)	+	+	+	
Cult.-Artistic societies	+	+		
Students	+		+	
Pioneers	+			
Local citizens	+	+	+	
Local musicians				
Jewish choir		+	+	+
Enterprises	+			
JNA			+	
Foreign guests	+			

(continued)

Table 3.3 *(continued)*

	Commemorations			
	Djakovo	*Ledine*	*Sajmište*	*Yom ha-Sho'ah*
Material Objects				
Spomenik (monument)	+	+	+	+
Spomen-ploča (tablet)	+			
Humka (burial mound/ mass grave)		+		
Individual graves	+			+
Wreaths	+	+	+	+
Flowers	+	+		+
Ritual vestments	+			+
Kipa	+			+
Jewish star	+			+
Wine	+			
Plum Brandy	+			
Eggs	+			
Tito image			+	
Red star			+	
Yugoslav flag			+	
Communist flag			+	
Banner			+	
Bust of National Hero		+		
Megile-zahvalnice (Certificates of thanks)	+			
Reference to Summarizing Symbols				
Partisan War	+	+	+	+
Tito	+	+	+	
The Party (KPJ, LKJ)		+	+	
Brotherhood & Unity	+	+	+	+
Self-Management	+			
Non-Alignment				
Reference to Elaborating Symbols (including combinations)				
fallen fighters	+	+	+	+
victims of fascism	+	+	+	+
liberation	+			
social liberation		+		
national liberation		+		
revolution				
revolutionary inheritance	+	+		
Borba (heroic struggle)		+		+
revolutionary hero				

(continued)

Table 3.3 *(continued)*

	Commemorations			
	Djakovo	*Ledine*	*Sajmište*	*Yom ha-Sho'ah*
National Hero		+	+	
Partisans				
prvoborci		+	+	
blood of fighters	+			
1,700,000 dead	+			
path created by KPJ & Tito	+			
obligation to stand with KPJ and/or Tito		+	+	
unity (jedinstvo)				
svetilište za mladu generaciju (shrine for young generation)		+		
independence			+	
progressive				
building new relationships		+		
chosen path		+		
true path		+		+
path of peace		+		
horrible past (description)		+	+	
for a beautiful future			+	
guarantee for future			+	
čast (honor)			+	
courage (hrabrost)		+		
homeland		+		
enemy (neprijatelj)				
freedom (sloboda)				
strength			+	
Spanish Civil War fighters			+	

(1) This table does not represent an exhaustive analysis. Features that are left unmarked may have been a part of the commemoration in a given year, but I have not come across them in the communal literature (*Jewish Review*, *Bilten* (JOB)).

Music, poetry, and dramatic readings were used regularly in commemorations, anniversary celebrations, and other performances. The Jewish community had two choirs, the Moša Pijade (now Lira) choir in Zagreb and the Braća Baruh choir in Belgrade. The names alone of these choirs indicated the Jewish community's transformation and submergence. The Belgrade choir has had a long history, most of it as the Serbian-Jewish Singing Society. After the war its name was changed to Braća Baruh Choir, honoring the famous

Table 3.5
Componential Comparison of Sarajevo 1966 and Zagreb 1986 *Proslave*

	Sarajevo 1966	*Zagreb 1986*
Fixed Order		
term of address	+	+
thanksgiving	+	+
govor (Jewish)	+	+
govor (non-Jewish)	+	+
počast/homage	+	+
pomen	+	+
spomen	+	+
music	+	+
poetry/reading	+	
state hymn		+
processional (povorka)		
wreath laying	+	+
flower laying		
Kaddish	+	+
El Male Rahamim	+	+
limud		
grave visitation	+	
commensality	+	+
prijem/reception	+	+
interaction w/ locals	+	+
Participants in Svečanosti		
SJOJ (Federation)	+	+
JOs	+	+
Jews from socialist countries	+	+
Jews from western countries	+	+
WJC	+	+
JOINT	+	+
YU Jews in Israel		+
Assoc. of YU Jews in USA	+	
Representatives from Israel	+	+
Local government	+	+
Republican government	+	+
Federal government		
League of Communists of YU		
socio-political organizations	+	+
SUBNOR (Partisan Veterans)	+	+
Representatives of major religions		+

(continued)

Table 3.5 *(continued)*

	Sarajevo 1966	*Zagreb 1986*
cultural-artistic societies		
local citizens	+	+
local musicians		
local artists	+	+
Jewish choir(s)	+	+
enterprise representatives		
Rabbi from Yugoslavia	+	+
Rabbis from abroad	+	
Material Objects		
spomenik (memorial monument)	+	+
spomen-ploča (memorial tablet)		+
wreath	+	+
flowers		
food	+	+
drink	+	+
photograph of Tito		
banner		
flag		
red star		
hammer & sickle		
ritual vestments	+	+
prayerbook/Torah scroll	+	
Reference to Key Summarizing Symbols		
Tito	+	+
NOB (Partisan War)	+	+
KPJ (LKJ)		
Brotherhood and Unity	+	
Self-Management	+	+
Non-Alignment		
Terms of Memorialism		
victims of fascism	+	+
fallen fighters	+	+
pokojnici (the deceased)		+
honorable ancestors		
martyrs	+	
pomen	+	+
spomen (remembrance)		
počast (paying homage to deceased)	+	
obligations of honor and respect		

(continued)

Table 3.5 *(continued)*

	Sarajevo 1966	*Zagreb 1986*
Elaborating Symbols		
liberation (oslobodjenje)	+	+
revolution (revolucija)	+	
revolutionary inheritance		
partisan fighters/fighters of NOB	+	+
uprising	+	
heroic call of Tito	+	
National heroes	+	+
unity (jedinstvo)	+	
equality (jednakost)		+
independence (nezavisnost)		
progressive (naprednost)	+	
national liberation	+	
social liberation		
borba	+	+
svetilište za mladu generaciju (shrine for the young generation)		
za lepu budućnost (for a beautiful future)	+	
describe horrible past (strasna proslost)	+	+
courage (hrabrost)		
honor (čast)		
homeland		
enemy (neprijatelj)	+	
destruction of fascism		
prewar revolutionaries		
new period of freedom	+	
freedom (sloboda)	+	+
prewar progressive	+	
new socialist society	+	
solution to the national question	+	
socialist ideals	+	
social justice	+	
our revolution	+	

revolutionary trio of brothers. Moša Pijade, as described above, was the most famous of Jewish revolutionaries and the postwar Vice President of Yugoslavia. The two choirs performed regularly at numerous communal and public events. For example, the Braća Baruh Choir sang at an event in honor of Tito's birthday. Both choirs included in their repertoires the state hymn and Partisan songs.

The ode that includes the oathlike words, "Comrade Tito, we promise not to turn from your path," was familiar to many Yugoslavs, and was used by the Jewish community as well.

During the war two Jews in particular played key roles connected with the music of the Partisans. The revolutionary leadership recognized early that music was a form that reached inside persons and helped to create emotional bonds. As co-Director of the Peoples' Theater of Liberation, Oskar Danon, a Jew from Sarajevo, often directed renditions of songs such as "Hej, Sloveni," arguably the favorite during the war. Besides his writing and painting talents, it seems that Moša Pijade tried his hand at musical composition, writing what he believed would serve as a worthy state hymn. During the war he sent his composition to Tito, but it was lost on the way (Pavlović 1986).

The events of 1941–1945, known around the world as the Second World War, are a part of history. There are certain facts about the war that were shared by all of its participants. Often, however, the actors in a historical event want to go beyond what is shared to create something that has utmost significance for them. The actors go on to either contract or expand history, or to select whatever they themselves deem significant. I am referring especially to literate populations, those which do not rely on oral tradition alone. What unfolds is a conscious process of mythologization and sacralization. A "sacred history" is created, with an origin myth, a pantheon of heroes, and a cluster of ideals and values that flow from the origin myth and the acts of the hero-warriors. When history is selectively contracted or expanded by particular actors who participated in the history it becomes mythologized. When myth is used by the rulers to help meet their goals it becomes a tool of ideology. If it can be shown that a broad consensus unites the rulers and the ruled, and this consensus becomes normalized, then perhaps it can be called culture.

The first step of the Jewish community in adopting the new symbolic order was not only to accept the myths propagated by the new rulers but also to participate in the process of myth propagation and elaboration. In regularly articulating the myths they also helped to legitimize the new Titoist order that rested on these myths. Having had key protagonist roles in the Partisan War, which became the origin myth of the new state, the Jews accepted the myth enthusiastically as their own. The origin myth ensured the surviving Jews, especially their organized community, of a place in the new order. They entered the new society with a sense of place.

As I describe below, this place in the new order was regularly reaffirmed in numerous symbolic activities that I have subsumed under a class of performances called *svečanosti*.

The Yugoslav Jews helped to propagate and elaborate the myths through books (e.g., *Jevreji Jugoslavije 1941–1945. Žrtve Genocida i Učesnici Narodnooslobodilačkog Rata* (The Jews of Yugoslavia 1941–1945. Victims of Fascism and Participants in the NOR)), articles, special supplements and brochures, speeches, museum exhibits, meetings, commemorations, and anniversary celebrations.

Tito satisfied the popular need of a hero. Tito himself was aware of this, according to his biographer (Dedijer 1981, cited in Magnusson 1987:74). The Tito myth extends back in time before the Partisan War and then extends well beyond it into the late 1980s. During my initial prolonged stay in Yugoslavia in the mid-1980s, more than five years after Tito's death, the Tito myth lived on, deeply entrenched in the symbolic order. Just one year before my arrival a "Law on Tito's Image" had been passed. Special commissions were established to ensure proper adherence to the law (*NIN*, 1 October 1989, 21–23). Certain individuals even took it upon themselves to enforce the law. Even during my stay in 1989, when Tito's mythological stature was beginning to crumble, not everyone was prepared to contribute to the demise of this dominant symbol of the New Yugoslavia. As I walked along Belgrade's main promenade, a street closed to motorized traffic, a siren sounded signaling to all pedestrians that they should stop in their tracks and offer their silent honor and respect to the memory of Tito on this day in May, the anniversary of his death. The two Jewish women with whom I had been walking stopped, as did other pedestrians. Others, however, continued to walk, an act that would have met with some sort of public sanction only a year or two before and certainly as late as 1985. Did the women's stopping symbolize honor and respect? Did continued walking symbolize defiance or disrespect? Perhaps, or perhaps not. In this instance, the public acts of these individuals was all I had to go on. It is important to emphasize that submergence was a public form of consensus and symmetry with the rulers. What went on inside the mind of the actors or the meanings they attached to their acts may not have been symmetrical at all. Such variability and deviation are addressed in chapters 5 and 6.

Tito was both a legend and a myth. It is difficult to determine at what point fact stops and fiction takes over. The significant point is the Tito myth was accepted completely by the organized

Jewish community. His place as the dominant symbol was secure even after his death. This was quite apparent during the first ethnographic period of my research.

The Partisan or National War of Liberation myth served as the origin myth of the New Yugoslavia. Each society has a mythology detailing its origins and sanctifying its norms. Some, like that of the New Yugoslavia, revolve around notable events (NOB) and great persons (Tito) defined through a web of symbolically constructed meaning (Kertzer 1988:12). It was the basis of all that came later during the years of socialist construction and state-building. The Partisan War was portrayed as the determinant of the new order.

The National Liberation Struggle served as the guiding metaphor of the New Yugoslavia, both conceptually and behaviorally. It was the new point of origin. Everything that came after was "determined by" the National Liberation Struggle. The cultural models (e.g., brotherhood and unity, equality, heroic struggle, strength, humanism) were said to be derived from the NOB, though in fact many had their roots in the traditional cultures of the region. Society was built upon the heroic struggles of diverse but united Yugoslav peoples. Those who fell in the original struggle, in the war itself, were venerated as heroes. Monuments were raised to these heroes, and they became the shrines for the future generations which did not experience the original struggle and thus required such visible objects to strengthen their resolve to "guard the inheritance" of the revolutionary struggle.

This myth proclaimed the successful resolution of the "National Question" in Yugoslavia: that is, the solution to the divisive ethnic antagonisms, conflicts, and atrocities that were committed during the war. Since the "National Question" had been declared solved, there could be no "Jewish Question." Indeed, after the war the president of the Federation of Jewish Communities of Yugoslavia declared that "there is no "Jewish Problem"" in the New Yugoslavia (Vajs 1954).

The myths of socialist construction[7] included (1) Brotherhood and Equality, Self-Management (called the second "founding myth"), and (3) Non-Alignment, which was a movement and a policy. Of particular significance for the Jews of Yugoslavia was the ideology and policy of non-alignment, particularly after Tito severed diplomatic relations with Israel in 1967 when pressured by Nassar to do so. Despite the potential for asymmetry that the absence of diplomatic relations between Yugoslavia and Israel held, the Jewish community refused to oppose publicly its country's foreign policy.

The Objects of Submergence

Tito was an object of commitment and veneration. This was manifested materially by photographs, sculpture, and publications showing reprints of telegrams sent from Tito to the Jewish community. In the Federation's library-meeting room sat a bronze bust of Tito. It was a prominent fixture in the room. Below the Federation, in the Belgrade Jewish community, a large photograph of Tito hung front and center in the main meeting room. Tito looked out over all the participants in every meeting held in this room where most gatherings of Belgrade Jews occurred. As this room was the secular equivalent of the synagogue hall, Tito's image was located in the section of the room where the ark is situated in the synagogue, the holiest of places. It was not unusual to find representations of Tito in the Jewish community, for various representations of Tito were ubiquitous in Yugoslav public and private spheres. What is worth noting about Tito's visual presence in the Jewish community was the fact that the community remained officially and legally a religious community. It is especially when this fact is considered that Tito's representation becomes a matter of symbolic contradiction or opposition.

The Jewish Historical Museum in Belgrade is operated by the Federation of Jewish Communities, while the Jewish museum in Sarajevo fell under the auspices of the city. Both museums displayed and revealed much of what these Jews deem to be significant about their past and present existence. The two museums exhibited permanent displays and temporary special exhibits on selected topics and individuals (e.g., the revolutionary Baruh family). Both museums were open to the general public, with the Sarajevo museum more accessible because it was on the advertised tourist route in Old Sarajevo. The exhibits in these museums displayed submergence by presenting visually and chronologically the processes and major events that led to submergence. In the prewar years this meant the tradition of the progressive movement (*napredni pokret*) which had various surface manifestations. The NOR occupied a prominent place in the museums' permanent displays. Photographs, documents, newspaper clippings, and various artifacts individually and collectively portrayed the tragic suffering and genocide upon the Jews and the Jewish contribution to the resistance and successful Yugoslav revolution.

The Jewish Historical Museum and the Federation of Jewish Communities of Yugoslavia presented the exhibit "The Baruh

Family—A Family of Revolutionaries" in January and February 1976. This Jewish family was among the most famous and celebrated of revolutionary families in postwar Yugoslavia. The exhibit on the heroic Baruh family was organized to mark the thirtieth anniversary of the victory over fascism and at the same time to evoke "the memory of all freedom fighters of the National Liberation War and all victims of Nazi genocide" (*Jevrejski Istorijski Muzej,* 1976). A special opening (*svečano otvaranje*) was held in the form of an *Akademija,* a formal meeting to mark an important event, in the hall of the museum. A speech was given on the revolutionary work of the Baruh family. As part of the *Akademija* the Jewish choir, *Braća Baruh* (Baruh Brothers), named after the three famous revolutionary brothers in the family, participated, as did two Jewish dramatic artists. Students from the *Braća Baruh* elementary school also took part in the festivities. A thirty-eight-page catalogue was published for the occasion. The booklet contains historical and biographical information on all members of the family. Photographs and several paintings by Joza Baruh, who was an artist, are included. All of the exhibit's artifacts spoke about the members of a Belgrade Jewish family "who excelled themselves as active fighters against fascism already before World War II. All three brothers and three sisters were engaged in progressive or revolutionary activities before the Second World War. The mother, Bulina, supported her children's endeavors." Sonja Baruh, the surviving sibling, served as a consultant for the exhibit catalogue.

Memorial objects include monuments (*spomenici*), tablets (*spomen-ploče*), and other memorial markings (*spomen-obeležje*) of various form. A large part of postwar activity went into materially marking and erecting various memorial objects in memory and honor of victims of fascism and fallen fighters of the National Liberation Struggle (see Levi 1954). In almost all commemorations, the commemorative focus was on both of these categories. This reflected and symbolized the balance between, or perhaps fusion of, the tragic and the victorious in Yugoslav memorialism.

For such a tiny community the Jews of Yugoslavia published an extraordinary amount of material about their past and present. A great volume of the historical material describes the fate of Yugoslav Jews in World War II, both as victims of genocide and as participants in the National Liberation Movement and the National Liberation War. This material was published in Federation serial publications (*Jevrejski Pregled*, *Jevrejski Almanah*, *Zbornik*), books, and exhibit catalogues. Individual articles and books on

Jewish participation in the NOB and prewar revolutionary movement also were published outside of the Jewish community. In addition, numerous unpublished accounts were and continue to be kept in the Jewish archive in the Jewish Historical Museum in Belgrade and in other archives.

The Performances of Submergence

Yugoslav Jewish life in the postwar period abounded with various kinds of performances and activities through which the organized community collectively presented itself to the rulers, to the public, and to its own members. These performances included a broad class of symbolic activity commonly called *svečanosti*, described in detail below.

The term *svečanost* (sg.) is derived from the root morpheme *svečan,* which can mean either festive, solemn, or formal. As its etymology suggests, *svečanosti* (pl.) may take the form of either solemn, festive, or formal performances. An entire ritual lexicon can be created from the terms *svečan* (adj.) and *svečanost*. The following are actual examples of different morphological usages: *svečana akademija* (formal meeting to mark an important event), *svečani trenutak* (solemn/festive moment), and as an adverb *svečano obeležan* (solemnly/festively marked or decorated), *proslavljen najsvečanije* (celebrated most festively). Additional examples include: *svečan prijem* (formal reception), *svečanost ljubavi i pravde* (commemoration of love and justice), *tužna svečanost* (sad commemoration), *svečanom otkrivanju spomenika* (commemorative unveiling of a monument), *svečana atmosfera* (solemn/festive atmosphere or mood).

Below, I describe three kinds of *svečanosti*. As an example of solemn *svečanosti*, I describe commemorations (*komemorativne svečanosti).* Anniversary celebrations (*svečanosti proslave godišnjice*) combine solemn, festive, and formal activities. The third kind, the formal gathering (*svečana akademija)* used to mark an important event, can stand alone or be a part of an anniversary commemoration. The *svečanost* was the most common class of symbolic activity or performance in which the organized Jewish community participated with other groups and through which the community exhibited symbolic symmetry with the new order. A separate class of performance described more briefly was the cultural gatherings and activities within the community referred to as *kulturne manifestacije* ("cultural manifestations"). Whereas most of the commemorations and anniversary celebrations described below involve actors representing different ethnic populations and official organizations, cultural manifestations were held for members of the Jewish community, though they were open to non-members.

It is important to connect the *svečanost* performance to its source or antecedent context. The postwar *svečanost* was a synthesis of ethnic and political features, and as such draws its significata from Jewish, non-Jewish, and Yugoslav socialist domains. Not all of these domains were mutually exclusive. Some overlap existed.

In the case of Yugoslav postwar *svečanosti*, the Yugoslav socialist domains included the National Liberation Struggle, Yugoslav Communist revolution, prewar political history and myth, Tito, resolution of the national question through brotherhood and unity, socialist construction of the New Yugoslavia, and Soviet (socialist) ceremonial and symbolism. Jewish domains included the Judaic religious tradition, internal traditions (Sephardi, Ashkenazi), the organized Jewish community (Federation, local communities), the progressive Yugoslav Jewish prewar tradition, participation in the NOB, the Holocaust, and the Jewish community.

Traditional Yugoslav cultures provided additional domains from which the new socialist rulers borrowed preexisting cultural values and norms. These traditional values and norms provided cultural models for the National Liberation Movement and War, the socialist revolution, and the postwar socialist construction. *Borba* ("struggle") was a word familiar to all Yugoslavs, young and old alike, one they saw daily. It was and remains the name of a major newspaper. For the Yugoslavs there is war, and then there is *borba*, heroic struggle. The Second World War as fought on Yugoslav territory was most commonly referred to as the *Narodnooslobodilačka Borba* (National Liberation Struggle). *Borba* as heroic struggle, however, was not invented by Tito's ideologues, nor did it first emerge during the war. Rather, the ideologues borrowed the term from Yugoslav cultural history and myth. The term is associated with the continuous Serbian rebellion from 1389 when they were defeated by the Ottoman Turks on their holy ground of Kosovo Polje and their medieval kingdom came to an end to the emergence of the modern Serbian state in 1878. It is said that this continuous struggle instilled in the Serbs *borbenost*, the quality of being able to struggle. The Partisans of Tito, thus, can trace their inspiration to the Serbian *borac*, the heroic warrior. These historical and mythical *borci* were immortalized in epics and in ballads performed by the *guslar*.[8] The rulers of the New Yugoslavia applied the terms *borba* and *borac* to the postwar period as well. In *svečanosti*, for example, the *govornik* or orator exhorted the crowd to carry on the struggle for Tito's brand of communism. In the ideology of self-management, the self-manager was conceptualized as a fighter (*borac*) (Zukin 1975:218–219). Other examples of traditional values borrowed by the socialist rulers include *čast* (honor), *čojstvo* (manliness), and *hrabrost* (courage). All of these can be read in Jewish communal publications and were heard at performances in which the community participated.

Svečanost performances had several explicit and implicit goals. What must be kept in mind is that there were at least two levels of collective presentation. Each level was represented by a different audience. On one level, the community presented itself to the rulers and to the public. Symbolic symmetry and inclusiveness were emphasized, hence the emphasis on such key symbols as brotherhood and unity or, simply, unity. On another level the performance was directed inward. The community presented itself to itself. It was an ethnic rather than a political orientation. It was the organized Jewish community that represented the Jews of Yugoslavia in these performances, and thus its most frequent representatives in these events, its leaders, controlled the impression that was presented to the audiences. It presented the collective impression of who the Yugoslav Jews were, where they fit in the new order, why they belonged, what was significant to them, how they contributed during the war-revolution, and how they were contributing to ongoing socialist construction. Potential contradictions abounded in such performances in which two contrasting traditions or domains met and where symbolic amalgamation occurred (Handelman 1990; Eisenstadt 1974). As they attempted to express discontinuity, inclusiveness, and submergence on one level, they expressed ethnic continuity and distinctiveness on another. These contradictions were partly resolved by the nature of the participants and audience in a given performance. Where ethnic heterogeneity predominated Jewish distinctiveness and exclusivity were undercommunicated. However, the situation was further complicated because of contradictions and incongruities between social reality as constructed by the rulers and the social reality as experienced by the actors and as institutionalized in the increasingly decentralized structure of the state. As unity and brotherhood and unity continued to be invoked, the Yugoslav peoples became increasingly divided because of the complicity of the rulers and the peoples themselves. While the ethnic (Jewish) intent was to memorialize the dead, the political intent called for an ordering of reality as constructed by the rulers, even if that meant that Brotherhood and Unity was solely a ritual construction.

The *svečanost* could be a single ceremony or performance or a complex series of events and activities. A fixed order or set of activities characterized the *svečanost*. It was not spontaneously generated. Hence, communitas[9] was more difficult to attain. Ideally, the performance should have recreated or given the appearance of the popular front solidarity that coalesced in the National War of Liberation but no longer existed. Social roles were not discarded when entering into ritual space or time. Adding to the complexity were the characteristics of the actors participating in the *svečanost*. Besides the friends and acquaintances who participated, there were many strangers who brought to the *svečanosti* "diverse experiences, characteristics, and personal histories" (Myerhoff 1977:200–201; cf. Cohen 1985).

Having a standardized order or set of activities, the *svečanost* was characterized by repetition and predictability. The performance, in Goffman's terms, was scripted; in Myerhoff's terms, it was closed. There was little room for innovation or spontaneity. For regular participants and congregants the performance scene was familiar in terms of who the actors were, what language was used, what acts were performed, what objects were visible, and which speech themes were communicated. Annual performances (e.g., commemorations), in particular, were regular events and thus showed continuity and reaffirmation of the political and symbolic orders of the rulers.

Submergence, in the form and performance of *svečanosti*, had many of the characteristics of dramaturgical performance. Form was emphasized. The rituals and ceremonies of the Yugoslav socialist state can be likened to a performance on a stage. Impression management was staged for various audiences during the same performance (e.g., the Sajmište commemoration which identified multiple victim groups—Serbs, Jews, Gypsies, Communists—in a single event) or at certain phases of the performance (e.g., the Djakovo commemoration in which there was a phase for the general public and one for the Jewish participants, as when the memorial prayer Kaddish was recited in the small Jewish chapel).

Although individual actors played different roles in the performance, as speakers, singers, and wreath layers, the emphasis was on the collective performance. Deviations or disruptions fell outside the boundary of collective performance because they distracted from the intent of the performance. The organizers of these events, which included members of the Jewish community, served as impression managers in staging the performances. The Jewish role as "stage managers," however, was limited or nonexistent in certain performances. In 1989, for example, Jewish leaders were surprised when they received their formal invitations to the Sajmište commemoration only one day before the event.

Dramaturgical performance need not always be public and dramatic. Such a performance may be carried out in private without an audience. I was a participant in one such drama. The context for the drama was provided by the terrorist murder of a Jewish tourist on a cruise ship in the Mediterranean Sea. As I played the role of prosecutor, one of the community's leaders adopted the role of defense attorney. He sat on one side of a desk, and I sat on the other. As defense attorney this individual began defending the actions of the state in allowing a known terrorist, one who had just murdered a Jewish tourist, to pass through the country. This leader was not defending the terrorist. That was abundantly clear. But he was dispassionately defending the action taken by the rulers of the Yugoslav state. This was only one example of an overall pattern of never designating the state (i.e., the Titoist rulers) as the target of criticism.

The Jewish community succeeded in fostering the impression that it possessed the ideal qualifications for the role of presenting certain key symbols. First, there was Jewish participation in the progressive movement (*napredni pokret*) before the Second World War, painstakingly documented by individual members and published by the community in books and journals. Second, during the war Jews contributed to the resistance and revolution above their proportion of the population. The community took upon itself the task of massive documentation of Jewish victims of fascism and of Jewish fighters and organizers. They indicated in this documentation that they were rewarded for their contributions. Third, Tito's right-hand man, Moša Pijade, was a Jew who felt no need to hide his Jewish origins or to avoid contact with the Jewish community. Fourth, most considered themselves secular Jews, and their behavior reflected this. For the most part, they discarded traditional practices, particularly those they defined as religious. For example, when one of my informants asked a middle generation leader of the Belgrade community whether he would be attending the community *Seder*, the individual replied, "No, it's religious." His was not an isolated case. Fifth, the Jews continued to be dispersed throughout the country and thus could not be associated with one particular majority nation or *nacija*. Moreover, they displayed a strong Yugoslavist orientation, especially through the Federation of Jewish Communities of Yugoslavia. Sixth, given their transformed (out of private businesses and into government service) and leveled socioeconomic position in a nationalized (socialized) economic system, they could not be targeted as class enemies. Finally, given their demographic impotence and their public enthusiasm for the new Yugoslav state, they presented no real political threat. They had no political agenda other than securing for themselves a place in the new order and a safe haven from those who might still inflict harm upon them.

Furthermore, they presented themselves as an indigenous, not a foreign, element. They were recognized as national and revolutionary heroes who had not been afraid of undertaking the most dangerous assignments during the National Liberation Struggle. They were fighters (*borci*) and fallen warriors (*pale borce*) who had sacrificed their lives, but also who had been victims of fascism (*žrtve fašizma*). These contributions and experiences had secured for them a place among the peoples in the "brotherhood and unity" of Yugoslav peoples. They presented themselves as a free and happy people living for the first time in a truly free country, and as a community that was free to pursue ethnic aims without interference or interruption from the state.

Although continuous participation as an economic or political player was no longer possible for the Jews collectively, it cannot be said that they were not motivated by any interest. For example, by remaining officially a religious community when in terms of beliefs and practice they were largely a secular community, they retained the kind of maneuverability that benefitted them most. They wanted a place in the new society, and religion would not secure that place for them. To be recognized by one's significant others was to exist. Visibility was associated with structure, invisibility with anti-structure. Given their demographic composition they could not attain such visibility in the power order, other than through association with the loci of power. Such visibility was more attainable, however, by seeking "a place close to the sacred center of the common values or [key symbols] of society" (Goffman 1957:36). As previously indicated, they possessed the credentials, the ideal qualifications for attaining and occupying such a place. They regularly reaffirmed their place by repeating the myths and by acting out proper performances. Proper performances were those that maintained the "front," which, in postwar Yugoslavia meant showing cultural interest in and not questioning the key symbols of the New Yugoslavia. In presenting these key symbols through language, performance, and material culture, and by living according to the calendar of Yugoslav socialist festivities and memorial days (*spomen-dani*), the organized Jewish community manifested the components of submergence: loyalty, conformity, unity, inclusiveness, amalgamation, ideological orthodoxy.

It was their participation in the cycle of commemoration that above all else made them visible players in postwar Yugoslav society. Otherwise there existed few if any venues of collective visibility in public, non-Jewish arenas. As participants in the cycle of commemoration, they could meet the obligation of memorializing their own dead and in the same arena reaffirm their place in the new order by displaying the key symbols that they ostensibly shared with the rulers and the other nations and nationalities of socialist Yugoslavia. "To the degree that a performance highlights the common official values of the society in which it occurs, we may look upon it, in the manner of Durkheim and Radcliffe-Brown, as a ceremony—as an expressive rejuvenation and reaffirmation of the moral values of the community" (ibid:35). Paradoxically, participants in such ceremonies were taken out of the profane world and placed into the other world of genocide victims, fallen fighters, and revolutionary heroes, but they did not discard their ordinary social roles. The participant placed one foot into the other world, but the other stayed behind. Participants thus straddled both the ordinary and memorial worlds. This limited what kind of a transformation could take place, and thus communitas was difficult if not impossible to create. There were spheres in which it may have been attained, such as the chartered bus in which I traveled with the Belgrade Jewish pilgrims to and from the Djakovo commemoration. This structure and process appears to reverse Victor Turner's model. The Jews, when participating in these ceremonies, gained structure rather than liminality. They seemed to be more liminal in the everyday world than in the ceremonial. The *svečanosti* gave them visibility, association with the dominant political and symbolic structure, and the clear symbolic statuses of victims of fascism and fallen warriors of the Partisan War.

All participants in the performances need not have been members of the Party or even sympathetic supporters to have participated in the commemoration cycle. In fact, by the time I conducted research in the mid-1980s, and certainly by the late 1980s, the political dimension had worn thin for many of the participants. Nevertheless, it continued as part of the scripted language and the fixed order of the performances. Something spurred continued participation even after disillusionment had set in and over-saturation made the political symbols invisible to the participants. The president of the Belgrade community told me that they did not even notice the symbols anymore. Part of the new cycle's attraction and sustained place in Yugoslav life came from the subsequent conceptual and performative synthesis of what had been simultaneously a resistance to a hated foreign occupier and an indigenous and independent political revolution. Individual actors could draw on either or both experiences while performing a role or occupying ritual space as a spectator in the commemoration ceremony. Moreover, a reference to one of the key symbols did not mean it was interpreted uniformly. By describing Jewish involvement as performance, I am not judging motivation for every participant. Participants may have been motivated by belief or some other stimulus. One thing is certain. Individuals were careful to adhere to the script in order not to detract from the collective performance which reflected on the Jewish community as a whole.

The stated intent of the rulers was to create unity. *Svečanost* performances created a temporary ritual unity. The speakers in these *svečanosti* often spoke of unity. The problem with achieving unity in the mundane ordinary world of postwar Yugoslavia was twofold. First, the institutional structure of society precluded such unity from ever taking shape. Second, the rulers failed to control the conflicting perceptions and meanings held by different actors and groups. People from different regions of the country saw in print and heard in endless speeches the same word symbol of *jedinstvo* (unity). They recognized *jedinstvo* as a key symbol of the Yugoslav state; it was a part of the lexicon of the political and symbolic orders. It was a part of that ambiguous domain referred to as "Yugoslav culture," "shared cultural territory," or "common socialist aspirations." In the language of symbolic anthropologists it can be described as part of the "dominant, though fractured, symbolic universe." Each of the peoples of Yugoslavia had its own symbolic universe. Constituting these universes at any one time were the collective memories of the past and the perceptions and orientations of the present. These were the lenses through which such symbols as *jedinstvo* were perceived and then given meaning. Where the Jews of postwar Yugoslavia, and even those of interwar

Yugoslavia, diverged from Yugoslavia's larger ethnic populations was in their Yugoslavist and federalist orientation. That the Jews were dispersed throughout much of the country contributed to that orientation. The Federation, as the single central institution and official patron-protector, led the way in exhibiting a strong federalist orientation. Whereas other populations diverged from the intent of unity, even while regularly reiterating the word-symbol of unity, the Jewish community oriented itself toward it. The creation of the Kingdom of Serbs, Croats, and Slovenes in 1918 was the first experiment to create unity out of diversity. The socialist rulers had borrowed from traditional cultures cultural models that were familiar and successful, such as *borbenost*, but *jedinstvo* was not one of these. This aspiration which grew out of the Yugoslav Idea of the nineteenth century had been a dismal failure between 1918 and 1941 when the political framework existed. The only alternative was to draw once again from the myth of the Partisan War and find their cultural model there. Unity would be modeled on the "brotherhood and unity" model of the National Liberation Struggle. But the abandonment of Yugoslavism (*Jugoslavenstvo*) and structural decentralization precluded the development of countrywide commonality and unity. Yugoslavia and Yugoslavism were contradictions to most Yugoslav peoples, but not to the Jews. Being without a territory and dispersed throughout the country, and having their own Yugoslav oriented federal organization, many of the Jews of Yugoslavia, especially those in the capital of Belgrade, saw Yugoslavia and Yugoslav unity as a real possibility and pursued it to a much greater extent than did other Yugoslav peoples.

In these performances dramaturgical discipline served as a mechanism of social control. This can be illustrated by the official foreign policy of non-alignment. Given Tito's leading role in the non-aligned movement, non-alignment was added to the list of key symbols of the Titoist symbolic order. The Yugoslav Jews may have responded to this symbol in different ways. After Yugoslavia severed diplomatic relations with Israel in 1967, a potential existed for deviation and disruption, which was behavior to be avoided in a collective performance. With non-alignment occupying such a prominent place in the order, the Yugoslav state placed a wedge between the Jews of Yugoslavia and the state of Israel. Despite the official wedge, a strong tie between the Yugoslav Jews and Israeli Jews of Yugoslav descent continued. Speaking out publicly on such issues as Zionism, Israeli politics, Israeli-Arab conflicts, and the Palestinian problem was potentially disruptive. If an impression was made that some of the performers ("stage team") had aligned themselves with the opposition ("competitor," "enemy"), it made the whole "team" (Yugoslav state) look bad to its "friends" (other audiences—e.g., non-aligned, particularly Arab, states). Conversely, keeping silent and avoiding a clash showed the community's loyalty. Complicating any neat analysis was the fact that the Jewish-Arab conflict was not entirely avoided in community publications. Significantly, however, the Yugoslav state was never the target of attack. The Jewish community was trusted to perform in the proper manner. As trusted members they were even allowed to stage their own performances (e.g., anniversary celebrations) and to perform with other non-Jewish participants on front and center stage (e.g., Ledine commemoration). In either case they could not exploit their presence on the stage (Goffman 1957:212–214). The Yugoslav Jews were excellent dramaturgical performers, as Goffman defines the term. They played their part to critical success by reciting the proper word-symbols and themes, uttering the performer's oath, and acting out their designated roles.

Dramaturgical control was possible only through the organized community, that is, the Federation and the local communities. Collective expressions of Jewishness were necessarily accomplished through these state-recognized organizations which were fully integrated and committed to not upsetting the ideological plumcart. Their freedom, compared to Jewish organizations in Eastern Europe and the former Soviet Union, made the performance even more convincing to the audience. No coercion was involved. For a while, at least, many of the Jewish actors believed in the characters and in the "front" they were presenting.

Their visibility was a controlled visibility. As a collectivity the Jews were more invisible than visible in the mundane spheres of life. Even in commemorative performances their visibility was one part of a visibility shared with other "victims of fascism." It was not a genocide upon the Jews, but upon the Serbs, Jews, Gypsies, and even Communists. They were even in death, as the president of the Belgrade community put it in the spring of 1989, "in the shadow of the Serbs." A voluntary association such as the Society of Serbian-Jewish Friendship established in 1989 would not have been possible any earlier, for it would have carried the potential of uncontrolled visibility, a performance in which the symbols might be new and different, perhaps even oppositional. However, even after the formation of the Society in 1988 and its first public gathering in March 1989, dramaturgical discipline continued to function in the organized Jewish community. The public statements of any individual member of the Society when speaking as a private citizen were not to be interpreted as representative of the organized Jewish community, even though the president of the Federation welcomed at the time the formation of the Society. Another case involved statements made by the Rabbi of Yugoslavia. His statements, too, were to be understood as representing his personal views as an individual in Yugoslav society and not as the Rabbi of Yugoslavia or as an official spokesperson for the Jewish community. Such dramaturgical discipline as late as 1989 revealed the depth of the Jewish community's submergence.

In the following sections I describe (1) commemorations (*komemorativne svečanosti*) and (2) anniversary celebrations (*proslave godišnjice*). In analyzing the intent, structure, content, and outcome of these performances, my primary objective was to determine to what extent such performances exhibited symbolic symmetry with the new symbolic order and how they functioned to meet ethnic aims. My presentation and analysis of the predictable structure and content of these performances should be contrasted with the openness and variability of the individual narratives in chapters 5 and 6.

The main method that I use in operationalizing symbolic symmetry is determining whether a key symbol or a referent of a key symbol was present in or absent from any phase of the performance, including the post-ceremonial phases. I examine the structure, activities, language, and concrete objects that were part of the performance. In analyzing speech content, I examine key single words, phrases, and themes that make direct reference to a key summarizing symbol or that clearly were an elaborating component of a such a symbol. For example, the National Liberation Struggle was a key summarizing symbol. Elaborating components of this symbol might include the following: struggle (*borba*), revolution, revolutionary inheritance, revolutionary heroes, fallen warriors. Given the interrelatedness of the key symbols, elaborating symbols overlapped considerably.

Commemorations

Commemorations are by definition past-oriented. Their primary focus is on death and remembrance, particularly on individuals of special significance or status, or on categories of individuals that died in association with a particular event in history. Death, however, is more than the biological demise of the human body. Cultural meanings are attached to death. Yugoslav commemorations operate on more than one level of meaning. They are rituals of social and psychological support for bereaved individuals, kin units, communities, and even entire nations and the state. They are also rituals of remembrance, and of honor and respect for the dead.

Knowing that bereavement is an emotion that can be channeled, the rulers also exploited these rituals for political purposes. They crafted these rituals into political tools that allowed them not only to incorporate political symbols of their choosing but also to manipulate the cultural symbols of the participating groups. For example, the rulers of postwar Yugoslavia first expropriated the dead of all the Yugoslav ethnic populations and then transformed them into the two inclusive commemorative categories of "victims" and "fallen warriors" without any ethnic labels attached. Through such symbolic manipulation they attempted to manifest the "brotherhood and unity" and "brotherhood and equality" of the Yugoslav nations and nationalities. Furthermore, no one people contributed more or less to the resistance and revolutionary struggle. The rulers attempted to sustain an ideology of egalitarianism in this manner. As I describe below, the politicization of commemorations took other, more overt, forms.

The great emphasis on memorialism must be understood with the following factors in mind. First, the conceptions and activities of memorialism and commemoration are not new creations. They have long been a part of the universal cultural domain(s) of death and mourning. They deal with an ultimate concern—death. For many people the tie to their ancestors does not cease with the burial and initial mourning period. Many people feel an obligation to remember their dead. This sense of obligation is very strong among the Jews who have experienced numerous tragedies in their history. I describe this obligation in Jewish tradition in the section that follows. Next, over eighty percent of the Jewish population died during the Second World War. This was a catastrophe, a cataclysmic event that changed them forever. The more tragic and devastating the loss to a people the more likely that this loss will be collectively marked and remembered. Surviving members of the Yugoslav Jewish community believed that the generation of the Holocaust and the NOB ought to objectify their "obligation of respect and reverence" while witnesses from that period remained alive. In fact, they believed that the entire community shared that obligation. Third, the Yugoslav population as a whole suffered a great loss of life, proportionately one of the greatest in the war. During the Titoist period the official figure was 1,700,000. Today, this figure is debated among different individuals and groups. Fourth, the Serbs, Gypsies, and Communists were also categorized as targets of genocide, which deliberately was used to show that the Yugoslav people were victimized rather than just one population. Thus, memorialism could be made an integral part of the new symbolic order in which all of the "nations and nationalities of socialist Yugoslavia" could participate. By fusing memorialism with political components, commemorations could also be used as mechanisms of symbolic manipulation and control whose intent was to legitimate and reinforce the new political and symbolic orders. Political messages in isolation may lose their potency, but when fused with the emotions evoked by memorialism then perhaps there is a greater inclination to listen to and remember them. Enthusiasm waxes and wanes depending on the stimuli from without and from within a particular social unit. Immediately after the victory of the National Liberation Struggle, there was widespread and spontaneous enthusiasm for having overcome the enemy and liberated the homeland. The new rulers seized this link between the Partisan victory and spontaneous enthusiasm to promote the legitimacy of the popular and indigenous revolution that brought them to power and established the legitimacy of their rule in the New Yugoslavia. The rulers soon discovered that such exuberance could not be maintained indefinitely from within the individual or the collectivity itself. The transformation of the National War of Liberation into the origin myth of the New Yugoslavia and the institution of a new calendar and cycle of commemoration were means by which the spontaneous enthusiasm that emanated from direct experience could be regularly energized or stimulated by the commemorations. Commemorations thus became rites of political legitimation and political reaffirmation.

Memorialism and Commemoration in the New Yugoslavia

The postwar Yugoslav Jews met their obligations of reverence and respect for their ancestors. They did this not only as individuals paying respect and homage to their own kin, but as a community of persons remembering and honoring its ancestors. Death and its consequences have long involved the entire community (Savishinsky and Wimberley 1974). Specifically in the Yugoslav

Jewish community, this collective expression was visible in attendance at funerals and death anniversaries, at numerous commemorations in the cycle of commemoration, in special anniversary commemorations, in printed form (e.g., "In Memoriam" eulogies published in the *Jevrejsi Pregled*), in the synagogue (*pomen, limud*), and at the unveilings of memorial monuments and plaques. Even a special commission was established to oversee the material aspects of memorialism.

Commemoration ceremonies were not new symbolic creations. They were not the creations of the socialist rulers or commemoration organizers. What were new and deserved attention were the structure, forms, and content of these postwar ceremonies, their referents, and the political context in which the ceremonies occurred.

Table 3.3 shows the structure, forms, and content of submergence in and across four commemorations by means of a simple componential analysis. If a feature such as a category of actor or a key summarizing symbol is present, it is indicated by the sign "+." If it is either absent or I have not substantiated its presence, the space is left blank. The table functions also to compare different events and speeches to show stability of structure, form, and content and to show differences where they exist. Table 3.5 serves the same purpose in describing anniversary celebrations.

The new cycle of commemoration was oriented to a specific period of the past marked by the historical events that transpired between 1941 and 1945. As fought on the territory of Yugoslavia, this period was commonly referred to as the National Liberation Struggle, which, in turn, is divided by its antifascist resistance side and its political revolution side. The participants and the audience were encouraged to reflect on this period and remember what took place. Images of a horrible past brought about by the forces of fascism and nationalism were conveyed. This horrible past was connected to the fascist occupation and also to the period of the Old Yugoslavia. In remembering they recalled a period when a true transition did occur. Thus, they simultaneously commemorated the dead victims and heroes and celebrated the passage from the Old Yugoslavia to the New Yugoslavia. Both continuity and transformation were experienced in that passage. In conveying images of the past and those of the present, participants and audience were encouraged to compare and contrast the two periods.

The principle of determinacy was communicated. The National Liberation Struggle was portrayed as determining the present phase of socialist construction, founded on the new guiding key symbol of self-management, which will usher in the "beautiful future." The structure of the *svečanost* itself was concerned less with transition and more with reflecting the constructed and controlled political stability of the present and reinforcing the present order. What existed in the structure of society was evident in the *svečanost*. Certain key participants never discarded their social roles; badges of status were not stripped away and key institutions were recognized. On the surface, at least, there appeared to be little interplay between structure and anti-structure in these performances. Structure predominated.

In 1985 the Jews observed the "Year of Commemoration," marking the fortieth anniversary of the victory over fascism. Representatives of the Yugoslav Jewish community participated in numerous commemorations in Yugoslavia and abroad.

Commemorations making up the cycle were held at different sites: Jewish and non-Jewish cemeteries, mass extermination sites, sites of previous concentration camps, public halls, schools, and other public sites. Sites on which memorial objects sit have been called shrines for the younger generation. The Djakovo commemoration, which I observed on one occasion, took place at several sites during the course of the entire commemoration. In the city of Djakovo itself, it began in the general cemetery and then moved by procession to the Jewish cemetery. A Jewish rite was conducted in the Jewish chapel that sits at the entrance to the area of the individual graves. Following the religious ritual in the chapel, the participants visited the individual graves of the genocide victims. The commemoration group of pilgrims then moved to the third ritual site, where the Ustasha concentration camp operated. Other sites can also be considered. I traveled with Jewish pilgrims from Belgrade on a chartered bus. The bus ride to and from Djakovo must be included as phases of the entire ritual process. There were also the post-ceremonial sites in Djakovo itself (restaurants, receptions) that must be considered.

The old, prewar cycle of life was disrupted. Religious holidays could no longer be celebrated as state holidays. This act on the part of the rulers affected the Jews as well. Before the war the government authorities recognized the Jewish holiday cycle as well as the Orthodox and Catholic cycles. Jewish students and military personnel were released from their regular activity on certain Jewish holidays (Freidenreich 1979). A new calendar encompassing all of the significant memorial dates (*spomen-dani*) and socialist holidays (*socijalistički praznici*) was instituted, creating a new calendrical rhythm for all Yugoslav citizens, regardless of their religious or national affiliation. This act to temporally reorient the population was consciously done in order to help uproot the traditional orders and rhythms by which people lived their lives and to replace them with a single order and rhythm that would unite all the Yugoslav peoples. Its impact was probably greater on the South Slavic peoples than the Jews, for the direct targets of the reordering were the Roman Catholic Church and the Serbian Orthodox Church. Given the size of these institutions and their place in Croat and Serb history, it was inevitable that the official negation of their calendars would become politicized. In contrast to the former peoples, the Jews did not politicize what they had been denied, which was not the case for the Jews of the Soviet Union, who represented a much larger percentage of the population and whose religion was directly targeted for attack. Furthermore, as I will show, although the Jews of Yugoslavia stopped living according to the rhythm of the Jewish calendar, the traditional Jewish holiday cycle continued to operate. Jewish individuals did feel pressure to work on Jewish holidays. One of my informants, whom I estimate to be in his late thirties or early forties, who was not among the twenty or so synagogue regulars of the Belgrade synagogue, took time off from work every year to attend Yom Kippur day services in the synagogue. He was an exception for those of his generation. The synagogue was far from full when I attended day services during the High Holidays. On the eve of Yom Kippur the synagogue was filled to capacity, but attendance at this evening service did not disrupt the rhythm of one's mundane activities. This was also true for Jewish holidays celebrated outside of the synagogue, in the communal hall. Events associated with Jewish holidays, which took place in the communal hall, were held in the evening and thus did not disrupt the flow of mundane activities. Moreover, ever since the holiday observances were moved from the home, only a small group of activists were needed to prepare for the holiday. There were no symbolic activities of preparation and anticipation. Except for a few holidays, with one or two of these celebrated in a full synagogue (Rosh Hashanah and Yom Kippur), many Jews in Yugoslavia were ignorant of the Jewish cycle or, if they were cognizant of certain holidays, did nothing special on those days. For Shabbat, about twenty-three people gathered in the Belgrade synagogue on Friday evening, and not all of these were Jews.

The new state holidays included dates honoring significant persons, events, and organizations. The Day of the Republic

(November 29), which celebrated the founding of the new socialist Yugoslavia (29 November 1943 in Jajce, Bosnia) was the country's most significant holiday. Workers were given two days off. Workers also received two working days off during the socialist holiday of May Day or International Workers' Day. Associated with the new state's hero-founder Tito were Youth Day (*Dan Mladosti,* Tito's birthday) and later his death anniversary. Both were working days. Holidays or memorial days associated with special organizations or categories of person included Fighters' Day, Yugoslav National Army (JNA) Day, and International Women's Day. Each republic and province had its own Day of the Uprising holiday. The dates differed according to when a particular nation people joined the uprising. This holiday may have hindered rather than contributed to the unity of Yugoslav peoples, since the implication was that the earlier the uprising date, the earlier the participating nation or people joined the NOB. Perhaps the creators of the cycle failed to see the contradiction between brotherhood and unity and brotherhood and equality (including the proclamation that among the people there was no greater hero or villain), on the one hand, and the implication of the different uprising dates, on the other.

Each year the Federation of Jewish Communities of Yugoslavia published a Jewish Calendar (*Jevrejski Kalendar* or *Luach*). The Rabbi of Yugoslavia prepared the contents of the calendar. Both the Gregorian and corresponding Jewish lunar calendar days were printed together on each page. In this complete calendar both Yugoslav and Jewish holidays and memorial days were marked. Events associated with the Holocaust were marked extensively. In addition to the Jewish traditional holidays, the dates of significance in the Yugoslav Jewish community's *Jevrejski Kalendar*[10] included the following:

Yugoslav state holidays (not working):
- Day of the Republic (29 Nov.)
- New Year's Day (1 Jan.)

Yugoslav state holidays (working):
- Fighters' Day (7 July)
- Day of JN Army (22 Dec.)
- Day of Youth (Tito's Birthday) (25 May)

Republic/Autonomous Province holidays:
- Day of Uprising (various) (7 July, Serbia)

Socialist holidays (not working):
- International Day of Work (1 May)

Socialist holidays (working):
- International Day of Women (8 March)

Memorial Dates (spomen-dani) (selective list):
- Novi Sad Massacre (January)
- Skopje (11 March)
- Ledine (April)
- Djakovo (June)
- Tito's Death Anniversary (4 May)
- Sajmište (9 May)
- Zemun (July)

Jewish Memorial Dates:
- Yom ha-Sho'ah (Day of Remembrance) (27 Nisan)

Significant differences existed among the commemoration sites. Commemorations held in Jewish cemeteries incorporated traditional Jewish rituals, such as Kaddish. It was in these sites that the Jewish pilgrims, among whom only a few would say they were religious, came into contact with the Judaic Tradition. Since few Jews had regular contact with the Judaic Tradition, and what contact they did have was often fragmented and initiated not from within themselves, particular components of the Tradition served as the mediating symbols between the individual and the Tradition. It may have been the rabbi, or the Kaddish prayer, or the act of putting on a *kipa*. The only place in which a *kipa* was compulsory was in the synagogue, although there were individuals whom I never saw in the synagogue, yet who donned a *kipa* while the Kaddish prayer was recited. Mediating acts that put the individual and the ritual group in contact with the Judaic Tradition are acts of authentication. They are unmistakably Jewish acts. Only a Jewish male can be counted in a prayer quorum; only a Jewish male was asked to open the ark where the Torah scrolls are kept; and only a Jew reads the Kaddish prayer. Generally in these commemorations in socialist Yugoslavia, Jewish ritual was not conducted outside Jewish sites, although there were exceptions. For example, the Jasenovac commemoration was by far the largest attended commemoration in Yugoslavia, attracting fifty thousand people on 21 April 1985, perhaps more in other years. This commemoration was also televised. I remember watching it in 1986. The Jewish pilgrims held their own ritual, at least in that year. The prayer leader from the Zagreb community recited the *El Male Rahamim* and Kaddish prayers in front of the large monument. Even though more Jews died in Jasenovac than anywhere else, this site was not the most significant pilgrimage site in the Jewish community's annual cycle of commemoration.

The following actors usually filled a participant or spectator role in the commemorative *svečanost*: representatives of different ethnic populations, representatives of the government (one or more levels), representatives of socio-political organizations, especially from SUBNOR (veterans' association), representatives of the Party, representatives of religious organizations, men and women, older and younger persons, representatives of the organized Jewish community (Federation and local communit(ies) send separate representatives), school children and pioneers (mobilized for the performance). From this list it is clear that commemoration gatherings were heterogeneous affairs.

Along with the Jewish community, among the regular organizers of the commemorations were local SUBNOR organizations and local government communes (*mesna zajednice*). For special occasions, such as an anniversary commemoration, or when there were plans to construct a memorial object of some kind, a special committee composed of members of various organizations was formed.

The structure of commemorative *svečanosti* was characterized by a fixed or closed order (Moore and Myerhoff 1977) (see Table 3.3). They were "finished performances" (MacAloon 1984:2). An open order that might encourage spontaneity, deviation, evaluation, and criticism was avoided. The fixed order refers to the activities that constituted most commemorations: *pozdrav*—"greeting"; *govor*—formal speech; *počast*—giving honor and respect to the dead; *povorka*—"processional"; music; poetry or dramatic reading; wreath and flower laying; the concrete objects (e.g., memorial monument), the language used, the actors involved, the temporal orientation, the symbols manifested, and the messages communicated. The closed order refers to the content that was communicated (Table 3.3). Although individuals may have undergone personal transformations during the commemorations and assigned personal meanings to the constituent symbols, the emphasis was on the collective features and functions of these performances.

Since I spent most of my time in Belgrade, I pay closest attention here to those commemorations in which Belgrade Jews participated regularly. The Federation of Jewish Communities of Yugoslavia, being located in Belgrade, was included in this social category of Belgrade Jews. The Jews of Belgrade participate regularly in an annual cycle of commemoration. Since 1985 was designated the "Year of Commemoration," the occasion of the fortieth anniversary of the war's end, participation in commemorations was even more widespread. My description and analysis of the symbolic forms, techniques, and functions of commemorative *svečanosti* draws from both the narrower and broader spheres of participation.

Certain activities were common to all or most of the commemorative *svečanosti*. Two speech activities were the *pozdrav* (greeting) and the *govor* (speech). Several words and terms appear repeatedly in connection with commemorations. These can be called memorial words or *spomen-reci*. The domain of *spomen-reci* included the following: *spomen* (remembrance), *pomen*, *sećanje*, komemoracija (commemoration), *počast* (honor, respect), *pijetetne obaveze* (obligations of reverence and respect), (*večna*) *slava mu* (masc.) or *slava je* (fem.). The same components were repeated by speakers and were manifested at different sites and times.

The *pozdrav* was the greeting that opened the commemorative *svečanost*. The participants and congregants were greeted as *drugarice* (fem.) and *drugovi* (masc.); that is, as "comrades," which was a common term of address in the socialist world. Used in such a way it identified the actors and, by association, their activities as socialist. It matters not whether certain individual actors did not consider themselves as such. Because of its widespread and long-term usage, this term of address had lost much of its political meaning at the time of my research. It remained, however, significant in the formal structure of these performances and was especially salient in anniversary celebrations in which both Yugoslav and foreigners greeted the congregants. As a general rule, only speakers from socialist countries used "comrades" as a term of address.

A second important component of the *pozdrav* was the recognition of the participants. Designating the performance "team" helped to set the scene. Actors who were familiar with the commemorations did not need this reminder, for the same categories of participants were recognized from year to year, and also from one commemoration to another. These categories included representatives of at least the local government (*vlasti*, *Mesna zajednice*—commune), the socio-political organizations (e.g., SUBNOR) and local citizens. In addition, representatives of the Party, the Alliance of Working Peoples of Yugoslavia, local enterprises, school children, cultural-artistic societies, and the Yugoslav National Army could often be seen in attendance.

The *govor* is a formal ritual speech. Usually the congregants listened to more than one *govor* presented during a commemoration. In some commemorations, like the Ledine and Djakovo commemorations, a Jewish and a non-Jewish representative both spoke. Regular Jewish speakers were long-term leaders and activists in the Federation and local community. The two institutions each sent their own representatives to the commemorations. There was little variation in speech content among speakers. A rather small group of men represented the Federation and the local communities in commemorations. Such representation reflected the general pattern of leadership in the organized community. By examining leadership positions and activist roles over at least ten years, I found considerable stability in these areas. Stability was particularly evident in the case of the Federation president who held the position of president for over twenty-five years. He was the principal speaker, representing the Federation in numerous commemorations and other *svečanosti* over the span of his leadership. The Federation's deputy presidents were also key participants, representing the Federation in numerous events.

A speaker often opened the ceremony by giving the *pozdrav.* The *govor* was sometimes referred to as the *spomen-govor* (speech of remembrance), and the words of the *govor* as *spomen-reci* (words of remembrance). The language used and imagery conveyed to the congregants was intended to evoke memories (*evocirati uspomena*) of both the tragic and the victorious past. The commemorative focus of the *spomen* (commemorative remembrance or commemoration of) was on the "victims of fascism" and the "fallen fighters." In remembering these victims and fallen fighters, the participants paid their honors and respects (*odati počast*). The speaker usually called for a "minute of silence." This act is called a *počast.* The "fallen fighters," in particular, having given their lives during a heroic struggle (*Borba*), were elevated to hero status.

Govors were vehicles of closed communication. Spontaneity and innovation were not their primary features. The same or similar words, phrases, and themes recur in different *govors* which give the appearance of scripting by the same source.

Commemoration speeches were vehicles of political communication and legitimation. In that sense they were conservative instruments that communicated a sense of unquestionability and

Table 3.4
The Djakovo Commemoration: Political and Cultural Dimensions

Political/Yugoslav	*Ethnic/Jewish*
NOB	Holocaust
fallen fighters	victims of fascism
Red Star	Jewish Star
General Cemetery	Jewish Cemetery
wreaths placed on monument	flower placed on each individual grave
SUBNOR representative's govor	Rabbi reading Kaddish
Local citizens	Jewish pilgrims
Slavonia	Jews from Serbia, Croatia, Bosnia
melodies by group of local musicians	El Male Rahamim prayer by rabbi

immutability with regard to the present order. *Govors* verbally negated what the rulers defined as antithetical to the new order. This included anything from the past or present that was labeled as an "enemy" of the New Yugoslavia. Conversely, *govors* were vehicles for presenting what the rulers defined as positive, good, and friendly. What was positive and good was usually related in some way to the key symbols of the state, starting with the National Liberation Struggle and followed by the process of constructing a new, unique, and independent socialist tradition. The intent was to indicate determinacy between the NOB past and the socialist present.

In addition, *govors* were instruments of fusion or synthesis. They help to synthesize certain cultural and political features (see Table 3.4). Below is a translation of a *govor* by a veteran, a non-Jewish participant, in the Djakovo commemoration. I requested and was given the actual document. This document is a representative example of the kind of commemorative speech (*spomen-govor*) presented during a commemoration. The following *govor* was read at the Djakovo commemoration that I attended. Sprinkled liberally throughout the *govor* were references to key summarizing and elaborating symbols of socialist Yugoslavia. The following is my translation of that document:

> This *spomenik* [monument] before us, this five-pointed red star, the monument is to the warriors of the NOR who . . .

died in battles for the liberation of Djakovo and Djakovstine in April 1945. On this place, in the *spomen-kosturnici* [memorial charnel], besides the fallen warriors, the liberators of the city and commune of Djakovo, one Jew is also buried, Regal Vajs, a prewar Communist and one of the first organizers of the uprising in Djakovstine. In battles for the liberation of Djakovo, 172 warriors of the NOR fell, and 300 more fell in battles for the liberation of Djakovstine. For the national and social liberation of our entire land, for the freedom of all our nations and nationalities, a total of 411 warriors of this region gave their lives and 1,785 were victims of fascist terror. Sad is the memory of those days of the NOB, the days when blood and ashes built this land, when brotherhood and unity was tempered, when 1,700,000 sons and daughters of our homeland lost their lives. Hundreds of thousands of people lost their lives on different places of execution in fascist prisons and concentration camps. One of these places of execution was the concentration camp in Djakovo. In that camp about 3,000 people were interned, and 560 of them were liquidated. The rest were taken to the even more horrible camp of Jasenovac. More will be said about the horrors of that concentration camp in Djakovo at the very site of that onetime place of agony and suffering of the Jewish population, women, and children. Those 560 innocent Jews who died in the Djakovo camp are also buried in the cemetery. In memory of all of them, as well as all the warriors of the NOR and victims of fascist terror, we bow with respect and hope that it will never happen again. We are deeply conscious of that time, the NOB, when we were writing the sad, but also the brightest pages of our history; when struck with the firm foundation of our brotherhood and unity and other inheritances of our socialist revolution, we are building the new relations among our peoples and nations, we are building and developing self-managing socialist social relations. The path that we have chosen and on which we travel is not easy, but we are deeply convinced that it is the true path of peace and human prosperity, for it is in fact the path of our Party and Tito, the path of complete pride built upon our greatest inheritance—the brotherhood and unity of our nations and nationalities. I call on you for a minute of silence to give honor to the fallen warriors of the NOR and to all Jews—

> victims of fascist terror, and especially these who were killed in the camp in Djakovo and are buried in this cemetery. To them be eternal glory and thanks!

Music and other artistic forms such as poetry and dramatic readings often played an important part of the commemoration. Music appeals to what Turner calls the sensory pole. It stimulates the emotions and sets the mood. Instrumental and/or choral music was performed in commemorations. A funeral march was played during the processional and wreath-laying activities. Singing was also used. Both Jewish choirs, *Braća Baruh* from Belgrade and *Moša Pijade* from Zagreb, participated in commemorations.

The *počast* was the act of paying honor and respect to the *pokojnici* (the deceased). I have already described the *počast* as a component of the *govor*.

The *povorka* can refer to two kinds of processional. The first refers to the processional to the memorial monument at which wreaths were laid. In commemorations where there were multiple sacred sites, the second processional involved the ritual walk from one site to the next.

Wreath laying was a major part of the commemorative ceremonies. In the Sajmište ceremony at the site of the former concentration camp, representatives of various organizations participated in this ritual activity.

The Kaddish mourners' prayer or *molitva* was a specifically Jewish part of the commemoration. In general, the Kaddish prayer was only a part of those commemorations or phases of commemorations held in Jewish cemeteries (Djakovo, Yom ha-Sh'oah in the Belgrade), but it was "the most distinctive feature of the Jewish observance of mourning" (Kertzer 1988:96). "According to some authorities, saying Kaddish makes one still a Jew no matter what else of the heritage one has relinquished" (Myerhoff 1984:171). In addition to the Kaddish mourners' prayer, the memorial prayer *El Male Rahamim* was recited or sung. Where a qualified ritual specialist was unavailable, a recording of the prayer was played.

On sites with individual graves, the participants visited the graves of kin and friends. Sometimes a separate commemoration was held at the gravesite of an esteemed Jewish individual. Grave visitation had special significance in the Djakovo commemoration. About six hundred Jewish women and children were killed by the Nazis in Djakovo and buried there. Thanks to the efforts of a local gravedigger in recording the burial sites of the victims, the graves are named. I have been told that this is the only site in Europe where the graves of individual Jewish victims are named. In other commemorations there was only a mass common burial mound (*humka; gubilište,* "site of mass execution") or a monument without any physical remains buried under it.

The various commemorative objects and markings that are associated with memorialism can be subsumed under the complex term, *spomen-obeležje.* The shapes of or markings on some of these objects are specifically ethnic (e.g., Jewish menorah or Star of David) or political (e.g., Communist red star). Yugoslav Jewish sculptor Nandor Glid, whom I call a ritual specialist in addition to the artist he is, has constructed several memorial works of sculpture in Yugoslavia and abroad.

There were also noncommemorative objects that were displayed in certain commemorations. These would include Tito images, Yugoslav flag (with red star), Communist flag (with hammer and sickle), banners, military uniforms, and medals. Of the commemorations that I have examined, the Sajmište commemoration was the only one in which there was such an abundance of political symbols: a photograph of Marshall Tito, a banner with the oath-like words, "Tito, we promise never to turn from your path," and a Communist red star on the small monument, which had no ethnic symbols.

Post-ceremonial activities sometimes included a reception (*prijem*), informal social interaction with the locals, and commensality. Commensality could be in the form of a snack sometimes prepared by local citizens, as in Ledine, or eating together in a local restaurant following the commemoration, as in Djakovo. This was a joyous, festive phase of the commemoration, a celebration for the living.

Commensality was sometimes a part of the commemorative ceremony itself. Specially prepared, Sephardi-style boiled eggs, small, round pita pastries stuffed with cheese (*pogačice*), and wine and/or plum brandy (*šljivovica*) were consumed by the participants.

At times the Federation of Jewish Communities of Yugoslavia distributed certificates of thanks (*megile zahvalnice*) to individuals and organizations that played a key role in commemorations or in the maintenance of Jewish memorial markers and sites.

Anniversary Celebrations

The anniversary celebration (*proslava godišnjice*) can be classified as a festive *svečanost* or a combination festive-solemn *svečanost.* In the case of the latter, the primary intent was to celebrate festively, but during the course of the celebration solemn, commemorative activities were included. It also included the formal meeting, or *svečana sednica*, among its events.

The objects of the anniversary celebrations in the Yugoslav Jewish community have included: (1) local and regional Jewish communities (e.g., Zagreb Jewish community; Jews of Bosnia and Hercegovina); (2) Jewish organizations (e.g., Federation of Jewish Communities of Yugoslavia); and (3) non-Jewish organizations (e.g., League of Communists of Yugoslavia).

Anniversary celebrations were complex performances. They were rituals that were composed of a number of "performance taxa" (Turner 1982)—formal meetings (*svečana sednica*), commemorations, theater, concerts, exhibitions, receptions, banquets, refreshments, receptions, inaugurations, unveilings, excursions, religious rites, and award ceremonies. Some of these events or activities were classified as *svečanosti* and others as *kulturne manifestacije*. In fact, such an explicit classificatory distinction was made in the memorial book that describes the Sarajevo 1966 celebration. These multi-event performances were performed over the course of two or more days. The ceremonial activities took place on several sites, both Jewish and non-Jewish. It was an occasion that focused on the ultimate concern of death but it also celebrated life. The living and the dead were linked by the performances. There was thus, as noted above, a combination of the festive and the solemn in these performances. Emotions ranged from the sad and somber to the joyous and jubilant. These celebrations were both commemorations and jubilees.

Anniversary celebrations were public events that were national and sometimes even international in scope. Jewish guests arrived from all over the country and from abroad. After being recognized by their Yugoslav Jewish hosts by means of a formal greeting, many of these guests reciprocated by giving short greetings and speeches. Higher-level Yugoslav government officials made appearances, gave speeches, and held receptions for the participants. Many local residents attended the public events. In addition, representatives from Yugoslavia's religious communities were invited and attended some of the events. Specifically, this meant that representatives of the Roman Catholic, Serbian Orthodox, and Muslim religious communities attended the celebration. International Jewish organizations such as the World Jewish Congress, of which the Yugoslav Jewish community was a member, sent high-level representatives. Other features added to the extraordinary character of these celebrations. One such feature was the special Memorial Book or *Spomenica* that was published to mark the celebration. Other special features included exhibit openings, unveilings of a memorial monument or plaque, or inaugurations, such as that of the Jewish Historical Museum in Sarajevo or the Šik Library in Zagreb.

As was the case with commemorations described above, the anniversary celebrations were characterized by a fixed order and closed content. However, there was greater potential for deviation from these fixed and closed patterns, and indeed such unstructured deviation occurred. I suggest the following two reasons for such deviation in order and content. First, foreign guests attended and participated in the celebration. There was less control over what they said and did as formal participants in ceremonial events and as informal participants in various informal social interactions. The latter as well as the former occasions have found their way into the written historical record. For example, a private conversation that deviated from the public image of the Yugoslav Jewish collectivity's symbolic symmetry was published by a guest who attended the Sarajevo 1966 celebration. Secondly, since the celebration was spread out over two to four days, there were many opportunities for informal social interaction. These may have been scheduled, but they were unscripted occasions, open spaces in an otherwise closed structure.

Such celebrations can also be considered as rites of reversal. Whereas the Jews of Yugoslavia were more socially invisible than visible in the ordinary flow of time and usually kept a low profile, the public nature of such anniversary celebrations gave them high visibility. The mass media played a key role in this process. Furthermore, although anniversary celebrations, like commemorations, were a fusion of ethnic (Jewish) and political events, Jewishness was displayed much more in the former than in the latter.

Comparison of Two Anniversary *Proslave*

The Sarajevo *proslava* held in 1966 and the Zagreb *proslava* held twenty years later in 1986 were two extraordinary anniversary celebrations in the postwar Jewish community. They transformed a socially invisible collectivity into a highly visible collectivity for the duration of the celebrations. The anniversary celebrations described below share many features common to the simple *svečanosti* described above and with each other, but they also exhibit important differences. First, I will briefly describe each celebration separately, and then I will compare and contrast the two anniversary celebrations.

The Sarajevo 1966 Proslava

Over a four-day period, from Friday to Monday, in October 1966 in the city of Sarajevo, the Jews of Yugoslavia, their domestic and foreign guests, local citizens, and local and republican politicians celebrated the 400th anniversary of the settlement of the Jews in Bosnia and Hercegovina. This four-day celebration was actually a part of seven days of events that occurred in Skopje and Belgrade as well as in Sarajevo. It was written that these celebrative and commemorative events "filled with pride and happiness not only the whole Jewish community of Yugoslavia, but, too, the broad Yugoslav public and guests from a great number of foreign countries" (*Skopje-Sarajevo October 1966*, 109). One visitor reflected that the "appearance of Jewish delegations from all over the world . . . inspired a resurgence of spirit in the hearts of this remnant of a Jewish community" (Sitton 1985:249–250). Furthermore, "it was a seven-day meeting of human friendship, mutual cooperation and esteem, and *the reflection of the honorable and dedicated solution of the national problem in the frame of the contemporary Yugoslav trends*" (ibid, emphasis mine). As is evident from this statement in the Memorial Book published after these events and from statements made by Jewish and non-Jewish participants during the events themselves, the key symbol of Brotherhood and Unity was the guiding paradigm of the Sarajevo *proslava*.

The anniversary celebration opened with a formal meeting (*svečana sednica*) of the Plenary Board of the Federation of Jewish Communities of Yugoslavia. Attending the formal session were foreign guests, representatives of international Jewish organizations and communities, and members of the Sarajevo and other Jewish communities from around the country. It was perhaps significant that there were no representatives from Spain, the country from which the Yugoslav Sephardim had come, or from neighboring Italy, the country through which many of the Sephardim had passed. There also were no representatives from the Soviet Union. Two formal greetings were extended at the opening of the celebration. The Federation president opened the meeting by greeting and recognizing the Sarajevo community and the Board for their part in planning and organizing the celebration. The president of the Sarajevo Jewish community then greeted the gathering in the name of his community (*Skopje-Sarajevo October 1966*). The formal greeting was an important component of the entire celebration for it recognized the participants and by association the organizations and entities that they represented. Among the guests were representatives from Eastern European and Western Jewish communities and from Israel, the first time that such a united gathering had taken place. This in itself was highly significant for Yugoslavia, a co-founder of the non-Aligned movement only four years before. The greeting also served as a rite of incorporation, for it transformed the various participants, many or most of whom were strangers, into a ritual group.

A key component of both *pozdravi* was that of *čast* (*kavod* in Hebrew, "honor" in English). In publicly recognizing the Sarajevo Jewish community and the efforts of its activists in creating and staging this public celebration of Yugoslav-wide and international scope, the Federation president elevated the status of the Sarajevo Jews and thereby conferred honor upon them. Honor was a trait that was highly valued in Yugoslav and South Slavic history, and one that touched on traditional Sephardi pride exibited by the Sarajevo Sephardim. The Sarajevo community had been predominantly Sephardi in composition, style, and outlook. However, given that the primary guiding paradigm of the celebration was Brotherhood and Unity, the president went on to state that "the entire [Yugoslav Jewish] community can be truly proud of what happened here and proud of what we see. . . . All the effort that went into this was a picture of Jewish activism. We can be most proud of that (*najviše nam služi na čast*)" (ibid:20).

Revealed in the *pozdrav* of the Sarajevo community's president were certain local intents of the celebration. "The decision to organize the celebration, made several years ago, had in view that the possibilities of carrying out such a project were becoming smaller and smaller because our number is dropping. Every day we lose a witness to the past, a vital and active Jewish worker. Consequently we hurried to publish a Memorial Book for the celebration that would present a historiography of Yugoslav Jews, and at the same time would leave for our youth the permanent facts about our past and that the pages of this book would inspire them to be active in the future" (ibid:21). There was a sense of urgency among the elder activists to stimulate their children and grandchildren to be active and to eventually replace them and thus ensure the continuity of Sarajevo and Bosnian Jewry. Although somewhat pessimistic they saw the possibility of revitalization, not in a return to religion or tradition but in maintaining an organizational framework that would continue to indicate that there were still Jews in Bosnia and Hercegovina four hundred years after the initial settlement. Revitalization was to come from the celebration itself and from the history that would be written and published in the special memorial volume called *Spomenica: 400 godina od dolaska Jevreja u Bosni i Hercegovini* (Commemorative volume: 400 years since the arrival of Jews in Bosnia and Hercegovina). Since most of their recorded past had been destroyed or lost during the war, these Jews decided that in preparation for the celebration they would write their history and leave a written representation of themselves for their descendants and for other Yugoslavs. This representation would include as its most significant material the "latest chapter" of the Holocaust and the National Struggle of Liberation, a history which they believed had found its culmination in socialist Yugoslavia.

The *govori* followed the two greetings. Twenty-three individuals gave speeches—three from Yugoslavia and twenty from other countries. As in the commemorative *svečanosti*, the *govor* was a primary medium of expressing both the specifically ethnic and the key political symbols of socialist Yugoslavia. Verbal utterances helped to fuse the ethnic and political (ideological) domains.

In his *govor*, Federation President Dr. Lavoslav Kadelburg set the tone for the entire celebration when he emphasized the key symbol of "Brotherhood and Unity" as realized within Yugoslav society and in the Jewish community. The Sarajevo 1966 *proslava* celebrated the resolution of what has been referred to in Eastern Europe as the "National Question," that is, the problem of ethnic divisions, conflicts, animosities, prejudices, and discriminations. The implication was that the resolution was based on the Brotherhood and Unity that was forged during the National Liberation Struggle and subsequently institutionalized in the federal structure and sociopolitical organizations of socialist Yugoslavia. President Kadelburg declared that "the culmination of all that has been attained appears to be clear: a free life in a free land, free activity of the Jewish community in free Yugoslavia, the brotherhood and unity of Yugoslav peoples, and maybe something more if we are talking about our own community—brotherhood and unity among ourselves" (ibid:22). When contrasting the past with the future, Kadelburg used an approach common to many postwar speeches. The past was usually depicted in a negative way, whereas the present was described as positive. Just as the peoples of Yugoslavia were divided by conflicts and animosities before the Partisan War, so too were the various segments of the Jewish population. First, Kadelburg referred to the past: "I can remember conflicts and battles here. Just 30 years ago there were conflicts between two parts of our single community. These were among Jews who had the same ideals and aims but in certain moments did not speak the same language" (ibid.). He then continued by focusing on the present. He expressed the contrast in the following way:

> In this place and in this moment we must say, with great pride and pathos that the differences between Sephardim and Ashkenazim have disappeared. When today we speak about the successes of Jews in Bosnia and Hercegovina, we do not differentiate whether they were Sephardi or Ashkenazi successes; they were the successes of one living Jewish organism which contributed not only to its own development but participated in the development of its surroundings, in the entire social community in which it found itself and in which, in dialectical fashion, it influenced and was influenced by its environment. That is the basic characteristic of all that which we can conclude today: that with common efforts and strength, after a huge cataclysm which befell us, in this place in this *svečanom trenutku* [festive or solemn moment], in the presence of many delegates and foreign guests, we can say—we are one, we gravitate toward each other, and you can count on us being like that. I think that nothing else needs to be added in this *svečanoj atmosferi* [festive atmosphere] which begins at this moment (ibid:22–23).

From these statements of the Yugoslav Jewish community's most influential individual, it is clear that the focus of the celebration certainly went beyond celebrating the arrival of the Jews in Bosnia and Hercegovina four hundred years before and beyond the intentions stated by the Sarajevo community's president. It was a celebration of the resolution of the "National Question" by means of the Brotherhood and Unity of Yugoslav peoples, begun during the Partisan War and carried over into the phase of socialist construction of the New Yugoslavia.

The General-Secretary of the World Jewish Congress (WJC) spoke on behalf of the Congress's president, Nahum Goldmann, a man who was held in high esteem by the Yugoslav Jewish community (his visit in 1967 was proclaimed one of the four most significant events of the decade) and who had met with Tito on several occasions. The General-Secretary of the WJC continued the session's focus on Brotherhood and Unity, though from the position and perspective of a non-Yugoslav. He first spoke about unity among Jews everywhere. "We came in the spirit of solidarity and brotherhood and are happy that among us are delegations from Jewish communities of Eastern Europe. The WJC is conscious of the fact that it will become truly a worldwide Jewish organism only when all Jewish organizations and organisms are a part of a single organization which represents all Jewry. He then turned his focus on Sarajevo and how this multiethnic and multi-religious city symbolized the solution of the National Question for the Jews and all the Yugoslav peoples.

> From three different aspects Sarajevo is a symbol of that which we have in common and love. Sarajevo is one of the Jewish communities which has an old Jewish tradition . . . we are very proud of the great Jewish culture of this region which was predominantly Sephardi. . . . The Sarajevo *Haggadah* is known in the entire Jewish world as the fruit of Jewish tradition and culture. It is ours, common to us. This land, this city and this community represent a symbol of harmony and unity in the midst of different civilizations, nationalities, and religions. [We] do not see anywhere in Europe the harmonious common existence between Jews and Muslims as here in this city. This gives us hope not only for the Jews of Sarajevo, for we know that [there] exists here a centuries-long tradition of Jewish-Muslim cooperation and coexistence, . . . (ibid:25–26).

In addition to the formal meeting or *svečana sednica* described above, the Sarajevo 1966 celebration encompassed several other ceremonial occasions (*svečanosti*) and several events classified as "cultural manifestations." The ceremonial events included a reception by the president of the Republican Assembly of Bosnia and Hercegovina, the official inauguration of the Museum of the Jews of Bosnia and Hercegovina, a commemoration to the fallen warriors and victims of fascism in the Jewish cemetery, a reception by the mayor of Sarajevo, an *Akademija*, and a banquet for one hundred fifty people. I would also include in this first category of events the Torah gift ceremony, the spontaneous *Simhat Torah* celebration, and the Sabbath service in the synagogue. The latter two events were not reported by the Yugoslav Jewish community in its Memorial Book that otherwise described the celebration in detail. The cultural manifestations included an opera, an exhibition of works created by Jewish artists, a lecture and film on the Sarajevo *Haggadah*, and a symphony concert with the participation of the Braća Baruh and Moša Pijade Jewish choirs.

One of the most significant events of the anniversary celebration was the inauguration of the Museum of the Jews of Bosnia and Hercegovina. Among the dignitaries attending the opening was the president of the Parliament of the Socialist Republic of Bosnia and Hercegovina. The president of the Executive Council of Sarajevo gave a *govor* in which he noted the Jewish contribution to revolutionary movements and their progressive aspirations that were expressed in the struggle for socialist ideals even before the Second World War. This struggle came to its fullest expression during the National Liberation Struggle (ibid:47). He continued:

> Many Jews, the citizens of Sarajevo, together with their Serbian, Croatian and Muslim comrades and members of other nationalities, became partisan fighters and heroically spilled their blood for the defense of human dignity, for a new era of freedom and social justice. . . . Because of this we are convinced that many of the elements of the *svečanosti* in which we are participating represent dignified contributions in the celebration of the 25th jubilee anniversary of the people's uprising (ibid:47–48).

The museum occupies the space of the Sephardi synagogue first built in 1581 with the permission of Pasha Sijavuš. The synagogue was built adjacent to the central market area of Sarajevo, which today is called *Stari Grad* (Old Town). Before the tragic war and seige of Sarajevo, tourists walked the cobblestone streets of this district. Among the tourist signs they saw was the one for the Jewish Museum.

The commemoration held in the Jewish cemetery in Kovačići, on whose hillside sit unusual tombstones from the sixteenth century, was another significant event attended by thousands of people. One observer described it as "the most impressive of the week's events" (Sitton 1985:247).

The *Svećana Akademija* was a formal meeting that marked an important event. Such gatherings were a common type that most often characterized the central event of an anniversary celebration. Sometimes they were the sole event, as was the case for the Rom-Jewish *Akademija* that I attended in Belgrade in the fall of 1985. The *Akademija* consisted of formal speeches and an artistic program with music and poetry. The program of the *Akademija* held during the Sarajevo celebration included a historical lecture on the significance of the 400th anniversary of the arrival of Jews in Bosnia and Hercegovina, followed by an artistic program (*Skopje-Sarajevo October 1966*, 56–71; 128–129).

The Unscheduled and Spontaneous Simhat Torah. The spontaneous *Simhat Torah* celebration in the Sarajevo synagogue was an unscheduled event that fell outside the fixed order of the celebration's program. It is significant that this event was not recorded in the special volume published after the celebration. This book described in some detail the scheduled events of the celebration, but it excludes any mention of the *Simhat Torah* celebration. Spontaneous activities were not scheduled and thus cannot be controlled. They were not encouraged. It is therefore not surprising that the spontaneous *Simhat Torah* was generated by outsiders, specifically by a group of foreign rabbis. My source for the description of this event is a written account by David Sitton who attended the celebration in the capacity of Chairman of the Executive of the Jerusalem Council of the Sephardi Community. From Sitton's account it appears that the spontaneous *Simhat Torah* occurred on the Sabbath following the gift giving ceremony in which the Head Rabbi of Romania presented two Torah scrolls to the Sarajevo community. This gift giving ceremony was reported in the memorial book as "a rare and interesting ceremony" (1966). Sitton described the spontaneous *Simhat Torah* as follows:

> The new scrolls elicited much enthusiasm among the community, particularly the elderly. The guest rabbis decided to hold a *Simchat Torah* and to put the scrolls into the ark after seven circuits and dancing, as is the custom. The news of the rejoicing quickly spread, and in no time many people streamed to the synagogue and filled it. Rabbi Pardes [Sephardi rabbi from Israel] organized the ceremony and for two hours there was *Simchat Torah* in song and dance. The Rabbis bore the Torah scrolls aloft dancing and singing. Rabbi Pardes chanted aloud: "*Simchat Torah Yesh Yesh!*

Simchat Gila Yesh Yesh!" and the congregants chanted loudly in response (1985:247–248).

The Zagreb 1986 Proslava[11]

In November 1986 the Jews of Zagreb hosted a four-day (Thursday to Sunday) anniversary celebration to mark the 180th anniversary of the Zagreb Jewish community. About two hundred Jewish guests from around the country and thirty foreign guests attended.

Before the anniversary celebration officially began, a press conference attended by twenty journalists was held. Two representatives from the Zagreb community and one representative from the Federation of Jewish Communities of Yugoslavia responded to the reporters' questions. The celebration continued to receive considerable print and broadcast media attention, helping to make it even more of a public event.

The official opening of the anniversary celebration was marked by a *pozdrav* extended at the outset of the *Svečana Izvedba,* a festive performance of a Verdi opera held in the Croatian National Theater in Zagreb. On the second day, Friday, a *Svečana Sednica* of the Zagreb Jewish communal council was held. In the evening, as part of the official program of the anniversary celebration, a *Svečana Sluzba* was held in the synagogue. About three hundred people packed the synagogue beyond its capacity, the largest synagogue gathering in Zagreb since 1941. The Rabbi of Yugoslavia, Cadik Danon, conducted the liturgy. Assisting the rabbi were four young men training to become prayer leaders and three individuals from the Zagreb community. Following the Erev Shabbat service, the rabbi was awarded the *Medal of the Jewish Educator* for his longtime successful service in spreading knowledge about Jewish tradition. Later that evening a special lecture was presented on the history of the Jews in the Habsburg Empire. The final event of the day was a reception (*prijem*) in the Skupština of the city of Zagreb. During the reception members of the Zagreb Jewish community and local politicians discussed future cooperation.

On day three of the celebration the inauguration of the Šik Library was held. A *govor* was given. That the community chose to name the library after a rabbi is significant. Lavoslav Šik was a Zagreb rabbi who was killed in Auschwitz. This was a deviation from the general pattern of postwar naming practices, which had been to select the names of Jewish individuals who had been associated with the revolution and resistance. The names of the two Jewish choirs were examples of this pattern. The main event of the entire celebration was the *Svečana Akademija*, which, like other *akademije*, included formal speeches and an artistic program during which ethnic and political compositions and recitations were presented by Jewish and non-Jewish participants.

Commemorative events and activities were integral parts of all anniversary celebrations and meetings, and the Zagreb 1986 *proslava* was no exception. In particular, three commemorative events were part of the fixed schedule of the four-day celebration. On the fourth day, before television cameras, the Rabbi of Yugoslavia unveiled a memorial tablet for the Jewish victims of fascism on the site of the synagogue that had been destroyed in the war. A *govor* was given. A special commemoration service was then held on the premises of the Zagreb community. Again, a formal speech was given. A three-person delegation was then sent to the Jewish cemetery to lay a wreath on the monument to the Jewish victims of fascism and the fallen warriors. The Kaddish prayer was recited there as well.

Similarities and Differences

The Sarajevo 1966 and Zagreb 1986 anniversary celebrations as complex *svečanosti* share many features. In comparing the two celebrations I extracted the following similarities that characterize large-scale anniversary celebrations in the Jewish community:

1. multi-event and multi-activity
2. multi-day
3. multi-site
4. primarily festive
5. contain solemn activities (commemorations)
6. predominantly secular
7. contain religious features (e.g., Kaddish prayer)
8. Jewish guests from throughout Yugoslavia
9. foreign Jewish guests
10. government representatives
11. representatives from socio-political organizations
12. representatives from major religions

13. Yugoslav and foreign speakers
14. synthesis/fusion of the ethnic and political
15. publication of *Spomenica*, a special memorial book
16. an inauguration (a museum in Sarajevo; a library in Zagreb)
17. rite of revitalization (intent)
18. greater emphasis on Jewishness compared to commemorations
19. mass media plays a prominent role in making the celebration an even greater public event

There were also marked differences between the two anniversary celebrations (see Table 3.5). Two different communities, situated in two very different republics and regions of Yugoslavia, were the focus of the celebrations. Sarajevo is located in Bosnia-Hercegovina, the territory that was held by the Ottoman Turks for about five hundred years. Sephardi Jews lived there together with Muslim Slavs, Orthodox Serbs, and Catholic Croats in this heterogeneous region for four centuries. Ashkenazi Jews began arriving in significant numbers only after Bosnia's occupation by Austria in 1878. Sarajevo itself was a microcosm of that ethnic and religious heterogeneity, and it remained so until the recent collapse of Yugoslavia. Zagreb is the capital of Croatia. It is part of the Habsburg past. Having been expelled for three hundred years from the region in the medieval period, the Ashkenazi Jews settled in Zagreb early in the nineteenth century. Thus, their presence in Zagreb has been considerably shorter than has been the Sephardi presence in Sarajevo.

Twenty years passed from the Sarajevo celebration in 1966 to the Zagreb celebration in 1986. In the 1960s Tito was alive and Titoism was very strong, especially in Bosnia, which reputedly was one of the most politically conservative of the Yugoslav republics. During the war Bosnia had been a stronghold of the Partisans, and the New Yugoslavia was founded in the Bosnian town of Jajce on 29 November 1943, which became celebrated as the Day of the Republic. The participation of Bosnian Jews reflects the fact that the Partisan movement was strong in Bosnia. For example, of the one hundred fifty Jewish survivors who joined the Partisan uprising at the outset, the greatest number came from Bosnia and Hercegovina. The political climate was quite different in 1986. Tito had been dead for six years, and no one had emerged to replace him. Although Tito's mythological stature and position as a dominant symbol remained relatively strong, it was beginning to crack slightly. In 1986 this was not so apparent in the organized community. More apparent in 1986 was the deepening crises into which the country had fallen. The economic crisis was uncontrollable. Politicians talked more and more, but acted decisively less and less. People were talking about a moral crisis. Ramet (1985) has described this period as a time of "apocalyptic culture." Many individuals sought a way out of the crisis and moral vacuum created by a quickly decaying Marxist-Titoist order by returning to organized religion or other forms of spiritual activity. The Jews as a collectivity, however, showed little interest in returning to Judaism.

The difference in political and social conditions is reflected in the intent, content, some of the forms, and in the outcomes of the two celebrations. Table 3.5 shows both the similarities and the differences between them. Given Titoism's far greater stability in 1966, particularly in Bosnia-Hercegovina as opposed to Croatia, it is not surprising that the Sarajevo celebration exhibited greater symbolic symmetry and hence submergence.

The two celebrations were also different in terms of their Jewish orientation. The Sarajevo *proslava* was clearly past-oriented, but the senior generation expressed a desire for Jewish revitalization among the younger generations. The seniors were showing signs of pessimism, believing that Jewish life in Sarajevo would soon come to an end unless they acted to revitalize their children and grandchildren who had moved further away from Jewish tradition in a city where Jewish life may have been the most vibrant of traditional communities before the war. Revitalization did not mean a return to the Jewish religion or even to Jewish tradition, but rather a continuation of Jewish life by means of an organized communal existence. Most vital was the continuation of Jewish existence, not the particular form of that existence. Certainly the structure of the anniversary celebration as designed by the organizers was not intended to stimulate interest in traditional forms. Apparently, given the course of communal life over the next twenty years, the secular continued to predominate, so that by the mid-1980s, and perhaps much earlier, it was difficult to mobilize enough men to form a prayer quorum for the Friday evening service. The Zagreb *proslava* also celebrated the past, but it clearly served as a rite of revitalization for both younger and older generations. The celebration, while looking back into the past, also looked forward to the future. In fact, the main temporal orientation seems to have been the future. Already during the celebration there was talk of rebuilding the synagogue destroyed by the Nazis. In Sarajevo, in contrast, a ceremony was held to transform a synagogue into a museum. During the inauguration one of the speakers referred to the synagogue-turned-museum as a "temple of piety," retaining religious language to describe it. The supernatural orientation of the synagogue, however, gave way to the natural orientation of the temple of piety, as the victims of fascism and the fallen warriors of the Partisan War became the central objects of ceremonial focus. Although the Ashkenazi synagogue continued to be used in Sarajevo, the symbolic contrast throws light on the different temporal orientations of the two communities at the time of their anniversary celebrations.

The Persistent Sephardi Worldview in Submergence

Submergence as an ethnic response reflects several features of the traditional Sephardi worldview and ethos. Like the Jews of Medieval Spain who did not seek to isolate themselves from broader society and its pursuits, the postwar Jews of socialist Yugoslavia sought a balance between their Jewishness and their degree of submergence. They did not adopt the either-isolation-or-assimilation approach that some writers associate with the Ashkenazim.[12]

Historically, there have been significant differences between the Sephardi and Ashkenazi Jews in terms of life style and worldview. The Sephardi Jews "have been more likely to integrate into the somewhat pluralistic" Islamic cultures [where they lived], whereas the Ashkenazim as a group, have been more likely to live separately from the Christian cultures, and as individuals, have been more likely to choose between either separatism or assimilation" (Lavender 1981:25). One possible explanation for this difference is the relative amount of opposition and oppression faced by each of these Jewish branches. Despite the Spanish Inquisition and the expulsion from the Iberian Peninsula, Sephardi Jews have suffered less than their Ashkenazi counterparts, who have experienced the Crusades, numerous massacres, and the Holocaust of World War Two. Although the Jews of Yugoslav lands did not escape suffering, they were not constantly the direct targets of the rulers and local oppressors. This was especially true for Jews living in the Ottoman Empire. In socialist Yugoslavia Jews and non-Jews alike boasted about how Yugoslavia, until the Second World War, had a tradition relatively free of anti-Jewishness. Perhaps the Sephardi view of the world is predicated on a relatively low amount of opposition that makes integration desirable and attainable. Of course, one can always point to exceptional periods when opposition intensified.

The Sephardim emphasized form. For example, they exhibited a structured collective form of prayer in the synagogue, as opposed to forms in which self-expression becomes the foremost value. The Sephardi emphasis on a structured collective form of ritual performance, which frowned upon idiosyncratic public deviations, appears to have been more conducive to an ethnicity of submergence. This emphasis on form carried over into other spheres of life. Any internal factions or social dramas played out within the community tended not to reach an outside audience. Instead, the community tended to project a common and united front to outsiders. This was true to a lesser extent during the interwar period in Yugoslavia when Jews were divided over integrationism and Jewish nationalism, and it was a dominant characteristic of the ethnicity of submergence (e.g., in the *svečanosti*) in the postwar period. What transpired inside an individual was certainly important to him or her, but of overriding importance was the presentation of a structured collective performance that reflected what the group intended to show about itself and its place in the larger society.

During their difficult years in Spain, the Sephardim were able to maintain what Liebman (1975:146, quoted in Lavender 1981:28) calls "an almost schizophrenic existence: outwardly and publicly Catholics, but inwardly and privately practicing Jews." The Jews of Yugoslavia were by no means schizophrenic, but there remained in the postwar more than traces of this private-versus-public past. It need not be a matter of polarization. The majority of Jews who remained to rebuild their lives in postwar Yugoslavia were content with, if not enthusiastic about, the new political and social conditions. They joined the Communist Party in substantial numbers, perhaps twenty percent according to one community leader. They joined with others in praising Tito and other revolutionary heroes for their collective exploits of liberation and revolution. They recited the politically correct slogan of brotherhood and unity. They participated in the cycle of commemoration. And they performed these acts publicly, as individuals as a community of Jews, and as part of the community of Yugoslav peoples. After all was said and done, they were still Jews but they had become Yugoslavs as Tito had envisioned Yugoslavs to be—in his image. The joke that Tito was Yugoslavia's only true Yugoslav requires a postscript. A case could be argued for an additional several thousand Yugoslavs who were also members of the Jewish community. The Yugoslav Jewish community had become a part of the new order. They had found a structure in which they could ease the tensions, ambiguities, and contradictions of being a tiny minority-religious group in a land composed of many poles which, in a paradoxical way, the new rulers tried to eliminate but reinforced instead.

The emphasis on simplicity is associated with a search for clarity of style and expression. Given the diversity and complexity of Yugoslavia's past and present, the Yugoslav Jewish community and its leaders strived to order some of the complexity. For example, they revealed a tendency to simplify the past by focusing on what had shaped their postwar collective identity rather than on features that did not fit their representation of themselves. One community member, an ex-POW and postwar functionary of the Yugoslav Foreign Ministry, described the Jewish POW experience in Nazi Germany "from an exclusively Communist angle" (Loker 1977:115). Zvi Loker, who left Yugoslavia for Palestine before the Second World War and has conducted historical research on the Jews of Yugoslavia, was in a position to know why Jews left Yugoslavia after the war. He (ibid:115–116) writes:

> The reader is led to believe that all Jewish war prisoners were eventually integrated in the New Yugoslavia (i.e., Tito's Yugoslavia). Many of them were, of course, so integrated, which is perfectly normal. However, a fairly large percentage, about half of the total, chose to emigrate to Israel after its creation. The reason for this emigration is, most probably, twofold: flight from Communism and the desire to participate in the building of a Jewish state. This fact is well known to the ex-POWs but is missing from Pressburger's otherwise interesting article.

The emphasis on proportion involves taking the middle way and avoiding extremes. There were few if any occasions for displaying unbridled exuberance and certainly no place for fanaticism, especially in religious expression. There was a tendency to avoid strong polarities (Lavender 1981:27). Balance was important. It was believed that men and women should strike a balance between their lives as Jews and as part of larger society. Living as a Jew should not involve compartmentalization, or an either-integrationism-or-assimilationism proposition. That would disturb the balance. The individual and the community did not flee all contacts with the outside world. At least some degree of integration, but not assimilation, was sought. Ritual was thus more an end-in-itself, performed because they were Jews, and not as a means-to-an-end (e.g., boundary maintenance).

The Sephardi Jews "captured the stimuli of [their] times and adapted them to the specifics of the community. [They] thus created something which was part and parcel of the general intellectual and cultural climate of [their] times and at the same time uniquely and distinctly Jewish" (Faur 1972:6, quoted in Lavender 1981:27). The postwar Yugoslav Jewish community followed the same pattern, even if they did not succeed in creating a new form of Jewishness that would stand the test of time by crossing over into a new historical period. Jews have been captivated by ideas and their relationship to social conditions associated with specific historical periods. In the interwar period Sephardi Jews were captivated by Jewish nationalism, but they viewed it differently than did the Ashkenazim. They were also captivated by socialism and what the synthesis of socialism and Zionism might produce. Those who remained after the war were excited by the prospects socialist Yugoslavia afforded them, including the opportunity to reformulate and restructure Jewishness as they envisioned it, as a kind of synthesis between a particular variant of socialism (Titoism) and an updated brand of Sephardi nationalism which advocated the viability of Jewish life outside of Israel.

Sephardi Jews were "usually allowed to maintain [their] uniqueness as [Jews] while integrating at least to some extent into the larger society" (Lavender 1981:27). The postwar Jewish community took this route further than at any time in the past. They wanted to remain Jews, but at the same time to be integrated into something larger and more powerful—socialist Yugoslavia. To become part of this entity, they chose to reformulate Jewish identity to the point where they felt integration and distinction were not contradictory. To the communal leaders it was plausible that to remain Jews in what they considered their homeland they had to become part of something larger, for Jews as Jews could best attain their goals in a single state defined by brotherhood and unity than in states defined by nationality and political chauvinism. The Sephardi worldview facilitated the decision and the process of integration. Those who led the restructuring were, in their minds, just as Jewish as those who wanted to retain traditional religious ways; they felt no clash or contradiction between the sacred and secular and thus felt no inhibition in setting a new course for Jewish life in the Diaspora. Any doubts they may have had were kept to themselves.

They did not feel that Jews must be religious in order to remain Jews. Adding to this was the fact that they faced no internal opposition from an ecclesiastical structure or numerically strong religious segment, for no such structure or segment existed. Nor did they feel a push from a younger generation that had not directly experienced the war. Again, balance is important for understanding how the sacred spheres of Jewish life were handled in the postwar period. Whereas in the larger ethnic populations a more concerted effort was made to abandon traditional rituals and symbols, the traditional cycle, albeit eroded, remained in place. In not abandoning the traditional cycle, Jewish rituals were essentially depoliticized. This was not the case for other ethnic populations, especially the Roman Catholic and Serbian Orthodox religious communities against which the state directed most of its anti-religious attacks. In time the rituals of these larger communities took on greater political significance. Obviously, size and other demographic variables had had a constraining influence.

Sephardi Jews tended not to polarize the religious and the secular and "thus were able to perpetuate [their] Jewishness even when 'neglectful of their duties' " (Corre 1973:20, quoted in Lavender 1981:27). Faur (1972:6, quoted in Lavender 1981:27) states that "it [is] the political dimension of Judaism rather than the religious dimension that 'is essential to the Jewish mind.' "[13] Integration is impossible to those Jews who polarize these dimensions. The Sephardim, however, do not see "a contradiction and because . . . when [they] did participate in [their] synagogue [they] did so intensely despite [their] integration into the larger secular culture" (Lavender 1981:27). It is their "ideals of decorousness, high standards of performance, and respect for tradition that help counter the casualness approach" (Corre 1973:20, quoted in Lavender 1981:27). In my description of submergence, I have tried to show how the Jewish community emphasized forms that may have served both to integrate them into Yugoslav society and to maintain their Jewish identity.

4

AN EXPERIMENT IN SECULAR JEWISHNESS[1]

> 1977 We are drowning into one impersonal mass. This is our advantage over others . . . . [We are moving] towards a world in which boundaries will have been wiped away. Therefore it is funny to talk about renewal of religious rituals and customs. It is hypocritical to do what you do not believe in. We want to find our faith in progress, in advancement (*Kadima* 38 (1977)).
>
> 1989 The small remnant of the Yugoslav Jews [is] so assimilated that [it] will disappear as Jews in 2–3 generations or even sooner. The only thing that can save the ethnic group is *religion*. Personally I feel myself as a Jew and was from childhood proud of it. But I am definitely a secular Jew and a nonbeliever. [But this kind of] belonging to the people and nation cannot regenerate a small community!

If evaluated as a collective movement away from the Judaic tradition of belief and ritual, the process of secularization of Yugoslav Jewry was well underway before the Second World War, particularly in the northern parts of the country. As a distinct generational phenomenon, the Jewish young people of the 1930s manifested it in different ways. Many were secular left-wing Zionists influenced by Marxist instruction in Jewish clubs and camps, some were Communists, and others were apolitical career-minded professionals. The individuals who became the leaders of the postwar Jewish community belonged primarily to the first of these categories. After the Second World War, with the rule of the Communist Party firmly in place and the Jewish ritual structure virually wiped out, secularization accelerated and manifested distinct qualitative and quantitative differences from its prewar forms, which reflected Jewish and societal transformations. From the surviving members of the secularized, progressive youth generation of the 1930s emerged the postwar leaders of the Jewish community. A significant number of them entered the postwar period as secularists with a passion to change society. Their loss of faith in the God of their fathers or grandfathers, if they ever had such faith, and their adoption of new objects of faith had occurred in ever-increasing numbers, for some during the 1920s, others in the 1930s, and for a greater number during the war years. Their worldview had undergone a major transformation. Furthermore, no longer were their more tradition oriented parents or grandparents, most of whom had perished in the Holocaust, the leaders of the Jewish community. The surviving sons and daughters largely controlled communal affairs. When the secular engulfed the sacred in this generational cohort, there was no need to restrain the transformation of the community itself. What the new leaders set in motion was essentially an experiment in secular Jewishness. Their intent was to construct a secular Jewish community and a secular Jewishness. As Fenn (1978:78, quoted in Lyon 1985:17) has stated, "secularization proceeds or fails because particular groups or organizations want secularization to proceed or fail." Certainly the postwar leaders wanted it to succeed.

One essential ingredient of an experiment is the experimenter's ability to control the environment and manipulate the treatment. Of course, the "experiment in secular Jewishness" was not a scientific experiment. Nor am I using the term "experiment" in a strictly metaphorical sense. I argue that the relatively small and stable core of leaders maintained such control over the secular path the organized community selected. There were no power struggles to obtain control of the leadership. Given the radically changed societal conditions and the size of the Jewish population that had been reduced to a twelfth of its prewar size, those who occupied leadership positions were among those who chose to remain in socialist Yugoslavia and rebuild the community and the new state. They were assisted by a voluntary core of long-term activists who, on the whole, felt the same inclination. Moreover, the internal transformation of the community and the political transformation of Yugoslav society created conditions, such as the loss of the old structural supports for religion, conducive to such experimentation. One significant question is, how successfully did the secular forms replace the traditional forms in maintaining and perpetuating Jewish life and identity? Can secular forms be the symbolic vehicles that effectively carry persistent Jewish meaning? Can Jews remain

Jews without the traditional forms, that is, without forms associated with the Judaic religion or, more broadly, the Jewish Great Tradition? The postwar leaders of the community were believers in the functional equivalence of secular forms. One observer has written that the role of the Yugoslav Jews "in world history is an interesting and important one since it directly confronts the issue as to whether the Jewish people can survive independently of their religious base" (Perlmutter 1973).

Submergence and the experiment in secular Jewishness were interrelated conceptions and processes that not only fed off each other, but also blended together, each serving the other. In fact, they often used the same forms. Submergence can be understood as a part of the experiment in secular Jewishness, for the latter was a long-term goal, while much of the former can be understood as an ethnic strategy or response to a particular political and ideological system that, according to historical precedent, sooner or later would be replaced by another system of rule and symbolic management. At the time, constructing a secular Jewishness was believed to be a unidirectional, irreversible process, one that would lead to a more progressive level of human and Jewish development. Whereas submergence was a process that was intended, among other things, to ensure Jewish maintenance and continuity and thus keep the chain of tradition intact, the experiment in secular Jewishness also sought to transform Jewish being. Of course, the experiment in secular Jewishness contributed to the community's submergence, for it effectively removed the ideological opposition of a religious worldview.

The Secularization Thesis and Debate

The secularization thesis follows the Weberian theory that the forces of modernization will lead to the eventual demise of the overarching place of religion in society. In Berger's terms, religion will lose its place as a plausibility structure for the collective. Religion may continue in privatized forms but without "a common binding quality" (1967:133). No longer will it regulate and guide every major facet of human existence. The secularization thesis has been challenged (see reviews of the debate in Davidman (1991) and Lyon (1988)). "The description of an inevitable, inexorable, unilinear process of religious decline stems from flawed understanding of religion, society, and human nature, past and present," writes

Davidman (1991:29) in her review of the debate surrounding the secularization thesis. Perhaps what needs to be distinguished is religion and the religious (Glasner 1977, cited in Lyon 1988:146). The decline of certain forms of religion can be demonstrated, but so can their replacement by new forms and objects of commitment or faith (see Binns 1979, 1980; Lane 1981). In Yugoslavia Titoism was ultimately a failed attempt to "provide a new plausibility structure, a new overarching transcendent universe of norms" and meaning (Lyon 1988:144) . Nationalism, the kind in which one worships at the altar of the Nation, is another example of such an attempt to attain symbolic immortality. In his review of the debate, Lyon has concluded that the "triumph of the secular" is itself a "myth that represents rather than reflects reality" (ibid:138).

First, I concur with those who have challenged the thesis that the decline of certain institutions of religion has not resulted in the disappearance of the religious or the sacred. In much of the Western world the religious has been relegated to a separate sphere of life and it has been privatized. Men and women remain religious beings, but the objects of their faith do change, as do the forms and meanings associated with their faith. This does not mean that movement away from traditional forms was not highly significant for the population under investigation. For the Jews, whose religion had long been the basis of their collective identity, the removal of that foundation and core resulted in a crisis of identity. Ambivalence is felt when, on the one hand, there is conscious abandonment of religion or tradition, and selected features are retained deliberately or remain a part of the consciousness, on the other (Kokosalakis 1982).

Where does the Jewish community of Yugoslavia fit into this debate? Was it or was it not a secular community? By what standards or criteria can these questions be answered? Was secularization a unilinear process that had accelerated under conditions less favorable to religion? To answer these and other questions it is necessary to define such terms as secular and religious. Must religion be associated with the supernatural, for instance? Or, can it be defined in terms of a broader definition of what is of ultimate concern to the group and its individual members? As shown in chapter 6, the reaction of Yugoslavia's Jews to what they perceived as the profanation of the Star of David symbol reveals that they did have conceptions of the sacred and the profane, though these conceptions were not necessarily manifested in forms associated with the Jewish religion. Conceptions of the sacred perhaps extended

Table 4.1
Standards to Evaluate Level of Secularization

	Level of Secularization				
	Low				*High*
Standards	*1*	*2*	*3*	*4*	*5*
1. Jewish Halakhic Law					5
2. Jewish Tradition (broader than (1))				4	
3. Self-ascription					5
4. Beliefs			3		5*
5. Other inner states:					
a. feeling of belonging (affective)		2	3*		
b. level of Jewish knowledge (cognitive)			3		5*
6. Conception of sacred-profane (Jewish)			3		
7. Conception of sacred-profane (e.g., Titoist)		2			
8. Ritual-symbolic behavior			3		
9. Objects of faith		2			
10. Privatized religion (in relation to (1) above and (2))					5
11. Pursuit of transcendent meaning		2			

Figures that appear with a "*" pertain to < 50 years of age.

beyond distinctly Jewish symbols to the key symbols of Titoist Yugoslavia. As shown, Tito became an object of veneration for the Jews and other Yugoslavs. Were the acts, words, and objects of Tito veneration religious in nature? Were the *svečanosti*, the ritual and symbolic activities described earlier, religious behavior? The commemorative *svečanosti* performed in socialist Yugoslavia society were rituals that may not have been religious in terms of traditional definitions, but they shared the ritual focus on death. In a similar sense, the anniversary celebrations (*proslave*) were rites of intensification; they focused ritually on life as well as death. Finally, privatized religion must be considered. There were individuals who were believers, who held a supernaturalistic worldview, yet who did not participate in collective rituals. An even broader view of privatized religion would include all individual quests for transcendent meaning. Victor Turner would agree with Lyon (1988) that all men and women need and search for transcendent meaning and as such they are religious beings.

Table 4.2
Secularization Evaluated According to the Standard of Jewish Tradition

Features of Judaic Tradition	*Prewar*	*Postwar*
1. circumcision	+	
2. Bar mitzvah	+	
Bat mitzvah	+	
3. synagogue wedding	+	
4. Jewish burial	+	+(1)
5. Kaddish	+	+(2)
6. pomen (7,30 day, 1 year)	+	+(2)
7. Sabbath synagogue attendance	+	+(3)
8. light candles	+	*
9. mezuzah on door post	+	*
10. menorah in home	+	*
11. Sabbath meal in home	+	
12. Seder in home	+	
13. observe dietary laws	+(2)	
14. purification rites	+(2,3)	
15. fast	+	
16. visit graves of kin	+	+
17. High Holiday synagogue attendance	+	+

Based on an internal scale:
(1) = high; (2) = mid; (3) = low; * = very few or rare cases

In short, depending on one's definition of such terms as religion, religious and sacred, one's standards for evaluating secularization will vary. I recognize this variation and accommodate it in answering the questions asked above. To evaluate the secularization and secularism of the Yugoslav Jews, I have used the standards and scale shown in Table 4.1. The assessments in Tables 4.1 and 4.2 are based primarily on my own "expert knowledge" drawn from long-term participant observation, pertinent literature, and survey data.

As a population the Yugoslav Jews were highly secular if secularization is defined in terms of movement away from Halakhic law more narrowly and from their own Great Tradition more broadly. They were secular by their own admission (what they said), by the degree of their ritual performance compared to other Jewish populations and other Yugoslav populations (what they did and did not do), and according to my own observations and investigation (see

Tables 4.1 and 4.2). In addition, their ritual infrastructure was so reduced by the catastrophe of 1941–1945 that even larger communities have been forced to import ritual specialists for certain holidays.

Adopting many of the criteria used in other studies (e.g., Sharot et al. 1986) to determine the degree of secularization or traditionalism is almost nonsensical when applied to Yugoslav Jewry. The anthropologist or even casual observer need not spend months in the field to discover that even those considered religious do not perform most of the traditional rituals and customs associated with the Jewish religion. According to standard #1, thus, the Yugoslav Jewish community was highly secular, and according to standard #2, it was still highly secular but less when judged according to the stricter standard of Jewish law. The Jewish calendar may not have had great significance for the majority of Yugoslav Jews, but certain holidays in the annual cycle continued to be observed in the operating synagogues and in the community.

Secularization is also an internal process. Peter Berger (1967) refers to this as cultural-ideological secularization, or the "secularization of consciousness," which is associated with the "decline of religious content in various spheres of cultural thought and manifestations of a secular worldview." Below I present available quantitative data on dimensions of the internal state of the Yugoslav Jews, particularly religious belief, feeling of belonging, and degree of knowledge.

In the 1985 survey (*Demographic Survey*, 1985) administered by the Federation of Jewish Communities of Yugoslavia, fifty-five percent of the respondents fifty years of age and older described themselves as atheists (Table 4.3). An analysis of responses of those at least sixty-five years of age would reduce the fifty-five percent figure, given the overall age trends in the population. The majority of those who were old enough to have attended school before the war received at least some religious instruction. The fact that forty percent of the Belgrade respondents fifty and older and fifty-seven percent of the Zagreb respondents fifty and older reported they were religious seems to reveal a different picture from that of the collective self-representation of the organized community. These results for the older Jews suggest that the Jews of Yugoslavia were not as secular as some of their leaders claimed, at least when the standard of evaluation is belief (#4). As with almost everything related to the Jews of multiethnic Yugoslavia, one must proceed with extreme caution when generalizing from survey data. Usually

Table 4.3 Standard: Self-Reported Religious Belief and Practice

	Religious Belief and Practice (%)			
	Atheist	*Religious*	*Religious Non-Pract.*	*Religious Practicing*
Belgrade				
Age 20–50	77	23	18	5
Age >50	60	40	23	17
Zagreb				
Age 20–50	75	24	18	6
Age >50	43	57	40	17
Sarajevo				
Age 20–50	95	4	3	1
Age >50	70	19	15	4
Subotica				
Age 20–50	70	28	17	11
Age >50	31	68	23	45

all such statements must be qualified with other kinds of data and explanation. In the survey results considerable variation emerged across local communities as well as between age segments (see Table 4.3). Once one of the most traditional Jewish communities, the Sarajevo community deviated considerably not only from the Subotica community, as expected, but also from the other large communities of Belgrade and Zagreb. In the Sarajevo case, the responses of the older group matched their secular representation of themselves (seventy-nine percent atheist, nineteen percent religious). The percentage of self-reported atheists jumped to eighty-one percent for those between twenty and fifty years of age. How can this generational decrease in religious belief be explained? One explanation lies in Jewish socialization or, better, its absence in the postwar generations. As noted, most of the older Jews received formal Jewish education, and virtually all of them received informal Jewish socialization. The younger Jews received little or no formal or informal Jewish instruction. They never had the option of abandoning tradition because it was never theirs to abandon. In terms of Jewish tradition, theirs was a deculturated rather than an assimilated or acculturated generation.

Both the fifty and older and ten to twenty age groups had a similar percentage of respondents with "little" or "no" Jewish knowledge (twenty percent, twenty-four percent). The dramatic difference

Table 4.4 Standard: Self-Reported Level of Jewish Knowledge by Community and Age

	Level of Jewish Knowledge (%)			
	Know Enough	*Some-what*	*Want to Know More*	*None*
Total				
Age 10–20	5	13	70	11
Age 20–50	19	16	60	5
Age >50	53	17	26	3
Belgrade				
Age 10–20	0	16	76	9
Age 20–50	4	14	70	2
Age >50	45	20	31	4
Zagreb				
Age 10–20	8	22	52	22
Age 20–50	16	17	62	5
Age >50	53	21	24	2
Sarajevo				
Age 10–20	15	9	67	9
Age 20–50	35	15	45	4
Age >50	63	16	17	1
Subotica				
Age 10–20	0	11	78	11
Age 20–50	35	15	45	4
Age >50	71	15	13	0

between these generational segments was in "satisfaction with what they already know" and in "wanting to know more." Whereas fifty-three percent of the older segment indicated they "knew enough," only five percent of the younger group indicated the same response. Seventy percent of the younger segment responded that they "wanted to know more," compared to twenty-six percent of the older segment. In these figures a dramatic difference between the generational segments can be seen in the degree of knowledge each segment claimed to possess and in the desire to learn more (see Table 4.4). The sharp decline in knowledge of Jewish subjects divided the older Jews who were born before the war and raised in Jewish families, and who often received some Jewish education (seventy-four percent), and the Jews belonging to the postwar generations who lacked Jewish socialization in the home and formal Jewish education outside the home.

Does the absence of knowledge have any relationship to the strength of one's Jewish identity? Without knowledge the individual

Table 4.5
Standard: Self-Reported Feeling of Jewish Belonging by Community and Age

	Feeling of Jewish Belonging (%)		
	Yes	*Sometimes*	*No*
Total			
Age 10–20	47	40	12
Age >10	72	19	8
Belgrade			
Age 10–20	45	48	7
Age >10	70	22	7
Zagreb			
Age 10–20	41	52	7
Age >10	75	20	4
Sarajevo			
Age 10–20	50	35	15
Age >10	57	22	13
Subotica			
Age 10–20	56	44	0
Age >10	91	8	1

relies heavily on feelings of Jewish belonging (#5a). In the case of these Jews, the 1985 survey responses show that Jewish feeling in the younger generations was unstable (see Table 4.5). In the ten to twenty age segment, twelve percent indicated they "do not feel Jewish" and forty percent indicated "some feeling." When the two responses are combined, fifty-two percent had only some or no feeling of Jewish belonging. These results suggest that knowledge and affect are both needed for a strong and stable Jewish identity. One should not outweigh the other to the point where identity is based solely on knowledge without affect or vice-versa. When all respondents ten and older were examined for feeling of Jewish belonging, eight percent reported "no feeling;" nineteen percent reported "some feeling;" seventy-two percent reported "yes," they had a feeling of Jewish belonging. When the generational segments are collapsed in this manner, the results are misleading, with each segment either inflating the percentages or deflating them, depending on the question or particular response category. The prewar and postwar generations were two radically different segments, as the comparison of the prewar and postwar population profiles in chapter 3 demonstrates. This difference persists when other standards are applied.

One informant, a woman of Yugoslav Jewish descent who had come from Israel to work as an educator in the Zagreb community, argued that knowledge is necessary for individual Jewish identity, for the individual cannot choose if she or he first does not have the choice. To have the choice the individual must know what it is he or she is rejecting or selecting.

The Old and the New in the Cycles of Jewish Life

A Jewish calendar continued to be published after the war by the Federation of the Jewish Communities of Yugoslavia. Rabbi Cadik Danon was the compiler of the calendar since the 1970s. Included in the calendar were: holidays, memorial days, days on which Jews were taken away or killed during the Second World War, information on Jewish tradition and religion, candle lighting times for all of Yugoslavia, and a listing of Jewish communities with numbers of registered members.

Only three synagogues operated on a weekly basis. Two held a Friday evening *Arvit* service, while one held a Sabbath day service. An average of twenty-three people gathered for the Shabbat eve service in the Belgrade synagogue during my initial stay. Among these was a core of regulars, mostly males and a few women, and several semi-regular attendees. In 1985–1986 five or six of the regulars were not Jews: a mother and son, a young woman in her twenties, an ex-seminarian, and a university student who eventually converted.

Saturday was the day when the children's and youth clubs met in the community. The activity of the few youths that gather was largely unorganized. At the annual youth Inter-Club meetings, one could hear lively discussion about structuring the local clubs with organized programs. It appears that the enthusiasm generated by these well-attended gatherings only temporarily revitalized local youth clubs.

One site in which there was an conscious effort to reintroduce a degree of ritual authenticity into Jewish life was the summer camp during the children's program. One of the camp's leaders expressed the following to me:

> Shabbat . . . became a very strong institution in the camp. It's one of the rare places, or unique places, in the country where Shabbat is conducted . . . in the way it should be done

in homes. Which means, we do not feel the religious connotation of Shabbat in the way that we pray and read the prayers and bless the God that gives us Shabbat. But we feel the day is different. We feel it in the way we dress. We feel it in the way the camp is decorated. We feel it in the songs. [Every Shabbat?] Yes, every Shabbat. We feel it in how the food is on the table. We sing songs. We have a dance. And we feel that the next day. . . . We feel the next day is Sunday because it is a day like Monday, Tuesday, other days. The food, it is better on Shabbat. I don't say it is worse on Mondays. But it is better. Better cake. Table cloths on the table. We have hallah. We have wine. We have the [blessing]. Each table has flowers. We dress in white. We prepare. We have feelings of things like that. I enjoy this. And the kids enjoy this. I tell you that people, if somebody would be able to conduct these kinds of things here in the community [in Belgrade], people would come. They would come because they would have a feeling of unity, of family unity, which they don't have. The youngsters for sure would come. You know what the reason is they don't have [it] here? Because Friday night is the time when the choir has its meetings. In this building [the synagogue building, which has several apartments] you cannot organize [Shabbat]. There is no place to organize Shabbat, you know what I mean? If I say to the people, "Let's go to the synagogue and after let us have dinner together. You bring this, I bring that. We will make this, you make this. And let's sing together, I guarantee I will have 10–15 kids every Friday. I will have a kind of traditional way of celebrating Shabbat. [Why just the kids? The others won't?] I am talking about kids because I take care of kids. I tell you, the kids know more songs about Shabbat than the others, because they know them from the camp. Because I continue things which they learned in the camp. Because in the camp they do it. The elders do not. The elders used to do it. The elders have forgotten. It is in their memory, somewhere in the back [of their memory]. . . . Now we introduced many other things which are dealing with the traditional way of life—the life cycle, *bar mitzvah*, *brit mila*, Jewish holidays. I'm talking about rituals. So we slowly introduced many things. Many things we do not, sometimes we do not, put on paper at the Federation, but I do it at the

> camp. Not because I am afraid but because . . . I am confident I will do it in a way that it will not harm. But people were offended. People were saying, "Marko, you pushed my kids to put a *kipa* on their heads, to [light] candles." It is to show how the rituals [are done] and it is part of tradition. It is not theater. We cannot do it 100 percent how it [should be] done. We are doing it the way we can. . . . People cannot feel it in other places. . . . So I think this traditional cycle we started to talk about is coming back. . . . [The parents] know that they didn't have it, and they know that they cannot do it, but no one says one of their kids will not do it one day. I don't know when [my daughter] will do it, but, for example, one of the things "Ana" [from Israel] asked me was, "Teach [your daughter] to give the blessing with candles for Friday night," which I will do. I will be happy if [my daughter] starts to light the candles here [in my apartment] on Friday night.

During my fieldwork I witnessed a full synagogue for the Erev Rosh Hashanah (New Year) service. In addition to the liturgy, the president of the Belgrade community gave a speech, which is customary for this event. Rosh Hashanah was celebrated in the community hall at three different times by different age groups—once for the general membership (many senior generation members), once for the middle generation, and once for the children. For the Erev Yom Kippur service in which *Kol Nidrei* was performed congregants again filled the synagogue. A choir participated during this evening service. On the day of Yom Kippur synagogue services were held. More people attended than for the weekly Shabbat services, but the synagogue was far from full.

A *sukkah* was constructed in the courtyard of the Belgrade synagogue for the Sukkot holiday. After the service in the synagogue, there was a time of commensality in the *sukkah*. The holiday of Simhat Torah was festively celebrated in the Belgrade synagogue. The Torah scrolls were paraded around the synagogue. The young people joined in this celebration of the Torah. Congregants reached out and touched the Torah scroll, then put their fingers to their mouths.

Hanukkah and Purim were the two holidays most celebrated in the Belgrade community. For Hanukkah a large menorah, the hanukkiya, was lighted. *Maoz zur* was sung. A placard with the words of the song was held up for people who did not know the words. In between Hanukkah and Purim, Tu Bishvat was celebrated especially for the children who attend the Saturday clubs in the community. Probably the most festive celebration held in the community was Purim. The Purim celebration attracted large crowds, and for this reason had been held for some time in a local hotel. The Purim celebrations that I attended in Belgrade and Zagreb were held on different days.

For Pesah (Passover), a communal Seder was held in the community hall. The religious Jews were in charge of the celebration. They sat at the head table in the hall. On the two occasions I attended the seder in Belgrade, the community hall was full, with many new people attending. However, the Seder was avoided my many leaders in the Federation and local community. The following is how one of my informants saw the 1989 seder:

> I would like [the Seder] to be on a higher level, not just a show. For example, last night it was for me not a show but half a show. The people who I saw there were supposed to be in, [to] see, a real Pesah. Every single person who is sitting around the table has to . . . feel the meaning of the words, but he didn't because for him it is, first, a social evening, to see and to hear something. But how much did he feel? He felt uneasy because it was hot, it was too tight, he could not smoke, couldn't move. To [have it at home] he could have really enjoyed the evening—to have a good dinner, with the reading of a nice story. He doesn't know the language, doesn't know the tradition, doesn't know the customs; he doesn't know why it is like this or like that, but he knows that something goes around and something is connected with the Jewish exile from Egypt. [Can that happen again in the home?] No. I don't think so. No, but what can happen and where we can be a power is that we build it up, that this what happens in the community is less theater . . . which means that people are provided with books in Serbo-Croatian, know what it is about, more people [become] involved in this, that they read together, maybe sing together. To get a more communal gathering.

Yom ha-Sho'ah is observed by Jews around the world. In Belgrade a special commemoration ceremony held in the Jewish cemetery attracted quite a large gathering. A secular phase initiated the commemoration ceremony, with music by the Belgrade

Jewish community's Braća Baruh choir and a *govor*. Next, Rabbi Cadik Danon led a procession to the great memorial monument to the victims of fascism and fallen warriors. While standing by the monument the rabbi recited the Kaddish prayer.

I refer the reader to an earlier part of this chapter for a list and a description of the other memorial days marked in the Jewish calendar published by the Federation and observed by a segment of the membership. As I mention there, these memorial days together constituted the cycle of commemoration. Except for Yom ha-Sho'ah, all of the other commemoration rites were multi-ethnic gatherings that memorialized both victims of fascism and fallen warriors of all the ethnic groups.

The opening event of every annual cycle in the Belgrade Jewish community was Federation President Kadelburg's talk about current events relating to world and Yugoslav Jewry. The cycle corresponded with the Jewish year, and so the talk was given in September or October.

The annual women's conference was held in a different city every year. The Women's Sections in the various communities had been the most active of the various sections, committees, and commissions that composed the local community. In addition to the business affairs discussed at these conferences, individuals read papers that they had written. Each year the papers reflected a new theme.

During the Day of the Republic holiday, on 29–30 November, the Jewish youth of Yugoslavia gathered in a different city each year for the *Medjuklupski Susret*, the Inter-Club Meeting. Every January or February, a group of youth from various cities gathered for the *Zimski Seminar*, the Winter Seminar. Leaders from the community and specialists from abroad lectured and provided practical instruction to the youth on numerous topics related to Jewish life. The seminar prepared Jewish youth to work with younger children, particularly in the summer camp in Pirovac.

An annual event that attracted gatherings of up to four hundred or more was the Little Maccabiah, loosely patterned after the Maccabiah Games held in Israel, which attracts Jewish athletes from around the world. For its part, the Little Maccabiah Games of the Yugoslav Jews attracted Jews from all parts of Yugoslavia. Sports competitions were held in soccer, running, table tennis, and chess. The function of the event, however, went far beyond athletic competition. Both the young and the old attended. Large meetings were held. Lively discussions were held. Representatives from

Jewish patron organizations attended. This event took place on the International Workers' Day holiday (May Day), and was held in resort towns on the Adriatic coast.

Finally, each operating community held its own annual conference in the spring. These separate conferences are followed by the Conference of Communities held in Belgrade.

The rites of passage associated with the life cycle of an individual were almost altogether absent, with the exception of the stage of death. There remained considerable ritual focus on death, even though the funerals could not all be classified as religious events. Although the rabbi may not have been present or Kaddish not recited, the funeral took place in a specifically and unmistakably Jewish sphere. In no other physical sphere was the ethnic boundary so tightly drawn as in the Jewish cemetery. Sometimes, as the president of the Belgrade community told me, the Jewish identity of an individual became evident to the general community only in death, when he or she was buried in the Jewish cemetery.

The Yugoslav Jews did not regularly observe food prescriptions and proscriptions. I heard about only one Jewish man from the Bosnian town of Višegrad on the Drina River who attempted to maintain Jewish dietary laws, or kashrut. Occasionally kosher meals were prepared for visiting guests. Since there was no ritual slaughterer or shohet in Yugoslavia during the period of my research, I do not know where or how, or if any ritually pure meat was procured for such occasions. Another exception was the kosher wine, brandy, and mazzah used for Passover. The wine and brandy were produced in a factory located in the Adriatic town of Zadar. Cadik Danon, the sole rabbi, visited the factory in which these beverages were produced in order to carry out the purification rite that made them acceptable (i.e., kosher, pure) for consumption. In 1986 the mazzah were obtained from Holland, and in 1989 from Israel. The infrastructure to maintain such dietary laws was absent, with the exception of the rabbi's visit to the Zadar factory. Perhaps most importantly, the Jews themselves chose not to observe such laws. Neither, apparently, was fasting a common ritual observance among the Jews of Yugoslavia, not even on the day of Yom Kippur. In addition, they did not abstain from pork meat, although it may have been eaten less regularly than other meats. They stopped using pork meat in the summer camp. Sometimes, however, when chicken or some other meat was unavailable, pork in the form of *pašteta* (pate) would be served. The individual responsible for food procurement did not classify pork pate as pork meat, because, as one individual explained, it did not come out of the butcher's knife. Still, the camp leaders attempted to start *kashrut* in the camp: "We started *kashrut* in the camp. A few years ago. There was no pork schnitzel on the table. But we are far away from *kashrut*, from real *kashrut*. Real far away. We are not accustomed to it. The life we have here, it is very hard [to have it]. People don't feel it."

Were They as Secular as They Purported To Be?

Were the Yugoslav Jews as secular as they purported to be? The answer is an ambivalent, yes and no. Part of the ambiguity of this answer derives from the fact that it is extremely difficult to separate completely every feature of the Jewish Great Tradition from Jewish life. As Finestein (1977) has noted in his article "What is a Secular Jew?" secular Jews continue to live from the capital of Judaism. That was true to a significant extent in the Yugoslav Jewish community. The holiday observances during the postwar years may have moved out of the homes and synagogues and into the community halls, but the fact remains that some Jews gathered together on Jewish holidays and thereby maintained the Jewish annual cycle. Another example is on those occasions when the Kaddish prayer was recited. Even some of the secularists could be seen wearing a *kipa* or a hat. If Table 4.3 is examined once again, it is clear that the percentage of respondents who answered they were religious (practicing and/or non-practicing) was much higher among the fifty and older segment, which is not surprising at all. The generational split is yet another explanation for an ambivalent response. Of interest is that the number of "religious" in the older segment, whether practicing or not, was nearly fifty percent for the total sample, and certainly it was higher for those who were sixty and older. However, I do not have the raw data to support that conclusion. The fact of variation across the ten individual communities examined in the 1985 Survey is interesting. I rank them in order of religiosity as measured by this item: Subotica (68%), Zagreb (57%), Rijeka (56%), Osijek (50%), Ljubljana (50%), Novi Sad (41%), Belgrade (40%), Skopje (39%), Sarajevo (19%), Split (8%).

Whereas before the war there was a discernible difference between the older and younger generations on the issue of traditionalism versus secularization, in the postwar years many of the young people continued on the secular path set by the revolutionary generation of their parents. Within the youth generation there was an anti-religious orientation that was very evident in the 1970s in the Jewish youth publication *Kadima*. Consider the following statements:

> Who today will talk about ethnic origins or religion? No young person will. That is the way it should be. . . . [We are moving] towards a world without boundaries (*Kadima* 38 (1977)).
>
> We are drowning into one impersonal mass. This is our advantage over others . . . [We are moving] towards a world in which boundaries will have been wiped away. Therefore it is funny to talk about renewal of religious rituals and customs. It is hypocritical to do what you do not believe in. We want to find our faith in progress, in advancement (ibid.).
>
> The young Jew does not believe, does not know Hebrew, does not differ in any way from others (ibid.).
>
> If we begin to ask who had a Bar Mitzvah or who celebrated a seder in the home, or who even once in his lifetime saw the inside of a synagogue, we would have to come to the sad conclusion that we can count such young Jews among us on our fingers. But we are, nevertheless, some kind of Jews (ibid.).

Explaining Secularization

Secularization as a collective movement away from Jewish law and the Judaic tradition was a historical process underway before the war. As a generational phenomenon it became quite distinctive by the 1930s, particularly in Sarajevo. The older generations continued practicing Judaic ritual right until the war, while the youth generation was largely secularized and many were secularist. It is important to add that, on the whole, the secularized generation failed to transmit Jewish tradition to their children in the household setting.

The impact of the war accelerated secularization in different ways. The catastrophe of the Holocaust nearly annihilated the population, including many of the religious Jews and, among them, the ritual specialists. These were never replaced. From about 1948 until 1968 and between 1973 and 1992, only one rabbi served the religious needs of the population. In the intervening years there were no practicing rabbis in the country. More than one attempt to train young men abroad ended in failure. That there were religious Jews among the survivors is evident from some of the religious observances that took place immediately after return from various places of internment, hiding, and fighting (e.g., in Novi Sad). Of these religious Jews, some no doubt emigrated to Israel; some others were probably among the older Jews that stayed but did not become part of the leadership. In terms of belief they belonged to the "silent segment" described above. On the last census on which religion was listed, the census of 1953, about half of those who declared as Jews did so according to religion. The catastrophe of the Second World War also devastated the religious infrastructure of the community. Synagogues and many ritual articles were either destroyed or carried away as spoil.

The social and political transformation of Yugoslavia contributed to secularization. Religion was associated with the old order, the Old Yugoslavia, and thus was seen as potentially dangerous to the new order, the New Yugoslavia.

Usually the secularization of the family lags behind in the secularization process, but this was not true in the case of the Yugoslav Jews. As demonstrated in chapter 2, the family ceased to function as an agent and sphere of Jewish socialization and ritual activity. Some parents even became anti-religious, expressing their displeasure when Jewish rituals were taught to their children in the Jewish summer camp in Pirovac.

Secularization was a leader-directed process. Many of the communal leaders had ties to the prewar progressive tradition, particularly in the Jewish youth movement, to the National War of Liberation, and to the postwar *struktura* (honors and awards, Party membership, government employment). As I have shown, they were highly sympathetic to the New Yugoslavia. Secularization as a movement away from the Judaic Tradition was one way of showing how progressive they were. Their statements regarding the decline of religion and the pursuit of a secular line were explicit. Among some of these leaders there existed a general bias against religion. Part of this bias was rooted in how one perceived history. One prominent leader revealed his reasons. First, clerics participated in genocide during World War II. He went so far as calling them "the greatest criminals." Second, he referred to the tie between the Catholic

Church/Vatican and the fascist Ustasha regime in the Independent State of Croatia. He next noted that Islam contributed the most severe indoctrination in Yugoslavia. Nor did he exclude the Serbian Orthodox Church from his list. He stated that the Orthodox Church's dogma against the Jews is "still in the books." The same individual remarked, "Where there is indoctrination there is also collusion between the state and the church. Where religion indoctrinates there the state must intervene. Indoctrination is blind faith in all the comes from religious dogma or the lips of the clergy. That is a very dangerous philosophy and teaching that causes a man not to be tolerant towards others, neither to the members of other religious communities nor to the political system in general."

Above I noted that the leaders engaged in some symbolic manipulation and control. They helped set the "experimental" conditions for the experiment in secular Jewishness. In directing the cultural program they controlled which influences reached the Jews in the context of the organized community. For example, ritual was treated as theatrical performance outside the spheres of the synagogue and cemetery. In fairness, I must say that they were not devoid of self-criticism, nor beyond trying different "treatments." They made decisions accepting or rejecting whether a particular "treatment" made a difference, that is, whether or not it was effective. It was not a matter of padding the results, or predetermining them. They were rational pragmatists and optimists, not militant atheists or even militant secularists. They faced no opposition from other Jews in the country. In fact, they made the few practicing traditionalists dependent upon them. They had faith, but it was now in socialism and humanism. They passed on an unbalanced view of Jewishness, for they rejected the religious elements of Jewishness. They declared, "This is what Jewishness is," or, at least, "This is what is good and positive about Jewishness. This is what we will retain."

How did the experiment in secular Jewishness succeed or fail? Certainly some of the leaders of the organized Jewish community would proclaim the success of the experiment in secular Jewishness. They would point to the successful maintenance of organized Jewish life over a 45 year span in the face of demographic vulnerability and significant assimilation. Not every leader, however, took such an optimistic view. One prominent communal leader, who was the president of the Cultural Commission of the Federation of Jewish Communities of Yugoslavia, wrote the following on a questionnaire he had returned to me:

The small remnant of the Yugoslav Jews [is] so assimilated that [it] will disappear as Jews in 2–3 generations or even sooner. The only thing that can save the ethnic group is *religion* [emphasis his]. Personally I feel myself as a Jew and was from childhood proud of it. But I am definitely a secular Jew and a nonbeliever. [But this kind of] belonging to the people and nation cannot regenerate a small community!

5

VOICES OF YUGOSLAV JEWRY

> But for me, now, it's really not important what Jews think or what Serbs think. I have my own life and feelings. . . . I forgot this word We. It doesn't mean anything to me. I can only say I.

The aim of this chapter is to explore several individuated forms and meanings of Yugoslav Jewish identity. Unlike the pattern of submergence which emphasizes public uniformity, stability and a fixed order, individuation reflects variability, flexibility, fragmentation, and the characteristics of being betwixt-and-between fixed structures and meanings. For those unwavering in their definitions of ethnic identity, individuation may entail commitment to one or more selected objects and spheres of Jewish life. Such commitment is affirmed and reaffirmed by social acts of ethnic authentication within the social parameters of an organized and dialogical community, one that retains at least some of the features of *gemeinschaft*. The core of stable leaders and activists belonging to the senior generation exhibited such commitment. Other individuals, especially those born after the Second World War who were without the experience and memory of a Jewish past, were less secure in situating or constituting their Jewishness. Having been cut off from the Jewish past, they tended to be divided among several things in the present, beginning with their descent. Some of these individuals actively pursued resolutions to the metaphysical (being) and epistemological (knowing) dilemmas they faced, while others actively moved away from what they perceived to be Jewish, or they passively allowed the Jewish thread, be it social, cognitive, moral, or affective, to attenuate.

The purpose of this chapter is to present both individuals who were committed to performing acts of authentication and individuals who moved either closer to or further away from Jewishness in terms of behavior, conceptualization, affect, and, perhaps, moral commitment. In short, the course of this chapter is to go inside the tri-level model and to explore a small part of the variability that was manifested on the individual level of the Yugoslav Jewish population. Many questions come to mind. What did it mean to be a Jew in Yugoslavia? Who were these individuals who were at least partly Jewish by descent? Why were they Jewish? What made them Jewish? How did they know they were Jewish? How did others know? How did they know they knew? What were the sources of their fragmented Jewishness? How did individuals actively seek and select fragments of Jewishness? How were these fragments of Jewishness integrated, actively or passively, into their consciousness, their conceptions and perceptions, and perhaps even into their behavior? What motivated them to pursue Jewishness at all? Was it culture, or the lack of it? Was it the psycho-cultural desire to be different? Or was it the need for transcendent meaning? Was it the non-Jew who categorized the Jew as "someone else" and "something else?" Or, was it outside of the human motivation that stems from being a cultural, social, and psychological being? Did Jewishness, at least for certain individuals, transcend these human facets of everyday life?

Individuation

Individuation, as defined here, is of two major kinds. First, there is the external form whereby the individual articulates or displays ethnic identity. Meyer Fortes (1983:395) argues that "to know is to show." To Fortes, showing identity means demonstrating commitment, which he defined as "accepting obligations" and "putting out an objective product" (ibid.). Eliade (1961;1957, quoted in Myerhoff 1978:190) wrote that "one becomes what one displays." There are individuals, however, who do not know what or how to show. Committed individuals may feel they are without the dilemmas of being and knowing, even though certain tensions may persist because of the political or social environment in which they display their Jewishness. They, too, must live with disjuncture and fragmentation. However active they may be within the sphere of the organized community, they must live their lives where there is no ongoing Jewish life, no Jewish neighborhood, no Jewish shops, no Jewish restaurants or theaters. Individuation also entails the manner and means of pursuing meaning and identity. Individuation need not be only performative or action-oriented. It may be a pursuit played out in the conscience, mind, or emotions of the individual.

The identity of the individual is examined primarily through his or her own words. Much of Jewishness in Yugoslavia was "feeling Jewish" and "talking Jewish" but not "acting Jewish." But, it is important to understand that such articulation was set within the broader context of historical life experiences and of contemporary life in Yugoslav society. Identity is not some static concept, but rather a dynamic process of construction, of rearrangement of the "givens," of negotiation, of presentation that at times involves impression management, even of dispute. Seen thusly, identity formations and transformations involved "a continuous process of working out [one's] own definition of who [one is] vis-à-vis the surrounding non-Jewish world" (Kugelmass 1988:8). Placing the individual in Yugoslav context entails consideration of where he or she was situated vis-à-vis the various poles of Yugoslav life and the concentric layers which indicated degree of identification with the Jewish community itself.

Not even those most secure in their ethnic identity arrived at a point of ethnic inertia. This was where external influences and constraints initiated a response. For some, Jewishness meant continuous flight or movement; one remains in a transitional or suspended state of anti-structure. The famous writer Danilo Kiš, the product of a Jewish father and Montenegrin mother, who called himself an ethnographic rarity, was an example of such Jewishness. If reality is always associated with movement, as another Yugoslav Jewish writer contends, then does it follow that to be an authentic Jew means to be in constant movement? The connotation here does not necessarily pertain to geographical movement but rather to movements within the person. One of my informants spoke of great spiritual movements within him.

My focus on the individual, a form of person-centered ethnography (see Hollan and Wellenkamp 1994), shows what occurs when external impositions and pressures, followed by the responses of the membership itself, radically alter a sociocultural collectivity. Individual variation and individuation result. Examining individuals in this case was an ethnographic necessity because it reflected the ethnographic reality of the Yugoslav Jewish population.

How does one go about describing the underdeveloped territory of individuation? I looked for help in the literature and found such potentially useful terms as private symbols (Firth 1973), personal symbols (Obeyesekere 1982), intimate culture (Epstein 1981), webs of significance (Geertz 1973), quest (e.g., Native American), odyssey (Meyer 1990), subjectivization (Berger 1967), acts of authentication (Sartre), *ikigai* (Matthews 1996), succession of autonomous moments (Alter 1971), liminality (Turner 1969), experience of commitment (Stromberg 1987), authoring oneself (Myerhoff 1986), personal myths (Myerhoff 1978), and bricolage (ibid.).

Recently I discovered that Robert Jay Lifton's (1993) concept of the protean self shares many characteristics with the concept of bricolage as I apply it below. In my reading of Lifton's delineation of the protean self, I found that many of the postwar Jewish selves described below have been or are associated with the characteristics of the protean self. It is often given birth by chaotic and dislocating and often irreversible historical conditions. One's primary community may have faced or may continue to face extinction, leaving its individual members without a guiding tradition. Lifton is no pessimist when discussing the possibilities of the protean self. He tells us that in the aftermath of these conditions "the self turns out to be surprisingly resilient" (ibid:1). Despite the breakdown and fragmentation of the community and the authority that it provided individual lives, the self actively responds to fragmentation by becoming malleable, which in turn allows for continual recreation (ibid:3). As Lifton describes it,

> Though variation is the essence of the protean self, that self has certain relatively consistent features. Central to its function is a capacity for bringing together disparate and seemingly incompatible elements of identity and involvement in what I call "odd combinations," and for continuous transformation of these elements. At the same time, the protean self must cope with, and sometimes even cultivate, feelings of fatherlessness and homelessness, associated with shifts in authority and mentorship. One may take on the psychology of a survivor and undergo symbolic forms of death and rebirth that contribute further to shapeshifting. At the same time, one always seeks a degree of form, grounding, and cohesion.
>
> Mockery and self-mockery, irony, absurdity, and humor enable the protean self to lubricate its experiences and to

> express the absence of "fit" between the way the world presents itself and the way one actually feels about it. The emotions of the protean self tend to be free-floating, not clearly tied to cause or target. . . . The protean self has an uneasy relationship to the holding of ideas. . . . Idea systems can be embraced, modified, let go, and re-embraced, all with a new ease that stands in sharp contrast to the inner struggle people in the past endured with such shifts. . . .
>
> One seeks lasting human ties and sustained ethical commitments; while these, too, can be uncertain and susceptible to their own shifts, they can also be subject to various kinds of renewal. Indeed, a large question for the protean self, and one that cannot be answered simply, concerns its capacity to sustain and live out moral principles in the midst of psychological flux. For the entire life cycle, no longer governed by formal rites of passage, tends to be subject to considerable improvisation. . . . The overall quest involves a struggle for larger human connectedness, for ways of symbolizing immortality in the form of attachments that transcend one's limited life span (ibid:4–6).

Admittedly, my approach to understanding and describing individuation is eclectic, fragmentary, and exploratory, drawing from a variety of anthropological and other disciplinary sources that may possibly illuminate some aspect of inner and external individuation. It is an expedition of encounter and discovery more than an exercise in explanation, although the latter is attempted. Perhaps in this regard I acknowledge Lifton's remark that the proteanism of the researcher himself must also be considered in an exploration of this kind (ibid:7). However, I (more than Lifton) tend to see the debilitating nature of this kind of self. Neither most of my informants nor I, it is my contention, embrace disjunction and fragmentation.

Moreover, it is not sufficient to find cohesion in the self alone. In Lifton's words above, we "struggle for larger human connectedness" (ibid.). He writes that we human beings do not end our quest at this point. Here Lifton seems to share Ernest Becker's "notion that we search for ways of symbolizing immortality in the form of attachments that transcend [our] limited life span" (ibid.). A major significance of both Lifton's and Becker's work is that Becker (1975) contends that the immortality striving principle is at work in strong, intact and cohesive communities while Lifton argues that this principle is also at work in fragmented communities and individuals. There is a dark side to such strivings when the collective or individual self becomes or continues to be "a self detachable from its social and historical roles and statuses," that is, from its own historical narrative and the historical narratives of others (MacIntyre 1984:220–221). This may be the self without accountability. The philosopher Alisdair MacIntyre writes that "we can only answer the question, 'What am I to do?' if we can answer the prior question, 'Of what story or stories do I find myself a part?'" (ibid:216). But it may also be the self that does not seek to move from a place of dislocation and fragmentation toward relocation, connectedness, and renewal (Lifton 1993:15; see MacIntyre 1984: 218). Lifton recognizes that the lack of such movement can be dangerous for the self (ibid:14).

Individuation involves a process by which individuals engage in private symbolization. They either select or create private symbols that have personal significance and serve as reference points or as a mnemonic (Myerhoff 1978:189). Without these, individuals will lack "a vision of coherence and continuity [and will] become utterly vulnerable and disoriented" (ibid:222). Although Abner Cohen focuses on collective forms of ethnicity, he has recognized that

> we are all potential creators of symbols . . . through our dreams, illusions, spontaneous activities, moments of reflection and in the general flow of our consciousness, we continually proliferate symbols and manipulate them. Many mean to keep their symbolic creativity to themselves. Others externalize it and try to share their symbols with other men. This symbolic proliferation within each one of us is not entirely our autonomous creation, but is the product of a dialectical interaction between ourselves and our social reality (1976:30).

Critical here is the context of such symbolization, that is, how collective and personal history, population profile, and social context facilitate or constrain the process. The Yugoslav Jewish case can be contrasted, for example with the process of private symbolization Obeyesekere (1982) describes. Obeyesekere posits a relationship between cultural ideology and private (personal) symbols. This is not problematic. The contrast lies in the strength of culture over the individual. In describing the case of a key Indian informant, Obeyesekere demonstrated the strength of culture. I still look for the relationship but culture, plus overall population profile, in the Yugoslav Jewish case, as I have indicated, is fragmented and exercises limited and variable degrees of constraint on individuals. As Fischer (1986:173) has stated, "Certain ethnicities cannot be encompassed by discussions of group solidarity, traditional values, family, or other categories of sociological analysis applied to ethnicity." Can the Yugoslav Jews be categorized as a "people without culture," a de-culturated or post-cultural rather than an assimilated or acculturated population (Rosaldo 1988)? To de-culturated and post-cultural I would add supra-cultural, which refers to phenomena that appear to be outside of the sociocultural realm. As I show in the cases below, and as Boyarin (1991:56–57) discovered in his study of the Polish Jews in Paris, not everything is normative, rational, and predictable in the life experiences of individuals. Furthermore, "being a Jew" may be what Victor Turner has described as "a matter of the heart," that is, "what circumvents cognitive processes and formal training" and is "ineradicable and ineffable" (1978:xii). One important question is, how are life experiences, especially extraordinary ones, to be explained? Can experience alone be the "touchstone for truth" (Bell 1980:15)? Are meaning and identity simply self-created? Not everyone is willing to cede to approaches to ethnicity and identity based on extreme subjectivism. Katz (1992:36) argues that "if the self creates the world it inhabits, then the only result can be an unacceptable subjectivism, a knowing only of "appearances" or the "appearances" of "appearances." Do all collective and individual patterns necessarily reflect reinterpretation and reinvention (Fischer 1986), or can they reflect disjuncture, fragmentation, erosion, decay, and attenuation?

Fragmentation and Bricolage

Many Yugoslav Jewish individuals live divided among and along the interstices of several fragmented symbolic universes. Kugelmass (1988:2) writes that "the search for Jewishness and for identity itself has been particularly acute because of the fragmented universes in which they have moved." Being divided and fragmented is a reflection of individual Jewishness outside the organized community or, perhaps, for an unknown number, it is because of the kind of community that did exist under state socialism, one that had lost its institutional and ideological diversity and offered a cultural program that divided those present into performers and spectators.[1] Yugoslav Jewishness was not some autonomous semiotic code or a unified, integrated cultural whole or an ongoing dialogical community, but rather for most it was and continues to be a shreds-and-patches conception and an irregular manifestation, especially without any commitment or effort to become part of a dialogical community. Each individual constructed his or her own web of significance. Each pursued, more or less aggressively, what he or she believed or conceived to be his or her own significance. Each sought answers to what are the basic philosophical, religious and cultural questions of life by working his or her way through the diasporic labyrinth and, in choosing from among the (fragmented) contingencies confronted along the way, each constructed an individuated Jewishness. Many refused to become the yielding clay, to be passively molded by societal "trends" and "forces." Instead, as individuals they acted upon their environment or in spite of it, thereby manifesting a constant movement that resisted both totalizing ideologies and accommodating host cultures. Some resisted more, some resist less. Some remained *u strukturi* ("in structure," i.e., submerged), while others fell clearly outside of it.

Following Myerhoff's (1978) usage, I will call this individuated process, together with its source, process, and product, ethnic bricolage, and its individuals, bricoleurs. Bricolage begets bricolage, unless a major transformation or revitalization returns an entire collectivity to a stable and normative structure that has the capacity to provide individual members with cultural models that facilitate cultural maintenance, transmission, and reproduction from one generation to the next. But was this possible in a community that described itself as maimed and crippled and kept asking itself, "Are we the final generation of Jews?" Jonathan Boyarin also conducted an ethnography of a fragmented community. He quotes a line from an unpublished and unproduced screenplay that fit his ethnographic experience and mine as well: "We cannot put ourselves together; how could you" (Szalat n.d., quoted in Boyarin 1991:173)? I confronted a different Jewish population, but one that was likewise fragmented and unable to return to its former state. For me to portray the Yugoslav Jews as anything but fragmented and consequently individuated is to portray them falsely. Certainly not every Yugoslav Jew conceived of his or her Jewishness as bricolage and him- or herself as a bricoleur. Indeed, some fragments were more fragmented than others. Abner Cohen (1974:xiv) has stated that there is ethnicity and there is ethnicity. Likewise, there is bricolage and there is bricolage. Individuals selected different fragments. Some could select from the past, while others could not. Even the most committed members had to confront the reality of this form of Jewishness in postwar Yugoslavia, if not in themselves then in others, including in their own children. Sometimes, it was the children who had to confront it in their parents or parent.

According to the *Concise Oxford Dictionary of Literary Terms* (1990), bricolage means "improvisation or a piece of makeshift handiwork. Sometimes applied to artistic works in a sense similar to a collage: an assemblage improvised from materials ready to hand, or the practice of transforming 'found' materials by incorporating them in a new work." The term bricolage has been previously used by anthropologists. In *The Savage Mind* (1966) Claude Levi-Strauss "used the word *bricolage* to describe the process through which myths are constructed in preliterate societies. Odds and ends, fragments offered up by chance or the environment—almost anything will do—are taken up by a group and incorporated into a tale, used by a people to explain themselves and their world. No intrinsic order or system has dictated the materials employed. In such an inelegant fashion does the *bricoleur* or handyman meet his needs" (Myerhoff 1978:10). Barbara Myerhoff (1978) adapted the term bricolage to characterize the Center culture of the elderly Jews of Venice, California. The following are several descriptions of bricolage that I have extracted from her own description in *Number Our Days*:

> [Center culture is] in some respects thin and fragile, but its very existence must be seen as a major accomplishment, emerging spontaneously as a result of . . . continuities between past and present circumstance, and social isolation [of the members] made up of bits and pieces of people's common history; revitalized selected features . . . adding and amending without concern for consistency, priority, or authenticity; occasionally disorderly and illogical amalgam of forms and sentiments, memories and wishes, rotating around a few stable, strong symbols and premises; eclectic, it shifted and stretched to meet immediate needs—private, collective, secular, and sacred; no explicit plan or internal integration can be detected; untidy assemblages . . . focused only in crisis, systematized after the fact; made up of many small

> pieces sewn together by necessity, intended to be serviceable and to last. It was sufficient for the people's remaining years (1978:9–10).

Applied to individuated Yugoslav Jewishness, bricolage was even more fragmented. There were significant sociocultural and demographic differences between the Yugoslav Jews and the Center culture Barbara Myerhoff describes. Center culture was richer. The population of elderly Venice Jews was more homogeneous. Many shared a common history, and there were continuities between past and present. In the Yugoslav Jewish case, for example, a distinct break divided prewar and postwar generations. There was no Yiddishkeit. In fact, there was no true secular cultural variant of Jewishness in Yugoslavia, only a "cultural program" organized by the activists in the organized community. Yiddish was never widespread or strong, and Sephardi culture had become mostly nostalgic folklore. In addition, the political conditions in Titoist Yugoslavia precluded Zionist or political activity common to many Jewish communities, including the Polish Jewish immigrants studied by Boyarin. Thus, there were no alternatives for collective expressions of Jewishness outside the sphere of the organized community and its cultural program. Where did that leave Jewishness for the individual, particularly the one who was either outside the community altogether or was looking for something beyond or in place of the cultural program that had significance for her or him? Jewishness was a creation, a construction, an authoring of oneself; it was an improvisation or "piece of makeshift handiwork" in the sense that the individual was not situated within a single culture that regulated how she or he thought, believed, felt, and acted. Rather the individual was situated or moved between different symbolic universes, themselves fragmented, and along their interstices (see Handelman 1990). As one moved though the labyrinth or matrix, or however else this social and symbolic complexity might be described, one selected, or sometimes discarded, fragments from the different universes and engaged in conceptual, perceptual, and symbolic juxtaposition, reordering, negation, and synthesis to construct or redefine one's Jewishness. The individual constructed a web of personal significance. Once an element was added did not mean it would be retained forever, and once an element was discarded did not mean it would never again be selected. To most Jews in Yugoslavia who were without the experience and memory of an integrated Jewish tradition, they perceived Jewishness as a bricolage, and therefore they constructed an ethnic (Jewish) bricolage. Sometimes, however, the fragments that reached them and became a part of their conscious self were not actively pursued. They reached them in the form of dreams, transference (Fischer 1986), and transcendent experiences that they did not seek. Other times they selected for themselves elements that were within their reach. What they saw, heard, sensed internally, and imagined must be considered when examining the sources, the processes of selection and integration, and the outcomes of such individuation. It is only when the individual chooses to become a part of a collectivity whose members interact regularly and in which there is the potential for cultural reproduction and to which he or she is committed can Jewishness begin to take on a different form.

The data and their presentation in this chapter reflect the fragmented nature of Yugoslav Jewishness on the individual level. Because of this ethnographic reality I present a few of the many voices of individual Jews while interjecting an interpretive and analytical structure. By providing such a structure, which itself rests on the social context in which these individuals are situated (though the data are limited here), I try to avoid presenting an ethnic cacophony or a self-standing or undirected polyphony of Yugoslav Jewish voices.

In constructing a bricolage Jewishness, individuals draw from outside of themselves, that is, from what they have been told, read, seen and from personal ties. They also draw from within themselves those significances attached somehow to Jewish descent, Jewish narratives and symbols, and Jewish imagery, and to imagination, conscience, and affect. The process of integration of the various fragments involves unconscious incorporation, conscious but passive incorporation, imposition, and active pursuit and selection. The outcome may involve a display of their Jewishness through cultural production (e.g., a book, a diary) or, for example, acting out the behavioral patterns of one's parents (see Fischer 1986).

As an anthropologist, and as the author of this chapter, I bring my own set of presuppositions and framework to my work, but at the same time attempt to present just a few of the many voices within the Yugoslav Jewish population.[2] I do not adopt a structuralist or post(anti)-structuralist approach. If anything, I try to give visibility to what may be for many the invisible individual Yugoslav Jew. An argument can be made that it is precisely individual Jews, outside the context of the organized community, who gave visibility to the Yugoslav Jews as a whole.

I recognize that they were a post-traditionalist population, and the ethnographic reality of the postwar Jews of Yugoslavia reflected not one but many Jewish minds, not an integrated and unified Jewishness but an ethnic bricolage, and not one voice but many voices. I am not referring to multiple interpretations of a single voice, but to many voices, each with its own set of meanings that must be understood in terms of where the individuals were socially, culturally, and psychologically situated. My aim is to show how these individuals constituted or situated themselves (i.e., how they engaged in private and public symbolization), how they were situated by others and the external factors that touched their lives, and how I analytically and interpretively situated them within the framework of my research problem and assumptions. In addition, I assume that there is commonality that underlied or potentially underlied (e.g., when Jewishness became visible in times of crisis, when there was a perception of threat to the Jews collectively) the diverse particulars found in the narratives that follow. One unfulfilled analytical task is to locate the common strands in all of the individual webs. This is problematic because I do not have the well-developed webs or the life histories of these individuals. A subsequent research objective would be to collect life histories and many more strands of the individual webs. In contrast to the collective forms described in chapters 3 and 4, whose structures and patterns are more apparent and amenable to traditional anthropological analyses, my understanding of individuated Jewishness is very partial and tenuous. Hence, my presentation of the individual narratives that follow is fragmented just as their Jewishness is fragmented to them.[3]

I have been asked, Are these typical individuals in the narratives? How typical are they? I am not sure I know what typical means. Certainly I make no claims for any individuals being typical of some "existing type." Instead, what the individuals in the following narratives reflect in varying degrees are the strands of significance within the Yugoslav Jewish population. Some of the strands are structural, such as generation and gender; some are experiential, such as whether or not an individual experienced prewar Jewish life, the Holocaust, and the National Liberation Struggle; some are ideological, such as whether or not an individual supported the politics of the state. If one was a member of the senior generation, he or she carried the experiences and memories of a vibrant Jewish past, whereas members of the middle and youth generations could not draw upon that which they never knew or experienced. All generations, however, felt an acute sense of disjuncture. The following narratives show how individuals, each different from the others, have confronted and dealt with this disjuncture.

Voices of Yugoslav Jewry

Commitment to a Secular Jewish Community in Socialist Yugoslavia

Individuals who were committed to a secular and unified Yugoslav Jewish community in socialist Yugoslavia tended to know who they were and what they wanted to accomplish. Many of the committed members of the senior generation acted out their commitment by performing leadership roles within the context of what organized Jewish life remained in Yugoslavia. Perhaps because their commitment was action oriented, their own Jewish identity tended to be less ambivalent. Concretized commitment accomplishes this. Commitment was strong, as it was for those few men and women committed to Jewish religious tradition (see following narrative), but the objects of commitment were different or differently defined. For example, both secular and religious Jews share a commitment to the the institution and the symbol, "the Jewish community," but they attach different meanings to this symbol. The leaders of the Yugoslav Jewish community were Jews committed to a particular kind of community—a secular Jewish community. In their minds, there were only a few, elderly Jews in the community who simply could not let go of the religious sentiments inculcated in them when they were children. In their efforts to create a secular community and a secular Jewishness, the leaders chose not to base their existence and that of the organized community on forms of the Judaic Tradition. Instead, they introduced functional replacements that had significance for all members of the community. Memorialism surrounding the Holocaust and National Liberation Struggle became the focus of their collective ritual observance. These were Jews who continued to invoke "Tradition" but did not attempt to live according the rhythm of the Jewish calendar. Many avoided attending the communal Passover seder and the High Holiday services in the synagogue, but they could not avoid entirely contact with the Judaic Tradition, such as the recitation of the Kaddish prayer in commemorations. In invoking "Tradition," however, they belied their own secularist position. As Finestein (1977) has pointed out, secular Jews find it difficult to discard the so-called cultural baggage entirely.

Rather than work with the Jewish tradition to interpret the Jewish community's new circumstances in socialist Yugoslavia, the leaders of the community attempted to redefine their tradition through the lens of the key symbols of socialist Yugoslavia. Their approach reflected a degree of divided loyalty to which they had to attend constantly.

The activist and leadership core was largely composed of individuals who fit into this category. They led the organized Jewish community in the postwar period. Most had never been political radicals, but they had moved among radicals or had been exposed to radical ideas. A significant number participated in one of several Jewish organizations that together formed the progressive paths of the prewar Jewish youth movement. Their intent even in their youth was not to repudiate their Jewishness or abandon the Jewish community, but rather to redefine and reorient their Jewishness toward secular Zionism and socialism.

Individuation here is worked out within the only institutionalized sphere of activity, the organized community.

Lavoslav Kadelburg: Yugoslav Jewry's "Ambassador to the Outside World"

Dr. Lavoslav Kadelburg was in many ways a microcosm of the postwar organized Yugoslav Jewish community, particularly of its small but persistent activist core and within that of its highly stable leadership elite. Since assuming the presidency of the Federation of Jewish Communities of Yugoslavia until retiring from the post in 1992, he molded the community as much as it molded him. It bore his image. Both exhibited intellectuality, moderation, secularness, persistence, and integration with the Yugoslav state and the Jewish world.

Lavoslav Kadelburg was born in 1910 in the Slavonian town of Vinkovci which had a Jewish population of about six hundred, one of the smaller communities in interwar Yugoslavia. His parents, Tobias and Jolan, named him after a dead grandfather, as was the Ashkenazi custom. Kadelburg represented the Slavonian variant of the Jews of Croatia and Yugoslavia, which was a mixture of German and Hungarian Jews, a result of intermarriage between the two linguistic units. These polyglot Jews spoke Hungarian, German, and Serbo-Croatian. Dr. Kadelburg speaks all three of these languages and several others. Making a living as small industrialists, merchants and craftsmen, these Jews belonged to the middle and upper-middle classes of society. Virtually no poor Jews inhabited this region. Their high socioeconomic status helped them to place their children even further into the mainstream of society. Consequently, the pattern of occupational distribution began to change. Their children received a university education in Yugoslavia and abroad. Vienna and Prague were two popular places for such study. Many of them, like Kadelburg, entered the free professions. Medical and law departments, for example, had disproportionate numbers of Jews. After completing classical secondary school (*gimnazija*) in Vinkovci, Dr. Kadelburg studied law in Zagreb University from which he obtained his Doctor of Jurisprudence degree in 1935. Significantly, many of the leaders of the Jewish community in socialist Yugoslavia were lawyers and physicians.

Dr. Kadelburg always declared and identified himself as Jewish and almost never as anything else. Since his middle school days in his hometown of Vinkovci, he was involved continuously in Jewish communal life. Between 1925–1929 he was president of *Herut*, a Jewish youth association and a member of the *Radni odbor* of the Federation of Jewish Youth Associations. He admits that perhaps during one period in his life, while in the military, he tried to assimilate. "I am ashamed to admit, but I did try to assimilate. This was a slight betrayal (on my part), but I did not succeed," he confessed to me. Apparently, the non-Jewish soldiers under his command never saw him as anything but Jewish. This and other accounts that I heard only reinforces the validity of Fredrik Barth's early emphasis that ethnic categorization entails both self-ascription and ascription-by-others. Later, while interned as a prisoner-of-war in Germany, he was surrounded by many other Jewish officers of varying degrees of radical persuasion. In such surroundings it was easier to retain strong Jewish identification while simultaneously being influenced by the radicals in the camp. In those days and later I think that he was more anti-fascist than communist in orientation. In contrast, those Jews who fought among either Croatian or Serbian Partisan detachments were often isolated as Jews and consequently felt a stronger desire to assimilate or hide their Jewish identity (Loker 1977).

Dr. Kadelburg served as the president of the Federation of Jewish Communities of Yugoslavia for twenty-eight years (1964–1992). Having occupied this position for so many years, he became the most powerful individual in the organized Jewish community, though he would never admit this. The Federation was the only supralocal Jewish organization in the country. It had no competitors. While the state of Yugoslavia was intact the Federation controlled the individual local communities (opština/općina), at least until the late 1980s when the Zagreb community began exerting more autonomy. The Federation was recognized by the state and foreign Jewish organizations as the representative of the entire Jewish community (*zajednica*) of Yugoslavia. Dr. Kadelburg was the foremost representative of the Federation and entire organized community both within Yugoslavia and abroad. Historian Harriet Pass Freidenreich (1984:47, 51) has described him as Yugoslav Jewry's "ambassador to the outside world" and "by far the most influential figure in the community." One local community member acknowledged Dr. Kadelburg's power within the community in noting his ability to make a decision against the entire Executive Committee of the Federation. Though stating to me that decision making within the Executive Committee was democratic, a Deputy President of the Federation acknowledged that Dr. Kadelburg was accustomed to feeling that his opinion would be accepted in the majority of cases.

Dr. Kadelburg possessed the characteristics that made him an excellent broker between the Jewish community and the state, and also among the local Jewish communities (*opštine*). From the standpoint of the Titoist rulers, they saw a man who was politically active in the anti-fascist movement while interned as a prisoner-of-war in Germany, who served in the Popular Front transition government (NOO) in Vršac immediately after the war, who served in a number of top-level government positions, and who actively participated in various sociopolitical organizations. He was a member of the Communist Party and other prestigious organizations in the country. The rulers also saw a man who served in several prestigious international Jewish organizations, including the World Jewish Congress as vice-president. He was a personal friend of World Jewish Congress President Nahum Goldmann who happened to know Tito well. In his role as Federation president, Lavoslav Kadelburg was influenced by Nahum Goldmann whose visit to Yugoslavia in 1967 he named as one of the four most significant events of the decade in the Yugoslav Jewish community. As president of the Federation of Jewish Communities of Yugoslavia, Kadelburg appears to have followed the same Talmudic concept in Yugoslavia as Goldmann did on a global level: "The law of the state (where you live) is the law" (Abramowicz 1978:5).

From the perspective of the Yugoslav Jews, Lavoslav Kadelburg possessed the necessary characteristics of a Jewish leader. He had been raised in a "good Jewish home," as another community leader put it. Although secular, he knew Jewish tradition. In his student days before the war he had served in several organizations, including the Zionist-Marxist youth organization Hashomer Hatzair described earlier. A significant number of the postwar communal leadership came out of Hashomer Hatzair. After the war Dr. Kadelburg served as president of the Autonomous Aid Committee from 1945–1952, vice-president of the Federation of Jewish Communities of Yugoslavia from 1948–1964, and president from 1964 to 1992. He was exceptional in that he simultaneously served as vice-president and president of the Federation while occupying high positions in the government at the federal and republic levels. Especially among those in government service, the usual practice was to return to Jewish communal life only following retirement. There was no doubt, then, that he held Jewish interests as a priority. As one community worker expressed it, Lavoslav Kadelburg was a great Jew and a great Yugoslav. Interestingly, however, he identifies himself as a Jew and not as a Yugoslav Jew.

In summary, several characteristics helped Dr. Kadelburg maintain his position and influence in the community. He did not originate from one of the three main communities of Belgrade, Zagreb, or Sarajevo. Rather, he was raised in a Jewish family from Slavonia where there was a mix of of different Jewish linguistic groups. This fact of origin perhaps gave him broader acceptance, at least in the beginning of his tenure as president. Since his teenage years he had been active continuously in Jewish communal life and had occupied leadership positions. Having been a member of the prewar Zionist youth movement, particularly of Hashomer Hatzair, he had strong associations with the prewar progressive tradition. His was not a wartime or postwar ideological conversion. He had studied law and later practiced in the field. After the war he became a state authority in this field. He served as a prosecutor and a supreme court judge. As a prisoner-of-war in Germany during the Second World War, he participated actively in the antifascist movement within the camps. Although I would not classify him as politically radical, he cooperated with other Jews who were, such as the art historian and essayist Oto Bihalji-Merin, the boyhood friend of Kadelburg's predecessor, Albert Vajs. There were Jews of his generation who held a worldview and operated in a sphere of activity that was no longer Jewish. Kadelburg never belonged to this group of Jews who opted out of the community. Although he attained very high posts in the government, he never abandoned his Jewish outlook and activity. His predecessor Albert Vajs exhibited the same sense of obligation to the ethnic community. Such men were more antifascist and socialist in orientation than hard-core communists, even though many joined the Communist Party during or after the war. Significant also with regard to his being a POW were the ties that were formed during internment and carried over into the postwar years. Vajs and Kadelburg, having been POWs, had the support of others who had been POWs with them, many of whom also became activists in the postwar community. Other leaders and members of the community acknowledged that Dr. Kadelburg had a deep knowledge of and was an expert in Jewish affairs. He also possessed extensive knowledge of Jewish history, philosophy, and tradition. Outside the country, he held high positions in international Jewish organizations, including the World Jewish Congress. From the beginning Lavolslav Kadelburg was no mere titular head. For seven years immediately after the war, he served as president of the Committee on Autonomous Aid, leading the community's humanitarian efforts. He was an excellent administrator, paying attention to detail. Possessing great energy and memory, he achieved significant results in Jewish public work.

Dr. Kadelburg displayed the proper ascribed characteristics, a high level of Jewish knowledge, considerable intellectual and technical skills, a long record of activism and positions in both Jewish communal and Yugoslav government spheres, prewar progressive and wartime antifascist experience, brokership qualities, and he was an acknowledged authority within the Jewish community. A community leader described him as being an excellent authority, experienced practitioner, experienced organizer, and as having great energy, methodicalness, a love toward work, consideration for everyone, a willingness to listen to and advise everyone, a great memory, boundless patience, and balanced pedantry (Levi, A. *Jevrejski Pregled*, year unknown).

I can only present the public side of Lavoslav Kadelburg. This is the only side I observed and knew. He did not often shed this public side, neither to outsiders like me nor to all but his closest friends. Perhaps the exceptions were those times he exposed his sense of humor to me and others. In any case, it is his public Jewishness that is most significant here. What I want to show is that his Jewishness was largely what was public, what he chose to display, his style of leadership, his aims stated in the form of communal aims, and his formal positions in Jewish organizations. That is where his own Jewishness impacted the Jewish Community of Yugoslavia. Whether one agreed or disagreed with his position and policies, one tangible outcome was his role in successfully maintaining Jewish life for at least another generation by strengthening what was already a strong, central Jewish organization. He saw his task as one of providing and maintaining the organization for Jewish life, within whose sphere of influence a cultural program was provided for those who were interested. He realized that the family no longer transmitted Jewish culture to its members. The organized community, with Dr. Kadelburg at the helm, assumed that function and thereby maintained the Jewish community (Freidenreich 1984). Another aim, which is better described as one of Dr. Kadelburg's passions, was to maintain the unity of the Yugoslav Jewish community. Whereas the Yugoslav rulers failed to establish unity among the Yugoslav peoples under Titoism, the Jewish leadership under President Kadelburg was largely successful in uniting the Jewish communities. On the other hand, the structure of socialist Yugoslavia and the position of the Jewish community within it may have facilitated this unity. Even as socialist Yugoslavia was disintegrating beginning in 1989–1990, Dr. Kadelburg displayed his passion for keeping the Jewish community intact and united.

A significant part of Dr. Kadelburg's Jewishness was defined in terms of the relationship between the organized Jewish community and the state and the position of the Yugoslav Jewish community in the Jewish world. His role in this relationship was that of rational broker. He was an excellent broker because he possessed the traits and positions that both the community and the state regarded highly. His contacts were immediate. He was rational in the sense that he felt no compunction to retain or give priority to those cultural elements that fit less well into the new societal conditions. Unlike certain groups which, in post-revolutionary periods, interpret their new political and economic conditions through their traditional lens, the Yugoslav Jews with Dr. Kadelburg leading the way interpreted their tradition through the new conditions they had helped to create. Despite the emphasis on a rationalist approach to deciding how to react to change, a new idiom of belief was inevitably created, with Kadelburg subsequently reasoning excellently in the idiom of this belief (Polanyi 1958:288). Religious faith may have been discarded, but a secular faith replaced it. His faith was a kind of socialist optimism and a driven commitment, one, however, that required a central organization behind it.

Having been one of the chief architects of the experiment in secular Jewishness, and being an optimistic pragmatist, Dr. Kadelburg believed that Jewish life in Yugoslavia was more than just individual feelings or ascriptions; he believed it was a social reality. On this he differed with other prominent Yugoslav Jews. Of the latter, one told me that there was no Jewish social reality in socialist Yugoslavia. Another, an activist in the Federation, asked me, "Have you found any ethnicity yet?" It is significant that Lavoslav Kadelburg believed that what he had helped to construct had an existence, a reality of its own.

Commitment to the Great Tradition: Living by the Rhythm of the Jewish Calendar—in the Yugoslav Sense

Only a few Jewish individuals tried to live according to the traditional Jewish rhythm of life as it existed and could be lived in Yugoslavia. These Jews knew that they were Jews and were a part of a continuous Jewish Tradition. As a remnant of this tradition, they were committed to keeping the tradition alive in a community that was predominantly secular and whose members tended to avoid regular contact with the tradition. They exhibited this commitment by participating regularly in ritual activity that occurred on at least a weekly cycle (attending a high holiday service once a year does not meet this standard) and/or performing ritual roles associated with the Jewish Tradition.

The traditional rhythm of life must be defined as it was actually practiced by the small remnant of ritualists in Yugoslavia. Life cycle rituals pertaining to the stages of birth, puberty, and marriage were extremely rare in postwar Yugoslavia. Only rituals associated with death remained strong. Thus, when determining the degree of an individual's commitment to Jewish Tradition, it would be unrealistic to consider the first three life stages. Observances according to the Jewish calendar continued to be observed on the communal level. Here, however, there was a clear division between how religious and non-religious Jews observed these rituals. Only a handful of practicing religious Jews attended weekly services in the synagogue in Belgrade, Zagreb, and Subotica. An Erev Shabbat (Friday evening) service was held in Belgrade and Zagreb, and a Sabbath day service in Subotica, which was home to many Orthodox Jews before the war and after the war remained the most religious of all the Yugoslav Jewish communities, at least by reputation. Several other cities had a sufficient number of males who claimed to be religious but either failed to mobilize the minimum ten males who would attend regularly and thus ensure the necessary prayer quorum (*minyan*) or did not have a qualified prayer leader (*predmolitelj*). This potentially creates a problem for my definition of commitment. Even though every city which had a Jewish community included individuals characterized by a personal state of commitment to the Jewish religion, only in those places that allowed for regular participation could this commitment be acted out and thereby contribute to the continuation of this tradition in Yugoslavia. From this category I have excluded individuals who, for example, light candles in their home on Friday evening but perform this act alone.

Bencion Pinto: Imam Srce Jevreja—"I Have the Heart of a Jew"

Bencion Pinto fascinated many, including me. Small of girth, fast in gait, most found it difficult to keep pace with this man in his eighties. Bencion was born in 1906 in Belgrade into a religious Sephardi family of nine children. His father, David, was a grain merchant. Milena Estera, his mother, helped establish the Jewish Women's Society. On the day that I interviewed Bencion Pinto in the Sephardi cemetery, he wanted desperately to show me his mother's grave, but he could not find it right away. I followed him as he kept searching and giving voice to his growing agitation. He complained that everything in the cemetery was overgrown: "The cemetery is so overgrown that I can't find the grave of my birth mother. The grave of my mother must be here." He called for the custodian of the cemetery. "Is Jovica not here?" He must clean this. He is paid to clean this. I can't find the grave of my mother. I will find it." As I followed him through the overgrown maze of memorial stones, he eventually did find the grave. I photographed the tombstone, on which there was inlaid a photograph of his mother. Pinto's persistence in looking for the grave of his mother showed me firsthand its obvious significance in his life as one of the several private symbols that hold personal significance and give meaning to his existence as a Jew in a once thriving community, indicated by the large and elaborate grave markers, and now reduced to a minuscule, weak and dependent community, indicated by the overgrown bush in the cemetery.

I last saw Bencion Pinto when he was nearly ninety years old. I had not seen him for several years. His face was gaunt and his eyesight had deteriorated. He mistook me for the president of the community. But his physical state failed to stop him from attending the synagogue and dropping in at the community. He remained as one of the few Jews in Belgrade who could be called "a child of Dorcól." As I described earlier, Dorcól was the old Jewish quarter in Belgrade where Jewish life once thrived. Pinto carried on the Jewish tradition of prewar Dorcól. He provided a concrete connecting thread to and from Dorcól's colorful past. To me he expressed pride in his Belgrade and Dorcól origin. Perhaps more than any other individual in the Belgrade Jewish community, Bencion Pinto served as a guardian of the Jewish Tradition, even though his status in the social hierarchy of the organized community did not reflect this critical role that he played. Those characterized by high traditionalism in the socialist Yugoslav did not generally occupy high leadership positions in the communal structure. This does not mean his service went unrecognized or that members did not worry about who could replace him. His service was recognized and people expressed such concern. Within his ritual sphere of the Jewish cemetery, Bencion Pinto had no equal.

The Jewish Great Tradition was his blueprint for action. Below I describe how he acted out his commitment in various ways. His father and father's father before him had served the Sephardi community as ritual practitioners. His father was also the one who ensured that Jewish tradition was maintained in the family. The family observed dietary prescriptions and proscriptions. Not only were all the necessary prayers said in the home, but the entire family attended the synagogue. Bencion Pinto fulfills his individual passion and obligation to his Belgrade community within this collective tradition (see Polanyi 1958). "I have the heart of a Jew and am carrying out that obligation (*dužnost*) as the Jewish religion prescribes it. I'm doing it because of religion, because of the laws of the Jewish religion. That is essential for me." . . . "I have worked without pay in the Jewish community [and] Federation for 35 years already. I work without pay. According to the Spanish saying, I have *kurazon djidjo*. Translated it means *imam srce Jevreja* —"I have the heart of a Jew." For these reasons I don't serve God for money."

Bencion Pinto represented that small segment of the Yugoslav Jewry whose cognitive map was neither a mazeway nor a "hodgepodge creation arising from intermittent, irregular, random experiences with other Jews" (Shweder and LeVine 1984). Rather his Jewish commitment as manifested by the ritual duties that he fulfilled without monetary compensation was not a part of some artificial construction. He knew what his past was. It was not merely an idea to him. Unlike almost every other Jew in Yugoslavia, Bencion chose to become what his father David and his grandfather Hajim had been before him, thereby feeling less the disjuncture that so strongly characterizes other Jews in the community. His father had served as a *predmolitelj* (prayer leader) in the Bet Israel Sephardi synagogue and his father's father as the director (*rukovodilac*) of the Sephardi cemetery. In this manner Pinto continued a historical tradition in the community and in his patrilineal line rather than created something entirely new. Pinto's Jewishness was individuated insofar as the ritual practitioner role he fulfilled had become an endangered category and practice. People had forgotten how to carry out the rituals according to Jewish law. People expressed concern about a replacement. Being in his eighties, he was aware that time was running out and was concerned with the matter of who would succeed him. He wished to instruct his successor as he once was taught by his predecessor, Ruben Rubenović. Pinto proudly showed me the old stone tablet on which are inscribed the names of all the cemetery's directors. The tablet is "an eternal memory of the members of the administration of the Jewish cemetery in Belgrade. Among them is one of the founders, my deceased grandfather Haim Pinto, who died in 1917. Bencion Pinto, the grandson of that Hajim Pinto, says this." Being the latest in the line of cemetery directors, which included his own paternal grandfather and his predecessor and ritual mentor, Ruben Rubenović, I photographed him standing in front of the tablet located on the cemetery wall just inside the entrance to the cemetery. He did not feel the need to become another kind of Jew or to redefine his Jewishness after the new political conditions in the country or even the restructured community. He had traditional models within his own family (his father) and outside his family (Ruben Rubenović) after which to pattern his own performance-based Jewishness. These models were there for him and others to see, inscribed in stone.

Bencion Pinto can be described as one who did not attempt to interweave his Jewishness with something else. As such, he is one who avoided the tensions and contradictions that inevitably arise when there is an attempt to integrate different worldviews and cultural practices. His idiom is an action idiom. Thereby he avoided entanglement in conceptual or ideological contradictions. However, the potential for such contradiction could not be avoided and did arise. For example, in his role as *rukovodilac groblja* (director of the cemetery), he directed both religious and secular funerals, including those for Jews who were atheists and agnostics in life. Being a religious Jew he faced potential conflict between his personal beliefs and adherence to Jewish law and his role in directing funerals for such Jews. But when I probed him about his personal opinions and attitudes, he refused to engage me in such a dialogue. "This and that is not interesting. What is essential are the facts," which to Pinto were the specific actions he undertook as the director of the cemetery in connection with the entire burial process. These he described for me in detail, occasionally struggling to remember everything he wanted to tell me. In those moments of mental struggle he would remind me that he was old, "in the depths of old age." But he added, after asking me how old he was, "I can still remember to tell you a few things."

The particulars were important to Pinto—particular ritual acts and sequences. Conceptually, however, it was not the separate categories of "religious funeral," "Communist funeral," "traditional funeral," or "modernistic funeral" that give meaning, but rather the ritual whole—the rite itself, that is, the fact that it remains a Jewish funeral in a Jewish cemetery, led by a Jew who has the heart of a Jew, whose father and grandfather before him had the heart of a Jew, that gives meaning. For Bencion Pinto, the presence of cremated remains in an urn during a "modern" burial, or the absence of the rabbi during a military funeral, did not negate the Jewishness of the funeral as a whole. For him, Jewish affirmation accomplished by burial in a Jewish cemetery overrode any particular negations, irregularities, or contradictions in this the most Jewish of spheres in Yugoslav Jewish life. If conditions a, b, and c of the regulations are met, then he should proceed with his duties. If the conditions are not met, the regulations are violated. The conditions cannot set new standards for the acts themselves, and the conditions that permit or do not permit a certain kind of funeral do not negate the Jewishness of this rite of passage.

When individuals died and were buried in the old Sephardi Jewish cemetery in Belgrade, where Bencion Pinto directed the ritual process, there was no equivocating about identity. The dead may have lived as Serbs or Hungarians, or as Communists or Yugoslavs, but they were buried as Jews. During their lives they may have undercommunicated, redefined, concealed, or switched their identity, but they were buried as Jews. They undertook their final passage as Jews in the domain of Bencion Pinto, *rukovodilac groblja*. Bencion Pinto was the guardian who accompanied Jews back within the walls of Jewishness. He facilitated the final passage. Within these walls they were buried as Jews, regardless of what they were during life.

In socialist Yugoslavia, death, not life, drew the strongest boundary of Jewishness. This boundary is symbolized by the wall (*zid*) that encircles and separates the Jewish cemetery from the outside world. The wall has been a historic reality and a powerful metaphor for the Jewish people. In Belgrade, the wall is an ironic form, for these are Jews, most of whose ancestors lived in quarters without walls, who went from living without walls to moving within a walled space in order to retrieve their Jewishness before the living who gather for the funeral.

Hevra Kaddisha is the Jewish burial society. When Jewish settlers established communities around the globe, they formed burial societies. Purchasing a plot of land for a cemetery was one of the first priorities, even before the construction of a synagogue. Before the war in Belgrade, both a men's and a women's Hevra Kaddish served the needs of the Sephardi and Ashkenazi communities. In Belgrade in the 1980s Bencion Pinto alone represented Hevra Kaddish. In fact, Bencion described himself to me as Hevra Kaddish. When I asked him what his title was as the director of the cemetery, he answered, "I am Bencion Pinto, I am the Hevra Kaddish of the Jewish cemetery." You alone? "I am. I am Hevra Kaddish. The only one. I inherited this after the death of Ruben Rubenović. . . . For 21 years I have been fulfilling the duty of Hevra Kaddish. Listen to what I tell you." At an earlier time he had told me that Hevra Kaddish did not exist "anywhere in Yugoslavia except in Belgrade. Not in Zagreb, not in Sarajevo. In this society there is only me. I alone accepted this duty." He described it for me:

> I especially can describe my function as Hevra Kaddish. I am the one who gives permission [to the family of the deceased]. I give them approval from the community. . . . I as Hevra Kaddish accept my duty to purchase a *sanduk* (casket) and to schedule a *sahrana* (funeral). I schedule all that. The Jewish community gives me this *dužnost* (duty). I am an employee of the Belgrade community. On that day the president of the Jewish community gives me the duty. My duty comes directly from the president of the Jewish community. Only the president gives me the duty. The Jewish cemetery is under the Jewish community, not under

> the Federation of Jewish Communities of Yugoslavia. The community is the god and *batil* of the cemetery. . . . My work is under the control of the president of the Jewish community of Belgrade. . . . What I do first for the family of the deceased is buy the most common casket. It is not that we are trying to save money. In Israel they still bury the dead without a casket. I purchase the least expensive casket. [The Serbian authorities] don't permit you to bury without a casket. And two linen sheets. . . . If you were to go to the Serbian cemetery, they will not sell you the cheapest casket. They will sell you one for about 100 million (old) dinars, while the cheapest one costs 30 million. But when I come to the Serbian cemetery, they know that I represent the Jewish community, that it is for a religious ritual. . . . Then, when I go, there must be everything: that, that, and that. And what do I buy? I buy the most common casket in the name of the family of the deceased. . . .

Bencion Pinto also occupies a key ritual position in the Belgrade synagogue. The position is that of *shammash* who in the past fulfilled various duties as an employee of the community, including walking through the Jewish quarter and shouting to the Jewish inhabitants to light their fires in preparation for the Sabbath.

Bencion Pinto performs at least two important duties in his role as shammash. The first begins outside the synagogue, before the Friday evening service, and concerns the *pomena mrtvima* or prayers that are made in memory of the dead (Yahrzeit is the annual *pomen*). He gathers all the names and amounts of the donations of individuals who want to hold a *pomen* in the synagogue. He then passes this information on to the rabbi who reads it during the Friday evening service. In my regular visits to these services I noticed that individuals, sometimes accompanied by other family members, attend when they hold a *pomen* on the anniversary of a parent's death. Even certain individuals who otherwise avoided the synagogue attended on those occasions. A rather large number of people hold a *pomen*. During the first year following a death, three *pomena* are held: at seven days, thirty days, and one year from the time of the burial. Thereafter one *pomen* is held annually on the death anniversary. According to Pinto, the person holding the thirty-day *pomen* is obligated to have a *limud*, a rite of commensality held in the synagogue immediately following the service. Wine and plum brandy are consumed. Food items include Sephardi eggs, which are boiled for three days in oil and with the skin of an onion, giving them a brown color, and small pita cakes with cheese called *pogačice*. If a wife survives her husband, she holds a *limud* for her husband, and vice-versa. I asked Pinto about Samuilo Kalderon, an elderly Sephardi Jew whose funeral I attended. He told me that Samuilo Kalderon "didn't have anyone. I took upon myself the entire *sahrana*. I bought the casket, etc. as a great friend." There was a *pomen*, with a donation, for the deceased at seven days and at thirty days following the burial. The Federation of Jewish Communities of Yugoslavia contributed the thirty-day donation. I remember that Samuilo Kalderon would sit dozing in a chair just outside the library-conference room of the Federation. That is where and how he would spend part of his day. Pinto covered the cost of the *limud* for him.

Bencion Pinto's second duty is to prepare the cup of wine and bring it to the rabbi at the proper time during the Friday night service. The cup of wine is for the Kiddush, the sanctification over wine.

Besides the individual graves and tombstones, the *spomenici* or memorial monuments in the Jewish Cemetery represent the significant past of the Jews—Yugoslav Jews, Serbian Jews, and Austrian Jews. These stones speak about the great tragedy of the Holocaust and about the patriotism and heroic contributions of Yugoslav and Serbian Jews in various wars. These monuments also say something significant about the communities that erected them. On my personal tour with Bencion Pinto, *rukovodilac groblja*, he pointed out these monuments to me and commented on their significance:

> Consider this . . . Bencion Buli. He was the best known banker. He had a bank in Belgrade. Bencion Buli. He [even] loaned the state money. Eh, people, there were powerful Jews here in Belgrade [before the war]. Bencion Buli loaned money to the Serbian state. I am Bencion Pinto. I say that is the way it is. Understand, then, that no money came from America. These were our contributions that created the monument. This is Bencion Buli. No one [of the family is alive today]. They all died. This kind of monument would cost 100 billion [old] dinars to build it today. It's monumental. You see the Star of David? Did you see it?
>
> I'll show you some other graves. I'll show you now the graves of the Viennese Jews. . . . [These were refugees who fled

from fascism only to be murdered by the Nazis in Yugoslavia.] We took their remains from Šabac and moved them here, and we raised this monument. We, the Jewish community of Belgrade. . . . Tell the Americans, when you see the American Jews, what we accomplish as Jews. . . . [We have] the heart and soul of a Jew. And we did it in very difficult economic circumstances, especially with . . . inflation, very small salaries, and very small pensions. But, again, we are holding on to our Jewishness. That is not to be extinguished.

Being a Jew as Moral Obligation

"This is how I learned to do it and I couldn't leave it."

Sami is a member of an age cohort referred to in the Jewish community as the *srednja generacija*, the "middle generation" encompassing those anywhere from their thirties to their fifties. He lives with his wife of Hungarian descent and their two sons in the quiet, mid-sized city of Subotica near the Hungarian border. His Jewish ancestors who have lived in Subotica can be traced back for about two hundred years, a line of descent he is very proud to continue. As his parents raised him to be a Jew, so Sami raises his sons to be Jews. Sami says that they both will have a bar mitzvah, a rather rare rite of passage in the postwar period. Sami is a not only a practicing religious Jew, but he also is the prayer leader in the Subotica synagogue, which is now located in the building occupied by the Jewish community. The grand synagogue in Subotica was deeded to the city years ago, being too large for the needs of the community and too expensive to maintain. Since the collapse of socialist Yugoslavia, there has been a campaign to restore the synagogue, which had fallen into great disrepair.

Sami is an individual who is representative of the Subotica Jewish community, which is recognized as the most religious and traditional of all the remaining Jewish communities in Yugoslavia. This recognition on the part of Jews living elsewhere seems to be supported by data gathered in the two surveys conducted by the Federation of Jewish Communities of Yugoslavia, the first conducted around 1970 (reported by Perić in several articles in the *Jewish Review* and in a chapter in a book (Perić 1980)) and the second in 1985. At this point, I will present some of these data, which are important for distinguishing this Jewish community from the other communities and for situating Sami as a representative of this community.

In the first survey 282 persons (94%) from the Subotica Jewish community responded. Of these 239 (85%) had parents who were both Jewish, 229 of them Ashkenazi. In the case of the twenty-seven of the thirty-two respondents with only one Jewish parent, the father is Jewish. According to Jewish law, 244 (87%) of the respondents are Jews. That is, they are Jews because both parents are Jews or, if only one parent is Jewish, it is the mother. The postwar Yugoslav Jewish community, as pointed out earlier, has a more inclusive membership policy that accepts individuals whose only Jewish parent is the father. Compared to the mean percentage for the entire Yugoslav Jewish sample and to the percentages of other local communities, 87 percent is exceptionally high. Seventy-three percent of the respondents were born in Subotica or some other place in Vojvodina. An additional 23 percent were born "abroad," which may mean that a considerable number were born in Hungary. That 79 percent are Hungarian speakers seems to support this. Seventy-seven percent of respondents fifteen and older indicated that they observe Jewish holidays and customs, while 70 percent (113 females, 78 males) reported that they attend synagogue. Most of these are older members of the community. Also, these high percentages do not reflect regular observance or attendance. An individual may attend only the Rosh Hashanah and/or Yom Kippur services once a year and still report that she or he attends synagogue.

I turn now to the data from the 1985 survey. With regard to religion, 68 percent of the respondents age fifty and older reported that they were religious, 45 percent practicing and 23 percent non-practicing. This combined percentage and the percentage of those who report they practice are much higher than the percentages reported for other local communities. Compared to the 68 percent who consider themselves religious in the Subotica community, 57 percent reported themselves religious in Zagreb, 40 percent in Belgrade, 35 percent in Skopje, and 19 percent in Sarajevo. In comparison to the Subotica community's 45 percent who indicated they were religious and practicing, 17 percent reported themselves as such in Zagreb and Belgrade, 13 percent in Skopje, and only four percent in Sarajevo, which was one of the most traditional communities until the Second World War. In the fifty and older subgroup, 31 percent responded they were atheists. Again, this figure reflecting religious belief is very different from the figures of other communities (Zagreb 43%, Belgrade 60%, Sarajevo 79%) and far below the mean percentage of 55 percent. When the younger age twenty to fifty subgroup is examined, there are higher percentages of declared atheists and lower percentages of religious, but the pattern that differentiates the Subotica community from the other Yugoslav Jewish communities holds. Even in this younger subgroup Subotica Jews tend to be less atheistic in belief, more religious, and more religiously active than other Yugoslav Jews. These statistical figures are strikingly different. They set Subotica apart, which begs for an explanation. Before attempting such an explanation there are additional statistical results that support the claim that the Subotica Jewish community exhibits greater religiosity and traditionalism.

Perhaps this process starts with the fact that 39 percent of the parents in the Subotica sample indicated they want their children to identify themselves as Jews, compared to 25 percent in Belgrade, 24 percent in Zagreb, and 17 percent in Sarajevo. Only in Novi Sad was there a similarly high percentage (38%). But, interestingly, 11 percent of the parents in the Subotica sample responded that they do not want their children to have Jewish identification, which is second only to the Osijek community (12.5%). The percentages for the largest three communities of Belgrade (2.5 percent), Zagreb (4.9 %) and Sarajevo (4.4 %) are all comparatively lower.

Sami is a natural and cultural product of this kind of Jewish community, which is, as the figures suggest, at least a statistically exceptional community in postwar Yugoslavia. As I have noted above, he had two Jewish parents who socialized him to be a Jew. Such generational cultural transmission in the home has been rare in the postwar Yugoslav Jewish population. Sami considers his Jewishness obligatory rather than something he himself has chosen or is in the process of creating. Furthermore, he is an agent of Jewish socialization in his role as a parent in the home and prayer leader in the Subotica synagogue. He received training for this ritual role in Budapest.

Sami does not search for the unique and personal meaning in Jewishness as much as he acknowledges its commonalities and constancy for all Jews. Essentially, for Sami, to be Jewish in Subotica is the same as for Jews anywhere in the world, whether in Israel, in Yugoslavia, or in some other country.

What exactly is this Jewishness? How does he conceive being Jewish? Most broadly, for Sami being Jewish is a way of life. More specifically, being Jewish is relational; it is a relation to the Other rather than to self. Particularly important are the relations within one's own family. For Sami, this means his relation to his wife, who is not Jewish, and to his two sons to whom he is passing on the Jewishness that was transmitted to him by his parents. Second, it is also the non-Jewish Other's relation to the Jew that defines Jewishness as it is felt, perceived, and manifested by Jews in any particular historical context. He refers to the surrounding population, particularly the host group, as potentially influencing Jewish life for the good or the bad. Once important, but not nearly as significant during the postwar, was the class position of the Jews vis-a-vis the surrounding population. The Ashkenazi Jews in this region north of the Sava and Danube Rivers belonged to the middle and upper classes, were literate and educated, and exhibited a [high] culture. The surrounding population envied them for their material well-being, perceiving them as the rich stratum of society. This contributed to antisemitism, according to Sami. Today, the class factor in the interethnic perceptions and relations is much weaker because of the class leveling that occurred in socialist Yugoslavia. In Yugoslavia, the influence of the surrounding population also meant religion, for the larger ethnic populations were divided and differentiated by religion. In Subotica, the Hungarian Catholics were and are the majority group. Sami also uses folk classifications to classify the surrounding population's relation to the Jews:

> It is not by original idea, but a Jewish proverb says: "Beware of the people (or nation) who don't drink milk." You can analyze [who is and is not antisemitic using this proverb]: the Danes drink milk—they aren't antisemites; the Germans drink beer—they're antisemites; Ukrainians drink vodka—they're antisemites; Romanians drink milk—they're not antisemites. Bulgarians drink milk—they're not antisemites; Serbs drink milk—they're not antisemites; Croats drink wine—they're antisemites; Hungarians drink rakija—they're antisemites. So it is. And it really is like this. It is so in Yugoslavia in various centers. It is like this today.

To be a Jew means to declare oneself a Jew, making it public, showing it, as Fortes (1983) wrote. Sami said that he knows of only two Jews in Subotica who do not want to declare themselves as

Jews, that is, they do not want to be members of the community. Nevertheless, they are Jews, he says. For him, however, Jewishness is not the private half of a dualistic self, but rather it is a part of the public self. In this way he appears to want to avoid any dualism within himself, which happens to be the state of being of many Jews in Yugoslavia, especially of those of his and younger generations. They are the products of divided pasts and have learned to exist in a divided state. Some actively pursue ways to bring a unity into their lives, to eliminate the divisions that create tensions for them, with variable degrees of success. For Sami, it appears that his Jewishness occupies both his private and his public self. But it also goes beyond the self. It is both backward looking toward his parents, grandparents, and ancestors who all trace their descent to Abraham, the founding ancestor, and forward looking toward his own two sons.

Sami feels and accepts his moral obligation to be a Jew and to live as a Jew because it is his duty to his ancestors who gave him the gift of life. The large oil paintings that hang on the wall in the large dining room of some of Sami's ancestors make their presence felt. They are more than just visual representations in the eye and mind of Sami. They are the representation of beings to whom he is obligated. Moreover, the ancestors are not just those who go back two generations, or even the two hundred years in Subotica, but back three thousand years. "I think I would behave immorally if I were to throw away these customs."

There are temporal, behavioral, and affective dimensions to his Jewishness. It is important to celebrate all of the Jewish holidays, including in the home. He does not say they are important. Rather, he says, celebrating all the holidays is necessary for his children and for him. It is necessary "to feel the spirit of the holiday."

> Among Jews time does not flow continuously. . . . That means that certain days of the year are distinguished from the other days. It's like this. At the creation of religion . . . my distant ancestors . . . arrived at this knowledge, but they determined the days and got the feeling that time is not the same for every day. Thus when the earth reaches a certain constellatory moment, then that day is here—time stops. Thus, it is not the same but it stops, and then something happens—a break, let's say, the New Year. Understand? So the New Year, it is different; the air is different, the smell of the air is different, everything is different. . . . You don't

> have this among the Muslims. Among the Muslims time flows homogeneously. . . . This year [Ramadan] will be in June, next year it will be September. So there is not that periodic repetition. I don't know [whether] nature influences me. I know that the Jewish calendar influences me. . . . I see on the calendar that it is Hanukkah today. I have a different feeling than I have on a usual day.

For Sami, the holiday cycle includes the weekly Sabbath celebration. He is the *predmolitelj* in the Subotica synagogue, where a service is held every Saturday. In the other two synagogues that have weekly services, in Belgrade and Zagreb, the weekly service is the Friday evening service.

Sami believes there are levels of Jewishness. One is at the higher levels when Jewishness permeates every day of one's life. It becomes part of conscious thought and "only then are you a Jew." Second, it is at this level that one has the ability to and does pass on Jewishness to one's children.

In summary, for Sami being Jewish means "a way of life" that was passed on to him by his parents. "This is how I learned to do it and I couldn't leave it." Choice does not play a part. Rather he believes he is morally obligated to continue a Jewish existence, both to his ancestors who extend back far beyond the family's two hundred-year sojourn in Subotica and to his two sons who he expects will continue the line. Culture overwhelms nature. He is fully aware of this when he states, "I don't know [whether] nature influences me. I know that the Jewish calendar influences me." In social terms, it means his relation to others, starting with those in his own family. Being Jewish entails avoiding any conceptual dualism within the self. Acting out one's Jewishness, showing it, in Fortes' (1983) terms, helps to do this.

Preserving Fragments of the Past: Guardians of Tradition

Šemaja Avramović: Cantor

Šemaja Avramović was in his eighties, but he looked much younger than his years. He told me that he owned three birth certificates, each with a different birthdate. He did not believe that age is important. Health is more important, he says. When people ask, "Šemaja, how old are you?" *Koliko vam godina?* Literally translated, "How many years do you have?" he responded by looking into his shirt pocket and saying, "None." He recited:

> Nemojte mi govorite o smrti. (Don't talk to me about death.)
> Nemojte mi govorite o starosti. (Don't talk to me about old age.)
> Nemojte me govorite o bolesti. (Don't talk to me about sickness.)
> Samo napred. (Only about going forward.)
> Barukh Hashem, Hvala Bogu. (Blessed be He. Thank God.)

Šemaja Avramović, the son of mother Šolci and father Josif, both Sephardi Jews, was born in Dorcól, the Jewish quarter of Belgrade. Thus, like Bencion Pinto, he was a "child of Dorcól." When I and another of my informants interviewed Šemaja Avramović in his and his third wife's Belgrade apartment, he gave me a copy of a typed autobiographical account of his life that he wanted to have published in the Federation's *Jewish Review*. A part of his case that I present here is directly based on this document, his own written story. In this three-and-one-half page abbreviated version of his past, it seems that Šemaja Avramović selected to include those elements (experiences, roles, awards) that have had and continue to have personal significance. One of these elements is his recollection of the festive Purim holiday celebrations that created such gaiety in the *Jevrejska mala*, the Jewish quarter of Dorcól. In the postwar years when such neighborhood and family celebrations were only nostalgic memories for the older Jews and not even stored in the memories of the younger Jews who had never lived in a Jewish neighborhood or experienced a Jewish holiday celebration in the family, Šemaja Avramović strove to infuse fragments of the *mala* Purim that he remembered into the organized community's Purim party. In the postwar the Purim celebration had to be created and staged as a party within the closed social sphere of the community.

> I was a member of the Cultural Section for many years. With my organizational help we organized Purim parties, *Mezas di Purim*, which included a dinner. There was also a humorous and entertaining program in which our eminent actors and singers participated on a voluntary basis. They received a token gift. The music was also good. . . . A lottery was organized with rich prizes, which were donated

> by members of our community. I donated several expensive textile articles, which I obtained from my friends, and some tortes as well. As a symbol of the holiday Purim, I also organized the wearing of masks, which created amusement. The Women's Section of the community made a great contribution. It organized the *bife*, serving sweet and salty pastries, including *Roskas Kindl*, a symbol of Purim. The Israeli ambassador came to the party. [This occurred before Yugoslavia severed diplomatic relations with Israel in 1967.] I welcomed him as well as the other guests. Everyone was very enthusiastic about the party, so that some stayed until three o'clock in the morning.

For the relatively few "children of Dorcól" that survived the war and remain alive today, Dorcól is more than a nostalgic memory of a once vibrant Jewish neighborhood. Dorcól, on one level, symbolizes the death of Belgrade Jewry. Its significance even today is manifested by the great commemoration held there in October 1990 and by the plans to turn *Jevrejska ulica* (Jewish Street), whose Jews are no more, into a cultural-memorial district. In the Belgrade community elections of 1989, which I happened to attend, the man who eventually won the election made this one of the key points of his campaign platform. Šemaja, however, did not live to see Dorcól returned, at least in a memorial sense, to the Jews of Belgrade. Until the October 1990 commemoration there was no memorial marker commemorating the Jewish victims of fascism to be found in Dorcól. Only some of the street names remained to give testimony of a Jewish past, but there were no more Jews on Jewish Street.

When the war broke out in Yugoslavia, Šemaja Avramović considered staying with his wife, son, and daughter in Belgrade. In May 1941, the month after the air bombing of Belgrade, the Germans held him as a hostage for two days. Had any German soldiers been killed during that period, he would have been killed. None was killed, and he was released. The Germans had taken away his shop, as they did to all the Jews. Šemaja and his wife decided then to flee Belgrade to the Serbian peasant countryside, but to be able to travel outside of Belgrade they had to pay a "contribution," in a rather large sum, to obtain the necessary travel papers from the Germans. Šemaja Avramović succeeded to procure such papers for all four family members. They ended up in the Serbian village of Jugovac, where they remained until the liberation, except for the son who was mistakenly shot by the Partisans on August 24, 1944.

From reading his story, it is clear that Šemaja Avramović's ritual activities in the postwar years are highly significant to him. He devotes most of the space describing them. Starting in 1948, at the request of the Jewish community of Belgrade, Šemaja Avramović began to lead the Friday evening service in the synagogue, as a cantor. He fulfilled the same function for all of the high holidays. In addition, he conducted funeral services in Belgrade and other cities.

> During the time of our High Holidays, Rosh Ashana and Yom Kippur, I sang spiritual, synagogal religious songs (choir melodies) with the accompaniment of the accordion, so that those who attended were very pleased. These and other religious activities I carried out for many years, without any kind of honorarium, because it was voluntary on my part. For my service that I carried out for many years I was awarded the diploma *Keren Kajemet* and my name was written into the *Zlatnu Knjigu* (Golden Book). The diploma was presented by the president of the community, Mr. Stevan Levi, in the presence of about 100 people, during the holiday of Erev Pesah in the hall of the community.

Šemaja Avramović also describes his activities as president of the Religious Section, as president of the Cemetery Committee, and as a member of the Cultural Section of the Belgrade community.

> For many years I was the president of the Religious Section. During that period I strove to beautify the temple, inside and outside, so that it would be more beautiful and becoming. . . . A new cloth covering was bought for the altar. . . . We could have done more but there was no money. I was the president of the Cultural Committee. The entire building [chapel] in the cemetery was whitewashed. . . . The entire cemetery wall was repaired. . . . I was a member of the Cultural Section for many years, and with my involvement the Purim. . . . The Israeli ambassador came to the party. I welcomed him and other guests. Everyone was very pleased with the party, so much so that people stayed until three o'clock in the morning. I was one of the founders of

the Braća Baruh choirs. . . . Today I help support the choir financially.

The following account illustrates that Šemaja Avramović's conceptions about who and what is a rabbi were fragmented, despite his having served for many years as a ritual practitioner. What knowledge he did have came from his father and from his observations of synagogue ritual before the war. He admitted his lack of formal training and his limitations, though he was a proud man. My inclusion of the following text is not meant to disparage Šemaja Avramović or anyone else. After all, since 1948 he performed multiple ritual roles in a city without a practicing rabbi or cantor. He performed these roles because he was asked, because the community desperately needed such practitioners, and, I believe, because he enjoyed the roles. The current rabbi, who carries the title, Rabbi of Yugoslavia, had served as a *hazzan* (prayer leader, cantor) before the war, and only began serving again in the early 1970s after his retirement from government service. After the current rabbi's reentry into Jewish life, Šemaja continued to serve when and where needed, particularly in Sarajevo during the High Holidays after 1968, the year Sarajevo Rabbi Menahem Romano died. In particular, the immediate discussion refers to the actual ritual status of the Rabbi of Yugoslavia and Semaja's disagreements and conflict with him. There is some disagreement concerning whether or not he can be called a rabbi. In an interview with two men from Sarajevo, one told me he was a rabbi, while the other said he could not be because he was a member of the Communist Party.

[Will you lead Kol Nidrei this year?]

Šemaja: No, this year I will be like every *yachid*. I cooperated with [X], this *pop*. I call him a *pop* (clergy, priest).

[Why?]

Šemaja: Because he has no qualifications, not even for a *haham*. And for a rabbi? He completed theological school, as Jaša Romano tells me. [X] was born in Sarajevo. He completed theological school, nothing more. Besides that, they gave him the title of rabbi here for political reasons. Otherwise, the knowledge a rabbi must have—Do you know what it means to be a rabbi? First, there must be the step

> that leads to a *haham* [hakham]. Do you know what a *haham* is?
>
> [What?]
>
> Šemaja: I will explain what a *haham* is. [A haham] is between a rabbi and a *pop*.
>
> Šemaja's wife: Yes, but I heard that he received it in Budapest.
>
> Šemaja: No. He didn't receive it for a rabbi.
>
> Marko: He got it from Gaon, from London.
>
> Šemaja: He got it (laughs) from London, and from here to become a rabbi. But the knowledge for a rabbi—
>
> [What must I know to be a rabbi?]
>
> Šemaja: To be a rabbi, you first must have theological seminary [university level or higher than high school]. Second, wait, not for a rabbi, but rather to first be a *pop* [you must have] theological seminary. And after you have completed theological seminary and have become a *pop*, after becoming a *pop*, you must be in Israel. They observe how he reads. Those are the *hahami*. They know theology. They are old people, rabbis; they are *hahami*. They are the ones with the beards. When the *pop* reads the *hahami* follow to see if he makes a mistake. The place where they say *barukh* he says *berukh*. They control his reading. These are the *hahami*. If he gets to be a rabbi . . . a *haham* and then a *rabiner* (rabbi). Those are the steps. From a rabbi he goes further, to a high rabbi.

Where one might question whether or not he is a cantor, Šemaja Avramović says, [The rabbi] "can say that I am a cantor. I do not have the qualifications for a cantor. Am I a cantor? I do not have the qualifications. . . . But I gave myself the title because I sing the songs of a cantor. And thus I am a cantor."

The average size of the weekly synagogue congregation in Belgrade was about twenty-three people during my fieldwork. Of these twenty-three, five were not Jewish. For certain holidays this number doubled. Only for Erev Rosh Hashanah and for Erev Yom Kippur, when *Kol Nidrei* was sung, did Belgrade's Jews fill the synagogue to capacity. Tiny congregations do not necessarily preclude the appearance of conflict. That was the case between Šemaja and the current rabbi.

There was a meeting of the Religious Section in the Belgrade community. Šemaja Avramović happened to walk into the meeting. The rabbi, "that *pop,*" as Šemaja refers to him, was there, along with about six other persons. They asked Šemaja to join the meeting. It was the day before Sukkot. They asked Šemaja, "Do you want to be the Hozan-Hatan?" Šemaja answered that he did. When the meeting was over he approached the rabbi, "Listen [X], this evening [for Erev Sukkot] I will make [the temple] more beautiful by singing songs for Sukkot." The rabbi replied, "No, it can't be." Šemaja: "What can't be?" Rabbi: "No, it can't be." Šemaja then asked the others in the Religious Section: "I ask you, what is bothering him about my singing tonight in order to beautify the temple. . . ? Why doesn't he allow me?" One of the men answered, "You shouldn't be surprised. He is a *Bosanac*" (he is a Bosnian). I personally heard this label used by one of the Ashkenazi regulars in referring to the synagogue regulars who migrated to Belgrade from Bosnia after the war. When the label is used in this manner outside of Bosnia, it is a stereotypical pejorative. Here it is also used to mark an outsider.

Šemaja Avramović described for me his "home synagogue" where he performed the rituals *po starinski*, the "old way":

> I don't go to the temple. I only go for Rosh Hashanah and Yom Kippur, and when someone requests that I come for a *pomen*. I hold prayer every Friday evening, on the eve of Shabbat, here in my apartment. See, here are the candles, *kapa*, tallit, shofar, 12 books for different holidays. All Jewish. [He sings Kol Nidrei.] I'm a bass, but I can also sing tenor. Sometimes I smoke but when I have to sing I don't smoke for a month beforehand. Then my voice is like a bell. On Erev Rosh Hashanah I go to the temple, but on the day of Rosh Hashanah I am in the house. . . . [You celebrate alone?] Yes, alone. [Šemaja Avramovic's wife]: I help. [Šemaja Avramović]: She helps, assists. In all of the places where a response is required, she responds. Every Friday evening. My wife lights the candles. One time when I was in Israel, when they gave me the *počast* (honor) of leading the prayers, I was going to light the candles, but a man is not permitted to light the candles there. Only the women light the candles there, not the men. And I see how the

> women there light the candles, . . . [Jewish education continued, even for 86-year-old Šemaja Avramović.] My wife performs this way in the house for many years. "Barukh atai Adonai. . . ." We light the candles precisely when they should be lighted, when there is Minhah. Do you know what a Minhah is? It means before the main prayer there comes the Minhah, and afterwards comes Arvit. For Minhah the candles must be lighted on time. Arvit can be read even after eight at night. That is not important. We do it every Friday, here, in the evening. But for Pesah, in the evening, we have guests, and I hold the entire prayer, Haggadah, which lasts for more than [unclear] minutes. The Haggadah. That is history, one history. But I have a lot of Psalms that are translated. Unfortunately, I'm not a professional, as I said before. What I know I know from my father and from [unclear]. But I don't know how to translate what it means, I don't know. I only read and know how to read.

I asked Šemaja Avramović if other people come to his home synagogue. He identified several people who come or once came. "His father and mother come [referring to the individual who accompanied me to the apartment], and M and his wife. B came with his wife. Now J comes here. He has no one anywhere. I call him since he is alone."

Preserving Fragments of the Past: Narrating Jewishness

In postwar Yugoslavia, where Jews have been distinguished less by what they do and more by what they say, "talking Jewish" has taken on added significance as a means of signalling and preserving Jewish identity. "Talking Jewish" can take various forms, and these are dealt with throughout this chapter. Storytelling is a form by which the memory of culture is carried, preserved, and transmitted by an individual to one or more persons. In postwar Yugoslavia, where behavioral patterns and material objects of Jewish culture are absent altogether or highly eroded and fragmented, language is the carrier of the memory of an integrated, vibrant culture (Schaeffer 1968:57). In some cases the language forms or word symbols become the focus, for what they once stood for is absent or eroded. Here I examine how one individual preserved fragments from the past by narrating these fragments to her listeners. This form goes beyond mere casual conversation and internal private reflection (Turner 1978:xii). It does not involve philosophical musing about identity, nor is it particularly introspective. Rather, it is about real people, real relationships, real events, and the joys, sorrows, loyalties, and prejudices of these people. It is the stuff of real life mixed together with the larger-than-life legends of the ancestors who have lived on through oral transmissions and the preservation and display of material objects. My informant, Katarina Adanja, described to me fragments from Jewish life when it was thick and tasteful, when it could be seen and heard, smelled and tasted.

Katarina Adanja: "There are so many stories"

Katarina Adanja was born and grew up in Hungarian-speaking Subotica where the Ashkenazi Jews were divided between the Orthodox and the Neologue (Reformed) branches of Judaism. Her Neologue family was highly acculturated. Her father was completely non-religious, while her mother tried to preserve some customs in the home, such as fasting on Yom Kippur and performing the *kapara* rite of sacrifice. Her father "found [the rite] very comic, . . . very unusual." Katarina's mother also lighted candles in the house, and for Rosh Hashanah, the New Year, she gave the children "a piece of bread and honey to make the coming New Year as good and sweet. . . . That evening we had a nice supper. Oh, my father was always for eating. And, there were nice dishes on the table. But [father] was not for the religious part." It was a neighbor, who was religious but not Orthodox, who provided Katarina with the opportunity to observe many features of Jewish tradition. She would go to this neighbor's home to see how Rosh Hashanah, Yom Kippur, and Pesah were celebrated. At her mother's urging, she participated in a neighbor's Seder.

By descent, Katarina was one-quarter Sephardi and three-quarters Ashkenazi. Her parents were Hungarian Jews who felt strongly, even absolutely, she said, Hungarian. In the home, the family spoke both Hungarian and German. The family was economically well-off. The father owned a business which employed more than one hundred workers in season. The family lived a very cosmopolitan life. According to Katarina it was not a typical southeast European Jewish family. She attended school in Switzerland and Vienna. As with virtually all other Jewish family units in Yugoslavia, her family fell victim to fascism. Her mother and sister died in the Auschwitz concentration camp in Poland. Her father was taken to Belgen Belsen but managed to survive. Katarina was also taken to a camp. She and her husband gave their oldest daughter Mira, who became a well-known television journalist, to non-Jews in order to save her life during the war. It was Mira who informed me that her mother had died.

When Katarina married her husband whose family had lived in Serbian Belgrade for several centuries, she had to cross a cultural boundary into the Sephardi local tradition in Belgrade. Ethnocentrism existed among Sephardi and Ashkenazi Jews. Quite strong earlier in the century, it can still be heard on occasion today in the comments of individuals, even among the youth. Whatever her immediate feelings were at those moments in the past, Katarina Adanja retained and incorporated them into the family tales that she is so adept at narrating. There was little she could say when hearing her father-in-law describe her native Hungarian as "that fox language of yours." It was when she married, and she remembers that she started to cry.

> Father-in-law: "If I should have grandchildren from you, they must not know that fox language [Hungarian] of yours."
>
> Katarina: "Papa, my parents don't speak Serbian."
>
> Father-in-law: "They have enough time to learn."

Her husband later explained to her: "You must understand my father. He was with the [Serbian] troops near Šabac. He was among those who took down the Serbs who had been hanged from the trees [by] the Hungarians. He can't forget it." Also, the Jews of Belgrade considered themselves "Serbs of the Mosaic faith." Another example involved an exchange with her mother-in-law, who asked her, "Look, Katarina, you have a Christian name—Katarina. Are you Jewish?" Katarina answered, "Yes, because in the Neologues we have a normal name. . . . My mother was Olga." To which Katarina's mother-in-law expressed her doubt. "But you told me you keep swine. . . . You are Jews and you had pigs?" One day Katarina came home and saw that her mother-in-law had a piece of ham on her plate. She was eating ham. Katarina was surprised and said, "Mama, excuse me, but you were so shocked that we have our own ham [pigs]. . . . " Her mother-in-law replied, "Yes, of course, but you see, I don't put it [directly] on my dish." She had placed a piece of paper between the ham and the dish.

It is difficult to say how much Katarina as storyteller reconstructed the events of her narration. The significance is that Katarina's memories and reconstructions in the form of stories, and especially her stylistic narration of these stories, comprised an integral part of her Jewishness that she selected to display. At different times, she would say: "There are so many, many stories," "We have three kinds of stories in the family [see below]," "There are many legends in my family," "My husband told me how he decided to be a doctor," "There is a nice little story," "I had a very interesting aunt," "There is another little story about," and she could go on and on, drawing deep from the well of her memory.

Katarina talked about her family's ties to aristocracy in her stories, or, as she called them, the family legends. The setting and style of her presentation, together with the material objects that she displayed, were important components that lent credence to the stories themselves. They are not just stories that stand by themselves, but are intimately linked to the narrator herself and to the material culture that she managed to preserve and display. To step into her apartment was to step into what appeared to be a fragment of the aristocratic past that she described—paintings, porcelain, and old documents preserved from the family's past. And then there was Katarina herself. Even her kin from Australia were astonished by her style of impression management. They perceived her to be a wealthy woman and asked her how she managed to live the way she did. Her reply to them was that "it is a big Yugoslav secret," further adding to the mystique of the setting she has constructed and of the person herself.

Katarina's storytelling ability flowed from the memory of her rich cultural past in prewar Yugoslavia, colored by the diversity of the country and the Jews themselves, which she experienced firsthand moving from an acculturated Ashkenazi milieu in the midst of a Hungarian-speaking population to the Sephardi milieu of Serbian Belgrade. She also retold the stories once told to her by other family members. Narrating the stories was not a chore for her. She exuded pleasure from narrating them. To me, it seems a perfect fit that she was by profession an art historian, which enabled her to interweave the artistic and the historical into her presentation. Besides the content of what was being presented, the representations were important. The setting, the objects displayed, and the narrator herself were all very important components of the presentation of the narratives.

> There are many legends in my family. You see these crowns and perhaps you are asking, "We are a Jewish family and we have crowns?"
>
> The first story. . . . Many years ago, during the Thirty Year War one of my ancestors was a "home Jew" [court Jew] of one of the dukes—Wallerstein. He lived a great life, spent a lot of money, but sometimes he had some financial trouble. So then he asked his "home Jew" to solve his problems. Many times he did. Once he told the duke, "Your Highness, there is no more money. . . ." So he took out all the gold from the money box and he added his own gold. He made a little circumcision on all the gold pieces, and then he made other pieces from it. The duke could then pay back his debt. Duke Wallerstein then wrote to Emperor Rudolph of Germany to say that he has the best "home Jew" in the world. He is so intelligent, so devoted, and he would like to get a fine noble name for his "home Jew.". . . And so they got the name Bashevi. . . . So they got that noble title. It wasn't very fair play to cut all of those gold pieces. In the family we all laughed so hard.
>
> The second story is from my mother's side. My mother was Horvat. There was a very big family in Hungary. . . .
>
> The third story. . . .

Katarina could continue narrating on and on, from one story to the next.

Lending credence to the family legends were the various material objects that were in the room and which she wove into the stories. Among them was the large portrait of Moric Fišer, who had been the house doctor of the Banus of Croatia. The latter had asked the court of Vienna to bestow a noble title upon the physician. Also there were the royal blue dishes displayed prominently in the same room. She directed my attention to them as she told the Moric Fišer story. She walked to a chest and took out a heavy album. She showed me, "Even Count Bijašević signed it." In 1861. Here is Count Ladislav Bijašević. And here, here is my father," thereby establishing the generational link between the ancestors' aristocratic past and her own father and herself.

In addition to the "family legends," there are stories about family members, particularly about her Sephardi affines in Belgrade.

When she married her husband she married into an old Belgrade Sephardi family.

> My husband's family came directly to Belgrade from the Pyrennian Peninsula after the Inquisition in the sixteenth century. Straight to Belgrade. There are no data or recollections of whether they stopped anywhere on the way. They told me that they came directly to Belgrade. All the Adanjas were born here. Only my grandson D was born in Pancevo, where my daughter-in-law is from. She wanted to go to her own doctor. Of course, I told her you must go, [not] to risk [the child] for the sake of family tradition. I said, "Go where you feel better."

Katarina Adanja's mother-in-law is a central figure in her stories and also a primary source of the some of the stories that Katarina now narrates.

> The wedding of my mother-in-law took place before World War One. It was held on 7th of July Street [then and now again called Kralja Petra], where the Jewish community is today. Before the war it was the main business street in Belgrade. Then you could immediately recognize who is Serbian, who is Jewish, and who is Turkish. The Serbian women had their beautiful *libade*; it was part of their clothes. You can see them in the Museum of Urban and Applied Art. So the Serbian woman had her *libade*, her gold pieces around her neck. The Jewish woman had the same *libade*, but she also had a little cap, and the jewelry pieces were on the cap. The Serbs had a beautiful *grana* (branch) made from gold and diamonds. Mine is now the property of my eldest daughter. The Serbian women wore it here, on the *libade*, and the Jewish women covered [it?]. So you always knew whom you were meeting.
>
> My mother-in-law was a very sweet person. I can't understand those who say they don't like their mother-in-law, because I loved her very much. She had a fantastic sense of humor. She was always very good to me. I liked when she told me all those things [about the past] because they were, for me, so fantastic, very oriental and very exotic, if I may say so. She couldn't marry my father-in-law because

> he had one unmarried sister. While a man had an unmarried sister, he couldn't marry because he had to take care of every member of his family. That was between the Jews, and the Turks. I think it was pure Turkish influence. I think so. It's an oriental influence. She was 25 years old, a very [old] age to be single at that time. She waited seven years for my father-in-law, like in the Bible [referring to Jacob and Rachel].
>
> The only place where women and men could meet in old Belgrade before World War One was in the singing house. There the young girls went with their mothers and aunts. You absolutely needed a chaperon. And there my mother-in-law and father-in-law met. The Jewish Singing Association (*Jevrejsko Pevačko Društvo*) prepared a very famous Czech opera. It was the first performance of this opera in Belgrade. There they were always together. My mother-in-law sang very well. My father-in-law couldn't sing. He was lifting something, like in the circus.

Before World War I among the Sephardim, the bride was subjected to a test of her virginity. If the bride was found to not be a virgin, the husband had grounds for divorcing her (Pinto 1987). But one generation later the custom had been discontinued. Katarina considered the custom barbaric. She narrated the following account transmitted to her by her mother-in-law:

> It was in the house. There was a big supper. Then the young couple had to retire to their room. There was no wedding trip. All the women went home. Only the men stayed there. And the mother-in-law, she stayed in front of the door [to the married couple's room]. Awful. Then when the "big thing" happened, you know, then K, my father-in-law, came out with the linen sheets. The mother-in-law took the sheet and she showed it. Then there was *vruća rakija*, hot cooked rakija—brandy [with] water [and] sugar, sometimes. It was served hot. I don't know, perhaps it was a tradition. It was served, and it was over. My mother-in-law told me [this account] as we were escaping from Belgrade to Arandjelovac during the bombardment. She was telling me the [wedding story]. "Mama, how could they touch into

your private life, into your intimacy, in such a harsh way?" I asked her. "But why dear? I was a virgin, no problem." She didn't feel how awful it is. She was a virgin, everything was ok. It was a habit. And I looked at her like this. She was not offended at that. She was expecting that, and she was even proud somehow that everything went so well. She told me that that was a custom here. Perhaps even in non-Jewish circles. I was deeply shocked when she told me. I felt like it was a terrible assault, an offense to my mother-in-law.

Katarina's Jewishness is past-oriented in other ways. She regularly lighted a candle in memory of her mother. "It is only a memory for my mother because she was the only person who was really religious." But she also lighted a candle because God answered a prayer when she asked for a grandchild for one of her two daughters. This ritual act, which was a very private act, evoked memories and provided a link to the past. Katarina immediately associated this with yet another story from the past.

Preserving Fragments of the Past: Sephardi Folklore

Samuel Elazar: Preserving the Fragments of Sevdah

Samuel Elazar was born in 1902 in Gračanica, a town in northern Bosnia. His large traditional Sephardi family, unlike most of the other Jewish families, subsisted on their small plot of land and a few head of cattle. This early tie to the land contributed to the development of Samuel Elazar's lifelong interest in herbs and their curing properties. Before the war he also lived in Tuzla, just to the southeast of his birthplace, and later in Sarajevo, where he spent most of his postwar life as an *apotekar* (pharmacist).

Samuel Elazar was a very lucid eighty-four years old when I interviewed him, still very active and intellectually productive in his second career as a folklorist and writer, which was his way of individuating his Jewishness at a time when he thought the Jews of Yugoslavia and the entire Jewish diaspora, except for the Orthodox Jews, were becoming "neither wine nor water," that is, ceasing to be Jews but not yet being something else. Part of Samuel Elazar's daily routine was to sit down at his table and write. He presented me with a photograph of himself doing just that. "I started collecting

Sephardi songs when I began to go deaf and started to write after I developed cataracts," he joked, though his words reflected the physical reality of his elderly years.

The room in which we sat together on three different occasions revealed its share of clues to Samuel Elazar's ethnic identity—the Federation of Jewish Communities of Yugoslavia periodical, *Jewish Review*, miniature scrolls or *megile* [megillah] (*svici*, Serbo-Croatian), a small statue of Michelangelo's Moses, and a metal cover for a Hebrew prayerbook that belonged to his father's father. Another manifestation of his Jewish ancestors, besides his grandfather's prayerbook cover, was the picture hanging on the wall of his mother's maternal grandmother, who had been a midwife and folk healer.

As I write about Samuel Elazar, Sarajevo and all of Bosnia-Hercegovina is in the chaos of war and "ethnic cleansing," which for the Jews are words that denote the horror of the Holocaust. Since Samuel Elazar died in 1989, he departed this world with his perceptions of interethnic harmony in Sarajevo and Yugoslavia intact. As I was asking him about interethnic relations, he wanted to make sure that I walked away convinced that good relations existed among the ethnic groups in Sarajevo. Back in 1986 Samuel told me in that he preferred the one-party system because it eliminated animosities and hatreds among the ethnic groups, at least compared to how they were before the Second World War. He pointed to the relationships in his own apartment building and neighborhood, located outside the center of old Sarajevo, near the Miljačka River that bisects the city. "Members of various ethnic groups sit and drink coffee together. *Komšija* (neighbors) come to check on my sick wife. It's not like in the United States. Isn't that so?" "A good neighbor is better than a brother." Samuel Elazar was affirming what is called *komšiluk*, the "cult of good neighborliness" that had developed in Bosnia in centuries past and was still alive, given all of the interethnic intermingling (Burg 1983). In her ethnography of a mixed Muslim-Croat village in central Bosnia, Tone Bringa (1995) demonstrates that, although ties between neighbors were strongest among members of the same ethnic group, *komšiluk* operated interethnically as well. It was not solely an urban phenomenon. While he talks Samuel Elazar enjoys interjecting various sayings and such proverbs, which he selects perhaps from the body of Sephardi wisdom he has gathered in the last twenty-five years. Here he shares with me a saying about neighbors:

> A man wanted to sell his house. Another man came to the house, wanting to purchase it. He asks the owner, "How much is it?" "One thousand five hundred gold Napoleon dollars." He says, "That's a lot. The owner says, "It isn't much. I value the house at 500 Napoleon dollars, and the neighbor at 1,000 Napoleon dollars. I have good neighbors, and that is worth more than a brother.

We spoke about what it meant to be a Jew in Yugoslavia in the present (in 1986). Samuel Elazar held a very pessimistic view of Jewish life in the present, and his forecast for the future was even more grim. The Second World War had wiped out almost completely the Sarajevo Jewish population. Before the war over 8,000 Jews lived in Sarajevo, more than 7,000 of them Sephardi, to whose branch Samuel Elazar belonged (Pinto 1987). Samuel Elazar's figures seem somewhat exaggerated, as he told me there were 12,000 Jews in Sarajevo before the war. When I spoke with Samuel Elazar only about 1,000 Jews who were registered with the community lived in the city. The demographic bleakness indicated by this tiny remnant, together with other factors, had turned Samuel Elazar into a pessimist about a Jewish future in Sarajevo and everywhere else in the Diaspora. He explained the reasons for his pessimism in the following way:

> With regard to the anthropological, national, racial, and religious status of the Jews—not only in Sarajevo, Bosnia, and Yugoslavia but in all of Europe, and in America—I am a great skeptic. . . . This comes from the following reasons. Until the Second World War the Jewish family, most of the time, was completely characterized by monolithic marriages, which means Jewish marriages, not mixed marriages. Second, there were more children and more descendants (*potomstva*). Third, there was greater maintenance of national and religious tradition in the family. The Jewish family fell apart. Those who remained alive . . . had to abandon the traditional way of life. Many were left without families after the war, husbands without wives and wives without husbands. . . . But unfortunately there was no opportunity to always have Jewish marriages, but rather there were mixed marriages. There are not enough numbers in those marriages; there are not enough children. And there

> is neither any national nor religious tradition. . . . I am a pessimist. I compare this to a wine cellar with 1,000 liters of wine, where every day you would release half a liter of wine and pour in half a liter of water. After three or five years will you still have wine in that bottle? It will be neither water nor wine. . . . Among us here in Sarajevo, about half of the marriages are mixed [actually closer to three-quarters]. The children of these mixed marriages are not Jews. They come to the community (*općina*). [If the mother is Jewish?] But even the mother born after the war no longer saw Jewish tradition, neither religious nor national, in the parental home. She did not see it. . . . I have two daughters and a son. The oldest daughter did not marry. The younger daughter was married; she is divorced. And the son is married. He has two daughters. It is a mixed marriage. I can no longer give my son some kind of Jewish upbringing. I cannot. [You did not want to or you could not?] It could not be done. After the war it could not be done.

Samuel Elazar's statements support what I describe as the pattern of truncation. Having been raised in a traditional family, Samuel Elazar believed that he was unable to socialize his own children to be Jews in the present social circumstances. How then can those Jewish parents who never even saw any Jewish tradition in their homes transmit it to their children? Samuel Elazar believes they cannot. Thus, the individual Jew, particularly the Jew who has never observed Jewish tradition in the parental home, is especially vulnerable to losing all contact with his or her Jewishness. If the individual desires to actively pursue Jewishness, it is most likely that he or she must engage in that pursuit outside the family.

According to Samuel Elazar that pursuit will not be productive in the realm of what remains of organized ritual life. "My parents were traditional. I, too, was traditional. But now we do not have the possibility to hold Sabbath prayer in the temple on Friday evening and on Saturday. We do not have those 10 persons, nor do we have a *molitelj* (prayer leader) who will pray the prayer." If the family is removed as an agent and setting of Jewish ritual and socialization, and much of organized ritual life is either highly eroded or altogether absent, where does that leave the individual? Samuel Elazar answers that he remains a member of the Jewish community of Sarajevo and he is a Jew by nationality.

Although Samuel Elazar, like most of his generation, did not confront his Jewishness in the same manner as do his children's and grandchildren's generations, in the postwar period it, too, was fragmented. His prewar past may not have been a bricolage, but his Jewish present certainly was. He acknowledged his own inability to adopt the parental role of an active agent of Jewish socialization. Once a traditional Jew, he lost the possibility of being a member of a prayer quorum. Sarajevo was once the most traditional of Jewish communities. It had the country's only Jewish theological school, which produced several esteemed rabbis and cantors. The irony is that while the individuals who were once students in that institution were practicing around the world no rabbis remained in Sarajevo after 1968. None remained in all of Bosnia.

What was Samuel Elazar's solution to these dilemmas? By engaging in a daily routine of gathering material and writing about the past, he partially solved the dilemmas. It connected him to his Jewish past. For example, for twenty-five years he gathered Sephardi songs called *romanses*. This task did not involve just gathering the words. It also entailed hearing the sounds, the melodies of these songs, which probably evoked various memories and emotions connected with growing up in Bosnia.

> The love songs, in which the love of a boy for a girl, and vice versa, is proclaimed, are filled with the feeling of what we call sevdah. This passionate feeling, unparalleled in its depth of sentiment, is expressed in its most delicate and noble form in the ballads we call, with full right, 'our (i.e. Jewish) sevdahlinkas'. . . It is certain that we can speak of no Western inspiration in these Sephardic melodies. . . The Sephardi songs, which were almost always sung individually, reproduce Arab, Turkish, and other Oriental musical motifs. When we hear them, we cannot stop our souls from being transported to a romantic Oriental sphere, to quietude and a placidity of being, to this unique, delicious languor we call sevdah (Elazar 1987, quoted in Schwartz 1990:156).

Bosnian Jewish women were the preservers and guardians, the gatekeepers, of this longstanding tradition, which was carried from Spain and Portugal and then exposed to local cultures from which it borrowed various elements, such as particular words and melodies.

Again, it was mostly women who were able to assist Samuel Elazar most in his efforts to rescue these songs, ballads (*sevdahlinkas*), dances, etc. from obscurity and oblivion. An oral archive was established. "Our good aunts and grandmothers jealously preserved and guarded, with almost a religious devotion the entire cultural heritage brought from Spain" (Elazar 1987, quoted in Schwartz 1990:156).

The culmination of Samuel Elazar's more than a quarter century of research is his production of a cultural product, *El Romancero Judeo-Español*, a two-volume work published in the Ladino and Serbo-Croatian languages. In this 400-page collection, Samuel Elazar provides examples from various genres, such as old Spanish ballads, Sephardi poems in Spanish, Ladino poems written in Bosnia, Shabbos and festive verses, songs of pilgrims to Eretz Israel, etc. (Schwartz 1990:156–157). Thus, the process, with all of the knowledge and feelings associated with it, went beyond Samuel Elazar alone. The private symbols of his Jewishness, which to him included the very act of sitting down at his table and writing daily, in the post-Jewish world of Sarajevo, a city in which perhaps as many as fifteen percent of the inhabitants were at one time Jewish, are now a part of the public domain, available to the current and to subsequent generations of Jews and others who show an interest in the Sephardim of Bosnia. To Samuel Elazar, producing such a text may have been a mitzvah, but it also brought honor (*kavod* (Hebrew), *čast* (Serbo-Croatian)) in the form of recognition. He was proud of his cultural and scientific production and the recognition it brought him from members of different nationalities who knew him as a Jew and respected him as a man.

Identity Imposed, Imagined, and Sought

An unknown number of individuals of the postwar generations had their Jewishness imposed on them. For them, becoming Jewish was not a process of cultural transmission starting at birth. The fact of Jewishness by descent was withheld from these individuals until a point in time when this information was suddenly imposed upon them without prior ethnic socialization or preparation of any kind. Below I present two cases of imposition. The circumstances of each of the two cases, however, are different, as are the responses the individuals took and their outcomes. What they share is a quest for their Jewishness, although the timing of a physical quest was delayed in the čase of Zlata Klajn.

Zlata Klajn. "They told me the terrible stories from the past"

Zlata Klajn is a woman in her thirties, a Jew by patrilineal descent. She does not participate in the program of the organized Jewish community. She may occasionally attend a Shabbat service in the synagogue, a sphere that is largely avoided by most of the secular-oriented community leaders and by most of the membership, except for Rosh Hashanah (New Year) and Yom Kippur (Day of Atonement). I first met Zlata in the courtyard of the Belgrade synagogue after a Friday evening Shabbat service. Although estranged from the community, as I explain below, she does maintain at least a few personal ties with other Jews, such as with my key informant who arranged my interview with Zlata, and with the rabbi.

I include Zlata Klajn among my cases because she is both modal and unique for the immediate postwar generation, what is referred to in the community as the middle generation (roughly thirties through fifties). She is modal insofar as she is a self-ascribed Jew without a Jewish past. She has no memory of a Jewish life that once was because she never experienced such a life. But being a Jew without a Jewish past (and present) extends for Zlata and others like her to the ascending generation, for the parents of individuals born in the postwar years either transmitted only certain fragments of their personal histories or they kept silent altogether about the past, especially the Jewish past (see author Ana Šomlo's description of the father-daughter relationship in *Glasovi Dijaspore*). For many older Jews, part of this Jewish past is too painful to talk about, even (especially?) with their children (because they want to protect them?) and close friends. Some also reject all or much of the traditional past of their personal histories, choosing instead to retain the memory of their involvement in the progressive tradition of interwar Yugoslavia. In much of this pattern of no explicit Jewish socialization, Zlata Klajn is not atypical. The manner in which she was told she is Jewish, the content of that oral transmission, and her conscious and unconscious responses since, however, are very much a part of her own story.

The first fragments to consider are associated with Zlata Klajn's descent and earliest childhood years. She is the product of an ethnically mixed marriage. Her father is an Ashkenazi Jew whose upper class ancestors lived in the former Habsburg lands, while her mother is patrilineally Serbian and matrilineally Italian. Born in Belgrade where she lived with her parents until she was four years old, she then spent time (at least one continuous year) in Naples, Italy with her maternal grandmother and mother's half-sister. Her grandmother took Zlata with her to a Catholic church in Naples, where she had her baptized. "I forgot Serbian. I was a Catholic child. I loved to go to the church," Zlata told me. Fearing Zlata's father, who was a Communist, her grandmother told her that the ritual activities she was seeing in the church were theater. It was her father's political orientation and not his Jewishness that her grandmother feared. Later, Zlata came to conclude that her father was not serious about anything, not Communism, not religion, and not anti-religion, which, as I point out below, was a non-committal view of the world that came to characterize Zlata's own political, though not religious, view of the world. She says that she was a Catholic until she was eleven, and then she rejected religion altogether. The fact that she was religious as a child distinguishes her from the Yugoslav Jews of her generation. But the religion was not the Judaic religion of her patrilineal line.

Like so many others of her generation, Zlata was not born into a Jewish family in which any semblance of Jewish life, traditional or secular, was practiced or even casually discussed. Beginning with her mixed descent, subsequently having lived in different countries under the supervision of different caretaker kin, and having been exposed to different cultural influences and opposing ideologies (her father's and Yugoslavia's communism and her grandmother's Catholicism), Zlata was an individual divided among several things before she reached her adolescence. For some time before she reached the age of twelve, she did not know that she was patrilineally Jewish, which, which when she did find out, added yet another dividing element into her life. As another of my informants of mixed ethnic descent told me when I asked him what it means to be Jewish in Yugoslavia, he answered that being a Jew in Yugoslavia means to learn how to be divided among several things. Parents are among the agents who have taught their children to live a double life.

Eventually her parents decided to disclose to Zlata that she was Jewish. This encounter is etched in her memory. She remembers that it was in the kitchen that they suddenly revealed the past of the patrilineal side of the family.

> The first time my parents told me I was Jewish [was] in the kitchen. They told me in a terrible way. They couldn't calm me all night. They told me I am Jewish. They told me the terrible stories from the past. They told me to be Jewish is that.

What embedded this experience in her consciousness was the timing, setting, and content of this ethnic imposition, which became equated with Jewishness itself. For Zlata Klajn, Jewishness became the tragic and the terrible, all in relation to the patrilineal Jewish past. Her parents imposed on her only this imbalanced view of Jewishness, tied to the divided and tragic lives of individual family members. She was emotionally traumatized by the stories.

To impress on the reader how traumatizing the content might have been to a child, particularly one with a fertile imagination, I will share a few details. First, divisions characterized the family, which included strained and broken relationships that involved her own father. Ideological differences separated family members. Some were Communists, others anti-Communists. The Holocaust expanded the family to all Jews. But the horror went beyond the collective suffering and the individual Holocaust victims in the family. There had been a spy in the family, and also a Nazi collaborator. One family member had betrayed another family member to the Nazis, resulting in the latter's death. This individual survived the war, but soon after committed suicide because he could not bear to live and work in a Communist system. This act of collaboration and betrayal is only one of very few documented cases involving Yugoslav Jews (Levntal 1957). The sudden imposition of this past into Zlata's consciousness was her very first orally transmitted and imaginatively received violent encounter with what it means to be Jewish.

Once Zlata was told she was Jewish and had encountered the patrilineal past, how did she respond? How did this shape her own conception of what it means to be Jewish? At first, as a child, she began to use her fertile imagination to construct her own stories about what had happened. Thus, the early formation of her Jewishness was an internal process of integration. As she says below, she wanted to reject what had been imposed on her and instead reconstruct what had happened in her mind. She began a process of "imaginative intimacy" (Alter 1971:30) with her Jewish past. As far as her Jewishness was concerned, the stories and her imagination were all that she had. She could not use memory, perceptions, or existing conceptions of what a Jew was.

> They told me I'm Jewish. They told me the terrible stories from the past. they told me to be Jewish is that. So I lied a lot; [I] invented stories about my uncle in my imagination. Such a terrible impression these stories made on me. Nothing about Biblical stories, only the terrible stories were told to me.

As noted above, Zlata Klajn abandoned religion when she was twelve years old. In her teenage years she began to adopt a leftist orientation (an anarchist, in her terms), a tradition in her father's family from before the Second World War. She was too young to be directly involved in the 1968 student movement, but she worked for the demonstrators in the student newspaper. Although by then she had rejected her Catholicism, she recognizes now that the first impulse of the leftists is religious, because they, too, want to save. They have, according to Zlata, a messianic complex.

Zlata visited Israel twice. She first visited in 1973 during the Yom Kippur War. She stayed in a kibbutz. "It was nothing," she told me. This first trip either did not significantly transform her, or else she did not want to talk about it. In 1983 she returned. Israel was at war in Lebanon. At the time she was working as a journalist for one of the news magazines published in Belgrade. Because of the war in Lebanon and the Yugoslav state's support of the Arabs, the Jews in Yugoslavia were feeling some of the heat. Yugoslavs took to the streets of Belgrade to demonstrate against Israel. Another journalist working at the magazine told her, "Look what [you people (Jews)] are doing. We thought you are good. [You are] so terrible." This incident motivated her to return to Israel. She took an unpaid leave, supported by money from her father. She told me that she felt terrible because she was a leftist at the time. Being very emotional she took everything to heart. The 1983 visit became a four-month quest throughout Israel. "I searched with everyone—political people, leftists, rightists; [I] went to language school, [I] went to the *Jerusalem Post* to search. [I was] just searching, trying to understand." I still am not sure what it is she was trying to understand. Did she want to find a more "acceptable" line of continuity to replace the patrilineal line associated with the horrible and the tragic? Did she want to reject this past? But she certainly talked openly about it. It remains a part of her. Perhaps she did not seek to eliminate, but rather to overcome those elements known to exist but that are not completely understood (Fischer 1986:174).

One of her Israeli friends, an Orthodox Jew, suggested that she talk to an internationally recognized high-level Israeli official. The official agreed to an interview. At the outset of the interview the official began saying negative things about Yugoslavia and Communism. This touched her pride, she says, and they began to argue. "It was great. The official, the official's confidant, and my Orthodox Jewish friend, [all] against me." The official then told her that she could write whatever she wanted, but nothing against Jews. After returning to Yugoslavia and her magazine, Zlata had difficulty publishing the article at first. In her words, it was like "publishing the Devil." She had written a lengthy article on the Israeli official that the editor refused to print in its entirety. The editor cut out the beginning of the interview [which made it appear] that Zlata's accusation was actually a response to what the official had said previously. Because of the editing the reader got the opposite impression of what Zlata had intended. It appeared that Zlata Klajn had been arrogant with the official.

> I was aware [of the situation in Israel and Lebanon] and I wanted to publish [the article] because here in Yugoslavia they don't know what is going on. I was aware but I wanted to save the Jews. I was a leftist. It was very good because Yugoslav generals called me [and said], "Who are you to talk to such a brilliant general in this say?" It was a mess here. I wanted this. After that my name can't be published in any Jewish publication in Yugoslavia. Someone in the Jewish community wanted to beat me. [People] called, wrote me. I didn't cry then, but I did after. They didn't understand. There are different ways to tell facts. [It was] the only way to get my work published. The official political approach to the problem was: Jews—bad, Palestinians—good. I was able to at least explain to people what was going on. What I wrote about Israel, this approach you can find in the Israeli papers (at that time, in leftist anarchist organizations, the extreme left, the facts were thrown into that approach). It was a publishing trick. I didn't have a political opinion. Maybe sometimes I believe in something more, but the day after I'll doubt it. So I can be the perfect rightist, also.

The whole experience, Zlata recalls, was terrible for her. She had never been an active member of the Jewish community, but from that point on she felt estranged from the community, ostracized forever, she feels. "After that I never mixed in politics, never again," she noted. Given the tiny size of the community, but one with a sizable number of intellectuals, there is the danger that the process of private symbolization and the products of one's quests will become a part of the public domain, open to public scrutiny and (re)interpretation, which can have unpredictable ramifications as in Zlata's case. Her quest did not result in greater inclusion into the community, but in even greater exclusion, leaving her more alienated than ever from the organized community.

The transmission of ethnic identity may involve the process of transference whereby "cultural data fragments" (e.g., stories, relationships, customs) are . . . imposed without adequately explaining them . . . at critical points in the [individual's] development" (Fischer 1986:173). I have described above how Zlata Klajn passed through part of her childhood not knowing she was Jewish, and then how suddenly she was told in a manner that frightened her. The stories depicting the broken relationships, the betrayal, and the deaths were imposed upon her without balancing them with anything positive or with an integrated sense of what it means to be Jewish. How could the father have transmitted such an integrated Jewishness when he himself was first a dedicated Communist and, later, someone who, according to Zlata had no firm beliefs or objects of commitment? Any analysis of transference would require far more data than I have at this time.

Thus far in her life Zlata Klajn has had her Jewishness defined for her through imposition. She has imagined it. She has pursued it in her mind and in a physical four-month quest throughout Israel. Where was she positioned when I spoke with her? She had reclaimed her religious worldview in the form of a religious synthesis, though she did not want to discuss this aspect of her life. She said that a return to Israel "only has religious significance for me now."

Jaša: A Quest for True Identity and Ritual Incorporation

When I interviewed Jaša he was about twenty-two years of age. At the time he was one of several young university students who regularly attended the Belgrade synagogue. He lived the first seventeen years of his life unaware that his Serbian parents had adopted him. When they revealed this fact when he was seventeen, Jaša was, in his words, shocked. He had never doubted that the father and mother who had raised him were also his biological parents. Jaša began to judge his parents harshly for withholding this information, and thereafter he initiated his quest by searching for something within himself. He became detached from who and what he thought he was. Disorder came into his life. He calls it a horrible year in his life.

When they revealed that they had adopted him, Jaša's parents did not tell him that he was a Jew. Rather, they only disclosed his mother's name, and from her name he drew the conclusion of his own Jewish descent. Jaša then met the Serbian woman who had adopted his biological mother, and she proceeded to tell him the story of his mother's tragic past. He discovered that she was a Sephardi Jew from Macedonia whose parents had died as victims of fascism in a concentration camp. After the war this Serbian woman and Jaša's biological mother, whom she protected during the war and later adopted, settled in Belgrade. Later, sometime after Jaša was born, his biological mother moved to Italy where she later died.

Armed with this new knowledge of his Jewish descent, Jaša was not suddenly overwhelmed with an onslaught of Jewish feelings. Nevertheless he actively pursued his Jewishness by trying to contact other Jews in Belgrade. At first he went to the local community, the Jevrejska *opština*. He recalls how nervous he was. Upon arrival at the door of the community, he did not want to go inside. He did not feel very Jewish. In fact, at that time he was not sure who he was. When the fact of his adoption was imposed upon him, he felt stripped of his identity. His initial contact with the community did not encourage him to return. He felt unaccepted by the people he met there. People in the community were skeptical of his beliefs and story. In mulling over his reception, he reasoned that perhaps they had concluded he was only trying to gain access to some of the potential advantages enjoyed by young community members, such as receiving a stipend for studying abroad.

Because of his disappointing initial experience in the local community, Jaša decided to try the synagogue next. He began to attend the weekly Friday evening service regularly. Religion always had interested him. He expressed its attraction:

> I strongly believed in the Egyptian religion. I was obsessed with the Egyptians. Since I was 10 years old I was prepared

> to study Egypt. I read Freud afterward and was amazed. Now I think it just wasn't a coincidence. I think I was very closed. Pharaoh who let the Jews go—I was obsessed with that period—he changed everything. Then years later I discovered the Jewish [religion]. [The Jews] took the pattern from that monotheistic religion. I like Far Eastern religions—Buddhism [and the religions of] China, Japan. I even started to learn Japanese. . . . I was also interested in Zen Buddhism. It helps in manual things, for example, in playing the harp. [It is] a practical religion. . . . Then I started with Judaism. Actually, I don't think [it's so much that I] believe as I'm interested in customs . . . art for art's sake, because I like the past so much.

His first visit to the synagogue frightened him because all of the rites were unfamiliar to him. Jaša believes that as he learned more and more his fear subsided. It was a progressive process. Yet he stopped attending the Friday night Shabbat service in the synagogue after attending for about one year. The synagogue regulars were not counting him in the prayer quorum, and so he felt disappointed and unaccepted. Because he had not been born into the community, gaining acceptance was important to him. The synagogue would provide the ultimate acceptance, for ritual incorporation into the Belgrade minyan (prayer quorum) would erase any doubts of his Jewishness.

Jaša performed a significant act when he was nineteen years old. He changed his name legally. Both first and last name are now distinctly Jewish. People asked him why he did it. At that time, he recalls, he answered many questions about the Jewish people, Jewish life, and Jewish customs. He also notes that he heard many prejudicial remarks, but he lost no friends because of the name change.

A significant transformation occurred in Jaša when he traveled to Rome to meet his sister for the first time. It was there in Rome, with his sister, that he began to feel like a Jew. He felt free to talk to his sister about his ambivalent feelings, about his anger and how he blamed their mother for giving him up for adoption. His sister helped him to confront his feelings and to accept what had happened. She explained that it all happened because of bad circumstances in life. "Those things always happen to other people, and in the movies, so you don't believe they are true," Jaša told me.

It seems that Jaša returned to Yugoslavia with a new resolve to actively pursue his Jewishness. His trip to Rome had facilitated an internal process of coalescing the cognitive and affective domains of his Jewishness. He had left Yugoslavia with the knowledge of his Jewish descent; he returned with both the knowledge intact and the new feeling of being Jewish, strengthened by his newly established kinship tie with his Jewish sister and her family.

Sometime after his return to Yugoslavia Jaša renewed his contact with the Belgrade synagogue, which happened to coincide with the period of my fieldwork. It was near the end of my stay during the High Holidays of Rosh Hashanah and Yom Kippur that Jaša felt that he was finally accepted by the synagogue regulars. We talked at that time and he expressed to me the following:

> Yesterday [October 5, Yom Kippur] I read the blessing over the Torah, so officially, religiously, I'm finally accepted. I think they count me in the minyan now. . . . They were counting people in the minyan and they weren't counting me. I was disappointed. I wanted to become a part of the ritual. I stopped after going for one year [because] they didn't accept [me] as a member. Things have changed since I think I'm accepted. Now I have a relationship with God. I had a relationship with God [before], but I couldn't do certain things. I wasn't allowed to open the ark and read the blessing, and this means something when you are religious—to do some things. [It was] also a religion when I progressed in my own way, but I wanted to do it in the traditional way, to feel that. . . . Judaism, Buddhism, etc. gives you just the form to approach God. [Jaša also participated by carrying a Torah scroll around the synagogue.]

Jaša shared the following views on being Jewish in Yugoslavia:

> For example, you have a very old tree. It's getting old. Its leaves are falling, its branches are falling. That is also happening to the Jewish religion here. I don't know what will be left in 100 years. Even now most of the people are in mixed marriages. If a marriage is mixed—the man is a Jew and the woman isn't, and he is not religious and they have children—these children must choose whether or not to be religious. I think they will choose not to be.

> People here are losing Jewish blood. What is remaining is feeling only. Feeling is not enough. Religion is the only connection. That is the real feeling for me. For me, the real feeling of being Jewish is coming from yourself. It's also coming from other people. They tell you. Believing—[it's] not only religion; it's also customs [and] the history of your nation.
>
> If we all [two other young men who started attending] stay here in Yugoslavia, maybe we can change something in the synagogue (because we don't have any intention of working in the [secular] community). We don't have interest except in ritual and synagogue life. Unless I go abroad. Then I may become a part of another community. I felt beautiful in Amsterdam in the Sephardi synagogue. . . . I think we [three] will become [better] friends. We have some things in common. I don't know Mirko's ambitions. I think both of them want to become a rabbi. I don't. I think I would have to change my [whole] life [and] devote myself only to that. I don't think it's reasonable at the moment. I just want to know as much as possible about customs, religion. I want to be a member [in the synagogue]. I don't have the ambition to be a leader. We don't have the opportunity to get that knowledge here. It may be useful to go to Israel for a year to learn their language, customs, everything.

Spiritual Quest, Conversion, and Ritual Incorporation

I know of only one case of conversion to Judaism in postwar Yugoslavia, though there may be several. Two other young men I met over the course of my fieldwork expressed a desire to undergo the conversion rite, one a Serb and the other a Montenegrin, but I know of no formal conversions other than the case I describe below. One writer has stated that secular Jews must rely on the cultural capital of Jewish tradition for their identity (Finestein 1977). In cases of conversion the secular Yugoslav Jewish community, as all other Jewish communities, can only use a religious mechanism to transform a non-Jew into a Jew. It has no secular mechanism of inclusion into Jewish peoplehood, though it does permit non-Jews to be members of the local community (opština).

Mirko: The Quest for a Unified Spiritual Field

In presenting the case of Mirko, a convert to Judaism, I explore the possible motivations behind the quest, the personal significances along the way, and the transformations that occurred.

Mirko was born in 1964 in the Dalmatian region by the Adriatic Sea. He was born at a time when Yugoslavia, with the ouster of secret police chief Aleksandar Ranković just a year before, was setting out on a phase of increased liberalization, democratization and decentralization. When I met Mirko in 1985 he was a part of the *omladinska* (youth) generation whose collective experience and memory did not include the horrors of the Second World War (though he indicates below that an individual who has not experienced directly the horrors of the past can still feel them), the Partisan victory, the Yugo-Stalinist period, the initial, enthusiastic years of socialist state-building, or even the student riots of 1968. For this generation, which had yet to confront the realities of unemployment, growing up in the 1970s when the Yugoslav standard of living was relatively high meant a rather comfortable existence for most. Such conditions did not create dilemmas or crises for most of these young people. Mirko is one of the exceptions. Already by his mid-teenage years Mirko's internal tensions were growing in intensity rather than waning. It is precisely these tensions and how he went about trying to assuage or conquer them that ultimately brought Mirko to Judaism. It was the inner struggle with the epistemological and metaphysical dilemmas of life that brought him to the point of traditional Judaic ritual passage and practice. It was not practice that eventually led to belief, though practice may have strengthened belief. For Mirko, thus, his transformation to Jewishness and Judaism was primarily a spiritual and intellectual process of coming to terms with himself and his place in the world rather than a physical one that began with his circumcision in a Belgrade hospital at about twenty-one years of age.

Perhaps the initial source of his tension was the vagueness of his descent. Unsure of his lines of ethnic descent, Mirko claims they are unimportant to him. Indeed, his quest and ultimate conversion was primarily religious, but the fact that he talked about his mixed and uncertain ethnic descent indicates that its ambiguity was far from insignificant in his life.

> I never believed in blood, since my family is rather mixed . . . Turkish blood, Italian blood. . . . That there is Jewish blood, maybe it's accurate, maybe not. I don't know what Jewish blood means. This was the area by the [Adriatic] sea. Peoples mixed together. They weren't rich families; everyone was poor. And everything was all blended together. . . . I can't say, [these were] "my ancestors," when my own mother doesn't know who her grandfather was. . . . Every new generation of my family again mixed with other nationalities,. . . Constantly blood mixed with other blood, and so I grew up without any feeling of national membership.

Although he claims that descent is unimportant to him, what little he did know perhaps contributed to his search. Partly because of names like Jakov (Jacob) in his family, Mirko believes he has Jewish ancestors. However, he cannot prove any Jewish descent. His mother does not know her father's ethnic origin, and his grandfather and father died before he could question them about it. Consequently he just "didn't get to know all these things." According to Mirko, both of his parents were probably atheists. Even in those families in which descent was known, the atheistic beliefs of one or both parents sometimes precluded discussion of Jewish descent.

Mirko says his quest began when he was fifteen years old, after his father died. He began at that time to show an interest in the spiritual world or, as he put it, the "spiritual spirit."[4] First he read Freud's biography and Martin Buber's *I-Thou*. He also read philosophy very early. Others advised him to read Buber in parts, thinking it was too advanced for him, and so this was how he started reading Buber. But while reading Buber he says that he "really saw" that "it was written just for me." In his words, he then "swallowed" the entire book. From reading *I-Thou* he "got an entirely different frame of mind." I see this as the first transformation, or, the beginning of his transformation. On the other hand, since he at first acknowledged no specific ethnic or religious descent or connection, perhaps it was a process of becoming and of transformation.

Buber's *I-Thou* may have changed his entire way of looking at the world and seeing reality, but it was only when his conception of the I-Thou relationship became objectified in the form of a close personal relationship with a well-known Jewish composer of modernistic music that his quest took a leap forward. It was 1980, one year after his father died. He was sixteen. Patterned after Buber's *I-Thou*, the relationship facilitated the next major transformation or phase in the process of becoming. The year they met, Mirko dedicated a poem he had written to the composer. He was so moved that he even thought about writing a composition that year. Such a dyadic tie includes an element of trust. As Giddens writes, "trust can be mobilized by a process of mutual disclosure" (1991:6). Giddens calls such a tie a "pure relationship." In such a relationship "trust can no longer be anchored in criteria outside the pure relationship itself, such as criteria of kinship, social duty, or traditional obligation. . . . The relationship exists solely for whatever rewards that relationship as such can deliver (ibid.)." The relationship continued in full bloom during my stay. It was Mirko who arranged for me to meet his "thou." The two individuals feel that they can disclose the most intimate details of their experiences with each other. This is what happened between Mirko, the younger seeker, and his older thou. As Mirko describes it, his thou little by little began to come out of his conceptual world and began to share his thoughts with Mirko. But he never said, "It's like this; you must think like this." His thou expressed what he had experienced, and that disturbed Mirko. Both found that their experiences were very similar. They shared a feeling for horror, for hurt, for [God? unclear], and for suffering.

Mirko read more than Freud and Buber. Nor did these authors' works set the limits of his quest for transcendent meaning and identity. He explored the religions of the East. He read the works of Dostoevsky, Hesse, and Mann. Mirko spoke about his feelings of being a part of this world, that he was "closer to this world of suffering, . . . Which was abstract and cold, than to a transcendental world or a world that is to come, because he "experienced enough of these great horrors." Following his father's death he no longer had the support his father had given him, and he "had no spiritual contact with [his] mother." He began a friendship with the composer "J". Strengthening their *duhovna veza* (spiritual tie) was their mutual love for and involvement with music. Mirko had completed music secondary school, while "J" was already a well-known composer of modernistic music. Also, both liked the work of Martin Buber. In addition to sharing a love for music, other commonalities strengthened this dyadic tie: a similar level of abstract thinking, similar experiences, feelings for hurt and suffering, belief in a transcendent Creator and the fulfillment of the prophecies of the Hebrew prophets. Both had experienced personal transformations.

In his third year of music school, when he was seventeen years old, something was unclear to Mirko. It was the time when Israel was at war in Lebanon. He said:

> I was constantly asking myself, "What's going on there?" In the Books of Moses there is the verse, "Who blesses you I will bless, and who curses you I will curse." Also, in chapters 36, 37, and 38 in the book of Ezekiel, I see there the return of the nation of Israel to the land. . . . Maybe this is a little funny, but it was one verb that opened my eyes in a dreadful way. To some it comes through music, or through poetry, but to me it came through a verb. It is the verb "to be" (*biti*), from which is derived the name of that book, Buber's *I-Thou*. This I-Thou relationship appeared awesome to me. On the other hand, there is one story by Proust I read that says there was a young man who fell in love with this mysticism and wanted to completely lose himself in it and to remove himself from this world. Then one great teacher came and asked him, "Isn't this your world that you are throwing away? I don't know whether you recognize that this is your world". . . . I later saw that in Hebrew [. . .] means the world that is to come. It doesn't mean a transcendental world but rather the world that is close and this world here. That messianic time will encompass all of creation, the entire earth, all that is created. . . . and, yes, certainly that the Creator is present in history with his people, . . . [O]ne would have to be really blind not to believe in that. These themes were always close to me.

If the existential experience or the inner tensions can be verbally communicated to another person(s), that is, if one enters into a face-to-face relationship and thereby engages in social interaction with at least one other person, then it can be determined whether the experience and/or whatever else one feels within oneself is to remain a part of the distinctive self or is to become a part of the common self. Mirko and "J" were able to communicate their experiences, feelings and conceptions, and they were able to recognize in those what they shared. Thus their aspects of their lives are not entirely distinctive, but neither are they necessarily part of a broader, collective commonality.

Mirko's Terrible Illusion and the Quest for a Unified Spiritual Field

Mirko's quest did not exclude the Serbian Orthodox religion. His family had moved from Dalmatia to Belgrade in 1964. During the early part of my stay, as I recall, he had not yet abandoned entirely his efforts to find or forge some kind of synthesis between Christianity and Judaism. He called it experiencing the Christian and Jewish worlds as one. His significant other, "J", believed in it too for forty years, he told me. "I believed in it for a much shorter time, for three years." Later, as he related to me, he would refer to this effort at unity or synthesis as a terrible illusion (see Meyer 1990 on "tantalizing illusions"). According to Mirko, part of the illusion is that there has never existed any antisemitism in the Serbian Orthodox Church in Serbia. I should interject that these myths of the absence of antisemitism in Serbia and the uninterrupted friendship between Serbs and Jews have been propagated by both Serbs and Jews. Recently, however, both Jews and non-Jews, mostly Croats, have contested the myth (see Albahari interview in *Intervju* (Belgrade), 25 May 1990; Sekelj 1980). . . . I saw that that is antisemitism in the spiritual sense in that theological dimension, and all of this is inherited from Russia. . . .

Formalizing the Tie: Conversion and Circumcision

Ethnic boundaries differentiating Jews from non-Jews have been considerably loosened during the postwar period. The Jewish community permits non-Jewish relatives to be members of the Jewish community. Some even participate actively in communal activities. The position regarding one boundary, however, has remained intransigent. A non-Jew can become a member of the Jewish community, but a non-Jew cannot become a Jew except through religious conversion. For males, that process of passage entails answering questions in what remains of a spiritual court (Bet din) and undergoing the physical rite of circumcision. During my initial research stay, Mirko was one of two males who were circumcised in a Belgrade hospital by a doctor and subsequently became members of the Belgrade Jewish community. When an individual does approach the community about converting, he (I am personally unaware of any female requests) is discouraged from following through with his desire. He is told, among other things, that "it is hard to be a Jew."

> They held a spirtual court for Mirko.
>
> Everything was a surprise for me. We didn't devise a plan. . . . I didn't have time to prepare. . . . There were two rabbis, the president of the Jewish community of Zemun, and the president of the Religious Section. I spoke about the Jewish holidays, Jewish ethics, and whatever they asked me about. They told me that they accept people very reluctantly. All of this was, really, a little funny, I think, because in that moment they treated me like a Gentile. . . . They asked me what name I would like to adopt for use in the synagogue. Jakov (Jacob) pleases me the most, because Jakov became Israel. . . . However, since I already had enough Jakovs in my family, a grandfather Jakov and another relative with that name, I said, "Let it be *Icak* (Isaac)." So when I am called to read the Torah and Haftere, then it is Isaac. . . .

Circumcision of the Spirit and the Heart: Entrance into the Community and the People

When I asked Mirko if he felt any different following the rite of circumcision, he answered:

> Your heart is circumcised. [It is] a circumcision of the heart, a circumcision of the spirit, . . . You are marked with the same ghetto. Not a physical ghetto, but I think there exists a great spiritual ghetto. Not only the Jew feels this spiritual ghetto. Man in general can feel this horrible ghetto today from within his spirit. Almost every man who thinks in this way can be, today, in one moment of his life, can feel isolated here. There is a difference from Judaism, which is completely prepared for the fact that there will be a ghetto. Then it isn't difficult for you to bear your isolation. You know that there are others who also share this fate with you. But if you are separated somewhere, alone, then it is much more difficult for you. . . . What can I tell you? Nothing essentially has changed. I received this brit milah, but that which I wear inside myself is like it was before [the physical rite of circumcision]. Now I know that no one will create problems about any formalities. I think these aren't formalities . . . it's far from that. A religious man never dares to say that these are formalities; otherwise it would be

catastrophic. This is never just a circumcision of the body. Simultaneously it is a circumcision of the spirit and the heart. . . . Secondly, somehow it makes you equal. You enter through this into a community. You become a part of a whole. . . . It means, from that moment, you will also wear the packsaddle that they wear. You don't have to put it on; it's simply given to you to wear. . . . I don't know, it's very complicated. . . . I can't express it. And it is very fresh, and I'm afraid to tinker with it because it is so fresh. I simply rejoice that I wear this saddlepack, and that God gave it to me so I can feel it. . . . [He says the concentration camp, ghetto, and persecution are the three themes that are constantly with him.] When people hear this maybe it appears nihilistic to them, but it isn't. . . . When you experience one funeral, let's say the death of someone close to you, you encounter that death. It's not easy. Imagine 10, 20, 30,000, six million people. . . . The brain can't grasp it. . . . How don't you become a nihilist after this? Really, you naturally wait for man to be a nihilist. But you see from that war, out of those camps came Jews who in faith endured and became much wiser and stronger. They didn't say much, but it left a deep trace upon them. I think that it is terribly present and that it is one essential component in order to understand Judaism. In general one must understand this theme of persecution and that Shekinah, that one part of God that is always with Israel in persecution. . . .

Being a Jew in Yugoslavia

Society did not set the limits of Mirko's quest and search for personal identity or prohibit conversion to Judaism. It did not regulate what transpired within Mirko's self. Interestingly, however, Mirko acknowledges that Yugoslav society does set the limits regarding the practice of religion. "Society is like that and to go against that is to be really out of one's mind." To be religious beyond what society defines as fanatical is to be labeled a fanatic, and to be a fanatic is to be an abnormal person. To be a Jewish fanatic means living like a hasid. "That is already crazy," says Mirko. But it means much less. To wear a *kipa* in public is also to be a fanatic in Yugoslavia. Although the official view of the state, which the organized Jewish community vociferously reiterated, is that individuals are free to practice their religions without hindrance unless it becomes politicized, the view from the individual level is sometimes quite different. Perhaps the discrepancy arises because the community leaders are almost all secular. They do not practice and thus they feel no fear or hesitation. As Mirko told me, "Yugoslavia is still an atheistic country. The demonstration of religious feeling is always with a dose of fear, so that you don't get labeled as "that crazy religious person." You never dare to exaggerate your beliefs (religious faith). You don't dare to allow yourself to exaggerate your feelings, and when you have them, you hold them back. You don't express them publicly. You do so only before the one you know is your good friend. You know that he feels the same way, and that it is your intimate conversation."

Mirko married a young Yugoslav Jewish woman and adopted her family name. The couple went to Israel where Mirko began a five-year rabbinical study program. His intent was to return to Yugoslavia and serve the Jewish community. When I interviewed Mirko in Yugoslavia he, as a student of ethnology, felt like Jacob working off his seven years in order to finally get what he really wanted. Even back then he was seriously considering rabbinical study. When I returned to Yugoslavia three years after my initial fieldwork, Mirko was engaged in rabbinical study in Israel, and, without the extra seven years, he had his "Rachel" with him.

The Writers: Confronting and Writing Oneself into Jewishness

Despite the tiny size of the Jewish population in Yugoslavia, the contribution of Jewish intellectuals to public culture is considerable. The influence of these individuals in public life far outweighs their number or proportion in intellectual society. This is one reason for taking a closer look at how they pursue and display their Jewishness and their comprehensive identity. A second reason for examining this segment of the Yugoslav Jewish population is that its younger members belong to that generation which has been cut off from its Jewish past. Many have only one Jewish parent. Interestingly, it is the father in the case of several prominent writers. These writers have written about the Jewish father in their books. Most of their ancestors in the preceding generation were killed in the Holocaust. This, too, is a prominent theme in their writing, as is death in general. Having been cut off from the kin they might have known, from the sounds, sights, and smells of the Jewish world that was, and being of mixed ethnic descent, these individuals have struggled to find who they are and where they fit in. There is something inside them, they say, that causes some kind of discomfort. For some feel the discomfort more intensely, while others less. They write to bring relief to themselves. Writing is, thus, besides other things, a personal ritual of catharsis. But it can also be seen as something far more than relieving personal discomfort. The pain and discomfort is brought on, in part, because of the ethnic predicament they experience, part of which is learning how to be divided, and how this predicament or dilemma impinges on the self.

What is Jewishness to these writers? How do they pursue that "elusive character" that seems to elude all taxonomic classification (Meyer 1990)? Perhaps it is the very elusiveness of what Jewishness has become in the post-Enlightenment world that has made it so attractive to Jewish writers and academicians. Jews have long been fascinated by the topic of identity, even before it became fashionable in the academy. As I found out firsthand in Yugoslavia, Jews are a reflexive and self-critical population. They play sociologist and psychologist on themselves. Some have mystified the concept of identity even further. Others have sought to demystify it. Freud said that Jewish identity was "hard to grasp in words." Some of my informants concur that Jewishness is something that cannot be put into words. Freud further associated Jewishness with "many dark emotional forces," as "potent," as the "intimacy that comes from the same psychic structure" (Freud, quoted in Meyer 1990:4). Meyer writes that "Freud found Jewish identity present in individual consciousness, but deeply beyond definition" (Meyer 1990:4). The Yugoslav Jewish writer David Albahari (see following narrative) says that being a Jew in Yugoslavia also involves "something which for most of us is inexpressible." Much of the inability to put it into words stems from the absence of a Jewish existence that can be tasted, smelled, and handled. Such a life can only be imagined or observed elsewhere.

Writing is also an odyssey, a quest that can take the individual writer through many spheres and domains, some real and some imaginary. For David Albahari it included experimenting with the fascinations or "tantalizing illusions" of his own '60s generation. He entered, but ultimately did not remain enamored with the domains of rock music, drug culture, religions of the East. It is simultaneously an act of bondage, if one feels he or she must write to gain relief, and of ultimate freedom, especially when the society in which he or she lives is trying to create a certain kind of Yugoslav socialist person. Writing becomes in this context an act of resistance to all totalizing ideologies and systems, for there is no place for the individual in them. It resists existing categories and classifications and shows that boundaries are permeable, imperceptible, even illusionary. This is apparent in the writing of Danilo Kiš (1935–1989), David Albahari (b. 1948), and Filip David (b. 1935). For these writers, writing is foremost an individual and personal act. "I write only for myself," one of these writers has said. Danilo Kiš, the most famous of the Yugoslav Jewish writers, writes in *Homo Poeticus* (1983: 214, quoted in Matvejević 1988: 338), "As far as I personally am concerned, in my prose works I lie shamefully on the psychiatrist's couch, and attempt through words to reach my traumas, the source of my own anxiety." To some of these writers, this odyssey knows no boundaries. They move from reality to illusion, from this world to the other world, and then back again. It is a process of extreme flexibility, one that is less open to those who do not engage, or engage less, in creative thought and action. During the writing phase they engage in private symbolization.

Writing is not a continuous phase. It is an activity that the writer returns to time and time again. He or she must allow him- or herself to withdraw into the mundane world. This mundane world was at one time the Jewish world. One had Jewish parents, Jewish siblings, Jewish uncles and aunts, Jewish cousins. One lived beside other Jews. One shopped in Jewish stores. One knew who she was and where she fit in. Even if one chose to leave the Jewish milieu for a Gentile one, he knew that those familiar sounds, sights, and smells still could be sensed in the *mala*, the old Jewish quarter. Jewish time was continuous time, if not for oneself then for those other Jews in the quarter. But the postwar Jew no longer lives within the stream of continuous Jewish time, nor can she. That option does not exist. To enter the Jewish world that is a part of his or her writing he must create this moment. This moment is a segment of autonomous time. Jewishness becomes a "succession of autonomous moments" (Alter 1971). This applies to most other generations, but particularly in the postwar generation of Yugoslav Jews. "The sad caprice of history has cut us off from our past. Any attempt to pursue this past is probably futile," as one member of the youth generation put it (*Kadima* 38(1977)) These Jews can no longer be the Torah scholars their grandfathers or great-grandfathers were or the revolutionaries their parents were.

The themes of death, suffering, uselessness, despair, and so on are all symbolized in the scenes, characters, and language of their works. It is when these cultural products are shared with others, with the readers, that the private symbols become public symbols (Firth 1973).

The Writer David Albahari: "I write only for myself"

David Albahari was born in the Kosovo town of Peć. After his birth the family moved to a small Serbian town, where they lived for six years before moving to Zemun, located just across the Sava River from Belgrade. David's ancestors were a mobile Sephardi family that wandered around Serbia and Macedonia for about 150 years as traders and artisans. Now in his forties, he lives across the Sava River from Belgrade in Zemun, with his Serbian wife, their two children, and his mother. Zemun had a sizable Jewish community before the war. The community still operates an office, and has its own officers. It also sponsors a commemoration that is held in the Jewish cemetery in Zemun every July. The Jews of Zemun today participate in the Belgrade Jewish community.

David's deceased father, a Sephardi Jew who had been raised in a strong Jewish milieu, was an important influence on his life. The family name that his father passed on to him was one of the most common Sephardi names in Yugoslavia, especially in Bosnia, so that David cannot be mistaken for anything but a Jew. His mother is a Serb by descent, but she converted to Judaism in the 1930s after her marriage to her first husband, an Ashkenazi Jew. David has a sister who also enters his stories. Although David is very active in Jewish communal life and occupies a leadership position, and thus his Jewish network is extensive, most of his close friends are non-Jews. This is true of other Jews who are activists in the community. This can be explained partly by the small number of Jews and partly by one's sphere of work and the voluntary organizations to which one belongs.

To understand David Albahari, it is necessary to recognize the following spheres of his life: personal-private, vocational, communal, public. They are overlapping spheres in terms of actual living, but they nevertheless have certain discrete features. He separates his personal-private sphere even from his writing, which analytically I do not do. This sphere includes his family and the relationships within the family, his fascination with rock music culture and certain aspects of "Eastern" culture and religion (Zen Buddhism), the Jewish mystical tradition, and Israel. The vocational sphere includes not only his writing, but also considerable translation and editorial work. From 1973 to 1988 he wrote seven books, served as the editor on five publications, produced an anthology, and has published in various journals. He has translated the work of Singer, Bellow, Nabokov, Sholem, and Agnon. The years 1982 and 1983 transformed David into a public figure for all of Yugoslavia. His reputation and recognition extend far beyond the borders of the Serbian Republic. In October 1982 he spoke out for Israel during a year in which the Jews of Yugoslavia were placed in an uncomfortable position because of demonstrations against Israel's occupation of Lebanon. In 1983 a book of his short stories, which were sprinkled with Jewish themes and characters, won a prestigious literary award named after Ivo Andrić, the Yugoslav writer who had been awarded the Nobel Prize for literature. David's public persona has grown even more in the transition period. He was one of the twenty-two founding members of the Society for Serbian-Jewish Friendship, though he later withdrew from the Society because it became too politicized (see chapter 6). In 1992 David succeeded Dr. Lavoslav Kadelburg as president of the Federation of the Jewish Communities of Yugoslavia, which now encompasses only the territory of Serbian-controlled Yugoslavia. Before succeeding Dr. Kadelburg, David had been active in the communal sphere for many years.

On Becoming and Being Jewish

David here reveals the fragmented nature of being a Jew in postwar Yugoslavia: "It is not easy to define oneself as a Jew in Yugoslavia because I think that definition of being a Jew should be connected with some kind of roots, something deep down, something that doesn't exist among Yugoslav Jews as I see it. So, somehow being a Jew in Yugoslavia means to learn how to be divided among several things, between your belonging to a community where you were born and between something which for most of us cannot be put into words."

David passed through three phases of becoming Jewish. The first phase involved becoming aware of his descent and of his difference from other children. He describes the following early experience, which I combine from two different accounts, the one he related to me and another printed in *Kadima*, the journal of the Yugoslav Jewish youth:

> I once told a little story, that my first impression of being a Jew was a horrible one. It came to me when I was still

> a little boy in school, when all of us had to go to medical examinations, to be checked. I was circumcised at eight days. I didn't think of myself as someone special. I remember the scene today. There were 20 of us boys in class undressing. We had to take everything off for our medical checkup. Suddenly, I'm standing in the middle with everyone else all around me, dumbfounded. Besides everything else, the checkup required that she—the doctor was a woman—take our little things and examine them. I had a feeling that everybody just held their breath when my turn came, because they expected that I would be diagnosed as being ill. I'm convinced that they were disappointed when they didn't see a reaction by the doctor. From that time on checkups for me were difficult, tiring affairs. I was different. I was simply different from all the other little boys in my class, although this difference for a Yugoslav probably would not denote a Jew but a Moslem, I guess, because there are more Moslems in Yugoslavia than Jews. I also noticed the same thing later in the Army. So as a small boy, from the very beginning, I was somehow afraid of being a Jew, although at that time I spent every summer at the Jewish camp on the Yugoslav coast (date unknown).

Another early experience occurred in school. When he was about eight years old, the students were required to declare their nationality. David said that he was a Jew. The teacher's response was, "Why did you say a Jew? Why didn't you say a Serb?" The teacher did his best to encourage David to declare himself as a Serb. He thinks he wanted to declare himself as a Jew, but at the time he had no special feelings, only the feeling of being different, which in the beginning, as a boy, was very important for him because it made him different from other people. Later, he says, it became a problem because he no longer wanted to be different. But at the time he could not define what a Jew is, despite being taught from his youngest days that he belonged to the Jewish community, went with other Jewish children to the summer camp, and participated in various cultural events in the Jewish community (*Start*, October 1985).

In the second phase David moved from merely feeling different (sense awareness) to realizing that being a Jew is to know and understand one's Jewishness intellectually. This is the epistemological dilemma (knowing) he and other Jews must confront, particularly those of his postwar generation. David said that they know without really knowing that they are Jewish. His manner of intellectual probing was to write stories about what he knew best—his own family.

> As far as I'm concerned, the most important thing was actually an article published in *Kadima* [journal of Yugoslav Jewish youth] 15–20 years ago, before I became involved in editing *Kadima*. The article really made me aware in an intellectual sense. I was always constantly aware of being a Jew, of having a specific Jewish name. You always know, [but] you probably never think of it. That was the first time I became [intellectually] aware of being a Jew. It was in my twenties. . . . I guess trying to understand all those things intellectually made me write all those short stories on Jewish themes, on my family here in Zemun. The article in *Kadima*—maybe it wasn't a special article, but maybe I was ready at that time to think who I am and to solve whatever there was to be solved as far as my Jewish origin is concerned.

Writing Oneself into Jewishness

> My first [short] stories ran away from Jewishness as from a live fire. . . . Born into a mixed family, I accepted the title of "Jew" with unconcealed pride—there I was the only Jew in my class, the only Jew in my fieldball club, etc., etc. . . . Thus, [such were] those childhood years when all that stands out as wonderful and what separates you from rest of the heap. Naturally the transitional years followed, the period of doubting everything, including one's own body, etc. etc. . . . Now, at 24, when I am a university student who has satisfied all my course requirements in the School of Philosophy, things appear completely differently. My "Jewish" stories and poems, as I call them, appeared on the pages of *Savremenika*, *Književne novine*, *Mladosti*, *Student*, *Letopija Matice Srpske*, etc. But, now is the period when I am afraid that I will not have enough time to read everything, and maybe that is why I still never have time "to respond to invitations." But believe me, and perhaps this is more important, I am always there in my heart. I guess trying to understand all those things intellectually made

> me write all those short stories on Jewish themes, on my family here in Zemun.

David told me, "I try not to live with my identity as a writer. I think it is a very personal thing." Writing is the quest time, when the writer, as Danilo Kiš phrased it, puts himself on the psychiatrist's couch. To remain in quest time, which, when put together, constitutes a series of autonomous moments (Alter 1971), is to remain anti-structural, transitional. Who can remain constantly anti-structural? For David, writing relieves whatever hurt that he feels. He acknowledges that the moments of writing are outside the normal flow of time:

> I think a writer exists only in moments of creation, when the writer creates. I believe an artist is an artist only when he creates. So I try to avoid, in my private life, [spending] time with other writers, unless they are my very good friends with whom I don't discuss literature and writing . . . . Of course we discuss literature, but we meet not because of literature. I try to spend my time with people who are just normal people, with whom I can really show the identity I believe is my most important identity, the regular one, the normal one, where I see myself as a person influenced by the '60s, rock music, the hippy generation, and all those things. Actually, when I think of it, and when I'm talking about my friends, I do not have a lot of Jewish friends, in a way. I mean, I have a lot of Jewish friends, but I don't have Jewish friends among the friends I see almost everyday. Almost all of them are Serbs, Serbs who are inclined towards Jews and Judaism and who constantly are curious about Jewish things, constantly asking me questions connected with Judaism and Israel.

The third phase was becoming active. After he wrote the article in the Jewish youth journal *Kadima*, he "really became active in the Jewish community in Belgrade, in the Savez [Federation] as we call it, first in *Kadima* and then in all those commissions—student, cultural, summer holidays, etc. . . . I guess that the young Jew in Yugoslavia must become involved in, first of all, cultural projects, to develop his own Jewishness. Without it he or she will probably, as far as I can see it, there is only one way to have problems either in school or among people being accused of being a Jew: knowing you are a Jew without really knowing. Becoming active in all those different fields of work meant building up my own Jewishness. That was one side of it."

Blocks to Jewish Identity in Yugoslavia

First, the question of Israel affects many Yugoslav Jews, including David. He notes that he "broke with that problem" several years ago when he gave an interview in a leading weekly magazine. "I openly declared myself for Israel. . . . I just wanted to say that out loud [publicly]. But I guess for quite a number of [Jews in Yugoslavia in 1986] it still creates a problem that doesn't give them a real chance to define themselves as Jews."

The Writer Filip David: Living "in the shadow of ideological and national symbols"

During my last round of fieldwork I had the opportunity to interview the Jewish writer Filip David. I had seen David in the Jewish community on a previous visit but had never met him. At that time, in the mid-eighties, David was working in television drama and pursuing his writing. It seemed to be a quiet life, nothing like what it would become with the fall of Yugoslavia. By the time I saw him in 1994, Filip David was a recognizable figure in the political arena because of his opposition to the Serbian government of Slobodan Milošević and to all the forms of ethnic nationalism that contributed to Yugoslavia's collapse. The words that follow are mostly his.

> I'm fighting here [in Serbia, in the former Yugoslavia] not as a Jew but as a human being. I think the problem [rise of antisemitism] is with the rise of nationalism at the beginning of the destruction of Yugoslavia . . . . In the last 50 years, during Tito's regime, it was a dictatorship of course, but on the surface we had no antisemitism, no ethnic hate. It was forbidden by law. Of course, this state, this government during Tito's time, was a member of the Non-Aligned Movement. They didn't look at Israel. But the Jews here could live quite well. . . . In the last two years we have had a real wave of antisemitism. It is not against Jews here, but it's against Jews generally. But because it's against Jews generally, the Jews who live here must sense it in some way. It began with the printing of *The Protocols of the*

Elders of Zion. There were a lot of commentaries about it. You had articles everywhere. You had programs produced on government TV, official TV. They produced some stereotypes [of Jews]. One of the main stereotypes here is that there exists some international conspiracy against Yugoslavia, against Serbia. . . . They declared, in two or three programs of official TV, they declared openly, that Jews are the enemies of Serbs.

In the beginning of the war you had a philosemitic temperature. They said that we [Serbs and Jews] had the same destiny. From the first moment I must say that I was against the Society for Serbian-Jewish Frienship [see following chapter] because, as I said to some of my friends who were members of the Society, that kind of society must produce some kind of antisemitism, because the aim was not real friendship. I always had said that I was part of Serbian culture. What does it mean to be the friend of myself? The aim of this Society was to explain to the Jews, especially to the Jews in America, the Serbian aims in this war. They really believed that there exists a [central command post] and that the Jews are at the top of it. In [this] way they believed in the existence of *The Protocols of the Elders of Zion*. They had political aims. Many of the members of that Society became very nationalistic. You have that strange thing, you have Jews [in the Society] who are Serbian nationalists. But it is also not something that is all that strange because you have that syndrome, that pathology, Jewish self-hatred. You had it through history, in Europe especially. In this area you had it before the Second World War and the First World War. You had this syndrome. It means that Jews are afraid that they cannot assimilate enough into society. They try to show that they are more Serbian than the other Serbs, or more German than the other Germans. And we have that syndrome here. [How about those who don't seem to have this self-hatred?] They are not conscious of it. They think that they are fighting for the Serbian [unclear]. In the Jewish community, here [in Belgrade], the Jews are divided. I think on the one side are the younger generation which really knows what has happened and the older generation which doesn't want to know.

At the beginning they declared, and it was officially recognized here, that this is a continuation of the Second World War, that the antifascists are here in Serbia and that the others [in the former Yugoslavia] are fascist. Of course, it was only the official explanation of what happened. It was, we had that situation, we had the Yugoslav Army. The Yugoslav Army had to be a Yugoslav army. Very quickly it disintegrated into three Serbian armies. The Serbian army from here, from Krajina, and from the Serb Republic in Bosnia. It was destroyed completely, but from it came three armies. Serb communists lost their ideological, Marxistic, base. They were transformed in one night into Serb nationalists. It was a disaster. It was the real beginning of the war. Serbs were the most populous people in the past Yugoslavia. It depended on Serbia, whether we would have war or democracy. There were [mass] gatherings after the fall of communism in Europe. There was a rise of populism with the mass gatherings. At those meetings they didn't ask for democracy and human rights. They asked for arms to go to Kosovo, to arrest somebody in Kosovo, to go to Zagreb, to go to Ljubljana. In other parts of Yugoslavia everybody was afraid of the rising of this popular nationalism in Serbia. That is the reason why Serbia is so responsible. I am not saying you didn't have nationalism everywhere. But if you could have established democracy in Serbia, the war would have been impossible. You would have a democracy everywhere. You could then have found some solution, a confederation or federation, or maybe new states, separated in peace.

Yes, the *Memorandum* [written grievances of Serbian intellectuals, members of the Academy of Sciences and Arts] is in some way the beginning. Mr. Milošević, a communist, was against the *Memorandum*. But when he lost that communist base, he declared the *Memorandum* as his aim, [and as] a national aim—that all Serbs must live in one state. We see now it is impossible to divide Bosnia into two or three parts because everything is so mixed everywhere. Here in Serbia, in central Serbia, live inhabitants, 33 percent of whom are not ethnic Serbs. What if Croatia declared the same, and Albanians declared the same? You don't have enough territories for everybody. The main thing is that

Serbia is multicultural, completely. Thirty-three percent are not ethnic Serbs. [I am referring to] Serbia without Bosnia, without Krajina. It is impossible to create ethnically clean states. If you try to insist on that idea, it means one endless war, one war for generations. It's crazy, completely. But when you are in war, when you are obsessed with nationalism, then you lose your reason, your mind. I know very clever people whom I liked very much before this war, but now they are completely dumb persons with whom you can't speak about anything. They believe in the international conspiracy against Serbia. They believe in the new order in the world which is against, of course, Serbia. They believe that Croatians are genocidal, that Muslims are suicidal [peoples]. All these stereotypes are created by official TV, by government. Everybody has to think in the frame of these stereotypes. If not, you are an enemy of the people.

[Why were your intellectual friends from the community here so quick to change, so quick to convert?] Some of them really believed that Milošević's ideas are in the interest of Serbia. But very soon after, after six months or three or four months, they saw that Milošević is only a pragmatist. A pragmatist and a demogogue. He has not one idea which he will [continue to hold fast]. And some of our nationalists now are very ashamed. One of them, Mr. Z. Stojković, wrote in the newspaper some months ago that he is very ashamed. But at the beginning he supported Mr. Milošević. Now he is very ashamed. . . .

[We have] "three kinds of nationalism.The first one is populist, which is manipulated by the government; the second one is the nationalism of past communists, . . . and the third one is the extra-right, fascistic nationalism. . . . In this area nationalism always had a bad connotation. Maybe in France or England it means nothing bad, but here it always had a bad connotation because here we live in such a country in which you have a lot of cultures, languages, religions. If this balance would be [disturbed], it would be a disaster. We can live only in good balance. . . . We didn't have muhajedins and fundamentalists before the war. Now we have. Before, our Muslims didn't know what these things mean. We did not have Ustasha, we had no Chetniks, but now we have everything. We have real fascists. It's one pot in which you have everything. . . .

The place of the Jews—now the question is, what to do in this situation? To be quiet because you are afraid, or to speak loudly what you think about the situation? I choose to speak very loudly. I think it's the only way. Sometimes it is better to be louder than quieter. [It is] because we have the experience of the Second World War. Before the war people were afraid to speak, and the consequences were terrible. Of course, there are only 2,000 Jews in Serbia or in Yugoslavia. But it doesn't change anything. It's a question of morality, of principle. That's the reason why I speak, not only against antisemitism but against all kinds of irrational hate, ethnic cleansing, and about concentration camps. I can't believe that I live in this country. [What if] one day somebody asks me, "why were you so quiet, why didn't protest?" The problem is that people who protest and oppose are outsiders. We can speak freely. I have no problems. We are not dangerous for the government at this moment. But in the moment when you become dangerous for the government, for the ruling party, for Milošević, then they stop you. We have that experience.

I had been for 30, 35 years head of the drama department. It is one special part of TV. We had during Tito's time a problem [of censorship] which I opposed. In that department it was not so obvious. But . . . with war, war propaganda, and irrational hate, it became obvious, and then I openly opposed it in [the following] way. We journalists asked [the government] to respect our professional codex, because in our professional codex of rights it's forbidden to lie and to [incite] irrational hate; it's forbidden to have, to support, black lists. We asked only for this. We established the first independent union in Yugoslavia three years ago, at the beginning of the war. It was an independent union of journalists.[The government] did something against the law. They expelled us. Just suddently one day they declared that it's forbidden to come inside the radio and television building. After 28 years it was forbidden for me to come and take my books, my documents. We went to the court, and twice the court stated it was against the law. [It was so stated] in this country which is not based on the law. It was always like that—the law said, the courts said, but nobody expected [anything]. Some of the best journalists of TV, the best editors, have been without a job for one and a half years. Nobody asks them how they are surviving. We organized in some way. We have each other. And we continue our fight against the abuse of the media and censorship . . . by printing our magazine . . . and in some other ways. . . . I'm also one of the founders of the Belgrade Circle. I was co-president for long time. . . . I'm still close to them but I'm not so much involved. Belgrade Circle [Beogradski Krug] is an organization of individuals, of intellectuals—writers, musicians, architects, film directors, actors, various people, which opposed this regime from the beginning. They declared that they also oppose the *Memorandum*. And they declared a new option for Serbia, for a second Serbia; they are fighting for a second, or for a third Serbia. It means some other Serbia, not this kind of Serbia in which you have that kind of illness called strong or extreme nationalism. No. We are fighting for a European Serbia, for an open Serbia, where everybody can live well and respects human rights. . . the things without which you can't imagine a normal society. Sometimes you have a situation in which normal things are absent and are forbidden. People ask me why I don't go to live outside the country, since a lot of my friends, my best friends, writers, now live outside. I say I'm satisfied because I'm fighting. Tito had enough strength to fight. I suppose I would be unsatsified if I lived somewhere outside and I just had to look [from outside]. Maybe it's also contradictory, but I feel that this country is my country. I am born here. I am not part of this Serbia. I am part, maybe I'm also in some way Yugonostalgic—[meaning] that I'm part of former Yugoslavia because I was born there, I lived there. But now I know it is only a dream. We must forget it. But . . . I am a man without identity if I live in some other country because language gives you identity. I am connected with this place until my death. Was it better to be here and fight or to live some place where you are nothing, really nothing.

The Writer Ana Šomlo: "In my dreams I'm always a Jew"

Ana Šomlo belongs to the segment of postwar Jewish writers discussed above, although her literary reputation is not nearly as far-reaching. She was born in 1935 to a Hungarian Jewish father and a Serbian mother. Her father came to Serbia from Budapest. He came to build the railroads in Serbia. Ana classifies him as an assimilated Jew. Her mother was strongly Serbian and raised Ana as a Serb. While growing up the matrilineal side, which was Serbian, was much stronger than her father's Jewish side. There were significant differences between the two families and the two populations. To Ana these differences between Jews and others, particularly Serbs, are magnified in her own life because she herself is half Jewish and half Serbian and has experienced this division within her familial life.

As I have presented my argument in the preceding chapters, the reasons for the weakness of the Jewish side, besides being a tiny minority, stem from the catastrophe that the Jews experienced and its outcome in the demographic, sociocultural, and ideological spheres of life. Even if all the other variables were to be kept constant, the decimation of Jewish kinship units alone would account for the weakness of Jewish socialization in the postwar years. But other factors, such as ethnically mixed marriages in which one partner is a member of the host population, psychological trauma and perhaps repression, and political transformation, add to this weakness. There are other differences that she points out. For three hundred years everyone in her patrilineal line was literate. This was not the case in the matrilineal line. Even most urban Serbs are only one to three generations removed from the village. Ana's mother, in fact, received much of her education from her husband, Ana's father. Ana still carries Serbian and Yugoslav identities because she was born in Yugoslavia, Serbo-Croatian is her maternal language, and her mother is Serbian. But these identities are now overwhelmed by her Jewish identity, for it is through her Jewish grid, or prism as she calls it, that she sees the world around her. However, she remarks how she has had to resist strong Serbian pressures. After giving birth to her daughter in a Belgrade hospital, she gave her a Jewish name. An acquaintance approached her and asked, "Ana, why give your child such a name when there are so many beautiful [Serbian] names?"

Apparently her father did not talk much about his past or his Jewishness, which Ana reveals in the relationship between the fictional father Viktor and daughter Mirjana in her book, *Glasovi Dijaspore* (Voices of the Diaspora). In discussing Ana Šomlo I draw from this book. I feel free to do so because much of her writing is based on real people, including herself. In comparing the book and my interviews with her, I found several close parallels. In *Voices of the Diaspora* Ana accurately depicts, with a keen ethnographic eye, the reality of Jewish existence in postwar, 1980s, Yugoslavia. For the Jews in the book, Jewishness is largely individuated. Even within the family, as she shows in the relationship between father Viktor and daughter Mirjana, the discontinuity between the Jewish past and present is striking. The father says little about his Jewish past. The daughter, thus, must create her own Jewishness with very little or no help from her father. Ana sets her Jewish characters outside the context of the organized Jewish community, which adds to the ethnographic realism, for the organized community plays a minor or no part in the lives of the majority of Yugoslav Jews. Living without the rhythm of Jewish life, they meet other Jews in irregular encounters. Those who have retained an interest in Jewish subjects may send certain ethnic signals to those they meet in order to determine whether they are Jewish.[5]

In Ana's case, individuation involves more than one kind of process. Like so many others, she is the natural and cultural product of an ethnically mixed marriage. She was born divided and continues to carry this division within herself, even though the Jewish self has come not only to take precedence but to be the self through which she views the world. This Jewish self sensitizes her to see what is Jewish in a society where Jews are supposedly invisible.

The process of becoming a Jew has been both a conscious dimension in which she has actively, even aggressively, pursued and created her Jewishness, and an unconscious one that involves her dreams. The unconscious state of dreaming, however, meets the conscious state of awareness when she records all of her dreams in her diary, which she showed to me. Unfortunately, I have only the fragments of dreams which she described to me.

The Unconscious: Ana's Dreams

Ana Šomlo's dreams are very important to her. She records them all in a diary. Through the conscious act of writing down her dreams, what begins in her unconscious becomes embedded in her consciousness. Her dreams are the private symbols of her Jewishness.

> I had a very strange dream. I wrote it [in my diary of dreams]. I wrote it at night. I don't remember exactly what it was. I always, [since] I was a little child, wrote down my

> dreams—my dreams and my feelings and my thoughts. . . . I always think in this way now. In this dream [I] was [in] a very difficult situation. I saw two women. I was waiting. I didn't know what to do. I came to these women. I understood that I can't come back now, because now I'm sure that I'm the only Jew and it is my end. It is even very difficult for me. [Looks for the dream in her diary.] Almost in every dream I am a Jew. Always I'm on some way, in some situation, and I don't know where to go. Always I'm looking [for] something. Always in my dreams I have some old people who are Jews. I don't know why. They always recognize me, and invite me. I dreamed it even before, when I was a young girl. I always am between old people and the Jews, and they recognize me. When I had the promotion of my book on Knez Mihailova, I felt that it was my dream. It was the dream of my life to be among old Jews, and they recognized me. Because these people I met for the first time, many of them. How it is, and why, I don't know. Because I had more friends always, and more cousins, who are not Jews. All my [father's] family was lost in the war. Everywhere in my diary is a Jew, Jew, Jew—Jevrejin, Jevrejin. Why, I don't know. Even before the war I said, "I am Serbian," but something always was every way one way, and this way is through Jews.

First, the content of many of her dreams is constant. The people in the dreams, including Ana, are Jews. "I always in my dreams have some old people who are Jews." Second, this content has been a part of her dreams since childhood, even when she was saying, "I am Serbian." She says that she does not know why. She has, and perhaps had had as a child, a strong desire to be Jewish. Her dreams may be a means of compensating for being ethnically divided and being Jewish only by her father, which does not make her a Jew according to Jewish law. What the dreams do for her is provide confirmation that a Jewish core, which she wrote about and described as having been passed down across 2,000 years by the ancestors, is in her as well, a kind of ethnic genus. There is, thus this ethnic genus that exists, but whose existence can only be intuited. She says that she does not require any objective proof of its existence. Perhaps tied to this intuitive belief that she possesses a Jewish pre-existent core is the belief that "if I try not to be a Jew [i.e., who I am] I will have some punishment from God. Really, I am feeling it." This belief in a Jewish pre-existent has its basis in historical depth, which is antithetical to the position of many Jews of her parents' generation for whom the significant past began only with the prewar progressive movement.

> Many things exist but aren't seen. I don't think a person is conscious of all that which unfolds in a way he wishes it would or thinks he wishes it would. There exists a *pamćenje organizma*, a life of an organism that is irrational and that remembers and transmits itself. If someone knew the Bible by heart 2,000 years ago and if all of our ancestors read and remembered and behaved in a certain determined way, then I think that this exists in a certain way in individuals (in personality) and that it erupts like lava when the character emerges in a fixed moment. I personally do not require scientific evidence for this; I feel it and know it intuitively, and that is somehow my inspiration (*Kadima* 1986).

Ana Šomlo's Jewishness is not restricted to the unconscious realm of the dream or to the phenomenological realm of Jewish consciousness where she is aware of what is transpiring within her and uses this to order her world. Her Jewishness is also based in concrete human experiences, some of which predate her conscious state of Jewishness. Her experience during the Second World War would certainly be among these (see Jaša Almuli's series in *Politika*, April–May 1989).

Descent is a matter of individual choice, as I mentioned in chapter 2. But what seems to be an individual choice is influenced by the social and cultural environment in which one lives. This is illustrated by means of a dialogue between two Jewish characters, members of the postwar generation, in *Voices of the Diaspora*. The young man, David Hirshorn, is Jewish by patrilineal descent, while the young woman, Mirjana Crnić, is Jewish by matrilineal and patrilineal descent. Her father had changed his name from Švarc (German, meaning black; a common Jewish name) to Crnić (Serbian, meaning black) during the war to protect his first family, which was wiped out except for the father and the father's mother.

> David Hirshorn (DH): Your mother was called Sara?
>
> Mirjana Crnić (MC): Yes.
>
> DH: Was she. . . .?

> MC: Yes, she was a Jew. Why is that so essential?
>
> DH: It's not. My mother isn't Jewish; she is Serbian.
>
> MC: Why didn't you tell me yesterday you're Jewish?
>
> DH: What else could a David Hirshorn be but a Jew?
>
> MC: If your mother bore you, and she is a Serb, you are, first of all, a Serb. Jews reckon descent according to the mother. This is also the case in the Bible.
>
> DH: We Serbs reckon descent according to the father. According to that, I live in Serbia and I am a Jew.
>
> MC: That's not important. What is important is how you feel.
>
> DH: I know that story. It would be clever if it weren't so banal. You can be only what those in your surroundings see you as, and they have never seen me as a Serb.

In Ana's own experience, she has opted for a predominantly Jewish identity and line of descent. This is apparent from the way she talks about the depth of Jewish descent and the Jewish ancestors. How others see and classify her varies. Some see her as a Serb, while others as a Jew. "People never spoke about me as they do about the Serbs here. Even when I was a girl I heard my friends say, "this Jewish girl, this Jewish family." But for me it wasn't important. Still, they don't believe that I'm a Jew. On the other hand, when Jews choose to abandon their Jewishness, sometimes it takes being defined by others to bring them back or bring them to their Jewishness for the first time. The case of Ana Šomlo's sister provides an example. I paraphrase it as follows:

> My sister is a doctor of hematology. She always had Serbian friends, only Serbian friends. Both her first and last name are Serbian. She once asked me, "Why do you try always to be a Jew? Our own mother is a Serb, we are Serbs, our family is Serbian. Even our father says he's Serbian. And we live in Yugoslavia." I told her, "I studied Oriental languages and my husband is part Jewish." Then she said, "I don't think it's good. You have friends who are Jews, you don't celebrate a *slava* [the household's patron saint day, celebrated by Serbs]. Your husband is half Jewish and half

> Serbian. Why do you always think about Jews? It's not healthy."
>
> One day my sister came to see me. She cried. I listened to her describe an experience her son had had with other children during a party. They had called him a *Čifutić* ["little Jew." *Čifutin* is what the Ottoman Turks had called the Jews. Since that time the label has became a pejorative]. Her son was five years old at the time. At the party the children were competing to see who would jump the longest distance. My sister heard that one boy say, "You [son's name], *Čufutić*, will be first." He told them, "I'm not *Čifutić*, I'm [Serbian name]. He never had heard anything about *Čifut. M*y sister didn't want to believe what she had heard. When her son told the other children, "I'm [Serbian name]," and another the boy said, "No, you are *Čifut*," my sister saw that everybody knows she is a Jew and sees her as such. For my sister it wasn't important that others see them as Jews. She was unhappy that they didn't see her son as a Serb. Later, she experienced another unpleasant occurrence. Her friend, also a doctor, said, "We'll put you [Jews] into the sea. You [Jews] are against the Arabs. We will take you and put you in the sea." You know, it's what Nassar said. She couldn't understand why he said it. She didn't know that war had broken out in Israel. When she grasped the meaning of his words she said, "Don't tell me. The war is in Israel. I'm in Yugoslavia. It is my story, my life." The doctor said, "It is your life. You are all fools. You will be killed because you are this kind of people." It was then that she began to feel like a Jew. Now she is like me. She never had problems like I had. And she never had feelings like I had. But people put her in her own Jewish place.

"But for me, now, it is not really important what Jews think and what Serbs think. I have my own life and feelings. . . . I never said after this conference when they threw me out [of job], I never said "we." I forgot this word. It doesn't mean anything for me. I can say only "I."" For example, when there is some game, football or basketball, I never say, "We must, it's our victory." I never [say it]. . . . When somebody asked me, when Yugoslavia and Israel had some match, "For whom are you? Tell me. I said, "I can't say I am for us, for who is "us" for me? It is some kind of freedom. I am free now, because if "you" is some society then you must think like them, do what they suppose you must [do]. Now I'm free. I have never been in some society, never been a member of some party. It is a good feeling."

Marginality and Jewishness

Flora: The Ambiguity of Marginality: Resisting and Continuing the Past

Flora was born in 1949 to a Jewish mother and father. Reckoning descent is not problematic for her. She identifies herself as a Jew, though she says she thinks like a Serb. "I even can rationalize why I do it. But I would die if I had to stay in a Serbian village for half an hour." She is very conscious of her Jewish past, though she resists those patterns of the past (and present) that have torn families apart. Both her mother's and her father's parents' marriages ended in separation. Later her parents divorced. These broken relationships between husbands and wives made their mark on Flora. Her parents transmitted different versions of this past to her. Having heard about these failed conjugal relationships and directly experienced the dissolution of her own parents' marriage, Flora may have been intent on breaking this pattern, which is apparent in her feeling for family, her family life, and, I speculate, in her professional role (see below).

Flora is married to a Croat from the Adriatic city of Split. While taking her husband's name she also has retained her Sephardi Jewish name. Her mother's maiden name ties her to the famous Belgrade revolutionary family described in chapter 3, the Baruhs. Indeed, Flora is the niece of the famous trio of Baruh brothers and the two aunts who were all killed during the Second World War. A painting by Bora, one of the brothers who was an artist, hangs on a wall in her apartment. At one time, being a descendent of the famous Baruhs brought attention and perhaps some privilege, but by the 1980s people just were not interested. Her mother was the sole surviving sibling of the six children of Bulina Baruh, who also survived and became one of Flora's primary caretakers. Flora says that her grandmother imparted in her a feeling for family. As a child, Flora observed a strained relationship between her mother and grandmother. She describes it as growing up with two grieving, angry women, one who had lost all her children except one, and the other who had lost her five siblings. Being a member of the famous revolutionary family was both a blessing and a curse for Flora's mother.

> My mother was a middle female child. She was never loved . . . She was not a hero; she was not an intellectual . . . she was nothing. And she remained alive. . . . She didn't have guilt. That is the only guilt she doesn't have, because she really tried also, but she wasn't killed. . . . The thing that ruined her completely, I think, was one sentence. . . When my grandmother saw my mother and found out all the others were dead, she said, "From all of them that I loved it is only you that remained," which implied, . . . you whom I didn't love. [That is your father's story?] Yea. Which is not far from the truth, honestly speaking. I remember my grandmother. . . . They were like two women, both of them angry, grieving, and aggressive. . . . Grandmother . . . after all these dead people around her, I was the first living thing, so she put all her nice things into bringing me up. And my feeling for family life . . . is from her. And that's the difference between me and my (half) brother. He wasn't brought up by my grandmother.

Flora now is the mother of three boys. She has very little contact with the organized Jewish community. I would describe her as marginal to the organized community, which places her in the same category as many other Yugoslav Jews. She did pay the annual fee once when she wanted to vacation with the family in the community's camp, but her application was turned down. She is not sure why. Outside of the organized community she has several Jewish friends. Five of her best ten friends are Jews, she told me. She did not know they were Jewish when they struck up a friendship. She only discovered her best friend was Jewish after she got pregnant and named her child.

Similar to her mother's family before the war, Flora is socially located on the margins of the organized Jewish community. She has very little contact with the community. Without this contact she is located outside the only available form of collective Jewish activity. Her family of procreation cannot be the source, for its structure is what contributes to the pattern of truncation. Her husband is not a Jew. She does not send her sons to the community's summer camp or to the children's clubs that meet on Saturdays. Her eldest son, who is old enough to reflect on questions of "identity," is more Yugoslav than anything else (see below). Her mother who lives in the same city has no firm ties to the organized community. She was a committed Party member who not only kept the family's ideological zeal alive for the sake of her dead siblings but also because she was a Communist believer. She expected Flora to join the Party because it was "the tradition in the family." "Do you have anything against it?" she asked. Flora recalls the time her mother asked her about the family's Communist tradition. She felt like her son Martin when she asked him about Jewish tradition (see below). Flora joined the Party, but later dropped out, after the student demonstrations at Belgrade University in 1968, an event which left its mark on her life. Subsequently, she spent so much time outside the home that her mother lost influence over her. Her father, who did maintain his Jewishness, lived on the other side of the country, and then he moved abroad. Without these Jewish institutions she was left to stitch together the various shreds and patches of her Jewishness. Given her marginality to the organized community, it would follow that her Jewishness is even more fragmented, more of a bricolage, than the Jewishness of those who regularly engage in some activity within the organized community. First of all, she has to rely totally on herself for integrating Jewish fragments into her life. She participates in no "cultural program," nor does she passively observe such a program. As a marginal individual she must either passively await what may pass his or her way, or she must take the initiative and actively pursue her Jewishness, which is an especially difficult task where there is no Jewish culture in everyday life and where even Jews are hard to find. After the war, the sights, sounds, smells, and tastes never returned to the streets of Yugoslavia. Jewish culture, as I pointed out in chapters 3 and 4, became a Jewish cultural program, something to be created and staged within private spheres by the most active members of the community. Avoiding these communal spheres makes living Jewish life extremely difficult.

I lack the data to attempt a reconstruction of Flora's entire worldview, that is, how she perceives and conceptualizes her world. Although I know that her Jewishness is constructed from fragments, I, too, must work from the fragments that are available to me. Below I have extracted some of the fragments that, across time and space, have contributed to her sense of Jewishness.

One of Flora's earliest sources of Jewishness was her maternal grandmother, who lived in the same home until her death when Flora was eleven years old. Since Flora's own mother spent a considerable amount of time attending various political meetings, no doubt a considerable part of Flora's early socialization was left to her grandmother. Her grandmother cooked Jewish meals, but she was silent about her own Jewishness. She also took Flora with her to the Jewish community a couple of times. Flora remembers these visits as having a negative influence on her. "I felt others were from elite families in Belgrade. I was brought up to be non-snobbish. I didn't feel I belonged there. I belonged to the kids on my street."

Flora's mother transmitted very little that was specifically Jewish. She told Flora a few stories from her childhood. Importantly, she served a primary source of information about the family's past, including her own parents' failed marriage. Following the divorce (I do not know how old Flora was) her father lost a regular influence over her life. At some point he moved to the Adriatic side of Yugoslavia. He now lives in the United States. He, too, was a primary source on the family's past, including his wife's family history. Her mother and father transmitted two different versions of the past. Among her relatives, her father's sister visited Yugoslavia from the United States. She gave Flora Leon Uris' book *Exodus*, which Flora read in English.

Flora passed through what she refers to as her "Spanish period." She knew she was not Serbian. Her Spanish name distinguished her from those around her. She was not attracted to what other people enjoyed. She did not like Serbian folk music. She felt no special attraction for the Serbian ritual, the *slava*, except for the special cake called a *kolač* baked for it. At one point Flora recalls that she "fell in love" with Spanish music and language. She wanted to imagine herself as Spanish. She listened to Spanish music for hours at a time. Her fascination even included applying Spanish makeup. I was "trying to find out within myself what's going on," she told me. Some of the songs were old Jewish, Ladino songs. The fact that many Spanish films were playing in Belgrade cinemas at the time probably contributed to her fascination with Spanish culture. Nevertheless, Flora says it "was the first time that I was thinking about my origin." Her Jewishness had become a part of consciousness, beyond the state of mere awareness of difference.

Her descent and profession place her in the Sephardi tradition. Consciously or not, she is acting out a role that ties her to the women and men who proceeded her.

A Modern Kazamentero: "Matchmaker, Matchmaker, Make Me a Match"

Before the war the Jews of Yugoslavia hired matchmakers (*kazamenteros*, Seph; *sadten*, Ashk.; *provodadzija*, Serbo-Croatian) to arrange marriages. There were several well-known matchmakers in Sarajevo: Moso Isak Abinum, "Behor il Camal," "Modor Coso," "Tija Rufkula Cosa," and others (Pinto 1987:35). Flora follows in this tradition, for she is essentially a *kazamentero*, although her methods are more western, and she does not personally arrange marriages. With her half-Jewish partner and friend, Flora established Fortuna, a dating and marriage agency, which in 1986 was the only such service in Serbia. Only two, perhaps three, of these services existed in the entire country, the other being, I believe, in Slovenia. That same year Flora cast her entrepreneurial vision far beyond her own modest agency when she successfully organized IFOMAFA, an international conference that was held in Belgrade in October 1986. When I revisited her agency three years later, Flora had expanded the workspace and computerized the operation. To her print advertisements she added television advertisements in which she herself appeared, becoming a small media celebrity to her eldest son's classmates in the process.

It is tempting to speculate why Flora pursued the business of matchmaking. Unfortunately I did not ask her why she did. I will speculate. First, there was no such service available, and thus a person with entrepreneurial inclinations would consider the fact that such a gap existed and that she or he would be meeting a need. The image of socialist Yugoslavia was just the opposite, suggesting that traditional social mechanisms based on the values of the countryside and the new socialist system were meeting that need, and that individuals were not becoming increasingly atomized. The responses of individuals in turning to the agency indicated, however, that such a need did exist and that people would turn to this new social form for assistance. So there is this entrepreneurial motivation that may have contributed to the establishment of the agency. It is difficult to ignore the psycho-cultural components of what possibly motivated Flora. I have mentioned the failed relationships of her own parents and both sets of grandparents. Perhaps she consciously or subconsciously set out to engage in an activity that put men and women together rather than tore them apart. I am not stating this is what motivated her or that she was even conscious of any correlation. This psychological component begs for further interviewing of Flora. Finally, whether or not Flora realizes it, her agency is a cultural product, and her role as a modern day matchmaker is one way she displays a fragment of the Sephardi past.

Flora's Natural (Jewish?) Products

Flora has produced three sons who are Jews according to Jewish law, which reckons descent matrilineally. Beyond the principle of descent, however, her sons' Jewishness becomes problematic. Flora assumed the role of anthropologist and asked her eldest son, Martin, who was in his early teens, about being a Jew.

> I talked to Martin. I talked to him straight. Just asked him a couple questions. At first, he said he feels Yugoslav, not Croatian [his father is a Croat], not Jewish, not Serbian, or anything. He feels Yugoslav, by nationality. I asked, "What about your Jewish and Croat parts?" He said, "I know it only by name. I don't know anything more about it. And I'm not interested." [That] is the most interesting part. Then I asked him, "What and how much do you know about your being a Jew?" And he said, "Only what you told me." Then I told him, "Then it's not too much." He said, "It's almost nothing." Ach. He made me feel guilty. Then I asked him, "Would you like to go to Israel?" He said, "I would like to go anywhere." "To live?" I asked him. "No, for a visit because I don't know how it would be there." I told him, "It's a good climate there," and he said, "In Split [on the Adriatic coast] it's a good climate, too."
>
> I asked him, "Do your friends know that you are Jewish?" He said, "Yes." Flora: "How did they get to know that?" Martin: "Because you are very popular in my class." Imagine that! I felt very nice at that moment. . . . Because a couple of times I have been on TV because of Fortuna business, and they asked [Martin], "Why is [your mother] called Flora? It's not a Yugoslav name. Martin: "Then I explained to them that Flora is a Spanish name and M is your father's name and he was a Jew." So Martin gave me an explanation.

I didn't know they ever talked about such stupid things among themselves. I asked him, "What are their attitudes toward the whole point?" Martin: "They tease me." Flora: "In what sense, in what way?" And now comes an interesting thing. He said, "They tease me, but not viciously, more jokingly, saying, "You dirty Jew."" But it wasn't funny for me at all. Flora: "What do you mean? Why don't they call you "you stupid Jew" or "you bad Jew," but why "you dirty Jew?" OK, they just joke. "Does it bother you?" Martin: "No, we tease each other in different ways." He didn't seem to be upset at all about it. He didn't know the connotation at all, so that's why it didn't bother him. . . . So he would be, of course, much more disappointed if they would call him "fat Jew," because he is fat [laughs], or "stupid," because he has some bad marks [laughs], but it goes easier for him if they call him a "dirty Jew.". . . So, it means that kids know this slogan. That's my way of thinking. They know the slogan. They didn't call him a, a, I don't know, anything, anything that you can attribute to this [word] Jew, which you could say small, big, quick, slow, rich, poor, fat, thin, or something, but the word "dirty." So they must have heard it somewhere. They couldn't invent it. There are not any antisemitic films on Yugoslav television where you can say they picked it from the film. That's my observation. The discussion was almost, I told you almost word-[for]-word. So it made me think because I was never told anything like that in my 40 years of life. [He saw your reaction or he didn't?] No, I was drinking coffee, smoking, and chatting. . . .

I asked him, "Would you like to know some more information and facts about Jews and the Jewish way of life, tradition, and everything?" He said, "I'm not interested. I asked the question, "Would you like to know more about the Jewish and Croatian past and tradition?" Martin: "I'm not interested at all in all these things." Flora: "What about the good meals that Jews cook? Would you? Martin: "You want to make me fatter." I said, ""That's not the point. Would you like to go with the Jewish youth for a holiday? Martin: "Why not? I would like to." Flora: "But you don't know anyone from there?" He said, "I'd like to know them." [Flora tells me she will try to send him to the Jewish summer camp in Pirovac on the Adriatic coast.] [What if he comes back and is filled with new ideas?] Great. Any new ideas are welcome. Why not. Perhaps. But he's not good soil for good ideas that [aren't] based on either music. . . . He might if he feels he belongs to some group, [then] he could accept the idea, the whole thing. If he will find a friend or two, or a few, . . . he has very few friends at school, which is . . . [because] he's a type of lonely person. Not lonely in a bad sense, but he prefers being with one person, talking, listening to music. . . . He's not a crowd person. . . . That's [my husband's] part, in a way. . . . Going to the music school he had a chance to meet different kind of people, closer to his way of thinking. . . . The prospect of finding a similar companionship is less in any other school than in music school. But in the [Jewish] community perhaps he will find someone less aggressive or aggressive enough to take him and lead him, because he's not a leader. Maybe [it will] be okay, why not. I owe it to you [that] I got this idea to even ask. . . . It might turn [out] very well.

Aleksandar Najman. The Isolated Jew in a Place without Jews

I traveled to the Slavonian town of Vukovar situated on the Danube River and to the neighboring factory town of Borovo, to interview an elderly Jewish man who has lived most of his adult life in Yugoslavia apart from other Jews. Since my visit the town of Vukovar has been leveled in the interethnic fighting between the Serbs and Croats.

Aleksandar Najman was born in 1909 in what was then Hungarian territory and now belongs to Romania. Both parents were Jews who had come originally from different cities in Slovakia. The family lived in a workers' cottage in a Budapest quarter whose residents were not Jewish. Because his father was a state employee, the entire family spoke Hungarian at home. Aleksandar attended middle school and some secondary school in Budapest. The Jews were permitted to constitute only five percent of the students because of a quota in Hungary at the time. Perhaps this is why Aleksandar went to study in Bernow in Czechoslovakia, where he studied chemistry in a German technical high school.

Before the war it was as a student and a member of the Jewish sport club Makabi that he felt Jewish. In Hungary the Jews felt Hungarian."That is a big question—what we are." His childhood language was Hungarian, he went to a Hungarian school, and he received very little Jewish education."I grew up in a Christian environment. All my friends, from the street, were Christians." In the state school the Grand Rabbi in Budapest did come to the school to teach religion. Never having learned to read Hebrew, Aleksandar had difficulties with this course.

After the war in 1923 Aleksandar's father came to Kruševac in Serbia to work for the railroad. Upon Aleksandar's graduation the whole family joined the father in Kruševac, where they lived for three years before moving to Belgrade. Aleksandar continued his studies in Czechoslovakia. He visited home frequently, about once every two weeks. In Belgrade the family was not active in the Jewish community. Aleksandar thinks that his father may have made a few donations to the community. His father already had moved away from the religion of his father. Aleksandar's grandfather lived in Slovakia for ninety-one years. He never knew that his grandson, Aleksandar, never had a bar mitzvah.

Aleksandar came to Borovo in 1933, a year after the factory was established. He continued to work for the Borovo factory for forty years, until his retirement in the 1960s. Before the war there were only about two or three Jews in a workforce of two or three thousand. In 1940 he married his wife whose father was German. About seven thousand Germans lived in the Vukovar area at that time.

After the war started the Germans took control of the factory. During our time together I got the impression that Aleksandar did not want to discuss what exactly had happened to him. He did tell me, in response to my query, that he was necessary to the factory and that his wife was a Christian of German descent. Aleksandar did say of his wife, "She never was a bridge between me and the Volksdeutsche. She lived with me when it was most difficult to be a man." Like other Jews, he was required to wear the yellow badge. Today, all of the older people know he is a Jew because they saw him wearing the badge during the war. As for the Jews of Vukovar, they all "disappeared during the war." Aleksandar's parents and his brother died in Belgrade as Jewish genocide victims.

After the war Aleksandar continued to live isolated as a Jew without other Jews. The nearest Jewish community is thirty-five kilometers away in Osijek. While still alive the president of the Osijek community would occasionally visit Aleksandar. He "looked upon me as a member," Aleksandar told me. After the president's death, his son, a student, visited Aleksandar ten or fifteen years ago. Several years ago he also received matzot from the secretary of the Osijek Jewish community, but since then he has "lost all connections." Without the social connection with other Jews, he does not feel special on Jewish holidays. As a Jew he is alone. His friends today are not Jews. His sons' friends, also, are not Jews. They are Christians. There are no Jews. "What are those from a mixed family like we are? What are the children? Jews? They do not know.

Beyond Socialist Reality: Moris's Transcendent Experiences

Moris: The "Voice of God"

Moris was a 66-year-old man when I first interviewed him at the location of his choice, the Metropol Hotel, located on the Boulevard of the Revolution in Belgrade. I interviewed him a second time three years later in the same location. On other occasions I conversed with Moris less formally, and I have also corresponded with him. He was one of the "regulars" attending the weekly Arvit services held in the Belgrade synagogue.

Moris was born into an ethnically mixed household. His banker father was a Jew by descent who had been baptized as a child of four in the Roman Catholic Church, as were his father's father, father's mother, and others in the patrilineal line. Moris, too, was baptized in the Catholic Church. Although Moris's father was not a member of the local Jewish community (he would not have been accepted, unless he first renounced his Roman Catholicism), Moris said that he helped many Jews through his high-level position in banking. According to Moris, he "remained a Jew in his heart." When he died he received a Christian burial. Baptized Jews were not Moris's only ancestors. His paternal grandfather's uncle was the Grand Rabbi of Rome. His mother was a Serb by descent.

As an adolescent Moris's parents sent him to a German school. His socialization there must have been effective. He felt "very inclined toward German culture." Apparently this connection saved him from the fate suffered by nearly all of his patrilineal/lateral kinsmen during the Second World War. Only he and his sister, who had been baptized in the Greek Orthodox Church, survived from their family of orientation. Outside the family only four cousins survived.

Moris continues to be divided in various ways. He is married to a Serbian woman who he says does not understand his Jewishness. He has strong Serbian sentiments, which were made clear during our last meeting when we discussed the changing political situation in Serbia and Yugoslavia. His religious worldview not only sets him apart from society, but also from the organized Jewish community's secularism and submergence. When invited to join the Party on three different occasions, he answered openly that he was a believer. He did not lose his job over this, but he was kept from business travel abroad, which must have been a heavy price for someone who was the editor of the foreign section in a major weekly magazine. To complicate the situation further, Moris's religious worldview is syncretistic, with the ultimate component being the Judaic. Its ultimacy for Moris derives, partly, from his philosophic logic, which is "very reluctant to [any kind] of conception which is not strictly monistic, and from the suffering of the Jewish people throughout its history. For Moris, faith is "something beyond all linguistic and theological reflection, even if all rational arguments were against such a faith (see below)."

Some of the components of Moris's religious worldview are (1) a series of transcendent experiences, (2) beliefs that are syncretistic, but whose foundation is Judaic; (3) Jewish knowledge; (4) practice in the form of synagogue ritual and self-instruction, and (5) significant dyadic relationships with two other Jewish men who are religious and who, like Moris, have sought at some point in their lives a religious synthesis. I have stated above that for Moris the ultimacy of the Judaic religion derives from his philosophic logic and from the sufferings of the Jewish people.

> I came . . . to the conclusion that I must stay in my previous conception of God's unity.
>
> For me, as well for the other Jews who are attached to Judaism, the unity of God, the idea that excludes all differentiation within the essence of God, is the very base of the religion of my forefathers and I must not forget that they were ready to suffer all the persecutions and humiliation only not to betray their fidelity to the God Who on the mountain Horev in Sinai said: I am your only God.
>
> I admit that this is not the principal reason I can't accept the Christian conception of the Trinity of God. There is one other: also my philosophic logic is very reluctant to any kind of conception which is not strictly monistic. The Absolute can't be in any manner divided, because if divided, even in the Christian manner, he is no longer Absolute. . . .

> But in the last analysis all this has for me a linguistic or semantic, not a theological value. I don't deny that the subtle differentiations you quoted are of great importance for the Pauline Christians and for the comparative study of Christianity and Judaism. But the faith is something beyond all linguistic and theological reflection, even if all rational arguments were against such a faith.

Moris was twenty-one years old when Germany attacked Yugoslavia. He declared himself as a German. His name can be classified as either German or Jewish. As a boy he had attended the German school in Belgrade, so he spoke German fluently and was very inclined toward German culture. As mentioned, his parents had him baptized in the Roman Catholic Church. Although he had friends who were Jews, Moris was not raised as a Jew and he did not feel like a Jew. He felt Serbian before the war.

Although Moris grew up outside a Jewish milieu, the Jewishness of his prewar past is now a part of his significant past. After the war he discovered that even his Jewish kin who had been baptized died in Hitler's concentration camps as Jews. "It is the reason I also became a Jew, because I have seen that the Jews can never cease to be a Jew." Only Moris, his sister, and four cousins survived the war.

Moris's first transcendent experience occurred when he was a child of nine. He woke up at midnight and heard a voice say, "I am God. You are not a good child." He felt a slap on his cheek and then cried, "Father, father, God struck me." His father responded in German, "Fool, you have only dreamed." For many years this childhood experience was forgotten. Only after the war, when his Serbian wife was operated on for cancer, did he remember it—"in the moment of my highest desolation," he told me. "I didn't believe my wife could survive. I begged God for my wife. In that moment I remembered my [childhood] experience and felt at that moment my wife would survive. Twelve years have passed and she is still alive. My school friend who operated on her told me two years ago, ten years after the operation, "I can tell you now the truth about your wife. When I operated on her I believed she would live at the maximum six months. Her case was very bad. Moris, I'm sure it was the grace of God.""

Moris relates his third such transcendent experience:

> About 10 years ago I listened to Radio Jerusalem every morning. One day I turned on my radio one hour earlier, and it was a program in English. The program always began with the prayer, Sh'ma Yisrael. This was six–seven years ago. When I heard this program, at this moment I believed it was the same voice I heard when I was eight years old. It was from this moment that I began to feel like a Jew. It was the same voice. I have such an (impression?).

Michael Polanyi (1958:97) writes that life's experiences are not always evaluated individually; they are cumulative. Moris's case supports this. Following his third experience with the "voice of God," Moris began to aggressively pursue his Jewishness by seeking knowledge, studying Hebrew, practicing Jewish ritual, visiting Israel, and establishing a significant relationship with another religious Jew who does not attend the Belgrade synagogue. He began to read more about Judaism. After hearing the Sh'ma Yisrael prayer on the Radio Jerusalem program, he started to teach himself Hebrew. Although unable to speak Hebrew, he can read it with a dictionary. Moris has read the Old Testament in Hebrew. The same time that he heard the Sh'ma Yisrael prayer he had an urgent need to visit Israel. He went and calls the pilgrimage his greatest experience. Every Friday evening Moris can be found sitting among the synagogue regulars at the front left quadrant of the hall. He does not attend the synagogue to express or maintain his ethnic Jewishness. It is out of inner conviction that he participates in the collective form of worship.

Experiential, Propositional, and Natural Revelation

Enriko Josif: "This revelation that was given to me, I saw later that it exists in the Bible"

Enriko Josif has been called a prophet and a mystic. To some he is both, to others neither. He is a true intellectual who can speak on any number of subjects, which he takes to a new, hermeneutical level. I know he is a favorite speaker in the Belgrade community. People enjoy the verbal excursions they take with him. By vocation he is an artist, a composer of modernistic music. In Yugoslavia Enriko Josif is well-known for his compositions that are performed and, more recently, also for his public expressions of spiritual solidarity with the Serbian people. He is in his sixties. His home is a Belgrade apartment in a nondescript building near the center of the city. Having lived in Belgrade before the war, he is a true Belgrader. Although he is a religious man with a supernaturalistic worldview, he chooses not to participate in collective prayer and worship, at least not regularly. He did not attend any of the Shabbat services in the Belgrade synagogue when I attended over the course of a year. I did not see him at any other holiday service, although he may have been present for the Rosh Hashanah and or Yom Kippur services. The synagogue was full for services held on the eve of those holidays. I do not know what kind of privatized religion he may practice, besides studying the Bible and kabbala, and engaging in at least two dyadic relationships with other religious Jewish men, one in his early twenties and the other of his own generation.

His form of freedom is symbolized by the bird that flies freely in his apartment. In some ways the narrative that follows is like that bird. I asked few questions and with difficulty attempted to follow Enriko's flight into and out of the personal experiences and transformations, historical events, scientific discoveries, and passages of scripture that have deep significance for him and for, he believes, the Jewish People and all people. Although some might call him a mystic, as I heard one man say, he attempts to relate the mystical and existential, and the physical and metaphysical, to what is for him revealed truth, the Bible, particularly its eschatological aspects.

Wandering: "On the Way"

Enriko Josif did not always have a religious and supernaturalistic worldview, nor did he feel anything like a Jew. He says that he was a *tabula rasa* as far as his Jewishness was concerned. Before the war, like so many young people of his generation, Jews and non-Jews, Enriko's hope was in humanism, Marxism, Communism, and progress. The war, particularly what happened to him as a Jew, stripped him of his ideological baggage and lens. He became, in Victor Turner's terms, a liminar in an anti-structural phase. Enriko was in transition. First he was stripped of the past—of what he was, of his objects of commitment and hope, of his faith in humankind, and so on. These were all taken away. All were stripped away. It was while he was on the road, in passage, that he was separated from his past and began to undergo a transformation.

> I crossed through, as all of us have, much wandering. And during the war, of course, when man either is dying or close to death, then some ancient truth from his sleeping spiritual gene will be awakened. I also had an awakening of my sleeping spiritual gene. So I express it in a modern way. No, it's not; it's said in an impressionistic way, isn't it? Since my youth I grew up with . . . Plato, Dostoevski, Bergson. Since I was very young I always asked myself, "What does it mean to be a man?" Before the war I didn't feel like a Jew at all, that [being a Jew meant] I had something inside that was against me. Surely I did not feel that. Thus, I didn't grow up with the feeling that I live in some ghetto. [I lived in] one open community. Maybe I was spared [from feeling this], I don't know. But I associated with my Serbian friends andwith Jews, and I felt no differences. . . . I was protected then. You will see later that I have an impression that I was protected.

Enriko Josif grew up continuously asking the perennial and universalistic existential questions such as "What does it mean to be a man?" and not the particularistic question, "What does it mean to be a Jew?" He did not feel Jewish. He did not feel divided. There was no inner tension. Rather than being in a social or mental ghetto, he felt he belonged to "one free community of Serbs and Jews, not distinguishing one from the other. As far as his Jewishness was concerned, he was a *tabula rasa*." He does not know why, except to say that perhaps he was "spared from seeing this," "protected." As a student and a Jew he was required to take a religious class taught by a Jewish instructor, but he never went to the class. Every year his father had to plead with the teacher to give his son a passing grade.

Encounter, Revelation, Awakening, Transformation

> [During the war] there began inside of me some things that came from the depths of mystery. And that is one kind, I must call it this, I had one kind of revelation. Earlier, I was like this: I loved people; I felt that Marxism and Communism are the fundamental answers for the good of mankind. And then, suddenly, I began to gradually grasp, through experience, or through some [pre-existent] experience, or through heredity, that it is not possible to love man

> if there is no God; that every person is primarily a religious being, however much it has been said, or is a political [being] as Aristotle says, or . . . that he is . . . in all his own cells and in the smallest parts of the cells a religious being, that he really is that which the Bible says in an excellent way—that man is created not like but in the image of God. From that moment I, as a lover of several progressive ideas and beliefs in the power of mankind, which loves man but does not know God, I had one encounter in Italy which completely [changed] me. In that second it came to a transformation.

The first dilemma was solved, the dilemma of being, or, the metaphysical dilemma. Enriko received an answer to the question he had been asking since childhood. Only then did he confront the dilemma of his Jewish being. The answer that he received was that as a man he was created not like but in the image of God. This was basic to Enriko, before any dilemmas of religion, ethnicity, class, or ideology could be resolved.

> We were interned by the Italians near Parma. That was Borgo val di Taro, and, it is not that important, the place was called Betonja. They resettled us there, in an albergo. They interned us outside the village so that we wouldn't have the right to have contact with others. On the way to this albergo, an Italian child, 6 or 7 years of age, appeared with her sister. She was beautiful, red like one of Raphael's angels. After that, Raphael dropped a few notches in my eyes. He became for me merely one good photographer. It wasn't necessary to see angels in Raphael's paintings, when in Mussolini's time you had those same angels appearing in the Italian mountains. This child joyfully approaches me to kiss me. The child, feeling that I was excited with its beauty, comes to kiss me. The child comes into my arms and I to the child. Suddenly the child's sister, who was older, said to the child, "Go away, you can't kiss him. They are rich English." I wanted to say, "What kind of rich Englishman? I'm a poor Jew." And then I remembered, what if I was a rich Englishman at that moment? Did no one have the right to hug another in this period of starvation? [Being so] bitter that two beings kiss? So what if I'm a rich Englishman! In that moment, suddenly, it—the class struggle, class

> enemies—I felt this, that it began, with one small thing, but for me [really] one large thing. The entire lining of Marxist philosophy about progress, about progressive society, about the working class that has its rights, it all began to shake apart. This didn't happen quickly, but it was there. It all began in that moment. Slowly there began to occur in my life many strange (wonderful) things. . . .

From Personal Revelation (Transcendent Experience) to Revealed Propositional Revelation: A Return to Text

> This revelation that was given to me, I saw later that it exists in the Bible. . . . I never even read that book. . . . And now it happens that the events which occurred in me—I saw this after—coincide with the Old Testament.

Since he avoided religious class and never had read the Bible, a relationship between childhood socialization and his wartime experience is not clearly indicated. Enriko himself goes on to explain how he came to the Old Testament, how he moved from his personal transcendent experiences to the Bible. Following the capitulation of Italy in September 1943, Enriko and other Jews managed to find transport to Switzerland. While in Switzerland, two factors contributed significantly to the process that was transforming Enriko. First, he acquainted himself with the daughter of a Swiss pastor. He read his songs to her. While there he wrote music and songs. He wrote them in Serbian, German, French, Italian, and in all possible [languages]. The pastor's daughter told him, "What I hear from you is like the Old Testament". . . . Her words surprised Enriko. He replied to her,

> Old Testament? I also read Shakespeare and all, but the Old Testament. . . ? So in this way, which could be said [in] a literary way—no. . . . Suddenly I see there are some things which, with some experience, and an internal voice, and probably with [one's?] heritage, at that moment there began a great movement in my spiritual being and more. That I will not tell you about; it is too confessional. I experienced those kinds of things that monks experienced once they withdrew into a monk's cell. They hear a voice, but the true authentic voice, and then they leave. . . . And their entire vital metabolism changes. I experienced that.

To describe the experience Enriko uses natural symbolism.

> Let's say I was an average athlete. . . . Suddenly a distinct voice says, "Today you will stand from morning until the following day on one spot and look into the sun." I could never look into the light, and that for me would be senseless. . . . I never want to try that. But that voice was so strong that it simply dug me into one spot. Then I could no longer move, and I looked into the sun until the sun set and until the sun came up, and I saw that strange, wonderful things began to happen to me. On that level . . . wonderful things began to happen to me, great movements within me, which were completed with that. It's a long story, but I can't tell it now. There must be a moment when I am able to tell it. Not like this. . . . It was completed. . . . I saw that all the answers which in my time I had searched for are already expressed, in the Five Books of Moses, and, for whoever wishes, in the [Hebrew] Prophets. Do I need to show you? I am always bewildered from excitement. . . .

Text and Hermeneutics: From Metaphor to Reality

From his experiences of personal revelation Enriko moved to sacred text, to the Bible. He proceeded to read and explain hermeneutically several passages of biblical text. He read from the Torah, the Prophets, and from the book of Revelation in the New Testament.

> The complete prophecy, that which happened to us, . . . it's here, it's grandiose. That is the testament—Moses' song before his death. [He reads Deuteronomy 32 in the Croatian translation.] And now, of course, this is, seen like this, one hermeneutic. There is written here, in one place, that they will cast us into burning ovens. In the Books of Moses [it says] that we shall be thrown across Egypt into fiery ovens, but that we shall be returned, and that in the wilderness God will, when the nation shall return, settle accounts with Israel and with his enemies. In that time Hitler was on a rampage, concentration camps and all. And, of course, man asks, "Why? How is this possible?" Then I, since I was a lover of truth, searched for an answer and found it in the Bible. Here in one horrible, unheard of place of which

Honeggar wrote in his oratory, *Danske Macabre*, here in Ezekiel it is literally written about that which will come upon us in the last times. [In] Ezekiel, those are things described with a film camera. It is a well known passage. Many have written poems about it. [He reads Ezekiel 37.] So, how did Israel rise up? From concentration camps. The entire Zionist movement couldn't do anything until the destruction in the concentration camps. That is literal. There's no hedging here. It's unequivocal. Awesome.

[The prophecies] in Jeremiah and in Zechariah, today they are slowly being fulfilled. They are no longer metaphors. No longer are they even paradigms for all times. . . . "When I return you [to the land]." And where are we today? Today we are exactly at the moment of the most wonderful revelation, the return of Israel to the promised land. Here there is no equivocating; it's literally like what all these books say, thus how the Word of God says, which is the one truth.

It's described, what will happen to those who will rise up against Israel when it returns [to the land]. "All those who will rise up against you when you will return." It doesn't say, "I will punish you," but rather, "I will wipe you from the face of the earth. They will be no more." That is horrible. Look at what is happening. Wherever you look—Iran, Iraq—they are destroying themselves, just among themselves. Completely insane. They don't know what to do. The PLO, the talk about the Palestinians here, they will be scattered, will never return, because they rose up against their brother when he returned back to the promised land. It is no longer a joke. It makes no difference to me. I can be whatever I want, a Liberal, a Laborist, and a Shamirist. It's above everything. . . . As you know, there's no joking with the atom. When we opened the atom, it was finished, over. . . .

I see this. Israel didn't elect itself to be God's Chosen People. Rather it's all retrospective that God chose one of the peoples. It could have been any other people, but that was his will. "I will make an eternal covenant with you, and I will never leave you. When you are scattered throughout the whole earth, I'll never leave you, because I am God. . . . I saw that the Jews aren't narcissistic because they stay in the diaspora. . . . Not one people can, not one people could have survived when it lost food, lost its faith, and when it lost the state. All were assimilated, disappeared. That's normal. This is completely outside of historical fact. Not because the Jews earned this, but rather because God so determined. Here there's no equivocating. Through the most horrible situations to massacres. Thus, these aren't metaphors. That all happened. And in what time? In the most civilized, most cultured time. . . . Thus when it's said God is magnificent and terrible, simultaneously he is one and the other. There's no equivocation here. He really is terrible, but he is really magnificent. And he really is gracious without end.

Do you know German? I wanted to translate Buber's translation which is brilliant, which goes by the original text. There's no equivocating. These are exceptional things. Thus I say to you, Suddenly I had to see that all of my Marxism, Socialism, Humanism, all that is nice and good, but all of that is only one. It is, you know, like a free particle; it's no longer an atom in which wonders occur. . . . Before us are being fulfilled wonders of God for which we are unworthy. Rather, it has been decreed. That, for me, is something like this: someone who is contaminated with radiation. . . . If someone is contaminated with the terrible decree of God, he cannot be decontaminated. He must stay that way; there's no way out for him. You have a passage in Jeremiah that says [He reads Jeremiah 16]: "But now I will send for many fishermen, declares the Lord, and they will catch them. After that I will send for many hunters, and they will hunt them down on every mountain and hill and from the crevices of the rocks." I know the fourteenth and sixteenth chapters by heart. . . . "You will be called [by name]." Phenomenal. I, no, no, I'm exhilarated. . . . Now I saw. The Nobel Prize was given to one physicist [who said], "A majestic picture. We see the atom, [but] not it alone. Now it's clear through that electronic microscope. We see the paths of the atom. We see the particles. That's a majestic picture." And so what is this [in the Bible] when God says that he will send fishermen after us, and seek hunters to hunt for us. He says, "Watchfully I follow them, and my eye does not leave them." Those are grandiose things. I am saying this in a very simplified way. I grasped that we are helpless. I can thrash about as much as I want. There's one thing: there exists will, God's will which determines something. This is no kind of fatalism. We, within the framework of God's will, have great freedom, but we can never be what we are not. We cannot, that's impossible.

In that sense Israel is the people that is chosen. Not by their own "auto-suggestion" as Freud explains, or, I don't know, Jung. . . . We are chosen. It's not a privilege. To be chosen . . . is an earthly curse. Thus we are seen as cursed. Therefore everywhere we are persecuted. . . . If I have to choose between an earthly curse which is of God, it's a blessing. I'm not interested in earthly blessing. But a good part of the Jewish people are actually themselves inside first of all for this other [earthly blessing]. For us now there is emancipation. Of what use to us is emancipation when entire mankind today is going in the opposite direction?

Revelation in the Natural World: Physics and Metaphysics

We broke the atom today, scientifically, it's said, the nucleus. However, we don't understand that we didn't break the atom. We didn't penetrate the mystery of mysteries, the holy altar of [origins], because the temple, that is, the Jerusalem temple, is an atomic temple. First there was the destroyed Jerusalem temple which was the paradigm of external beauty. The barbarians destroyed the temple, . . . [It was] a marvelous internal nest in which wonders occur, completely incomprehensible to the mind. I heard one of those programs in which it was said that the free particles in the nucleus, . . . are no longer elementary particles, for there are so many of them. Besides electrons, protons, and neutrons, there is yet another element which is very interesting and wonderful, and scientists today are thus researching it. This element behaves completely differently from the rest. I forget how they call this element. Now begins a picture that's just too wonderful. They say the electron is, I don't know, one, two, or three dimensional, but this particle has 25 dimensions. Therefore, Einstein, with the fourth dimension, began the movement toward understanding. But what shall we do now with this conclusion that there is an element with 25 dimensions, and that it behaves differently? Now it's not known whether it is an integral part of the nucleus or flew in as a foreign element. Do you understand? But, it doesn't depend on all of that. We actually don't see that they destroyed that holy Jerusalem temple today. The [Hebrew] prophets foresaw what would happen when the temple was destroyed. Of course, [they saw] with the hermeneutics of their metaphors. But now we see that these are metaphors no longer, but are pure narration. Heizenberger, in his book *Physics and Metaphysics*, says that today, when we find ourselves before such views of the inside of the nucleus, we no longer can use scientific words, only poetic ones. . . . But today it's neither poetry nor metaphor any longer, but the essence of essence, encoded, stated, exegetically stated. But exegesis opens [it] only to oneself.

Chernobyl: "All bowed down before the Creator"

And now you must see what the point is. We are in this moment when Chernobyl occurred. That is a mild reminder to all of us. But nothing is of any use. We are going further. It was a mild reminder. I don't know if you know. Chernobyl's radiation in the period of four weeks, in relation to all atomic bombs tested, including Hiroshima and Nagasaki, is nothing, one one-thousandth. Maybe Sodom and Gomorra was a moment similar to *zakuzenjem* of the biosphere. I think that Sodom and Gomorra isn't just a spiritual story. Rather it was an incarnation of a war. It was the incarnation of the incarnate evil, certainly, . . . But Chernobyl is a fantastic warning. What happened there? In one passage the prophet says: "In the last days all the nations will bow down to him."

Now look, we have become numb, dull. When Chernobyl occurred it didn't depend on whether you were for or against atomic, nuclear energy. Everyone—look a little closer—bowed before God because they understood that this is something that is above us. Scientists said, "In the moment that such a thing happens . . . we are powerless." Do you hear the words? But before whom are we powerless? These powerful men? You are powerless before God. . . All the scientists of the world actually bowed before God. But he says that man should be able to see what he does. Moses says in prayer,"You are terrible, . . . I can't look at you."

This is what Moses says, "Let me see you." And God says, "You will see only my back. You shall not see me from the front. If you look at me you will die." They don't see that they did this. All bowed to God the Creator. Understand?

Then you have a phenomenal passage in the Revelation of John, the Apocalypse. Translations are wrong. Luther correctly translated it, and the Latin translations are accurate. [He reads Revelation 21.] "I saw a new heaven and a new earth. . . . Follow this. Not nations. It's now translated "with nations." Will all the nations enter . . . No, he says, Gentile. Goyim means one who knows not God. It's not a pejorative name. It's a name for those who don't believe in God. They believe in gods; they believe in power, in energetics, in progress. That's the idea. "You shall enter Jerusalem because God and those that know him . . . ." But we don't see that today we, and all scientists of the world, when Chernobyl occurred, bowed down to the Creator. Of course, not religiously, but fundamentally, in essence. Do you understand me? Fundamentally, metaphysically. We have all bowed down before him, whether or not we have believed in him. Because, they say, "That is a power which is stronger than all of us; we can't control it." Do you understand me? I always wondered how wonderful it sounds. All the nations, pagans and those who don't know God, will bow down. So, don't they see that that is happening today? On a fantastic level . . . on a wonderful marvelous level.

The Jews as Paradigm: A "Nation of Priests"

And now, I say, all the events that occur today in the world—let's say that struggle for peace, then humanism, and [the fight] against racial segregation—those aren't just phrases; they are sincere [efforts]. The other is that politicians create work from that. That doesn't interest me. But this is one sincere moment, the deepest moment in man, in intellectual man, in Christian man. I'm speaking about Christian nations. Christian nations accepted the yeast of Judaism, and simply say that suffering and sacrifice is something essentially sacred, the fundamental mystery on which begin all [unclear]. So they took that from Judaism. Thus, Christians were called first to feel the sense of suffering through Christ's crucifixion on the cross. It is not accidental that the Pope comes today to the church and says, "You are our dearest brothers." I don't know if you know this. I must show you. Just before his [Pope John 23] death he spoke his prayer of confession. It's written down. I'll retell it for you. He says, "Forgive us that for centuries we didn't grasp the beauty of your chosen people; rather we cursed it, cursed the name of the Jew. Forgive us for we didn't know that we crucified you, Christ, a second time. Forgive us for we didn't know what we were doing. Listen, that is Pope John the 23rd before his death, his prayer of confession. Do you know what a confessional is? It's what you pray just before death. Pope John the 23rd sees that Israel is the paradigm of the incarnate Christ who is crucified, and that Israel, like Christ, was innocently crucified . . . and he says, "Forgive us, we didn't know that we crucified you in the flesh for a second time.". . . Today that's no longer a literary story. That's so awesome.

Therefore today we find ourselves in a great moment when the Christian Church reveals to the nations the depth of such a crucifixion. That in the depth of this crucifixion an entire nation participates, but voluntarily. . . . What is essential is this: in the deepest depth, that which happened with Christ on the cross, it happened later with the entire nation of Israel, because they are one, they are inseparable. The fate of that nation is the same as the fate of the crucified Christ. Because he alone was crucified for the rest of the nations. All the great ideas—humanism, whatever you want, Christianity, the deepest theology of Christianity—all originates from there. Not because it's Jewish. It has nothing to do with that. They sin if they stir up things against the Jews. The Jews in general always wanted to be like the rest of the peoples, always, but then they got hit over the head, and so they were different. They weren't different because they wanted that. Wait, I'll translate for you a well-known place. . . . And there's no equivocating. Today we see that [these prophecies] are being fulfilled. Then, for us in retrospect they become eternal truth. Here is a marvelous place. I copied it. It's from Buber's translation. "So tell the house of Jacob and the sons of Israel, "You will be to me a kingdom of priests and a holy nation. . . . He, your God, is a fire (flame) which destroys, a jealous God, He is merciful." Therefore, simultaneously he is a fire which destroys and a merciful God. "He is your God. He will never leave you, and will not allow you to perish. He does not forget the Covenant which he made with your ancestors. . . ." Now it says, in the Book of Moses, not in the Prophets later, but already in the Book of Moses: "I will scatter you among all the nations of the world, and you will become people which . . . It's written, it says, the translation is bad—that means that you will be numerous. It's always said that Americans received the Nobel Prize, but those are Jews. They, again, are numerous. Do you understand? We're always taken out. "You will remain among the tribes of the nations, and then you will, when you are among them, again find me, because you will turn to me with your complete heart, and with your entire soul. In that time you will recognize me again in the last times." That is that apocalyptic time. "You will again hear his voice, you will follow his voice, and I will return you to the promised land." Thus, this can be what some psychologist or psychoanalyst states in [the following] way: in order that the nation survive, the priesthood of the nation instilled a suggestion that it be like this in order to survive. In order that the Jew survives he suggests this to himself. Psychoanalysis says this. Because it says that we have thought up God. Man is the great I. . . . If such things happen, outside of all historical laws, in the Prophets it says in one place—Where has it been seen that my people will be declared a nation in one day. In the United Nations on November 29 that happened. Nothing like this ever happened, that some people was declared a nation in one day. The prophet Isaiah says that, and this happened in the United Nations. . . . You know what kind of battle it was . . . Israel declared as Israel. He says that it will be called Israel when it has returned. It's not called the State of Palestine or State of Jewry, but Israel. And you know what Iraehet means—"warriors for God." . . . They must now fight for their land, but it's not seen that they fight for the Word of God. Sharon, Peres, it's not important. . . . They don't see that they are fulfilling God's decrees. Of course, they are broad, great. Man has a free choice. It doesn't mean that the will of God is deterministic fatalism. That's a lie; that's what we [humans] thought up. On the contrary, it's a terrible dynamism between the freedom of man and the will of God. The freedom of man and the will of God join together, and here great wonders occur. I still say, I was thrilled with that which we don't see, that after Chernobyl we all bowed down to the Creator. It's finished. Now it says there: "In the last times all will bow down and will see I Am Who I Am, I Am Who I Am; My name is "I Am," "Ich Bin," "Der Ich Bin." And now, we don't actually see that we are all joining together into (as) one, but in reality it is so. We are becoming Israel, consciously or unconsciously, because Israel means to give one's entire self to the Creator and to be with him. And now the fact that we are fighting against nuclear power, we don't see that this is a battle to be with him. Do you understand me? We don't see that all these movements—green belt, antinuclear, anti-racism, etc.—we don't see that it's a battle of all the peoples to be with God and in God. On the priestly level. . . . "From Zion shall come a new song; you will sing a new song. . . . This means, the ario of the priestly ceremonial, which is archaic, [it] became old, [it] falls, because it says: "In the New Jerusalem there will be no temple." You know, that's a fantastic place; there will be no temple. We have prepared ourselves. We have destroyed all authorities. But only one thing we haven't destroyed: the fear that we will destroy ourselves. Now, when we fight in order not to destroy ourselves, we don't see that we are fighting to be Israel and to be in God.

The Jews in Yugoslavia

No, you know what, it's not a wonder, after this horrible holocaust, all are set in concrete; the consciousness slowly awakens. I think that in this, our community such consciousness (in this sense) incredibly awakens. Of course, slowly, gradually, but it awakens. Secondly, . . . Something happens in people. Certainly, it happens slowly. And it must, it's more powerful than all of us. That's one thing. Secondly, we as a community, without regard to all that there is, nevertheless we find ourselves in a very privileged position, and we really are protected. No one persecutes us. Here and there, and always it must be, politics is politics. Today the politics [of Yugoslavia] is against the State of Israel. It's not antisemitic in the sense of being against

> Jews. Eli Wiesel, [there was] an article in the papers about him. I heard his announcement. He said, "I announced that I will fight my entire life so that it will not be forgotten what kind of horror it is to be an antisemite. A horror not for the Jew, rather for the other; it's a horror if they are antisemites. He wanted to say, in other words, "You don't know, you are against God if you are against the Jew." This has become a synonym. We can also be against us, and against God. . . I see in the prayer for Yom Kippur it says, "Lord, embrace those among us who don't know (believe in) God; forgive them." That's brilliant. I saw that in the prayer for Yom Kippur. . . . Listen, that is wonderful. Ha, Ha, . . . It doesn't mean anything to say you're an atheist. Can't be. Man is a creature of God.
>
> I think that huge, great things are happening, that still they haven't completely penetrated our consciousness. but they gradually sink deeper to the broadest layers of people. You have a wonderful example. One woman told me this. She's married to a Jew. She's a Serb. She says, "You know what happened to me a few days ago? I took some of my husband's clothes to the tailor to have mended." [The tailor asks], "For whom?" "Atijas." He says, "You're a Jew." She says, "No, but my husband is a Jew." He says, "You know, the Jews are mixed up with God; they will save us." Among the people it's like this. It's mixed together. He said it in folk way. They are mixed up with God. You must not touch them. . . . You see, it is ingrained, even in the average man. You see this more and more.

Ethnic and Political Man

Slavko Goldstein: "I have no dilemmas"

When conducting a week of fieldwork in Zagreb in the spring of 1989, I was fortunate to obtain two interviews with Slavko Goldstein who was a rising political star in Croatian political life. To members of the Jewish community he was a visible representative and good broker, while to outsiders he was perceived and used as valuable "symbolic capital" in the incipient democratizing phase. Community workers were becoming frustrated because they felt he was not giving them enough time to discuss their work in the community. At the time Goldstein was simultaneously the president of the Zagreb Jewish community and the president of an emerging quasi-political party called the Croatian Social-Liberal Association (HSLS). His dual role in the community and in the public political arena, together with other factors, make Slavko Goldstein an atypical case and this alone warrants his inclusion among the narratives. I draw upon my two interviews with Slavko Goldstein and sources that are a part of the public record.

Slavko Goldstein is not a typical Yugoslav Jew for the following reasons, which must be considered together rather than individually. First, he fought in the National Liberation War, joined the Communist Party of Yugoslavia, but unlike others he dropped out of the Party soon after the war. Second, he has had a strong Croatian orientation, even before the recent transition and collapse of socialist Yugoslavia (e.g., he was an advocate of the Croatian term for Jew, *Židov*, rather than *Jevrej*). Third, he played an instrumental role in bringing greater visibility to the Jews of Croatia and Yugoslavia as one of the conceivers of the successful exhibit, "The Jews of Yugoslavia," which contributed to the pre-transition feeling of philosemitism in the country. Fourth, as president of the Zagreb Jewish Community, Slavko Goldstein succeeded in establishing greater autonomy for the Zagreb community from the Federation of Jewish Communities of Yugoslavia. In seeking greater autonomy his and the Zagreb Jewish community's orientation reflected the broader societal orientation of the Croats vis-à-vis the Yugoslav Federation. Fifth, he had become a highly visible public figure beginning in 1985. This started with his public proposal for radical economic reform, whose stated solution was to join the European Community. His direct involvement in the push for a multi-party system in Croatia elevated his public visibility. Sixth, Slavko Goldstein was the president of the Zagreb Jewish community and the opposition quasi-party, the HSLS, simultaneously, a dual role that was not lost on either the Jews or Croats; lastly, because of his role within and outside the Jewish community, Slavko Goldstein has not escaped controversy. Both members of the Jewish community and non-Jews have criticized him. One of the controversial cases was called "the Goldstein Affair," in which he became entangled in the conflict over the number of genocide victims.

What do these factors say? First, Slavko Goldstein had positioned himself asymmetrically during the period of submergence. Second, he had exhibited a strong Croatian orientation long before the transition beginning in 1989. Third, he carries both a strong Jewish and a strong Croatian identity. Fourth, he was one of the earliest proponents and activists in the movement out of Titoist socialism and toward economic reform and a multiparty system. He was a public voice for change. Fifth, his dual role and his involvement in the genocide count conflict contributed to some bad feelings, and perhaps even a fracture in the Jewish community.

Slavko Goldstein was born in 1928 in Karlovac, near Zagreb, into a middle-class Ashkenazi Jewish family. Both of his parents were Jewish. Slavko Goldstein's father was a bookseller. The world of books would later become Slavko Goldstein's world as well. He became a publisher and publicist. Through his profession he met many leading intellectuals of different nationalities. With some he developed personal friendships, including the Communist-turned-dissident of Montenegrin descent, Milovan Djilas, whose wife requested books on Jewish subjects.

The fusion of Slavko Goldstein's Jewish identity, which became fixed during the twelve to thirteen years of his childhood before World War II erupted, and his Croatian identity began to take shape during the war years. "I am a Jew . . . when we had those [censuses] I always wrote that I am Jew. But I am a Croatian Jew and I am not ashamed of the Croat name. The reasons are mainly, but not only, from the wartime," he told me. That he developed a strong Croatian identity is highly significant for understanding Slavko Goldstein's motivation to enter the Croatian political arena beginning in the mid-1980s (see below). The Second World War erupted when Slavko Goldstein was thirteen years old. Soon afterward events separated him from his parents. The fascists took his father away and Slavko Goldstein never saw him again. His father eventually was killed in the Jasenovac concentration camp in the Independent State of Croatia. Early in the war Slavko Goldstein's mother was put into a prison. Slavko Goldstein then resided with an old Jewish widow. In November 1941 a Croat who was an official clerk in the financial department of the Karlovac municipality came to Slavko Goldstein and warned him that the day after tomorrow there would be a raid on all the Jews and they would be transported to a concentration camp. He then told Slavko Goldstein that a friend of his mother urged him to flee to a village twenty-two kilometers from Karlovac. Being thus forewarned, Slavko Goldstein tried to persuade other Jews to flee, but none heeded his warning. Slavko Goldstein fled to the village. The 300–400 inhabitants of the village that served as his temporary refuge were all

Croatian Catholics. They accepted Slavko Goldstein without questions and hid him for three weeks. All of the inhabitants knew that he was a Jew hiding in their village.

> I went to the village with my host Mata Kjerih. On the other side of the village was the school. We went to the school because the teacher was acquainted with my father. My father was a bookseller, and so the teacher knew him. Nobody in the village denounced me. And I didn't feel any danger in this Croat village. But after three weeks, less than a month later, I don't know the day, [although] I know the day when I came to the village—November 19, some time before the middle of December, the Partisans had an action about 10 kilometers away. And then the hosts came to me and said, "The teacher [said] that he hears the fascist army will make a strong hold here because of the [Partisan] action and it will be dangerous for you. I will bring you to . . . a Croatian family" [a family well acquainted with Slavko Goldstein's mother]. They told me they would take me to Karlovac and from there to the Italian zone. So they took me to Karlovac, dressed as a peasant. And it was true. The army would come and it would be dangerous for me, because somebody [among] the 300–400 people, a child will say, "There is a small Jew here." [In Karlovac] I was hidden four to five days in the flat of a Croatian family. In their store [we] hid many things from our house. They managed to get a false passport. It was not a passport, but it was a laze pasare, a document that says you are free to travel in this and that direction, not everywhere. They got it [with] a false name for me. I think I know who got it for me, but I never met him because during the war he disappeared. He was a very prominent official of the Croat Peasant Party. His wife helped. He wasn't in the Ustashi regime. He was in the majority Croat party before the war, the Croatian Peasant Party. He was a deputy for this party for the district near Karlovac.

Thus began Slavko Goldstein's formation of a bond with the Croatian people. The bond continued to solidify throughout the war years. In time his mother was released and joined him [in the Italian zone?], as did his brother. The three of them lived together for several months with a Croatian family.

A functionary of the illegal Communist Party, who knew Slavko Goldstein's father, provided the Goldsteins with a connection to the Partisans. They stayed where they were through the winter of 1941–1942, and then in April they set out to join the Partisans. The whole time they stayed with Croats who helped them. Slavko Goldstein was less than fourteen years old; his brother was ten. The Croats with whom they stayed warned them that a concentration camp was being prepared for Jews in Karlovac. His mother did not want to stay behind and be put into the camp, so she too asked for a connection to the Partisans. The liaison was a boy of seventeen who returned to them and informed them they could join. Their connection was with the Croatian Partisans. Slavko Goldstein did stay for eight months in a Serbian village, but then again rejoined a unit of Croatian Partisans. "That is [my] experience. Well, I have been persecuted. My father has been killed by Croatian people, but it is impossible for me to have feelings against the Croatian people as a whole because of such experiences. I think it is enough. It is pretty convincing, yes?" Various Croats had warned him of impending disaster, had provided refuge for him, a stranger, had transported him from one location to another, had provided illegal documents, and had connected him to the Croatian Partisans with whom he served. He has never forgotten this.

> I came to the Partisans at 14 years [of age]. My bar mitzvah I didn't celebrate because the [fascist] occupation came. My fourteenth birthday I celebrated in the Partisans. Two months before I became 14 years old I had been accepted. I didn't join. It was something like an honor to be accepted in the Communist youth. It was called SKOJ [Association of Communist Youth of Yugoslavia]. I became one of the youngest members of the Communist Party, one of the youngest officers in the Partisan Army. I commanded a *četa* [unit—a company]. I was 15-plus when I became a commander and also (later?) commissar of a bigger unit. I finished the war as a member of the Communist Party.

Given his war experiences among and in the Partisans, Slavko Goldstein became a member of the Communist Youth and then of the Party itself. Like many other Jews who had not been in the Party before the war, the war years served as a period of political transformation and socialization. Unlike most other Jews, however, he left the Party soon after the war.

> I was a member of the Communist Party [for] four years after the war, but I was a very bad member. I didn't like it. I was very enthusiastic during the war when I thought we were fighting for freedom and so one, [but] after the war became disappointed [because of the] totalitarian measures. I couldn't understand why, when [they got] complete power, why they [couldn't] give at least some freedom to others. They were punishing people without trials. So I didn't like it. I was brought up in a bourgeois family, a Jewish family, and couldn't approve of totalitarian measures after the war. So I broke with the Party. After four years I evaded [returning] to the Party. I went to Israel to my family and returned and never [re]joined the Party. My mother's complete family is in Israel. I visited them there, then I returned, and my mother returned.

Slavko Goldstein has been a catalyst for change in both the Zagreb Jewish community and in Croatian public life. In 1986 two young Jews in the community, one a representative of the middle generation and the other a representative of the youth generation, approached Slavko Goldstein and asked him to run for the presidency of the community. He agreed and in the election beat the incumbent, who, like Slavko Goldstein, also circulated in two social spheres, one within and the other outside the Jewish community. The incumbent's outside social sphere was that of his old Partisan network (he was a carrier of the Spomenica 1941, an award given only to Partisans who fought in the first days of the Uprisings). The year of Slavko Goldstein's ascendancy to the position of community president coincided with the community's 180th anniversary celebration. The two community members who had asked him to run wanted Slavko Goldstein to be the community's representative during the celebration, which would serve as both a rite of intensification and a rite of passage whereupon the community would open itself to the public. An even greater event that fulfilled the same functions was the exhibition, "The Jews of Yugoslavia" (see chapter 6). Again, Slavko Goldstein played an active and highly visible role. From the time of the anniversary celebration in 1986 the community under the leadership of Slavko Goldstein began to seek greater autonomy from the Federation of Jewish Communities of Yugoslavia, which had exerted great influence over the local communities throughout the Titoist period.

Beginning with the publication of a book in 1985 that brought him considerable public attention and with it his entrance into the political arena, Slavko Goldstein began to construct a narrative that opposed Jewish and societal submergence and the dramaturgical control that went along with it.

> After I was pensioned I started writing. I started writing some articles. I wrote a book, a critical book on the system. I think it was the first book—it was written in 1984—where there was a complete proposal of reform in the system of the enterprises. Yes, it was the first. . . . It was called "Proposal '85". . . . It was my personal experience. I wanted to put it down, about this system which doesn't function. Not only why the system can't function in other enterprises, and what it means in [for] the whole economy, but I also made new proposals. They were widely discussed. I was invited mostly to Slovenia, to the Marxist Center of the Central Committee, to explain. Also here in Zagreb, but much less. . . . And that was the turning point. I wrote it not because of any political ambitions but because I had a bad experience and wanted to put it on paper. I was free after pension and had time to write. This book became pretty well known in Yugoslavia, especially in Slovenia and Croatia. I think that all of those proposals have now [Spring 1989] been accepted in the Law of Enterprises, but not as my proposals. I am not jealous about it. . . But anyway it was the first complete proposal. And so I became very well known also in the political sphere and was invited by many newspapers, especially by weekly newspapers, to write and to [provide] interviews about this book.

He claims that he was the first person to actually write that the single way out of Yugoslavia's crises was to join the European Community. In 1987 he co-authored a ten-point proposal for economic change ("10 Points for an Open Economy"), which called for the free circulation of capital and in which the call to join the European Community was reiterated in the ninth point. At the time these points sounded very radical, but by 1989 they were all more or less accepted in Slovenia and Croatia.

During my visit to Zagreb in May 1989, the first public meeting of the Croatian Social-Liberal Alliance was held. Two friends of Slavko Goldstein asked him to serve as president of what was then a quasi-political party, the first noncommunist political organization in Croatia since the Second World War (*Danas*, 8 May 1990). They asked him to lead it because they thought that as a Jew no one would denounce him as Croatian nationalist. They saw his Partisan past and his recent writings as other advantages. In addition to Slavko Goldstein there were "several Jews and half-Jews in the leading group of the HSLS."

In the spring of 1989 when change was beginning to accelerate, both in terms of democratization and nationalism, Slavko Goldstein told me, "For me personally there are no dilemmas. I have no dilemmas." He continued:

> I think the Slovenian [path] is the way for all of Yugoslavia—democracy. I am not hesitating. I only think that I understand the Serbs better than the Slovenes do. [The Serbs and Slovenes were in the midst of a war of words.] We are nearer to the Serbs here in Zagreb. We have more connections. We have the same language. It doesn't mean that I accept the Serbian standpoint, but I understand it better than the Slovenians do. I think there are some [good] arguments that the Serbian Constitution wasn't fair towards the Serbs. And the Slovenes don't understand enough. But (concerning) the ideas of democracy I have no hesitation or dilemmas. . . .

Besides the motivating factors of his war experience and the initiative for democracy in Croatia, Slavko Goldstein expressed concern for his own children's future. "It is mostly because of my children who are living here that I decided to join this initiative. I think that [with] my reputation I can help. Not very much, but I can help. So I joined it. That is the reason. Not because of Jews. But [yes, also] because of Jews [laughs]. My children are also Jews."

During his involvement with the HSLS his life became increasingly divided between his communal duties and his political activism. The vice-president of the Jewish community told me in May 1989 that he saw no conflict of loyalties, but I saw that others were not pleased because they could not get his ear long enough. This displeasure grew to the point that it became an issue in the community. Slavko Goldstein decided not to run for another term (see *Bilten* (JOZ)). Slavko Goldstein himself believed that his involvement in the political arena could help reputations on both sides.

The Problem of Yugoslavia: Slavko Goldstein and the Jews as Broker

In the spring of 1989 Slavko Goldstein believed that some kind of an understanding between the Serbs and Croats was still possible, but that the formulaic "brotherhood and unity" was an illusion. When I interviewed him he already had a plan to work toward the goal of interethnic understanding in the form of a new program for Serbia and Croatia, which he believed was "the key for the solution of the Yugoslav situation. When I asked him whether this was just another resurrection of the Yugoslav Idea, he replied that it was not. Rather, he called it "searching for a new formula. . . .Perhaps it means divorce. But divorce is understanding." He added,

> In my opinion, it is not divorce [or] the Yugoslav Idea, but joining Europe. . . [Remaining as Yugoslavia is today?] Not important. Not important. It depends on the people. But if you are in Europe, then you are in the same state, [whether] you are Yugoslavia or not. You can be Serbia and Croatia. [You are talking about the European Community?] Yes, the EC. I am talking about the European state after 1992. That is what I think the program for Yugoslavia should be. . . Because of the mixed population, Serbian and Croatian, the problem of Yugoslavia has never been solved. When they lived in other states, the Yugoslav people, the Serbs and Croats, they longed to be together in the same state. And the Yugoslav Idea started here in Croatia, but it was well accepted in Serbia in the nineteenth century and especially at the beginning of the twentieth century. Immediately when they came [together] in the same state problems arose. They were never solved. . . Many people, among them the communists, felt it was impossible to solve it normally in such a frame of state. So the Communists proposed a Balkan Federation. It was an illusion that it, a broader federation, would diminish those frictions between Yugoslav nations. It was an illusion. . . .
>
> I think the first realistic idea was to join Europe. Because, in [the Yugoslav situation], for everything bad the Croats blame the Serbs, the Serbs blame the Croats. This play between Serbia and Slovenia is a play only. . . The real program [conflict] is between the Serbs and Croats. They live together. they live mixed in the same villages, but di-

vided. They don't marry between [themselves] and so on. That is the problem.

The Yugoslav Jews as Brokers

Goldstein believed that the Yugoslav Jewish possessed the necessary characteristics to serve as a broker between Yugoslavia's ethnic groups. He expressed the following:

> The possible role of the Jewish community in Yugoslavia is, although it is a very small community, as you know about 6,000, the possible role is to improve the understanding between Serbs and Croats. And the Jews can help. I will speak at the session of our Federation [of Jewish Communities of Yugoslavia] the day after tomorrow about it. I think that what I am doing personally, what I am doing with this group [HSLS], my main goal is more understanding between Croats and Serbs on a new basis. Not on a basis [as] Yugoslavs, but as Croats and as Serbs. It was always suppressed. Now you have the Serbs boasting, "We are Serbs," and the Croats [doing the same]. You can't suppress it. It is not normal [to suppress it]. You have to say, "We are not Yugoslavs. We can't be Yugoslavs. . . But we are Serbs and Croats, and please understand each other." The Jewish community can help. Nothing more. We can help because as a community we have a good reputation, as you know, here in Yugoslavia now. . . . We are in a situation where nobody can tell us we are nationalists, either Serbian or Croatian nationalists. So, that is one of the more important points of this discussion. The Jewish community can—it is not a must, but it can improve the Serb-Croat [relations]. It is in the interest of the Yugoslav nations and of the Jews. . . I don't want to be in politics, I think you understand me from all I said. At 60 years of age, to start [in] politics is not my ambition. But there is a danger even of a civil war, [although] I don't think there will be a civil war. You see the relations are bad and becoming worse, and that the Jews can be a very small but still existing bridge for more understanding. [Right now, where is the leadership going to come from, besides yourself, in the Jewish community? At the Federational level, is it important to have someone feel this way?] I don't think that such an activity can be

improved or implemented through the Federation [of Jewish Communities of Yugoslavia]. The Federation has other plans of action, activity, interest, mainly the Jewish. Especially such a leadership [of the Federation], which is very much dedicated to the Jewish cause. Now the present leadership [is] very capable of improving the Jewish cause but [does not give] enough thought towards the outside work. You know, the Jews are sometimes very much closed inside, and. . . they don't share the same opinions about such activities. So this is what I think the Jews can do. They can do it. First, reputationally, as good writers and as good lawyers, well known artists and university professors, journalists. [Second,] they can do it with the Socialist Alliance [of Working Peoples of Yugoslavia.

The Jewish Community Professional

Marko: A Change Agent for a Return to Ritual Authenticity

Marko is about forty years old. As a professional in the Jewish community, he served as an educational coordinator in the Federation of Jewish Communities of Yugoslavia. The foreign Jewish aid organization JOINT paid his salary. Marko was committed to the Jewish community and dedicated himself to serving it twenty-four hours a day.

Marko's father was a Sephardi Jew whose ancestors came to Bosnia from Salonika. His mother is a Slovene. Marko was born in Slovenia and says he admires "them"—the Slovenes. Both parents are members of the Communist Party. He was approached and asked to join on three different occasions but refused. In the last decade his father has become disenchanted with the political system. "He has lost his idealism of what the new society will become. His expectations weren't met." Now his father can be seen attending the Shabbat service in the Belgrade synagogue on occasion. His one sibling, a sister, is married to another Jewish activist. The family gathers together once a week, on Saturday, for lunch at the parents' home. Marko was married to a Jewish woman. The marriage produced a daughter who lives with Marko on weekends. He is raising her as a Jew, and the mother supports this kind of socialization. Marko's own father, who was a career officer in the Yugoslav National Army, did not raise him as a Jew. He did not pass on his Jewishness to his son. "But he didn't say, no. He didn't hide his Jewishness from me," Marko adds. His father was in his eighties during my fieldwork, retired for many years. Like others who had had careers in the military or other fields, Marko's father re-entered the Jewish community after his retirement and became active in communal affairs, serving on various committees and boards. Marko expressed the following:

> My father was a member of the Party, a colonel in the army, but you saw him last with a *kipa* [on his head]. My father became very strongly Jewish. He was always Jewish, but even before the war he was left-wing and he wasn't so interested in this. Many [parents], if they remember or don't remember from their childhood, they are not doing the most important thing. It's to pass (Jewishness on) to their children. . . . Many who have problems with their Jewish identity now in their 40s, it was because their parents hid their Jewish background. [They did so] because of troubles (they) had with the environment and with what happened during the war. So when you get this kind of people, you have to explain. The problem is how to bring something from the past which is called tradition, which (was) very vital and important in the community before the war, but you jump over the time because we are losing, we have 40 years, or let's say 30 years of a gap. Not only the wartime but for 30 years (after the war) things didn't happen that much. They did in a way, but [not] like before the war.

To Marko it is a gap because of truncation. The family has been removed as an agent and setting of Jewish socialization. "In this system here, in this world today, where people want to be in their own image, in certain moments, when it is to your benefit, you come as a Jew. [Otherwise] you neglect your Jewishness because it affects you in a negative way. I'm not that kind of person. I'm there (whether it is positive or negative). Even more (when it's negative) because I need to defend who I am."

Marko sees the older Jews as having a "ghetto mentality," which stems, partly, from what he calls the "Holocaust syndrome," the fear of being put on another list. For assimilated Jews, on the other hand, their Jewish identity is something that is irrelevant. "I'm the opposite. If I hide my Jewishness, if I close myself in(side) my walls, things will be more and more dangerous because I won't be able to see what's going on outside. . . I'm not always in the defending position. I'm not an aggressive Jew, but an open Jew." Despite his ethnically mixed background, particularly the fact that he was not born a Jew according to Jewish law [He was born to a Slovenian mother and circumcised when in his twenties], and despite not being raised as a Jew, his selection of his Jewish line of descent is clear and he shows no evidence of a dilemma regarding that choice. This is apparent when talking to Marko and observing him in the community, which I did for a year. At least in an ethnic sense, he is not divided. In fact, the Catholicism of his Slovenian mother's side is certainly foreign to him.

Marko worked for the major Yugoslav airline for four years. He also worked for a travel agency. He has traveled around the world directing tours. While working for the Yugoslav airline company JAT, he had some unpleasant experiences that remain embedded in his consciousness, reminding him that other Serbs, even those he worked with everyday, saw him as the Other, as different. One year he was collecting money to purchase gifts for women coworkers for the International Women's Day holiday. His attempts to solicit money from his male co-workers was unsuccessful. On the day of the celebration a drunk woman approached him and made an antisemitic remark that hurt him badly, even though he was trying to collect money for the women. She said, "You Jew, what do you have, a snake in your pocket?" He quit the company shortly after that, even though he was offered a promotion. He had another incident with an official at the airport with an identification card. They knew him and never before had asked Marko to show his identification card. Marko never wore it openly because of his name. He says he feared some kind of Palestinian action. The official, while refusing him entry, called him "Dayan." He never hid the fact that he was Jewish. People can identify him immediately because of his family name. Co-workers approached him differently, as if they were aware he was Jewish and therefore different. For example, a worker who was not a friend came up to him and said, "Heh Marko, come on and buy me a drink," which he translated as "Jews have a lot of money. You can afford it."

Marko has been deeply affected by his stays in Israel. He has been there about eight times. Once, when scheduled to go to Singapore with his wife, he told her, "We haven't been to Israel for two years. I'm going to Israel." He spent three months there alone after quitting his job at the Yugoslav airline company. In Israel he has stayed in kibbutzim and absorption centers. His experiences in Israel have profoundly influenced him. He feels that Israel is his real home, that he was born in Yugoslavia by accident.

Marko was in Israel during the Yom Kippur War in 1973. "I felt I am in danger, not as a human being who is in some place, but as a Jew, that something might happen to me that might have happened to my father or my grandfather, that I might be killed because I'm Jewish. . . . It was one of the points which was important in my life."

Position, Role, and Style in the Organized Community

Marko is a professional community worker in the Federation. He also freely gives of his time to the local Belgrade community. "In the Jewish community I am on my ground. Everybody knows me. . . . I feel very at ease in the Jewish environment. I can explain (things), be a leading person, and can talk." [You have to be a leading person, don't you?] "No. I don't want to be. You see, I am conscious of this. So I want to get involved with people for whom Judaism is not a main subject so we can talk about some other things, where I can learn something. But where I can give something, . . . I can give Judaism when somebody comes to talk to me about it. So I can also give and take." He works hard to use these personal network ties for various projects in the community. "Every single person is in my register for being used. I know I might have to get in touch because I might use you [for the community program]."

In recent years Marko has been one of those who attempted to reintroduce authentic Jewish tradition to children who attend the summer camp in Pirovac on the Adriatic coast. A professional community worker from the Zagreb community was like-minded about this aim, so the two acted as change agents for a return to authentic Jewish ritual expression. They opposed the leader who said that ritual expression was fine so long as it was performed in a theatrical form. In reintroducing Jewish ritual to the children they met with opposition. One local community president said that parents had told him that Marko was teaching the children religion, that he was trying to introduce religion. There was this fear of religion on the part of parents and Jewish community officials.

Marko believes that authentic ritual expression should also be introduced into the holiday celebrations in the local communities. "We started to do something. You know, we cannot build up the past. We cannot revive the past. But we can bring something from the past."

> I would like it to be on a higher level, not just a show. For example, last night [the Passover seder] was for me not a show but half a show. The people who I saw there were supposed to be in, to see, a real Pesah. Every single person who is sitting around the table has to feel the [?] of Pesah, has to feel the night, has to feel the meaning of the words, but he didn't because for him it is, first, a social evening, to see and to hear something. But how much did he feel? He felt uneasy because it was hot, it was too tight, he could not smoke, couldn't move. To (have it at home) he could have really enjoyed the evening—to have a good dinner, with the reading of a nice story. He doesn't know the language, doesn't know the tradition, doesn't know the customs, he doesn't know why it is like this or like that, but he knows that something goes around and something is connected with the Jewish exile from Egypt. [Can that happen again in the home?] No, I don't think so. No, but what can happen and where we can be a power is that we build it up, so that this what happens in the community is less theater . . . which means that people are provided with books in Serbo-Croatian, know what it is about, more people (become) involved in this, that they read together, maybe sing together. To get a more communal gathering. So it is not like people will sit and not know each other or what is going on. [Now] the rabbi has to explain it every time. This is something which I miss. I can explain to everybody what is going on, but if you go around and ask the people (whether) they can explain Pesah or Seder night, few of them will know. They don't know. . . The rabbi did it very fast because he knows people (don't know much). . . I think this could be done much better if it was prepared better. I'm not talking about food, not talking about the system of sitting, but I'm talking about the whole concept of it. People would be more involved if they were given some kind of material in advance.

During my last trip to Yugoslavia Marko appeared to me a somewhat frustrated individual. He felt frustrated because he believed he would not advance to the position in the Federation of

Jewish Communities of Yugoslavia to which he aspired. In the spring of 1989 he appeared hurt by being ignored in the general vote that elected the members of the Board in the Belgrade Jewish community. After all, he was a professional in the community, an enthusiastic and tireless worker who had never worked by the clock. To him, the vote was an index of how the members perceived him. Also, he was frustrated internally by his indecisiveness about making a break with his life in Yugoslavia and emigrating to Israel. For years he had been talking about making the move. In the last few months this plan was energized by a close relationship with A, an Israeli woman who had come to assist in the summer camp and then remained in Yugoslavia for almost one year. Lastly, the country was in a deep crisis and life was getting worse rather than better. Marko wrote:

> After this beautiful town [Marko was visiting in San Francisco.] Belgrade looks like the end of the world. I am out of the Jewish community. Still a solo player. Traveling is my work, love, adventure. Since October 1989 I am back in the tourist business. But I'm still seriously thinking about coming to Israel and . . . But when? Who knows? Everybody here is alive but in deep pit of national shit.

Subsequently he wrote:

> The situation [in Yugoslavia] is *hara*—Hebrew for shit.
>
> Imagine yourself sitting in a cozy armchair drinking whiskey and watching on TV the war in the Gulf. Thousands of miles away from you.
>
> Imagine me sitting in Yugo shit and going through the eighteenth century euphoria of nationalism, [childish] democracy fighting, the downfall of the economy, knowing that thousands of miles away and just across the street (in Italy, for example) people are entering into the sophisticated twenty-first century of mutual understanding, cooperation and friendly negotiation.
>
> I was born by destiny at this place, in this system of values and thinking. I am free. Yes, I am a cosmopolitan Yugo-Jew if there is such a combination. Free to leave. Do I have [what it takes] to leave this place, this system of life? I

don't have. Otherwise I would be in Israel, or USA or some place where life is also not a rose garden but this kind of stupidity is past. Maybe they have their own shit that I am not seeing on TV but I think mine is the worst: crisis of economy, political turbulence, nationalistic euphoria.

Milica: Curator of the Jewish Historical Museum

Milica can be found daily in the Jewish Historical Museum in Belgrade, where she quietly carries out her role as the Curator of the museum. Anyone who has ever spent any time in the museum, young or old, Jew or Gentile, knows how invaluable Milica is to many different individuals who utilize the museum in some way. In her quiet, unassuming but capable and productive manner, this woman of fifty, whose desire as a young student was to work in Belgrade's Museum of Modern Art, found herself first as the handmaiden-child and in time the parent of Belgrade's Community of Elderly Jews, always ready to help them in their projects. She admits that in the beginning it was not easy to let go of her passion with modern art. In time, Milica grew into the position which placed her into an unfamiliar world. Now, she says, she is very peaceful. "I'm looking now at all these people like children, like my children. . . . They are all so old. They need help. All their children are out of Yugoslavia. They need somebody and I need them. I don't know enough about my family, about my past. I can talk with them like with my parents. . . . Now it is like a big family."

The position in the museum was not an easy one to fill. Her new "family members" were all intellectuals with very high standards who expected a great deal from her. In Milica's words, they expected that "someone who works in this museum has to be a genius." Both she and her elderly friends have come to accept each other. They realize that she has done, without any formal training in history or Hebrew, everything that could be done.

Milica was a child of Tito's socialism. But she was no ordinary child. As Tito was giving birth to the New Yugoslavia, Milica's father, General Herbert Kraus, and her mother Blanka were giving birth to Milica. Her father was second in command in Tito's wartime medical staff. After the war he served as the Minister of Health. Although comfortable by the standards of postwar Yugoslavia, her parents avoided any ostentatious displays of wealth or status. In fact, Milica did not realize she had any special privileges that distinguished her from other children. Only now does she realize what she had in her childhood home, such as her own room, were counted as markers of privilege.

Although both parents were Jewish by descent, they did not raise Milica and her brother to be Jewish. Jewish themes were not the subject of conversation in the Kraus home. There were, however, certain clues that pointed to ethnic difference, but she only realized their significance years later. For example, her parents sometimes spoke when they did not want their children to understand them. Now Milica realizes that they also used Yiddish words. The first time that the family spoke about something Jewish was when Milica's father's brother who lived in Israel came to Belgrade for a visit. Milica recalls that one of the subjects they spoke about was the town of Vinkovci, the brothers' hometown. Her father never spoke about Jewish themes very much, but her mother started answering many of Milica's questions after Milica began working at the Jewish Historical Museum. By not talking about things Jewish, Milica thinks that her parents were trying to protect her. Even the name "Milica," she believes, was given to her in order to protect her. "They gave me the name "Milica" . . . . They even protected me with the name, but my family name was Kraus, so this "Milica" was no protection."

Yet another thing that Milica realized after taking the position at the museum was that all of her parents friends were Jews. She says, "I didn't know. I came here and I saw these old names, Jewish names. They were really close with these people. They spent their youth with them and [shared] a destiny. They have the same destiny. . . . I don't know how they could have survived all that has happened to them. They really were very close." One of these close friends was Dr. Lavoslav Kadelburg, who, like her father, also grew up in Vinkovci. She added these words about the former president of the Federation of Jewish Communities of Yugoslavia: "I thought he was [my father's] best friend, but now I see that he is best friends with everyone in Yugoslavia. He is the father of the whole community. He takes care of everybody. If somebody needs something, he can come to Kadelburg and ask him. . . . I think he is a genius."

As was true for many Jews around the war, the 1967 war in Israel began to transform Milica's life. She was twenty. It sparked an interest and made her realize difference. But it also instilled fear. "I started to think that somebody could kill me because I'm Jewish. . . . I am very sensitive and I was really afraid, because I didn't have any connection with the Jewish community. I never spoke with anybody about this. It was an absolutely new feeling for me."

As I described her above, Milica was a child of Yugoslav socialism. She was socialized into that world and felt a strong attachment to it. When Tito died her tears flowed. She now says that Yugoslav socialism offered one big idea. People could believe in something bigger and better. They believed in a communist future. You knew for what you were living. And there was any element of pride, of believing that you lived in the best country and the most beautiful country in the world.

The erosion and eventual collapse of socialist Yugoslavia erased such beliefs and dreams from the minds of even the so-called Yugo-nostalgics. Examining her own beliefs Milica now thinks differently. "Here we had a false picture that we are really free . . . that we are the best kind of communism . . . not capitalist as in the West . . . and in the East we are the best [she laughs]. But of course I didn't know that we weren't really free. . . . Now we see that we weren't free." I asked Milica when was it that her thinking began to change. She replied, "In 1989. I saw that newspapers wrote something that was not true. . . . It was wrong. Then I realized that the regime is lying."

Milica is not a political activist in any of the dramas that have been playing in the former Yugoslavia. However, because of her position in the museum, she must often consider the inquiries and requests of those who have involved themselves in ethnic politics. She must decide whom to help, and she thus tries to determine how individuals plan to use the archival material of the museum. If she decides that the material will be put to bad political use, she tries to avoid giving it out. Her motivation in this is to protect the museum and the Jewish community. She adamantly stated that she does not want any of her activity to help the war. On the other hand, she does not deny her attachment to the Serbian people. "I also don't want the picture of the Serbian people to be as bad as it is now, and I would always help to protect the picture of Serbia and the Serbian people. But I would like that the picture of Milošević and the regime to be right. I would like that the people abroad know that the war was started by the people who are absolutely sane—people who wanted power. All parts of Yugoslavia, all states, want their own power. . . . Milošević wanted to show that he is able to make a Big Serbia. Was it his idea, or Ćosić's or other people from the Academy [of Sciences and Arts] . . . I don't know. My husband says that people believe in a system. A system doesn't exist here. Things are happening by chaos. There is no system. There is no big idea. Everybody is doing what he thinks is best. Milošević is doing something. Ćosić is doing something. This Bulajić who was here in the museum, he established the Museum of Genocide [in Belgrade.] He also runs a kind of politics. He protects the picture of Serbia, [and] accuses Croats. This is his politics. He wants to show all the crimes of the Croats, and he believe if you show all their crimes people will see who the Croats are. That is the intention: always to show who the Croats were during the war, that everybody would like the help of Jews to show who were the Croats during the war, and that Serbs were protecting Jews. Jews are always between. Now in Croatia they want to show Croats were not so bad. And now we [in the Jewish community] are fighting between ourselves—was Nedic so bad or not so bad? For two years now we have been fighting among ourselves." Milica went on to say how she is always arguing with several prominent members of the Jewish community's senior generation, those who are active in the Society for Serbian-Jewish Friendship (see chapter 6). "What I would like them to understand but what they do not want to listen to is that everybody knows if someone is really writing something, if somebody is a real researcher, they have to look through the documents, [and then] they will see that [such] documents exist. He will see what were Croats and what were Ustasha and what crimes the Germans committed here. It is not critical to have Jews protect a regime like Nedić's regime. Jews really were victims of this regime. You don't have to protect Nedić. It is necessary to say that Serbs were not like Croats [Ustasha]. It is also ridiculous to protect Nedić, because he really was [unclear]. . . . You can't protect him. If he was a real friend of Jews, he should not have been in this regime. Chetniks also were not like Ustasha, but they killed so many Jews because they were communists. It doesn't matter for me if they were communists. Chetniks also killed Jews."

I asked Milica whether anyone was conducting research on this. She answered that "these days, when you have a war, real war, nothing is scientific research. Everything that is written is written for some [political] purpose. There is no real science in the university, in the history of the social sciences. In the social sciences there are only people who are against the war [or] people for the regime, because everything is now politics." About thirty years ago a professor of history wrote an article about the Jews of Belgrade in the seventeenth and eighteenth centuries. The director of the Jewish Historical Museum, Vidosava Nedomački, must have liked the article, for she asked him to write a book. He accepted her proposal. He never finished the book, even though a contract had been made. The museum had even given him money to work in the archives in Venice. He wrote articles, but no book was forthcoming. An article of his appeared in the sensationalist Belgrade magazine *Duga*. Nothing that this man had written earlier had prepared the members of the Belgrade Jewish community for what appeared in the *Duga* article. He wrote about the connections between Jews and Freemasons. At the beginning of the article, he stated that he was not Jewish, that nobody in his family was Jewish, ... More recently he published another article in a newspaper in which he claimed that the Jewish community of Belgrade was in the hands of the Freemasons, that Jews were always merchants of slavery, that Jews were always spies, that the Jewish Historical Museum in Belgrade does not want to publish his book, that we have a contract yet we do not want to publish the book. . . ." Milica could not believe what he had done. The next time they met she told him that all he needed to do was include Gypsies and it would have read like an article from 1941. It was fascistic article, she told him.

From Diaspora to Israel: An End to the Crisis of Identity?

Ivo: Israeli of Yugoslav Jewish Descent

The case of Ivo provides a contrast to the rest of the cases because Ivo lives in Israel. Before his retirement he was a diplomat in the Israeli government. For many years he engaged in historical research on the Jews of Yugoslavia. I present his case because it sheds some interesting light on the difference between being a Jew in Yugoslavia and Israel. The case presented is based on information from a questionnaire Ivo completed.

Ivo immigrated to Palestine in 1939 while in his early twenties. In prewar Yugoslavia he had lived in Novi Sad, a strongly Serbian city situated on the Danube River in the lower Vojvodina. His father had been a staunch, even militant, Zionist, notes Ivo. Their Zionism, apparently, did not cause them to break with their religious past. Both his father and mother regularly attended the synagogue. Like his father, Ivo became a firm and committed Zionist. He was a founding member of the Zionist youth organization, Hashomer Hatzair, in Yugoslavia. While living in Yugoslavia before the war he felt absolutely Jewish. A Jew could not feel anything else in a multinational country, he wrote on the questionnaire. I should interject that some Jews would have disagreed with him, although most of the younger Jews of his generation had moved far from the assimilationist tendencies that had characterized the Yugoslav Jews, particularly the Ashkenazi Neologues, before the 1930s. With the ascendancy of Zionism in the late 1920s and 1930s, Jews began to consider themselves Jews by nationality as well as by religion.

Ivo admits that he did carry a Yugoslav identity at times, though not as part of his everyday self. Asserting a Yugoslav identity was reserved for periods when traveling abroad, cheering on a Yugoslav soccer team in international matches, and while serving in the Yugoslav Army. There was also pride in his native town of Novi Sad, the "Serbian Athens," and an enjoyment of Serbian literature while in and out of school. It is clear, however, that in daily living his identity was exclusively Jewish. He faced no dilemma in terms of knowing who he was and of displaying who he was. Such displays were not religious, but rather secular, particularly involvement in Jewish organizations such as the Zionist-Marxist Hashomer Hatzair and the popular sport club Makabi.

Ivo first began to consider going to Palestine between 1931 and 1933, when he was a member of Hashomer Hatzair, the most Palestine-oriented of all the interwar Zionist organizations in Yugoslavia. Ivo identifies two reasons for his immigrating into what was then Palestine: Jewishness and Zionism. He was the first member of his family to immigrate to Israel. Subsequently his mother joined him in Israel. His father died of natural causes in Yugoslavia during the war.

Besides being a Jew by ethnic descent, what most defines Ivo's Jewishness now is (1) "the fact of living in my *own* (emphasis his) country" (contrast with Slavko Goldstein proclaiming Yugoslavia as homeland), (2) "speaking Hebrew (inside and outside the family circle)," (3) "having educated two children, born here, whose main language is Hebrew," and (4) "feeling "At Home" nowhere else!"

In response to the question, "What are the major differences between being a Jew in Yugoslavia and being a Jew in Israel?" Ivo responded that in Israel one can be free and proud as a Jew, while in Yugoslavia now [1986] being a Jew entails "living a tolerated, somewhat subdued existence. One would have to follow that country's pro-Arab and anti-Israel politics, either actively (militantly) or passively [and to] continue living among Gentiles and as members of a MINORITY group."

When asked to describe the most realistic optimistic scenario of the future of the Yugoslav Jewish community, Ivo responded as follows:

> If they can survive, despite the very limited numbers now (about 6,000 in all), in view of widespread mixed marriages and strong, local cultural pressures, without profoundly Jewish spheres of attraction, it is almost a "miracle"—a positive Jewish phenomenon—that there is a Jewish life in Y-slavia at all, at present.

In providing the most probable scenario, he responded as follows: "Survival as a secular branch of Judaism for another generation or so. Followed by decline for lack of adherents and lack of adequate leadership.

Ivo's tie to Yugoslavia did not end with his immigration to what was still Palestine before the war. He has traveled to Yugoslavia. He has written historical articles on the Jews of Yugoslavia. Also, he is a member of the Association of Yugoslav Jews in Israel.

Analysis of the Narratives

The narratives presented above represent some of the variability, fragmentation, and complexity that had been occurring on the individual level. The biographical vignettes reveal hints of the inner and outer dynamics of Jewish life in Yugoslavia and former Yugoslavia and identify some of the private symbols of real persons. As presented here, however, in textual form, these persons are what Myerhoff (1978) has called ethno-persons, subjects-turned-objects by means of the collaborative effort of the anthropologist and individual informants.

Yugoslav Jewish individuals shared certain features, but these features affected them in different ways depending on such mediating factors as generation, gender, descent, experience, significant social relations, region, beliefs, degree of participation in the organized community, and degree of submergence.

All of these individuals, in one form or another, have been cut off from the past. Many of them felt this sense of historical disjuncture that, above all else, was the outcome of a sudden and violent imposition—the Holocaust. Those that may not have felt this disjuncture as strongly were nevertheless its product. This may have been especially true for the postwar generations. I repeat the words of one of my informants as expressed in the Jewish youth journal *Kadima*: "We have been cut off from the past by the sad caprice of history, and any attempt to return is most likely to be futile" (38, 1977). Without an integrated culture to hold them together, it is, as Boyarin (1991:177) has observed among the Polish Jews of Paris, "ironically, their externally enforced shared experience [that] holds them together." "We are Jews because of the Holocaust," exclaimed a middle-generation member of the Zagreb Jewish community. The postwar focus on death and memorialism, thus, is what most united the living during the Titoist years. However, not every Jewish individual participated in ritual acts of memorialism.

The historical disjuncture was apparent in the disjuncture between the generations. It could be felt from either side. The older Jews may have regretted the "shortage of cultural heirs" (Boyarin 1991), while some of the younger Jews felt the "wound of cultural disinheritance" (Alter 1971). How, then, does one place oneself back into the line of inheritance? The Jews of postwar Yugoslavia, particularly those without the experience and memory of a Jewish culture, could not suddenly immerse themselves in a life that no longer existed. In some cases, parents did not tell their children that they were Jewish. Children discovered ethnic descent on their own. I met one such individual and heard about other cases. In other cases, parents told their children rather late into their childhood, as with Zlata Klajn. Still in other cases, the tragedies of the Holocaust and its aftermath sometimes caused parents to part with their children (Jaša). Yet in other cases, aptly illustrated by Ana Šomlo in her novel, *Voices of the Diaspora*, parents refused to talk about their Jewish past, at least that part outside the progressive tradition, which can be thought of as the prehistory of Yugoslav socialism. My key informant's father, who was a career officer in the Yugoslav National Army, began to share his past with his son only after his retirement, in his elderly years. How did individuals confront this disjuncture in their lives? Some tried to discard their Jewishness and immerse themselves in the host culture. Others tried to erase its relevance from their lives in Yugoslavia. Still other individuals confronted historical disjuncture by substituting what the writer Robert Alter calls a "succession of autonomous moments" (1971) for what was once the rhythm of Jewish life. Jewishness became something that was pursued, selected from available fragments, created, and displayed at intermittent and often irregular times. For some the interim periods were shorter, for others longer. Unlike for Sami, it was not the Jewish calendar that regulated one's existence but rather one's experiences and sensibilities. These were the touchstones of truth for many. In some cases Jewishness was not actively pursued but rather imposed upon the individual. Fischer (1986:173) writes that the parents can impose a series of fragments on the child, in the form of stories, myths, or customs, "without adequately explaining them at critical points of the child's development. It is left to the child to work through this legacy embedded in his consciousness, and to integrate it with his own experiences." This clearly happened in the case of Zlata Klajn. She first used her vivid imagination as a means of dealing with the horrible stories from the family's past.

The individuation of meaning and identity as a general postwar pattern demonstrates that when the particulars have been set free it is difficult to reunite them under the "common binding quality" (Berger 1967:133) that they abandoned or was taken from them. Efforts to bind the particulars—the individuals who turned to their own experiences, private symbols, and models of reality—entailed individually filling symbolic vessels such as "Jewish community, "Jewish tradition," and "Jewish identity" with the content derived from those real experiences or imaginative intimacies. Did they reestablish the historical sociocultural community, or merely a conceptual community or symbolic community (Cohen 1985) made visible by episodic commitment in times of crisis or threat, or by symbols interpreted idiosyncratically that require no shared commitment? A certain logocentrism was maintained, but the symbols were emptied of their content and stripped of their denotative meaning. They lost the critical feature of sharing.

Along with Victor Turner (1978) and A.L. Epstein (1978:88), I assume that the pursuit of meaning and creation of identity is a lifelong activity, and thus I looked for evidence of this process in the individual narratives. The means and forms used in such pursuit and creation varied. All searched for a way or ways to come to terms with their past, present and future, or at least one of these three historical orientations (see DeVos 1975). Epstein (1978) points out that this continuing quest "proceeds at the conscious and unconscious levels." In the cases above I examined, within the limits of the available data, both levels, as well as the movement from the unconscious to the conscious in the case of Ana Šomlo, who records all of her dreams in diaries. In Yugoslavia, this acuteness of the search for identity was felt especially by Jews of the younger generations. They were the "Jews without." Unlike their parents, the choice of retaining or abandoning Jewish tradition (the past) was not theirs. The only authority and tradition they knew were those of the state and Communist Party and Tito himself. If they resisted or rejected such authority and tradition, to what could they have turned? In this instance I would argue that "the individual himself becomes the source of all moral judgment. One's experience becomes the touchstone of truth" (Bell 1980:315). Certainly the postwar community as a voluntary organization could not exercise constraint upon them.

Among those represented in my sample were individuals who attempted to go beyond personal experience alone to transcendent sources of understanding and identity (Enriko Josif, Moris, Mirko). It is important to note that in so doing they had no social community from which to draw sustenance, for few shared their beliefs. Their experiences and sensibilities remained significant, but these were insufficient unless grounded in such transcendent sources as revelation, sacred text, and, to a lesser degree, in a significant other who served as a validating or corroborating source for their conceptions and feelings. After all, if others share one's beliefs and feelings, it is no longer just a matter of personal significance. There is communication and shared understanding. Bell writes that "individuals seek kinship with those who share their sensibility and experience" (ibid). I refer the reader to cases Mirko, Enriko, and Moris as exemplifying this kind of convergence.

Certain factors influenced individuals significantly in their pursuit and/or display of meaning and identity. I have already mentioned generation. There was distinct and abrupt generational discontinuity because of the events of 1941–1945, most notably the Holocaust. Individuals who were part of the prewar generation had radically different experiences from those of the postwar generations. In addition, those who grew up before the war were, for the most part, raised in homogeneous Jewish families that collectively formed a Jewish milieu. But those members of the postwar generations knew only a truncated pattern of Jewishness, most visible in the loss of the family as a distinctly Jewish unit.

Socialization was not a process whereby Jewishness was transmitted from one generation to the next in the household. It is not what made the postwar Jews, Jews. Jewishness ceased to be a given for many Jews-by-descent (cf. Zenner 1985). Becoming and being Jewish became a matter of individual choice. Neither were they forced to be nor could they be what their parents and grandparents were before them. The question to ask is, What were the effects of experience or personal history on the individual? Several individuals had significant experiences that changed how they thereafter perceived the world and how they acted within that world. When Enriko Josif told me that one cannot be decontaminated once God contaminates you, he included his own experiences which he classified as revelation. He was saying that he was no longer, nor could be, the person that he was before these experiences. It was a conversion, a complete transformation of his person and worldview. His language, which itself is a form of his individuated Jewishness, confirms his identity change. Other narratives also show how a supernaturalistic worldview influenced perceptions of reality and interpretations of experience.

Related to the belief system are an individual's object(s) and degree of commitment. The object of commitment is that which the individual believes has ultimate significance (Campolo 1983:91). I have shown how one individual was committed to the secular Jewish community and to a secular form of Jewishness, while another individual was just as committed to maintaining the ritual forms of Judaism. Although the objects of their commitment varied, they shared a broader commitment to the continuity of the Jewish people and their commitment was based on an action idiom. There were relatively few individuals in the entire population, or even registered membership, who demonstrated such a level of commitment. Committed individuals revealed little evidence of waffling or wavering where their Jewish identity was concerned.

Jewish individuals differed in their states of being and knowing. In some cases, there was a clear transformation of identity. Enriko Josif, for example, claimed that he was a *tabula rasa*, as far as his Jewishness was concerned, before his personal revelation and subsequent reading of the Bible. He did not feel Jewish at all before he experienced the war. Before he could come to terms with his Jewishness, he had to deal with the broader metaphysical dilemma of his being. He asked himself, "What does it mean to be a man?" Some individuals continued to confront division within themselves, such as the writer David Albahari whose definition of Jewishness is "to be divided among several things." Slavko Goldstein, on the other hand, had a strong Croatian component to his identity and was an active player in the politics of Croatia, but he told me, "I have no dilemmas."

The following are examples of states of being and sources of knowing in Yugoslav Jewish individuals:

life as pain
I write to bring relief to myself in some moment
great spiritual movements within me
divided among several things
For him life began with what he himself remembered
anxiety (in my prose works I lie shamefully on the psychiatrist's couch and attempt through word to reach my traumas, the source of my own anxiety)
I try in my books of the autobiographical genre to ask questions about the meaning of life—where am I from? Who am I? Where am I going? . . .
Before the fundamental questions we are all the same
something inexpressible
doubt in one's identity
feeling of vulnerability, that they are the last Jews
"something else" and "someone else"
flight: Maybe I'm a Jew, but only because I often had to flee
captivity/enslavement of the mind

Jewish individuals differed with regard to the sources and processes of becoming and being Jewish. For most Jews in the postwar years, the Jewish Great Tradition and the authority of Jewish texts (Torah, Tanakh, Talmud) as providing the charter for Jewish life and the touchstone for truth were replaced by experience (Bell 1980:315). Moreover, personal experience was most often not evaluated or interpreted against the sacred texts of the Jewish tradition, which not only reflected the eroded and fragmented state of Jewish tradition in the postwar period but also the political conditions of submergence. However, it should be apparent in these cases that individuals did not all reflect the forms or stated beliefs found on the collective level. As shown in chapter 3, the organized community publicly presented a uniform identity to others and even to themselves. Only particular kinds of spoken and written narrative were acceptable. What I have done here and in the following chapter is to present narratives that show a degree of opposition or resistance to submergence, or simply do not fit the pattern of submergence. There were many examples of this. For example, Moris talked about "the voice of God" and of rejecting invitations to join the Communist Party because he was a believer. Enriko talked about his conversion from Marxism and Humanism to a theistic belief system based on the Bible and his own experiences of revelation. Mirko talked about the "spiritual spirit." Jaša noted that he finally felt acceptance when the elderly synagogue regulars began to accept him. The actual sources of one's Jewishness vary. As in almost everything else, generation is significant. Those individuals who were raised in Jewish families and neighborhoods before the war carry within them at least the memory of a Jewish past. They, too, were the ones who participated in the Jewish Youth Movement and later in the National Liberation Struggle. The younger Jews had neither the memories nor the experiences that so radically altered the course of Jewish life in Yugoslavia. For individuals like Zlata Klajn and Jaša, their initial contact with their Jewishness reached them through the process of external imposition over which they had no control. In Ana Šomlo's life, her dreams, in which she was always a Jew and among many old Jews, were an example of how the unconscious influenced her conception of herself as a Jew. The conscious pursuit of Jewishness characterized the lives of these Jewish individuals. They actively sought and selected what had personal significance for them. Some individuals pursued meaning and identity more aggressively, others less so. Zlata Klajn, for instance, left her job and went on a four-month quest to Israel. The quest did not always take such a physical form. As I noted earlier, it could lead one into the contours of the mind and imagination. To illustrate this kind of pursuit, I turned especially to the case of the Writers, but it characterized others as well.

The following are several examples of private symbols of Jewishness:

The free particle
The spiritual gene
Voice of God (Moris)
The verb "to be" (Mirko)
The eschatological passages in the Bible
In my dreams I am always a Jew (Ana Šomlo)
Diaries (text) in which dreams recorded (Ana Šomlo)
There are so many, many stories (Katarina Adanja)
They only told me the horrible stories (Zlata Klajn)
The grave of my mother Ester Milena Pinto
Books: I belong to the generation for which
books became the first and only reality (Filip David)
Parent (see the writings of Kiš, Tišma, Albahari, and Šomlo)
The beautiful red-headed child, red like one of Raphael's angels
The heart and soul of a Jew (Bencion Pinto)

Time: The Jewish calendar influences me (Sami)
The true authentic voice
revelation (Enriko Josif)
Mirrors (Danilo Kiš)
The Jewish meals
Israel
Death
The ancestors

When these private symbols of Jewishness were shared with others through oral narration, as in the case of Katarina Adanja, or through written texts, as in the cases of the writers, Ana Šomlo, David Albahari, and others, they became public symbols, that is, ones that have significance for more than one person. One reader of Ana Šomlo's *Voices of the Diaspora* remarked that it was "the first book in the past 40 years in Yugoslavia that depicts Jews as characters. In it everyone can recognize them, young and old alike" (*Bilten* (JOZ) 9–10, 1989).

A Jewish parent produces a natural product—his or her child. The natural product does not automatically become a cultural (Jewish) product, as I have argued. One may be Jewish by descent, even self-ascription, but, as one of my informants put it, what does one do with the fact of one's Jewishness? Most individuals in the postwar years had to consciously pursue their Jewishness beyond self-ascription alone. For some individuals, particularly those who engage in creativity, this pursuit involved the creation of cultural products. In this study I examined this phenomenon in Jewish writers. They have created texts that contain Jewish characters and Jewish themes. Their works, which for some were very personal—David Albahari has said that he writes only for himself—nevertheless became part of the public domain. In this manner they have shown themselves through the products they have created. But displaying one's Jewishness was usually not so public. Katarina Adanja displayed her Jewishness through her stories, the objects that accompany and validate them, and her style of narration. Enriko Josif displayed his Jewishness through his eloquent and eschatological language. Those who attended the synagogue regularly (Moris, Jaša, Mirko) displayed their Jewishness by being counted in the prayer quorum and by performing ritual acts, such as opening and closing the ark or by handling a Torah scroll. Others displayed their Jewishness by participating in the various committees and events of the organized Jewish community.

6

FORWARD INTO THE PAST

> The situation [in Yugoslavia] is *hara*—Hebrew for shit. Everybody here is alive but in a deep pit of national shit.
>
> Imagine yourself sitting in a cozy armchair drinking whiskey and watching the Gulf War on TV. Thousands of miles away from you. Imagine me sitting in Yugo shit and going through the 18th c euphoria of nationalism, childish democracy fighting, the downfall of the economy, knowing that thousands of miles away and just across the street, in Italy for example, people are entering into the sophisticated 21st c of mutual understanding, cooperation and friendly negotiation.
>
> I was born by destiny at this place, in this system of values and thinking. I am free. Yes, I am a cosmopolitan Yugo-Jew if there is such a combination. Free to leave. Do I have the balls to leave this place, this system of life? I don't have. Otherwise I would be in Israel, or the USA, or some place where life is also not a rose garden but this kind of stupidity is past. Maybe they have their own shit that I am not seeing on TV, but I think mine is the worst: crisis of economy, political turbulence, nationalistic euphoria.

The bulk of the literature dealing with the collapse of the communist states in eastern Europe has described the impact of change on the majority populations and larger national minorities. Considerably less attention has been given to the small minorities of these former communist states—whom we may classify as the powerless people of eastern Europe (e.g., Gypsies, Jews, refugees).

This chapter shifts the focus and description of the outcome of the recent historic transformation to one such minority population, the Jews of Yugoslavia, who are now the Jews of Bosnia, Croatia, Macedonia, Serbia, and Slovenia. Examining the erosion and collapse of socialist Yugoslavia from the perspective of the Jewish minority can contribute to an understanding of how the past and the present, together with convergent and divergent visions of the future, intersect in the process of national identity (re)construction and in the disputes that arise over national symbols, myths, and the often contradictory collective images created for domestic and foreign consumption. More specifically, it furthers our understanding of how minority populations are often caught in the middle of interethnic confrontations when they are manipulated by the larger populations and are forced to adjust to changing criteria of national exclusion and inclusion.

This chapter examines how the Jewish population's status or place, once secure and deeply submerged in the symbolic order of the socialist state, began to be redefined and resituated when that order and its political supports entered a phase of chaotic transition. When faced with the uncertainties of such a transition, this minority population's vulnerability in the rapidly eroding socialist environment left it exposed to nationalist ideologies propagated and manipulated by the various contestants in the social drama that began in earnest in 1989. Specifically, this chapter describes how the Jews as individuals and as a population were affected by and responded to the erosion of the Titoist symbolic order, to changing power relations, and to the growing exclusivity of the "nation" peoples of Yugoslavia, particularly the Serbs, Croats, and Slovenes. Second, it shows how these larger ethnic populations, motivated by the hope of gaining strategic advantage and establishing themselves as morally superior communities in the interethnic conflict, appropriated the Jews and Jewish symbols to carry out these aims associated with processes of national socio-moral reconstruction. Furthermore, it describes how and why the Jews engaged in contesting encroachment upon their own symbolic space and that of their respective majority peoples.

This chapter approaches the Yugoslav transition as a process that sought to demolish the Titoist order and to (re)create and (re)define separate ethnic communities using distinctive moral categories. There is ample ethnographic data that supports the statement that "all people enter into vigorous moral judgment of others" (Priest 1993:294), even when their rhetoric and behavior violates the moral order of their respective social groups. These judgments become salient during periods of intergroup conflict, especially during phases of rapid and radical transition when one dominant power and symbolic order collapses and struggles ensue to replace it with new competing orders.

One common judgment is to accuse one's opponent of being the transgressor and thus of being defiled, evil, or guilty of committing various crimes against out-groups. From the perspective of the accusers, these judgments serve to essentialize the ethnic other as morally suspect, if not altogether inferior or evil. This essentialization is a kind of moral folk anthropology misapplied or gone bad. The conflict can be understood as one waged with symbolic weapons—symbols, images, single words, labels, mythico-historical narratives, statistics, dramatic performances played out in the streets, institutions, and the mass media, especially television. When appropriate or potent symbols cannot be found in one's own ethnic arsenal, which may be the case with symbols that do not pack the punch of defamiliarization, such symbols are appropriated from what are perceived at the time to be neutral and, perhaps, universal ethnic communities. I illustrate this process where it concerns Jews and highly recognizable Jewish symbols.

Why specifically have the Jews and Jewish symbols been appropriated? What meanings do they convey and what do they accomplish in the moral conflicts? I suggest that they have served to (1) create or exaggerate commonality or difference, (2) create association or distance, (3) subvert historical or official social categories, particularly those of the socialist period but also earlier historical periods, (4) contest others' versions of the past, (5) maintain a state of self-purity or defilement of the ethnic other by pointing to historical acts interpreted as collective martyrdom. Verdery (1993:197) suggests "that images of [minority] groups have become important symbols for discussing particular kinds of social dislocation attendant on the exit from socialism." Eastern European Jews, in particular, "seem everywhere to symbolize two things: socialism and cosmopolitan westernism" (ibid: 199). The former, association with socialism, has been less of a factor in Yugoslavia than in other east European countries. The latter association, however, has been a real factor. For example, Jews have been blamed for the plight of Serbia in the international order of nations.

In these symbolic contests, each group has sought to inflate the value of its own symbols and devalue those of ethnic others, and to seize certain symbols and transpose their meanings (Harrison 1996).

Is this not a form of immortality-striving described by Ernest Becker in *Escape From Evil* (1975)? Here, it is the glorious and eternal Nation that provides immortality, and thus anything that will achieve that aim, even if it entails stealing the life-force from others, will be deemed acceptable and moral. The language and activities of purification ("cleansing") have been intended to achieve this aim (see Nixon 1993). In late- and post-socialist Yugoslavia, Serbs, Croats, and Slovenes have all appropriated the Jews and/or Jewish symbols in order to convey such meanings and level judgments against one another, thereby hoping to achieve political and moral aims (see Verdery 1993; Braham 1994).

An understanding of both the past and the present is vital in order to trace the interconnections between contested histories and contemporary constructed realities. Actual documentation ceases to be important in this battle. Approaching the problem solely through political analyses of current events will not tell the whole story. It is from the histories and myths told by actors on all sides of the conflict that the symbolic complexes or the "signposts needed to understand what [is] happening now" (Poggioli 1993) will emerge.

It is perhaps more convenient to deal mainly with constructed realities in this chapter. This is not the same thing as stating there is no reality. One approach, taken by Loring Danforth (1995) in his analysis of the Greek, Bulgarian, and Macedonian-Slavic claims to Macedonian identity, is first to present insider narratives of the competing discourses and then to follow up with his own perspective. According to Danforth, his particular anthropological perspective deconstructs the nationalist discourses by revealing how identity is often a product of the intersection of historical events, social processes, and cultural constructions.

It is my contention that this conflict goes beyond rhethorical forms of regional difference, such as the form of Balkan "orientalization" described by Bakic-Hayden and Hayden (1993), to processes of a more universal form of moral judgment—that is, one of diminishment and eradication of the other, particularly of the one closest to oneself, the "brother" (see Kiš 1995; Volf 1996). We have been witnessing moral agents engaged in battle for more than resources such as land and more than the political rights of self-determination, however much a part of the conflict these ingredients are. To understand this battle on a level more fundamental to the human condition, we must approach each ethno-culture as a moral order, examining within it the moral vocabulary and symbolism of shame and guilt used in narratives, imagery, and rituals. In this battle of striving for self-justification and diminishment of others, little space is left for one's own guilt, one's own practices of defilement, exclusion, and eradication, and for admission of guilt, confession and forgiveness.

To demonstrate the symbolic appropriation and manipulation of the Jews and Jewish symbols, I present several examples below. The establishment of the Serbian-Jewish Friendship Society served to exaggerate the historical commonality of Serbs and Jews and helped propagate the myth of uninterrupted friendship between these two peoples. The Slovenian appropriation of the Star of David symbol illustrates how actors can attempt to subvert historical categories by transposing the historical victim as the current perpetrator of evil crimes against humanity. Author Slavenka Drakulić's story about Mira Furlan, whom she calls "Actress M," provides an example of how individuals who transgress the new moral order of the ethnic Nation are portrayed as defiled and thus contaminating to the Nation. Mira Furlan, who is Jewish and whose husband is Serbian, was no longer welcome as an actress or a person in her homeland of Croatia after performing in Serbia, the enemy camp. The means of dealing with such transgressors is to diminish or eradicate them. They can no longer enjoy membership. They can no longer be seen as a moral person within the Nation. When Croatian President Franjo Tudjman proposed to turn the Jasenovac concentration camp site, a symbol of martyrdom for Serbs, Jews, and Gypsies, into a "site of reconciliation" for all "victims" of the Second World War, regardless of the side they fought on, he was attempting to seize for himself the ownership of a major contested symbol. The victim groups of the Jasenovac camp rose up to defend against this encroachment whose end they perceived as eradication. This process of symbolic seizure and change of meaning is also illustrated by the case of the renaming of the Square of Victims of Fascism in Zagreb.

How have the radical changes affected the Jews? Answering this question is no easy task. One expert on the region has compared any attempt at analyzing recent events to hitting a moving target. It seems that everything in that part of the Balkans has been and continues to be in constant flux. The "Civil War of Words," as the Croatian magazine *Danas* once called the prewar heated language of argument, turned into war itself and the threat of war in other regions of the former Yugoslavia. Those of us who are following events in the region are trying to understand the complex dynamics and communicate results to various audiences. Following the ethnographic tradition in my discipline of anthropology, I try to avoid presenting an overabundance of my own biases by presenting a few of the voices of the Jews of the former Yugoslavia who themselves are influenced immensely by the political and cultural milieu in which they live and by what information reaches them. They must sift through the truths, half-truths, and outright lies that come their way. At the same time, however, everyone must confront the realities of violence, both the physical violence that wipes out human lives and the symbolic violence that obliterates collective memories and an objective knowledge of history, particularly about acts of human viciousness.

As the Yugoslav political order became increasingly paralyzed following Tito's death in 1980, and the Yugoslav people grew disillusioned with the Titoist experiment, intellectuals and journalists began to challenge the dominance and claimed moral superiority of Titoism. It was in this challenge to the dominant politico-symbolic order that precursors to the transition itself are found. The challenge of the 1980s used veiled and even overt attacks on the key symbols and myths of the dominant Titoist order. Subsequently, the disintegration of the Titoist system and its replacement by fields of rhetoric and action in which ethno-political actors actively engaged in constructing, presenting, and contesting emergent essentialist and epochalist (Geertz 1973) representations of themselves and their opponents created a highly charged environment of threat, confrontation, and conflict. The weight of historical memory, the highly charged atmosphere of political confrontation and symbolic contestation, and opposing visions of the future set the stage for a "a civil war of words" and for war itself. Below I show how the movement out of submergence and how living with the combustible mixture of democratization and conflicting nationalist ideologies began to transform Jewish ethnicity (i.e., the responses to change) and Jewish identities in a region in rapid transition.

History and the Uses of History

History and culture shape ethnic identity formation. I return to my earlier discussion of the historical processes that shape identities and continue to constrain what kind of responses are available to groups and individuals. First there is the history that actually happened. We can indeed know and describe the processes and events that tore apart the Jews of Yugoslavia. They did not describe themselves as "maimed and crippled" because present social circumstances dictated that they fashion themselves in that manner. Rather, historical processes beyond their control "maimed and crippled" this population of Jews. But there are also the kinds of histories that actors make in order to refashion their identities and suit present circumstances. There are growing numbers of examples of such refashionings (e.g., Lass 1988; Danforth 1995; Eriksen 1993; Goldstein 1993). In the chaotic and violent transition from socialist Yugoslavia to independent states, such remakings of the past have been the rage. Much of this activity is focused on the interethnic violences that occurred during the Second World War.

The Jews of Yugoslavia suffered extreme losses in the Second World War, mostly as victims of fascist terror. Of the 82,000 Jews who were on Yugoslav soil when the war broke out, about 60,000 died. Approximately 6,000 of these were refugees from countries to the north of Yugoslavia. Where and how did they die? How many died? Under what circumstances? Who did the killing? These questions are significant in their own right, but they have also been made significant in the context of the "civil war of words" referred to above and which is one of the foci of this chapter.

The fate of the Jews of Serbia was settled very early in the war, before the Final Solution was formally put into effect, and during the transition from reprisal shootings to the methods implemented in connection with Hitler's Final Solution. In Serbia, the German Wehrmacht was responsible for the large-scale murders of Jewish males. They were murdered under the pretext of carrying out reprisals for German soldiers who were killed or wounded. For every German soldier killed, 100 males were shot, while for every wounded, 50 were shot. In this manner most of the Jewish men and boys of Serbia were killed. The women and children were rounded up and transported to the fairgrounds called Semlin or Sajmište just across the river from downtown Belgrade. About 7,500 Jews who were in the Sajmište camp were killed. According to Christopher Browning (1985), who has meticulously researched genocide in wartime Serbia, the responsibility for carrying out these murders was on second-rate German SS men, with the exception of the officer Shaeffer. A gas van was shipped from Berlin. For each trip, about 150 women and children were squeezed into the death van. Children were sometimes enticed into the van by offers of candy. Seven Serbs were forced to unload the dead bodies after every trip. They, too, were killed after the final trip.

In the recent conflict over who was responsible for carrying out genocide upon whom, some Croats and Jews have stated that Belgrade was the first city to be declared *Judenrein*, cleansed of Jews—which, in fact, was the boast of a German officer in a communiqué. What these individualists have implied in such statements is that the Serbs were responsible for the genocide carried out upon the women and children of the Sajmište camp. According to Browning's research this is a false accusation. In fact, the fascist Ustasha regime of the Independent State of Croatia (NDH) insisted that the Sajmište camp be run by Germans and be supplied by Serbian goods (e.g., food). This is not to say that there were no Serbian fascists. Even before the war fascists were active on the Serbian political landscape. There were also Serbs who collaborated with the German occupiers during the war. The Serbian police force headed by the Serb Nedić assisted the Germans in finding and handing Jews to the Germans. However, can the Nedić regime in Serbia be equated with the Ustasha regime that controlled the NDH? Whereas one young Jewish woman in the Croatian Ministry of Information used this argument in a reply to an article in a London newspaper, basing her statement on a questionable source in the popular Belgrade magazine. Slavko Goldstein, former president of the Zagreb Jewish community, clearly makes the distinction, in the Zagreb community's newsletter, between the perpetrators of genocide in Croatia and those in Serbia, with the former being a domestic fascist group and the latter the German Nazis (Goldstein 1990:4). Perhaps the jury is still out on the extent to which the Nedić regime and certain Chetnik forces can be implicated in handing Jews over to the Germans. Recently, Philip Cohen (1996) has attempted to equalize Nedić's complicity with that of Pavelić in the Independent State of Croatia. However, Cohen's account is suspect because of its selective rendering of the literature. For example, he cites Christopher Browning's work, but he does so almost in passing, without addressing Browning's essential findings, which, I might add, do not support his own conclusions. Curiously, Cohen relies very little on the accounts provided by the Jews of the former Yugoslavia. It appears he did no work in the Jewish Historical Museum in Belgrade, an archival source that any serious work must consider.

In what is now Croatia and parts of Bosnia-Hercegovina, the puppet state of Independent State of Croatia ruled an ethnically and religiously mixed population with full German support. In fact, German support made the Independent State of Croatia possible.

The majority of Croats were not active supporters of the Ustasha. Significantly, a large number served as Partisans in the National Liberation Struggle. This minority group of Ustasha within the Croatian population carried out genocide upon the Jews. Many of their victims died in the Jasenovac concentration camp, which has become in recent times a contested symbol between the Serbs, who claim the Ustasha murdered hundreds of thousands of Serbs there, and the Croats, who have contested the official Communist and Serbian versions that claim at least 700,000 people were murdered at the Jasenovac camp alone.

The Collapse of Socialist Yugoslavia and Its Impact on the Jews

Where have the Jews fit into the process of the collapse of socialist Yugoslavia and the establishment of independent states? To answer this question, one must understand something about the setting and contexts of late-socialist (mid-1980s) and "transitional" (1989–91) Yugoslavia.

Antecedents and Conditions of the Erosion of Yugoslavia and Jewish Re-emergence

Political and cultural transition characterized the contexts of state erosion and Jewish re-emergence. All transitions, if not set against structure, are potentially dangerous processes. The Yugoslav transition is a case in point. The transition from Titoist Yugoslavia to fragmented Yugoslavia was fraught with intense verbal confrontation before breaking out into war itself.

Following Tito's death in 1980, intellectuals, journalists, and later, reform-minded or power-seeking politicians began to launch an assault on the dominant Titoist order. Several critical factors allowed such criticism of the key symbols and myths, whose place in Titoism had been guarded by sundry taboos, to take place. Tito, the great unifier, jokingly referred to as Yugoslavia's only Yugoslav, was dead. Before his death he constituted a rotating presidency of eight that failed to get the six republics and two autonomous provinces to act as a single federal entity. The controversial Constitution of 1974, applauded by the autonomy-oriented Croats but detested, mostly secretly at the time, by the integration-oriented Serbs, culminated in each of the eight federal units acting on behalf of its own interests. Such self-interest extended even into the literary and artistic domains. For instance, if a writer wanted to be known as a Yugoslav writer, no such category existed or was recognized. One could only be a Serbian writer, a Croatian writer, a Macedonian writer, and so on (but not a Jewish writer). It was difficult to be a Yugoslav in Yugoslavia. Given this growing centrifugalism, structurally supported by the federal constitution, political ineffectiveness and then paralysis ensued. The country was neither a federation nor a confederation. At the same time the economic crisis grew more grave. The foreign debt expanded to over twenty billion dollars. Inflation was rising. A large percentage of the population, especially the younger generation, was unemployed and foresaw a gloomy future. Living standards plummeted following the relatively prosperous 1970s, much of which had been financed by borrowed capital. Business scandals were commonplace. By the mid-1980s Yugoslavia was mired in a "permanent crisis." One observer has associated this period with what he calls "apocalypse culture" (Ramet 1985) which, in addition to the political and economic crises, added a moral and spiritual crisis to the general societal malaise. As Denitch (1990:52) puts it, "when God is dead and the largest secular secular world faith, Marxist socialist, is in crisis, a moral vacuum is created." Having become disillusioned with the Yugoslav system and even given up on it, many Yugoslavs harbored a kind of cultural, moral, and spiritual angst, which can be described as an intellectually and internal anti-structural state that either leaves one suspended in disillusionment or despair, or spurs one, in the language of Kierkegaardian existentialism, to make "a leap of faith." The Yugoslavs took both approaches. Some returned to institutional religions to try to fill the void or to move from their suspended state. Others tried non-institutional means.

Certain anti-structural features exist in Ramet's description of apocalypse culture. As Victor Turner (1967) has shown, anti-structure can spark creativity and quests of various kinds. In Yugoslavia during this phase writers and other intellectuals made their own leaps of faith or began spinning their own webs of significance by using their creative skills to describe an alternative version of Titoism and thereby challenge its symbolic and political dominance and the Communist Party's claims of moral superiority. It was at this time that the "secret histories" (Hayden 1991) that had been suppressed during Titoist rule began to appear in print, on film, on the stage, and, I can add, in conversations on the interpersonal level. In 1989 individuals revealed to me their own secret histories that to them belied such concepts as brotherhood, unity, and freedom. This apocalypse culture was creating or enlarging the capacity for societal change and radical transformation.

The erosion of Titoism, the emergence and pace of political pluralization, and the resurgence of nationalist ideologies did not occur uniformly throughout Yugoslavia. As noted above, the constitutional structure itself had contributed to decentralization along republic lines. The political elites in each republic, in order to retain power, began serving the interests of their bases of power, their own republics and nations. At the federal level political decision-making required a consensus, which had become a rarity. Political action beyond the level of endless dialogue came to a halt. Against this impasse on the federal level and with growing liberalization within the League of Communists, it was not long before politicians began to appeal to popular and romantic nationalism. The structural supports for ethnic conflict had been constituted and instituted long ago and by now were deeply entrenched and thus easily exploited. Given such political and ethnic polycentrism, the cross-cutting federal linkages were made ineffectual.

Yet another difficulty existed. With the Marxist-Titoist belief system in crisis and the vacuum created by its demise, the question was what would fill that vacuum. Structurally, as described above, cross-cutting linkages among the peoples of Yugoslavia had given way to autonomous political units. Denitch writes that "in the absence of a vibrant civil society (cf. Verdery 1991), that vacuum can be filled by xenophobic populist nationalism, the form of populist nationalism which puts forward one's own nation as the victim of history and oppression by 'others'" (1990:50). This is precisely what transpired in transitional Yugoslavia.

The Titoist system, which did not tolerate ideological diversity, has been replaced by another kind of ideology that tends to dominate everything else. I am referring to nationalism, both the ethnic or cultural dimension and the virulent kind that has led to name-calling, violence, and atrocities on all sides.

On all sides, those in power or with power have played the nationalist card. They have all played to their respective galleries. Each of the major ethnic populations has engaged in recreating and lifting up the Nation (see Golubović 1990; Verdery 1993a; 1993b). They have raised it above all else. This process has entailed negating much of the past, those parts that do not fit the new image. Each has presented a different image of itself to different audiences, playing up the nationalist image at home and the democratic image abroad. This process of image-making and unmaking has caused much conflict between ethnic populations. For example, the Croats have worked hard to dispel the myth that they are an antisemitic and genocidal people. At the same time, they have tried to dispel the myth of an unbroken line of friendship between the Serbs and the Jews and the myth that antisemitism never reared its ugly head in Serbia.

Another important factor to consider is that the various ethnic peoples of the former Yugoslavia perceived the past, the present, and the future differently. The New Yugoslavia and its elaborating symbols such as *jedinstvo* ("unity"), *bratstvo i jedinstvo* ("brotherhood and unity)," and *za l(ij)epu budućnost* ("for a beautiful future") carried different and even conflicting meanings for these peoples. The Yugo-Slav peoples had different aspirations as well, some of which are clearly manifested today for all to see. National self-determination for the Croats meant controlling their own destiny, apart from the Serbs.

Individual Movements out of Submergence: Asymmetrical Positioning

As expected, given the organized community's degree of submergence in socialist Yugoslavia until the late 1980s, individual Jews were the first to deviate from this general pattern of political and symbolic conformity to Titoism. These early deviations of individuals did not involve repudiations of the entire Titoist system. Usually the deviation occurred in relation to one or two key symbols which consequently positioned that individual in asymmetrical association with those particular symbols.

The impact and repercussions of these challenges and deviations varied from one individual to the next. For one Jewish individual, the initial repercussion was the loss of his academic position and the suppression of his book in which he criticized the key symbol of socialist self-management. This took place in the 1970s and is part of a well-known case that involved several professors from the University of Belgrade's Faculty of Law. I include this individual's case because his book was finally published in 1986 and won a prestigious award in 1987, and also because his personal history was used by the reformers as part of their overall effort to challenge the official history of Titoism by means of publishing "secret histories" of individuals who had suffered under the Titoist system (Hayden 1991). The secret histories or personal tribulations of other Jewish individuals have also been publicly revealed and discussed in the last few years. One of these is the travails of a young Jewish woman who was imprisoned after the Partisan War in the now infamous *Goli Otok* (Naked Island) concentration camp. This woman, who now lives in Israel, describes her experiences in an autobiographical book that was published in Yugoslavia (see "The Secret History of Ženi Lebl" below). Another Jewish woman's postwar travails in the postwar concentration camps became highly publicized because her husband, Andrija Hebrang, who occupied a high-level position in the hierarchy of the Communist Party in Croatia and was a personal friend of Tito, was accused of counter-revolutionary activities (meaning Croat nationalism) and soon after mysteriously disappeared, presumed to be executed. Other Jewish individuals have described for me their own secret histories, personal accounts that belied, at least for them and their families, such key summarizing and elaborating symbols as brotherhood and unity, freedom, and a beautiful future.

There were, it is fair to say, few Jews who suffered in such a public way during the Titoist period. It is equally fair to point out that most of the individuals who did suffer in some way were not singled out because they were Jews. No purges of Jews occurred in Yugoslavia as happened in other Eastern European states. Part of this may be attributable to the small number of Jews. Yugoslav peoples perceived no relationship between Jewish prewar status and postwar Jewish participation in the Titoist elite.

For most of the other Jewish individuals who contributed to erosion or to early re-emergence the sanctions were less drastic and immediate. One writer published a novel that happened to reach the bookstores during my fieldwork stay. Several sections of the book were quite critical of Yugoslav socialism, though this criticism was conveyed by means of dialogue between the characters in the book, many of whom are based on actual persons. The author told me that many people contacted her after they read the book. One reader expressed how brave the author was to have written the book. The author confided that her book was difficult to find in the bookstores and that it was not being reviewed by the press.

Case of David Albahari: Asymmetrical to the Key Symbol of Non-Alignment

In an interview he gave to Belgrade's weekly magazine *NIN* (10 October 1982) entitled "Israel and Me," the Jewish writer David Albahari deviated dramatically from the organized Jewish community's public position on the socialist state's key symbol of non-alignment. By publicly stating his support for the State of Israel, Albahari positioned himself in asymmetrical relation to this key symbol specifically where that symbol stood for the absence of diplomatic relations between Yugoslavia and Israel. He also deviated from the organized community's policy of presenting a rhetorical and dramaturgical united front to both the state's rulers and the non-Jewish public. Actually, David Albahari did not violate the letter of this communal norm. In the interview he clearly stated that he was expressing his personal feeling and position regarding Israel. Nevertheless, uniformity was broken because his deviation was so public.

What was especially dramatic about the interview was that he stated his support for Israel in 1982 when there were street demonstrations in Belgrade protesting the Israeli army's occupation of Lebanon. If there was a time, or set of circumstances, that caused Jews discomfort in Titoist Yugoslavia, it was then. By saying what he did so publicly he discarded the mechanism of dramaturgical discipline and placed himself in opposition to one of the pillars of Titoism.

David Albahari believed that in the period after the break in diplomatic relations Yugoslav Jewry had arrived at a point of stagnation. Because of this situation many members of the older generation, who still vividly remembered the hostility towards Jews during the war, simply thought that "they should be silent, that things related to the Jews of Yugoslavia should be decided within a closed family circle, that not much should be said and no public statements should be made" (*Bilten* (Tel Aviv), 1985). But with his increasing entrance into public life, Albahari felt the following:

> [I] could no longer . . . accept that kind of reaction to a reality which encircles us. . . . Of course, I would not want to be misunderstood. The Federation of Jewish Communities of Yugoslavia and the Jewish communities of Yugoslavia are very significant as institutions in maintaining the cultural identity of Jews in Yugoslavia, but in such a sociopolitical climate they cannot appear as the speakers and representatives of certain positions which concern Israel, because [these] are Jews who are first of all Yugoslavs and they must react in agreement with the position and politics of their country. [A good description of submergence.] But an individual can have his own personal position which

> radically differs from the general position . . . as an individual I have a political orientation which differs (ibid.).

Privately, the Jews of Yugoslavia disagreed with Tito's decision to sever diplomatic relations with Israel and were hurt by it in various ways. Many members of the community faced problems because of Yugoslav politics toward Israel. Some individuals exploited this situation in their own bad interpersonal relations with Jews, although there was no official sanction of such behavior. David Albahari resolved this problem for himself by stating his position publicly and thereby situating himself in the public arena. After this public act, there was, for him, no wavering or concealment.

Four years later, in 1986, this political situation continued to create a problem for many Jews because it did not give them a real chance to define themselves as Jews. Ever since the Six Day War in 1967 they were cautious about everything connected with Israel. Albahari expressed the following to me:

> All over the world Israel probably is the first thing on the list of possible agents creating Jewish identity or making it stronger, and if you cannot use that agent you have problems in creating Jewish identity. Somehow I feel people are more afraid than they should be. . . . I really don't know why people are so afraid. I'm talking about Jewish people in Yugoslavia. . . . The Federation has become more vocal. . . . They talk about such things but only [when] the TV program or article is [about] Yugoslav Jews and not about Israel. When something bad is written about Israel, the community will do nothing. The president wrote a letter of protest because of Yugoslavs, not because of Jews in general, especially not because of Israeli Jews. If there is a specific protest it is published in the *Jewish Review*. Every letter of protest is good, but how many people read the *Jewish Review*? No one outside [the community] except those guys who must read everything because it is their duty to read it. The Jewish community of Yugoslavia, if it would open its cultural programs, for example, to outsiders for people who are not Jews and who are not members of the community, would have open places for discussion on things such as Zionism, Israeli-Arab conflict, and those things. Whenever several people here tried to do a thing like that,

> there were always people who objected to it. They said, "Why should we open [our community] to other people? Who knows who would come?" The eternal fear is that somebody is ready to come [to the community]. . . . If somebody wants to come and destroy something, he can come anytime he wants. He wouldn't need an open discussion. I think that if the Jewish community and the Jews were louder, would speak more about what really hurts them, it would be much better for not only Jews but for other Yugoslavs, for it would help them to understand the whole situation.

Having appeared in the weekly magazine *NIN*, which then had the largest circulation of any news magazine in Yugoslavia, the interview with David Albahari reached a large audience throughout the country. Albahari believed that the significance of the interview was that non-Jews were exposed to a radically different perspective of Israel and some began to see things a little differently, and Jews, especially young Jews, received some moral support. In his case, no sanctions or adverse outcomes followed.

Case of Andrija Gams: Asymmetrical to the Key Symbols of the Communist Party, Socialist Self-Management, and Tito

Andrija Gams, now in his eighties and living in Belgrade, was raised in the home of Neologue Jewish parents in Subotica. His assimilated parents declared themselves as Hungarians. Although Gams believes that Jewishness is no longer a social reality in Yugoslavia, he nevertheless declares himself as a Jew. At one time he was active in the Belgrade Jewish community, particularly in the work of the Federation's Jewish Historical Museum. In addition, he has written books and lectured on Jewish themes.

In the early 1970s Andrija Gams criticized the founding myth of postwar Titoist Yugoslavia and the focus of international attention and prestige, the Yugoslav form of "socialism with a human face." Socialist self-management was lauded as an advanced form of socialism that pushed Yugoslavia years ahead of the rest of Eastern Europe and the Soviet Union. This was the myth propagated by the "infallible Party" (Hayden 1991). The Titoist variant of socialism rested on this founding myth and key summarizing symbol. It symbolized an epochalist accomplishment, which added to Yugoslavia's unique identity in the socialist world and made the entire world take notice of this little known Balkan state. Thus, anyone bold enough to criticize socialist self-management was playing in an arena with high stakes. Against this imposing political backdrop, here was this Belgrade law professor who participated in faculty discussions that criticized drafts of constitutional amendments and wrote a book called *Svojina* (1987) in which he criticized self-management's core conception of "social property." Gams theoretically attacked what supported "the entire structure in the blueprint of its main architect, Edvard Kardelj," Tito's principal ideologist (Miller 1989). He theoretically foresaw that this ideological conception in practice would lead to "various forms of abuse of law and corruption" (Gams 1987, quoted in Miller 1989: 437). Gams further noted that "in this connection, it is a characteristic phenomenon in our society that one's social position or public function is converted into a privilege and is monetarized" (ibid). He saw many contradictions in social property which, he later explained, he "could not in any way reconcile with the science of law and its general results in Yugoslavia and in the world. . . . It is incomprehensible . . . How in this conception and in these principles, which pretend to create a new democracy . . . there are traces and remains of Stalinism in our system . . . (*NIN*, 24 January 1988).[1] As a Party member himself and as a Marxist theoretician, Gams was acting the role of internal critic. His intention was not to undermine socialism in Yugoslavia, but it seems to me that he faced a dilemma of sorts. Certainly he was aware at the time of the enormous symbolic significance of socialist self-management and the possible repercussions that would surely follow any criticism. For many, socialist self-management had become Yugoslav socialism. The following statement, which Gams made after his book was finally published and he received a prestigious award for it in 1987, reveals the motivation that would have resolved any dilemma he might have faced in speaking out:

> Science was never just a source of wages for me, and I never saw science as a basis for social status. For me science was a calling. Fulfilling that calling meant serving an ideal which every person must have, for without an ideal man is empty, without any substance. Thus, I saw and see my scientific position as a calling and because of that I sincerely struggled for those scientific suppositions which I regarded as representing scientific truth (ibid:17).

Andrija Gams was also a member of the nineteen-member Committee for the Defense of Freedom of Thought and Expression, which at the time was composed of nonconformist artists and intellectuals, several of whom were also members of the Serbian-Jewish Friendship Society. The Committee released a letter to the Western media in June 1988 in which they called for an end to Tito's personality cult and asked that an "objective scientific and critical reappraisal" be conducted to determine Tito's "role in making crucial political decisions" (*RFE Research Report*, 11 November 1988, 6, quoted in *Naša Reč* (London) 412:11). As a participant in the Committee and in criticizing Tito, the central symbol of socialist Yugoslavia, Gams stepped almost completely out of the shadow of submergence.

Gams continues to live an active intellectual life. Recently he co-authored a book which serves as a rebuttal to a book, published in Croatia, which attempts to show that antisemitism was not absent from Serbia as some Serbs and Jews have claimed.

The Use of Secret Histories in the Process of Erosion

Political actors within the one-party system began to demystify the sacred pillars of the revolution and Titoist Yugoslavia as the Party's control was weakening and Yugoslavia was mired in a political and economic crisis in the 1980s. Yugoslav writers began to link this crisis with socialist self-management that Yugoslavia had institutionalized in the Constitution of 1974 and which, as indicated above, was a primary source of international prestige. Revealing "secret histories" served as a means of challenging the dominance, the claimed moral superiority and claimed successes, and the sacred myths and symbols of Titoism, including its hero-founder, Tito himself. Revealing the secret histories of Jewish individuals contributed to this challenge, with the cases of Andrija Gams and Olga Hebrang among the most prominent. The secret history that follows is significant and interesting because it was revealed through the form of an autobiographical book whose very appearance and contents challenged the official history that had been promulgated since the end of the Second World War.

The Secret History of Ženi Lebl. Ženi Lebl publicly revealed her own secret history in her book *Ljubičica Bela: Vic Dug Dve i Po Godine* (White Violet: A Two and a Half Year Old Joke), which was published in Yugoslavia in 1990.[2] She describes her two and a half year imprisonment in Tito's postwar Yugoslavia, which began in Belgrade's Glavnjača Jail, where the secret police interrogated her off and on for four months, and then was spent in other locations including the infamous Goli Otok (Naked Island) concentration camp in the Adriatic Sea. Lebl's book falls outside the genre of early to mid-1980s Yugoslav camp literature (Gruenwald 1989; Hayden 1989). Lebl's is a true autobiographical account. In the foreword to the book, Jakir Sade thanks Ženi Lebl for having written "without any malice (many would not have been able to—believe me!) this book of memories, the Naked Island book of the dead and the living . . . that which you have written does not fall into the domain of the dream; it is about real people who existed and who always continue to exist, somewhere here, beside us, who reside, who live in the same city, on the same street, and maybe even in the same house as we do. It is incredible that all that you have described is possible in our time—but it is a fact, it all happened, ... And for this, exactly for this, thank you, and thanks to others who speak the truth, however difficult it was. Continue to speak!"

Ženi Lebl opens her story with the following words:

> Perhaps I would not have written about Glavnjača, Ramski Rit, Zabela (in the eighth pavilion), and two unknown islands Sveti Grgur and Goli Otok had this thing been known, described, put into poetry, forgotten. But it hasn't. The hundreds of women who passed through all those places are silent. Even today they feel fear, after more than 40 years. Why? I will try to explain that here (ibid:9).

Ženi Lebl points out that all the truths about Naked Island, and not only it alone, have not yet been written by people who were there, with the exception of two memoirs written by two persons who had been prisoners in the Naked Island camp, and published in 1988. Almost all of "the truths about Naked Island," she notes, "have so far been written by those who heard only fragments of the truth, often only half-truths, and even lies." How people "fell into the abyss," as she describes it, often was not all that dramatic. Often more dramatic was the way people got out. Then they "fell into an even deeper abyss, into blib, bestiality, immorality, and so on. No one has described that yet. Why?" One well known writer gave Tito's biographer Vladimir Dedijer the following answer to this question: "We must be silent. The condition for release from Naked Island was to swear that you will not say anything about what you saw and experienced. And something else, which I will not tell you about." Lebl adds that "that "something" he indicated—that is the reason why so many hundreds and thousands are silent. That "something" is not something innocent; it is the center, the focus" (ibid:10).

It was 1949 and Ženi Lebl was working in Belgrade as a journalist for the newspaper *Politika*. She had survived the war. Early in the war she had been interrogated by the Germans and imprisoned by the Bulgarians. She spent the rest of the war in Berlin, passing as a non-Jew. Her mother and grandmother died in Serbia as victims of fascist genocide. Her father had survived the war. Ženi's brother, Aleksander, a journalist for *Borba* and *Financial Times* when I met him in his Belgrade home, had fought with Tito's Partisans. Ženi was an enthusiastic supporter of Tito. In the Communist Youth meetings during the 1940s, a time when a number of Yugoslav communists advocated closer ties to Stalin, she defended Tito in his conflict with the Cominform.

One day another journalist met her in New Belgrade. He began telling her one joke after another. As she remembers, he even told a few about Tito. "I didn't remember them all, but I remembered a joke about Yugoslavia winning the first prize at the international flower exhibition because it grew a white violet that weighed 100 kilograms." She wrote the joke down in order not to forget it. When she returned to the newspaper and retold the joke, everyone laughed (ibid:16–17).

On April 28, 1949 she was arrested by the secret police at *Politika*, where she worked, and taken to the Glavnjača Jail in Belgrade where she spent the next four months. For quite some time Ženi had no idea why she had been arrested. The jail authorities would only say, "You will tell us everything. We have the means and the time." "This is a real Kafka. . . ," she retorted. "You'll tell us all about him, too," they answered, without understanding her reference to Kafka (ibid:23–24).

""You're a Jew?" I heard, or did I only think I heard it. Was it a question or a statement?" It made her recall the time she was interrogated by the Nazi Germans in the city of Niš in southern Serbia. "Do you, Jews, have anything by which you can be recognized?" they asked her. "That, at the time, I remember, brought me to tears. . . ." To her current interrogator in Belgrade she replied, "I am a Jew, but the last time that was counted against me was in 1941."

> "They killed your mother, did they kill her?" . . . "Why didn't they kill you?" That was a question which I least expected on that late April night in 1949. Did I hear correctly? . . . [T]hose blue eyes of the German soldier once again were staring at me. . . . The last traces of hope that the war was over disappeared. Blood rushed to my head. . . . Then for the first time I felt a blow of fingers into my ear. . . .

The interrogator asked, "Why didn't you leave for your Palestine?" She thought to herself,

> Yes, I heard something about a Jewish state being created. . . . That didn't interest me. . . . What kind of ties did I have with the Jewish state? My father and brother were, it seemed to me, "declared" as Jews. But that was their private affair. I was a Serb, because there was no Yugoslavia then. But I wanted to be just a Yugoslav. But now, when I experienced this, it seemed that I was experiencing some kind of metamorphosis, that the burden of Jewishness was growing on my back, a burden that I successfully had concealed and succeeded to conceal from the Nazis for four years. Now I am becoming what I wanted to free myself from. I was overcome by a tide of defiance.

She answered the interrogator, "If that is the case, then after this stop I'm leaving for my Palestine." Again they didn't allow her to finish her sentence. "Eh bandit, first you will stay here for awhile" (ibid:32–36).

The interrogations in Glavnjača Jail continued. "Did you talk nonsense about Comrade Tito?" Ženi was asked. To this she replied,

> What kind of nonsense? About the 100 kilogram white violet? Oh, you're thinking about that joke? Yes, I said it. [Interrogator:] To whom did you tell it? [Lebl:] I don't remember. . . . [Interrogator:] Who told you the "joke"? [Ženi Lebl:] I don't know myself. Why is it so important? Is it forbidden to tell jokes? [Interrogator:] Joke? Why do you call curses jokes? Curses and lies!

Her interrogators attempted to extract from Ženi the name of the person who told her the joke (61–62). After a few days they called her for another interrogation. They asked about some papers on which was the handwriting of the journalist who had told her the joke about the white violet. Apparently, he had confessed and identified her. Ženi Lebl told them she did not recognize the handwriting.

> Eh, that's where the joke is: if someone tells you something against the people or the leaders, you must come immediately and tell us about him . . . Then your report will help to uncover an enemy of the people. If you don't report him it means that you too are an enemy of the people. In your case, you didn't come to report Vojo, which was your duty. . . . Call it what you want. But we aren't the kind of people that won't offer you the opportunity to atone for your sins. . . . What do you think, we know all of your movements, every step you take, everything you say, . . . Everyone's civil duty is to help the UDB [secret police] in uncovering anti-state elements. . . . Sign here and you go home immediately (ibid:62–63).

She retorted, "If that's the way it is, it means that my "crime" isn't a crime at all. . ." (ibid:63).

Her sentence was read to her: "In the name of the People, . . . [you are sentenced] for a period of one year . . . for cursing the people and the state. . ." (ibid:68). The director of the jail told her that the sentence "can be shortened to three months, but it can be [extended] to two years. It depends on you." She thought, "In the name of the People", they called it. . . . Do the People know what has been read in their name? We still didn't know. We didn't know what was waiting for us" (ibid:69).

At Ženi Lebl's first location of forced labor, the camp authorities informed the prisoners that they could write to their families. They were instructed to write that they were "alive and well." "But I'm not well. I'm barely alive!" is how Ženi felt. She and other women were then taken by train to the Eighth pavilion of the prison in Zabela (ibid:92–93). In Zabela she met women who had survived wartime concentration camps. There was Crna who had been in the Jasenovac concentration camp, Lala who had been in Ravensbrik, and Mira who had been in Auschwitz. Her yearlong sentence was coming to an end. Four more months, so she thought (ibid:94). Following her stay in Zabela Ženi was transported to Sveti Grgur island in the Adriatic Sea. From there she was taken to the infamous Naked Island camp, her final destination in a sentence that had been extended from one year to two and a half years.

Ženi, looking like a survivor of Auschwitz, saw her father again when she returned to Belgrade. Her father, overjoyed to see her, ran from neighbor to neighbor exclaiming, "My child has returned! My child has returned!" She could not tell him what really had happened. She was, however, required to report regularly to the secret police (ibid:148).

> In 1941 I "disappeared." I and my family, and many more Jewish families. June 1945 I reappeared. The most frequently asked question was, "Are you alive, child?" Then began the questions: where had I been, how did I remain alive, what happened to the rest of the family. I could tell them everything. . . (ibid:153). I began to heal the wounds, to "build a more beautiful future,' . . . . I participated in voluntary rebuilding activities, I went to school, I became a journalist. . . . In April 1949 I disappeared again. In August 1951 I reappeared once again. This time I was more alone than ever before, more than in 1941" (ibid:154).

However hard she tried Ženi could not find work. People refused to hire her. At her old work place in *Politika* newspaper, they told her, "You aren't a person. You are worse than a war criminal" (ibid:155)! She began to laugh at being called a war criminal. The same day she had been arrested she was thrown out of *Politika*, her name was erased from the list of the Association of Journalists of Serbia, she was expelled from the School of Journalism-Diplomacy, and her name was removed from the register of the veterans' association, SUBNOR (ibid:155–156). At first she reported to UDB, the secret police, but then stopped. Still, the UDB knew about her every movement. Everywhere she went to find work she had to reveal that she had been in prison.

Ženi began to think about going to Palestine. She went to the Federation of Jewish Communities on 7 July Street. In the Federation she met someone who asked her why she was not registered in the Jewish community.

> I didn't know how to answer him. I left and went to see Bencion Levi who at the time worked "in internal affairs." He informed me that there were no more requests for

> emigration. Who wanted to leave had left between 1948 and 1951. He was amazed that suddenly I felt Jewish. I filled out the form for membership in the Jewish community and a request for immigration to Palestine. They corrected me, telling me that that land is now called Israel. Whatever! Let it be Tunguzija.

Her request for emigration was denied. Ženi began reapplying every six months. For three years she kept getting denied. An explanation never accompanied the rejections. She began to drink, even to unconsciousness. "How can I live in a country where one person is a provocateur to another?" She thought of suicide . . . [of] going to Sajmište [the site of a concentration camp], to jump from the central tower. "But that would blaspheme the memory of those victims. . ., she told herself (ibid:153–159). One day she met an acquaintance and told him, "I was a person. Understand, a former person!" The man gave her a job, which she held until she left for Israel after her sixth application for emigration (ibid:159–160).

Jewish Euphoria in Yugoslavia: The Calm Before the Storm

The growth of a kind of philosemitism in Yugoslavia was associated with the grand exhibit, *The Jews in Yugoslavia*. This exhibit, which was shown in several cities, served as the rite that opened up the closed Jewish community to the Yugoslav public. The exhibit ran from 1988–1989. Still in the spring of 1989, a Serbian doctor commented to me in Belgrade, "It's a good time for the Jews." I sensed the popular fascination with things Jewish, having noted all the attention the media was giving them. Plus, I happened to be in Serbia where the Society for Serbian-Jewish Friendship held their first public meeting just before my arrival for carrying out more research.

Lavoslav Kadelburg, president of the Federation of Jewish Communities of Yugoslavia from 1964 to 1990, described it as a period of "Jewish euphoria." Euphoria, however, is a temporary state, as everyone soon experienced. The Jews of Yugoslavia, as early as that same spring of 1989, began to acquire a new public visibility, which cast them in the arena of interethnic political conflict, straight into the "civil war of words," exactly in the position most of them wanted to avoid, for they knew it would put a strain on the unity of the Yugoslav Jewish community as a whole. In multiethnic Yugoslavia, they had been playing the role of the acrobat, careful not to bring any imbalance to their relationship with any one particular ethnic population. In general, they had avoided entanglement in politics altogether. This is why Slavko Goldstein, a well-known Jewish and political activist from Zagreb, could tell me in the spring of 1989 that the Yugoslav Jews could serve as brokers in bringing together the conflicting groups in order to reach an understanding, an understanding which, for Goldstein, may have meant a political divorce. The Jews had the credentials for such brokership precisely because no one group could accuse them of being nationalists, either Jewish or any other kind.

The Beginning of the Collective Movement out of Submergence

Before the transition the organized community shared publicly much of its orientation with Titoist rulers in the party, the government, and the interest groups ("socio-political organizations"). During 1989–1990 the community's general political and symbolic-ideological orientation began shifting noticeably, although ties to Titoism certainly had not eroded or been severed completely. Publicly, communal representatives refrained from criticizing or repudiating the Titoist past. In fact, the community continued to cling to certain aspects of Titoism more than to others. After all, Yugoslavia had entered a phase of transition, but no one was quite certain what the outcome would be. The purpose here is to show that a shift was nevertheless occurring and beginning to reshape Yugoslav Jewish ethnicity and identity. There was a discernible movement out of submergence (an erosion of symbolic symmetry), a movement toward greater Jewish distinctiveness, toward reclaiming key symbols of the Jewish past (including Israel), toward greater performative authenticity (away from theatricalism in ritual), toward decentralization (local community autonomy, exemplified by the Zagreb community), and toward a public openness (away from dramaturgical concealment in 1989), politicization, and aggressiveness in guarding symbolic space and combating antisemitism. In private conversations and from a questionnaire, I heard statements and received responses in 1989 that I had not heard from leaders and activists in 1986. One interesting response, in light of the Jewish community's submergence, was that brotherhood and unity had never worked in Yugoslavia.

In the spring of 1989 a special conference was held in Belgrade in which sixty-seven Jewish representatives and activists from all over the country participated. About one month later the Presidency of the Federation adopted a text from this conference that was subsequently brought before the annual Conference of Communities. After an exhaustive discussion the participants of the special conference unanimously adopted certain conclusions, positions, and proposals for action that I will now present (*Jevrejski Pregled* 5–8(1989), 1–2(1990)).

According to the participants the increase in antisemitism in Yugoslavia was associated with the process of democratization and transition to a multiparty system. Antisemitism began to be used sporadically as an instrument in the battle for political power. For example, inflammatory statements were made in the heat of the pre-election campaigns in Croatia. The leader of the Croatian Democratic Community (HDZ), Franjo Tudjman, stated that "in Croatia all are equal, but one has to know who is the host, and who is the guest," implying that minorities could only hope to achieve the status of guest (Goldstein 1990:65). An assistant professor of History in the University of Zagreb, who has been an active member of the Zagreb Jewish community, criticized Tudjman for mixing "inconsistency and inarticulateness" with "statesmanship and moderation" in his public appearances. For instance, Tudjman once remarked, "We will not harm the interests of either Jews or Serbs, provided they are capable and loyal citizens. . . . Personally, I don't believe for a moment that Tudjman would persecute or punish someone on account of their opinions. But his words still give rise to unease" (ibid:66).

Tudjman's book, *Bespuća Povijesne Zbilnosti,* caused quite a stir in Yugoslavia and abroad. Whether or not some of the contents in the book are antisemitic has been debated. What is significant is that the contents have been construed as such, not only by supporters of the Serbs and by Jews in Serbia, but also by Jews in Croatia. The Zagreb Jewish community went so far as to sever its ties to the book's publishing house, Matica Hrvatska (*Bilten* (JOZ) 1990; *Jevrejski Pregled*, 1989). To the community participants, thus, the contemporary situation indicated the necessity of active struggle (they used the word *borba*) against antisemitism, which was said to be a dangerous aspect of national-chauvinism and racism. The members considered it necessary to form organizations for stopping the spread of antisemitism. These organizations, they agreed, could include non-Jewish citizens who were interested in and prepared to actively oppose manifestations of antisemitism, national-chauvinism, and racism. Thus, the call for mobilization went beyond Jews and beyond fighting only antisemitism. Furthermore, the text noted that it is necessary to inform the entire Yugoslav public and the world Jewish community about antisemitism in Yugoslavia. This marked a significant departure from the positions adopted during the period of submergence. Those positions varied from "there is no Jewish problem in Yugoslavia" to handling incidents of antisemitism as internal affairs that could be settled by the Yugoslav constitutional and legal system and by invoking "brotherhood and equality." The community never accused the state (i.e., the Communist Party and government institutions) of antisemitism. In fact, when the *London Chronicle* published charges of antisemitism in Yugoslavia, the Federation of Jewish Communities of Yugoslavia responded sharply against the accusations. Even as recently as 1986 the president of the Zagreb Jewish community stated publicly that antisemitism was no longer an issue in Croatia. Three or four years later he stated his concern over the antisemitism that had surfaced in the political arena in Croatia (*Danas,* 8 May 1990).

The erosion of Titoist Yugoslavia created political and symbolic vacuums and opportunities. Those vying for power began to use xenophobic nationalism as a political instrument of manipulation. Once in positions of power and authority, having been elected in free elections, the new rulers faced the challenge of constructing not only a new political infrastructure but also official and unofficial symbolic-ideological orders that would raise the "nation" as they and their supporters conceived it to its rightful place. In Croatia and Slovenia this first meant self-determination. Not only did the process of cultural objectification (Cohen 1974; Handler 1988; the difference between the two is that Cohen and I accept an existing tradition, while for Handler such a tradition is artificially created) entail restoring institutions, myths, and symbols that had been suppressed for about forty-five years, but also reconstructing and reinterpreting the past, establishing new criteria of distinctiveness, contesting other peoples over certain myths (e.g., Partisan War, Croats as a genocidal people) and symbols (e.g., Jasenovac, "victims"), and managing how this emergent symbolic order is institutionalized and weaved into the fabric of society.

Given the emerging political pluralism, the organized community did not question the right of its members to choose their own political affiliation. However, functionaries of the community were urged not to take a leading role in political movements, because such involvement would put the entire Jewish community at risk of being identified with a certain nation or a certain political party. Guarding the unity of the Jewish community in Yugoslavia remained the primary task of the Federation of Jewish Communities of Yugoslavia and many members of the community (*Jevrejski Pregled* 1–2 (1990); *Zapisnik* 1989). In this aim of unity there was no deviation from the position adopted under Titoism. The difference was in the activists' perception of social reality; that is, that open fragmentation and conflict between regions in which Jews live threatens Jewish unity. When some Jews publicly aligned themselves in the confrontational discourse, whether consciously or not, the unity of the Yugoslav Jewish community was exposed to strain. Such strain was already evident in the early part of 1989 and probably several years earlier in the Zagreb community's push for greater autonomy from the Federation. In some cases it was a matter of members of one Jewish community perceiving that members of another Jewish community had aligned themselves in the growing conflict because of certain statements they had made in the press. For instance, the Zagreb Jewish community objected to comments made by the Rabbi of Yugoslavia in an interview he gave to the Belgrade newspaper *Politika*. The interview took place at the beginning of March 1989, just following the Slovenian expropriation of the Star of David symbol (see below). The rabbi condemned that act by the Slovenes, and also the implied association of the Serbian people with Nazism and the symbolic transposition of the Kosovo Albanians into Jewish victims of fascist oppressors. Perhaps what the Jews of Zagreb found most objectionable was the rabbi's statement, "I think the rest of the Jews of Yugoslavia think this way" (*Politika*, 3 March 1989, 15). That same month two special sessions of the Zagreb community's Executive Council were convened in which the expropriation of the Star of David symbol and the interview with the rabbi were discussed. The session reached the following conclusion:

> The Executive Council of the Jewish community in Zagreb does not agree with part of the interview of Rabbi Cadik Danon in *Politika* on 3 March 1989, because it can be interpreted biasedly as the position of the entire community. Together, our position is that only the Federation, that is, the president of the Federation, can give statements and announcements in the name of the entire community (*Bilten* (JOZ) 11 (1989):4).

Having in view the delicate social and political situation in Yugoslavia, the Federation recommended taking action to protect all property belong to the Jewish community of Yugoslavia. This reorientation was a result of the start of de-nationalization and reprivatization of property. This indicated a change from relinquishing to reclaiming property. Also, a plan for material expansion was implemented in Zagreb. The community began campaigning actively after the anniversary celebration in 1986 to build a synagogue-cultural center directly on the site of the synagogue that was destroyed in the Second World War. Back in 1989, however, despite receiving wide support from the public and from government institutions, the community was faced with overcoming several formal obstacles. The people who opposed the project were using the formalities to derail it. One community official explained that it was not a matter of antisemitism, but a problem tied to other political games and tactics. The absence of an urban plan in the city of Zagreb since 1945 presented one such obstacle. Without such a plan the community could not build the center. "We're playing a game of everything or nothing," the same official told me. The community fought for a decision that would permit the site to be used only by the Jewish community. At the time it was prepared to take political action by arranging a meeting with the President of Croatia, to which other officials and Jewish leaders would be invited. The community, after three years of "nice behavior," was prepared to do battle, applying international pressure if necessary to realize their goal.

A distinct movement away from non-alignment and all that it entailed with regard to Yugoslav foreign policy in the Middle East was the call to strengthen efforts toward re-establishing diplomatic relations between Yugoslavia and Israel. In addition, the community called for a retraction of Yugoslavia's support for the United Nations' resolution condemning Zionism as racism. The community stated that this resolution was "aimed against the essential aspirations and interests of the Jewish people" (*Jevrejski Pregled,* 1989).

In the text that emerged from the special conference, it is clear that as early as March 1989 the Federation of Jewish Communities of Yugoslavia, the organization representing the entire registered membership of the Yugoslav Jewish community, was beginning to shift its orientation away from what it had been under Titoism, that is, away from submergence. With certain exceptions, the shift was not especially dramatic. There was no broad repudiation of the past. If there was any direct criticism of Titoism during the meeting, it is not indicated in the text except in connection with Israel and Zionism. It must be remembered that in the spring of 1989 the Socialist Federative Republic of Yugoslavia remained intact, and the League of Communists did not dissolve until the following year. The chief concerns of the Federation, thus, were fighting antisemitism (including its new political manifestations that would not have been tolerated earlier), maintaining the unity of the entire community during a time of societal fragmentation when Jews were used and participated voluntarily in new political movements, and campaigning for the renewal of diplomatic relations with Israel. The Federation was a conservative institution compared, for example, to the local Zagreb Jewish community whose path paralleled that of the Republic of Croatia in pursuing greater autonomy from the center of power. The Federation continued to strive to maintain a balance as ethnic strife began escalating out of control.

It is interesting that, in reference to this sensitive issue of Israel and Zionism which the organized community did not contest during the more than twenty year absence of diplomatic relations between Israel and Yugoslavia, most of the unconcealed and sharp criticism first came from Israelis of Yugoslav origin. Their remarks about events in Yugoslavia began to be published in the Serbian press. A Serbian journalist who interviewed Israelis of Yugoslav origin in Israel wrote:

> The Yugoslav Jews in Israel are disturbed by what is now happening in Yugoslavia's national regions. Their previous homeland took away much of their property, jobs, even their citizenship, but there is no tone of hatred in their remarks. There is shame. There is amazement. There is also astonishment at the actions of Yugoslav officials who after the break in diplomatic relations between Israel and Yugoslavia condemned "Israeli aggression" on Arabic lands, and chose a frigid posture and one of reproach towards Jews.
>
> No one in Israel understands why Yugoslavia does not reestablish diplomatic relations with their state. Egypt renewed them, a country with which Israel was at war, but Yugoslavia—out of friendship toward Egypt and the rest of the Arabic countries—will not do it! Hungary recently renewed diplomatic relations . . . (*NIN*, 19 November 1989, 57).

A commentator for *Maariv*, originally from Novi Sad, expressed that "until now I was bewildered, but now I am ashamed" (ibid.). The same individual relates a conversation he once had with an official from the Yugoslav Foreign Ministry. This official was born in the Yugoslav town of Apatin, a Yugoslav city that was once part of the Habsburg Empire. The Israeli of Yugoslav origin asked the Yugoslav diplomat: "When will Yugoslavia establish diplomatic relations with Israel?" The Yugoslav official: "I can tell you exactly when. When Israel leaves the occupied territories." Israeli: "And I can tell you exactly when we will leave." Yugoslav official: "When? Israeli: "When you return Apatin to the Habsburg Monarchy" (ibid.)!

It is unlikely that such an exchange between a Jew and a Yugoslav government official would have occurred in socialist Yugoslavia. But the fact that it was printed in a major weekly Yugoslav magazine placed it in the field of discourse associated with the phase of transition. The Israelis of Yugoslav origin thereby entered the field and become active players. As I will show, the subject of diplomatic relations was not the only part of the discourse in which they participated. In the same article from which the previous quotations are taken, individuals commented on Tito's mistakes, on *Goli Otok* concentration camp in which several Jews were imprisoned after the war, and on the general Yugoslav crisis. As far as I am aware, until 1989 no similar article appeared in which a number of Yugoslav Jews living in Israel freely expressed their views on such contested and sensitive subjects.

At the Thirtieth Conference of Communities held in Belgrade in 1990, the year following the Conference on the "Yugoslav Jews of the 1990s," antisemitism continued to be given priority in the collective discussion and motivated community members to form a plan of attack: "We must react with all our means to any appearance of antisemitism, taking preventative measures and energetic actions" (*Jevrejski Pregled* 1–2 (1990). The struggle was turned inward on Yugoslavia itself, a significant reorientation. This is reflected in the regular section on antisemitism published in the Federation's *Jewish Review*. Whereas previously antisemitism in Yugoslavia received scant attention in the *Jewish Review*, and when it did, it usually appeared at the end of the section, by 1990 antisemitism in Yugoslavia was receiving the most attention and being placed at the beginning of the section. The community was now prepared to inform foreign organizations, contrary to its earlier (public) apologetic stance toward the outside world. There was also continuity on this issue from before the Second World War. Then and now the Federation of Jewish (Religious) Communities led the fight against antisemitism (see Freidenreich 1979).

Second, the delegates to the Conference of Communities saw the transition and its goals as a threat to the unity of the Jewish community. Guarding communal unity was set forth as a major task, which was now necessary because of the failure of "brotherhood and unity" and the ongoing fragmentation of the state and society. They believed that the experiment of creating unity out of diversity had succeeded in the Jewish population, whereas the broader societal experiment of "brotherhood and unity" had failed or had never worked.

The aim of reestablishing diplomatic relations with Israel was more than reiterated. Now it became an obligation (the "ought") of the Jewish community to take decisive steps toward that goal. It is in the divergence from, or even repudiation of, the key symbol of non-alignment that re-emergence is most visible. From the writer David Albahari's public statement in support of Israel in 1982 to the organized community's first public declaration regarding the restoration of diplomatic relations more than six years elapsed. This is one indicator of the degree of the community's submergence within Titoism, and it shows how dramaturgical loyalty and concealment is used when there is dissonance between public and private orientations.

The ethno-political context made the campaign for restoring diplomatic relations with Israel possible. In fact, the campaign was led on several fronts. On one front the newly established Society for Serbian-Jewish Friendship called for the restoration of diplomatic relations with Israel. On the cultural level, which also served political aims, the Society played an instrumental role in establishing week-long cultural exchanges between Serbia and Israel and several sister-city relationships between Israeli and Serbian cities (e.g., Rehovot and Valjevo). The Serbian government actively engaged in preliminary discussions with Israeli diplomats, as did Croatian and Slovenian officials. The separate republics pursued their own foreign policies in relation to Israel. The Croats, in particular, aggressively contested the Serbian strategy. A Croatian journalist writing for the main Croatian daily newspaper accused Serbian politicians of pursuing resumed relations between Yugoslavia and Israel as "a carefully elaborated strategy" that "does not really have Israel and the Middle Eastern crisis in the center of attention at all, but they only serve as a means of realizing internal and foreign political aims of the present Serbian leadership" *(FBIS-EEU-70-71)*.

In response primarily, I believe, to the political activism of Slavko Goldstein, who was simultaneously in 1989 the president of the Jewish community in Zagreb, the Federation restated its position that functionaries of the community should not occupy leading positions in political parties and in the new political struggle. Goldstein, by the way, chose not to compete for a second presidential term in the Zagreb community, but he continued to be very active especially in areas where contemporary events affected the Jews of Zagreb and Croatia. When I spoke with him and others in the community in the spring of 1989, he and the vice-president of the Zagreb community stated (Goldstein turned to the vice-president and asked him to answer whether or not a conflict of interest existed) that until then there was no conflict of interest in performing his duties as the president of the community and as the president of the first opposition quasi-political party in Croatia. Goldstein himself wrote about his dual role and why he chose not to seek a second term as president of the Zagreb Jewish community in the community's *Bulletin* (*Bilten* (JOZ) 16(1990)).

The leaders of the Federation reaffirmed the position that the declaration of nationality was an individual matter, but they now added a warning about the possible repercussion of members not declaring themselves as Jews. It was stated that a "realistic (or actual) number of members provides the justification for the community's existence." Thus the previous policy of noninterference was abandoned in favor of applying slight pressure on individuals to decide to declare themselves as Jews on the next census (*Jevrejski Pregled*, 1990).

Although the Jewish community did not mirror the return to religion that occurred in other populations, certain significant turning points with regard to Jewish ritual took place, some of which I referred to earlier. More authentic ritual performance began to reenter Yugoslav Jewish life. Elsewhere I described how traditional ritual was reintroduced to Jewish children in the Pirovac summer camp (Gordiejew 1993). This return to ritual authenticity was apparent outside the camp as well, in the local communities. Ritual events that had been rare or had not occurred in many years began to take place. In the Zagreb community in 1988, Hanukkah was celebrated in a "new, different way—in a "family atmosphere . . . Gathered around tables were friends and in some places entire families from grandmothers to grandchildren" (*Bilten* (JOZ) 2(1988):7). Already in 1986 during my fieldwork the Rabbi of Yugoslavia began training several young men to serve as prayer leaders in the synagogues. In Zagreb an Israeli woman of Yugoslav Jewish descent started a Torah class (*Kružok Tore*) that attracted both Jews and non-Jews. She took the initiative entirely on her own, for at first she received very little support from the community. The most dramatic plan for material expansion has been to rebuild the Jewish synagogue in Zagreb.

The Symbolic Expropriation and Manipulation of the Jews and Jewish Symbols

In the process of the erosion of the Titoist state and its political and symbolic orders and their replacement by new states and symbolic orders that emphasized the ethno-nation, an intense interethnic verbal war intensified and physical violence ultimately erupted. This interethnic conflict has been waged on an international stage encompassing Europe, the Middle East, and North America. The movement away from the national repressions and suppression under state socialism and the movement towards democratization and nationalization have joined many national intellectuals to the side of their respective nationalistic political elites. In conjunction with certain journalists they have used the instruments of mass communication and cultural acts of symbolic manipulation (e.g., expropriation, association, negation, transposition) in the confrontational discourse to (1) (re)construct their respective collective identities as peoples, nations and states, (2) present particular images of themselves to their own peoples, to their ethnic opponents, and to international audiences, and (3) contest certain symbols, myths and images imposed upon them or their majority nations which they have deemed negative or inaccurate. The process of contestation involves defensive and offensive symbolic maneuvering and manipulation. As a particular people defends its symbolic space against encroachment, that is, against negative representations that are imposed upon it as a people, it in turn attacks the symbolic space of its opponents by imposing negative representations upon them. These maneuverings are part of the activities of justification of one's own group and diminishment and eradication of ethnic others, all working towards the end of attaining immortality for one's Nation.

The Jews have not been a major player in this ethno-political conflict, but neither have they been left out of the fields of rhetoric and action. In fact, given their tiny size in the population, their involvement, willing and unwilling, has been disproportionately great. At times they even have been the focus of attention. The negative aspect of their new visibility has been the rise of overt antisemitism in the post-Titoist context of essentialist politics and its servant, xenophobic nationalism. Instances of anti-semitism include statements made during the pre-election campaigns in Croatia, publication and/or reprinting of the *Protocols of the Elders of Zion* in Slovenia and Serbia, statements made by former Ustasha officials in the media in Croatia, vandalism of Jewish sites in Croatia and Serbia, and the same-day bombings of the Zagreb Jewish community and cemetery. From the perspective of certain political actors there is also a positive aspect to Jewish visibility. Among these are Serbs, Slovenes, and Croats who have vied for association with the Jews and/or who have used the Jews or Jewish symbols as an instrument of communication to send particular messages to various audiences at home and abroad (Krušelj 1989; Sekelj 1991; 1992). These actors have recontextualized Jewish symbols and meanings for their own aims. As such the Jews serve as a pawn in the broader conflict, with implications reaching far beyond themselves. However, the Jewish community has always been well aware of the potential implications for the Jews themselves, one being that any involvement or appearance of involvement with any particular national group automatically transposes the Jews from non-participants to participants to enemies of the opposing ethnic peoples. This, in the minds of the community leaders, puts Jews everywhere at risk.

The Yugoslav Jews, as a collective and as individuals, have reacted and responded to contested symbolic forms and meanings that they deem significant for the community and for all Jews. They have responded by discussing the various incidents among themselves and then by taking public action. Here they have not been without some power of their own, being a population that can draw on its resources from the realm of cultural production and distribution both in Yugoslavia and abroad, given their ties to such organizations as the World Jewish Congress. In this way they have become not only objects in the discursive conflict but also conscious actors who choose to enter the field of conflict in order to guard what is sacred to them (e.g., guard against attempts to redefine or negate Jewish history, especially in Yugoslavia) or contest what they perceive to be false symbolic transpositions (e.g., Albanians=Jews, Serbs=fascists, Croats= genocidal people).

The symbolic manipulation of the Jews and Jewish symbols occurred within the context of transition and radical historical change. First, the transition involves the erosion, collapse, and disintegration of socialist Yugoslavia. Second, the transition involves moving toward something else, ostensibly democratic states but ones which thus far have been dominated by essentialist aspirations and mechanisms of manipulation. Anthropologists have shown that transitions are anti-structural phases. The possibility of danger during these phases is increased. Consider a transition that includes what was an entire multiethnic state that was led by a single party, with a single political ideology, for about forty-five years. Begin to strip that away. There is transition but there are no "elders" to provide guidance. The transition is thus an uncontrolled, chaotic one. There is no one "in structure" to ensure that anti-structure does not turn into chaos. It is a dangerous phase for the rules have changed, and no longer are all the actors playing by the same rules. The position of the minorities, the powerless peoples, within this transition exposes them to even greater danger. They become vulnerable politically and symbolically, powerless and unable to defend their sacred symbolic space from becoming violated and used for profane activities. Once again, external history imposed on this population of Jews brought radical change and necessitated new forms of response. In the end, it was not a vulnerable population profile that dissolved the entity known as the Yugoslav Jewish community, but an external historical imposition by more powerful populations.

Symbolic Association with and Manipulation of the Jews and Jewish Symbols

Expropriation of the Star of David. In February 1989 striking Albanian miners in the Autonomous Province of Kosovo captured the attention of an international audience. On February 26, 1989, a television program broadcast throughout Yugoslavia presented Slovene politicians and intellectuals, gathered in Cankar Hall in Ljubljana, the capital of the Republic of Slovenia, promoting political pluralism and criticizing the Serbian repressive policy toward the Albanians in Kosovo. To communicate their message more forcefully they expropriated the Jewish Star of David symbol, which was juxtaposed with the words, "Kosovo—My Land."[3] Star of David badges with the same message were being sold on the streets of Ljubljana. The Slovenes used the symbol as a vehicle of communication. It had an instrumental use. The symbol's high recognizability in form and meaning endowed it with an interethnic communicative efficacy few symbols have. Many older Yugoslavs saw Jews wearing the Star of David badge during the war and knew what the symbol stood for. Its denotative meaning is that of Jewish suffering, particularly during the Holocaust (suffering, victimization, de-humanization). The intent of the Slovenes was to use the symbol in order to exercise an act of symbolic manipulation. Specifically, the intent was to symbolically transpose the Muslim Albanians of Kosovo, whom the Slovenes saw as repressed by the Serbs, and perhaps also, in the broader drama unfolding between the Slovenes and Serbs, the Slovenes themselves, into Jewish victims of the Serbian fascist repressors and hegemonists. Did the Jews occupy, in this case, the role of symbolic middlemen? A Jewish symbol was expropriated by a non-Jewish group, an act that was condemned by the Jewish community and individual Jews. The Jews themselves acted not as middlemen, though their symbol was used as a symbolic medium to communicate a politically charged message. The Jews perceived the symbolic borrowing as antagonistic. Thus it really was not an act of borrowing, but of expropriation.

The event in Cankar Hall triggered a passionate reaction from Serbs and Jews. Serbs in Belgrade came out into the streets. Serbs gathered outside the Federal Assembly in Belgrade. Amidst others, the following slogans could be seen in the crowd: "Kosovo is Serbian land;" "We will defend you, Yugoslavia;" "On whose behalf does the Slovene and Croatian leadership speak?" "Down with false brotherhood and unity;" "We do not give up Kosovo—we live in harmony;" "Yugoslavia, Serbia is defending you;" "Slovenes, remember Serbian bread;" "Slovenes, shame on you." More slogans were being shouted: "Serbia has risen;" "Slovenia lies;" "Let's go to Kosovo" (*FBIS*, 9 March 1989, 73, EEU-89-045). The reaction of the Jews was more rational and controlled, but also passionate. They perceived the expropriation and manipulation of the Star of David symbol as an abuse (*zloupotrebe*) of the symbol. Individual Jews communicated their anger through the popular media. The Jewish community of Belgrade and the Federation of Jewish Communities of Yugoslavia released statements condemning the act. In a press release the Federation condemned the abuse of the Star of David and stated that it served to widen the chasm between the peoples of Yugoslavia. The Federation filed criminal charges with the Ljubljana District

Public Prosecutor and City Secretariat for Internal Affairs in Ljubljana. "We are proposing that criminal proceedings be initiated against the people and creators responsible for the badge 'Kosovo—My Land' and are asking that its continued manufacture and distribution be banned," the report stated (*FBIS*, 16 March 1989, 59, EEU-89-050). The Federation informed international Jewish organizations of the actions. Thus began a more aggressive strategy of the Yugoslav Jewish community to defend its symbolic space and avoid being sucked into the nationalist vortex. In a meeting of the Federation's Workers' Council, the strong language of "struggle" (*borba*) began to be used: "If the distribution and selling of the badge does not stop, the Federation will begin a *borba* toward stopping this activity" (*Zapisnik*, 1989). In response to the Federation's actions, the Slovenian youth magazine *Mladina* printed the aphorism, "What do these Jews want? Money, probably." The Jewish community also criticized the Slovenian intellectual establishment for failing to condemn antisemitism in Slovenia, such as the aphorism in *Mladina* and the serial reprinting of *The Protocols of the Elders of Zion* in the magazine *Tribuna*. Laslo Sekelj, an intellectual and frequent contributor to the popular press, criticized the Slovene intellectuals for condemning Serbia's repressive policies against the Albanians in Kosovo while keeping silent about antisemitism in their own republic of Slovenia (see Sekelj 1991; 1992).

The symbolic expropriation of the Jews and Jewish symbols did not go unnoticed by the media in the Croatian and Serbian republics. Several articles dealt directly with this subject (see Krušelj 1990; Sekelj 1991; 1992).

A Deputy President of the Federation of Jewish Communities of Yugoslavia, Aleksandar Mošić, stated in a newspaper interview that nothing in Yugoslavia is strange for him. However, when he saw the Star of David badge, he said the hair on his head stood up.

In response to the Slovenian accusation that the Serbs were applying fascist measures against the Albanians in Kosovo, Mošić replied, "We all know very well, perfectly well, what persecution is, what a pogrom is, and what genocide is. The Star of David incident was a misuse; it was not an expression of antisemitism. It is a manipulation (cf. Sekelj 1991). This kind of combination [juxtaposition of the Jewish symbol and the political message] implies that the Albanians in Yugoslavia are under Nazism, and that the Serbs, that is, the Serbian authorities, are in the role of the Nazis" (*Politička Ekspres*, April 1989).

Mošić stated that many of his good friends do not have exact information concerning the events in Kosovo. The role of the media has been to proclaim half-truths. To support his case he shared an anecdote, which explains a lot about the problems in the former Yugoslavia, and which is even more accurate today. At one time Mošić lived in Sisak, a town near Zagreb, for twelve years. He had worked in Zagreb University. He had many friends there in Zagreb. It was the time of the Croatian nationalist awakening in 1971. A good friend told him, "It isn't possible to buy *KRAŠ* (a Croatian candy company) products in Belgrade." To this, Mošić answered, "Let's go, let's get in the train. I won't say a word. I'll take you to Belgrade, and you will come to believe that there are not one but four *KRAŠ* stores in Belgrade." The man just could not believe Mošić (ibid).

The six-pointed Star of David (*Magen David*) symbol is a sacred symbol of the Jews. That is clear from the passionate response of the Jews of Yugoslavia to what they perceived to be a profanation and desecration of this symbol. But was it always sacred to the Jews? This introduces the question of ownership? Do symbols fall in the private or public domain? If there are such things as symbolic space and symbolic ownership, then we can approach the problem of symbolic expropriation and manipulation as a process of encroachment upon and defense of symbolic space.

The history of the hexagram indicates that it was neither exclusively a Jewish symbol nor a sacred one. It was only in the nineteenth century Jews and Christians recognized it as an exclusively Jewish symbol. As Gershom Sholem (1971) points out, however, it was primarily used as an identifying ornament or sign. Otherwise its lack of substantive and especially sacred meaning made it an empty symbol. It was only when the Zionists, who were looking for a non-religious sign-symbol, chose the Star of David that the sign took on additional meaning. The most sacred meaning of the symbol derives from the experience of the Holocaust. Sholem (ibid:281) writes:

> But far more than the Zionists have done to provide the Shield of David with the sanctity of a genuine symbol has been done by those who made it for millions into a mark of shame and degradation. The yellow Jewish star, as a sign of exclusion and ultimately of annihilation, has accompanied the Jews on their path of humiliation and horror, of battle and heroic resistance. Under this sign they were

> murdered; under this sign they came to Israel . . . the sign which in our own days has been sanctified by suffering and dread has become worthy of illuminating the path to life and reconstruction. Before ascending, the path led down into the abyss; there the symbol received its ultimate humiliation and there it won its greatness.

Both Jews and non-Jews regard the Star of David as a Jewish symbol that communicates much of the same substance and meaning—the Holocaust of World War II and the State of Israel. The former of these two associations gives this symbol its most sacred qualities. The symbol embodies the collective experience of horror and humiliation and evokes the deepest of human emotions. It is on the historical connection between the humiliation and annihilation of the Jewish experience of World War Two and the Star of David symbol that the Jews of Yugoslavia based their claim to ownership. It was a key and dominant symbol in their symbolic space. When the Slovenes expropriated the symbol in February 1989 and used it in a manner that the Jews perceived as profanation, they reacted passionately. The fact that this act occurred within a much broader social drama made the impact far greater. This incident, more than the interethnic Society of Serbian-Jewish Friendship, brought the Jews of Yugoslavia into the public political arena. They recognized that they had crossed over into a historical phase in which they would have to fight their own battles within the countrywide arena. With the response of the Jews to what they perceived as an abuse of the Star of David symbol emerged the broader conceptual or symbolic Jewish community.

Serbs are conspicuously silent about this past event, once again brought to my attention by a Jewish informant. Brought to my attention during my visit to Zagreb in the fall of 1994 was an earlier expropriation of the Magen David during demonstrations by Serbs in Belgrade in 1982 against the Israeli occupation of Lebanon. In Belgrade's Marx and Engel's square, the crowd set ablaze an effigy with the symbol and the word "Jude." During my visit to Belgrade in 1989, soon after the symbol's expropriation by the Slovenes, I heard no references to the earlier Serbian expropriation. This incident recalls Ernest Renan's often quoted statement that nationalism entails not only remembering the past but also forgetting it and even getting it wrong.

Kosovo, the Serbian Zion. An additional comment on Kosovo may help place into perspective the sentiment many Serbs feel, or are said to feel, for this territory that today is about ninety percent Albanian. It is once again a site of interethnic violence. Kosovo was the seat of the great medieval Serbian kingdom and where the Serbian monasteries from that historical period still stand. Kosovo remains, for the Serbs, their holy land and Jerusalem. This symbolic association has been expressed explicitly by the Serbs, some of whom see themselves almost as the lost or 13th tribe of Israel. The Serbian writer-turned-politician (the main opposition leader in Serbia), Vuk Drašković, whom I interviewed before his ascent to political prominence, wrote an open letter to the writers of Israel in which he expressed the tie between the two peoples. He wrote how during the two world wars "every foot of Serbian land became Jerusalem and the tragedy of that City was enacted all over the country." Drašković further wrote:

> Our misfortune, however, continues. Just as in Turkish times, we are being impaled in Kosovo, the most sacred part of Serbian land,. . . And this does not happen in Kosovo only, although in that cursed and damned Zion of ours the anti-Serbian hysteria has reached its most violent peak. It is as if we were that 13th, lost, and most unhappy of all Israel's tribes. . . . Accept this letter, please, as a toast to suffering, for we at least, Jews and Serbs, have been used to drink[ing] out [of] such cups. At least we, Jews and Serbs, have learned and tasted the truth of the saying that there is no heavenly gift more precious than the suffering of the innocent (Drašković 1985).

Drašković concluded his open letter with the words: "I greet You as brothers with that oath which our ancestors heard from the Jews the meaning of which is carried by every single Serb banished from Kosovo: "If I ever should forget You, let my right hand forget me, o Jerusalem"" (Drašković 1985)! Drašković may be considered an extreme case by some (he certainly was before the collapse of Yugoslavia), but such comparisons and sentiments also have been uttered by other Serbian intellectuals. Even a sniper on a Sarajevo hillside told a Western reporter, "Serbs, we are just like Jews. We are God's people, chosen to suffer. Hungarians, Turks, Germans, Germans again. Now it is Croats and Muslims. So you see, always we are victims" (Horwitz 1993). Nor are the comparisons restricted to Serbs. Some Jews from Serbia have expressed the tie of Serbs and Jews based on the common histories of suffering of the two peoples (Ačin 1989; *Student* (Belgrade), 14 April 1989; Tanašić 1989). Given the state of interethnic conflict in the region, individuals have drawn parallels between Kosovo and Israel's West Bank (Denitch 1990; *FBIS,* 1990, 70–71, EEU-041). One Serbian intellectual, a member of the founding group of the Society for Serbian-Jewish Friendship, expressed his feelings as follows: "Kosovo is Serbia and this fact depends neither on the Albanian birthrate nor the Serbian mortality rate. There is so much Serbian blood and so many Serbian sacred objects there that it will remain a Serbian land even if not one Serb remains in it" (*Duga*, 1989: 37). Kosovo was the cradle of the medieval Serbian kingdom and Serbian Orthodox Church, and Kosovo Polje is where the Serbs lost a great battle against the Ottoman Turks but also, they proclaim, where they were reborn spiritually. Also, a highly significant act occurred in 1986 when members of the Serbian Academy of Sciences and Arts (SANU) prepared a document that listed the grievances of the Serbian people against the Titoist system. One of these long-held grievances was that Tito had deliberately parcelized Serbia into a republic and two adjoining provinces, with the latter exercising power in the federation equal to the six republics. The authors argued that no other republic or nation (*nacija*) had been so divided. The Serbs believed that Tito's policy was, "a weak Serbia—a strong Yugoslavia." Thus, when Milošević usurped power and proclaimed his intention of returning Kosovo to Serbia, he won wide popular support and, critically, the support of many intellectuals who otherwise would have opposed him as just another Serbian communist ruler. It is important to add that Milošević managed to gain control over most of the communications network in Serbia and thus controlled the resources of cultural production and presentation. Dissenters existed but they found it difficult to communicate their messages to a broad public audience because they lacked access to long-range communications technology and were weakened by factionalism within their ranks. In Serbia, therefore, even before any significant democratization emerged, the political manipulation of cultural sentiments and conceptions of peoplehood, together with that of the perceived threat of Islamic fundamentalism, was in the open and in full swing before 1989. Given the wide acceptance outside of Serbia of "Serbian hegemonism," itself a contested image built from a combination of prewar and postwar structural realities (after all, the king was a Serb, and, based on numerical data, the Serbs were overrepresented in key positions in the state, including in Croatia) and the perceptions and conceptions of non-Serbs, the Milošević government's constitutional reattachment of Kosovo and its repressive policies in that province struck fear among other Yugoslav people, particularly the Slovenes, Croats, and Bosnian Muslims. For these people Milošević's actions in Kosovo and his use of mass street demonstrations elsewhere confirmed their own perceptions and conceptions of just who the Serbs were and what the essence of *Srpstvo* was. Hence, in the context of change, the Kosovo of the 1980s did not remain a Serbian-Albanian conflict. It soon became a springboard for confrontation and symbolic contestation between Serbia and the two western republics of Croatia and Slovenia. Before long, the range of contestation extended to previous conflicts between these people, their present activities, and their future aspirations with regard to the federal structure of Yugoslavia. In addition to the contestation over specific symbols and myths, entire ethnic representations and images were contested (e.g., the Croats as an antisemitic and genocidal people and the Serbs as the eternal friends of the Jews). Anthony Smith (1991:18) tells us that "in such circumstances, it becomes impossible for ethnic minorities which have their own myths of chosenness not to become drawn into the nationalist vortex, irrespective of the inclinations of individuals."

Case of the Society for Serbian-Jewish Friendship. The Society of Serbian-Jewish Friendship (*Društvo Srpsko-Jevrejskog Prijateljstva*) was established in 1988. For eight months the police prohibited legal establishment of the Society. The police justified their decision by stating that such an interethnic alliance would undermine the brotherhood and unity ideology of socialist Yugoslavia. When a Serbian-Slovenian Society was established sometime thereafter, and the Miners' Strike in Kosovo gained the attention of an international audience, the Belgrade police backed down and allowed the Society to be formed.

The founding group of the Society was composed of twenty-two intellectuals, thirteen Serbs, and nine Jews. I have interviewed five of the nine Jewish members and met one other. All are males. Of these twenty-two, four Serbs and three Jews formed the Executive Council. These twenty-two individuals belonged to the echelon of the intellectual world of Serbia. Sixteen of the founders are members of the Serbian Academy of Sciences and Art. "That's a 'Little

Academy.' It has prestige," co-founder and President Ljubomir Tadić boasted. Tadić also noted, in the spring of 1989, that the Serbian intellectuals who were the founders of the Society were not popular with the state and were called "the opposition." Cultural intellectuals in Serbia are a highly visible group and have had considerable influence on public opinion. One of the founding members, an informant of mine and a member of the Jewish community, divided the group of twenty-two into two segments. The first group included those who were genuinely interested in friendship as explicitly stated in the Society's aims. He did not believe that the individuals in this group concealed a hidden political agenda. The second group, however, either had an unstated motive to begin with or saw an opportunity to use the symbolic association with the Jews for political purposes. "Friends use friends," another of the Jewish founding members told me. Tadić was not so forthcoming. He was one of the Belgrade University professors who had been removed from the university in the 1970s and had become a dissident in the Yugoslav sense of the word. Tadić told me that the Society was not formed for any instrumental or political uses, neither for Serbs nor for Jews, and not because of the increasing climate of interethnic hostility in the country. He did acknowledge one political aim: "We feel that the friendship between Serbs and Jews is not complete if there are no [diplomatic] relations with the State of Israel, which we believe were unjustly severed. We would like the friendship to extend to those Yugoslav Jews in Israel and not just to those in Yugoslavia." However, other informants, including members of the Society, believed certain actors harbored a political agenda, one that included showing who the enemy was. Klara Mandić, co-founder and Secretary of the Society, and a member of the Belgrade Jewish community, insisted that the Society have independent sections in the United States as well. Some of the members, including my informant, opposed this proposal because the Society would lose control over who could become a member. Those opposed did not want, for example, members of Serbian emigré groups in the Society. As my informant explained, "The reason [the others] wanted [sections of the Society in the United States] was because of the aims of the Serbian Lobby in the United States. Magljić [of the Serbian Lobby] spoke about uniting with Jews in the United States to solve the Kosovo problem. The main existence of this Society is not to solve the Kosovo crisis." Criticism also came from outside the Society. One argument of the critics was that only a handful of Jews joined the Society. I do not know how many Jews were or are members. What is clear is that prominent Jewish intellectuals from Serbia were among the members of the founding group.

The split within the founding group was also found among the Serbs and the Jews, and among the journalists who reported on the Society. In the Belgrade Jewish community there were those who thought that the Jews should throw all of their support behind the Serbs. When these same members of the Jewish community were asked about the Star of David incident described below, they gave long statements about how good the Serbs were to the Jews. They tended to exaggerate how good the relationship was in the past. In the second group were those who "tried to see things the way they were." They hoped that the Society would bring new possibilities to the community, given the limited resources of the community. The new possibilities they foresaw included the opportunity to develop Jewish culture and historical research.

What really pushed the Society into the increasingly hostile political arena was its first public gathering in March 1989. At that time relations between the Serbs and the two western republics of Croatia and particularly Slovenia were deteriorating quickly. The "civil war of words," as one major Croatian magazine described it, was beginning in earnest. The first public gathering of the Society was held in the Serbian Writers' Club in Belgrade, home of the Serbian Writers' Association, which had taken on the form of a quasi-political party before actual opposition parties emerged in the Republic of Serbia later that year. Thus, the Society chose a setting that was already highly politicized. Second, the timing of the gathering politicized the Society even more, for it occurred shortly after the gathering of Slovene politicians and intellectuals in Cankar Hall where the Star of David symbol was used (see Malisić 1989). In its public meeting, the Society sharply criticized the Slovenes, accusing them of abusing the symbol. This further politicized the Society, which caused one of its founding members, the Jewish writer Filip David, to withdraw. In his withdrawal letter to the Society, David accused the Society of becoming a political actor and of being guilty of the same expropriation and misuse for which it had attacked the Slovenes. David tried to convince another Jewish founding member to withdraw, but the latter opted to take a wait-and-see approach. When I spoke to the latter in 1989, he remained unconvinced and was unhappy with the slow development of the Society's program. Later, he also left the Society because he saw it as too politicized.

The Society received a mixed reception among the Jews of Yugoslavia. In the Belgrade community the membership was divided sharply, which was apparent in the interviews that I conducted in April and May 1989. When I asked Klara Mandić why some Jews in the Belgrade community did not immediately accept the Society, she replied that the community was a conservative organization. "The community has the following program: don't go to extremes with the state. Only that there be no excesses." "In order that there be no conflict," interjected Society President Tadić. Many Jews were afraid that association with the intellectual opposition would also place the Jews in a position against the government. Mandić said, "I can't say that the Jewish community is pro-state; it's not, but in every case it practices the politics of the norm." Later in my joint interview with the co-founders, Tadić noted, "Our Society was at first not permitted to operate, so [the Jews] were very afraid that we, that our Society, would be used in the political battle. When the people [in the community] saw that all was all right, that the Society was in their favor. . . . You know, it is very important that they know that they have among the Serbs . . . In every situation, that they will be protected, that they are not alone in the world. That is extremely important." Mandić noted, "This is the only Society, the only one in the world, of friendship with the Jewish people. It is not business, it is not religion; rather, friendship. Only about friendship."

The first public gathering held in the Writers' Club attracted such a large crowd that people were forced to stand outside the building. Both Serbian and Jewish intellectuals presented speeches. Society President Ljubomir Tadić gave me a copy of his entire speech, "On Friendship and Hatred," in which he expressed the following:

> We have established the Society of Serbian-Jewish Friendship in an unhappy time when hatred is spreading unrestrained throughout the country. We, the founders of this Society, believe that our aim, at this same time, is to call for reason and to oppose the troubled currents of irrationality that threaten to drown us. . . . It is said that friendship exists most often among people of the same nationality, although there exist experiences that completely contradict that. Today it is very difficult to speak, for example, about friendship between some South Slavic peoples. The Jews and Serbs do not share any kinship, but they represent two peoples who never fostered any unfriendly feelings between

> them. More specifically, among the Serbian populace, antisemitism as the most distinct form of enmity toward Jews never took root, regardless of the fact that in individual phases of the history of the emergent Serbian state, during the Obrenovic dynasty, there existed an unstable, even negative, orientation on the part of the rulers toward the Jews . . .[but] antisemitism among the Serbs was not widespread. . . (Tadić 1989).

Tadić then points out the historical bases for friendship between the two groups. Among these he notes the establishment, since the nineteenth century, of various associations and societies that fostered this interethnic tie. He proposed that the book *Naši Jevreji* (Our Jews), published in 1940, which was the collaborative effort of several Serbs and Jews who contributed chapters, should be published again. The strongest tie, Tadić noted, is the "common fate that the two peoples, including the Rom, suffered as victims of genocide during the Second World War. . . . All of the war criminals and all of the victims of genocide, unfortunately, have not yet been established, and this remains one of the most important aims of our Society" (ibid:2). Tadić then makes specific reference to the expropriation of the Star of David symbol.

> The [Society] is established at a time when intolerance and hatred is spreading throughout the land and when the propagandists of chauvinism in the Yugoslav northeast [a reference to the Slovenes and Croats], imaginary democrats, cynically hid their hatred, this time toward the Serbs, behind the Star of David, the symbol of the suffering of the Jewish people, completely forgetting that also in Kosovo the Nazis, from the ranks of the Albanian population, formed the notorious SS division *Skenderbeg*. But the Serbs and the Jews, this we ceremonially announce as our oath, have not established our Society in order to menace or alienate, nor that any of us, in the maelstrom of chauvinism, fish in troubled waters. We want to show by our example that friendship is a valuable virtue, and hatred is an evil vice" (ibid:2).

Whatever his stated intent, Tadić constructed an oppositional classification scheme that had the effect of further alienating the Croats and Slovenes. For example, in his use of Cicero's saying, "Friendship can exist only among the good," Tadić placed the Serbs and Jews on the side of the good and the others on the side of the evil. In so doing, he repeated the myth of the eternal friendship of Serbs and Jews. Elsewhere in the speech he states, "I hope that I will not be mistaken if in conclusion I say that only those peoples and individuals who felt, so to speak, something of the Jewish fate on their own skin can be, and remain, the friends of the Jewish people" (ibid: 8). This is a classification scheme that raises up one's own group and diminishes the other, even if not so intended.[4] In describing Johann Blumenbach's late eighteenth century classification of five races into what was a geometric model of racial hierarchy, Stephen Jay Gould (1994) demonstrates the enduring destructive power of certain classification schemes of which the classifier may be completely unaware. This may have been the case with Tadić in the spring of 1989.

Dr. Lavoslav Kadelburg, a former president of the Federation and one who had perfected the balancing act of the minority Jews in multiethnic Yugoslavia, responded that the Jews did not have such an overabundance of friends that gave them the luxury of turning down offers of friendship. This acceptance on the part of the Federation president was reflected in the positive coverage of the Society in the Federation's publication *Jevrejski Pregled* until it ceased publication at the end of 1990. Although his personal acceptance of the Society might have had a calming effect, the argument in the Belgrade community over the Society was silenced only when the Slovenes expropriated the Star of David symbol. This act silenced many of the critics in the Belgrade community, but doubters remained. One informant commented, "I don't see the necessity to organize and to explode. If you are a friend, you don't need to say you are a friend. You are a friend and that's it. They [in the Society] try [to present] another political opinion. I don't like Jews involved in politics." Another informant expressed the following opinion of the Society:

> In time intellectual people like writers and [academics] saw that our [foreign] policy isn't good. Inside Serbia, for the first time, you could say it, you could write it. It's the first time we can read and speak about it. It's the reason Serbs wanted to say, "We want to make friendship with the Jews, because we don't have a relationship with Israel." The main thing for the Serbian-Jewish Society is that Yugoslavia doesn't have diplomatic relations with Israel. And these intellectuals want to show their friendship not so much to

> Israel and the Jews, as they want to show who their enemy is—Muslims . . . and somewhat also the Slovenians. . . . It was the Serbs' idea for [a] friendship [society]. We spoke in the kehilla about that, and a lot were against this society. "Why do they want it? All those years they forgot we were in the war. They were against Israel. Now when they need our help, they suppose they will have help not from us but from Jews in the world." They did not believe in the sincerity of the Serbs.

The Jews of Zagreb greeted the Society of Serbian-Jewish Friendship less enthusiastically, even negatively. When asked about the Society during an interview for the Croatian weekly magazine *Danas*, Nenad Porges, who succeeded Slavko Goldstein as president of the Zagreb Jewish community in 1990, stated that it was clear that the Society was "strongly hitched" to Serbian political maneuvering. He pointed out that the "Society does not have a significant number of Jewish members, and the Jewish community in Belgrade does not have any formal ties with the Society and it is not the founder of the Society" (*Danas*, 13 November 1990, 39). Porges further stated:

> I would not want my narrower homeland, and that is Croatia, to fall into a similar noose. I especially do not see any reason for a Society of Croatian-Jewish Friendship because the Jews of this republic are not in conflict with the Croats, nor am I with my friends, and the Jewish community already insisted on the formation of the Miroslav Salom Freiberger Cultural Society, which is, judging by current membership, open to all people of good will. . . . [This] society is open to Jews and all others who are interested in widening their horizons [of] Judaism and Jewish culture. And then, I do not see a reason for establishing a special Society of Croatian-Jewish Friendship. I do not see any kind of reason why someone might not initiate the establishment of a Society of Israel-Croatia, but that could not be decided at the level of the Jewish community of Zagreb, but rather by Croatia as an integral part of Yugoslavia with regard to Israel" (ibid:39–40).

The Society's image was already quite tarnished by the time of my most recent visit in September 1994. It seems that most Jews were displeased with the nationalistic stance and displays by certain members of the Society. Depending on whom one speaks with, the size of the Jewish membership in the Society is substantial or negligible. For certain, the Jewish community of Belgrade has distanced itself from the Society. Key individuals have also left the Society, having opposed the increasingly nationalistic turn the Society had taken with the start of the war. In particular, both Jewish members and non-members have expressed their disagreement with the actions of the Society's secretary, Klara Mandić. Rumors circulated about her associations with individuals of the current Serbian government and of the Bosnian Serbs.

Pre-Election Campaigning and Antisemitism in Croatia. The pre-election campaigning in Croatia brought antisemitism to the surface. Slavko Goldstein, who was at the time president of the Zagreb Jewish community, expressed proudly in 1986 that antisemitism in Croatia virtually had disappeared. Three years later he was speaking out against the re-emergence of antisemitism. As a political player himself—Goldstein was the president of the first opposition group in postwar Croatia, subsequently a major player in a political coalition, and he continues to be a political voice—Goldstein became a target of attacks. When asked if his Jewishness was an advantage to him a few months ago, he replied:

> Yes. In the beginning my Jewishness was seen as a great advantage. A year and a half ago, when pluralistic life began, various groups invited me to cooperate with them or to join them. Even [Tudjman's] party invited me. . . . They believed my Jewishness would [have to] amortize labels like "Croatian chauvinism," "Neo-Ustashi," etc. . . . [U]ntil the legalization of the parties, my Jewishness was an advantage. At a time when in certain East European countries antisemitism emerged together with democratic processes, I was happy that as a Jew (I wasn't the only one) [I was] participating in the emergence of democracy in Croatia and that in general it was well accepted. Unfortunately, there began to appear, already in the fall [of 1989], contrary voices. Jewishness began to change from a desirable advantage into an undesirable defect. That doesn't serve democracy in Croatia, nor its image before the world. With antisemitism

> [Croatians] will not acquire a visa for entrance into Europe and the civilized world (*Danas*, 8 May 1989, 14).

Several inflammatory statements about Jews or minorities were made in the heat of the battle, including by the man who ultimately won the election and has been the president of the new Croatian state ever since—Franjo Tudjman, ex-Partisan, ex-Communist, ex-Yugoslav National Army general, and ex-dissident. Whether or not these statements had antisemitic intent behind them or were taken out of context and then used by Tudjman's opponents to characterize him as an antisemite, I cannot say for sure. From the perspective of the Jews of Yugoslavia, including the Jews of Croatia, there was enough there to upset them.

Back in the winter of 1990 Ivo Goldstein (1990:66–67), a member of the Zagreb Jewish community and a professor of history in Zagreb University, wrote the following about Tudjman:

> [T]he charisma of Franjo Tudjman is still enough for many to believe unreservedly that every move he makes is for the best.
>
> However, Tudjman has not won much trust in intellectual circles. In many of his frequent public appearances, statesmanship and moderation is mixed with inconsistency and inarticulateness. On one occasion he said: "We will not harm the interests of either Jews or Serbs, provided they are capable and loyal citizens." Immediately his critics wanted to know what it meant to be "loyal," who would determine the criteria, and how the "disloyal" would be punished. Personally, I don't believe for a moment that Tudjman would persecute or punish someone on account of their opinions. But his words still give rise to unease. Neither Tudjman nor the great majority of Croats for that matter are aware of the detrimental effect of statements like these, which are typical products of the way of thinking and speaking nurtured by the politics of the last 45 years. Actually, in spite of his claims to be influenced by Western political traditions, through his pursuit of image and spectacle and particularly his yearning to be "father of the homeland," Tudjman resembles [Tito] more and more. The difference between them is that Tudjman has traded in the commu-

nist ideal and class interpretation of history for the national ideal and nationalist view of the past.

Striving for and Contesting (Im)Mortality through Justification of the Ethnic Self and Diminishment and Eradication of the Ethnic Other

The events, sites, and persons associated with the wartime years between 1941–1945 became hotly contested symbols during the period of transition. The different sides in the conflict either supported the official Titoist version of that period where it suited them, or they challenged that version with their own.

The word symbol "genocide" has been one of the most contested symbols during the transition, along with the associated symbols of "victim" and the concentration camp of "Jasenovac" that was situated in the Independent State of Croatia. No small part in the battle over these symbols and their meanings has been played by Croatian President Franjo Tudjman. In his zeal to destroy the negative myth that the Croats are a genocidal people, imposed and held in place by some Serbs, Tudjman has written books challenging the Titoist and Serbian versions of the events of 1941–45. Although he admits that the Ustasha were fascists who conducted terrible crimes, he argues that they represented a minuscule part of the Croatian population and that they resorted to genocide as a response to Serbian hegemonistic goals during the interwar period and to Chetnik massacres of Croats during the war.[5]

Furthermore, Tudjman argues, the official numbers of genocide victims of the Ustasha were and continue to be deliberately inflated many times over. The official number of victims of the Jasenovac concentration camp, which has been called the "Yugoslav Auschwitz" (Dedijer 1992) and the "Serbian Golgatha," was 700,000. Tudjman refers to this as the "Jasenovac Myth." His own estimates have fluctuated, with the lowest estimate put at 30,000.[6]

Much of the early part of the interethnic conflict involved "counting of the graves," that is, various individuals on both sides putting forth estimates of the wartime losses of Yugoslavia's ethnic populations, particularly those attributed to genocide and mass executions (see Boban 1990; Hayden 1990; Pasic 1989). The Jews of Yugoslavia entered this polemic through what was referred to as the "Goldstein Affair." Slavko Goldstein, who was president of the Zagreb community at the time, contributed a foreword in a book by a Croatian author who estimated the losses were above the Tudjman figure but still far below the official figures favored by the Serbs. Leaders in the Federation of Jewish Communities of Yugoslavia were displeased with Goldstein's involvement in the polemic and stated in a communal meeting that Jews in the country should avoid any such entanglement. What was important to them was the fact that the estimate of Jewish losses was quite reliable and that was sufficient. Federation President Kadelburg stated this position in an interview for a weekly magazine. In the same article, Klara Mandić, secretary of the Serbian-Jewish Friendship Society, criticized Goldstein severely and said that his contribution to the book was the first sign of a split in the Yugoslav Jewish community (Nikolic 1989). Even within the Belgrade Jewish community, Mandić has become a controversial figure in the conflict because of her ultra-strong support of the Serbian position.

As Robert Hayden (1991; 1994) has demonstrated in "Recounting the Dead: The Rediscovery and Redefinition of Wartime Massacres in Late- and Post-Communist Yugoslavia," Serbs and Croats have gone way beyond hurling statistical accountings at each other. Hayden shows that the transitional phase of identity-making and unmaking involved a "discovery and celebration of martyrdom" expressed through the publicizing of the massacres in the mass media and in commemorative volumes, a displaying of the bodies in gory detail, and the performance of mass funerals. Official governments played a key role in these activities (Hayden 1994:172–175).

Tudjman has written that the genocide of the Second World War was not a unique occurrence, but only another in a long line of cruel acts that humans inflict upon one another. The Serbs, and some of the Jews of Serbia as well, have been outraged at Tudjman's revisionism of the official version of 1941–45 history as it was written during the Titoist period. One journalist, a member of the Belgrade Jewish community, responded critically in the popular press to Tudjman's writings and ideological approach (see Erenrajh 1989; 1990). To these Serbs and Jews, Tudjman himself became a symbol of neo-fascism and of a return to the Independent State of Croatia (NDH)-Ustasha past. One of my older informants, a prominent scholar from Belgrade, expressed his opinion to me in the following way:

> The elected regime today [October 1990] in Croatian works as a continuation of the "Ustasha" ideas. They are full of hatred and incite the hatred of the people against the Serbs. Their attitude toward the Jews . . . is a forgery. They show

> good will, but with their only purpose to win the support of the democratic West. The truth is that they have a deep contempt and hatred of the Jewish people.

Even within Croatia, Franjo Tudjman has his share of critics among the Croats and Jews. The difference is that in Croatia he is perceived by most not as an antisemite or a fascist, nor necessarily as a true historian or intellectual, but rather as a politician and a Croat patriot who is inept sometimes in his use of the cultural or communications resources at his disposal, especially in allowing the manipulation of certain symbols that have a great emotional effect on minority people. Critics like Ivo Goldstein (1992) have warned against any association with the symbols of the former Ustasha state, including allowing former officials of that state to return and express their views on television and in print.

President Tudjman has been an advocate of "national reconciliation," that is, the reconciliation of former Partisans and non-Partisans, including the Ustasha. He recently proposed that the Jasenovac memorial site be transformed into a memorial site for all the victims of World War II. This attempt to coopt a key symbol of ethnic and ideological others has the characteristics of symbolic encroachment and expansion. Whatever his personal motivation might have been, what we had was one group attempting to displace its competitors' symbol of identity and version of history with its own symbol and version of the past. *Pomiranje*, or the reconciliation of all "victims" of the war, would displace Jasenovac as a memorial site for Serbian, Jewish, and Gypsy victims of fascist terror.

The Jewish community of Zagreb was among those who rejected this proposal. In a letter to Tudjman, the Jewish Community of Zagreb supported 'in principle' the idea of national reconciliation, but through 'other means.' In the same letter it was stated that "all of us, including the Croatian government and political figures, should energetically oppose attempts at vindication and rehabilitation of the Independent State of Croatia" (Jajčinović 1990:28). On the other hand, the Jews of Croatia especially, but also the Federation of Jewish Communities of Yugoslavia, have acknowledged the steps President Tudjman has taken to assuage fears and unease about the position of minorities in general and of Jews in particular. He has stated in writing to the United States Congress and to the president of the World Jewish Congress his assurances that the Jews are in no danger and enjoy all civil rights in the new Croatian state.

Considerable argument has surrounded the word symbol "victims." During the entire Titoist period, it was only the Serbs, Jews, and Roma (Gypsies) who had victim status. In commemorations these three groups were always mentioned together as victims of fascism. Sometimes speakers would also mention that Communists and progressive Croats were among the victims. But the Croatian people were never classified under the Titoist regime as a victim people. Many Croats felt that their entire history was being deliberately reduced to the four years during which a fascist minority ruled. In this their feelings can be partly justified. They began to reveal one of the "secret histories" of the Titoist period—the massacres of Croats at Bleiburg by the Communist Partisans. They began to classify themselves as a "victim" people, thereby extending the category of victim beyond "victims of fascism" to encompass victims of Partisan atrocities as well. They also began to talk openly about how the Serbian Chetniks massacred Croats during the war, thus claiming the Serbs practiced genocide upon them. For a time the interethnic confrontation centered around claims and counterclaims and demonstrations of various Croatian and Serbian massacre sites.

Another example of the symbolic manipulations carried out by the ruling Croatian politicians in connection with the symbol "victims" was the renaming of the Square of Victims of Fascism to the Square of Croatian Rulers [or Great Men], an act that mobilized the Jews of Zagreb to form the first public demonstration by Jews in the postwar period. The Jews of Zagreb, the remaining left-wing (League of Social Democrats), and supportive journalists condemned this symbolic act as a negation of the anti-fascist past (Weiss 1990). Anti-Communism had come to mean anti-anti-fascism.

For the Jews the symbolic act involved an even greater kind of denial or negation—eradication. The vice president of the Zagreb Jewish community sent a letter to the mayor of Zagreb expressing the community's displeasure with the renaming of the square. He wrote:

> Among Zagreb's victims of fascism to whom this square is dedicated, there are more than 8,000 Jews who were members of our community. The Square of Victims of Fascism is the only marking in the city of Zagreb that with its name

> includes a remembrance of our onetime members, who significantly contributed to the development of Zagreb, and who died innocently. . . . We think that it is inappropriate to wipe away this memory, and it would have a very negative reverberation on many sides (*Jevrejski Pregled* 1990).

The Square of Victims of Fascism was one site of many sites selected in the campaign of renaming public places in Croatia. Just as the Communist rulers before them had attempted to reorder the past in their renaming campaigns, so now the new Croat rulers have attempted to reorder the past in a manner that diminishes or denies those parts of the past that do not fit the image of the new Nation. As the Croat writer Slavenka Drakulić puts it,

> [M]any antifascists had been tortured and killed in Ustashe prisons situated on the square and in nearby streets. The protesters wanted to honor the memory of the 50,000 Croats who participated in the antifascist movment during the war, 20,000 of whom died fighting fascism or as victims of its terror. Changing the square's name would, in their view, mean not only suppressing the antifascist past of Croatia, but rehabilitating the first independent Croatian state, an openly fascist state committed to a racist policy against people who were not Croats. Many thousands of Jews, Serbs, Gypsies, and Communists died in the Jasenovac concentration camp run by the Ustashe regime led by Ante Pavelić. Today it is simply a falsification of history to ignore that regime's fascism and emphasize only its independence (Drakulić 1989:21).

What reason did the renaming commission give for its renaming campaign? "Everything that would disturb the national being, the national identity and a rich Croatian heritage" would have to be removed (cited in Drakulić 1989). With the removal of names connected to the antifascist movement, does this mean "we might well conclude that only only Communists but antifascists "disturb the national being" of Croats? And if communists and antifascists become nonpersons, then who is left? Apparently only the fascists who supported the independent state of Croatia. Do the Croats really accept that they should be identified with the Ustashe, and if they don't, why don't they say so?" asks Drakulić (ibid.).

The Federation of Jewish Communities of Yugoslavia reprinted the Zagreb community's letter in its serial publication, the *Jewish Review* (*Jevrejski Pregled*). The Federation also released its own statement to the press and informed the World Jewish Congress in New York. The government of Croatia resisted all such efforts by the Jewish community and by groups of Croat citizens and held fast to its decision to change the name of the square.

The Case of Mira Furlan

In her book *The Balkan Express: Fragments From the Other Side of War*, Slavenka Drakulić, who happens to be a Croat, a not insignificant factor in the telling of this story, wrote a chapter called "An Actress Who Lost Her Homeland." She calls the actress "M," who I have since discovered is Mira Furlan.[7] I include the story of Mira Furlan for two reasons. Even though I never met Mira Furlan she is, as a Jew, a member of my broader sample of Yugoslav Jews. Hers is one of the voices of Yugoslav Jewry, a very public and unwelcome voice in her homeland of Croatia. Furlan's story illustrates in dramatic form what happens when an individual transgresses in the eyes of the Nation, that is, when an individual violates a moral norm of the ethnic Nation. In this case, the transgression involved Furlan's going from Zagreb to Belgrade, the territory of the enemy, in order to participate in *Bitef*, an international theatrical festival. From Furlan's perspective, magnifying the transgression were her statuses as a Jew, a woman, and a spouse to a Serb. Travelling to Belgrade was nothing new for her, for in the previous five years she had worked in both Zagreb and Belgrade. Before her transgression Mira Furlan was a celebrated actress in the eyes of the Croat Nation. She had received the accolades of the people of Zagreb.

Why did she choose to participate in a festival that had been boycotted by the theaters of Croatia? Furlan provided the answer in the *Bitef* festival's bulletin. Drakulić tells us that "she knew she was the only one, but nevertheless believed that art could remain unscathed, that even in war, art could preserve its freedom. In the festival bulletin she wrote that she had decided to appear at the festival in order not to lose faith in the possibility of us all working together and that in this way she was saving herself, at least temporarily, from utter despair. 'Not to play in this performance would mean signing one's own capitulation' " (1993:77). The Zagreb public spared no words when reacting viciously to what they perceived as her cavorting with the enemy. "M was parading her naked breasts on a Belgrade stage while people were being killed in Croatia" (ibid:78) wrote a woman journalist leading the attack on Furlan. Another accused her of being "a collaborator, a Mephisto, a Gustaf Grundgens who continued to perform in the theatre after Nazi occupation" (ibid.). The attack continued unabated, through letters and telephone calls. "The people who called her on the phone did not 'merely' threaten: they called her a 'Chetnik whore', they graphically, to a detail, described how they would torture her to death, which parts of the body they would cut off" (ibid.). Drakulić writes, "Overnight M became an enemy, publicly renounced by friends and colleagues" (ibid.).

Suffering through her dismissal from the Croatian National Theater and the endless verbal assault that served to diminish her and finally to eradicate her by forcing her to leave Croatia, Mira Furlan mustered her rapidly diminishing self in order to write an open letter, which was published in the magazine *Danas*. Here are her words:

> It seems that I've been chosen . . . to be the filthy rag everyone uses to wipe the mud off their shoes. . . .
>
> Listening to . . . the incredible quantities of indescribably disgusting messages from my co-citizens, I longed to hear at least one message from a friend. . . . But there was none. . . . Nevertheless, I am grateful to them, to those noble patriots who kindly promise me a 'massacre the Serbian way' . . . .
>
> I am grateful also to all my colleagues in the theatre . . . for their silence, I am grateful to them for not even trying to understand, let alone attempting to vindicate, my statement concerning my taking part in [the] BITEF Festival in Belgrade, the statement in which I tried to explain that taking part in that production at that moment was for me a defense of our profession which must not and cannot put itself in the service of any political or national ideas, which must not and cannot be bound by political or national limits because it is simply against its nature which must, even at the worst of times, establish bridges and ties . . . I cannot accept war as the only solution, I cannot force myself to hate, I cannot believe that weapons, killing, revenge, hatred, that such an accumulation of evil will ever solve anything. . . .

> There is nothing but despair, nausea and horror. I no longer have any decisions to make. [Others have] decided I must shut up, give up, vanish; . . . they have abolished my right to come home to my own city, ... Can the horror of war be used as a justification for every single nasty bit of filth we commit against our fellow man? Are we allowed . . . to justify our silence by the importance of the great bright national objective? . . . .
>
> It is hard to write without bitterness. I would like to be able to do that, because we should "Love Our Enemy." I wish we all could. Herein perhaps lies the solution for all of us. But I fear we are very far from the ways of the Lord. His is the way of love. Not hatred. . . .
>
> Everyone is so caught up by the great cause, that small personal fates are not important any more. How many friends do you have to betray to keep from committing the only socially acknowledged betrayal, the betrayal of the nation? How many petty treacheries, how many pathetic little dirty tricks must one do to remain "clean in the eyes of the nation"? . . . .
>
> I am sending this letter . . . without an inkling of who will read it and how, or how many different ways it will be misused or abused. . . . Perhaps someone with a pure heart will read it after all.
>
> I will be grateful for that someone (Furlan 1991).

The publication of the open letter failed to halt the public's assault. Drakulić summarizes several of the responses: "she may be a professional but she is no human being"; "Those in the know explained that her mother was Jewish and her husband Serbian: this suddenly became the key to her case, because if it wasn't for him—who had obviously made her do it—all this wouldn't have happened". Drakulić writes that what really upset her theater colleagues was Furlan "articulated a moral position, a position of non-compliance and individual choice. In fact, now it was those who saw her as a Mephisto whom M was accusing of condoning the war, of being accomplices, as it were. She did not doubt that a different option was possible. Claiming they could have opted for art, M turned from the accused into the accuser and therefore had to be dealt with mercilessly" (ibid:82).

The Fragmentation and End of the Yugoslav Jewish Community

The breakup of Yugoslavia has fragmented the Jews of that former country. No longer does a Yugoslav Jewish community exist. The three main Jewish communities are now part of separate states. One of those communities, the Sarajevo Jewish community, has only a few hundred people remaining in it, with the rest scattered among various countries.

The dismemberment of Yugoslavia proved to be a transnational drama that affected not only the Jews within that state but also those who live in other states, particularly Israel. There, too, Israeli Jews fell and continue to fall on different sides of the conflict. Within Yugoslavia, even Jews living in the same city became divided over the events that swept over them. In Belgrade, for example, some condemned the Slovenes, while others praised them.[8] Some have supported Milošević in Serbia and Tudjman in Croatia, while others have criticized these leaders. Thus, even the divisions within the former Yugoslav Jewish population were not neat and clear, thereby creating considerable ambiguity.

This chapter has placed the Jewish movement out of submergence and the phenomena associated with Jewish reemergence within the transitional processes of the erosion and ultimate collapse of Titoist Yugoslavia. The former process entailed an increasingly bold and broad demolition of the symbolic order of Titoism, while the latter involved the disintegration of the cross-cutting federal political institutions, followed by the dissolution of the state itself. Such disintegration of a unifying order was accompanied by increasing dislocation and distinctive reorientations of the nation peoples of Yugoslavia toward a separatist and xenophobic nationalism that emphasized ethnicity over citizenship. As Katherine Verdery has written, "part of what makes nationality so powerful is that it exists not just at the levels of political rhetoric, interest groups and constitutionalism, but as a basic element of people's self-conception" (Verdery 1993:194). She further notes that "something beyond concrete inter-group antagonisms is required if one is to account for how there can be hatred of groups like Jews and Gypsies in *countries where they are almost nonexistent*. . . . Other causes must be at work. I suggest that one of these causes is that people's identities are being defined, as before, in strict relation to unacceptable others, whom one excludes from one's moral community" (ibid.). Thus, for example, when the Serbs make Kosovo their central myth or symbol of *Srpstvo,* or perhaps Jasenovac, non-Serbs are excluded from the moral community being formed. Likewise when Croatian leaders try to rehabilitate certain individuals of the Ustasha or to equalize everyone they deem to be "victims" of the Second World War and then to call for *pomiranje* or reconciliation, the Jews and Serbs living in Croatia are excluded from the new moral community called the Croat nation. In short, minorities are excluded when criteria of ethnicity decide, in the words of Franjo Tudjman when he was campaigning for the presidency of Croatia, "who is the host and who is the guest."

Changes in minority status and orientation accompany radical political change. Minorities tend to occupy a more secure position within multiethnic states, where there is at least some space for maneuvering, than in so-called nation-states in which one ethnic population dominates (Rothschild 1993) and sets the criteria for national inclusion and exclusion. Given the dramatic disintegration of multinational and multiethnic Yugoslavia into several hostile independent nation-states in which the constituent ethnic populations were at war, it is not surprising that the Jewish minorities in each of the new states were forced to reorient themselves to new political and symbolic orders-in-the-making. The Jews have lost their secure place. No longer is there a single place for the Jews of former Yugoslavia. And no longer is there any kind of unified Jewish voice, which, I might add, was also very much a pan-Yugoslav voice.

I close this chapter with the apt words of the Jewish writer Filip David (1989) who has described the transition as "A false picture of the future and a false picture of the past. It is life in the shadow of ideological and national symbols. Both the future and the past are transformed into trash."

7

THEORETICAL MUSINGS: WHAT IS A (YUGOSLAV) JEW?

Have You Found Any Ethnicity Yet?

I went to Yugoslavia to find Jewish identity. Then I went again, and again. It was during the second of these research visits that one of my informants, a longtime leader in the Jewish community, rather casually asked me, "Have you found any ethnicity yet?" Indeed, had I found it? What was it? What did it look like? If it existed, had I seen it? How would I have recognized it? Was ethnicity something to be seen? I was confronting ethnographic dilemmas that I could not insert neatly into one theoretical framework in order for them suddenly to make sense. By now I am sure the reader, having engaged my and my informants' text, should be just as puzzled about the answer to the question, "Who is a Yugoslav Jew?" After my initial long-term fieldwork in socialist Yugoslavia, I would have been tempted to answer my informant's question ambivalently, "Well, maybe so, maybe not." Before returning for that second round of fieldwork, I had been questioning the existence of a Jewish community in Yugoslavia, at least one conceived in sociological terms. But he had not asked me the question during the still relatively politically stable period of the mid-1980s. Rather, he had asked me in 1989 as the country was beginning to quickly unravel from both the reality and veneer of brotherhood and unity and just as the Jews of Yugoslavia were being brought into the public political arena and caught in the middle of the escalating interethnic "civil war of words," as described in the preceding chapter. What was emerging in the new political mix of a late or dying state socialism was a different kind of Jewish community, one that perhaps had existed earlier but not in such a politicized form. It was a community whose boundaries went beyond the organized auspices of the Federation of Jewish Communities of Yugoslavia and its local Jewish communities. With the breakup of political and social order it became increasingly a community united by threat and fear of what the uncertain future could bring. However, for some individuals it was also an exhilarating time when they could join with others in seeing new visions and forming new movements, even if these entailed an amicable divorce of the marriage called the Federal Socialist Republic of Yugoslavia. For others, it was the excitement of a Jewish resurgence and the opportunity to be Jews, period. Was I finally seeing ethnicity? Was I witnessing yet another transformation of Jewish identity? What did the new historical conditions that I was observing tell me about the constancy and the fluidity of identity? Do identity and ethnicity, after all, involve just the maneuvering for or imposition of a structural place in society as responses to the historical events of any particular period of history?

The purpose of this book has been to delineate the complexities of Yugoslav Jewish identity formations and transformations both at times when and places where structure prevailed and at other junctures that were characterized by greater fragmentation, fluidity and human conflict. These processes, set within specific historical events and shifts of power, were linked to: political impositions (e.g., genocide) and the Jewish responses to them; broad social movements within (e.g., Zionism) and without (Communism) the Jewish community; the intentions of Jewish leaders (e.g., putting in motion the "experiment in secular Jewishness"); the constraints of a truncated population profile on biological and sociocultural reproduction; various collective and individual reimaginings; and the strategic and makeshift constructions of identity that followed in the wake of the destruction of old and emergence of new ways of seeing the world and struggling to establish a secure place in it. With regard to this last point, Jewish collective reimagining followed that of Tito and the rulers of the New Yugoslavia. The Yugoslav Jews too envisioned Jews and other ethnic peoples united in a land of brotherhood and unity of all Yugoslav peoples. If it meant that such unity was to be maintained by a ruling party that punished any ethnic intolerance, that was acceptable. But as socialist Yugoslavia began to fracture more and more along ethnic lines and then ruptured completely in 1991, the Titoist state, which had continued to proclaim brotherhood and unity when there was no brotherhood and unity, was shattered and replaced by the separate and conflicting identity projects of individual ethnic nations. These newly proclaimed imaginings saw one's own nation as independent and supreme, free from the imaginings of those who threatened one's own identity, that is, all outsiders who threatened one's very existence or diminished the collective self-concept of one's people. Present in these new visions of nationhood was the fear of nonexistence that arose from any internal and external threats to existence, no matter how slight, as perceived by members of the ingroup.

Approaches to the Study of Ethnicity and Identity

Earlier theories and approaches of the cultural and circumstantialist variety have described particular kinds and dimensions of ethnicity and identity (e.g., Barth 1969; Abner Cohen 1969, 1974; Despres 1975; Geertz 1973; Glazer and Moynihan 1975; Isaacs 1975; Nagata 1974; Naroll 1964; Royce 1981; Shils 1957; Smith 1981). These have contributed fundamentally to opening up diverse avenues of research regarding the forms, content, structural relations, and antecedents of ethnic phenomena. These approaches, which encompass various cultural, structural materialist and relational paradigms, cannot be disregarded in explaining Jewish identity in Yugoslavia. It is my contention, however, that applied individually none goes far enough in describing and explaining the dynamic processes of identity formation, maintenance, contestation, and change.

Anthropologists most often credit Edmund Leach (1954) and Fredrik Barth (1969) for initiating the shift toward a relational understanding of collective identity. Especially after the publication of *Ethnic Groups and Boundaries* (Barth 1969), the boundary clarity implicit in older ethnographies gave way to acknowledging that cultural features are often shared by different groups and change over time, thus making it more difficult to define groups by cultural features assumed to be discontinuous and static.[1] Thus anthropologists began seeking ethnic demarcation in the social boundary between groups, a boundary that is often solely maintained by ascriptions of identity. However, more recently the boundary concept itself has come under attack for several reasons. It does not always consider the complexities of interethnic interaction set in regional, and even global contexts. It has been criticized for being ahistorical and static, as well as for its inbuilt bias against culture, particularly against cultural continuity (see Wilson 1994).

The complexities of interethnic and state-ethnic group interactions and the hybridities, ambiguities, and complexities arising from them, have increased as more and more goods and services, information, and persons engage in voluntary and involuntary transnational and other boundary crossings. With such increased flow across a multitude of boundaries, we have to consider new definitions of identity characterized by such fluidity (Verdery 1996). Especially of interest here are those groups (e.g., diasporic and refugee) that fall outside social structures that are accepted as part of "the natural order of things" (see Malkki 1995). The Jewish community of Yugoslavia, which tried so hard and perhaps succeeded in winning a place for itself in socialist Yugoslavia, suddenly found itself divided among several new states in which the old "natural" order gave way to new "natural" orders in which finding a place became not only problematic but no longer necessarily desirable. One could more easily be both a Jew and a Yugoslav than both a Jew and a Croat or Serb in the new conditions of life. This was not always true, for at previous times many Jews were comfortable with the designation, "Serb (or Croat) of the Mosaic faith."

Ethnic Groups as Cultural Units?

Besides the factor of interaction between ethnic units or between the state and an ethnic population, there are such factors as social leveling, homogenization, and sociocultural erosion and fragmentation to consider, whatever the sources of such processes may be. Are ethnic collectivities that undergo such processes culture-bearing units? Can they be? If not, what are they? This is where ethnicity and identity enter the discussion. As Walter Zenner points out, "We have come to a point where not only is it necessary to view as separate aspects, race, language, and culture, but ethnicity and culture as well." He adds that "there is no one-to-one relationship between ethnicity and culture either. The connection between ethnic group and cultural unit is to be investigated rather than assumed" (Zenner 1978:329) These are significant reasons why anthropologists studying ethnicity have criticized Naroll's (1974) seemingly static approach.[2]

Naroll recognized the problem that the Jews as a group constitute in his approach, and he called them an "ex-tribe" or "ex-cultunit." An ex-cultunit is "a named group whose members have a common history and sense of common destiny and who are quite conscious of boundaries between themselves and others" (Naroll

1970, cited in Zenner 1978). Yet, as Zenner argues, modern Jews "are not distinguished by their speech, nor by political autonomy, which are among Naroll's most salient features" (ibid:328). Naroll himself describes the modern American Jews as those who "call themselves Jews but neither believe in the truth of the Jewish holy books nor attend Jewish religious services. They all however claim descent from people who did believe and did attend. These in turn claim descent from members of the ancient Jewish states of Israel or Judah." The "bonds of unity" of the Jews and other ex-cult-units are "the conditions of their forebears rather than their own condition" (Naroll 1970:731, cited in Zenner 1978:328). Because they deviate from his conception, Naroll, for the most part, ignores the Jews and other ex-cult-units. It is obvious that the Yugoslav Jews neither did meet nor now meet the criteria of a cult-unit. For example, they have no territory of their own, speak the languages of their host peoples, have no independent political power, and do not occupy a particular economic niche. In fact, even Zenner's definition appears problematic, for in pursuing submergence and other forms of integration these Jews blurred the boundaries between themselves and others. Moreover, many individuals probably had no conception of social boundary, and their cognitive boundary was either ill-defined or had no relevance in daily life. Rather than well-defined conceptions and social demarcations of boundary, the private symbols and life-path markers described in the individual narratives served to situate and guide individual lives.

Cultural Essentialism

Primordialism[3] has become a dirty word in the anthropological lexicon of ethnicity and identity. The tragedy, however, is not so much the avoidance of the word, but rather the refusal to acknowledge particular epistemologies. First, there continues to be a presentist bias among some anthropologists. Primoridialism connotes a sense of deep historical depth, which makes many anthropologists working from either modernist or postmodernist[4] assumptions uneasy. History itself is problematic for some anthropologists who choose not to deal with cultural continuities or who, like Clifford (1988), assume that the twentieth century is the era of inauthentic traditions (see Wilson (1994) for a critique of Clifford on this point.) Those who do write about "history" write not about a history that actually happened but rather about a history that is a construct in the minds of those who might use the past to meet present needs. In this latter use, history writing becomes a power tool that manipulatively asserts one's own identity and diminishes other identities. One's own identity is given all the cultural trappings of (new) life, but only by denying others their identity through some form of symbolic diminishment or defilement or, in the extreme, through physical eradication. Symbolic eradication can be accomplished by excising the part that other ethnic populations play in the historical narrative of one's own group and the evil parts that one's own group played in the narrative of other groups (see MacIntyre 1984). A better approach to adopt, I suggest, following the lead of certain other anthropologists (Comaroff and Comaroff 1992; Peel 1989; Wilson 1994), is to recognize that cultural essentialisms exist at some level, even if only in the conceptions of the in-group, and if nothing else we can trace historically how these essentials become essentialized, deessentialized, and reessentialized (see Comaroff and Comaroff 1992; Wilson 1994).

I would add that identities such as those of the Jews entail more than the basic belief in shared descent (Keyes 1976). The historical fact of Jewish persistence across radically different political and social contexts over two thousand years or more on the Balkan Peninsula alone begs for explanations beyond a particular set of political or economic conditions, or factors of interest and interaction. Even if I can argue that certain proponents of primordialism or cultural essentialism are not that far removed from those who advocate a subjectivist or circumstantialist approach insofar as their views are more dynamic than given credit for, a case also can be made for the stability of specific cultural features for certain ethnic and religious populations, particularly those with written charters. A less convincing case can be made for a view that sees every cultural form as stable. Consider, for example, the stability of Judaism, Christianity and Islam. Each has had its share of internal variation and deviation, but the core of each of these major religions persists. The form-meaning difference must be considered here. What may be the persistent cultural feature is a particular meaning rather than any particular form that serves as the symbolic vehicle for the meaning. The forms themselves can wax and wane depending on such contextual factors as perceived threat to the group, crisis, political change, demographic composition, and so on. Moreover, the traditional core of the charter or culture need not always be practiced, preserved, and passed on by a majority. In fact, the majority may have deviated so far from the core that they can be no longer defined as believers or adherents. In such cases preservation and perpetuation may pass to a remnant of believers or ritual adherents. This appears to be the case in the Yugoslav Jewish community. In Belgrade, for example, an approximate average of twenty-three people, not all of them Jews, attended the weekly synagogue service. These individuals contributed to keeping the Judaic tradition alive. The synagogue remained a living symbol, one filled with real content, for people continued to meet inside its walls and in its courtyard. Even for some secular Jews, the existence of the synagogue, though perhaps a symbol half-full, remained important. Even more important was the cultural attention devoted to death and the continuing significance of the Jewish cemetery.

Perhaps the basic difference is not whether cultural elements such as religion exist for the majority, or are stable or unstable, but whether or not they persist and carry meaning and explanatory power. Geertz (1973:259–260) assigns explanatory power to primordial elements when he writes that "the "givens" are "seen to have an ineffable, and at times overpowering, coerciveness in and of themselves . . . some unaccountable absolute import attributed to the very tie itself . . . some attachments seem to flow more from a sense of the natural—some would say spiritual—affinity than from social interaction." Admittedly, this quasi-mystical attachment can be difficult to describe. Various Jewish intellectuals have been at a loss to describe the primordial in Jewishness (see Meyer 1990) One of my informants expressed that it "cannot be put into words." How, for instance, can the attraction of the synagogue on Rosh Hashanah and Yom Kippur be explained? What coercive power do these have on the Yugoslav Jews and other secular Jews? Rather than interest, social contact, or belief, it seems it is "some unaccountable absolute import attributed to the tie itself," a sense of spiritual affinity, an acknowledgment of the "overpowering coerciveness" of the tie during the High Holidays. Perhaps this is what Peter Berger (1967) refers to as the ontological tie of generations. Some of the features subsumed by primordialism are essentially nonmaterialistic and thus, for certain social scientists, they can never be considered causal. What we have within the discipline is a clash of epistemological positions and the methodological assumptions that are derived from them.[5]

Relational Approach

In his relational conception of ethnicity, Barth (1969) moves the emphasis from material markers and specific content to ideological positions. Foremost it is the cognitive and behavioral processes of self-ascription that locate groups and individuals in society. In this conception, Jews are Jews not because they wear a particular style of hat or speak a particular language, but Jews are Jews because they say they are Jews and identify with other Jews (see Royce 1981). Is there a danger of excessive subjectivity here? What happens when all objective markers of distinction have disappeared (Moerman 1965)? Does that erase the relevance of self-ascription? It raises the question: when does ethnic group X stop being ethnic group X and become something else?

Gulliver (1971) questions whether it is the boundary or the basic value orientation of the enclosed group that is more important. Barth implies the former but gives evidence of the latter. For example, a Pathan becomes a Baluch only if he accepts a certain set of Baluch goals and organizational means. Boundaries are secondary features. One problem here is an unclear definition of culture. Is it an internal, cognitive process of ascription, or is it an external, behavioral phenomenon that arises in social relations, or is it a list of objective traits? Barth's lack of clarification was carried over into subsequent studies that adopted his framework. I would not go so far as to state the Yugoslav Jews had no boundary. But how significant was boundary, and what kind of boundary operated? There remained the boundary of who can be or cannot be a Jew. One was either born a Jew, though not only by a Jewish mother, or one had to go through a process of ritual conversion to become a Jew. At this level this boundary was significant, but not in everyday reality or in social interaction. Membership in the Jewish community, for example, was open to non-Jewish kin. The cognitive boundary, more than any social-behavioral boundary, categorized Jews and non-Jews. In fact, on occasions of multiethnic commemoration rituals, simultaneously a blurring and a demarcation of boundary often occurred when different ethnic groups were together.

Barth's conception of ethnicity and boundary is also too dualistic. As such, it does not consider the complexities of many multiethnic situations or situations in which the state or other nonethnic entities play a major role in creating identities and situating ethnic groups in the various structural arrangements of society.

Blurring the Boundaries of Identity

This study has delineated, for a particular minority population, what Geertz (1973) refers to as the area between politics and culture. It is the sphere in which the Yugoslav Jews confronted the aftermath of catastrophe and the impact of radical political and social change. The particular forms of their communal response during the socialist period I have subsumed under the term submergence. For the Jews of socialist Yugoslavia, submergence consisted of the forms manifested within the sphere that lies between the politico-symbolic order of Titoism and Jewishness. As described in chapter 4, it is a synthetic, multifaceted, somewhat paradoxical analytical concept that describes how the organized Jewish community of Yugoslavia sought simultaneously to integrate with the power and symbolic dimensions of Tito's socialist Yugoslavia while retaining their identity as Jews. The paradox lies in the intent and in the process itself, for these Jews sought both to remove the dichotomy between themselves and the dominant power structure outside of themselves, thereby not only blurring the boundary in the process but creating an ethnic-political amalgam (cf. Handelman 1990) that no longer could be distinctly Jewish. While intent on remaining Jews they blurred the boundaries. Submergence allows for various intersections and contradictions that inevitably result when the two domains meet. Bauman (1991:142) describes the ambivalence of such fusion. It occurs when there is an "obliteration of cultural distinctiveness and an acquisition of a different, power-assisted culture construed and perceived as the primary vehicle of political [and social] emancipation." This describes submergence beautifully.

Examined historically, as I have done, this postwar attempt at synthesis was not entirely new for the senior generation of this population, for they were, as described in chapter 3, the first generation that had attempted a synthesis of a Jewish form (Zionism) and a Marxist one. The postwar Jews, however, replaced Jewish tradition and Zionism with an experimental form of secular Jewishness that received sustenance from non-Jewish sources and forms. Rather than adjusting the Titoist system to their own, they adapted their own system to fit the Titoist model. This entailed a conceptual and symbolic reordering of Jewishness itself, which included retaining what they deemed "good" and "positive" in the Jewish tradition, and discarding, de-emphasizing, or relegating what they deemed archaic to the "few elderly Jews" who, the secular leadership believed, could not part with the traditional cultural forms because of childhood socialization.

Submergence has its conceptual dimension, but it is also readily susceptible to direct anthropological observation, for it is manifested through the general symbolic forms of language, material objects, and performances. When examined historically it is clear that these symbolic forms have changed along with radical political change. What persists is the fact that some of these forms reflect the power structure in society. Historically, the Jews have oriented themselves toward those in power. In Titoist Yugoslavia this meant an orientation not to one particular ethnic population but principally to the political elite, the Communist Party, and to the institutions of the state. It is clear that the manifestation of submergence is essentially a set of phenomena associated with a particular period in which politics and the policies of interaction it engendered, in this case the relationship between the organized Jewish community and the state, has the greatest influence on this form of ethnic response. On one level it is a strategy, a response to particular political and social conditions, but it is more than that. It has an inward-directed dimension that seeks to reformulate the being and forms of Jewishness itself, to abandon much of the past and to strive for the "beautiful future" promised by the rulers and reiterated by themselves. Having participated in the National Liberation Struggle and having experienced the horror of the Holocaust, they were given hope with this promise. They had begun to abandon their traditional past during the period of their radicalization before or during the war. What they did not abandon voluntarily, the Holocaust nearly completed the process for them. Declaring themselves "maimed and crippled," they believed that a return to the past was futile, even if desired. The future remained, but in time disillusionment set in and the future was lost as well (Boyarin 1991). At this juncture, perhaps, they entered what was for them a postmodern world—a world without a living tradition or a beautiful utopian future (ibid.). The constraints of population profile and the absence of a viable secular variant of Jewishness (e.g., Yiddishkeit and Zionism) outside the limited sphere of the organized community left their mark. This sense of liminality was quite apparent in their self-reflexive and self-critical statements. They felt their vulnerability to extinction. Otherwise, why would they have continued to ask themselves, "Are we the final generation of Jews?" Remarkably, they continued to display optimism. Explaining this optimism, however, is another matter on which I can only speculate. Right until the transition began in 1989 they continued to manifest submergence in their use of language and in their behavior, which demonstrates both the depth of their submergence and their dramaturgical loyalty to a system that recognized them and gave them place, security, and one with which they shared the values of ethnic tolerance. Even if certain freedoms were limited by the same system, perhaps they believed that a benevolent unifying force (West 1982) or even a temporary "militant cult of tolerance" (Lowie 1954) was preferable to what they had been imposed upon them between 1941–1945 and was now a part of their collective consciousness. If nothing else, and I would include in this the idea of shared descent (Keyes 1976), which has become problematic itself because of the extensive practice of ethnic exogamy, it was this experience and the consciousness of kind based on it that resisted total integration into a larger or more powerful entity.

Memorialism became the focus and the center of collective identity. It is ironic that the catastrophe that nearly annihilated these Jews and nearly completed the process of abandonment of tradition taken up voluntarily before the war, was the very thing that kept them together.

The Role of the State

Glazer and Moynihan (1975) point out the importance of the multiethnic state in ethnic dynamics, particularly in regard to interest and the conflict that it often engenders. Gladney (1991), introducing what he calls a dialogical approach, theoretically expands on the role of the state in ethnic dynamics, supporting his argument with his own ethnographic study of the Muslim Hui minority in the People's Republic of China. He shows how the socialist one-party state exercises its power of ascription over minority groups. Where the state wields this power, it can go so far as either recognizing or refusing to recognize the ethnic group by means of its policies on nationalities, and by direct actions. Certainly it can limit or raise the visibility of the ethnic group. Gladney demonstrates that a significant dimension of identity manifestation and representation, if not ethnic formation, falls outside the control of the ethnic group and into the domain of power relations as they are controlled by a single political elite. In understanding the postwar Yugoslav Jewish community, the state is an important factor influencing the forms of Jewish collective identity. The process is bi-directional. Using Abner Cohen's (1976) dimensions of the political order and the symbolic order (see *Two-Dimensional Man*), I have shown that the Jewish community strived to integrate itself in both of these orders. In socialist Yugoslavia it was primarily toward the state rather than toward various ethnic groups that the community sought integration. On its part, the state recognized the minuscule community in different ways. Although legally the Jews remained a religious community, they were also recognized as a nationality, which was clear in the state census. The state also gave the community visibility by conferring on the Jews the memorial statuses of victims of fascism and fallen fighters.

Frequently associated with state systems is the factor of interest and how the state serves as an arbiter between ethnic groups competing for real or perceived scarce resources. The factor of interest, if it is to be usefully applied to the Jews of Yugoslavia, must be expanded beyond its economic and more narrow political usages, or as a factor that organizes social relations between ethnic groups. It is difficult to conceive the Jewish community as an interest group vying for scarce resources (Despres 1975), fighting to maintain its occupation of an ecological niche, or being a significant actor in the ongoing political arena within socialist Yugoslavia. Rather, the occupational distribution of the Jews has changed so radically that they can be referred to as a post-economic group. As a collectivity, their influence on power relations was insignificant, making them politically powerless, at least on their own. If the factor of interest is connected to such concepts and values as place in the new order, security, tolerance, and the freedom to pursue organized Jewish activity, then it becomes relevant. However, interest is not described this way in the literature.

Are Conflict and Opposition Necessary Components of Ethnic Persistence

Both conflict and opposition are important factors in understanding ethnic perceptions and relations in former Yugoslavia. They are much less helpful in understanding the situation of the Yugoslav Jews in relation to the state and in relation to other ethnic populations. While submerging itself in Titoism the Jewish community sought to avoid conflict and any clash of ideas with the Titoist rulers. Internal factors that mitigated against such a conflict included (1) class leveling within the Jewish population, (2) the presence of only one central organization to represent the community, (3) a core of leaders and activists very sympathetic to the norms and goals of socialist Yugoslavia, (4) a weak ecclesiastic structure and a small number of religious believers, and (5) the emigration of those who may have been less sympathetic to the political and social changes in the country. Those who remained in

Yugoslavia wanted to be there. Even in specifically Jewish spheres, the organized community represented itself as *u strukturi*, "in structure." If opposition can be defined as an internal state, it has more relevance for the Jews of Yugoslavia. The break in diplomatic relations with Israel was a sore point among the Jews, but any underlying opposition was not made public until the transition phase. Another source of opposition was the rise of anti-Semitic incidents. To these incidents, the Federation of Jewish Communities of Yugoslavia responded, but the target of their attack was not the state and its organizations. Plus, actions taken against anti-Semitism were carried out within "the brotherhood of Yugoslav peoples;" criticism from outside the country was not welcomed by the Jewish community. Conflict and open opposition become a part of Yugoslav Jewish ethnicity and identity, once again, beginning in the transition phase that began in 1989. In response to the changing political conditions in the country, the individual Jews and then the community itself began to move away from the structure and field of submergence to being in opposition. Opposition and conflict began to characterize the Jews themselves, although many continued to advocate Jewish unity and uniformity in the face of the political and social fragmentation of the socialist state of Yugoslavia.

Ethnicity and Socio-Moral Orders

Dahrendorf (1968, cited in Glazer & Moynihan 1975:12) proposes that stratification and inequality arise from differential success in achieving the social norms which the society establishes. Members of different ethnic groups have different levels of success in achieving these norms. Given the plural complexion of many states, we have to ask, who establishes the norms? In socialist Yugoslavia the political elite established a normative structure that it expected its citizens to follow. The dominant group was until recently the Communist Party, together with the state's sociopolitical institutions and organizations. Many individuals thought that by adopting or achieving the norms set by the Party elite they could advance themselves economically, socially, and politically. One might surmise that this behavior is frequently associated with self-interest rather than with collective ethnic interest, though it is interesting to examine the exceptions. Facilitating the process of norm achievement within the organized Jewish community was a sympathetic leadership that carried out this integrative process within the framework of a well-organized central organization that could draw upon its own intellectual resources and that were supported materially by foreign Jewish organizations. These were very competent men and women, many of whom came out of the prewar Jewish Youth Movement, who fought in the National Liberation Struggle or were POWs in Germany, and who wanted to remain in and contribute to the building of the New Yugoslavia. As postwar Federation president Albert Vajs stated, "only a few [Jews] stood on the side." Significantly, their status and claim of being a Jewish community were acknowledged by the state and by foreign Jewish organizations.

We are now witnessing the making of new moral orders by the different ethnic communities. Rather than the proclaimed ethnically tolerant and open order of socialist Yugoslavia, the construction of the new moral orders go hand in hand with the construction of new moral communities. In the process there was an enlargement of the kind of suspicion David Rheubottom (1985) found among households in Yugoslav Macedonia. Now the entity to be protected is not the household but the ethnic nation. Furthermore, all those under suspicion include all members of outgroups and ingroup members who transgress the new ethno-moral order. In an effort to purify the moral community, the ruling political leaders have redressed such transgressions by means such as ostracism, denial of material resources, and demonization, which work to marginalize or remove individuals from the moral community known as the nation. Such were the actions taken against the actress Mira Furlan. The redefinition and reconfiguration of the relational aspect of the new moral orders is another point to consider. The new "enemy" is not someone from outside the borders of Tito's Yugoslavia or the cleric or nationalist within, but all those who are not members of one's own ethnic group. In this form of relativistic relational morality, such acts as rape, plunder, and homicide became acceptable when directed toward the "enemy."

The Individual as a Necessary Unit of Analysis

The place of the Jewish community and the forms Jewishness has taken have been influenced extensively by political factors. As I have made evident elsewhere, Abner Cohen's work has informed my own approach, particularly in delineating submergence as related to relations of power and their legitimation and expression in the key symbols and myths of Titoist Yugoslavia. One problem with using this approach as the only model for explaining Yugoslav Jewish ethnicity and identity is that he does not consider the degree of sociocultural erosion and fragmentation. The dissolution or erosion of symbolic formations and activities encourages self-ascription as the means of ethnic categorization, though it is not a necessary outcome in all contexts as Barth (1969) has shown. But Cohen does not consider self-ascription or identification with a set of cognitive categories to be ethnicity. Nor does he focus on individuals, who are primary units of analysis in this study.

The individual has become a necessary unit of analysis. One reason that the individual has become a unit of analysis in ethnographic studies is precisely because once-integrated collectivities are in various states of demographic and sociocultural erosion and fragmentation, and some are even in danger of dissolution. These factors characterize the Jews of postwar Yugoslavia. If the symbolic formations and actions of an ethnic collectivity are fragmented and eroded, either by choice or imposition, individuals are forced to select for themselves the norms, beliefs, and values that they believe will help them in everyday social life and bring some order and meaning to their existence (see Bell 1980). The dilemma of the individual is in selecting or adhering to norms, beliefs, and values outside of a collective reality, at least of one's ethnic origin. What do I choose? How do I choose? Why do I choose? Are my choices satisfactory? What are the consequences of my choices? Do they help me to answer the universal questions of life? Some of the choices will be closer to the charter or way of one's own ethnic population, while others may stand in opposition. In making choices an individual might turn to his or her own local group, a broader unit of one's group, other ethnic populations, and/or the ruling group of the state, or to all or none of these. The problem is the same for the researcher who tries to uncover the choices individuals make and the reasons for them. It is a problematic and interpretive endeavor to make sense of the numerous particulars of a once cohesive collectivity. The unity, previously assured by the power of authority and tradition, together with regular social contact, has given way to the particulars. Communal authority was undermined and the individual was confronting choice (Berger's "heretical imperative") more than ever before. With choice came increased deviation from communal values and norms. Subjectivist approaches recognize such deviations from tradition, and this is where they potentially are powerful. The danger is in not recognizing objective standards when they exist. If there are no objective standards, then it is difficult if not impossible to delineate distinct collectivities, consciousness of kind, and anything else that extends beyond the individual and his or her private world. With Cohen (1974) I agree that one does not evaluate whether or not something is collective by the same number of standards as there are members of the group.

If the traditional cultural forms, content, meanings, and practices of Yugoslav Jewry are in dissolution (in the traditional symbol system symbols may be multivocal, but they also carry a high degree of shared denotative meaning among members, thus permitting them to stand for collective representations and allowing communication), the symbol system will begin to break down. If there is more disagreement and an excessive amount or range of connotative meaning (intracultural and/or interindividual variation regarding symbolic meaning), then how can any become obligatory, which is one of Cohen's conditions? And, if none is or very few are obligatory, how can they "exercise constraint" on individuals (1974:xiii)? Perhaps the members of an ethnic population share a set of values, which are partly universal and partly particularistic, but can it be demonstrated that they share common beliefs and norms? Given historical antecedents and current conditions, it is presumed that they do not share, or at least are not consciously aware of what is shared. It must be shown that "representations" are not products only of individual memories, experiences, and perceptions, but are indeed collective, that is, shared. Ethnic "symbols essentially are objective, not subjective, forms. They attain an existence outside the individual and eventually become obligatory and exercise constraint on individual behavior" (ibid: x–xi). In addition, Cohen writes that these collective representations are supported by the pressures of the collectivity, which implies that the individual members recognize that the collectivity has authority over them and can sanction behavior (ibid:xiii). What pressures, then, can exist if there are no formal pressures or sanctions?

Ethnicity of Experience

Bentley (1987) has contributed the "ethnicity of experience" approach to the literature on ethnicity and identity. In Bentley's view, experience embeds itself in unconscious memory which, in turn, results in a conscious cognitive orientation and particular patterns of behavior. Experience then becomes symbolized and the "symbols of experience" are what determine behavior. Bentley assumes that the objective context of environmental constraints determines the nature of the experience.

At least part of Bentley's model can be applied to the Yugoslav Jews, if its theoretical assumptions are clear and understood. For example, this ethnic population can be divided into different segments according to whether or not they were directly exposed to a traumatic historical event, the Holocaust. One segment is characterized by its exposure to the event, and the other segment is characterized by the absence of such an experience. The next step is to determine whether the former segment's experience, now in the form of common memories, has been effectively symbolized. To find out, we can examine language, objects, events, and activities that indicate whether symbolization has taken place. When comparing the latter segment with the former, we can look for any divergence of patterns. If the second segment lacks the traumatic experience, its common memory cannot be exactly the same as those who experienced it. Their consciousness of the event, however strongly felt, is indirect. Thus, to start with, we might want to look within this younger segment for a change in time orientation from the past to the present or future. If put into practice this new orientation would alter the existing ritual cycle associated with memorialism, and probably the symbolic order that undergirds it as well.

Bentley's approach raises the questions: Does experience alone make an individual or a group an X individual or an X group? Did the experience of genocide upon the people called Jews make them Jews? One of my informants from Zagreb told me, "We are Jews because of the Holocaust." Is that because traditional cultural forms were abandoned and replaced by the cultural complex of memorialism, which became the center of their collective identity? Did the Holocaust transform them into something else? Is that what constitutes their collective consciousness or ethnic identity? Even more problematic is the application of this approach on the individual or sub-group level. What makes an individual experience an ethnic experience? Moreover, individual experiences, to be meaningful, must be communicated and shared with the collectivity at some point; otherwise it is neither a cultural nor an ethnic experience. The reference point is always greater than the individual. The Jewish patriarch Abraham and Moses had personal transcendent experiences that did not remain privatized but eventually were shared, even in written form. An experience that is noncommunicable to nonmembers may be an ethnic experience, but if it is noncommunicable to members, how can it be shared and become a part of the collective consciousness?

In her study of Hutu camp and town refugees in Tanzania, Liisa Malkki (1995:232) tries to show that it is "the lived, experiential circumstances which [made] it possible for historical and historicizing forms of consciousness to become dominant in the everyday social action of some Hutu groups and not of others." In her analysis, Malkki describes the two groups of refugees with the shared past experience of massacres in Burundi, but their present "lived, experiential circumstances" are what contributed to the camp refugees' obsession with historical and historicizing forms in regulating their social action and to the town refugees' cosmopolitan orientation that was much less concerned with the past and a desire to construct a homogenous Hutu nation. In the case of the Jews of Yugoslavia, it is the past experiential circumstances of World War II that were not shared by all members, while the experiential circumstances of living in the socialist Yugoslav state were, at some levels, shared by all. The refugees described by Malkki, then, shared memories, but these memories were worked out differently in the contemporary circumstances in which they found themselves. For the Hutu refugees, the "ethnicity of experience" approach is not problematic where instilling memory is concerned, for they all experienced the atrocities in Burundi. The problem with the approach surfaces in what is supposed to follow—a conscious cognitive orientation, a symbolization of the past experience, and particular action. We can see the camp refugees engaged in such activities, especially in telling particular stories, what Malkki has called mythico-histories. But, according to Malkki, this did not take place among the town refugees. Theirs was a present and future orientation.

The Symbolic Community

Both Edward Spicer's (1971) persistent identity system model and Anthony Cohen's (1985) symbolic community concept have relevance for the Jews of Yugoslavia. Neither Spicer's nor Cohen's concept requires an intact, integrated cultural system. Rather, as Spicer suggests, a cluster of key symbols can provide the necessary cultural dimension to a group's collective identity. Moreover, these symbols need not be a part of daily life. In describing the construction of a symbolic community, Cohen indicates that individual members of communities may continue to share key cultural forms (symbols), but they assign different meanings to them. For instance, when many sociocultural units and practices no longer are integral to the cycles of life, individuals may retain word symbols such as "tradition," "Jewish culture" and "Jewish community," but they interpret them differently. In this sense the Jews of Yugoslavia are a symbolic community. In the Yugoslav Jewish case, the Jewish community was not in opposition (one of Spicer's criteria for a persistent identity system), which further reduced any social visibility they had. As shown in chapter 6, the Yugoslav Jewish symbolic community, which included Jews who had minimal or irregular contact with the organized community, emerged in times of perceived threat or crisis.

However powerful in explaining certain ethnic groups and situations, no single existing approach adequately explains the ethnicity and identity of the postwar Jews of Yugoslavia. Precipitated by radical and rapid change in the forms of major historical swings and a sudden, violent imposition, the factors of disjuncture and fragmentation began to characterize the collective and individual lives of the Jews of Yugoslavia. Disjuncture and the resulting fragmentation and bricolage are what placed these Jews much earlier into a postmodern world. Having lost the connecting link of the Jewish family and household and the multi-institutional and multi-ideological structure that characterized the prewar Jewish community, Jewish individuals were left to pursue and construct their own Jewishness.

Narrative Approach to Identity

I agree with the philosopher Alisdair MacIntyre (1984) that "man is essentially a story-telling animal." Human beings tell many kinds of narratives—histories, myths, legends, fables, anecdotes, and so on. Anthropologists then do their bit in producing yet another kind of narrative about the narratives produced by particular cultural groups. It is my contention that the identities of the peoples anthropologists describe are most completely comprehensible through a corpus of such narratives, and less so when relying solely on any one of the approaches discussed above which appear reductionistic when placed against the breadth and depth of cultural histories. These narratives, the indigenous ones and those reproduced by anthropologists, do many things. They describe beginnings long before the time of anthropologists. Despite the current fascination with history in anthropology, many anthropologists continue the Malinowskian bias in viewing such accounts as inherently speculative, as inauthentic traditions (Clifford 1988), or as present-day constructions for manipulating social statuses. If identity is primarily a consciousness of being and secondarily the cognitive, affective and behavioral orientations that maintain and defend that consciousness from extinction, then it is important to know how that identity first emerged. Many narratives describe such a genesis in both/either cosmic and/or historical terms, including the account in the book of Genesis. Some narratives also describe the various threats to identity (being) and the recreations that occurred across time and place in its defense. A reading of the biblical narrative, for example, describes significant transformations of the Jewish people that resulted from internal and external threats. Above all, perhaps, such narratives are apt to describe what moves a people most, which anthropologists sometimes ignore or never see because of how they, as the primary instrument of the anthropological method, are calibrated (see Priest 1987). And it is in grasping what moves people most that we can look for answers to why they do the things they do and why their senses respond the way they do in relation to certain objects, events, and behaviors (see Wilson 1994). For example, the 607-year-old narrative of Kosovo evokes awe in many Serbs, but a radically different emotional response in Muslims and Croats. It is in these narratives that the unspoken becomes told, the mysterious becomes revealed, and, if we include within our corpus the narratives of others about ourselves, both the virtues and sins of a people are described in full detail.[6] There is, after all, a strong moral component to identity, both collective and individual.

To possess a particular identity, to be a member of a community, is to know the grand narrative of one's people and to make that story one's own. This is partially accomplished by making it part of the present through participation in a ritual cycle or in ongoing communal life. Being part of the narrative is "to produce a sense" "of being a single people in whatever place" (Meeks 1993:212) and, I would add, whatever time. The conditions and structures may change a ethnic people, but they do not make them.

From the anthropologist's perspective a cultural history would most closely follow the pattern of a story with a beginning(s), a middle, and perhaps even an end(s). It is in such narratives produced by indigenes and anthropologists that we can begin to understand that identity at any given historical moment is often reconfigured by relations of power, demographic processes, economic status, and interethnic interaction but that it cannot be reduced to any of these. For example, a major feature of the grand narrative known as Jewish history and what has the most significance for these Balkan Jews is not a single period of exile, slavery, or dispersion, but the consciousness that exile itself is a key ingredient of the Jewish narrative. They not only know that this is a key ingredient, but they, being part of the Jewish Diaspora, continue to experience it to some degree, perhaps in the form of a consciousness of always having to accommodate to larger, more powerful groups and of being prepared for the worst. Thus, the answer the question, "What is a Jew?" cannot stop with the question, "What is a Yugoslav (or Croatian or Serbian or Macedonian or Bosnian) Jew?" Rather, the latter question must proceed to the broader question, and the narratives of the latter must be understood as part of the larger Jewish narrative.

Appropriation and Manipulation of Identity

As this study has demonstrated, the identity features of a particular ethnic people can be appropriated and manipulated in various ways by outgroups of different size. In such instances these multivocal features are valued as symbolic capital capable of attracting attention and of evoking both a cognitive and sensory response from the intended audience. With the collapse of Yugoslavia, the Jews and Jewish symbols were used in this way. Specifically, they were used to show moral proximity or association ("only the good can be friends"), to subvert existing socio-moral categories (e.g., the Serbs as victims of fascism transposed to Serbs as fascist oppressors; Kosovo Albanians transposed to Jewish victims of fascist oppression), and to show difference (e.g., blaming Jewish congressmen in the United States for Serbia's plight; the rise in anti-Semitic rhetoric and vandalism of Jewish sites) with one aim being to move the Jews to the margins where they will be outside the "natural order of things" (see Malkki 1995). Whereas they once occupied a secure place in the brotherhood and unity of Yugoslav peoples, what such place is possible in "natural" orders defined and molded by each Nation?

The More Things Change the More They Remain the Same

One of the unsolved problems of anthropology is an explanation of the simultaneous presence of significant cultural change and continuity. The present can be seen as a hinge between the past and the future (Peel 1989). Since everything is in process it is often difficult to sort out the changes and the continuities.

What exactly do I mean by, "the more things change, the more they remain the same?" When we focus on any given historical moment, we are focusing solely on the hinge, the structural part of what is a process. We tend to assign greater import to the structures, categories, and ascriptions of identity. But when we consider identity within the process of cultural history or histories, we can question those theoretical assertions that reduce identity to particular structures or particular ideological or material conditions. They "remain the same" not in the sense that there is no change or that the "constants" or "continuities" are perceived and interpreted in the same manner. Rather, it is often the case that such "constants" or "continuities" play a prominent part in different historical periods, sometimes surfacing after years, decades, even centures of submergence. For the Jews, we can single out the Hebrew language, the Torah, and the contract known as the Covenant, and the condition known as exile. The ethnographic literature contains other cases. Recently, Richard Wilson (1994) has described the central place of the mountain spirits in the tumultuous history of the Q'eqchi' of Guatemala. The cultural significance of the mountain spirit has persisted across conquest and colonization, civil war, state terror, ideological and religious infiltration, and economic change.

A Final Word . . . For Now

No longer is there a Yugoslav Jewish community that includes the Jews of Croatia, Slovenia, Bosnia-Hercegovina, and Macedonia with the Jews of Serbia and its provinces. It was not their population profile, which projected a rather bleak future, that brought an end to the entity known as the Jewish community of Yugoslavia, but the collapse of state socialism and the violent political dissolution of the Yugoslav state. Again, the long-familiar pattern was reasserted: the pressures of external history intervened to radically transform this population of Jews. At the same time we must recognize that although once again the material and structural conditions have changed, Jews still live on the territories of what was until a few years ago a single country, and they struggle to refashion themselves yet another time.

An examination of the literature uncovers a plethora of definitions of Jewish identity. There is no consensus to be found. What is a Jew? Who is a Jew? The answers to these questions remain debatable. While recognizing the myriad of definitions and characterizations and the lack of agreement in answer to the question, "What is a Jew?", my intent has been to plunge into the murky waters of Jewish identity by asking "What is a Yugoslav Jew?" and proceeding to answer both questions through the lens of anthropology. My answer is that, for many Jews, Jewishness is a bricolage.

As a final word on Jewish identity, at least for now, perhaps those of us who have been struggling to answer the question "What is a Jew?" might agree with the words of the writer Nessa Rapoport (1993:44) and settle with "the temporary compromise that Jewish identity is a matter of *teiku,* which is a Talmudic term that means an unresolved debate whose outcome must await the Messiah."

APPENDIX

Table 2.
Contrasts Between Prewar and Postwar Population Profiles

Features	*Prewar*	*Postwar*
Demographic Composition		
Overall strength	weak (significant % in several cities)	weak
Absolute size	76,000 (82,000 w/refugees)	c. 8,000 (true number unknown)
Total proportion	0.46 4–9% in certain cities	0.03 0.09 (Belgrade, 1,600/2 mill.)
Geographical distribution	more widely; regionally and in more smaller towns; c. 40% in Belgrade, Zagreb, Sarajevo	less widely; c. 75% in Belgrade, Zagreb, Sarajevo
Sex ratio	fairly even	138(F):100(M) 186(F):100(M) in senior generation
Age distribution	normal distribution	markedly elderly; missing half-generations (between senior and middle and middle and youngest generations)

(continued)

Table 2 *(continued)*

Features	*Prewar*	*Postwar*
Fertility	low (significant decline since 1900, especially among Ashkenazim)	low
Mortality	low (lower than other YU populations)	high
Socioeconomic Composition		
Class	mostly middle; fewer wealthy and poor; regional variation (wealthier N; many poor Jews in Macedonia and Sarajevo)	class leveling
Settlement	urban (in contrast to 80% rural-peasant population)	urban (loss of contrast following postwar migrations to the cities)
Occupational categories	increasing no. in free professions; most in business; several hundred bankers/industrialists	govt. employees, administrators; free professions, arts, sciences; military; v. few left in business
Educational fields	overrep. in medicine, law, engin., music, arts and sciences	
Literacy	almost 100% (great contrast to other populs., except Slovenes)	100% (loss of contrast to most other urban populs.)
Social Composition		
Number of Jewish communities (JOs)	121	32 (only 10 with representatives in Federation/Conference of Communities)

(continued)

Table 2 *(continued)*

Features	*Prewar*	*Postwar*
Size of larger JOs	3–10,000	3 JOs with over 1,000
Organizational framework	multi-institutional; extra-communal voluntary organizations by gender, age, interest, political orientation; rabbinate	uni-institutional; JOs are dependent on Federation which, in turn, is dependent on foreign aid
Membership	compulsory (though there were non-members) communal taxation and ritual fees	voluntary; nominal annual membership fee
Communal revenue	taxation (gradated by class), ritual fees, donations, property, state	dependent on foreign Jewish aid, individual donations, state
Budget allotment	allotment for religion declined but still significant, particularly in Orthodox community	allotment for religion low (religion ranked low by priority); however, high number of individual donations to cemetery and synagogue
Family and Household	intact; homogeneous	truncation; no longer a viable Jewish institution or link between collective and individual levels
Marriage	ideology and practice of ethnic endogamy	practice of ethnic exogamy
Descent	both parents Jewish; birth ascription via matrilineal line	52% both parents Jewish; individual selects line of descent
Residence	concentrated areas of Jewish settlement (Jewish quarters dissolving); class; majority conc. in center ("Old Town")	no Jewish neighborhoods; many in center and adj. districts; move to high-rise suburbs

(continued)

Table 2 *(continued)*

Features	*Prewar*	*Postwar*
Sociocultural Composition		
Religious-Ritual infrastructure	relatively intact and strong, despite movement away from Judaic tradition	eroded and weak (e.g., 1 rabbi)
Ritual specialists	ritual specialists (rabbis, cantors, mohalim, shohetim, available	1 rabbi, several prayer leaders; need to import for special services
Operating synagogues	where synagogues existed they operated; several in the larger cities	3 operate regularly for Sabbath, a few others on major holidays
Maintenance of Jewish customs	strongly maintained	of those >20 yrs. old, 48% do not observe and 16% do not know them
Kashrut (dietary laws)	perhaps 50% (based on nonrepres. subsample)	none (occasional meals for foreign guests)
Purification rites	except for Orthodox and absent part of older Sephardim, in decline; kashrut, hand washing, kapara, hammez cleansing	
Commensality rites	familial commensality (Sabbath, Passover, etc.); limudim	communal Seder; limudim
Rites of passage	all life cycle stages	only death stage

NOTES

Preface

1. In *Works and Lives* Clifford Geertz (1988) writes about "Being There," that is, about the anthropologist conveying to the readers of his ethnographic text a sense that he was actually in the particular ethnographic space being described. At first I chose to borrow Geertz's phrase in introducing the study, but then dropped it in favor of "Being Where?", for I came to question what exactly was the ethnographic space occupied by the Jews of Yugoslavia. Can we even speak of them collectively occupying such a space? These questions are not easily answered, hence the new phrase.

2. During my last visit to Belgrade in 1994, a new bold inscription could be seen.

3. Church of the Serbian Orthodox Patriarchate.

4. Translated, Jevrejska ulica is "Jewish Street."

Introduction

1. When I refer to the "traditional" before the Second World War, I mean a life that was visibly regulated by Jewish rituals and customs associated with a particular rhythm of life. Furthermore, although there had been a significant movement away from religion and ritual practice before World War II, a ritual infrastructure was in place to meet the needs of all who wanted to participate. In addition, the Jewish family and household remained a place where even the non-religious came into contact with at least a few Jewish customs. After the war tradition lost its ritual-symbolic infrastructure and the rhythm of Jewish life was disrupted. Tradition took on connotative meaning.

2. I follow Victor Turner (1969) in my use of the term anti-structural. Anti-structure is a transitional state of being betwixt-and-between two fixed states or statuses.

3. Eugene Hammel (1993) shows that these divisions were not always distinct and stable.

4. In Yugoslavia, *veza* meant social "connections" that obligated the receiving party to reciprocate at some point in the future. In operation were several degrees of *veza* connections, with the *veza* connection of *poznanstvo* based on acquaintanceship.

5. Even before the Second World War some Jews in Yugoslavia were situated "on the fringe" or margins of Jewish communal life. I borrow this phrase from a translation of Nobel laureate Ivo Andrić's short story about Mento Papo, the Jewish owner of a small cafe in Sarajevo. This translation, with an afterword on the Jews of Bosnia by the present author, can be found in *Irish Slavonic Studies* 7 (September 1986).

Chapter One

1. It seems unlikely that he received such an orientation in Hashomer Hatzair, an organization influenced heavily by Marxist ideology. Alexander Orbach noted this discrepancy to me.

2. Interested readers can start with Harriet Pass Freidenreich's *The Jews of Yugoslavia: A Quest for Community*, an excellent interwar history of the Jewish communities of Belgrade, Zagreb, and Sarajevo. In relation to the present work, her treatment of ethnic identity during the years of the first Yugoslavia is especially interesting and worth examining. In some respects the current work serves as a complement to Freidenreich's, particularly in understanding ethnicity and identity as concepts rooted in historical structures and processes. One significant difference between the two works is Freidenreich's extensive description of the structure and various institutions of organized Jewish life. Readers interested in the histories of the Jews of Yugoslavia can see her extensive bibliography. Zvi Loker, who left Novi Sad for Palestine in the late 1930s and subsequently served the Israeli state as a diplomat, has written several works in English, two of which are cited in this book. Christopher Browning, an American historian of the Holocaust, has written a meticulously documented book on the Holocaust in Serbia, *Fateful Months: The Final Solution in Serbia*. In Serbian/Croatian the following sources are recommended. Ignjat Šlang, a former Ashkenazi rabbi in Belgrade wrote *Jevreji u Beogradu* (The Jews in Belgrade), a book published in 1926. Moric Levi, a former rabbi in Sarajevo, wrote his doctoral dissertation on the Jews of Bosnia. Originally published in German, his book was later translated into Serbian/Croatian. The Jewish community of Yugoslavia has published several serial publications that include valuable historical material—*Zbornik*; *Jevrejski Almanah*; *Jevrejski Pregled*; *Biltens* of the Belgrade, Sarajevo and Zagreb communities; *Židov* serial published in prewar Zagreb; various *Spomenice* (Memorial Books) and exhibit catalogues. Ženi Lebl has pub-

lished historical works in Hebrew and in Serbian on the Jews of Macedonia. Zdenko Levntal's (1957) book is an invaluable source on the Holocaust in Yugoslavia, as is Jaša Romano's *Jevreji Jugoslavije 1941–1945. Žrtve Genocida i Učesnici Narodnooslobodilačkog Rata* (The Jews of Yugoslavia 1941–1945. Victims of Genocide and Participants in the National Liberation War). There exists no more comprehensive source than Romano's on Jewish participation in all phases of the war. Romano himself was a career military officer who received a military funeral in Belgrade's Jewish cemetery. Several novels help bring to life Jewish existence in this part of the Balkans. Among the postwar writers, two of Aleksandar Tišma's novels have been translated into English. I highly recommend his *The Use of Man,* which shows that Jewish life in the city of Novi Sad before the Second World War was not without its share of ethnically heterogenous and ambiguous features, even within single families. Tišma's work is also valuable for providing narratives that deviate from those written by the organized Jewish community in describing the darker, even nihilistic, side of Jewish lives after the Second World War. Also translated into English are several of the works of Danilo Kiš, the most famous of the group of postwar Jewish writers. A selection of David Albahari's short stories have recently been published in English by Northwestern University Press under the title *Words Are Something Else.*

3. Raya (Turkish, literally means "cattle") designated the non-Muslim peoples within the Ottoman Empire.

4. Moric Levi, who was a rabbi in Sarajevo before the Second World War, describes several such cases in the book that served as his dissertation, *The Sephardim in Bosnia,* 1969 (1926).

5. As described by Braude (1982) foundation myths were constructed and used by minorities within the Ottoman Empire as a way of placing themselves closer to the rulers and thereby winning favor.

6. See Ankica Petrović's (1982) ethnomusicological work on Sephardi chants in Bosnia.

7. This law classified Sephardi and Ashkenazi Neologue communities together.

8. Simhat Torah is one of the gayest Jewish holiday celebrations that celebrates the completion of the annual reading of the Torah scroll, which begins again in the synagogue immediately. It means, literally, "rejoicing of the Torah" (*The Jews of Yugoslavia,* 1989, 144).

9. The story of Rav Moša Danon is an important part of Yugoslav Jewish, especially Bosnian Sephardi, history, and mythology.

10. Limud means "to instruct." When used by Jews in Yugoslavia, it referred also to the ritual of commensality held on the thirty-day anniversary of death and during certain commemorations.

11. For an account of the life of Jehuda Alkalaj, who may have influenced Herzl, see Jevrejski Almanah, 1968–1970, 55–65.

12. Slavko Goldstein (1989:13), Jewish activist and former president of the Zagreb Jewish community, wrote the following in regard to Jewish

persistence: "Older generations that credited all this to faith and not to nation were contradicted by the secularization of Jewry in the 19 c. and 20 c., when religious bonds became loose but national identity survived. A sense of being Jewish did not disintegrate and was not replaced by cosmopolitanism, which might have seemed an inevitable result of dispersal in the diaspora, for Jews never ceased jealously to cherish their unique identity."

Chapter Two

1. This model was derived from conversations with Arthur Tuden, Department of Anthropology, University of Pittsburgh.

2. *Jalija* means, literally, "coast," "bank." The Belgrade Jews lived near the banks of the Danube River and sometimes called this area *Jalija*.

3. Laslo Sekelj's (1980) article on antisemitism in Yugoslavia between the two world wars refutes the myth that there was no antisemitism in Serbia. See also Sekelj's article in *Vreme* (1992) in which he addresses the postwar years as well.

4. The strength of this tie is visible today in the four hundred Jews who have refused to leave war-torn Sarajevo, even though several evacuations of Jews took place in 1992.

5. In Sarajevo, a significant shift in voting pattern occurred after King Alexander's dictatorship. Sarajevo's Jews began to cast more votes for the opposition (*Jews in Yugoslavia*, 1989; Freidenreich 1979).

6. See Alex Dragnich (1989; 1991) for a Serbian view and Ivo Goldstein (1990), a history professor at the University of Zagreb and an active member of the Zagreb Jewish community, for a minority view from Croatia.

7. According to Robert Hayden, Zionism as a post-assimilationist movement can be compared to the American Indian Movement (AIM) in the 1970s. AIM involved urban Native Americans, not those from the reservations (Robert Hayden, personal communication, 1992).

8. Hashomer Hatzair represented the strongest and most important Zionist youth organization in the 1930s, but other, less socialist and political organizations existed (e.g., Tehelet Lavan in the Vojvodina). Some provided a Jewish nationalist education that was less intensive (e.g., Kadima). Akiba was the only General Zionist youth association in the country. It had no class ideology and placed less emphasis on Palestine (Freidenreich 1979:167). For an English-language summation of the Zionist movement in Yugoslavia, see Harriet Pass Freidenreich's (1979) historical study of Yugoslav Jewry during the interwar. An excellent source in the Croatian language is the serial *Židov*, which was published in Zagreb earlier in this century.

9. The size of the Ashkenazi community in Belgrade and in Sarajevo was much smaller than the Sephardi community in those cities.

10. The Vojvodina includes Subotica, which has the highest percentage of Jews whose parents are both Jewish.

11. The figures in the Jewish calendar include non-Jewish members of local communities.

12. Halakhah: "the traditions, stemming from the time of the Talmud and onward, which deal with ritual, ethnical, civil, and criminal law" (Goldberg 1986:332).

Chapter Three

1. My initial fieldwork was conducted when socialist Yugoslavia was intact and submergence was very evident. The process of submergence into Tito's Yugoslavia, described in this chapter, is now, of course, a part of the past.

2. Of course, Jewish individuals who participated in the NOB were more likely to survive than those taken to concentration camps.

3. Perhaps the same statement holds for the Jews of prewar Czechoslovakia. Masryk said about them, "In Czechoslovakia (1918–1938) there were Czechs and there were Slovaks, but only the Jews were truly Czechoslovakians" (Alexander Orbach, personal communication, April 1993).

4. See Christopher Boehm's *Montenegrin Social Organization and Values* (1983).

5. Albert Vajs actually used the phrases "constant in aim" and "elastic in method" much earlier, in connection with Jewish activism among the Jewish youth before the war.

6. Slobodan Nešović, Pijade's official biographer, told me during an interview that Pijade's co-translator of *Das Kapital* was merely an apprentice to Pijade.

7. For an in-depth understanding of these, I refer the reader to Dennison Rusinow (1977), Bogdan Denitch (1976), Pedro Ramet (1985), Aleksa Djilas (1991), Nora Beloff (1985), Kjell Magnusson (1987), and Dunja Richtman-Auguštin (1991).

8. The *guslar* sang epic poems while playing the stringed instrument called the *gusla* (see Boehm 1983:75–77).

9. That is, a community of equals sharing a common experience.

10. Differences exist between the calendar compiled by Rabbi Romano, who died in 1968, and current Rabbi Cadik Danon, who assumed the post of Rabbi in Yugoslavia around 1973. Romano, for example, did not mark Holocaust dates. He did include such dates as the birthdates of Israel's first president, Herzl's anniversary, Human Right's Day, Fighter's Day, and Day of the JNA. None of these is included by Danon in the 1985–86 calendar.

11. The following analysis is based on material in *200 Godina Židova u Zagrebu: Referati i Govori sa proslave 180-godišnjice Jevrejske općine Zagreb* (1988).

12. In her study of Jewish women in ninenteenth century Germany, Marion Kaplan (1991) describes how they strived simultaneously for integration into German society and for a distinctive Jewish identity.

13. In his study of turn-of-the-century Viennese Jewry, Steven Beller (1989) argues that there is no Jewish Mind, only Jewish minds.

Chapter Four

1. This has not been the only experiment to create a secular Jewishness. In the USSR in the 1920s, Soviet Jews attempted to create a non-religious, non-Zionist, Jewishness (Alexander Orbach, personal communication).

Chapter Five

1. On the other hand, it was due to the resilience of the organized community and some of its leaders that there was any organized Jewish life at all in Yugoslavia.

2. The present tense has been retained in much of the narratives, most of which are set in the historical context of socialist Yugoslavia.

3. Given the paucity of opportunities to collect data using participant observation, I had to construct much of the cases, both the quotations and the rest of the text, directly from interview data. Thus, my informants share the authorship of parts of the non-quoted text. I have also taken the liberty, out of fairness to my highly literate informants, to adjust grammatically interviews that were conducted in English.

4. Compare the use of "spiritual spirit" in a case in William James, *The Varieties of Religious Experience*, 1961, 70.

5. See Plotnicov and Silverman (1978) on ethnic signalling.

Chapter Six

1. Because the Titoist system remained in place, such changes introduced more contradictions. For example, the Constitution required that a certain individual be awarded the Lenin Prize for his achievements, even though he had been found guilty of orchestrating one of the country's greatest economic scandals.

2. The white violet was a reference to Tito.

3. The expropriation and recontextualization of the Star of David symbol operated on several levels of meaning, from the more specific event of the Albanian miners' strike in Kosovo and the general Kosovo conflict, and the rupture of Serb-Slovene economic ties, to the broader confronta-

tion between the Serbs and Slovenes (and Croats) over the definition of Yugoslavia and the future aspirations of the nation peoples of Yugoslavia (e.g., "self-determination" for the Slovenes and Croats).

4. When I interviewed Tadić in 1989, I sensed no hatred or malice toward non-Serbs. Tadić had been one of the most respected dissident intellectuals in socialist Yugoslavia, one of the founders of the Praxis group. He had fought for the freedom of other reformers, among them Albanians from Kosovo.

5. See Tudjman (1981) for a presentation of Serbian hegemonistic motivations from an ultra-nationalistic perspective. For a Serbian perspective, see Dragnich (1991) and the sources he cites. See Banac (1992) and Djilas (1993) regarding the perception and use of fear in Serb-Croat perceptions, politics, and relations.

6. In 1971 and again in 1981, Tudjman was sentenced for publishing secret documentation on the war losses.

7. Mira Furlan was an accomplished actress in the former Yugoslavia. Now living in the United States, she is best known for her starring role in the science fiction television series *Babylon Five*.

8. Certainly not all Jews in Belgrade perceived the Slovenes negatively. One informant remarked, "The Slovenes were the most democratic in speech, but other peoples were conditioned to reject anything that came out of Slovenia. If the same proposal emerged later from somewhere else, it was accepted." In the spring of 1989 another informant expressed the following to me: "Thank God for the Slovenian youth. They had the strength to lift the veil from false politics and to tell the truth. Still there are people who don't want to listen. They are confused with politics. . . . Our [Federation of Jewish Communities of Yugoslavia] president is against Milošević, because Milošević is an ambitious, bad man and a great nationalist. He will destroy Yugoslavia. If it comes to separation, civil war, it will be his fault. The younger people [in mixed marriages] are on one side. They are happy to be together with the Serbs because it would make it impossible for antisemitism to arise. Older ones know what Milošević wants. We all know how it will go. He will betray us, as Tito did. In fact, it is only for himself; he wants to be Number One. I am for pluralism, the only democracy. For example, if I say the Slovenian youth are right, X, here, would say, "What?! You like Slovenes and don't like Serbs." No. I want people who are honest."

Chapter Seven

1. In *Being Muslim the Bosnian Way*, anthropologist Tone Bringa (1995) notes Ernest Gellner's remark that the ethno-religious basis of identity in Yugoslavia was based on what people believed and did in the past rather than what they believe and do in the present. It is with such

an identity orientation that there existed such categories as "Muslim Communists."

2. Even though Naroll's cultunit approach has been shown to be inadequate and is not even referred to much in the anthropological literature, it remains a part of a general non-Jewish false perception of Jews as a closed, encapsulated group with impenetrable boundaries.

3. Not all writers use the term primordialism in the same way. For some, a primordial identity is one that includes a racial/ethnic/cultural essence that is ascribed at birth and remains essentially unchanged throughout the life of the individual or group. It is particularly this usage that has come under attack by anthropologists.

4. The postmodernist view in anthropology assumes that the past cannot really be known. History is instead a construction of present-day persons who are motivated by interests associated with their position in the social structure.

5. In *Chihamba, The White Spirit*, Victor Turner (1962) commented on how social scientific grids sometimes dismiss the religious features of life. See also Priest (1987).

6. A major difference between some of these older narratives and some of the new nationalistic ones is that the latter describe the evil acts of outgroups while omitting their own evil acts.

BIBLIOGRAPHY

Abraham, M. 1989. "Ethnic Identity and Marginality among Indian Jews in Contemporary India." *Ethnic Groups* 9:33–60.

Abramowicz, L. 1978. "Introduction." In Nahum Goldmann, *A Jewish Paradox* 1–6. New York: Fred Jordan Books/Grosset and Dunlap.

Ačin, Z. 1989. "Malo Nesrečniji od Drugih. Srbi i Jevreji: Prijateljstvo po Duši i Žrtvama." [A Little Unluckier Than the Rest. Serbs and Jews: Friendship According to Souls and Victims.] *Duga* (Belgrade), March, 25–27, 34.

Albahari, D. 1982. "Israel i Ja." [Israel and I. Interview with David Albahari.] *NIN* (Belgrade), 10 October.

———. 1983. *Opis Smrti*. [Description of Death.] Belgrade: Rad.

———. 1985. "Prepolovljeno Ogledalo Davida Albaharija." [An Interview with David Albahari.] *Start* (Zagreb) October, 55–57.

———. 1990. "Stvarnost—više od bedža." [Reality—Greater than the Badge. An Interview with David Albahari]. *Intervju* (Belgrade) 25 May, 22–24.

———. 1992. "Budučnost svih: Jevreja. Spremnost na nerazumevanje." [The Future of All Jews. Readiness for Misunderstanding. An Interview with David Albahari by Ejub Stitkovac.] *Borba* (Belgrade), March.

———. 1992. "Nacija Ne Nudi Spas." [Interview with David Albahari.] *Svetlost*, 12 March, 20–21.

———. 1996. *Words Are Something Else*. Translated by Ellen Elias-Bursac. Evanston, IL: Northwestern University Press.

Albahari, N. 1984. "Osobenosti Istorijskog Razvoja Bosanskohercegovačkih Jevreja." [The Particularities of the Historical Development of Bosno-Hercegovian Jews]. *Sveske* (Sarajevo) 7–8: 19–24.

———, ed. 1988. *Sarajevo u Socijalističkoj Jugoslaviji*. Sarajevo: Istorijski Arhiv. Alkalaj, A. 1961–1962. "Život i Običaji u Nekadašnjoj Jevrejskoj Mahali." [Life and Customs in the Former Jewish Quarter.] *Jevrejski Almanah,* 82–97.

Almuli, J. 1989. "Život i Strandanja Naših Jevreja." [Series on The Life and Suffering of Our Jews]. *Politika* (Belgrade), April–May.

Alter, R. 1971. *After the Tradition: Essays on Modern Jewish Writing*. New York: Dutton.

Anderson, B. 1991. *Imagined Communities: Reflections on the Origin and Spread of Nationalism*. London: Verso and New Left Books.

Andrić, I. 1986. "On the Fringe." Translated by Herbert Butler. *Irish Slavonic Studies* 7 (September):97–101.

Antić, D. 1989. "Srbi Nisu Uskogrudi i Nikada Nisu Ugrožavali Druge Narode" [Serbs Aren't Narrow-minded and Never Endangered Other Peoples. Interview with Rabbi Cadik Danon.] *Politika* (Belgrade), 3 March.

Arvidsson, C., and Blomqvist, L.E., eds. 1987. *Symbols of Power: the Esthetics of Political Legitimation in the Soviet Union and Eastern Europe*. Stockholm: Almqvist and Wiksell International.

Bakic-Hayden, M., and Hayden, R.M. 1992. "Orientalist Variations on the Theme "Balkans": Symbolic Geography in Recent Yugoslav Cultural Politics." *Slavic Review* 51(1):1–15.

Banac, I. 1984. *The National Question in Yugoslavia: Origins, History, Politics*. Ithaca: Cornell University Press.

———. 1992. "The Fearful Symmetry of War: The Causes and Consequences of Yugoslavia's Demise." *Daedalus* 121(2): 141–171.

Barth, F. 1969. *Ethnic Groups and Boundaries*. Boston: Little, Brown.

Bauman, Z. 1991. *Modernity and Ambivalence*. Ithaca: Cornell University Press.

Becker, E. 1975. *Escape from Evil*. New York: The Free Press.

Bell, D. 1980. *The Winding Passage: Essays and Sociological Journeys 1960–1989*. Cambridge, MA: ABT Books.

Beller, S. 1989. *Vienna and the Jews, 1867–1938: A Cultural History*. Cambridge, MA: Harvard University Press.

Beloff, N. 1985. *Tito's Flawed Legacy: Yugoslavia and the West, 1939–84*. London: Gollancz.

Bentley, G. Carter. 1987. "Ethnicity and Practice." *Comparative Studies in Society and History* 29 (1): 24–55.

Berger, P. 1967. *The Sacred Canopy: Elements of a Sociological Theory of Religion*. Garden City, NY: Doubleday.

Berger, P., Berger, B., and H. Kellner. 1974. *The Homeless Mind: Modernization and Consciousness*. New York: Vintage Books.

Bilten. [Bulletin.] Hitahdut Olej Jugoslavije. 1985. "David Albahari u Izraelu." [David Albahari in Israel. Excerpt from an interview published in *Iton* 77, IX, 1985 "Otkrivati se i medjusobno upoznati," D. Katan Ben-Cion.] Ž. Lebl. *Bilten* 5(1 November): 20–22.

Bilten. Jevrejske Opštine u Beogradu. [Bulletin. Jewish Community in Belgrade]. Belgrade.

Bilten. Jevrejske Opštine u Sarajevu. [Bulletin. Jewish Community in Sarajevo.] Sarajevo.

———. 1989. "Nekoliko Uspomena Sa Izložbe." [A Few Memories from the Exhibit.] 3:40–42.

Bilten. Jevrejske Općine u Zagrebu. [Bulletin. Jewish Community in Zagreb.] Zagreb.

———. 1988. "Židovi na tlu Jugoslavije." U Ogledalu Domaće Štampe." 6–7:4

———. 1988. "Vijesti . . . Konferencija općina." [News . . . Conference of the Communities.] 6–7:5.

———. 1989. "Izvanredna sjednica Izvršnog odbora JOZ." [A Special Session of the Executive Committee of the Zagreb Jewish Community.] 11:4.

———. 1990. "Intervju S Mihajlom Montiljom." [An Interview with Mihajlo Montiljo.] 16:7.

———. 1990. [On the Renaming of the Square of Victims of Fascism.] 16:3.

Binns, C.A.P. 1979. "The Changing Face of Power and Revolution and Accomodation in the Development of the Soviet Ceremonial System: Part I." *Man*, n.s., 14(4):585–608.

———. 1980. "The Changing Face of Power and Revolution and Accomodation in the Development of the Soviet Ceremonial Ceremonial System: Part II." *Man*, n.s., 15(1):170–187.

Boban, L. 1990. "Jasenovac and the Manipulation of History." *East European Politics and Societies* 4: 580–592.

Boehm, C. 1983. *Montenegrin Social Organization and Values*. New York: AMS Press.

Boyarin, J. 1991. *Polish Jews in Paris: the Ethnography of Memory*. Bloomington and Indianapolis: Indiana University Press.

Braham, R. 1994. "Anti-Semitism and the Holocaust in the Politics of East Central Europe." In *Anti-Semitism in the Treatment of the Holocaust in Postcommunist Eastern Europe*, ed. R. Braham, 1–30. New York: Rosenthal Institute for Holocaust Studies, Graduate Center/The City University of New York; Boulder, CO: Social Science Monographs. New York: Distributed by Columbia University Press.

Braude, B. 1982. "Foundation Myths and the Millet System." In *Christians and Jews in the Ottoman Empire: The Functioning of Plural Society*, Vol. I. eds., B. Braude and B. Lewis, 69–88. New York: Holmes & Meier.

Bringa, T. 1995. *Being Muslim the Bosnian Way: Identity and Community in a Central Bosnian Village*. Princeton: Princeton University Press.

Browning, C. 1985. *Fateful Months: Essays in the Emergence of the Final Solution*. New York & London: Holmes & Meier.

Buchwald, R. 1936. "Kroz Jevrejske Mahale Južne Srbije" [Through the Jewish Quarters of Southern Serbia.] *Židov*, 13 November. Quoted in U. Oren. *A Town Called Monastir*, 36. Translated by Mark Segal. Tel Aviv: Dror Publications, 1971.

Burg, S. 1983. *The Political Integration of Yugoslavia's Muslims: Determinanta of Success and Failure.* Pittsburgh: University of Pittsburgh Press.

Campolo, T. 1983. *A Reasonable Faith: Responding to Secularism*. Waco, TX: Word Books.

Clifford, J. 1988. *The Predicament of Culture. Twentieth Century Ethnography, Literature, and Art*. Cambridge: Harvard University Press.

Cohen, A. 1974. "Introduction: The Lessons of Ethnicity." In *Urban Ethnicity*, ed. A. Cohen, ix–xxiv. ASA Monography No. 12. Tavistock Publications.

———. 1976. *Two-Dimensional Man: An Essay on the Anthropology of Power and Symbolism in Complex Society*. Berkeley and Los Angeles: University of California Press.

Cohen, A. 1985. *The Symbolic Construction of Community*. London and New York: Tavistock Publications.

Cohen, P. 1996. *Serbia's Secret War: Propaganda and the Deceit of History*. College Station, TX: Texas A & M University Press.

Comaroff, J. and J. Comaroff. 1992. *Ethnography and the Historical Imagination*. Boulder: Westview Press.

The Concise Oxford Dictionary of Literary Terms. 1991. C. Baldick. Oxford and New York: Oxford University Press.

Corre, A. D. 1973. "The 60 Percent Minority." *The Sephardic World* 1(2):20. Quoted in A.D. Lavender. "Arabic-Islamic and Spanish-Mediterranean Influences on 'The Jewish Mind': A Comparison to European-Christian Influence." *Journal of Ethnic Studies* 8(4).

Dahrendorf, R. 1969. "On the Origins of Inequality Among Men." In A. Beteille, ed. Social Inequality. Baltimore: Penguin Books. Cited in N. Glazer and D.P. Moynihan, eds. *Ethnicity: Theory and Experience*. Cambridge, MA: Harvard University Press.

Danas (Zagreb).

———. 1990. Intervju: Slavko Goldstein. 8 May, 12–14.

———. 1990. "Neizbrisivi Tragovi Duha. Razgovori: Mr. Nenad Porges." [The Indelible Tracks of the Spirit. Conversations: Mr. Nenad Porges.] 13 November, 39–41.

———. 1993. "Jasenovac Će Biti Mjesto Pomirbe." [Jasenovac Will Be a Place of Reconciliation. Interview with Franjo Tudjman.] 26 October, 8–11.

Danforth, L. 1995. *The Macedonian Conflict. Ethnic Nationalism in a Transnational World*. Princeton, NJ: Princeton University Press.

Start (Zagreb). 1989. "Intervju: Cadik Danon." 15 April, 16–21.

David, F. 1994. *Fragmenti Iz Mračnih Vremena*. Belgrade: Beogradski Krug.

———. 1989. "Dnevnik." *Danas*, 26 September, 28–29.

Davidman, L. 1991. *Tradition in a Rootless World: Women Turn to Orthodox Judaism*. Berkeley: University of California Press.

Dedijer, V. 1961. *The Beloved Land*. New York: Simon & Schuster.

———. 1981. *Novi Prilozi za Biografiju Josipa Broza Tita, Knjiga II*. [New Contributions to the Biography of Josip Broz Tito, Book II.] Zagreb: Mladost; Rijeka: Liburnija. Quoted in Magnusson 1987, 74.

———. 1992. *The Yugoslav Auschwitz and the Vatican. The Croatian Masssacre of the Serbs During World War II*. Translated by Harvey L. Kendall. Buffalo, NY: Prometheus Books and Freiburg, Germany: Ahriman-Verlag.

Demographic Survey. 1985. Computer Printout of Survey Responses. Belgrade: Savez Jevrejskih Opština Jugoslavije.

Denitch, B. 1976. *The Legitimation of a Revolution*. New Haven: Yale University Press.

———. 1990. *Limits and Possibilities: the Crisis of Yugoslav Socialism and State Socialist Systems*. Minneapolis: University of Minnesota Press.

Despres, L. 1975. "Toward a Theory of Ethnic Phenomena." In *Ethnicity and Resource Competition in Plural Societies*, ed. L.A. Despres, 87–117. Chicago: Aldine.

DeVos, G. 1975. "Ethnic Pluralism: Conflict and Accomodation." In *Ethnic Identity: Cultural Continuities and Change*, eds. G. DeVos and L. Romanucci-Ross. Berkeley: University of California Press.

DeVos, G., & Romanucci-Ross, L. 1975. "Ethnicity: Vessel of Meaning and Emblems of Contrast." In *Ethnic Identity: Cultural Continuities and Change*, eds. G. DeVos and L. Romanucci-Ross. Berkeley: University of California Press.

Dimitrijević, M. and Stojanović, eds. 1940. *Naši Jevreji, Jevrejsko Pitanje Kod Nas*. [Our Jews, the Jewish Question Among Us.] Belgrade: Stamparija Minerva.

Djilas, A. 1991. *The Contested Country: Yugoslav Unity and Communist Revolution, 1919–1953*. Cambridge: Harvard University Press.

———. 1993. "A Profile of Slobodan Milošević." *Foreign Affairs* 72(3): 81–96.

Dorst, J. 1989. *The Written Suburb: An American Site, An Ethnographic Dilemma*. Philadelphia: University of Pennsylvania Press.

Douglas, M. 1973. *Natural Symbols*. New York: Penguin Books.

———. 1979 (1966). *Purity and Danger: An Analysis of the Concepts of Pollution and Taboo*. London and Boston: Routledge and Kegan Paul.

Dragnich, A.N. 1989. "Rise and Fall of Yugoslavia: Omen of Upsurge of Serbian Nationalism." *East European Quarterly* 23(2):183–198.

———. 1991. "The Anatomy of a Myth: Serbian Hegemony." *Slavic Review* 50(3):659–662.

Drakulić, S. 1993. "Nazis Among Us." *New York Review of Books*, 27 May, 21–22.

———. 1993. *The Balkan Express. Fragments from the Other Side of War*. New York and London: W.W. Norton and Company.

Drašković, V. 1985. "To the Writers of Israel." An Open Letter. Belgrade, 17 December.

Dumont, J. 1992. *Visayan Vignettes. Ethnographic Traces of a Philippine Island*. London and Chicago: University of Chicago Press.

Džumhur, Z. 1986. "Prije Četrdesetodvije Godine." [Forty-four Years Ago.] *Jevrejski Pregled* 11–12:51–52

Eisenstadt, S.N. 1974. "Preface." In *The Predicament of Homecoming*, S. Deshen and M. Shokeid. Ithaca, NY: Cornell University Press.

Elazar, D.J. 1989. *The Other Jews: the Sephardim Today*. New York: Basic Books.

Elazar, S. 1966. "Narodna Medicina Sefardskih Jevreja u Bosni." [The Folk Medicine of the Sephardic Jews in Bosnia.] In *Spomenica 400*, 155–156.

———. 1987. *El Romancero Judeo-Espanol*, 2 vols., Sarajevo: Svjetlost.

Eliade, M. 1957. *The Sacred and the Profane: The Nature of Religion*. Translated by William R. Trask. New York: Harcourt, Brace and World, Inc. Quoted in B. Myerhoff, *Number Our Days*, 190.

———. 1961. *Images and Symbols: Studies in Religious Symbolism*. Translated by Philip Mairet. New York: Sheed and Word. Quoted in B. Myerhoff, *Number Our Days*, 190.

Epstein, A. L. 1978. *Ethos and Identity: Three Studies in Ethnicity*. London: Tavistock Publications and Chicago: Aldine Publishing Co.

Erenrajh, M. 1989. "Jasenovac (Franjo Tudjman i Ernet Nolte)." *Duga* (Belgrade), 28 October–10 November, 20.

———. 1990. "Tudjmanova Bespuća [Tudjman's Tracklessness]. *NIN* (Belgrade), 28 September, 47.

Eriksen, T.H. 1993. *Ethnicity and Nationalism: Anthropological Perspectives*. London; Boulder, CO: Pluto Press.

Faur, J. 1972. "The Sephardim: Yesterday, Today and Tomorrow." *The Sephardic World* 1(1):6.

FBIS. Daily Report, Eastern Europe.

———. 1989. "Slogans, Banners at Belgrade Meeting Noted." 9 March, 72–73. Translated from *Politika* (Belgrade), 1 March 1989, 3. EEU-89-045.

———. 1989. "Jewish Association Files Charges in Ljubljana." 16 March, 59. Translated from Politika, 3 March, 1. EEU-89-050.

———. 1990. EEU-041, 70–71.

Fenn, R. 1978. "Toward a Theory of Secularization." Storrs, CT: *Journal for the Scientific Study of Religion Monograph*, 78. Quoted in D. Lyon, *The Steeple's Shadow: On the Myths and Realities of Secularization*, 17. Grand Rapids, MI: Eerdmans.

Finci, E. 1966. "U Avangardi Društvenog Progresa." [In the Vanguard of Social Progress.] In *Spomenica 1966*, 189–204.

Finestein, I. 1977. "The Secular Jew: Does He Exist and Why?" *Jewish Journal of Social Sociology* 19 (2):185–195.

Firth, R. 1973. *Symbols: Public and Private*. Ithaca: Cornell University Press.

Fischer, M. M. 1986. "Appendix. Ethnicity as Text and Model." *Anthropology as Cultural Critique: An Experimental Moment in the Social Sciences*, eds. G. E. Marcus & M. M. Fischer, 173–177. Chicago: University of Chicago Press.

Fortes, M. 1983. "Problems of Identity and Person." In *Identity: Personal and Socio-Cultural*, ed. A. Jakobson-Widding, 389–401. Uppsala, Sweden: Almqvist and Wiksell.

Freidenreich, H.P. 1979. *The Jews of Yugoslavia: A Quest for Community*. Philadelphia: The Jewish Publication Society of America.

———. 1984. "The Jewish Community of Yugoslavia." In *The Balkan Jewish Communities: Yugoslavia, Bulgaria, Greece and Turkey*, 12–58. Lanham, New York and London: University Press of America.

Furlan, M. 1991. "A Letter to My Co-Citizens." Website: The Mira Furlan Page. http://www.hookup.net/~bjust/B5/ Copyright, Mira Furlan.

Gams, A. 1975. "Napomene uz Rad "Prilog Izučavanju Učešća Bačkih Jevreja u NOR-u Naroda Jugoslavije." *Zbornik* 3: 45–52. Belgrade: Jevrejski Istorijski Muzej, Savez Jevrejskih Opština Jugoslavije.

———. 1987. *Svojina*. [Property.] Belgrade: Centar za Filosofiju i Društvenu Teoriju, Institut Društvenih Nauka, Univerzitet u Beogradu.

Geertz, C. 1973. *The Interpretation of Cultures*. New York: Basic Books.

———. 1988. *Works and Lives: The Anthropologist as Author*. Stanford: Stanford University Press.

Giddens, A. 1991. *Modernity and Self-Identity: Self and Society in the Late Modern Age*. Stanford: Stanford University Press.

Gladney, D. C. 1991. *Muslim Chinese: Ethnic Nationalism in the People's Republic of China*. Cambridge, MA & London: Council on East Asian Studies, Harvard University Press.

Glasner, P. 1977. *The Sociology of Secularization: A Critique of a Concept*, 8. London and Boston: Routledge and Kegan Paul. Cited in Lyon 1988.

Glazer, N., and D.P. Moynihan. 1975. "Introduction." In *Ethnicity: Theory and Experience*, eds. N. Glazer and D.P. Moynihan, 1–26. Cambridge, MA: Harvard University Press.

Glesinger, L. 1954. "Iz Povijesti Jevreja u Hrvatskoj." [From the History of the Jews in Croatia.] *Jevrejski Almanah*, n.s., 48–59.

Goffman, E. 1957. *The Presentation of Self in Everyday Life*. Garden City, NY: Doubleday.

Goldberg, H. 1987. *Judaism Viewed from Within and from Without*. Albany: State University of New York Press.

Goldstein, I. 1990. "Serbs in Croatia, Croatia in Yugoslavia." *East European Reporter* 4 (3):64–67.

———. 1992. "Ustaša Na Ekranu." [Ustasha on the Television Screen.] *Danas*, 31 March, 22.

———. 1993 "Uptreba Povijesti." [The Use of History.] *Erasmus* 1 April, 52–61.

Goldstein, S. 1988. "200 Godina Zagrebačke Židovske Zajednice." Referat na svečanoj akademiji u Hrvatskom glazbenom zavodu 8.XI 1986. In *200 Godina Židova u Zagrebu*, 16–22. Zagreb: Jevrejska Općina Zagreba and Savez Jevrejskih Općina Jugoslavije.

———. 1990. "Aktivnosti Židovske Zajednice Zagreba. Izvještaj Predsjednika Jevrejske Općine Za Razdoblje May 1986–May 1990." [The Activities of the Jewish Community of Zagreb. Report of the President of the Jewish Community for the Period May 1986—May 1990.] *Bilten* (JOZ) 16:2–3.

———. 1990. "Prijedlog Novi Hrvatski Ustav." [A Proposal for the New Croatian Constitution.] *Bilten* (JOZ) 16:4. (The proposal printed in its entirety in *Vjesnik* (Zagreb), 14–15 September 1990.)

———. 1990. "Sto je rekao Serge Zweigenbaum." [What Serge Zweigenbaum Said. Reprint of Slavko Goldstein's letter to Belgrade newspaper *Politika*.] Bilten (JOZ) 11(1989):1, 4.

———. 1991. "Jesu Li Ustaše Zaista Bile Džentlmeni?" [Were the Ustasha Really Gentlemen? Interview with Slavko Goldstein.] *Globus*, 23 August, 14.

Golubović, Z. 1990. "The Impact of Nationalist Antagonisms Upon the Perception of Present-Day Yugoslavia." *East European Reporter* 4(2):82–84.

Gordiejew, P. 1986. "Afterword. The Jews of Bosnia-Hercegovina." *Irish Slavonic Studies* 7(September):101–107.

———. 1993. *The Effects of History, Disjuncture, and Imposition on the Phases of Yugoslav Jewish Ethnicity*. Ph.D Dissertation, University of Pittsburgh.

Gould, S.J. 1994. "The Geometer of Race." *Discover* (November) 65–69.

Gross, M. 1988. "Židovi u Habsburškoj Monarhiji u 19. Stoljecu." [Jews in the Habsburg Monarchy in the 19th Century.] In *200 Godina Židova u Zagrebu*, 37–52. Zagreb: Jevrejska Općina Zagreba and Savez Jevrejskih Opština Jugoslavije.

Gruenwald, O. 1989. "Response: Camp Literature: Archetype for Dissent." *Slavic Review* 48(2):280–283.

Gulliver, P.H. 1971. "Review of Ethnic Groups and Boundaries (1969)." *Man* 6:308.

Hammel, E. 1993. "The Yugoslav Labyrinth." In *Anthropology of East Europe Review*. Special Issue, Vol. 11(1–2): 35–42.

———. 1993. "Demography and the Origin of the Yugoslov Civil War." *Anthropology Today* 9(1): 4–9.

Handelman, D. 1990. *Models and Mirrors: Towards an Anthropology of Public Events*. Cambridge; New York: Cambridge University Press.

Handelman, D. and L. Shanger-Handelman. 1990. "Shaping Time: The Choice of the National Emblem of Israel." In *Culture Through Time: Anthropological Approaches*, ed. E. Ohnuki Tierney, 155–193. Stanford: Stanford University Press.

Handler, R. 1988. *Nationalism and the Politics of Culture in Quebec*. Madison: University of Wisconsin Press.

Harrison, S. 1995. "Four Types of Symbolic Conflict." *Journal of the Royal Anthropological Institute* (N.S.) 1:255–272.

Haskell, G. 1994. *From Sofija to Jaffa. The Jews of Bulgaria and Israel*. Detroit: Wayne State University Press.

Hayden, R.M. 1989. "Using a Microscope to Scan the Horizon." *Slavic Review* 48(2):275–279.

———. 1991. "Recounting the Dead: The Rediscovery and Redefinition of Wartime Massacres in Late- and Post-Communist Yugoslavia." Paper prepared for an advanced seminar on Secret Histories: The Politics of Memory under Socialism, held at the School of American Research, Santa Fe, New Mexico, October 20–24, 1991.

———. 1992. "Constitutional Nationalism in the Formerly Yugoslav Republics." *Slavic Review* 51:654–673.

———. 1992. "Balancing Discussion of Jasenovac and the Manipulation of History." *East European Politics and Societies* 6(2): 207–212.

———. 1992. Personal Communication.

———. 1993. "Triumph of Chauvinistic Nationalisms in Yugoslavia: Bleak Implications for Anthropology." In *Anthropology of East Europe Review*, Special Issue,Vol. 11(1–2):63–67.

———. 1994. "Recounting the Dead: The Rediscovery and Redefinition of Wartime Massacres in Late- and Post-Communist Yugoslavia." In *Memory, History, and Opposition Under State Socialism*, ed. R. Watson, 167–184. Santa Fe, NM: School of American Research Press.

Heim, O. 1919. "Reforme u Hramu" [Reforms in the Temple]. *Židov* 3 (6): 4, 10 February. Quoted in H.P. Freidenreich 1979, 89–90.

Hobsbawm, E. 1983. "Introduction: Inventing Traditions." In *The Invention of Tradition*, eds. E. Hobsbawm & T. Ranger, 1–14. New York: Cambridge University Press.

Hollan, D.W., and J.C. Wellenkamp. 1994. *Contentment and Suffering: Culture and Experience in Toraja*. New York: Columbia University Press.

Horwitz, T. 1993. "Balkan Death Trap. Scenes from a Futile War." *Harper's* 286 (1714), March, 35–41, 44–45.

Isaacs, H. 1975. *Idols of the Tribe: Group Identity and Political Change*. New York: Harper and Row.

Jajčinović, M. 1990. "Grad i Politika: Zagrebačke Ulične Krstitke." *Danas* (Zagreb), 25 September, 28–29.

James, W. 1961. *The Varieties of Religious Experience*. New York: Collier; London: Collier Macmillan.

Jelić, D. 1984. "Subotički Jevreji i NOR." [Subotica Jews and the NOR.] *Rukovet* 2:130–161.

Jevreji u Jugoslaviji. 1988. [The Jews in Yugoslavia. Exhibit Catalogue.] Ed. Slavko Goldstein. Zagreb: MTM.

Jevrejski Almanah. [Jewish Almanac]. Belgrade: Savez Jevrejskih Opština Jugoslavije, 1954–1970.

Jevrejski Istorijski Muzej. Vezane Tkanine iz Jevrejskih Zbirki u Jugoslaviji. Belgrade: Savez Jevrejskih Opština Jugoslavije.

———. 1976. *Porodica Baruh—Porodica Revolucionara. Izložba*. [The Baruh Family—Family of Revolutionaries. Exhibit]. Belgrade: Jevrejski Istorijski Muzej.

———. 1979. *Jezik, Knjiga i Pismo Jevreja u Jugoslaviji*. [Language, Book and Letter in Yugoslavia.] Belgrade: Savez Jevrejskih Opština Jugoslavije.

———. 1986. *Praznični Običaji Jugoslavenskih Jevreja. Izložba*. [Holiday Customs of the Yugoslav Jews.] Belgrade: Savez Jevrejskih Opština Jugoslavije.

Jevrejski Kalendar. [Jewish Calendar.] Compiled by Cadik Danon. Belgrade: Savez Jevrejskih Opština Jugoslavije.

Jevrejska Opština Jewish Community Sarajevo. 1984. Sarajevo: Jevrejska Opština Sarajevo.

Jevrejski Pregled. [Jewish Review.] Belgrade: Savez Jevrejskih Opština Jugoslavije.

———. 1980. Special Supplement on Tito.

———. 1982. "Mr. ph. Samuel Elazar—osamdesetgodišnjak," 11–12:34–35.

———. 1986. "Prije Četrdesetodvije Godine." 11–12:51–52.

———. 1989. "Vaskrsnuće "Protokola . . . "; "Povampireni "Protokoli Sionskih Modrecev," 5–8:7–9.

———. 1989. "Nacizam, Antisemitizam—Juće i Danas. Nije Moguć Prekršajni Postupak Protiv Kolektivnog Organa," 9–12:30–31; "Da Li Áe "Mladina" Krivično Odgovarati?" 9–12:31.

———. 1989. "U Beogradu Održana Konferencija Saveza Jevrejskih Opština Jugoslavije." [The Conference of the Federation of Jewish Communities of Yugoslavia Held in Belgrade.] 5–8:1–4.

———. 1989. "Pismo Jevrejske Općine u Zagrebu Nakladnom Zavodu Matice Hrvatske." [The Zagreb Jewish Community's Letter to the Hrvatska Matica Publishing House.] 9–12:31–34.

———. 1990. "Zaključci XXX Konferencije Opština." [Conclusions of the 30th Conference of Communities.] 1–2:1–4.

———. 1990. "Nacizam, Antisemitizam—Juče i Danas. Povodom Preimenovanja Trga Žrtava Fašizma u Zagrebu." [Nazism, Antisemitism—Yesterday and Today. On the Occasion of the Renaming of the Square of Victims of Fascism in Zagreb.] 3–6:19–22; "Otvoreno Pismo Preživelih Logoraša Jasenovca i Stare Gradiške." [Open Letter of the Survivors of the Jasenovac and Stara Gradiška Concentration Camps.] 22–24; "Još iz Jugoslavije." [More from Yugoslavia.] 24–29.

———. 1990. "Židovi u Javnoj Upotrebi." [The Public Appropriation of the Jews.] 3–6.

———. 1990. "Nacizam, Antisemitizam—Juče i Danas. Jugoslavija." [Nazism, Antisemitism—Yesterday and Today. Yugoslavia.] 7–12:31–35.

Jews in Yugoslavia. 1989. [English-language edition of exhibit catalogue, *Jevreji u Jugoslaviji*.] Ed. S. Goldstein. Zagreb: MTM.

Kadelburg, L. 1970. "Položaj i Perspektive Jevrejske Zajednice u Jugoslaviji." [Position and Perspective of the Jewish Community in Yugoslavia.] *Jevrejski Almanah* n.s. 1968–70, 9–17.

Kadima. [Journal of Jewish Youth.] Belgrade: Savez Jevrejskih Opština Jugoslavije.

———. 1970. "Za Kadimu Govori Enriko Josif." 23:17–19.

———. 1977. "Naša polemika: Jevrejin ili ne? 38:2–4.

———. 1986. "Glas Ane Šomlo." 47:61–68.

Kaplan, M. 1991. *The Making of the Jewish Middle Class: Women, Family, and Identity in Imperial Germany*. New York: Oxford University Press.

Katz, S.T. 1992. *Historicism, the Holocaust, and Zionism. Critical Studies in Modern Jewish Thought and History*. New York and London: New York University Press.

Keyes, C.F. 1976. "Toward a New Formulation of the Concept of Ethnic Group." *Ethnicity* 3:202–213.

Kertzer, D. 1988. *Ritual, Politics, and Power*. New Haven and London: Yale University Press.

Kiš, D. 1985. *Homo Poeticus. Essays and Interviews*. Edited and an Introduction by Susan Sontag. New York: Farrar, Straus and Giroux.

Kokosalakis, N. 1982. *Ethnic Identity and Religion: Tradition and Change in Liverpool Jewry*. Lanham, MD: University Press of America.

Koš, E. 1976. "Djelatnost KPJ u Oblasti Kulturi." [Activity of the CPY in the Field of Culture.] In *Sarajevo u Revoluciji*, ed. N. Albahari, 189–196. Sarajevo: Istorijski Arhiv.

Kovač, T. 1975. "Neka Sećanja na Hašomer Hacair Prvih Meseci Okupacije u Novom Sadu." [Some Memories of Hashomer Hatzair During the First Months of the Occupation in Novi Sad.] *Zbornik* 3:213–222. Belgrade: Savez Jevrejskih Opština Jugoslavije.

Kovačević, B. 1959–1960. "O Jevrejima u Srbiji od XVIII do Početka XX Veka." [On the Jews in Serbia From the 18th to the Beginning of the 20th Century.] *Jevrejski Almanah*, n.s., 105–112.

Krušelj, Z. 1990. "Židovi u Jugoslaviji. Otvaranja Starih Rana." [The Jews in Yugoslavia. The Opening of Old Wounds.] *Danas* 3 April.

Kugelmass, J. 1988. "Introduction." *Between Two Worlds: Ethnographic Essays on American Jewry*, ed. J. Kugelmass, 1–29. Ithaca and London: Cornell University Press.

Lane, C. 1981. *The Rites of Rulers and Ritual in Industrial Society in the Soviet Case*. Cambridge: Cambridge University Press.

Lass, A. 1988. "Romantic Documents and Political Monuments: The Meaning-Fulfillment of History in 19th Century Czech Nationalism." *American Ethnologist* 15(3):456–471.

Lavender, A.D. 1981. "Arabic-Islamic and Spanish-Mediterranean Influences on 'The Jewish Mind': A Comparison to European-Christian Influence." *Journal of Ethnic Studies* 8(4):25–35.

Leach, E. 1954. *Political Systems of Highland Burma*. Cambridge: Harvard University Press.

Lebl, Ž. 1990. *Ljubičica Bela. Vic Dug Dve i Po Godine*. [The White Violet. A Two and a Half Year Old Joke.] Novi Sad: Dečje Novine.

Levi, A. 1954. "Spomenici Jevrejima i Žrtvama Fašizma." [Monuments to the Jews and Victims of Fascism.] *Jevrejski Almanah*, n.s., 117–120.

———. 1989. "Ponovo Zajedno." [Together Again.] *Zavičaj* 342–343 (March–April): 20–21.

Levi, M. 1969 [1926]. *Sefardi u Bosni*. [The Sephardim in Bosnia.] Belgrade: Savez Jevrejskih Opština Jugoslavije.

Levi, S. 1983. "Struktura i Karakteristike Naše Jevrejske Zajednice Danas: Starosna Struktura, Mešoviti Brakovi i Deca iz Tih Brakova, Podmladak." [The Structure and Characteristics of Our Jewish Community Today: Age Structure, Mixed Marriages and Children from Those Marriages.] Unpublished Paper, Belgrade.

Levi-Strauss, C. 1966. *The Savage Mind*. Chicago: University of Chicago Press.

Levntal, Z., ed. 1957. *The Crimes of the Fascist Occupants and Their Collaborators Against Jews in Yugoslavia*. Belgrade: Federation of Jewish Communities of Federative People's Republic of Yugoslavia.

Liebman, S.B. 1975. "Sephardic Ethnicity in the Spanish New World." *Jewish Social Studies* 37 (2):146.

Lifton, R.J. 1968. *Revolutionary Immortality: Mao Tse-tung and the Chinese Revolution*. New York: Random House.

———. 1993. *The Protean Self: Human Resilience in an Age of Fragmentation*. New York: Basic Books.

Loker, Z. 1976. "The Jewish Volunteers in the Spanish Civil War." *Soviet Jewish Affairs* 6 (2): 71–82.

———. 1977. "Radicalism, Heroism, Martyrdom." *Jewish Quarterly Review* 68 (2):104–116.

Longinović, T. 1996. "Afterword. Words and Things: David Albahari's Prose in the Context of the Former Yugoslavia." In D. Albahari. *Words Are Something Else*, 207–215. Evanston, IL: Northwestern University Press.

Lowie, R. 1954. *Toward Understanding Germany*. Chicago: University of Chicago Press.

Lyon, D. 1985. *The Steeple's Shadow: On the Myths and Realities of Secularization*. Grand Rapids, MI: Eerdmans.

———. 1988. "Secularization: Processes and Interpretations." In *Social Science in Christian Perspective*, eds. P. Marshall and R.E. Vander-

Vennan, 129–152. Lanham, New York and London: University Press of America.

MacAloon, J.J., ed. 1984. *Rite, Drama, Festival, Spectacle. Rehearsals Toward a Theory of Cultural Performance*. Philadelphia: Institute for the Study of Human Issues.

———. 1984. "Introduction: Cultural Performance, Cultural Theory." In *Rite, Drama, Festival, Spectacle. Rehearsals Toward a Theory of Cultural Performance*, ed. J.J. MacAloon. Philadelphia: Institute for the Study of Human Issues, Inc.

MacIntyre, A. 1984. *After Virtue*. Notre Dame, IN: Notre Dame University Press.

Magnusson, K. 1987. "Secularization of Ideology: the Yugoslav Case." In *Symbols of Power: the Esthetics of Political Legitimation in the Soviet Union and Eastern Europe*, eds. C. Arvidsson and L.E. Blomqvist, 73–84.

Malisić, V. 1989. "Cankarjev Dom u Francuskoj Sedam." [Cankarjev Hall in Francuskoj 7.] *Duga* 18–31 March, 36–39.

Malkki, L. 1995. *Purity and Exile*. Chicago and London: University of Chicago Press.

Mandić, K. Interview with Klara Mandić. "U Ime Oba Moja Naroda." [In the Name of Both of My Peoples.] *Radio TV Revija* (Belgrade), March 1989, 30–31.

Matić, S. 1993. "Pijetet Samo Žrtvama." [Paying Homage Only to the Victims.] *Danas* (Zagreb), 2 November 1993, 7.

Matthews, G. 1996. *What Makes Life Worth Living? How Japanese and Americans Make Sense of Their Worlds*. Berkeley: University of California Press.

Matvejević, P. 1988. "Danilo Kiš: Encyclopedia of the Dead." *Cross Currents* 7: 337–349. Ann Arbor: University of Michigan.

Meeks, W. 1993. *The Origins of Christian Morality: The First Two Centuries*. New Haven: Yale University Press.

Meyer, M.A. 1990. *Jewish Identity in the Modern World*. Seattle: University of Washington Press.

Milić, R. 1989. "Vek Srpskog-Jevrejskog Prijateljstva." [A Century of Serbian-Jewish Friendship. Interviews with Tadić, Popović, Gams, Josif, Medenica.] *Student*, 14 April.

Miller, R.F. 1989. "Theoretical and Ideological Issues of Reform in Socialist Systems: Some Yugoslav and Soviet Examples. *Soviet Studies* 49 (3):430–448.

Mirč, M. 1957–1958. "Jevreji na Balkanskom Poluostrvu i u Staroj Srpskoj Državi do Dolaska Jevreja." [Jews on the Balkan Peninsula in the Old Serbian State until the Arrival of the Jews.] *Jevrejski Almanah* n.s., 49–58.

Moerman, M. 1965. "Ethnic Identification in a Complex Society: Who are the Lue?" *American Anthropologist* 67:1215.

Moore, S.F., and B. Myerhoff. 1977. "Introduction: Forms and Meanings." In *Secular Ritual*, eds. S. Moore and B. Myerhoff, 3–24. Amsterdam: Van Gorcum.

Mošić, A. 1987. "I Mi Jugoslovenski Jevreji Ličimo na Ostale Jugoslaveni." [We Yugoslav Jews Also Resemble Other Yugoslavs.] *Jevrejski Pregled* 5–8:45.

Mosse, G. 1980. *Toward the Final Solution. A History of European Racism.* Madison: University of Wisconsin Press.

Myerhoff, B. 1977. "We Don't Wrap Herring in a Printed Page: Fusion, Fictions and Continuity in Secular Ritual." In *Secular Ritual*, eds. S. Moore and B. Myerhoff, 199–224. Amsterdam: Van Gorcum.

———. 1978. *Number Our Days*. New York: Dutton.

———. 1986. ""Life Not Death in Venice": Its Second Life." In *The Anthropology of Experience*, eds. V. Turner and E. Bruner, 261–286. Urbana and Chicago: University of Illinois Press.

Nagata, J. 1974. "What is a Malay? Situational Selection of Ethnic Identity in a Plural Society." *American Ethnologist* 1:331–350.

Naroll, R. 1964. "Ethnic Unit Classification." *Current Anthropology* 5:282–312.

Naša Reč [Our Word. A Serbian emigre magazine. London.] 1988. "Committee for the Defense of Freedom of Thought and Expression." 412:11.

Neal, F.W. 1984. "Yugoslav Approaches to the Nationalities Problem: The Politics of Circumvention." *East European Quarterly* 18 (3):327–334.

Nešović, S. 1968. *Moša Pijade i Njegovo Vreme*. [Moša Pijade and His Time.] Belgrade: Prosveta; Ljubljana: Mladinska Knjiga.

———. 1994. Personal Communication. Belgrade.

Nikolić, M. 1989. "Jevreji i Nacionalno Pitanje. Antisemitizam u Jugoslaviji. [The Jews and the National Question. Antisemitism in Yugoslavia.] *NIN* (Belgrade), 15 October, 30–33.

NIN (Belgrade).

———. 1988. "Čija je Naša Svojina?" [Interview with Andrija Gams.] 24 January, 15–17.

———. "Politika. Ikonografija i Tito." [Politics. Iconography and Tito.] *NIN*, 1 October 1989, 21–23.

———. "Jevreji sa Jugoslovenskim Uspomena." [Jews with Yugoslav Memories.] 19 November 1989, 57–58.

———. "Jugo-Jevreji. Egzodus?" [Yugo-Jews. Exodus?] 2 April 1993, 30.

Nixon, R. 1993. "Of Balkans and Bantustans." *Transition* 60:4–26.

Nova Hrvatska. 1989. [New Croatia. A Croatian emigre magazine. London.] "Opovrgnuta licitacija Jasenovcem."10, 21 May.

Obeyesekere, G. 1982. "After "Medusa's Hair": Progression and Regression in Personal Symbols." Lecture I in The Lewis Henry Morgan Lectures, University of Rochester, New York.

O'Meara, J. T. 1989. "Anthropology as Empirical Science." *American Anthropologist* 9(2):354–369.

Orbach, A. 1993. Personal Communication.

Oren, U. 1971. *A Town Called Monastir*. Translated by Mark Segal. Tel Aviv: Dror Publications.

Ortner, S. 1973. "On Key Symbols." *American Anthropologist* 75(7):1338–1346.

Papo, I. 1983. "Sjećanje na Tri Decenije Života u Našoj Porodici (1915–1945)." [Memories of Three Decades of Life in Our Family (1915–1945).] Unpublished Paper.

Papo, J. 1988. "Ponovom u Svom Gradu." [Back in My City.] In *Sarajevo u Socijalističkoj Jugoslaviji*, ed. N. Albahari, 45–48. Sarajevo: Istorijski Arhiv.

Parkin, D. 1974. "Congregational and Interpersonal Ideologies in Political Ethnicity." In *Urban Ethnicity*, ed. A. Cohen, 119–157. London: Tavistock.

Pasic, N. 1989. "In Search of the True Number of World War II Victims in Yugoslavia." *Serbian Studies* 5(1):65–81.

Pavlović, M. 1986. "Ovaj Zemlji je Potrebna Himna (2). Muza Medju Mitraljezima." [This Country Needs a Hymn (2).] *Duga* (Belgrade), 27 June, 73–77.

Peel, J.D.Y. 1989. "The Cultural Work of Yoruba Ethnogenesis." In *History and Ethnicity*, eds. E. Tonkin, M. McDonald, M. Chapman, 198–215. London and New York: Routledge.

Perera, D. 1968–1970. "Neki Statistički Podaci o Jevrejima u Jugoslaviji u Periodu od 1938 do 1965 godine." [Some Statistics on Jews in Yugoslavia in the Period from 1938 to 1965.] *Jevrejski Almanah* n.s., 135–147.

Perić, M. 1970. *Jevrejski Pregled* 5–6 :21.

———. 1972. "Prvi Rezultati Našeg Demografskog Istraživanja" [First Results of Our Demographic Research]. *Jevrejski Pregled* 23(11–12): 2–7.

———. 1973. "Dalnji Rezultati Našeg Demografskog Istraživanja" [Further Results of Our Demographic Research]. *Jevrejski Pregled* 24(1–2): 16–21; 24(3–4): 31–34; 24(5–6): 3–7; 24(7–8):3–6.

———. 1980. "Demographic Study of the Jewish Community of Yugoslavia, 1971–1972." In *Papers in Jewish Demography, 1973*, eds. U.O. Schmelz, P. Glikson, and S. Della Pergola. Jerusalem: Institute of Contemporary Jewry.

Perlmutter, F. 1973. "The Jewish Community of Yugoslavia." *Jewish Journal of Communal Service* 49(4):297–302.

Petrović, A. 1982. "Sacred Sephardi Chants in Bosnia." *Intercultural Music Studies* 3:35–48.

Petrović, N. 1989. "Povodom Smrti Danila Kiša" [On the Occasion of the Death of Danilo Kiš]. *Naša Reč* (London) 410, 12.

Pinto, A. 1987. *Jevreji Sarajeva i Bosne i Hercegovine*. [The Jews of Sarajevo and Bosnia and Hercegovina.] Sarajevo: Veselin Masleša.

Pinto, A. and D. Pinto. 1972. *Dokumenti o Stradanja Jevreja u Logorima NDH*. Sarajevo: Jevrejska Opština Sarajeva.

———. 1974. *Stradanja Sarajevskih Jevreja Pod Ustaškom Režimom*. Sarajevo: Jevrejska Opština Sarajeva.

Pinto, S. 1954. "Položaj Bosanskih Jevreja Pod Turskom Vladavinom." [The Position of the Bosnian Jews Under Turkish Rule.] *Jevrejski Almanah*, n.s., 48–59.

Plotnicov, L. and M. Silverman. 1978. "Jewish Ethnic Signalling: Social Bonding in Contemporary American Society." *Ethnology* 17(4):407–423.

Polanyi, M. 1958. *Personal Knowledge: Towards a Post-Critical Philosophy*. Chicago: University of Chicago Press.

Politika. 1989. "Aleksandar Mošić o Zloupotrebi Davidove Zvezde na Skupu u Ljubljani. Žrtvama se ne Može Podvaliti." 2 March.

Politika Ekspres. 1989. [Interview with Aleksandar Mošić.] April.

Presburger, J. 1975. "Oficiri Jevreji u Zarobljeničkim Logorima u Nemackoj." [Jewish Officers in Prisoner-of-War Camps in Germany.] *Zbornik* 3:225–275.

Priest, R. 1987. In *Current Concerns of Anthropologists and Missionaires*, ed. Karl Franklin. Dallas, TX: International Museum of Cultures.

———. 1993. "Missionary Elenctics: Conscience and Culture." *Missiology: An International Review* 22(3):291–315.

Radio Free Europe Research Reports, 11 November, 1988, 6. [Committee for the Defense of Freedom of Thought and Expression.] Cited in *Naša Reč* 412:11.

Ramet, P. 1985. "Apocalypse Culture and Social Change in Yugoslavia." In *Yugoslavia in the 1980s*, ed. P. Ramet. Boulder and London: Westview Press.

Rapoport, N. 1993. "Text, Language, and the Hope of Redemption." In *The Writer in the Jewish Community: An Israeli-North American Dialogue*, eds. Richard Siegel and Tamar Sofer, 41–44. Rutherford, NJ: Fairleigh Dickinson University Press.

Rhee, S. N. 1973. "Jewish Assimilation: The Case of the Chinese Jews." *Comparative Studies in Society and History* 15(1):115–126.

Rheubottom, D. 1985. "The Seed of Evil Within." In *The Anthropology of Evil*, ed. David Parkin, 77–91. Oxford: B. Blackwell.

Richtman-Auguštin, D. 1991. "The Metamorphosis of Festivals in a Socialist Country." *Ethnologia Europaea* 20(2):97–106.

Romano, J. 1980. *Jevreji Jugoslavije 1941–1945. Žrtve Genocida i Ucešnici Narodnooslobodilačkog Rata [The Jews of Yugoslavia 1941–1945.* Victims of Genocide and Participants in the National Liberation War.] Belgrade: Jevrejski Istorijski Muzej, Savez Jevrejskih Opština Jugoslavije.

Rosaldo, R. 1988. "Ideology, Place, and People Without Culture." *Cultural Anthropology* 3(1):77–87.

Rothschild, J. 1993. *Return to Diversity: A Political History of East Central Europe Since World War II*, 2nd edition. New York: Oxford University Press.

Royce, A. 1981. *Ethnic Identity: Strategies of Diversity*. Bloomington: Indiana University Press.

Rusinow, D. 1977. *The Yugoslav Experiment, 1948–1974*. Berkeley: University of California Press.

———, ed. 1989. *Yugoslavia, a Fractured Federalism*. Washington: Wilson Center Press.

Savishinsky, J.S., and H. Wimberley. 1974. "The Living and the Dead: A Cross-Cultural Perspective on Jewish Memorial Observances." *Jewish Social Studies* 36:281–300.

Scaglion, R. 1993. Personal Communication.

Schaeffer, F. 1968. *Escape from Reason*. Lecester: Inter-Varsity Press.

Schatz, J. 1991. *The Generation: The Rise and Fall of the Jewish Communists of Poland*. Berkeley: University of California Press.

Schwartz, S. 1990. "Yo Soy Una Rosa: I am a Rose. Bosnian Jewry's Present and Past." *Journal of Croatian Studies* 31: 151–175.

———. 1992. Personal Communication, December 1992.

Sekelj, L. 1980. "Anti-Semitism in Yugoslavia, 1918–1945." *East European Quarterly* 22(2):59–172.

———. 1991. "Obračun kod Davidove Zvezda." *Borba*, 24–25 August.

———. 1992. "Podlistak Vremena. Slobodna Upotreba Jevreja. Antisemitizam u Jugoslaviji" [Feuilleton of the Times. The Free Use of the Jews. Antisemitism in Yugoslavia]. *Vreme*, 31 August, 50–54.

———. 1994. "Budučnost je Počela?" *NIN*, 2 September, 18.

Sharot, S., and H. Ayalon and E. Ben-Rafael. 1986. "Secularization and the Diminishing Decline of Religion." *Review of Religious Research* 27(3):193–207.

Shils, E. 1957. "Primordial, Personal, Sacred and Civil Ties." *British Journal of Sociology* 8:130–145.

Sholem, G. 1971. *The Messianic Idea in Judaism*. New York: Schocken Books.

Shweder, R. and R.A. LeVine. 1984. *Culture Theory: Essays on Mind, Self and Emotion. Cambridge; NY: Cambridge University Press.*

Sindik, D., ed. 1972. "Sećanja Jevreja Na Logor Jasenovac." [Jewish Memories of Jasenovac.] Belgrade: Savez Jevrejskih Opština Jugoslavije.

Sion, I. 1985. "Jevreji Štipa u Miru i Ratu." [The Jews of Štip in Peace and War.] Paper read at the meeting of the Coordinating Committee of the Women's Sections of the Federation of Jewish Communities of Yugoslavia, Skopje.

Sitton, D. 1985. "Meeting in Sarajevo on the 400th Anniversary of the Bosnian Community." In *Sephardic Communities Today* (translated from Hebrew), 245–250. Jerusalem: Council of Sephardi and Oriental Communities.

Skopje-Sarajevo 1966. 1966. Belgrade: Savez Jevrejskih Opština Jugoslavije.

Šlang, I. 1926. *Jevreji u Beogradu*. [The Jews in Belgrade]. Belgrade: M. Karić.

Smith, A.D. 1991. "State and Peoples: Ethnic Nationalisms in Multi-Ethnic Societies." *Soviet Jewish Affairs* 21(1):7–21.

Šomlo, A. 1985. *Glasovi Dijaspore*. [Voices of the Diaspora]. Belgrade: Književne Novine.

Spicer, E. 1971. "Persistent Cultural Systems." Science 174 (19 November):795–800.

Spomenica Savez Jevrejskih Opština Jugoslavije, 1919–1969. 1970. [Commemorative Volume of the Federation of Jewish Communities of Yugoslavia, 1919–1969.] Belgrade: Savez Jevrejskih Opština Jugoslavije.

Spomenica 400 Godina od Dolaska Jevreja u Bosnu i Hercegovinu, 1566–1966. 1966. [Commemorative Volume of the Four Hundredth Anniversary of the Arrival of Jews in Bosnia and Hercegovina, 1566–1966]. Sarajevo: Odbor za Proslavu 400-Godišnjice Dolaska Jevreja u Bosnu i Hercegovinu, Oslobodjenje.

Štajner, A. 1968–1970. "Jehuda Haj Alkalaj (1798–1878)." *Jevrejski Almanah*, n.s., 55–56.

Starr, R. 1982. "Socialist Federated Republic of Yugoslavia." *Communist Regimes in Eastern Europe*, fifth edition, 221–259. Stanford, CA: Stanford University, Hoover Institution Press.

Stromberg, P. 1986. *Symbols of Community: The Cultural System of a Swedish Church*. Tucson: University of Arizona Press.

Sveske 7–8. 1984. "Stvaralaštvo Jevreja u Kulturnoj Baštini i Razvoju Bosne i Hercegovine." Sarajevo: Institute for the Study of National Relations, Marxist Study Center of CK SKBiH.

Sugar, P.F. 1969. *Nationalism in Eastern Europe*. Seattle: University of Washington Press.

Szalat, A. n.d. *Il Suffit d'une minute pour traverser un siecle*. Unpublished, unproduced screenplay. Quoted in J. Boyarin 1991, 173.

Tadić, L. 1989. "O Prijateljstvu i Mržnji." [On Friendship and Hatred.] Paper read at the first official (public) meeting of the Society for Serbian-Jewish Friendship, March, Belgrade.

Tanašić, D. 1989. "Čas Himničkog Iskupljenja." Prva Zvanična Skupština Društva Srpsko-Jevrejskog Prijateljstva" [The Moment of Hymn-like Redemption. The First Official Meeting of the Society of Serbian-Jewish Friendship]. *Intervju* (Belgrade), 17 March, 46–48.

Taylor, P.A. 1987. "The Celebration of Heroes Under Communism: On Honors and the Reproduction of Inequality." *American Sociological Review* 52(2).

Tišma, A. 1988. *The Use of Man*. Translated by Bernnar Johnson. San Diego: Harcourt Brace Jovanovich.

———. 1980. *Knjiga o Blama.* Belgrade: Nolit.

Tuden, A. Personal Communication.

Tudjman, F. 1981. *Nationalism in Contemporary Europe.* Boulder, CO: East European Monographs.

———. 1990. *Bespuća Povijesne Zbilnosti.* Zagreb: Nakladni Zavod Matice Hrvatske.

Turner, V. 1962. *Chihamba, The White Spirit: A Ritual Drama of the Ndembu.* Manchester: Published on behalf of the Rhodes-Livingstone Institute by the Manchester University Press; New York: Humanities Press.

———. 1969. *The Ritual Process.* Chicago: Aldine.

———. 1978. "Foreword." In *Number Our Days.* New York: Dutton.

———. 1982. *Celebration, Studies in Festivity and Ritual.* Washington, D.C.: Smithsonian Institution Press.

———. 1984. "Liminality and the Peformative Genres." In *Rite, Drama, Festival, Spectacle,* ed. J.J. MacAloon, 19–41. Philadelphia: Institute for the Study of Human Issues, Inc.

200 Godina Židova u Zagrebu: Referati i Govori sa Proslave 180-Godišnjice Jevrejske Općine Zagreb. 1980. [200 Years of Jews in Zagreb: Articles and Speeches from the Celebration of the 180th Anniversary of the Jewish Community of Zagreb.] Zagreb: Jevrejska Općina Zagreba and Savez Jevrejskih Opština Jugoslavije.

Vajs, A. 1954. "Jevreji u Novoj Jugoslaviji." [Jews in the New Yugoslavia.] *Jevrejski Almanah,* n.s., 5–47.

———. 1955–1956. "Na Kraju Prve i na Početku Druge Decenije." [At the End of the First and the Beginning of the Second Decade.] *Jevrejski Almanah,* n.s., 7–16.

Verdery, K. 1991. "Theorizing Socialism: A Prologue to the "Transition."" *American Ethnologist* 18 (3):419–439.

———. 1993a. "Nationalism and National Sentiment in Post-socialist Romania." *Slavic Review* 52(2):179–203.

———. 1993b. "Whither "Nation" and "Nationalism"? *Daedalus* 122(3): 37–46.

———. 1996. Invited Lecture, University of Pittsburgh.

Vinaver, V. 1955–1956. "Jevreji u Srbiji Početkom XIX Veka." [Jews in Serbia at the Beginning of the 19th Century.] *Jevrejski Almanah,* n.s., 28–34.

Volf, M. 1996. *Exclusion and Embrace: A Theological Exploration of Identity, Otherness, and Reconciliation*. Nashville: Abingdon Press.

Watson, J. 1974. "Restaurants and Remittances: Chinese Emigrant Workers in London." In *Anthropologists in Cities*, eds. G. Foster and R.V. Kemper, 201–222. Boston: Little, Brown and Co.

Weiss, L. 1990. "Stara Bolest u Novim Vremena." [An Old Sickness in New Times.] *Danas* (Zagreb) 22 May, 54.

———. 1990. "Trg Žrtava Fašizma Ostaje Za Nas Trg Žrtava Fašizma." [The Square of Victims of Fascism Remains for Us the Square of Victims of Fascism.] *Bilten* (JOZ) 16: 3.

———. 1990. "Neizbrisivi Tragovi Duha. Razgovori: Mr. Nenad Porges." [The Indelible Tracks of the Spirit. Conversations: Mr. Nenad Porges.] *Danas* (Zagreb), 11 November, 39–41.

West, R. 1982 [1940]. *Black Lamb and Grey Falcon, A Journey Through Yugoslavia*. New York: Penguin.

Wilson, R. 1994. *Maya Resurgence in Guatemala. Q'eqchi' Experiences*. Norman and London: University of Oklahoma Press.

Zapisnik. [Minutes.] 1984 (26 May); 1989 (2 February; 16 March).Belgrade: Savez Jevrejskih Opština Jugoslavije,

Zenner, W.P. 1978. "Jewish Communities as Cultural Units." In *Perspectives on Ethnicity*, ed. Serghei A. Arutiunov, 327–338. The Hague: Mouton.

———, ed. 1988. *Persistence and Flexibility: Anthropological Perspectives on the American Jewish Experience*. Albany: State University of New York Press.

Zimmels, H. J. 1958. *Ashkenazim and Sephardim: Their Relationships, Differences and Problems as Reflected in the Rabbinical Responsa*. London: Oxford University Press.

Zukin, S. 1975. *Beyond Marx and Tito: Theory and Practice in Yugoslav Socialism*. London and New York: Cambridge University Press.

INDEX

Age: and movement to the left, 61; and synagogue attendance, 72; group celebration of Rosh Hashanah, 191; structure, 17, 71, 75–76, 228; survey data by, 185–188, 229–230

Albahari, David, 439n.2, 39, 267, 271, 272, 273–278, 342, 359–362

Albanians, 6, 280, 374, 382, 383, 384

Andrić, Ivo, 274, 438n.5,

Alter, R., 204, 255, 272, 277, 339

Anniversary celebrations, 112, 159, 159–173, 441n.11, 183, 325. *See also* Performance(s)

Antisemitism, 118, 316; rise of nationalism and, 279; before World War II, 56, 60, 67; fighting against, 278, 282, 358, 371–373, 376–378, 384; in Croatia, 381, 396; in Serbia, 267, 279–280, 358, 393; in socialist Yugoslavia, 278; proverb about, 231

Arabs, 8, 113, 143, 144, 256, 289, 361, 376

Ashkenazi Jews: arrival and settlement of, 26–28; and Sephardi Jews, 13, 225, 239, 241–244; assimilationist tendencies of Neologues, 337; class statuses of, 318; in Subotica, 229–231; naming custom of, 214

Atheism, 185, 186, 198, 224, 229, 230, 242, 259, 279, 264, 270, 316

Balkan Jews, 22–26, 30–32

Barth, F., 411, 416–417

Baruh family, 52, 58, 133–134, 290

Bauman, Z., 417

Becker, E., 205, 350

Belgrade, 239, 256, 283, 331, 354; Ashkenazi and Sephardi relations in, 242–243; commemoration in, 192–193; Dorćol, 42, 220–228, 233–240; ethnic cleansing in, 10; Jewish Historical Museum in, 332; Jews of, 25–26, 34, 42, 80, 153–154, 303; markers of Jewish life in, xiii; Passover Seder, 192, 330; Sephardi milieu and culture in, 245–247; synagogue, 150, 189, 190–191; under the Ottomans and Habsburgs, 9, 31, 42

Beller, S., 442n.13

Bentley, G. C., 425–426

Berger, P., xvi, 37, 181, 184, 204, 340, 415, 424

Bible, 35, 246, 287; and (or as) revelation, 302–315, 342; and reckoning descent, 288; as authority and basis of belief, 343; eschatological passages in, 302, 344
Borba, 133, 372, 384
Bosnia, 5, 6, 24, 28, 29, 171–173, 248, 273, 280; Jews of, 165, 239, 247–252
Boundary, 11, 12, 196, 225, 242, 267
Boyarin, J., xiv, 207, 208, 210, 339, 418
Bricolage, xiv, 204, 207–212, 251, 292
Bringa, T., 248, 443n.1
Brotherhood and unity, 5, 143, 151, 324, 356, 358, 371, 378, 383, 389; as created by Tito, 121; as a cultural construction, 109, 116, 138, 146; as guiding paradigm of the Sarajevo anniversary celebration, 162–166; as inheritance, 157; as Partisan War rallying slogan, 120; securing a place in, 140, 176; as the solution to the National Question, 104, 111–112, 123, 136, 165; as summarizing symbol, 100–102; within the Yugoslav Jewish population, 164
Browning, C., 438n.2, 103, 353, 354
Bulgarian Jews, 30–32. *See also* Haskell, Guy
Burial society, 44, 225. *See also* Hevra Kaddisha

Calendar, Jewish, 185, 189–194, 213, 220, 232–233, 340, 345; of socialist Yugoslavia, 141, 147, 149–152
Cantor, 233, 236, 237, 238, 340
Catholic, Roman, 3, 6, 7, 27, 150, 197–198, 231, 254, 256, 299, 301, 319, 328
Cemetery, 167, 194, 221–227, 236, 273, 381
Census, 69, 86–89, 197, 318, 379
Chernobyl, 311–312, 315
Chetniks, 281, 335, 401
Chinese Jews, 36, 114
Christianity, 6, 28, 173, 267, 301, 303, 313
Christians, 24, 31, 242, 258, 267, 298, 299, 300–301, 312, 313. *See also* Catholic
Circumcision, 244, 263, 267, 268, 269
Class: and prewar movement to the left, 52, 54, 58, 62, 64; interpretation of history: shaking apart the, 304–306; substituting the nationalist for the, 398; leveling in socialist Yugoslavia, 72, 85, 231; priority of the dilemma of being over the dilemma of, 305; structure of Jewish communities before World War I, 26, 28, 54, 57, 59, 82, 215, 231
Clifford, J., 413, 428
Cohen, Abner, 206, 208, 373, 411, 420, 423–425
Cohen, Anthony, 33, 340
Collapse of socialist Yugoslavia, 347, 348, 349, 355–358, 380, 382, 406
Comaroff, J., 4, 414
Commemoration, 134, 138, 141, 145–147, 213, 235, 273, 401; categories, 86, 134, 138, 145–146, 151, 154; cycle, 148, 151, 153–154, 174; fixed order, 124, 153–159; objects, 103, 125, 128, 132, 133–135, 145, 149, 159; participants, 124, 153; phases, 138; rites and ceremonies, 148,

155; sites, 10, 16, 144, 149, 192–193; speeches, 154–158, 164–165; Year of, 149, 154. *See also* Memorialism
Communism, 37, 254, 257, 303, 304; belief in the future of, 334; fall of, 280; Jewish flight from, 175; Tito's brand of, 137
Communist Party, 8, 97; as authority, 341; as summarizing symbol, 100, 123, 125; attraction of, 59, 60, 64; beyond criticism of, 373; claims of moral superiority, 356; criticism of, 362–363; illegal, 53, 54, 60; Jews in the Central Committee of, 94, 116; leaving or refusing to join, 300, 320–321; membership in, 52, 54, 62, 65–66, 92, 99, 101, 114, 108, 117–118, 170, 216, 218, 237, 317, 320–321, 326; representatives in commemorations, 152
Constitution, 8, 119, 364
Contestation, 3, 380; contested histories, 350; contested images, 388, 389; contested symbols, 351, 355, 373, 381, 398. *See also* Symbols
Counting of the dead, 398, 399
Conversion, 217, 262–263, 267–268, 269, 342–343
Covenant, 34, 35, 308, 314
Cycles of Jewish life, 112, 151–152, 189–195

Dahrendorf, R., 422
Danforth, L., 7, 350, 353
Danon, Cadik, 117, 118, 441n.10, 169, 189, 193, 194. *See also* Rabbi of Yugoslavia
David, Filip, 272, 278–283, 391, 407
Davidman, L., 181–182
Death: as private symbol of Jewishness, 345; as the boundary of Jewishness, 225; and destruction in Jewish history, 109, 269; commemorative focus on, 145–148, 183, 339; experience of being close to, 304; stage in life cycle, 194, 220; and remembrance, 226; symbolic forms of, 204, 235; theme in Jewish writing, 270, 272; Tito's, 100, 121, 131–132, 151, 152, 334
Defilement, 349, 351
Demography. *See* Population
Denitch, B., 99, 356, 357, 358
Descent, 338, 345; continuity of, 232; data, postwar, 80; hidden and revealed, 252, 259, 261, 339; individual choice in reckoning, 89, 287–288, 328, 341; insufficiency of, 333, 345; mixed or fragmented, 48, 81, 201–202, 228, 254, 274; reckoning in Yugoslavia, 88–89; religion as marker of, 32; vagueness of, 263–264; without dilemmas, 47, 290, 337
Despres, L., 411, 420
Diaspora, 9, 35, 42, 247, 249, 284, 308, 336
Disjuncture, xiv, xv, 202, 207, 213, 223, 338, 339
Djakovo, 124–126, 138, 141, 149, 155, 156–159. *See* Commemoration
Dorćol, xiii, 26; child of, 220–228. *See also* Belgrade
Dragnich, A., 440n.6
Drakulić, S., 351, 402–405
Dramaturgical discipline, 96, 143–145
Dramaturgical performance, 96, 138–139, 349, 379
Drašković, Vuk, 387
Dumont, J., xiv

Elaborating symbols, 102–103, 358, 359
Elite, 8, 19, 116, 214, 357, 359, 380
Emigration, 68, 77
Enemies of the state, 99
Epistemological dilemmas, 201, 263, 275
Epistemological framework, 16–18
Eschatology, 303, 344, 345
Ethnic cleansing, 2, 10, 248, 282, 350, 354
Ethnic map, 3, 10
Ethnic nationalism. *See* Nationalism
Ethnogenesis, 32–33
Ethnographic reality, 10–12, 18, 203, 211, 212
Exilic condition, 36
Experience, transcendent, 301–302, 306–307
Exogamy, 78–80

Family, 75, 207, 217, 226, 231, 233, 273, 337, 379; absence of the specifically Jewish, 18–19, 39, 78, 85–86, 197, 219, 234, 249–251, 254, 285, 291–293, 299, 327, 332–333, 341; and life path, 58, 255, 292; Baruh, 52, 58, 133–134, 290–291; cultural models in the, 223; in Israel, 321; loss of, 78–81, 106, 241–242, 249, 286, 369; pre-World War II, 46–50, 222, 241, 249; secularization of, 197; stories, 242–247, 254–255, 276–277, 340
Fallen fighters, 140, 146
Fascism, 60, 67
Federation of Jewish Communities of Yugoslavia, 11, 72, 84, 140, 162, 360, 361, 369, 370, 372, 373, 374, 375, 376, 377, 378, 379, 383, 384, 394, 399, 400, 403
Final Solution, 103, 353
Finestein, I., 195
Fortes, M., 202, 232, 233
Fragmentation, 210, 202, 204, 205, 206, 207, 207–212, 338, 406–407, 374, 376, 378
Freidenreich, H. P., 9, 438n.2, 25–29, 32–33, 41, 42, 43, 45–46, 47, 52, 55–56, 57, 58, 60, 62–63, 440n.8, 64, 65, 83
Funerals, 118, 194, 224, 225, 227, 236, 269, 399
Furlan, Mira, 351, 403–405, 443n.7

Gams, Andrija, 65, 362–364
Gatekeepers of tradition, 68, 71, 81
Geertz, C., 437n.1, 352, 411, 415, 417
Generation(s): contrast between prewar and postwar, 68; of the Holocaust and NOB, 146; middle, 139, 212, 228, 232, 253; missing half-generation, 68, 76–77; post-Partisan, 117; progressive, 53, 62–63, 195; senior, 21, 51, 53, 56, 69, 75, 76, 87, 117, 172; youth, 61, 212, 263
Generational shift and fracture, 18, 43, 45, 51–54, 56, 61, 68–69, 195, 196
Genocide, 5, 39, 68, 103, 134, 141, 144, 147, 149, 197, 318, 353, 354, 355, 384, 393, 398, 401. *See also* Victims
Gladney, D., 419–420
Glazer, N., 411, 419
God, 180, 222, 247, 261, 269, 286, 299–302, 304, 305, 308, 309, 310, 311, 312, 313, 314, 315, 316, 342, 343, 344, 356, 387
Goffman, E., 96, 138, 140, 144
Goldmann, Nahum, 165
Goldstein, Ivo, 6, 440n.6, 353, 372, 397, 400

Goldstein, Slavko, 35, 439–440n.12, 316–326, 337, 342, 354, 371, 379, 395, 396, 398, 399
Goli Otok, 359, 365, 377. *See* also Naked Island
Gould, S. J., 394
Gypsies, 138, 144, 147, 342, 351, 401, 406, 407

Habsburg Empire, 9, 26, 27, 42, 45, 377
Halakhah, 52, 441n
Hammel, E., 3, 438n.3
Handelman, D., 137, 417
Hanukkah, 191
Harrison, S., 349
Hashomer Hatzair, 21, 43, 62, 440n.8, 65, 217, 336, 337
Haskell, G., 30–32
Hayden, R., 440n.7, 350, 356, 358, 362, 365, 398, 399
Hevra Kaddisha. *See* burial society
History: and identity, 1, 2, 18, 22, 352, 412–413, 444n.4, 429; biblical, 35, 240; construction and eradication of, 6, 18, 130, 136, 164, 197, 381, 398, 400, 401–402, 413–414; continuities and discontinuities in, 210, 277, 413; evil in, 414; imposition of external, 382, 431; Jewish, 2, 21, 23, 31, 34, 39, 97, 113, 146, 218, 266, 279, 300, 429; narrative conception of, 34, 414, 429; national(ist), 357, 398, 401, 402; of the Star of David, 385–386; personal, 206, 342, 358; secret, 364–370; two kinds of, 18, 21–22; Yugoslav, 23, 157, 339, 358, 399
Holidays, Jewish, 46–47, 83, 150, 185, 189, 190–192, 195
Holocaust, xiii, 18, 21, 39, 67, 136, 151, 156, 164, 180, 196, 212, 213, 227, 248, 255, 270, 327, 338, 339, 341, 418, 426
Identity: construction, 18, 348, 380, 399; crisis, 182; individual, 188, 189, 194, 422–424; transformation, 410
Imagined community, 109, 410
Immortality striving, 100, 205, 350, 380
Incorporation into socialist Yugoslavia, 103–109
Independent State of Croatia (NDH), 68, 354, 398, 399, 400, 402
Individuation, 201, 202–214, 285, 340
Integration, 50, 175–177
Invented tradition, 19, 91, 96, 97, 100
Islam, 6, 388
Israel: and Jewish identity, 278, 360; and Zionism, 63, 376; as paradigm, 313; as sacred land, 35, 58; being a Jew in, 337; in the Bible, 307–310, 314–315; Jews of Yugoslav origin in, 338, 376–377, 390, 394, 406; mazzah from, 194; on diplomatic relations with, 375–378, 390; postwar emigration to, 77, 113, 175, 197; radio broadcast from, 302; socialist Yugoslavia's politics toward, 113, 114, 132, 143, 315, 337, 375; speaking publicly in support of, 274, 359–360; street demonstrations against, 256, 274, 360; Star of David and, 385–386; symbolic association between Serbia and, 387–388; visits and longer stays in, 239, 256–257, 270, 302, 321, 328–329, 344

Jasenovac, 151, 152–153, 157, 351, 355, 373, 398, 400, 407
Jerusalem, 310, 312, 315, 387

Jewish calendar. *See* Calendar, Jewish
Jewish communal leaders, 51, 82, 91–96, 155, 175, 176, 180, 192, 193, 410
Jewish community, 2, 10, 12, 16, 18, 19, 434; local (opština, općina), 13, 50; membership, 13, 32, 70, 73, 77, 80, 90, 114, 435; organized, 11, 85, 86, 89, 91, 112, 198, 442n; secular, 76, 96
Jewish family, 39, 46–47, 58, 78, 79, 197, 437. *See also* Family
Jewish Historical Museum, 161, 167, 173
Jewish history. *See* History
Jewish writers, 270–273
Jewish Youth Movement, 53, 65
Judgment, moral, 348–350, 403–405

Kaddish, 138, 152, 153, 158, 170, 195, 213
Kadelburg, Lavoslav, 110, 113, 118, 164–165, 214–220, 370, 394, 399
Kashrut, 50, 194–195, 436
Katz, S., 207
Kertzer, D., 91
Key symbols, xvi, 19, 99–103, 120–121, 140–142, 352, 355, 358, 359, 364, 371, 400
Kipa, 152, 191, 195, 269, 327
Kiš, Danilo, 203, 272, 277, 344, 345, 350, 439n
Komšiluk, 248
Kosovo, 4, 6, 10, 73, 136, 280, 374, 382–385, 442n.3, 387–390, 393, 428
Knowledge, Jewish, 76, 186–187
Kugelmass, J., 120, 203, 207

Landscape, xiii, xv, xvi, 35
Language, 240, 283, 337, 342, 345, 350, 351, 384; of submergence, 123–132
Law, 32, 34, 52, 112, 131, 184; dietary, 184, 194; Halakhic, 183; movement away from Jewish, 184, 196
Lebl, Ženi, 438n.2, 364–370
Left-wing movement, 53–62
Levntal, Z., 439n
Lifton, R. J., 100, 204–206
Limud, 36, 439n.10, 226, 227
Loker, Zvi, 438n.2, 61, 67, 175, 215
Lowie, R., 419
Lyon, D., 183

Maccabiah, Little, 193–194
Macedonia, 6–7, 23, 28, 29, 59, 350; Jews in, 23–24, 28–29, 73
MacIntyre, A., 21, 34, 206, 414, 428
Malkki, L., 36, 412, 426–427, 430
Marriage, 48, 49, 220, 249, 250, 261, 290, 294, 435
Matatja, 62, 64
Matchmaker, 48, 294
Memorialism, 134, 146–159, 213, 339, 419; eulogies, 148; memorial books, 162, 167; memorial days, 141; memorial objects, 134; memorial speeches, 155–158; memorial words, 128–129, 154; memorial worlds, 141
Memory, 134, 190, 201, 210, 223, 226, 235, 240, 243, 247, 253, 254, 256, 263, 339, 344, 352, 370, 402
Metaphysical dilemma, 201, 263, 305, 342
Meyer, M., 204, 267, 271, 415
Milošević, Slobodan, 278, 280–282, 334, 335, 388, 389, 406, 443n
Minyan, 71, 221, 260, 261
Moral community, 398, 406, 407
Mošić, Aleksandar, 38, 384–385
Muslims, 6, 7, 24, 67, 233, 281
Myerhoff, B., xiv, xv, 138, 153,

158, 202, 204, 206, 208–210, 338
Mythology, 1, 53
Myth(s), 1, 4, 53, 92, 131, 304; foundation, 25, 51; making, 5, 55, 130; national patriotic, 100; origin, 130; Tito, 131; of absence of anti-Semitism, 267; of socialist Yugoslavia, 121, 123, 132; triumph of the secular, 182

Naked Island, 369. *See also* Goli Otok
Naming, 85, 93
Naroll, R., 411, 412–413, 444n.2
Narration, 243, 311, 345
Narrative, xiv, xv, xvi, 21, 23, 33–34, 206, 211, 212, 322, 338–345, 350, 373, 444n.6
Nation, 4, 5, 7, 182, 231, 262, 266, 307, 312, 313, 314, 350, 351, 357, 373, 380, 388, 402, 403, 405, 406, 407, 411, 414, 427–429
National Heroes of Yugoslavia, 67, 92, 120
National images, 357–358
Nationalism, 5, 7, 8, 9, 182, 176, 278, 280, 281, 283, 323, 331, 347, 357, 381, 386, 406
National Liberation Struggle (NOB), 21, 53, 62, 92, 98, 100, 101, 102, 132, 134, 136, 143, 148, 164, 167, 212, 213, 344, 355
Neologues, 27, 45, 83
Nešović, Slobodan, 441n
New Yugoslavia, xiii, 21, 51, 96, 101, 112, 113, 148, 332, 358
Non-Aligned Movement, 7–8, 113, 143, 163, 278, 359–362, 375, 378

O'Meara, J., xvi
Old Testament, 302, 306
Orbach, A., 438n, 441n, 442n
Orthodox Jews, 46, 50
Ortner, S., 99–102, 120
Ottoman Empire, 6, 9, 24, 27, 30–31
Ottomans, 4, 9, 289, 388

Palestine, 35, 59, 632, 67, 314, 336, 337, 338, 367, 369–370
Papo, Jakob, 105–109
Parkin, D., 44
Partisans, 67, 92, 93, 105, 106, 130, 132, 136, 171, 319, 320, 321, 355, 400, 401
Partisan War, 8, 97, 98, 116, 123, 130, 132, 143, 165. 173, 373
Peel, J. D. Y., 414, 430–431
Performance(s), 5, 103, 114, 121, 126, 131, 141, 154, 223, 349, 379, 399; of submergence, 135–145; commemoration, 135–159; anniversary celebration, 159–173. *See also* Dramaturgical performance; Svečanosti
Pesah (Passover), 192, 236, 240, 241, 330
Persistent people, 37, 414
Philosemitism, 317, 370
Pijade, Moša, 54, 58, 94, 104, 116, 118, 139
Pilgrimage, 10, 16, 36, 141, 149, 152–153, 302
Place, 111, 348, 406
Polish Jews, xiv, 53, 207, 339
Political order, 8, 97–99, 114–119
Politics, 47, 212, 258, 315, 325, 334, 335, 337, 342
Pope, 312, 313
Population, xv, 1, 11, 19; of study, 13–15; profile: 2, 17, 18, 40; prewar: demographic composition and trends, 41–42; profile and ethnic capacity, 42–50; postwar: demographic composition, 69–77; profile and ethnic capacity, 78–85

Poverty, 28, 59
Power, 4, 8, 20, 33, 35, 59, 76, 98–99, 114–119, 216, 305, 312, 321, 330, 334, 347, 348, 349, 355, 357, 372, 373, 376, 381, 382, 388, 417, 418
Priest, R., 348, 429
Prisoners of war (POW), 94, 96, 218
Progressive, 53, 55, 214, 217, 218, 253, 287, 305, 306, 339; movement, 53, 61, 113, 133, 139; tradition, 117, 136
Prophecy, 307
Protean self, 20, 204–205
Protocols of the Elders of Zion, 279, 381, 384
Purim, 191, 234, 235, 236

Rabbi, 21, 35–36, 44, 83–84, 193, 194, 224, 226, 227, 237, 238, 239, 251, 262, 330; at funerals, 194; Danon, myth of, 35–36; of Yugoslavia, 83, 117, 145, 151, 169, 237, 374, 380. *See* Danon, Cadik
Racism, 1, 112, 38, 315, 372, 375
Radicals, Jewish, 53, 57
Ramet, S, 356, 441n
Rapoport, N., 431
Reconciliation, 351, 400, 407
Refugees, 60, 67, 347, 353
Religion(s): and the crisis of survival, 179, 182, 199; and the state, 198; as traditional marker of ethnic identity, 6, 32, 443–444n.1; assigned low priority by postwar communal leaders, 83, 85; attraction of other, 259–260, 265, 271, 273; before World War II, 7, 42–50, 298; census declaration by, 85, 87, 197; given low priority after World War II, 86; in socialist Yugoslavia, practicing, 269–270; prewar legal status of Jewish community defined by, 89; prewar youth movement away from, 61; privatization of, 72, 181, 183, 263, 303; leaders' symbolic manipulation of, 121, 122
Renaming, 351, 401–402
Reproduction, capacity for, 40, 70, 71, 78
Revelation, 302–315, 341, 342, 344, 345; Book of, 312
Ritual(s), Jewish: and degree of ethnic integration, 40, 46, 50, 68; avoidance of, 139–140; bath, 46, 49, 50; candlelighting, 247; circumcision, 267–269; decimation and absence of, 71, 78, 83–84, 179, 185, 194–197, 250; ethnic preservation and perpetuation through, 415; food prescriptions and proscriptions, 194–195; impact of secularization on, 179–180; importation of specialists to conduct, 83, 185; in summer camp, 379; incorporation into the minyan, 260–262; memorialism as focus of, 183, 194, 213, 426; movement toward more authentic, 189–191, 329, 371, 379; of the life cycle (rites of passage), 12, 48–49, 78, 84–85, 194, 205, 223–226, 436; place of the family in, 46–47, 50, 78; practitioners and roles, 220, 222–223, 226–236; self-sufficiency before World War II, 29, 43–44, 83; spheres of, 222
Romano, Jaša, 439n.2, 53, 58, 66, 68
Rosh Hashanah, 150, 191, 229, 238, 239, 241, 253, 261, 303
Rothschild, J., 407
Rusinow, D., 5, 441n

Sajmište, 10, 138, 139, 353, 354, 370. *See* Commemoration
SANU Memorandum, 388
Sarajevo, 5, 9, 10, 44, 64, 106–109, 160, 166, 229, 230, 237, 248–252
Savez Jevrejskih Opština Jugoslavije (SJOJ). *See* Federation of Jewish Communities of Yugoslavia
Schwartz, S., 5, 251, 252
Sekelj, L., 440n.3
Secret histories. *See* History
Secular: Jewishness, experiment in, 19, 37, 68, 121–122, 179–199, 442n; faith, 219; funerals, 224; Jews, 36, 139, 179, 180, 195–196, 214, 262; Jewish community, 34, 182, 213, 220, 262, 342; Jewishness, 2, 15, 19, 220, 338, 342; leaders, 253, 270
Secularism, 37, 214, 300
Secularization thesis, 181–185
Seder, 139, 192, 213, 241, 330
Self-hatred, 279
Self-management, 121, 123, 132, 137, 149, 358, 362, 363, 364; as summarizing symbol, 100
Sephardi Jews, xiii, 13, 24–32, 38, 44–45, 47–48, 56, 57, 64, 162, 166, 210, 226, 242, 246, 247–252, 262, 294, 295; worldview of, 173–177
Serbian lobby, 390
Settlement, 22–26, 434
Shabbat (Sabbath), 39, 45–47, 83, 150, 189–191, 220, 239–240, 253, 260, 303, 326
Sholem, G., 385–386
Simhat Torah, 34, 439n.8, 168, 191
Society of Serbian-Jewish Friendship, 144, 279, 351, 378
Soviet Union, 6, 8
Spanish Civil War, 66
Spicer, E., 37, 427
Star of David, 182, 374, 382–386, 442n
State, 1, 6, 7, 8, 19, 71, 112, 139, 144, 212, 214, 216, 219, 256, 269, 278, 281, 334, 341, 373, 419–420; holidays, 150–152
Stories, 2, 34, 35, 206, 241, 243, 244, 245, 253, 255, 256, 273, 276, 293, 340, 344, 345. *See* narrative, narration
Submergence: as symbolic symmetry, 120–123; capacity for, 50–69; collective movement out of, 371–380; definition of, 96–97; individual movement out of, 358–363; into socialist Yugoslavia, 114–119; language of, 123, 125–126, 128–132; objects of, 133–135; performances of, 135–173
SUBNOR, 96–98, 119, 138, 153
Subotica, 220, 228, 229, 230, 231–232, 233
Sukkot, 191, 239
Summarizing symbols, 99–100
Summer camp, 189–191, 275, 292, 296, 329
Svečanosti, 135–138. *See also* Anniversary celebrations; Performances
Symbolic appropriation and manipulation, 80, 84, 122–123, 146, 198, 349, 351, 429, 442–443n
Symbolic capital, 316, 429
Symbolic community, xv, 340, 427
Symbolic eradication, 350, 414
Symbolic order, 99–103, 120–122
Symbolic symmetry. *See* Submergence
Symbolic violence, 352
Symbolic weapons, 349
Symbol(s), xiv, xvi; creators of, 206; dominant, 131–132, 172; empty, 385; historical, 4;

Symbol(s) *(Continued)*
Jewish, 3, 12, 211; key, 19, 426; linguistic or word, 213, 240, 427; living, 45; national, 278, 348; natural, 307; of death and rebirth, 204, 235, 272; of identity; of socialist Yugoslavia, 214; personal, of personal significance, 16, 204; private, 12, 19, 204, 205, 206, 212, 221, 252, 258, 272, 273, 285, 338, 340, 344, 345. *See also* Elaborating symbols; Summarizing symbols
Synagogue, 14, 16, 29, 34, 36, 44, 45, 83, 104, 150, 167, 168, 189, 415, 436

Tadić, Ljubomir, 14, 390, 392–394, 443n
Talmud, 216, 343, 431
Tanakh, 35, 343
Time, 4, 47, 50, 68, 86, 232, 233, 240, 266, 272, 277, 345
Tišma, Aleksander, 439n.2, 344
Tito, xiii, 5, 7, 8, 98, 100, 105, 115–116, 121, 131–132, 133, 172, 183, 334, 341, 352, 355, 362, 364, 388, 397
Titoism, xvi, 2, 5, 8, 20, 38, 100–102, 171, 172, 182, 348, 352, 355, 371, 374, 375, 388, 398, 399, 401, 406
Torah, 34, 35, 39, 168–169, 261, 268, 272, 307, 343, 380
Transition, 382, 398, 399, 406, 407
Truncation, 18, 78, 85, 250, 291, 327
Tuden, A., 440n
Tudjman, Franjo, 351, 372, 396, 397, 398, 443n.6, 399, 400, 406, 443n.8, 407
Turkish coffee, 10
Turner, V., 437n.2, 141, 158, 160, 183, 204, 207, 241, 303, 340, 356, 444n.5

Ustasha, 4, 68, 92, 107, 149, 281, 354, 355, 381, 398, 399, 400, 407

Vajs, Albert, 14, 32–33, 91, 96–97, 110–111, 441n.5, 112, 113, 212, 218
Verdery, K., 349, 350, 357, 406, 412
Victims: of fascism, 139, 140, 144, 193, 235, 241, 259, 351, 353, 366, 401, 402; of genocide, 67, 134, 298, 317, 393, 429; Holocaust, 255; of history, 357; of Jasenovac, 351, 355, 398; of Partisan atrocities, 401; call for reconciliation of all, 351, 400; of the Ustasha, 398
Vojvodina, 73, 441n
Volf, M., 350
Vukovar, 297–298

War: civil, 1, 109, 325, 351, 355, 396, 403, 405, 407; of words, civil, 323, 351–353, 370, 380, 391. World, xiii, 1, 4, 5, 46, 67, 67, 201, 249, 280, 286, 298, 304, 320, 353. *See* Partisan War
Watson, J., 12
West, R., 61
Wilson, R., 4, 411, 413, 414, 429, 431
World Jewish Congress, 160, 165, 166

Yiddish, 27, 210, 323
Yiddishkeit, 418
Yom ha'Sho'ah, 192–193
Yom Kippur, 150, 191, 229, 238, 239, 241, 253, 261, 303, 316
Yugoslav Experiment, 5. *See* Rusinow, Dennison
Yugoslav Idea, 9

Yugoslav Jews in Israel, 110, 112, 127, 143, 359, 376–377, 380, 390
Yugoslavism, 7, 61, 113, 143

Zagreb, 9, 10, 229, 230, 233, 317, 323, 329, 351, 403; Jews of, 45, 169, 441n.11, 371, 372, 374, 375, 376, 379, 381, 395, 400, 401, 403
Zenner, Walter, 341, 412–413
Zion, 315, 387
Zionism, 35, 36, 51, 55–59, 61–65, 143, 179, 336, 337, 361, 375–376; Zionist organizations, 53, 55, 63, 440n
Zukin, S., 136–137